Pauline Frommer's

ITALY

SPEND LESS ★ SEE MORE ™

1st Edition

by Keith Bain, Reid Bramblett, Pippa de Bruyn,
Bill Fink & Barbie Latza Nadeau

Series Editor: Pauline Frommer

WILEY
Wiley Publishing, Inc.

Published by:

Wiley Publishing, Inc.

111 River St.
Hoboken, NJ 07030-5774

ISBN-13: 978-0-471-77860-8
ISBN-10: 0-471-77860-5

Editor: Matthew Brown
Production Editor: Suzanna R. Thompson
Cartographer: Andrew Murphy
Photo Editor: Richard Fox
Interior Design: Lissa Auciello-Brogan
Production by Wiley Indianapolis Composition Services

For information on our other products and services or to obtain technical support,
please contact our Customer Care Department within the U.S. at 800/762-2974,
outside the U.S. at 317/572-3993 or fax 317/572-4002.

Wiley also publishes its books in a variety of electronic formats. Some content that
appears in print may not be available in electronic formats.

Manufactured in the United States of America

5   4   3   2   1

Contents

SPEND LESS SEE MORE

List of Maps

Acknowledgments

I wish to thank April Orcutt (for forwarding me the gig) and Brett Rugroden (for tag-teaming Florence restaurants). Thanks also to my dad, who left me home from his trips to Italy, but always brought back slide shows and, more importantly, stories of travel. Finally, thanks to Heather McGinnis, a good little navigator.

—Bill Fink

An Invitation to the Reader

In researching this book, we discovered many wonderful places—hotels, restaurants, shops, and more. We're sure you'll find others. Please tell us about them, so we can share the information with your fellow travelers in upcoming editions. If you were disappointed with a recommendation, we'd love to know that, too. Please write to:

Pauline Frommer's Italy, 1st Edition
Wiley Publishing, Inc. • 111 River St. • Hoboken, NJ 07030-5774

An Additional Note

Please be advised that travel information is subject to change at any time—and this is especially true of prices. We therefore suggest that you write or call ahead for confirmation when making your travel plans. The authors, editors, and publisher cannot be held responsible for the experiences of readers while traveling. Your safety is important to us, however, so we encourage you to stay alert and be aware of your surroundings. Keep a close eye on cameras, purses, and wallets, all favorite targets of thieves and pickpockets.

About the Authors

Born, bred, and living in South Africa, **Keith Bain** holds a doctorate in contemporary cinema studies. He has enjoyed such diverse activities as stage acting, skydiving, trance-partying, and bungee-jumping (although the latter, only once). He is passionate about travel, and when he's not exploring the world in search of social and cultural adventure, he lectures at a film school in Johannesburg. Keith is a co-author of *Frommer's India* and is a contributor to the most recent edition of *Frommer's South Africa*.

Reid Bramblett is the author of 10 guidebooks—7 of them to Italy, where he has lived on and off since the age of 11. He writes the weekly "The Intrepid Traveler" adventure column and is a contributing editor to *Budget Travel* magazine and Concierge. com. A Philadelphia native, he now lives in Brooklyn, New York, where he maintains the award-winning Reidsguides.com, recommended by CNN, *USA Today,* and *National Geographic Traveler.*

Pippa de Bruyn is an award-winning journalist, seasoned travel writer (author of *Frommer's South Africa* and *Frommer's India*), and oenophile (contributor to *John Platter's South African Wine Guide*). Her toughest assignment? Trying to fit the sybaritic pleasures of the Italian Riviera into 35 pages.

Bill Fink is a freelance writer based in San Francisco, covering topics ranging from trash-dump volleyball in Burma to helicopter-skiing in Nevada. His writing appears regularly in the *San Francisco Chronicle* and other publications, including Travelers' Tales Guides *30 Days in Italy* and *The Best Travel Writing 2006.*

American freelance writer **Barbie Latza Nadeau** has been based in Rome since 1996. She writes for a variety of publications including *Newsweek, Budget Travel,* and the World Monument Fund's *ICON.*

Star Ratings, Icons & Abbreviations

Every restaurant, hotel, and attraction is rated with stars ★, indicating our opinion of that facility's desirability; this relates not to price, but to the value you receive for the price you pay. The stars mean:

No stars: Good
★ Very good
★★ Great
★★★ Outstanding! A must!

Accommodations within each neighborhood are listed in ascending order of cost, starting with the cheapest and increasing to the occasional "splurge." Each hotel review is preceded by one, two, three, or four dollar signs, indicating the price range per double room. Restaurants work on a similar system, with dollar signs indicating the price range per three-course meal.

Accommodations	
€	Up to €50/night
€€	€51–€100
€€€	€101–€150
€€€€	Over €150 per night

Dining	
€	Primi courses for €7 or less
€€	€8–€14
€€€	€15–€19
€€€€	€20 and up

In addition, we've included a kids icon (kids) to denote attractions, restaurants, and lodgings that are particularly child friendly.

Frommers.com

Now that you have the guidebook to a great trip, visit our website at **www.frommers.com** for travel information on more than 3,000 destinations. With features updated regularly, we give you instant access to the most current trip-planning information available. At Frommers.com, you'll also find the best prices on airfares, accommodations, and car rentals—and you can even book travel online through our travel booking partners. At Frommers.com, you'll also find the following:

- Online updates to our most popular guidebooks
- Vacation sweepstakes and contest giveaways
- Newsletter highlighting the hottest travel trends
- Online travel message boards with featured travel discussions

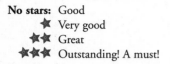

A Note from Pauline

I STARTED TRAVELING WITH MY GUIDEBOOK-WRITING PARENTS, ARTHUR Frommer and Hope Arthur, when I was just 4 months old. To avoid lugging around a crib, they would simply swaddle me and stick me in an open drawer for the night. For half of my childhood, my home was a succession of hotels and B&Bs throughout Europe, as we dashed around every year to update *Europe on $5 a Day* (and then $10 a day, and then $20 . . .).

We always traveled on a budget, staying at the mom-and-pop joints Dad featured in the guide, getting around by public transportation, eating where the locals ate. And that's still the way I travel today because I learned—from the master—that these types of vacations not only save you money, but they also give you a richer, deeper experience of the culture. You spend time in local neighborhoods, and you meet and talk with the people who live there. For me, making friends and having meaningful exchanges is always the highlight of my trip—and the main reason I decided to become a travel writer and editor as well.

I've conceived these books as budget guides for a new generation. They have all the outspoken commentary and detailed pricing information that you've come to expect from the Frommer's guides, but they take bargain hunting into the 21st century, with more information on how you can effectively use the Internet and air/hotel packages to save money. Most importantly, these guides stress the availability of "alternative accommodations," not simply to save you money but also to give you a more authentic experience in the places you visit.

In this Italy book, for example, we tell you about light-filled apartments in the historic Trastevere neighborhood of Rome, from just €100 a night (p. 27); guest-accepting convents and monasteries in Assisi, Florence, Rome, and other areas that allow a fascinating peek into the monastic life, for as little as €25 a night (p. 209, 99, and 21); and oceanview guesthouses in the Cinque Terre, where you can toast the sunset from your own private balcony for as little as €50 a night (p. 454).

The individual chapter sections on "The Other Rome," "The Other Florence," and so on immerse you in the life that residents of a particular place enjoy: the courses they take, the work they do, the crafts they practice. Page through this guide and you'll find 1-day paper-marbling and gondola-making classes in Venice (p. 329), soccer mania in Florence (p. 131), and intense cooking classes in Bologna (p. 244), among other experiences.

The result, I hope, is a valuable new addition to the world of guidebooks. Please let us know how we've done! I encourage you to e-mail me at editor@frommers.com or write to me, care of Frommer's, 111 River St., Hoboken, NJ, 07030.

Happy traveling!

Pauline Frommer

Pauline Frommer

1 The Best of Italy

From ancient ruins to tasty *trattorie* and from urban verve to rural charm—how do you choose?

by Reid Bramblett

WHEN IT COMES DOWN TO IT, NEARLY EVERY REGION IN ITALY HAS QUAINT hill towns, picturesque countryside, magnificent art cities, ancient ruins, exquisite food, sublime wines, and just about any other travel cliché you want to throw in there. It's wonderful, it's incredible, and it's why Italy remains one of the most popular destinations on the planet—but it's not going to help you plan your trip.

You probably have only 1 or 2 precious weeks of vacation time, and we suspect you have your own ideas about how to spend it. That's why we're going to cut through the brochure-speak and help you home in on the best of the best, right from the start.

THE BEST OF THE BEST

While there are **ancient ruins** across the peninsula, from the Alps of the Valle d'Aosta to the very southern tip of Sicily, the real showstoppers lie in the southern half of the country. You'll find the best Roman remains in—surprise, surprise—Rome (the Colosseum, Roman Forum, Imperial Fori, and several top museums), and get the best sense of what life was like 2 millennia ago in the ancient ghost towns of Pompeii and Herculaneum, both just outside Naples, or in Ostia Antica, just a subway ride from the center of Rome.

What few folks realize is that, before the Romans, everything from Naples south was actually part of Greece (back in the 5th c. B.C., when *Magna Graecia* was much, much bigger), and that some of the best-preserved ancient Greek ruins anywhere are actually in Sicily (Agrigento, Siracusa, Segesta, Selinunte), and on the coast south of Naples (Paestum).

When it comes to **medieval hill towns,** you have plenty of options. However, the hill-town heartland really is central Italy, particularly in Tuscany (Siena, Montepulciano, Montalcino, and especially San Gimignano, bristling with stone towers like a medieval Manhattan) and neighboring Umbria (from its capital, Perugia, to smaller cities and towns such as Gubbio, Todi, and Spoleto).

Of course, you can't swing a paintbrush in Italy without spattering it on some of the finest **Renaissance art** in the world. This is where Italy's Big Three—Rome, Venice, and Florence—really live up to their reputations. Florence (the Uffizi and Pitti Palace), Rome (the Vatican), and Venice (the Accademia) collectively have more works by Old Masters like Michelangelo, Donatello, Leonardo da Vinci, Raphael, Botticelli, and Titian than you could hope to see in three lifetimes. And the artwork is not limited to just the major museums. There are dozens of smaller collections, as well as countless churches where the walls (not to mention the ceilings—Sistine Chapel, anyone?) sometimes seem to be little more than grand settings on which to display masterpieces of fresco, painting, and sculpture.

LIVING LA DOLCE VITA

Perhaps all that's simply too much sightseeing. An endless litany of ruins, churches, and museums can make for a dull vacation. You've come to sample that Italian *dolce vita* (sweet life)—or even better, *la dolce far niente* (the sweetness of doing nothing). And with Italy's 8,475km (5,264 miles) of coastline, there are few better places to find that sweetness than at the **beach.** You just have to pick which kind of seaside vacation—or 2-day break from the relentless sightseeing—you want. Do you want to hang with the jet-set (the Amalfi Coast), join the ever-increasing tourist hordes that hike from one fishing village to the next (the Cinque Terre), grab an umbrella and beach chair alongside vacationing Italian families (the Italian Riviera), or get off the beaten path and see what all those places looked like before they were discovered (Puglia's Gargano Peninsula)?

Or, you can opt for an **island**—no, not Sicily: the tiny islands. Now you just have to decide: Will you follow the Americans and Brits to the storied isle of Capri and its Blue Grotto; the Germans to Capri's lesser-known neighbor, Ischia; or the Italians down to the string of Aeolian Islands off the north coast of Sicily, where the isle of Stromboli erupts regularly throughout the day and night like some kind of volcanic Old Faithful?

Then again, there are always the elaborate villas and sumptuous gardens of the **Lake District**—Lake Como, Lake Maggiore, Lake Garda—where the plains of Lombardy meet the Italian Alps. Speaking of which, plenty of people prefer to seek *la dolce vita* at a higher altitude. It doesn't get any higher than 3,300m (11,000 ft.) at Punta Hellbrunner atop Monte Bianco, Europe's tallest **mountain,** shared by France (which calls it Mont Blanc), and the northwestern Italian region of Valle d'Aosta. On the other side of the country, just a few hours north of Venice, rise the craggy peaks of the Dolomites, into which are tucked tony ski resorts such as Cortina d'Ampezzo.

THE BEST EATS

And, of course, there's the **food.** Don't ask us to single out just one place in Italy for its cuisine. We can't do it. That would be like choosing a favorite child. With extremely rare exceptions (usually around the biggest tourist sights and in beach resorts), it's nearly impossible to have a bad meal in Italy. These people live to eat. Their idea of an ideal evening out is not dinner, a movie, and maybe dancing; it's appetizer, main course, and dessert—preferably strung out over 3 or 4 hours. Wherever you go, you'll find regional specialties to knock out your taste buds: pizza in Naples, spaghetti carbonara in Rome, Adriatic fish in Venice, juicy steaks in Florence, swordfish in Sicily, *osso buco* in Milan, prosciutto and parmigiano in Parma, calamari in Puglia, polenta in Alpine villages, and pasta absolutely everywhere you turn. Oh, and for dessert: gelato, which makes every other frozen dairy treat ashamed to call itself ice cream. (Here's a fun travel game: Race to see who can be the first to sample all three kinds of Italian gelato—the ice milk of Sicily, often delicately flavored with fresh fruits and nuts; the dense milk-and-egg-yolk-based product of Florence, which gives new meaning to the phrase "death by chocolate"; and the cream-and-custard-based gelato of Northern Italy.)

To wash it all down? **Wine** from the folks who taught the French how to tend grapes. Again, every region in Italy produces phenomenal wines, from the earthy, purple-black *Salice Salentino* in Puglia to the light, fruity *tocai* in the Friuli. But, if you had to pick just two regions that are constantly trying to outdo each other in the prodigious production of truly great wines, those would have to be Tuscany (the short-short list of varietals includes Chianti, Brunello di Montalcino, and Vino Nobile di Montepulciano) and the northern region of Piemonte (from which the mighty Barolo, Barbera, Barbaresco, and Nebbiolo hail—not to mention Asti spumanti, the champagne of Italian sparkling whites).

Now let's get down to specifics. You will, of course, tailor your trip to your own tastes and interest, but there are a few things no one should miss. What follow are the greatest Italian attractions and experiences—plus ways to get off the beaten path and discover the "other Italy."

THE BEST CHURCHES

ST. PETER'S & THE VATICAN (ROME)   The capital of Christendom and the Pope's personal pulpit is St. Peter's Basilica, one of the most spectacular assemblages of art and architecture on the planet, and a pilgrimage point for Catholics from around the world. The world's smallest country—Vatican City—is also home to one of the grandest museum complexes in Europe, of which Michelangelo's ceiling in the Sistine Chapel is just a teensy part. See p. 67.

THE DUOMO (FLORENCE)   Florence's cathedral is a study in the origins of the Renaissance, from the doors on the baptistery out front, which set the tone and style for all later Renaissance art; to the frescoes in the church by Paolo Uccello, one of the first masters of perspective; to Brunelleschi's ingenious dome, which revolutionized architecture. Bonus: You can climb up between the two layers of that dome and see Brunelleschi's genius up close as well as the brilliant panorama of the city. See p. 119.

ST. FRANCIS'S BASILICA (ASSISI)   This massive home of the Franciscan order is a major pilgrimage destination, both for devout Catholics and art aficionados, who arrive in droves and tour buses to view the famous frescoes by Giotto—though don't miss the equally brilliant frescoes by early Sienese masters Simone Martini and the Lorenzetti brothers in the lower church of this double-decker basilica. See p. 211.

ST. MARK'S BASILICA (VENICE)   Grafted together from bits of military plunder, coated inside with golden mosaics, and sporting a quintet of vaguely Eastern-looking domes, the cathedral of Venice epitomizes this city's obsession with beauty and religious ritual, and its style reflects its ancient trading connections with the Oriental world. See p. 309.

CAPPELLA DEGLI SCROVEGNI (VENETO)   For every 100 people who visit the Giotto frescoes in Assisi, maybe one makes it to the university town of Padova, which the Gothic master painter—widely considered to be the father of Western art—also blessed with an amazing, colorful fresco cycle in this small chapel. Bonus: It's an easy day trip from Venice. See p. 347.

THE DUOMO (MILAN)   The fourth-largest church in the world is also Italy's grandest Gothic structure, and even though it took 500-odd years to complete, the city fathers resolutely stuck by their original, medieval-looking plans. The result is stupendous: 135 marble spires, some 3,400 statues adorning the exterior, and a nave that feels like a forest of columns. The real treat is to clamber up onto the roof for close-up looks at the buttresses and a lovely city panorama. See p. 394.

THE CATHEDRAL OF MONREALE (OUTSIDE PALERMO)   If you thought the mosaics of Palermo's churches were something else, wait until you get to this village above the city and see the sparkling golden interior of its cathedral— not to mention the amazing Romanesque carvings and inlay work on the columns surrounding its quiet cloisters. See p. 556.

THE BEST NON-ECCLESIASTICAL ARCHITECTURAL SIGHTS

THE COLOSSEUM (ROME)   Every modern stadium in the world is but a feeble imitation of Rome's Colosseum. Wander amid its ramparts and imagine the cheering crowds, roaring beasts, and clash of swords as gladiators battled for the amusement of Caesar and the masses alike. See p. 53.

ROMAN FORUM (ROME)   Walk in the footsteps of the Caesars amid the remnants and ruins of what was once the center of the Roman world, puzzling together a picture of the ancient city from the remaining fallen pillars, corners of temples, triumphal arches, and slices of statues that fill this (free) archaeological park in the heart of Rome. See p. 51.

THE CAMPO DI MIRACOLI (PISA)   Sure, it's got a famous Leaning Tower— but the brilliant green grass of Pisa's Campo di Miracoli (Field of Miracles) is also backdrop to the massive cathedral that the titling tower goes with, an amazing Gothic baptistery with perfect acoustics and a brilliant carved pulpit, a serene holy cemetery with ruinous but fascinating frescoes, and two intriguing museums devoted to the church treasures of this once mighty maritime power. See p. 155.

IL CAMPO (SIENA)   The main piazza in Siena is a gorgeous sloping semicircle of brick that, on nice days, is scattered with people sunning themselves, couples sipping cappuccino at cafes, kids playing soccer, and groups strolling and chatting. The whole thing is bounded at the bottom by Siena's medieval city hall, with its amazing Gothic frescoes and 100m (330-ft.) tower. See p. 173.

THE PALLADIAN ARCHITECTURE OF VICENZA (VENETO)   Vicenza's hometown hero, Andrea Palladio, is generally considered the father of High Renaissance architecture in all its geometrically precise, classically inspired glory (think Monticello in Virginia, or the marble buildings of Washington, D.C.). Vicenza has done a superb job of preserving the cobblestone streets and fine buildings of its urban fabric, including several structures designed by the master himself—though Palladio's real masterpieces are the *palazzi* in the hills around town. See p. 354.

POMPEII & HERCULANEUM (CAMPANIA)   The view of Mt. Vesuvius from the narrow streets of these ancient Roman ghost towns destroyed by the volcano in a.d. 79 is as eerie as it gets. You can almost smell the ashen lava, but concentrate instead on the remarkable glimpses into the daily life of those who lived—and died—here nearly 2,000 years ago. See p. 508.

THE LECCESE BAROQUE (LECCE)   Often called the Florence of the South, Lecce is overflowing with churches and palaces built of honey-colored stone along the lines of the city's unique, gorgeous take on baroque architecture—a profusion of symbolic animals, elaborate carved motifs, and complex curlicues. See p. 538.

CASTEL DEL MONTE (PUGLIA)   Like a cut-stone wedding cake atop a barren hill, this old fortress of Frederick II is a lesson in octagonal geometry and medieval architecture, with unbeatable views across the gentle plains of olive groves. See p. 532.

NORMAN ARCHITECTURE (PALERMO)   Sicily was Greek, Arab, Norman, French, and Spanish long before it ever became a part of Italy. The medieval Norman rulers in particular—yes, those Normans, the ones who came from northern France—adopted a syncretic style of architecture that freely mixed Byzantine mosaics, Arabic domes, and Romanesque details, to which later rulers often added baroque flourishes and facades. See p. 548.

ANCIENT GREEK TEMPLES (AGRIGENTO)   The 5th-century b.c. temples on a hillside of olives and cherry trees just below the southern Sicilian city of Agrigento are among the best-preserved ancient Greek ruins in the entire world— Sicily was once part of *Magna Graecia,* the ancient "Greater Greece." See p. 563.

THE BEST MUSEUMS

THE UFFIZI GALLERIES (FLORENCE)   The 16th-century offices of the Medici family, with frescoed halls lined by ancient statuary, house their collection of some of the Renaissance's finest artworks. Don't let this museum's small size fool you: It's right up there with the Louvre, Metropolitan, and Vatican, housing some of the greatest artistic masterpieces in the world, including Botticelli's *Birth of Venus,* da Vinci's *Annunciation,* and Michelangelo's *Holy Family.* See p. 116.

THE ACCADEMIA (FLORENCE)   The art academy of Florence always has a long line outside. Why? Because this is where they keep Michelangelo's *David*— along with his unfinished (and far more fascinating) statues of slaves, the full-scale model for Giambologna's *Rape of the Sabines,* and a passel of fine paintings. See p. 125.

THE BYZANTINE MOSAICS OF RAVENNA (RAVENNA)   On an easy day trip from Bologna you can gaze at the glittering medieval mosaics slathered on the interiors of churches and tombs in Ravenna, Western Europe's last bastion of the Byzantine empire. See p. 256.

GALLERIE DELL'ACCADEMIA (VENICE)   The world's most extensive collection of Venetian art is kept in a glorious Venetian *palazzo* on the Grand Canal. From the Byzantine-inspired technique of using gold leaf for decorative effect, to the masterful embrace of color, mood, and movement by Titian, Tintoretto, and Veronese, the Accademia provides an opportunity to penetrate beneath the surface of a vast number of superbly rendered canvases. See p. 321.

THE PEGGY GUGGENHEIM COLLECTION (VENICE)   The only truly worthwhile modern-art gallery in Italy is installed in Peggy Guggenheim's former (unfinished) *palazzo* on the Grand Canal. It's a who's who of 20th-century artists: Max Ernst, Salvador Dalí, Joan Miró, Pablo Picasso, Constantin Brancusi, Marc Chagall, Piet Mondrian, Jackson Pollock, Alberto Giacometti, Henry Moore, Marcel Duchamp, and René Magritte. See p. 320.

THE EGYPTIAN MUSEUM (TURIN)   Who would've thought that the single greatest collection of Egyptian artifacts outside of Cairo is not London's British Museum or New York's Metropolitan, but this remarkable museum in the genteel Italian industrial capital of Turin? Hey, if nothing else, it makes for a nice break from all that Italian art. See p. 437.

NATIONAL ARCHAEOLOGICAL MUSEUM (NAPLES)   The artifacts housed in Naples's archaeological museum are among Western Civilization's most significant, including rare finds from the ruins of Pompeii and Herculaneum, and Greek, Etruscan, and Roman artifacts that are simply unmatched in historical significance. See p. 491.

THE BEST TRAVEL EXPERIENCES

DESCEND INTO THE CATACOMBS (ROME)   The web of ancient Christian burial tunnels under the Via Appia Antica park just outside Rome's city walls is an important stop for religious pilgrims and the historically curious. There are miles upon miles of these earthen corridors stacked with tombs, underground mausoleums, and marble chapels—a bit spooky, and with cheesy tour guides, but endlessly fascinating. See p. 77.

ENJOY A MARATHON DINNER (FLORENCE)   We already talked about the Italian penchant for lingering over a meal for 3 or 4 hours, with all the courses—*antipasto* (appetizer), *primo* (pasta, soup, or risotto), *secondo* (meat or fish), *contorno* (side dish), *dolce* (dessert)—plenty of wine to lubricate the meal, and a grappa and espresso to finish it off. You could experience that anywhere in Italy, but if we had to pick one place to set aside the whole evening (and all plans of eating again for 24 hr.) for that marathon meal, it'd be Florence—probably at Il Latini or Cibreo Ristorante. See p. 107.

PICK A FESTIVAL, ANY FESTIVAL (TUSCANY & UMBRIA)   The heart of Central Italy is a festival-happy place, hosting everything from pagan parties masquerading as Christian rites to modern music fests. Tops are Gubbio's 800-year-old race of saints' shrines; the contemporary music and arts festivals of Perugia, Spoleto, and Arezzo; and Perugia's delicious "Eurochocolate '06." See chapters 4 and 5.

TOUR THE CHIANTI VINEYARDS (TUSCANY) These vine-covered hills between Florence and Siena have dozens of wineries you can tour, usually for free (tippling of the product included), as well as plenty of picturesque hill towns where you can pick up picnic supplies to accompany the bottles you buy directly from the source. See p. 168.

RIDE THE *VAPORETTO* DOWN THE GRAND CANAL (VENICE) For a fraction of the cost of a gondola ride, you can ply the Grand Canal on the *vaporetti* no. 1 or 82—the motor launches that act as the public bus system in this city built on water. It's like watching a scrolling postcard of hundreds of Gothic and Byzantine *palazzi,* redolent of the days when Venice was a powerful maritime republic. Angle for a seat on the open-air deck up front. See p. 272.

LEARN THE SECRETS OF THE DOGES (VENICE) The "Secret Itineraries Tour" of Venice's Palazzo Ducale takes small groups of visitors into the many rooms in the palace normally locked to the public—and often hidden behind false walls, tapestries, and Renaissance paintings. This warren of secret rooms, passages, and stairways allowed the vast, often shadowy machinery of the Venetian state to continue to operate for 900 years behind the pretense of unhinged luxury that still greets visitors in the official spaces of the palace. See p. 314.

SKI THE DOLOMITES (CORTINA D'AMPEZZO) Italy's top ski resort is a thoroughly Italian medieval village coupled with access to excellent slopes and top-notch facilities. For winter visitors, Cortina has eight ski areas; there are another ten within easy reach of the town. In summer, there's mountain scenery and great sports facilities to keep active types engaged. See p. 375.

ATTEND THE OPERA (VENICE, MILAN, NAPLES & VERONA) Italy is home to some of the grandest opera houses the world has ever known—and two of the greatest each emerged in 2005 from many years of restoration. Venice's Teatro La Fenice (The Phoenix) has risen from the ashes of a disastrous fire to reclaim its status as one of the world's most spectacular operatic venues. Milan's famed La Scala opera house—where Verdi was the house composer and Toscanini once waved the baton—has also finally reopened following years of restoration. Then there's the Teatro San Carlo in Naples, where the term *prima donna* (which just means "first woman," or, in other words, the female lead) was born, and the magnificent 2,000-year-old Arena in Verona, the world's third-largest amphitheater, which has long since replaced gladiators with divas and become world-renowned for its productions of *Aïda* under the stars. See chapters 7, 8, 9, and 12.

HIKE THE CINQUE TERRE (ITALIAN RIVIERA) While away your time on the southern end of the Italian Riviera by strolling from one lovely fishing village to another along old goat trails through terraced vineyards, gardens, and scrubby mountaintops with breathtaking views over the Mediterranean. See chapter 11.

EXPLORE THE ISLANDS OF LAKE MAGGIORE (THE LAKES) Ferry-hop your way from Isola Bella, with its ornate gardens; to Isola Madre, where peacocks stroll the exotic grounds around the Borromean palace; to Isola Superiore, a fishing village where you can dine on fresh lake trout at a table not 1.5m (5 ft.) from the water. See p. 416.

HEAD TO THE TOP OF EUROPE (THE ALPS)   Ride a series of cable cars up snowy slopes and ski gondolas dangling high above glaciers to arrive at Europe's highest peak, Monte Bianco—and then continue on down the French side (call it "Mont Blanc" now) to the chichi resort of Chamonix and take a bus ride back to Italy through one of the world's longest tunnels. See p. 440.

CLIMB MT. VESUVIUS (NAPLES)   You may never again get this close to a natural disaster in waiting. Climb to the top of Mt. Vesuvius and stare down into the crater created in A.D. 79 when it destroyed Pompeii. Then turn to look out to the bay of Naples across the crusty lava fields overgrown with vineyards and dotted with houses and the Naples suburbs. All of it is smack in the path of the lava, should another major eruption occur . . . an event that's long overdue. See p. 508.

ATTEND A PERFORMANCE IN AN ANCIENT THEATER (SICILY)   The ancient theaters of Taormina (Greco-Roman), Siracusa (Greek), and Segesta (Greek) all host summertime series of concerts, operas, and ancient plays under the stars—and, since they're all set atop hills, if you arrive before dusk, you get to watch the sun set over the Sicilian countryside (or, in the case of Siracusa, the city). See p. 568.

PICNIC (ANYWHERE)   Some of your most memorable meals will undoubtedly be picnics, with wonderful (and cheap!) ingredients culled from the *alimentari* (deli/grocery store), *panetteria* (bakery), *fruttivendolo* (fruit-and-veggie shop), and *vineria* (wine shop) that line the streets of every city and village. Just pick an appropriate venue—church steps, stone wall around an olive grove or vineyard, bench by the beach, even just the terrace back at your hotel room—and get ready to have a feast fit for a king on a pauper's budget. (Just don't forget the corkscrew.)

THE BEST OF THE "OTHER" ITALY

SHOP THE PORTA PORTESE MARKET (ROME)   Join the crowds of locals who religiously flock to this massive flea market each Sunday morning in search of elusive bargains or just to meet friends. See p. 83.

GET CAUGHT UP IN *CALCIO* (TUSCANY—OR ANYWHERE)   Share the locals' passion at a professional sports event—Florence and Siena have top division Serie A (first division) soccer teams, and Siena's pro basketball team is a champion. See p. 178.

VISIT THE OLTRARNO ARTISANS (FLORENCE)   Head to the Oltrarno neighborhood to see fifth-generation craftsmen at work in ceramics, woodcarving, goldsmithing, mosaics, cobbling, and other specialties. See p. 134.

TAKE COOKING LESSONS IN A TUSCAN VILLA (TUSCANY)   You could simply rave about the food in Italy when you get home—or you can learn to re-create it for your jealous friends. Try your hand at a cooking class in a Tuscan villa or Florence restaurant—or stick around for a couple of weeks and attend a formal culinary school. See p. 166.

MAKE A PILGRIMAGE TO ASSISI (UMBRIA)   Though most Italians are not overtly devout, faith remains one of the cornerstones of Italian culture and society, and there are few better places to see it in action than at the Basilica of St. Francis in Assisi. Masses run constantly, and are best on a Sunday—and if you can swing it to be here on Easter, you just might have a transcendent experience. See p. 211.

LEARN TO MAKE THE PERFECT SPAGHETTI BOLOGNESE (BOLOGNA)
Every Italian is proud of his or her local cuisine, but every Italian also agrees that the best cooking in Italy is done in Bologna. But don't just dine there; take a morning stroll through the food markets and gourmet shops, and then learn how to prepare its signature dishes with an afternoon cooking lesson. See p. 244.

MASTER AN ANCIENT CRAFT (VENICE)   Tourists shell out big bucks for marbleized paper in Italy, but instead of bringing home a trinket you can bring home a whole new skill learned from a master craftsman. And besides: How many teachers do you know who serve snacks and wine at the lessons? See p. 330.

GO BACK TO SCHOOL (ITALIAN RIVIERA)   Genoa University's annual summer school is aimed at improving foreigners' spoken Italian and grammar, and also acts as a crash course on Italian culture and history, with guest speakers from various faculties lecturing on anything from Italian cinema and art to contemporary politics. Best of all, the course, which is usually 2 weeks in September, is held at the beautiful Villa Durazzo in Santa Margherita Ligure, with gorgeous vistas of the Ligurian sea. See p. 478.

GET INTO THE UNDERBELLY OF NAPLES (NAPLES)   You need to dig deep to really understand a city's history, and Napoli Sotterranea (Underground Naples) does it better than anyone else. Take one of the winding tours through the complex of ancient underground aqueducts and cisterns that have been bomb shelters and modern-art venues. See p. 495.

SLEEP IN A *TRULLO* (PUGLIA)   Every visitor spends half the time in central Puglia snapping endless photos of its iconic whitewashed round huts with conical stone roofs. But *trulli* can be more than just a postcard sight; you can actually set up temporary housekeeping in one and feel what it's really like to live in one of these ancient structures. See p. 534.

2 Rome: Where All Roads Lead

Every traveler to Italy should visit the capital.

by Barbie Latza Nadeau

ONCE IT RULED THE WESTERN WORLD. AND EVEN THE PARTIAL, SCATTERED ruins of that awesome empire, of which Rome was the capital, are today among the most overpowering sights on earth. To walk the Roman Forum, to view the Colosseum, the Pantheon, and the Appian Way—these are among the most memorable, instructive, and chilling experiences in all of travel. To see evidence of a once-great civilization that no longer exists is a humbling experience that everyone should have.

Thrilling, too, are the sights of Christian Rome, which speak to the long and complex domination by Rome of one of the world's major religions. I am a resident of Rome, and I am constantly reminded of its extraordinary history, which sets the stage for your own visit.

It is virtually impossible to visit Rome without harboring at least a few expectations. After all, most people have seen pictures of St. Peter's Square and the Colosseum. There is a certain preconception that's hard to shake about dining alfresco and wandering through the narrow cobblestone streets. In fact, Rome has been described and typecast in such tedious detail that it may seem inconceivable that you could have a unique experience here. But Rome is precisely the type of place you can easily make your own—no matter how much you've heard or read about the city.

With that in mind, it's important to remember that Rome is much more than a place in which to be a tourist. Walk across the same stones that Julius Caesar once traversed in the Roman Forum and imagine what it was like to rule the world from here. Stare at the ceiling of the Sistine Chapel on a lonely winter's day, or imagine Federico Fellini filming Anita Ekberg in *La Dolce Vita* as she splashed in the shallow water of the Trevi Fountain. Or better yet, go to the center of St. Peter's Square at dusk, when it is nearly empty, and try to remember the historical scene of the recent election of Pope Benedict XVI that was shown across the globe; or look down between the square's cobblestones, at the candle wax left there from prayer vigils when Pope John Paul II passed away. These experiences can be intensely emotive, and they are so easy to include in your visit to Rome. As Renaissance artist Giotto di Bondone said, "Rome is the city of echoes, the city of illusions, and the city of yearning." And as a visitor here, it is all yours for the taking.

DON'T LEAVE ROME WITHOUT . . .

CATCHING A VIEW FROM THE TOP   The best place to look out over the eternal city depends entirely on the time of day. Sunset is best from **Gianicolo**

(p. 66) because of the way the light catches the terra-cotta rooftops of Trastevere. Sunrise, on the other hand, is better from the terrace behind the **Campidoglio** (p. 56) overlooking the ancient forum, where the columns glisten in the day's first light. The midday view is best from the top of **St. Peter's cupola** (p. 70), where you can sometimes see the sun's reflection on the Mediterranean Sea in the distance, or from on top of the **Vittoriano** (p. 55) in the middle of Piazza Venezia, where all of ancient Rome is laid out before you. Late afternoon is best from the terrace of **Castel Sant'Angelo** (p. 72), from which you can see the warm golden colors of the city below.

SEEING ROME FROM BELOW   Rome is a city of layers, and digging down is as easy as tripping over a cobblestone. The **Pantheon** (p. 58), the **Piazza Navona** (p. 60), and the ruins at Largo Argentina, where Julius Caesar was assassinated, are all easy vantage points from which to see how modern Rome has been plunked on top of its ancient past. To dig deeper, you need only check out the **Balbi Crypt** (p. 62) or visit the fascinating church of **St. Clemente** (p. 80), which has three distinct layers to explore. But if you really want to go far below, head out along the Appian Way to explore the massive network of underground **Catacombs** (p. 77).

VIEWING A MASTERPIECE FOR FREE   It's absolutely essential (and practically unavoidable) to see a masterpiece for free in Rome. Michelangelo's statue of Moses sits in the quiet church of **San Pietro in Vincoli** (p. 55). You can find Raphael's *Sibyls and Angels* fresco in the church of **Santa Maria della Pace** (p. 61). Caravaggio's depiction of *St. Francis* contemplating death is free in **Santa Maria della Concezione** (the Capuchin Church; p. 75), and his *Crucifixion of St. Peter* is in **Santa Maria del Popolo** (p. 73). For the best of Bernini's masterpieces, try **Santa Maria della Vittoria** (p. 80) for the *Ecstasy of St. Teresa;* walk behind the Pantheon to the Piazza della Minerva for his beloved elephant carrying an obelisk; or simply stroll through **Piazza Navona** (p. 60) for his *Fountain of the Four Rivers.*

GETTING LOST IN TRASTEVERE   There is perhaps no city in the world where getting lost is more fun. Dive into the confusing labyrinth of streets in the quaint district of **Trastevere** (p. 63) and follow the winding maze until you run into the Tiber River, the Gianicolo Hill, or the busy Viale Trastevere. Peek through any door that is open, browse the tiny shops, and drink cappuccino until you are dizzy. Sit on the fountain steps of a piazza, then cross over to the "other side" of the Viale Trastevere and do it all over again.

SPLURGING ON A FIVE-COURSE MEAL IN A TINY TRATTORIA   It's much easier (and cheaper) than it looks, especially if you go to a friendly place like **Perilli** (p. 35) in Testaccio. Start with a simple fried zucchini flower for your *antipasto,* have the pasta carbonara or the cannelloni for your *primo,* glide through the suckling pork roast or grilled lamb as your *secondo,* and then pause—for just a minute—before diving into a fresh green salad for your *contorno.* Follow that up with a tiramisu or fresh Nemi strawberries on vanilla ice cream before shocking your system with a late-night espresso. With any luck, the house will offer you a *limoncello* to help you digest it all. And you won't have spent much more than €25.

LIGHTING A CANDLE It doesn't matter what your religious beliefs are, lighting a candle in a Roman Catholic Church is a non-denominational must-do. Avoid any churches that offer only electric candles and, instead, head directly for the medieval churches like **Santa Maria** (p. 64) in Trastevere or **Santa Maria della Pace** (p. 61) behind Piazza Navona, where the smell of burning wax is intoxicating. The procedure is simple: You must make a monetary offering (like half a euro) before lighting a candle from those already burning, and it's recommended that you light it with a cause or person in mind before sticking it into a bowl of sand or mesh holder.

DRESSING UP Go to the clothing market at **San Giovanni** (p. 79) and, for next to nothing, pick up a new dress or a jacket that looks great. You will never feel overdressed in Rome; in fact, dressing up is a sign of cultural respect, even for a simple meal out. It is, quite simply, a matter of adhering to the idea of the *bella figura*—putting forth your best image. Women here still believe they can be feminine and flirtatious, and men are still chivalrous. So why not do as the Romans do?

A BRIEF HISTORY OF ROME

"Roma, Caput mundi, tenet orbis fren rotundi (Rome, Head of the World, holds the reins of the round orb)," wrote a medieval poet, summing up the high esteem in which Rome was once held. No other Western city has ever embodied such power, such wealth, such majesty.

As you go from the Forum—a large part of it now buried beneath Mussolini's folly, the Victor Emmanuel II monument—to the church of San Clemente, where archaeologists have unearthed finely wrought pagan sculptures, you'll be reminded of how cultures inevitably cannibalize each other.

The Palatine Hill, one of the seven hills on which Rome was founded, bears evidence of Iron Age huts from the mid–8th century B.C. The Etruscans conquered Rome around 660 B.C. and established it as the capital of their empire. By 250 B.C., Latin tribes finally purged the Etruscans from Italy.

Rome flourished as a republic, the center of a huge, growing empire. In 44 B.C., Julius Caesar was assassinated and his successor, Augustus, transformed Rome from a city of brick to a city of marble and solidified Rome's status as a dictatorship. By 40 B.C., Rome and its armies controlled the entire Mediterranean world. Because of overexpansion and a series of corrupt and incompetent rulers, Rome declined in the 3rd century.

In 395, under Constantine, the empire split and a "new Rome" was established in Constantinople. From 410 to 455, Rome was sacked by barbarian tribes and the population dwindled. In 475, Rome fell, leaving only the primate of the Catholic Church in control. In the following decades, the Pope slowly adopted many of the responsibilities and the prestige once reserved for the Roman emperors. The classical city was literally stripped of its stone and marble to build the Christian city we see today. From the ruins of antiquity came the splendor of Christian Rome in the late Middle Ages and the Renaissance.

The Romans' building acumen is still evident today. The first of many great Roman roads, the Appian Way, still stands, lined with tombs. You can climb to the top of the ancient fortification wall that surrounds the city core at the tiny Wall Museum. The first Roman aqueducts streak across the nearby countryside.

A visit to the port of Ostia, which opened in 380 B.C. to bring supplies into Rome via the Tiber River, is a wonderfully educational day trip.

Today Rome continues to make history. It was the site of the signing of the Treaty of Rome, in 1957, establishing the European Economic Community, and it is where the same member states signed a draft European constitution in 2002. Papal deaths and elections still capture the world's attention, and events in Rome rarely go unnoticed.

LAY OF THE LAND

Rome is divided in many ways. Officially it is cut up into 22 *rioni,* or central districts, which extend out from the historical center. In modern-day Rome, though, most residents describe locations as either "inside the walls" or "outside the walls," referring to the ancient fortification walls that surround the city's core. Zones are more often divided loosely, mostly owing to real-estate definitions such as:

Inside the Walls
- The historical center (from Piazza del Popolo to Piazza Venezia)
- Campo de' Fiori and the Jewish Ghetto (bordering the Tiber River on the east)
- Trastevere (bordering the Tiber River on the west) and adjacent Testaccio (bordering the Tiber River on the east)
- The Colosseo (including Monti and Esquilino)
- The Vatican and Prati
- San Saba and Aventino (the area between Circus Maximus and Testaccio)

Outside the Walls
- Monteverde Vecchio and Monteverde Nuovo
- The Appian Way
- San Giovanni
- San Lorenzo

Historically speaking, Rome is divided into time frames, and every geographic zone has at least a small sampling of the vast array of historical offerings. Highlights from each era include:
- **Ancient Rome** (the Forum, Ara Pacis, Colosseum, Pantheon, Castel Sant'Angelo, Baths of Caracalla and Diocletian, and the walls)
- **Early-Christian and Medieval Rome** (Catacombs, churches of San Giovanni, Santa Maria Maggiore, and San Clemente)
- **Renaissance Rome** (Raphael, St. Peter's Basilica, Sistine Chapel)
- **Baroque Rome** (Caravaggio, Bernini, Trevi Fountain)
- **Modern Rome** (tends to include everything built from the late 1800s to the present)

GETTING THERE & AROUND

Rome has two international airports: **Leonardo da Vinci (FCO)** in Fiumicino, 26km (16 miles) from the city center, and the smaller **GB Pastine (CIA)** in Ciampino, located 15km (9⅓ miles) from the center. Both are run by **Aeroporti di Roma** (☎ 06-65951; www.adr.it). Visitors coming from North America generally arrive in Fiumicino and those arriving via European budget carriers land at Ciampino, though bad weather and strikes have been known to divert major flights to Ciampino.

The Art of Crossing Streets

Traffic lights in Rome are sometimes merely a suggestion. In fact, it's a safe bet to assume that motorists and moped drivers will go through a red light rather than stop, even in the busiest parts of town. Yellow lights are actually more dangerous because drivers often speed up to try to make it through before the light changes to red.

Designated pedestrian crossings mean absolutely nothing unless you are a nun or are with a group of school children in tow (so if you see either of these, cross the street with them). Despite a surprisingly low incidence of car-pedestrian accidents in Rome, there are plenty of close calls.

Some rules:

1. Never run across the street; if you trip over a cobblestone and fall, you will become a human speed bump.
2. Never, ever try to jaywalk unless you have lived here for many years. Instead, cross at the lights and zebra crossings (painted on the street), though keep in mind that these won't necessarily stop traffic.
3. Don't be offended if a car honks at you to get out of the way even if you are crossing at a zebra crossing or at a green light.
4. When you do begin to cross, walk authoritatively and confidently, and, if you can, look the motorists in the eye.
5. If you are crossing a busy traffic square like Piazza Venezia or Piazza della Repubblica, go to the outer perimeter and cross the streets individually that lead into the piazza, even if this means you must double your distance.

The fastest and most economical route into the city from Fiumicino is by the **FR1** (www.trenitalia.it), which runs an hourly, eight-stop, €4 train from the airport terminal to Fara Sabina station from 6:28am to just after midnight; or the faster €8 direct line from Fiumicino to Termini, which makes hourly runs from 7:38am to 10:08pm. Tickets are available from agents or at yellow self-service stands, both found in the airport terminal train station (lower level). There is no direct train service from Ciampino.

Bus service is not as reliable as train travel from Fiumicino, but it is the only public-transportation option to and from Ciampino. **COTRAL** (☎ 800-150008; www.cotralspa.it) and **Terravision** (☎ 06-65958646; www.terravision.it) offer regular routes.

The fastest but least economical choice is **taxi service** from the taxi stand outside the departure doors of both airports. The fare from Fiumicino to the center of Rome runs about €50, depending on supplemental charges for luggage, nights, or weekends. The fare from Ciampino to the center of Rome is around €30, again depending on supplemental charges for luggage, nights, or weekends.

Rome As a Clock

Make your central point of reference the Piazza Venezia, with its giant white monument to Victor Emmanuel II (often called the wedding cake or the typewriter, but officially known as the Vittoriano).

- From here, imagine that the Vittoriano is the center of a clock and Piazza del Popolo to the north is 12 o'clock.
- Trevi Fountain, the Spanish Steps, and Villa Borghese are in a line at 1 o'clock.
- Piazza Barberini and the Via Veneto are at 2 o'clock.
- Termini Station is at 3 o'clock.
- The Colle Oppio and Domus Aurea are at 4 o'clock.
- The Imperial Forums, Palatine Hill, and Colosseum are at 5 o'clock.
- The Roman Forum and the Circus Maximus are at 6 o'clock.
- Testaccio is at 7 o'clock.
- The Jewish Ghetto and Trastevere are at 8 o'clock.
- The Gianicolo is at 9 o'clock.
- Campo de' Fiori is at 10 o'clock.
- The Pantheon, Piazza Navona, and Vatican City are at 11 o'clock.

The long, straight street that extends north from the Vittoriano is the Via del Corso, which slices through the historical center, ending at Piazza del Popolo and the far gate into the city. This is a noisy, smog-infested thoroughfare that you don't ever really need to walk down, but you should always know where you are in relation to it. To get your bearings, you can always see the Vittoriano from Via del Corso.

WALKING

Getting around the center of Rome is best done on foot. There is so much to see en route to the various museums and antiquities. Never mind that the streets wind around each other and street names are hard to find—it's actually a very easy city to navigate.

PUBLIC TRANSPORTATION

Public transportation within the city of Rome is comprehensive, though not very reliable if you are in a hurry. Efforts to enforce a timetable for buses in particular have proven impossible because of heavy and unpredictable traffic. In general, buses in the city center should run at 15-minute intervals, but often several buses from the same line are backed up at various stops and the wait can be up to 45 minutes for others.

Buses & Trams

Bus and tram transportation is operated by **ATAC** (☎ 800-431784; www.atac. roma.it), which has a comprehensive multilingual website to help you decipher the routes. Each bus or tram stop has an ATAC board listing relevant bus lines. Tickets are available at green self-service kiosks at Termini, Largo Argentina, and Piazza San Silvestro; they are also sold by news agents displaying the ATAC sign, as well as at all tobacco shops with a brown-and-white T sign. You can also buy tickets

via your mobile phone if you have GSM capability—send a text message to 48299 with the message BIT; the reply you'll receive serves as your ticket. The charges will show up on your phone bill. You cannot buy tickets on the bus or tram.

Four types of tickets are available:

* **BIT** (Biglietto Integrato a Tempo) €1 for multiple rides on any tram or bus and a one-way route on the underground metro system within a 75-minute time frame.
* **BIG** (Biglietto Integrato Giornaliero) €4 for multiple rides on all buses, trams, and the underground metro system for 24 hours.
* **BTI** (Giglietto Turistico Integrato) ★★★ €11 for all bus, tram, and metro lines, including regional trains to Ostia, for 3 days.
* **CIS** (Carta Integrate Settimanale) €16 for all bus, tram, and metro lines, including regional trains to Ostia, for 7 days.

Monthly passes are also available for €30. Children under 10 or under .9m (3 ft.) tall travel free on all transportation networks. You must validate your ticket in the yellow machines on each bus or tram once you get on. Tickets are rarely checked, though if you are caught without one, you will be fined €51 on the spot. Validate your ticket for the underground system at turnstiles leading down to the trains.

Touring Rome

An excursion accompanied by a Roman is a viable option, but you've got to be a discerning customer when it comes to choosing what's right for you. Rome has an overabundance of umbrella-wielding tour guides who regurgitate snippets from guidebooks. To avoid a superficial tour, rent an audioguide from the specific site you are interested in seeing.

It's a much better idea to look for guides who will personalize your visit based on your interests and knowledge of art, religion, or history, or those who offer niche services like culinary or photo journeys. One of the best enterprises in Rome is **As The Romans Do** ★★★ (no phone; www.astheromansdo.com), the brainchild of historian and author Dr. Alan Epstein, who also wrote a wonderful companion book by the same title; it's a must read for anyone curious about local culture. Alan's wife, Diane Epstein, directs the culinary and photography adventures. They have lived in the city for a decade, and have a knack for sprinkling interesting trivia into their excursions. Their private explorations are very comprehensive, worthy of the higher fees, and the most personalized of any listing here.

Another of the better guide companies is **Context Rome** ★★ (☎ 06-4820911; www.scalareale.com), run by a group of architects and art historians who take small groups through the local museums. These tours are extremely focused but less personalized than those led by As The Romans Do, though they will deviate from the agenda upon request. If you are especially interested in architecture, these folks will not disappoint.

Through Eternity ★★ (☎ 06-7009336; www.througheternity.com) is an entirely different (read: nonstandard) type of tour company—but worth your consideration. It is also staffed by a group of art historians and architects (plus the added bonus of theater experts), and offers niche tours like Angels and Demons, inspired by Dan Brown's best-selling novel, and a wonderful Feast of Bacchus wine tasting and culinary extravaganza. Similar to the folks at Through Eternity, **Enjoy Rome** (☎ 06-4451843; info@enjoyrome.com; see p. 33), offers niche tours with an emphasis on night walks.

Personal excursion prices vary greatly depending on the number of people in the group and the length of time the guide spends with you. Most are around €300 to €500 for a 4-hour tour, split by the number of people, which generally ranges from 2 to 10 in most cases, meaning that these tours can be extremely economical.

Both Context Rome and Through Eternity also offer pick-up tours of 2 to 3 hours that you can take on an ad hoc basis for about €12.

At just €7.75, Rome's **Archeobus** (Piazza Venezia; ☎ 06-46954695; www.atac.roma.it; daily 9am–8pm) is the most economical way to reach the significant sights outside the city walls. You can get on at any of the stops listed below, but the best place to start is at the beginning, on Piazza Venezia near the ticket kiosk. Stops include the Bocca della Verità (p. 63), Baths of Caracalla (p. 79), Porta S. Sebastiano and the Wall Museum (p. 76), the base of the Appia Antica (p. 76), the Catacombs (p. 77), and tombs along the Appia Antica (p. 77).

Metro

Rome has two underground metro lines (see the map on p. 21), **Red line A** and **Blue line B,** which are somewhat limited and constantly impeded from expansion by the multitude of protected ruins under the city. The metro system in Rome is useful for straight shots across town, and it is generally efficient, but not as encompassing as the bus network. The cars on the red line are old and not air-conditioned. In the summer, the red line in particular is best avoided because of stifling heat and overcrowding. Pickpockets are also common, but less so than they used to be.

River Boat

An innovative addition to the public-transportation scene is the **Battelli di Roma** (☎ 06-6789361; www.battellidiroma.it), or Tiber Taxi, as most residents call the river boats that glide through the muddy waters of the Tiber river. A 1-hour, multistop commuter trip is just €1 from Tiber Island down to the northern part of Rome at Ponte Duca d'Aosta, with hourly stops at each docking point (which vary depending on the season and water levels of the river). There isn't much to see past the Castel Sant'Angelo stop. There are also seasonal options for guided tours on the river boats, starting with a 1-hour guided tour for €10 that departs from Ponte Sant'Angelo at 10, 11:30am, 3:30, and 5pm; or a 2½-hour dinner boat tour for €43, which departs from Ponte Sant'Angelo at 8pm (reservations required).

Top-Down Buses

You can't miss the bright red convertible **110 Open** (Piazza dei Cinquecento Termini Station; ☎ 06-46952252; www.trambus.com; €13; 9am–10pm) tour buses that barrel through the city. Get on or off at any of the stops (Termini, Quirinale, Colosseo, Bocca della Verità, Piazza Venezia, Piazza Navona, Vatican City, Piazza Cavour, Ara Pacis, Piazza Navona, Fontana di Trevi, or Via Veneto).

The Vatican and the city bus company also offer a joint bus tour called **Christian Rome** (Piazza dei Cinquecento, Termini Station; €15; 9am–10pm), which stops at St. Peter's Basilica, Colosseo, Santa Maria Maggiore, San Giovanni in Laterano, St. Pietro in Vincoli, San Clemente, and Santa Maria in Aracoeli. These tours are focused on Rome's Christian heritage and are generally filled with religious pilgrims.

These stop-and-go bus tours come with an audioguide and can be useful if you are in a hurry to get around town or are otherwise unable to navigate the cobblestone streets on foot. The drawback of bus tours is that ideally Rome should be discovered by ambling through its streets and these buses don't allow any real self-guided exploration.

A Definition of SPQR

One set of initials that you cannot avoid while visiting Rome is SPQR, emblazoned on manhole covers, water fountains, and building facades. It means "Senatus Populus Que Romanus," or "The Senate and the People of Rome." It was unveiled 24 centuries ago, making it the oldest acronym still in use. It's on Trajan's Column and is still found on public-works projects.

Taxis

Licensed taxis in Rome are white and always have a meter. They are difficult to hail from the street and almost impossible to find around midnight, when Italians are finishing up the evening meal or moving from restaurant to discothèque. Taxi stands are well indicated, but not always staffed with taxis. The base fare during the day should be €2.35 (€4.90 after 10pm). The most you should be charged for luggage is €1.05 per piece.

DRIVING

Driving in Rome is not as hard as it looks, but it's also not necessary. Getting around the city is easy on foot, and the public transportation system for both local and regional travel is comprehensive. An additional consideration is a recent rash of vehicle arsons, which have made it necessary to either add fire protection to your car-rental policy or park in a secure garage, which costs from €10 to €25 a day. A car is, of course, useful for day trips and jaunts to the seaside or neighboring towns.

If you drive in Rome, don't try to do so as you would in other cities. The best analogy is perhaps to think of Roman cars as grains of sand tumbling through the small funnel of an hourglass. What this means is that, in general, you should do as other Roman drivers do; you're actually more likely to have an accident if you try to follow conventional driving rules.

That said, Italian police will stop you for talking on a cellphone while driving, for speeding, or for blowing a red light—though traffic cops are a rare breed in the city center. Much of the city is also closed to all but resident traffic and monitored by electronic cameras that pick up signals from residents' permits. Your rental car won't have one of these, and you risk getting a ticket if you drive into a zone that is closed.

REGIONAL TRANSPORTATION

Regional buses to neighboring towns like Tivoli (p. 85), Ostia (p. 86), and Viterbo (p. 85) are run by **CoTral** (☎ 800-150008; www.cotralspa.it). CoTral does not have a presence at Termini, so you generally have to travel by metro to an outlying station (Tiburtina and Anagnina are the largest) to get on your bus. Ticket agents are always near the CoTral terminus stations. Bus tickets to Ostia, Viterbo, or Tivoli are under €5.

Train travel in and out of Rome is very easy. For trains to other European countries, check schedules at www.trenitalia.com; for regional trains, check www.ferroviedellostato.it. You can buy tickets online and pick them up at self-service kiosks at any of Rome's train stations. An economy ticket from Rome to Naples is around €22, to Florence around €14, and to Venice €45.

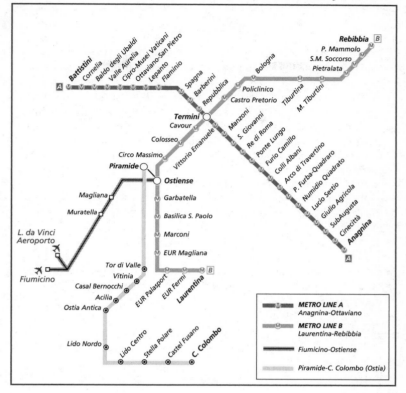

ACCOMMODATIONS, BOTH STANDARD & NOT

Though the bulk of my lodging recommendations are regular hotels, I'll start with the untraditional choices that transform tourists into travelers. In Rome, these unusual choices have two great virtues: They are cheaper than standard facilities and, in almost all cases, more memorable. When you make a decision to stay in a convent or monastery, a rental apartment, or a B&B found through an *affittacamere* (rooms for rent) organization, you're gaining a perspective on the city that most visitors lack.

MONASTERIES & CONVENTS

Staying in a convent or a monastery can be more than a religious experience; it is also a great bargain. But remember, these are religious houses, which means that the decor is most often stark and simple, and the rules are extensive. Cohabiting is almost always frowned upon (though marriage licenses are rarely required), and unruly behavior is not tolerated. Plus there is usually a curfew. Most rooms in convents and monasteries do not have private bathrooms, but ask when making your reservation in case some are available. Prices are per person unless otherwise noted.

Credit Cards, Banks & Change

Many services in Rome do not accept credit cards. Cash is preferred—though counterfeiting in Italy is a big business: Italians were the first to counterfeit the euro currency, even before it was issued. Museums generally do not take credit cards, except in the bookshops; taxis do have the capability in some cases, but always ask first. Most drivers keep their credit card machines in the trunk, so don't be alarmed if the driver suddenly stops to get something out of the back. Most restaurants will now take cards, but they almost always prefer cash. There are also stores in the center of Rome that will give a discount for cash (or an extra charge for credit depending on how you look at it).

Bank machines, called Bancomat, are plentiful in the center, though on Monday mornings they are usually empty because the employees who fill the machines have Sundays off. In general, there seems to be a shortage of change in Rome. It's often hard to break big bills such as a €50 note, and in some not-so-rare cases, the clerks will forfeit the sale before giving up all their precious change. If you pay for a small item with a big note, you will almost always get a *"Madonna!"* cry out of the cashier. If the clerk asks for *spici,* he wants exact or small change, even though in some cases you end up getting all your change in small currency.

While the religious lodgings that follow are for the most part rather similar in price, quality, and amenities, what distinguishes each of them is location—the factor you'll most want to consider.

Near the Vatican

Staying this close to Vatican City, at **Casa D'Accoglienza S. Spirito, Franciscan sisters** ★★ (Borgo S. Spirito, 41; ☎ 06-6861076; ssmsanpietro@libero.it), may actually make you convert. The rooms are spartan, but you'll hear the bells of St. Peter's Basilica. It's €40 for a double, €35 for a triple or quadruple, €12 children under 12, €25 students under 25. Curfew is at 11pm in summer, 10pm in winter.

Just across the street from the entrance to the Vatican Museums, **Suore Sacra Famiglia** (Viale Vaticano, 92; ☎ 06-39091411) is perfect for exploring this area, though there is a definite religious undertone to this place. Rooms are larger than most of the others listed here. Price per room (not per person): €30 single, €52 double, €70 triple, €83 quadruple. No breakfast, and curfew is at midnight.

In Gianicolo

Much more a hotel than a convent in feel, **Suore Dorotee** (Via del Gianicolo, 4A; ☎ 06-68803349; casafatima@libero.it) offers great views from the top of the Janiculum Hill, tucked in a green area perfect for those who want to appreciate Rome without the noise. It's €65 per person for full-board double, €60 half-board. A half-board single is €62, €72 for full-board single. All rooms have private baths. Curfew is at 11pm.

Near the Spanish Steps

You couldn't ask for a better spot than **Le Suore di Lourdes** (Via Sistina, 113; ☎ 06-4745324), a convent tucked among the hotels near the Spanish Steps. The drawback is the price, which is about the same as that for a small-hotel room, plus Le Suore de Lourde's rooms are convent-conservative and the curfew is among the earliest of those listed here. It's €70 for a single room without bathroom; €35 per person for a double room. Breakfast is included. Curfew is at 10:30pm.

In Campo de' Fiori

Casa Di Santa Brigida (Piazza Farnese, 96; ☎ 06-68892596; brigida@mclink.it) is the least religious of the convents listed here and the rooms are tastefully decorated with antiques and even carpet on the upper floors. The price is more, but the lack of curfew may just make this worth it. It's €100 for a single, €180 for a double.

Near Piazza Venezia

You cannot beat the price for such a centrally located bed in Rome, but you may not get into **Casa Il Rosario** (Via S. Agata dei Goti, 10; ☎ 06-6792346; irodopre@tin.it). First choice goes to pilgrims, then families and unmarried couples are scrutinized. A single with bathroom is €46, €38 for a single without bathroom. A double is €80. Single handicap-accessible rooms are available. Breakfast is included; curfew is at 11pm.

Near Piazza Navona

You definitely get what you pay for at **Fraterna Domus** (Via del Monte Brianza, 62; ☎ 06-68802727; domusrm@tin.it), but the rooms are miniscule (you may actually have to keep your luggage closed in order to navigate around the slim double beds). The bathrooms are even smaller, and the shower is a spout hanging on the wall (no stall, so the entire bathroom gets soaked the minute the water is

---

Deal Alert: Going with a Package

Rome is one of the top destinations in the world for travel packages, which bundle airfare, hotel, and sometimes car rental at one reasonable price. The cheapest of these packages generally offer somewhat traditional, somewhat dull hotels, but there's no denying the savings: In some cases, a vacation to Italy can cost as little as $100 a day or less for airfare (not including taxes) and hotel.

The following companies are particularly recommended for travelers to Rome (all have offered weeklong, off-season deals with airfares from the U.S. and accommodations for $600 per person): **Go-Today** (☎ 800/227-3235; www.gotoday.com), **Virgin Vacations** (☎ 888/937-8474; www.virgin-vacations.com), **Gate 1 Travel** (☎ 800/682-3333; www.gate1travel.com), and **Europe ASAP** (☎ 415/750-5499; www.europeasap.com). See p. 578 for more on travel packages.

Rome Accommodations & Dining

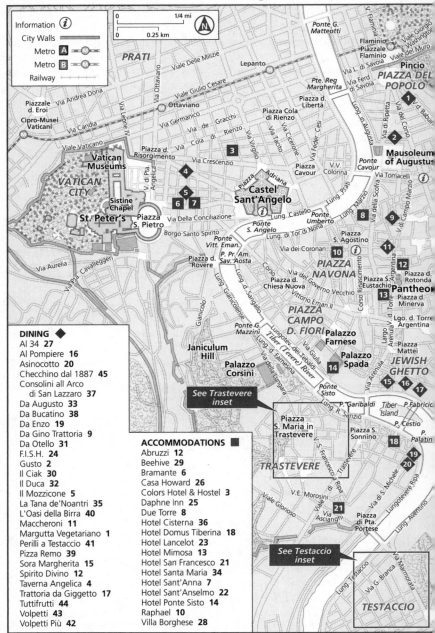

Legend:
Information ⓘ
City Walls ▬▬▬
Metro Ⓐ ═Ⓜ═
Metro Ⓑ ═Ⓜ═
Railway ┼─┼─┼─┼

0 — 1/4 mi
0 — 0.25 km
N

PRATI

Ponte G. Matteotti

Flaminio Piazzale Flaminio
Lepanto
Pincio
PIAZZA DEL POPOLO

Pte. Reg Margherita
Piazza d. Libertà

Piazzale d. Eroi
Via Andrea Doria
Ottaviano

Cipro-Musei Vaticani
Via Candia

Via Germanico
Via de Gracchi
Piazza Cola di Rienzo

Piazza d. Risorgimento
3
Piazza Cavour
V.V. Colonna
Ponte Cavour

Mausoleum of Augustus ⓘ
Via Tomacelli

Vatican Museums
4

VATICAN CITY
5
Adriana
Castel Sant'Angelo
ⓘ

Sistine Chapel
6 **7**
Via Della Conciliazione

St. Peter's Piazza S. Pietro
Lung. Castello
Ponte Umberto
8
9
Piazza S. Agostino

Borgo Santo Spirito
Ponte S. Angelo
Lung. di Tor di Nona

Ponte Vitt. Eman.
Via dei Coronari
10 ⓘ
11

Piazza d. Rovere
P. Pr. Am. Sav. Aosta
PIAZZA NAVONA
Piazza S. Eustachio
12
Piazza d. Rotonda
Pantheon

Via Aurelia
Piazza d. Chiesa Nuova
Vittorio Eman. II
13
Piazza d. Minerva

Janiculum Hill
Ponte G. Mazzini
PIAZZA CAMPO D. FIORI
Lgo. d. Torre Argentina
Piazza Mattei

Palazzo Corsini
Palazzo Farnese
Palazzo Spada
14
JEWISH GHETTO
15 **16** **17**

See Trastevere inset

Ponte Sisto
P. Garibaldi
Tiber Island
P. Fabricio
P. Cestio
P. Palatin

Piazza S. Maria in Trastevere
Piazza S. Sonnino
18
19
20

TRASTEVERE
V.E. Morosini
21
Piazza di Pta. Portese

See Testaccio inset

TESTACCIO

DINING ◆

Al 34 **27**
Al Pompiere **16**
Asinocotto **20**
Checchino dal 1887 **45**
Consoli all Arco
  di San Lazzaro **37**
Da Augusto **33**
Da Bucatino **38**
Da Enzo **19**
Da Gino Trattoria **9**
Da Otello **31**
F.I.S.H. **24**
Gusto **2**
Il Ciak **30**
Il Duca **32**
Il Mozzicone **5**
La Tana de'Noantri **35**
L'Oasi della Birra **40**
Maccheroni **11**
Margutta Vegetariano **1**
Perilli a Testaccio **41**
Pizza Remo **39**
Sora Margherita **15**
Spirito Divino **12**
Taverna Angelica **4**
Trattoria da Giggetto **17**
Tuttifrutti **44**
Volpetti **43**
Volpetti Più **42**

ACCOMMODATIONS ■

Abruzzi **12**
Beehive **29**
Bramante **6**
Casa Howard **26**
Colors Hotel & Hostel **3**
Daphne Inn **25**
Due Torre **8**
Hotel Cisterna **36**
Hotel Domus Tiberina **18**
Hotel Lancelot **23**
Hotel Mimosa **13**
Hotel San Francesco **21**
Hotel Santa Maria **34**
Hotel Sant'Anna **7**
Hotel Sant'Anselmo **22**
Hotel Ponte Sisto **14**
Raphael **10**
Villa Borghese **28**

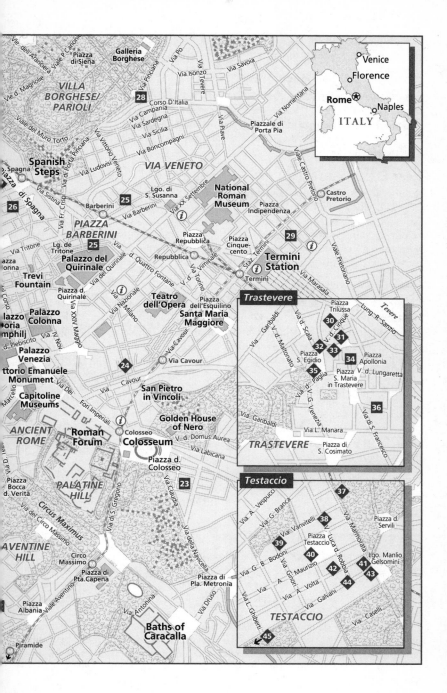

turned on). It's €48 for a single, €78 for a double. All rooms have private bathrooms, and breakfast is included (additional meals on request). Curfew is at 11pm.

Near Santa Maria Maggiore

Casa Unione Misterium Christi (Via Merulana, 174; ☎ 06-70492421) is definitely off the beaten track, close to the patriarchal church of Santa Maria Maggiore, and not far from Termini train station. The rooms (€40 per person, including breakfast) are clean and comfortable, and the service is exceptional. Curfew is at 11pm.

Near Circus Maximus

Staying at the **Villa Rosa, Dominican Sisters** (Via Terme Deciane, 5; ☎ 06-5717091; villarosa2000@libero.it) is much more like communal living with the Dominican sisters than independent accommodations. There is a real sense of belonging and, for this reason, religious pilgrims, especially those traveling alone, flock to this lovely convent. The location is serene atop the Aventine Hill. It's €50 for a single, €85 for a double, including breakfast.

Near the Colosseum

Run by Portuguese- and Spanish-speaking nuns from the Ukraine, **Santa Sofia** (Piazza Madonna dei Monti, 3; ☎ 06-485778; santasofia@tiscalinet.it) is definitely a multicultural stop. The rooms (€42 single, €67 double, including breakfast) are very tidy and the nuns keep their distance, giving you much more privacy than many of the other convents. The location is just a few blocks from the Colosseum in an area that is brimming with ethnic restaurants and Italian favorites. Curfew is at midnight.

In Trastevere

Casa Santa Francesca Romana (Via dei Vascellari, 61; ☎ 06-5812125; www.sfromana.it) is undergoing a gradual transition from convent to hotel, so while it does neither perfectly, it is a great way to have the best of both worlds. The rooms (€105 double, €135 triple) are barren, but they do have air-conditioning. The location is superb, right in the hub of some of the best restaurants in Trastevere, and the curfew is generous (2am) though, if you miss it, don't expect anyone to answer the door to let you in.

SELF-CATERING APARTMENTS

In the Jubilee Year of 2000, when Rome was inundated with pilgrims, many owners cut up their larger Roman apartments into small, self-catering flats for rental to tourists. As a result, the city now has an over-abundance of these quaint little one- and two-bedroom apartments all over town—and they have become real values for budget-minded travelers.

They also can be charming places to stay, though the decor and tone vary by neighborhood. A tiny apartment in Trastevere, for example, will generally have original wood-beam ceilings, terra-cotta floor tiles, and tasteful antique furnishings. Air-conditioners, TVs, and telephones are rare in the rentals of this neighborhood, but you won't lack for entertainment: In almost every case, your shuttered windows will open out into the lively streets.

Self-catering apartments near the Vatican are designed for religious types, so expect a somewhat plainer decor with a crucifix on the wall and a Bible on the table. It's a newer neighborhood—white marble will usually replace the quaint terra cotta found in Trastevere and the historical center. On the plus side, though, these apartments are generally larger (and you may even score air-conditioning). In the neighborhoods between these two, expect a blend of elements. All self-catering apartments have weekly linen service, kitchens, bathrooms, and sleeping quarters, and the best have balconies and extras like airport pickup and drop-off.

The only real way to book an apartment for the first time is through an agency, which generally charges a small commission, included in the prices listed. On future visits you can always call the landlord directly, but even then some will insist you use an agency as a go-between.

The best way to search the listings is via the Internet so that you can see photos. **Rome Accom** (www.rome-accom.com) has a vast selection of good apartments in the center of Rome, many of which start as low as €100 a night. The staff will arrange for airport pickup and drop-off as well. This agency is selective about what properties it lists and will even act as an intermediary between you and the landlord once you are in Rome.

Accommodations Index

€   **Rooms €50 or less a night**

The Beehive (Train Station, p. 30)

Papa Germano (Train Station, p. 32)

Also, see "Monasteries & Convents," above

€€   **Rooms €51 to €100 a night**

Colors Hotel & Hostel (Center, p. 33)

Daphne Inn ✮✮✮ (Center, p. 28)

Hotel Domus Tiberina (Trastevere, p. 31)

Hotel Mimosa ✮✮✮ (Center, p. 28)

€€€   **Rooms €101 to €150 a night**

Albergo del Sole (Center, p. 29)

Casa Howard ✮✮ (Center, p. 29)

Hotel Lancelot ✮✮ (Colosseum, p. 34)

Hotel San Francesco ✮✮ (Trastevere, p. 31)

€€€€   **Rooms more than €150 a night**

Abruzzi (Center, p. 29)

Bramante (Vatican, p. 33)

Due Torri (Center, p. 30)

Hotel Aventino (Aventine Hill, p. 32)

Hotel Cisterna (Trastevere, p. 31)

Hotel Ponte Sisto (Center, p. 30)

Hotel Santa Maria ✮✮✮ (Trastevere, p. 31)

Hotel Sant'Anna (Vatican, p. 33)

Hotel Sant'Anselmo (Aventine Hill, p. 32)

Raphael (Center, p. 30)

Villa Borghese (Center, p. 29)

Domus Connect (www.domusconnect.com) has one of the largest selections of apartment listings, but it isn't as discerning as Rome Accom and thus should be used only as a backup. This agency also lists some B&B options and small hotels.

Bed & Breakfast Association of Rome (www.b-b.rm.it) handles both self-catering apartments and rooms for rent within private apartments, some of which charge as little as €30. Pauline Frommer used this service on her last visit to Rome and reports that "our apartment was a charmer, right in the old Jewish Ghetto area on a street where tourists rarely ventured. From our balcony in the evenings, we'd look down on our neighbors feasting in the garden below, and it became a nightly ritual for them to toast us after we toasted them and wished them a good evening. We had two large rooms and a kitchen for less than €150 a night, perfect for my husband and our two small daughters."

Pauline's experience points up the hidden value of these types of accommodations: Not only will you spend less, but you'll also be much more likely to meet actual Romans and see what the life of the city is like.

HOTELS IN THE HISTORICAL CENTER

Most visitors attempt to stay in this area for the simple fact that it puts them within walking distance of most of the important sights of Rome. It is not, however, always the best area for affordable, authentic food, so if you travel on your stomach (as Napoleon said that his army did), you may want to choose Trastevere or one of the more residential neighborhoods for your stay.

€€   At first glance, the **Hotel Mimosa** ★★★ (Via di Santa Chiara, 61; ☎ 06-68801753; www.hotelmimosa.net) may make you wonder how it can charge so little for such a great location. Doubles without bathroom start at €65, €85 with bathroom. The mystery continues: The rooms are spacious by Rome standards, cleaner than a church, and nicely appointed, albeit hardly fancy. This is a hotel for those who need a place to sleep, *basta,* without the bells and whistles and velvet curtains. The breakfast is hearty (think scrambled eggs rather than standard European continental) and the rooms are all air-conditioned. Because this hotel was converted from an army barracks, the walls between some of the 12 rooms are thin, but visitors keep coming back and noise usually isn't a problem.

€€–€€€€   The **Daphne Inn** ★★ (Via degli Avignonesi, 20, and Via di San Basilio, 55; ☎ 06-47823529; www.daphne-rome.com) provides an experience that is something like staying with friends, or at least friends of friends. When you arrive, the owners sit down on the worn leather sofa in the makeshift lobby and explain the city layout; they offer suggestions and exude a sense of hospitality that is unheard of in most hotels. They offer a wide range of room choices with shared bathrooms or private bathrooms not in the room (€80–€120), or with in-room bathrooms (€110–€180). All the rooms are clean and feature new mattresses on the beds, and there's free Wi-Fi access and a lending library on-site. ***One caution:*** Staying here is not for those who relish their privacy. There is a sense that you are part of the family and an expectation that you'll sit and talk about your day when you arrive home each evening (which can make it a superb spot for those traveling alone).

Two Splurges with Amazing Views

€€€€   Of all the views you might wish to enjoy from your hotel room, the ancient Pantheon has got to top the list. You can have this view at the **Abruzzi** (Piazza della Rotonda, 69; ☎ 06-679-2021; www.hotel abruzzi.it) for €160 a night for a comfortable double room. The view is worth the price alone—every room faces the ancient ruin, but there are other reasons to stay here. The rooms are bigger than many others in Rome, especially in the historical center. And the location, not just the view, is optimum for exploring the city center. It's only 15 minutes to the Vatican, the Spanish Steps, and the Colosseum.

€€€€   The location among the grand hotels of this area makes the **Villa Borghese** (Via Pinciana, 31; ☎ 06-85300919; www.hotelvillaborghese.it) another good choice and a surprisingly fair deal at €160 a night for a double (you'll probably pay twice that at nearby hotels). Rooms overlook the lush greenery of the Villa Borghese, and as the former home of Italian author Alberto Moravia, this hotel has a sense of history. The rooms are dark and cozy and strategically arranged to capture the natural light.

€€€   The **Albergo del Sole** (Via del Biscione, 76; ☎ 06-688-06873; www.sole albiscione.it) is a fine choice when the weather is mild; doubles here start at a mighty reasonable €110. But because it faces the noisy Campo de' Fiori, the deal turns sour when the weather is hot and you're forced to keep your windows open. You can pay €40 more and move up to the fifth-floor doubles, which are air-conditioned and sound-proofed, but then it isn't so great a deal. All in all, the rooms are very comfortable with ample space by Roman hotel standards, but the real perk is the top-floor terrace, where you can gaze out above the rooftops over a glass of wine after a day of touring.

€€€€   If you're looking for a bit of style, the ultrafunky **Casa Howard** ★★, (Via Capo le Case, 18, or Via Sistina, 149; ☎ 06-69924555; www.casahoward.com) is a welcome respite from the tiny, bland budget hotels that seem to dominate the center of Rome. The two locations of the Casa Howard—both true guesthouses in the sense that they are homes within a larger structure—have real flair, each room decorated with a different theme. At the Capo le Case address, my favorite is the Chinese room, complete with Shanghai Tang silk curtains; at the Via Sistina locale, there's the stark black-and-white Zebra room with its own balcony. All rooms have satellite TV and high wood-beam ceilings. Another nice touch is the Turkish *hammams* (steam baths) available for guests' use. The cheapest rooms start at €150 and have a private bathroom (but it's down the hall from the bedroom); those with bathrooms in the room go for €20 to €50 more.

€€€€   If you're willing to sacrifice space for location, and if you're looking for luxury at a much lower price than you'd pay for similar rooms on the Via Veneto, the **Due Torri** (Vicolo del Leonetto, 23–25; ☎ 06-68806956; www.hotelduetorri roma.com) is a good bet. Doubles, which start at €172, are very tiny but well appointed with very comfortable beds. And the showers are quite strong, though the bathrooms are small. When you book, request a room with a balcony. They also offer four apartments with kitchenettes, perfect for people traveling with children or a large group.

€€€€   The **Hotel Ponte Sisto** (Via dei Pettinari, 64; ☎ 06-686310; www.hotel pontesisto.it) has undergone a major renovation that has made its price, starting at €180 for a double, worth the splurge. The location near the bridge from Campo de' Fiori to Trastevere, makes it an easy launching pad for exploring the Vatican and the historical center. The rooms are elegant, and the bathrooms have been upgraded to luxury status.

€€€€   Tucked behind Piazza Navona, **Raphael** (Largo Febo, 2; ☎ 06-682831; www.raphaelhotelrome.com) is a true oasis with an ivy-covered facade. Starting at €250 a night for a double, this is the lowest priced of Rome's luxury hotels. The rooms are high-tech and well suited for business travel, but the location is what makes this hotel worth the price. The roof terrace overlooks many of the city's major churches.

HOTELS NEAR THE TRAIN STATION

You stay in this area because it is cheap. Period. As in most European cities, the area around the train station is not where you want to dine or really hang out. Still, if you're looking for bargains, you'll find them at either of the places I recommend below, or at the dozens of little hotels that line the streets here (it's possible to simply go door to door and bargain during slow periods).

€-€€   Part hostel, part hotel, **The Beehive** ★★★ (Via Marghera, 8, near Termini; ☎ 06-44704553) falls squarely in the realm of the odd but wonderful (and the price is perfect). The American owners say they conceived of this lodging–cum–art show as a "kooky dream," and they've achieved it. Rooms are decorated with art pieces and flea-market treasures and are available for a variety of budgets: €24 for a bed in the dorm, €70 to €84 for a double with shared bathroom; it's €30 to €36 per bed in a double, triple, or four-person apartment with shared bathroom. Apartments sleeping between 8 and 10 people start at €180 a night. Cash only and highly recommended.

€-€€   The warmth and gracious welcome that Gino, of **Papa Germano** (Via Calatimi, 14a, 4 blocks west of the Stazione Termini; ☎ 06-486919; www.hotel papagermano.com), extends to guests is legendary in budget-travel circles. He's simply one of the nicest guys in Rome, always ready to help out a lost or confused traveler, and his modest guesthouse is spotless. It's also inexpensive, especially for those willing to share bathroomless rooms with a couple of others, dorm-style (€23 in low season, €30 in high season). Doubles with their own bathroom and satellite TV are also available for those who require a tad more privacy (expect to pay €75–€105). Call well in advance—this is a very popular hotel.

HOTELS IN TRASTEVERE

Akin to New York's Greenwich Village in its festive atmosphere, abundant street life, and superb restaurants, Trastevere is one of my favorite neighborhoods and highly recommended. The downsides to a stay here involve the nighttime noise, which can be problematic (especially if you're staying above a popular bar or restaurant), and the neighborhood's considerable distance from the historical center.

€€   It's amazing to find a boutique hotel room in the heart of popular Trastevere for around €90, but **Hotel Domus Tiberina** (Via in Piscinula, 37; ☎ 06-5803033; www.domustiberina.it) doesn't come without some sacrifices. It used to be rented by the *New York Times* correspondents, until the owners realized what a tourism gold mine they were sitting on. Now, as a 10-room hotel, it offers a prime location in the heart of Trastevere, just 5 minutes from the Jewish Ghetto. But the rooms are very, very small and the service is marginal.

€€€   An option that takes you to the very edge of Trastevere, closer to the Porta Portese Gate than the church of Santa Maria, is the **Hotel San Francesco** ★★ (Via Jacopa de'Settesoli, 7; ☎ 06-58300051; fax 06-58333413; www.hotelsan francesco.net), which is new to the area and will soon likely be a favorite for return visitors. The doubles, which start at €110, are small, even by local hotel standards, but the bathrooms are downright palatial. The San Francesco oozes character; one of its best features is a top-floor garden that overlooks the other terra-cotta rooftops and church bell towers of this district.

€€€–€€€€   The best accommodations in the heart of Trastevere are found at the picturesque **Hotel Santa Maria** ★★★ (Vicolo del Piede, 2; ☎ 06-5894626; www.htlsantamaria.com). Staying here is a little like living in Trastevere; you feel very much part of the local scene, thanks in part to the terrific staff. The rooms are not large, but they don't feel cramped, either. And the showers have excellent water pressure, which is hard to find in the older parts of Rome. There is a great courtyard where you can unwind with a glass of wine before hitting the restaurant circuit, and the hotel coffee bar has free Internet access. At €135 to €155, this is a bargain in Trastevere.

€€€   Finally, the **Hotel Cisterna** (Via della Cisterna, 7–9; ☎ 06-5817212) has been a standby for many travelers returning to Rome. Rooms are modestly furnished with original beamed ceilings and low doors; room 57 is the largest and room 40 has a terrace. There is a small garden with a fountain for visitors, but the area, close to the busy Viale Trastevere, is often noisy and dusty. While the hotel could use a few refurbishments, and it is not as nice as others in this list, it's still a decent value at €140 a night.

HOTELS IN AVENTINE HILL

If you are actually hoping to sleep while staying in central Rome, there is perhaps no better neighborhood than the Aventine Hill, just minutes from the Roman Forum and Colosseum.

Seasons & Agencies

As you may have noted from the above discussion, Roman hotel rooms are noto-riously small and often extremely expensive. Rates change and the low season seems to get shorter each year. Normally Easter kicks off the high season, which runs through October, though lately an extension of the high season to Christmas has kept prices inflated from April through December.

Rome-based **www.venere.com** is a reliable **online booking agency** that spe-cializes in non-chain hotels across the country and can check vacancies and spe-cial deals on the spot. The city's **Hotel Information Center,** which operates info points at both airports, also has an online service for checking availability and prices: **www.hotelreservation.it.** They access the same network as the agents at the airport desks, and availability and special deals are up-to-the-minute.

€€€€   A pair of adjacent hotels under the same moniker offer very good value for the rooms: **Hotel Sant'Anselmo** (Piazza S. Anselmo, 2; ☎ 06-5745174) and its annex, **Hotel Aventino** (Via S. Domenico, 10; ☎ 06-5783214; www.aventino hotels.com). The neighborhood is an upscale district where the residents demand quiet and decorum, which makes it a perfectly tranquil oasis in the center of the city. Here you are just minutes from the great restaurants of Testaccio and across the river from the nightlife of Trastevere. The rooms are elegant with replicated period decorations that successfully give it an aristocratic touch. There are very expensive rooms in the main hotel Sant'Anselmo (doubles from €160), where celebrities and diplomats stay, but everyone comes together in the morning for breakfast in the garden. Rooms at the Aventino start at €114.

A HOTEL NEAR THE COLOSSEUM

Staying near the Colosseum is a favorite of large tour groups, and, as a result, almost everything in this neighborhood has been diluted—from the fare at the local restaurants to the character of the area, which seems to be dwindling at an alarming speed. Still, waking up with a view of the Flavian Amphitheater is a thrill.

€€€-€€€€   **Hotel Lancelot** ★★ (Via Capo d'Africa, 47; ☎ 06-70450615; www.lancelothotel.com) is a mainstay for consultants to the Food and Agriculture Organization of the United Nations, which is down the road. Lancelot is a great option for singles or longer stays; there is a community feel to the restaurant, which serves family-style meals at fixed times, and diners tend to visit more with those sitting nearby than with their own companions. The rooms, €105 for a sin-gle to €165 for a double, are comfortable and unspectacular, but they are reliably clean and the service is top-notch. You can relax on the rooftop bar overlooking the Colosseum after a day of touring.

HOTELS NEAR THE VATICAN

The worst deals in town are around Vatican City, where hoteliers pilfer the pilgrims' pockets. Many of the hotels here cater to large tour groups and the prices are almost always too high for what they are getting. The exceptions to this rule are the nonstandard options (p. 33) like monasteries and self-catering apartments, where the prices are fair. Another strike against this district: The neighborhood is not within walking distance of Rome's historical center and thus is convenient only if you plan to spend the bulk of your time at the Vatican.

€€€€   The **Bramante** (Via delle Palline, 24; ☎ 06-68806426; www.hotel bramante.com) will at least make you feel as if you are getting what you pay for. The rooms, which start at €150 for a double, are modestly furnished, but the walls are soundproofed, the beds are large, and the bathrooms are bigger than most (though none have bathtubs). Plus, the included breakfast here is spectacular, complete with eggs and toast.

€€€€   Another fairly good deal is, unfortunately, often fully booked. Why? Well, the **Hotel Sant'Anna** (Borgo Pio, 133–134; ☎ 06-68308717; www.hotel santanna.com) is not all that economical, but its rooms are spacious and modern with rare amenities like dataports and room service. Doubles start at €130, but you're more likely to spend €175 because the cheaper rooms go to regular customers like cardinals and journalists who have long-standing agreements with the hotel. There is a small courtyard in the back for summer relaxation, and the location, literally 1 block from St. Peter's Square, is unbeatable for those who are centering their attentions on the Vatican.

Staying with the Guides

€-€€€   Visitors owe a debt of thanks to the multifaceted **Enjoy Rome** travel agency (www.enjoyrome.com), with its innovative and always-fascinating walking tours (including a night tour, a bike tour, and some very interesting niche tours like "Fascist Rome: The Urban Planning of Mussolini"). Now the company also has its own accommodations to offer. The recently opened hybrid hotel and youth hostel **Colors Hotel & Hostel** (Via Boeszio, 31; ☎ 06-6874030; www.colorshotel.com) is as delightful a place as you'll find near Vatican City. Here you can choose from dorm beds or private rooms, some with bathrooms and others with shared bathroom facilities in the hall. The most economical option is a dorm bed for €18; the most expensive is a private triple room with bathroom for €145. The establishment is clean, the owners are friendly and helpful, and the place has a fully equipped kitchen for cooking your own meals; there are also laundry facilities and Internet access. Enjoy Rome also offers two larger self-catering apartments (called Valerio's Flat and Granny's Flat) with rates starting around €100 a night. These folks are on to something, and even if you don't stay in their hotel, definitely try one of their walking tours, which are around €20 a person for 2 to 4 hours.

DINING FOR ALL TASTES

The closest you can come to living like a true Roman is to eat at a local trattoria. Dining out in the evening is the preeminent social activity for Romans, and they have made an art of it.

It's wise to remember that tourist menus are for tourists, and Italians invariably avoid these. The best way to approach an Italian meal is to experiment. Ask the waiter for his recommendation: *"Cosa mi consiglia?"* Bear in mind, too, that you will always find better deals if you move off the main squares and try the quieter restaurants around the back corners, down the narrow alleyways, and even in neighborhoods without a single tourist site or monument.

Italian menus are often quite standardized. They usually include a first course known as the *primo* and more often than not consisting of pasta plates, and a second course (meat or fish) known as the *secondo* (second plate). You are not obliged to order both, and many residents confine their meals to simply the first course and a glass of wine. Doing so is the way to live on a budget in Rome.

I've classified selections according to the price of the *primo*. And if *primi* are cheap, *secondi* at the same restaurant also tend to be cheap. For a detailed **map of Rome's restaurants,** see p. 24.

Dining Index

Al Pompiere (near the Ghetto, €€, p. 40)

Al 34 (near the Spanish Steps, €€€, p. 40)

Asinocotto ★★★ (Trastevere, €€€€, p. 39)

Checchino dal 1887 (Testaccio, €€, p. 36)

Consolini all Arco di San Lazzaro (Testaccio, €€€, p. 36)

Da Augusto (Trastevere, €, p. 37)

Da Bucatino (Testaccio, €, p. 35)

Da Enzo ★★★ (Trastevere, €, p. 37)

Da Gino Trattoria (near the Pantheon, €, p. 41)

Da Otello (Trastevere, €€, p. 38)

F.I.S.H. (near the Colosseum, €€, p. 42)

Gusto (near the Spanish Steps, €€€, p. 41)

Il Ciak (Trastevere, €€€, p. 39)

Il Duca (Trastevere, €€, p. 38)

Il Mozzicone (near the Vatican, €, p. 42)

La Tana de'Noantri (Trastevere, €€, p. 38)

L'Oasi della Birra (Testaccio, €, p. 37)

Maccheroni (near the Pantheon, €, p. 41)

Margutta Vegetariano Ristorante (near the Spanish Steps, €€€, p. 41)

Perilli a Testaccio ★★★ (Testaccio, €, p. 35)

Pizza Remo (Testaccio, €, p. 37)

Roma Sparita [kids] (Trastevere, €€, p. 39)

Sora Margherita (near the Ghetto, €€, p. 40)

Price for a *primo* course: € = €7 or less; €€ = €8–€14; €€€ = €15–€19; €€€€ = €20 or more

Spirito Divino ✪✪ (Trastevere, €€, p. 38)
Taverna Angelica (near the Vatican, €€, p. 42)

Trattoria da Giggetto (near the Ghetto, €€€, p. 40)
Tuttifrutti (Testaccio, €€, p. 36)
Volpetti (Testaccio, €, p. 36)
Volpetti Piu (Testaccio, €, p. 36)

RESTAURANTS IN TESTACCIO

If you're looking for very good food and willing to sacrifice ambience, go straight to Testaccio. This neighborhood has the best meals for the price in the city. It's just a short walk from the historical center and adjacent to Trastevere. Formerly an area given over to slaughterhouses (now transformed into the MACRO museum), restaurants here specialize in meats from the *quinto quarto* (fifth quarter), the leftover segments of an animal after the slaughter, like sweetbreads, tripe, entrails, and other goodies you won't find on most American menus (though you also find the standard cuts). You come here for food, and it's always worth it.

€   **Perilli a Testaccio** ✪✪✪ (Via Marmorata, 39; ☎ 06-5742145; closed Wed) has been a reliable favorite of Italians and foreigners living in Rome since it opened in 1911. It's a classic noisy restaurant with terrible murals on the walls and a bustling male-only waitstaff. It was a favorite restaurant of Federico Fellini, and even now it's not uncommon to see local celebrities at the cramped tables inside. Not that they're afforded any special treatment; instead, all patrons are treated like regulars. As soon as you enter, you'll notice seasonal fruits and vegetables stacked in baskets and plates on a table in the back corner by the kitchen; the chef leans out from time to time to pluck what he needs as he prepares the meals. I especially enjoy Perilli on a winter's day when the hearty *cannelloni* (€8) warms your insides before you get down to the serious business of devouring the superb *abbacchio al forno* (roast lamb) or the *maialino* (roast suckling pork). Both of these second plates start at €10 and generally include roast potatoes. There is no outdoor seating, and this restaurant is always packed for dinner, so reservations for the evening meal are compulsory, though you can almost always get a table for lunch if you are at the door by 12:30pm, when they open.

€   If Perilli's is full, a good second choice is **Da Bucatino** ✪✪ (Via Luca della Robbia, 84; ☎ 06-5746886). This is a true home-style restaurant, with garlic garlands and dusty Chianti bottles, not to mention the head of a wild boar, on the walls. You can almost always get a table, either in the main dining room or in the basement under whitewashed arches. And in the summer you sit right on the cobblestone streets, often between parked cars. The waitstaff are anchored by two married couples and their sons, who are as delightful to watch as any sitcom. The food here is always satisfying, and the *antipasti* buffet is certainly enough for lunch. Da Bucatino offers some of the best *secondi* in the area and most start under €10, with such standards as *pollo con peperoni* and *abbacchio*, which are worth coming back for. The restaurant's namesake pasta, *Bucatini all'Amatriciana* at €6, is so sloppy good that the gentle waiters are known to affix a napkin-bib to you if you are wearing a white shirt.

€€   New to the restaurant mecca in Testaccio is **Tuttifrutti** (Via Luca della Robbia, 3A; ☎ 06-5757902; closed for lunch), an eatery that has great potential, though it's not yet a regular stop for the Italians. Its multilingual owner Michele enjoys translating the menu in truly colorful, animated English (and you'll enjoy listening to him do it). The menu, which changes several times a week depending on market offerings, has some creative dishes, often utilizing curry or mint to spice up usual Roman fare, and most first plates start at €8. The food is always satisfying, and some items like the fried pizza balls *(pizzelle)* are truly exceptional. This is an upbeat alternative to the working-class digs nearby. Come on a Monday when the chef offers a fixed theme menu (not to be confused with his tourist menu) based on seasonal market offerings.

€€€   If you are looking for something more "dressed up" in this neighborhood, there are two solid options. **Checchino dal 1887** (Via di Monte Testaccio, 30; ☎ 06-5746318; www.checchino-dal-1887.com; Tues–Sat), as the name implies, has been around for a very long time. This is a meat-lover's paradise, set directly across from the old slaughterhouse on the far end of the district along the slopes of the man-made Monte Testaccio. A more expensive choice than most of the other restaurants in this area, with pastas starting at almost €10, it draws Romans from all over the city.

€€€   Another elegant alternative is the very romantic **Consolini all Arco di San Lazzaro** (Via Marmorata, 28; ☎ 06-57300145), which is literally attached to the San Sabina hill (with an entrance on Via Marmorata next to the Porsche dealership). In summer, ask to sit on the flowered terraces. Seafood is the specialty here, and a favorite is gnocchi with lobster sauce at €12. But this is not a family-friendly place, so don't bring the kids with you.

Places to Snack in Testaccio

€   Rome's finest delicatessen, **Volpetti** (Via Marmorata, 47; ☎ 06-5742352; www.volpetti.com), is a massive barrage to the senses. If you even feign the slightest interest in a product, the helpful crew behind the counter will have you sampling goodies, tasting the various olive oils and vinegars until you beg for mercy. This is the place to buy vinegars and oils (in small, packable bottles that start around €5), cheeses, or cured meats to take back home. The owners here will vacuum seal and pack everything for you, including special gift boxes with local samples. You can also buy a slice of pizza or order a special deli sandwich to take away.

€   If you prefer to sit to eat, go around the corner to the delicious **Volpetti Piu** (Via A. Volta, 8; ☎ 06-57301439), a self-service *tavola calda* (cafe or diner) with products from the deli. They make the best potato pizza in the city, bar none, and you can walk away satisfied for under €5. The menu here changes depending on the season; other than extraordinarily tasty pizza by the slice, the specialties are lasagna (vegetarian or buffalo mozzarella) and interesting cold pasta dishes, as well as rice-and-chickpea salads.

€   **Pizza Remo** (Piazza Santa Maria Liberatrice, 44; ☎ 06-5746270; Mon–Sat, dinner only) is a Roman institution. In the summer, reservations at least 2 days in advance are compulsory (imagine that at your hometown pizzeria!). The bruschetta here melts in your mouth, and every pizza is made lovingly for all to see behind the open marble counters; the most basic start at just €5. If it's too crowded on a summer evening, order your pizza as takeout and eat it in the quaint park across the street.

€   Finally, Testaccio has lately made a noble attempt to shed its grungy every-man image with some funky wine bars under track lighting. Skip 'em (the wine bars in the historical center are far more interesting) and go instead to the always-interesting **L'Oasi della Birra** (Piazza Testaccio, 41; ☎ 06-5746122), which offers over 500 types of beer, including obscure Italian microbrews and lesser-known European offerings. The meals here are either super-light (cheese and salami plates for €5) or beer-worthy heavy (goulash, bratwurst, and cabbage-based salads starting around €8). And the wine list is almost as impressive as the beer offering, with many vintages served generously by the glass for €3.50.

RESTAURANTS IN TRASTEVERE

Dining in the medieval enclave of Trastevere, just across the river from the city's historical center, is always a boisterous affair. Patrons of the restaurants here are young and loud (mostly), reveling in a neighborhood that is positively ancient.

Most people consider the heart of Trastevere to be the area around Piazza Santa Maria, but the restaurants around Piazza di Santa Cecilia on the other side of the busy Viale Trastevere are actually better. In particular, the Via Genovesi and Via Vascellari are havens for good food, and eight distinctively different restaurants suit all tastes.

€   **Da Enzo** ✸✸✸ (Via dei Vascellari, 26; ☎ 06-5818355) is as far a cry from some of the costlier selections as you can imagine, except for its genuinely tasty food. The tables are smashed together, covered with paper runners; the shelves inside the dining room are lined with cleaning supplies; and the lighting is hospital-fluorescent—as far from romantic as you can get. But the food here is so delicious that Giuliano Brenna, the chef of the high-priced Asinocotto (see below) eats here on his days off. Portions are hefty, with specialties like *polpette al limone* (meat-balls in lemon sauce) costing just €7, and the simple ravioli and carbonara are even cheaper and just as savory. In summer, tables are set out on the cobblestone streets, at the base of an intersection, which means you may have to move your chair if an oversize car needs to pass by. This restaurant is pure Roman enjoyment and no secret to the locals, so reservations for both lunch and dinner are recommended.

€   Back across the Viale Trastevere, on the notably busier side of this district, restaurants seem to ooze out of the decaying facades. Of the vast array, the most wonderful (the only word for it) is the tiny trattoria **Da Augusto** (Piazza Renzi; ☎ 06-5896848), tucked between Piazza Santa Maria in Trastevere and the Via del Moro. This is one of the last original *trattorie* in Rome, and no doubt someone will ruin it soon by redecorating its crumbling interior. In the meantime, enjoy the ambience. Tables here are tiny squares covered with white paper on which the waitstaff will eventually write your bill. Have what they recommend because the menu is basically for show, and whatever they've got simmering in the back is freshly made with ingredients direct from the morning market. Most plates are around €6. The soups here are addictive, and if you eat here early on in your visit to Rome, you will be tempted to come back "just one more time" for another bite. Reservations are hard to make because no one ever seems to answer the phone, but try anyway because it fills up. Lunch is a better option than dinner, though only because the Piazza Renzi attracts a large crowd at night.

€€ **Spirito Divino** ★★★ (Via dei Genovesi, 31 A/B, Vicolo Dell'Atleta, 13–15; ☎ 06-5896689; www.spiritodivino.com) is tourist-friendly, but never touristy. The name, which translates to "divine spirit" or "spirit of the wine," is not accidental—the building sits on the site of Rome's original synagogue. At the end of the meal the owner gives a guided tour—in English and Italian—of the basement excavations, which now house the restaurant's extensive wine cellar (sculptures that were found here are now in the Vatican Museums). Mamma is the cook in the kitchen and polyglot dad takes care of the customers, explaining each item on the menu in French, German, or Russian, among other languages. Their son Francesco is the sommelier who keeps one of the most interesting Roman-age wine cellars in the city, and he is an expert at finding a wine that matches both your budget and your meal. The menu flits from such imaginative fare as coriander-spiced meatballs (€10) to succulent pork in "the style of Matius" (€12), which was a favorite with Julius Caesar and Augustus. The latter dish follows an ancient recipe, requiring that the pork be marinated for 24 hours in red wine with apple slices. There is nothing better on the menu and you will be tempted to come back to Rome just to eat it again.

€€ It's difficult to know whether to recommend **Il Duca** (Vicolo del Cinque, 56; ☎ 06-5817706), but it is such a favorite for tourists and locals alike that I'd probably be negligent to leave it out. What's good about the place is very good: The classic Roman dishes like ravioli and Amatriciana are more than satisfying and cost just €8, and the waiters are helpful and animated. But in the summer, when the tables line the streets, the restaurant becomes a magnet for flower vendors and strolling minstrels. In the winter, things are almost as bad because the restaurant has its own musicians. Quaint it is—there is no question. But the activity is often distracting and conversation at the table almost impossible.

€€ A better choice for similar food is **La Tana de'Noantri** (Via della Paglia, 1/2/3; ☎ 06-5806404), which is much less quaint, to be sure, but if you sit inside, rather than in the piazza across the street from the restaurant, you will be left alone to enjoy the meal. In the winter months, it's the coziest restaurant in all of Trastevere thanks to the fireplace, but in summer it is very busy and you likely won't get in without a reservation. Pizza (under €10) is the specialty—try the Gorgonzola and tomato or the Quattro Stagione.

€€ Another solid choice, though not recommended for vegetarians, is **Da Otello** ★ (Via della Pelliccia, 47–53; ☎ 06-5896848), which places a heavy emphasis on grilled-meat dishes (starting around €12). It's a festive place, always filled with groups of Italians who crowd into the tiny dining room. Here's how they order (and you should do the same): Skip the *primi,* which are largely unexceptional, and head directly to the wonderful antipasto bar (you'll spot it as you enter). There's an extensive dessert menu featuring some of the best tiramisu in town, so be sure to save room. As with other restaurants in the neighborhood, you will not get a table on a summer night without a reservation or an hour wait, and the outdoor tables are the usual magnet for peddlers, beggars, and musicians.

€€   **Roma Sparita** 🧒 (Piazza di Santa Cecilia, 24; ☎ 06-5800757) is simply the best family restaurant-pizzeria in this part of Rome. The owner, Ugo, makes you feel as if you're a longtime family friend, and the setting, tucked in a corner of the car-free Piazza di Santa Cecilia, is a great place for the kids to run around while you wait for your meal or linger over a *limoncello.* This place is packed for Sunday lunch when the weather is nice and Ugo sets out long lines of tables. His own family is always anchored there first. On summer nights, reservations are mandatory, and it's not uncommon to find long lines of regulars milling around the piazza waiting for a table. But this restaurant is really just as delightful on a cold winter day, when the fireplace inside warms the intimate lower dining room. If it's crowded, you may be shunted up to the larger cafeteria-style dining room adjacent to the restaurant and church, but it's better to offer to wait so that you can sit down in the smaller dining area below. Pizza here is made in a classic wood-burning oven; the best is the rughetta with baby tomatoes. The tasty *farfalle alla ghiottona* (butterfly pasta with Sicilian pesto and pine nuts) for €8 is also perfect in the winter and the spaghetti *alla vongole* (€10) is spiced with bits of hot pepper, just the way it should be.

€€€   Not far away is **Il Ciak** (Vicolo del Cinque, 21; ☎ 06-5894774), which hasn't changed in 40 years, during which time it's been frequented by movie stars and local celebrities, thus giving it the name Ciak (the sound a signboard makes when clapped before filming). Note the autographed photo on the wall of Francis Ford Coppola from the 1970s. Even though reservations are mandatory, there is always a line of regulars outside who just didn't have time to call. And even if you did call, they will get the table first. This is a place that many tourists avoid for several reasons, perhaps most of all because the front windows look more like a taxidermist shop's than those of a quaint trattoria. It's a restaurant for meat lovers only, especially those who love wild game cooked, with Tuscan flair, over an open grill by Sammy the chef, whom you must squeeze by on the way in. Ask to sit in the back "garden," which is a walled room covered with vines on the ceiling, away from the fire, and ask the waitress/owner what she recommends, as sometimes the game is a little too wild-tasting, depending on the season and origin of the meat. There is almost no reason to have a *primo* plate here. Instead, try one of the innovative bruschetta offerings like *funghi* porcini paste or hot pepper paste, and just sip your Chianti while Sammy prepares your feast. Most second plates are around €12, but they are generous and come with roast potatoes.

€€€€   A worthy splurge is the darkly romantic **Asinocotto** ★★★ (Via dei Vascellari, 48; ☎ 06-5898985; www.giulianobrenna.com). The food here is original and outstanding, and the owner and chef, Giuliano Brenna, has built a culinary reputation that has made him a local celebrity. He is a master, trained at some of the best five-star restaurants in Italy, yet he personally takes your order and delivers the food to the table. He explains the menu in English and he will answer any questions you have in terms of the subtle flavors in his innovative dishes. Downstairs in the grotto is an intimate wine bar for an aperitif or after-dinner drink, or better yet, just linger in the medieval dining room after your meal. (They never double-book a table, so you won't feel rushed.) This is not a cheap restaurant and most first plates are over €15, but it is one of the few in Trastevere where you actually feel that you have eaten a meal worthy of the bill. The restaurant prides itself as gay-owned and gay-friendly, but the clientele is positively mixed, and the Italian couples of all orientations who come here are faithful regulars.

RESTAURANTS IN THE JEWISH GHETTO

The Jewish Ghetto is a quieter version of the quaint Trastevere, and the clientele (and overall aura of the area) is about 10 years older. It's also slightly more subdued and sophisticated. No one gets very excited here about anything, except about the genuinely good food you're served. This neighborhood's restaurants often possess a casual charm that turns one-time visitors into repeat customers.

€€   The choices at my first selection are not as ample as in other parts of town, but the dishes are solid and dependable. **Al Pompiere** (Via Santa Maria dei Calderari, 38; ☎ 06-6868377; Mon–Sat) is a casual *osteria* frequented by locals. There are no surprises on the menu, but they do the standard Roman dishes like fried zucchini flowers and batter-dipped salt cod better than most, in addition to preparing top-notch seafood pastas, which start at €10 and are always fresh. It's a tossup between this gem and **Sora Margherita** (Piazza delle Cinque Scole, 30; ☎ 06-6874216; Tues–Sun lunch, Fri–Sat dinner), which is as charming as a hole-in-the-wall gets, literally, since that's exactly what this delightful *osteria* looks like from the outside. There is no sign outside and the entrance makes you feel as though you are coming in through the kitchen door. But luckily, first impressions mean nothing. The food here is classic Roman-Jewish cuisine, done with style and predictable grace. Try the *Tonnarelli Cacio Pepe* or the chickpea-and-pasta soup for under €10. This is a better choice for lunch since it is open for dinner only on the weekends, when reservations are compulsory.

€€€   A worthy splurge in the Jewish Ghetto is the **Trattoria da Giggetto** (Via del Portico d'Ottavia, 21/a; ☎ 06-6861105), which isn't necessarily even a splurge because the prices generally reflect both the quality and quantity of the food. Here you are in the very heart of the historical Jewish Ghetto, a stone's throw away from the ruins of the Portico d'Ottavia. This is a classic Roman-Jewish restaurant that has been run by the same family for three generations. The fried zucchini flowers are stuffed with mouth-watering mozzarella and the seafood pastas are exquisite. First plates here start at over €12. They also specialize in the hot oil-boiled (not deep-fried, mind you) artichokes in the Roman-Jewish style.

RESTAURANTS IN THE HISTORICAL CENTER

Dining close to the Spanish Steps and deep inside the historical center is all about style. Restaurants here are trendy and intentionally chic in appearance; there is absolutely nothing spontaneous about them, but I've managed to find a handful of worthy choices.

Near the Spanish Steps

€€€ **Gusto** (Piazza Augusto Imperatore, 9; ☎ 06-3226273) has succeeded in making the experience of dining en masse both enjoyable and Italian in feel. This enormous restaurant complex, which includes a wine bar, a pizzeria, a drink bar with the Italian version of bar food, and an upscale restaurant, is, perhaps as trendy as Rome gets. Most dishes are around €12. It is a popular hangout for Italians and local expats who want to escape the monotony of the quaint *trattorie,* and it is a magnet for Rome's glitterati, who flock here on the weekends to be seen. It is also a gastronomically pleasing place to eat and a wonderful environment in which to meet friends, but the question that begs to be asked is: Who comes to Rome for trendy eats? If you are only in Rome for a few days, give this one a skip and head to one of the more authentic Italian restaurants. But do visit the cookbook-and-gift shop.

€€€ **Al 34** (Via Mario de' Fiori, 34; ☎ 06-6795091) is one of the most consistently tasty restaurants in this area. There are regional Italian dishes, and the chef offers up very creative fare by mixing and matching pasta shapes with sauces that don't generally go together. Favorites include the sepia fettuccine with seafood, verzino pasta with garlic, and the tonnarelli with scampi and radicchio, all €12. The decor has a distinctively romantic feel (red velvet tends to do that), and the tables are dark and intimate. Reservations are recommended.

€€€ **Margutta Vegetariano Ristorante** (Via Margutta, 118; ☎ 06-32650577; www.ilmargutta.it) is widely touted as the city's leading spot for creative vegetarian fare. What this restaurant can do with a simple zucchini flower is amazing, to be sure. Established in 1979, Margutta continues to attract many non-vegetarians simply because the food is so reliably delicious. Try the monster salads for lunch, or tuck in for the famous *Garfagnana* soup (€12), with chestnuts, pumpkin, and mushrooms, or sample the vegetable chickpea couscous.

Near the Pantheon

€ Eating near the Pantheon is synonymous with spending money—with two exceptions. The wonderful and ever-so-rustic **Maccheroni** (Piazza delle Coppelle, 44; ☎ 06-68307895; www.ristorantemaccheroni.com) is the first. Reservations here are compulsory and the place is always packed with boisterous Italians who come for the good value and good food. The waiters are flirtatious and pinup cute, but it's the food that makes the visit worthwhile. Start your meal with the buffalo mozzarella, which comes sprinkled with bread crumbs and olive oil, and move on to the *rigatoni alla gricia* (bacon, sheep's cheese, and pepper) for just €6.50. The house wine is Chianti, and the menu looks like it hasn't been updated (or reprinted) since the 1960s—which is lucky for anyone dining there.

€ Not far away is **Da Gino Trattoria** (Vicolo Rosini, 4; ☎ 06-68734341), which will give you as authentic an Italian experience as you might hope for in the center of Rome. Ask the matron of the restaurant for advice on what to have and she'll likely suggest the specialty *coniglio al vino bianco* (rabbit cooked in white wine). It is almost impossible to find bastions like this tried-and-true trattoria in the historical center, where an increasing number of restaurants cater to the trend-setters. Don't miss it.

RESTAURANTS NEAR THE VATICAN

Across the river, into the area around the Vatican, dining is a mixed bag. By day, the restaurants here cater to large groups that are moved through at lightning speed. By night, the restaurants are inhabited primarily by priests and cardinals, and, not surprisingly, eavesdropping Vatican journalists. The residential district of Prati, near St. Peter's Square, is vibrant, and the dining choices here cater to the area's international population.

€   **Il Mozzicone** (Borgo Pio, 180; ☎ 06-6861500) is a tiny little getaway just a stone's throw from the Vatican City gates. There are no surprises on the menu here, and you will almost always find the usual dishes like *fettuccini ragù* for €6 and tripe for €8, but considering its location, it is the best deal around. This restaurant is miniscule, so book a table if you don't want to wait for one.

€€   **Taverna Angelica** (Piazza A. Capponi, 6; ☎ 06-6874514) is a standard Vatican City–area trattoria specializing in fowl-based dishes like lentil soup with pigeon breast for €10, and duck breast with balsamic vinegar for €15. This is a popular spot for priests with higher budgets, and it's not uncommon to overhear heated debates on church policy.

A RESTAURANT NEAR THE COLOSSEUM

€€   It's possible you will not have better seafood in Rome than at the appropri-ately named **F.I.S.H.** (Via dei Serpenti, 16; ☎ 06-47824962; www.f-i-s-h.it). The menu is divided into Mediterranean, Asian, and oceanic categories, and it's about the best ethnic food you can get in the city when it comes to sushi and *nasi goring*. But the Mediterranean menu is by far the most interesting, with the house dish being *volcano di riso nero*—seafood cooked in a bed of mixed rice for €12. The atmosphere in this restaurant is sleek and non-trattoria style.

WHY YOU'RE HERE: THE TOP SIGHTS & ATTRACTIONS

If I were to describe each and every one of the really important historical sights, structures, museums, exhibits, and attractions of Rome, I'd fill an entire book; you could tour Rome for a year and still not experience everything worthwhile and memorable. However, I've confined this chapter to 36 such places, and I've preceded that discussion with recommendations on allocating your time, depend-ing on the number of days you'll be in the Eternal City. Following that treatment of the sights, I've dealt with nightlife and shopping, out-of-town excursions, and other miscellaneous, but important, aspects of a trip to Rome.

The Question of Museum Reservations

If you've only got a short time in Rome, don't waste it in long lines, even if that means paying twice the entrance fee to book a guided tour at places like the Vatican Museums and Sistine Chapel. During most of the year, and especially around Easter time, the line to get into the Vatican Museums starts forming at daybreak and the wait can exceed 3 hours just to get to the ticket booth. You've got to seriously weigh whether it's worth the wait when those 2 or 3 hours could be so much more rewarding—especially if you are only in Rome for a day or two.

The best option is to make the worthy splurge, **reserve ahead at the Vatican Museums,** and forgo the long wait. Unfortunately, you cannot just reserve a ticket; instead, you must book a 2-hour guided tour (with audio-guide). The cost is €22 (regular admission is €12) and you can reserve by fax (06-69885100) at least 7 days and no more than 1 month before you will be visiting the museums. You'll receive a confirmation fax that you must bring with you to the exit gate of the Vatican Museums (right beside the ticket booth) 15 minutes before your reservation time (Mar–Oct Mon–Fri 10:30am, noon, and 2pm and Sat 10:30am and 11:15am; Nov–Feb Mon–Sat 10:30am). It may seem like a lot of extra money to spend on a ticket, but you will easily justify it as you walk past the massive lines that snake from the entrance door all the way around the perimeter of Vatican City. For more information on the tour, visit www.vatican.va.

Warning: Be wary of private companies that offer to get you these reservations; some charge as much as €75 for the service, but you can just as easily reserve it yourself for a fraction of that.

Beating lines is a tough game elsewhere in Rome, too. It is generally advisable to **book ahead for the Colosseum,** where the lines are often torturous, especially in the summer months under the blazing sun. Both the Domus Aurea (p. 54) and the Borghese Galleries (p. 75) require manda-tory booking. Many of the other museums and galleries can only be booked by faxing **Rome's Cultural Ministry** (☎ 06-69885100), which handles the Vatican Museums, Colosseum, and Roman Forum as well as Domus Aurea bookings, and through **Ticketeria** (☎ 06-32810; www.ticketeria.it), which handles the Borghese Galleries.

If you are interested in seeing excavations in progress that are not open to the public, call **Ripartizione X** (☎ 06-67103819; fax 06-6892115). But be aware that these tours are often expensive, depending on the site you wish to tour. It usually takes 5 days to get a response for your request, and you'll need to leave your hotel information with them so they can con-firm your tour.

Rome Attractions

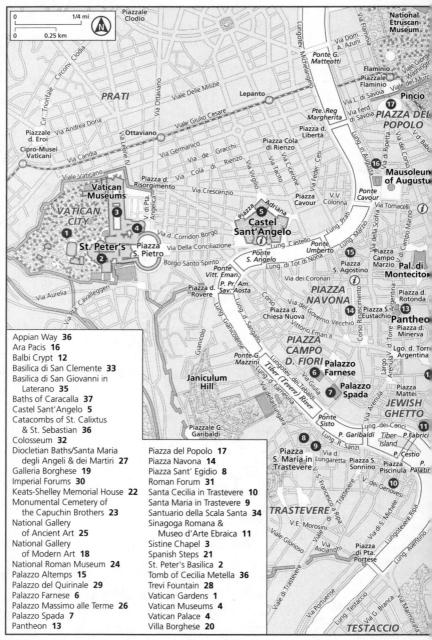

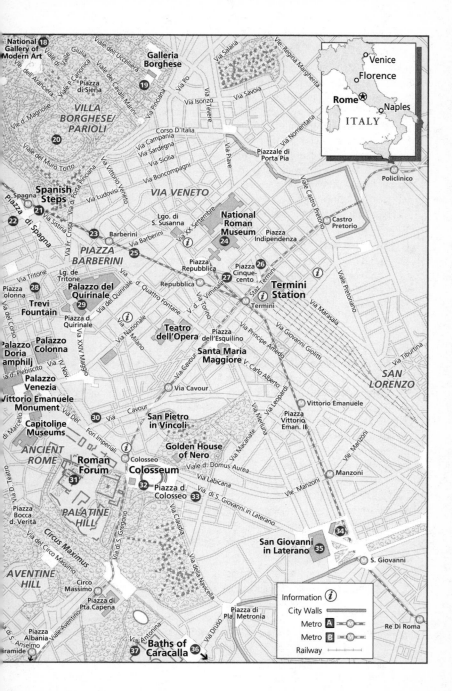

National
Gallery of
Modern Art (18)

Galleria
Borghese

Piazza
di Siena (19)

VILLA
BORGHESE/
PARIOLI

(20)

Corso D'Italia

Piazzale di
Porta Pia

VIA VENETO

Policlinico

Spanish
Steps

Piazza
di Spagna (21)(22)

Lgo. di
S. Susanna

National
Roman
Museum (24)

Piazza
Indipendenza

Castro
Pretorio

PIAZZA
BARBERINI (23)(25)

Barberini

Piazza
Repubblica

Piazza
Cinque-
cento (26)

Trevi
Fountain

Piazza
Colonna (28)

Palazzo del
Quirinale (29)

Repubblica (27)

Termini
Station

Termini

Palazzo
Doria
amphilj

Palazzo
Colonna

Piazza d.
Quirinale

Teatro
dell'Opera

Piazza
dell'Esquilino

Santa Maria
Maggiore

SAN
LORENZO

Palazzo
Venezia

Via Cavour

Vittorio Emanuele
Monument

Capitoline
Museums

Vittorio Emanuele

Piazza
Vittorio
Eman. II

ANCIENT
ROME

San Pietro
in Vincoli

Golden House
of Nero

Roman
Forum (31)

Colosseo

Colosseum (32)

Manzoni

Piazza d.
Colosseo (33)

PALATINE
HILL

Circus Maximus

(34)

AVENTINE
HILL

Circo
Massimo

San Giovanni
in Laterano (35)

S. Giovanni

Piazza di
Pta.Capena

Piazza di
Pla. Metronia

Piazza
Albania

Baths of
Caracalla (37)(36)

Re Di Roma

Information (i)
City Walls
Metro A
Metro B
Railway

ITALY

Venice
Florence
Rome
Naples

45

Rome Itineraries

Rome is a city that can be sampled and savored according to your personal tastes. Instead of making sure you do five museums, three churches, and two ruins, follow your instincts. Try a little baroque, gaze over some antiquities, and wander through a few churches. Sample the art, taste the food, feel the culture. If you see an open courtyard, stroll inside. If you happen upon a particularly charming ivy-laden street, walk down it. If there is an inviting table at a sidewalk cafe, sit at it. Look up at the buildings for the Roman faces in the windows. Look down the streets for cats sunning themselves in the alleyways.

Following are suggested itineraries for short trips that touch on all aspects of what there is to see here, from ancient Rome through Holy Rome.

If you have only 1 day in Rome

The best thing you can do is change your ticket so that you can spend more time here. Otherwise, get up very early and, from the terrace behind the Campidoglio square off Piazza Venezia, watch the sun rise over the **Roman Forum.** You likely won't have time to explore these ruins in full, but from here, you can see the entirety of what was once the heart of ancient Rome, set against the backdrop of the Colosseum and cast in the day's best light. Next, walk the few blocks through the historical center to the **Pantheon** and be one of the first in when the doors open at 8:30am. From there, walk to St. Peter's Square by way of **Piazza Navona** and over the Bridge of Angels. Once through the security lines into St. Peter's Basilica, wander around until your reservation time—10:30am—at the **Vatican Museums.** (Book 1 week ahead so you can waltz through the entrance, confirmation fax in hand, 15 min. early.) When you are out of the museum at 12:30pm, dash over to Castel Sant'Angelo for a quick lunch and a view of the city below. From here, wind your way to the Via del Corso, taking side streets and quaint alleyways around Campo de' Fiori and the Pantheon. After stopping for an ice-cream pick-me-up, make your way to the **Spanish Steps** and cross over to the **Trevi Fountain** to throw in your coin, which will ensure your return to Rome. End your afternoon at the **Colosseum** and have dinner in Trastevere.

If you have only 2 days in Rome

Two days are better than one, but not by much. Start the first day by getting in line at the **Vatican Museums** by 7am at the latest so you are among the first inside when the doors open at 8:45am. You'll still have to rush, but you can take in a few extra highlights like the **Raphael Rooms** in addition to the **Sistine Chapel** and be out in less than the 2-hour tour you get with a reserved ticket. When you walk out of the Sistine Chapel, duck through the exit marked FOR AUTHORIZED TOUR GROUPS ONLY before the string of gift shops and you'll find yourself in St. Peter's Square, where you'll be able to bypass the metal detector (because you'll have gone through security at the museums). Tour the church and then head to **Castel Sant'Angelo** for a late lunch and view of the city below from the terrace. From here, you can take a more leisurely walk through the center core, including **Campo de' Fiori** and the **Jewish Ghetto,** before heading up toward **Piazza del Popolo.** From Piazza del Popolo, make your way to **Piazza di Spagna,** and after you've ascended the Spanish Steps, walk down the back way to the **Trevi Fountain.** Head to **Trastevere** for dinner and take a guided night walking tour.

Wake up very early the second day to watch the sun rise over the **forums** from the terrace behind the **Campidoglio.** Spend the morning touring the **Colosseum** and **forums** and take your lunch in the neighborhood directly behind the Colosseum. Start the afternoon at the **Pantheon** and plan to spend the rest of the day wandering around the historical center. There are several lovely museums to choose from here. For antiquities, go to the **Balbi Crypt** on the edge of the Jewish Ghetto. The recently reopened **Ara Pacis** is a modern jewel in the ancient city, and the charming **Palazzo Altemps** offers some lovely art in a quaint and cozy setting. If you are not into art museums, spend this time ducking in and out of churches like the **Santa Maria della Pace** or the church of **St. Ignatius** near the Pantheon. Have dinner in **Testaccio** and wind up your evening with a late-night view of Rome from Orange Park on the **Aventine Hill** (p. 78).

If you have only 3 days in Rome

If you have 3 days in Rome, follow the itineraries above and add a trip outside the walls on your third (or middle) day. In the morning, either add the **Borghese Galleries** (advance booking is compulsory) or the ancient Catacombs along the **Appian Way.** In the afternoon, take a bus to **Tivoli** to see the ruins of Hadrian's Villa or take the train to **Ostia** to see the ruins of Rome's original seaport. On the third night, have dinner in the Jewish Ghetto.

If you have 4 days or more in Rome

After following the above itineraries, fill your last few days with what you like best. For example, if antiquities are for you, spend an entire day searching for ancient Rome by visiting the **Church of San Clemente,** exploring the **Domus Aurea,** and checking out the **Wall Museum.** If art is more your style, dizzy yourself with Rome's wonderful museum offerings like the **Capitoline Museums** and **National Roman Museums,** near Termini. If you are interested in the Catholic Church or religious architecture, visit the five patriarchal parish churches and duck into any basilica that looks interesting.

Cutting the Cost of Museum Admissions

For all there is to see and do in Rome, the city doesn't do a great job of making it easy or convenient. Unlike in, say, Naples and Florence, there are no all-encompassing tourist passes that integrate museum admission and public transportation. Instead, Rome's visitors have to pick and choose their deals, juggling a handful of different tickets to enjoy savings. The integrated tickets that do exist are available at any of the sites they cover, or through **APT Azienda per il Turismo Roma** (Via Parigi, 5, or inside Fiumicino Airport; ☎ 06-48899200 or 06-36004399; www.roma turismo.com). It's important to note that most museums are closed on Mondays, with the exception of the Vatican Museums and the Museum of Modern Art, which makes taking advantage of a 3-day ticket purchased on a Saturday or Sunday nearly impossible.

Consider the following:

- ◆ **Capitolini Card** Adults €8.30, seniors and students €6.20, 7 days: Capitoline Museums and Montemartini.
- ◆ **Museo Nazionale Romano Card** Adults €7, seniors and students €3.50, 3 days: Palazzo Massimo alle Terme, Baths of Diocletian, Palazzo Altemps, and Balbi Crypt.
- ◆ **Appia Antica Card** Adults €6, no discounts, 7 days: Baths of Caracalla, Tomb of Cecilia Metella, and Villa dei Quintili.
- ◆ **Archeologia Card** Adults €20, seniors and students €10, 7 days: Colosseum, Palatine Hill, Terme di Caracalla, Palazzo Altemps, Palazzo Massimo alle Terme, Baths of Diocletian, Balbi Crypt, Tomb of Cecilia Metella, and Villa dei Quintili.
- ◆ **Go.Card** (www.gocard.org) Adults 18 to 30 €6, good from July 1– June 30 (no matter when you buy it), supplying discounts to tourist sites, movie theaters, art showings, and some shops.

ANCIENT ROME

Ancient Rome may look like a jumble of fallen columns and confusing ruins, but this area, which is the most historically significant in the city, is quite easy to navigate and decipher with a good map and a good imagination. You will not see full buildings here; in fact, the most complete ruin in the antiquity park is the Colosseum, which is essentially just a shell.

The Capitoline Hill

Start exploring the many gems here from the government center of modern Rome, atop the Capitoline Hill just behind city hall. Head straight up the *cordonata* ramplike stairs from Piazza Venezia to Piazza del Campidoglio. Though it's open 24 hours, it's best to come here right before dawn (you'll want to avoid this area at night). Watching the sun rise over the ancient forums is perhaps the most magical moment you'll experience in this city, and well worth the sacrifice of a little

The Colosseum, the Forum & Ancient Rome Attractions

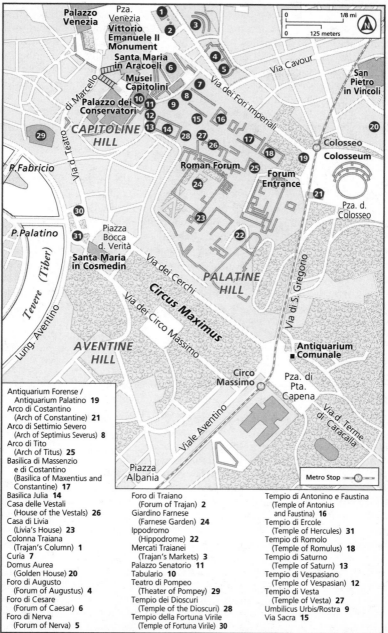

sleep. In this first light, the ancient pillars sparkle and the shadows dance below the columns.

At the top of the ramp stairs, walk past the massive statues of the mythical twins Castor and Pollux and the replica of the emperor Marcus Aurelius in the center (the original is just a few feet away behind glass in the museum courtyard). This square, designed by Michelangelo in the 1530s, is now flanked on either side by the glorious Capitoline Museums, which you should come back to visit after you've fully explored the ruins below. Most of what's in the museums comes from there, so it's more fulfilling to first visit the source.

For now, head around the back of City Hall to see the entire spread of the **forum complex** below, which is divided broadly into four segments: the Imperial Fora (Fori Imperiali), the Roman Forum (Foro Romano), the Palatine Hill (Palatino), and the Colosseum (Colosseo; www.capitolium.org). It is vital to see the outlines of these buildings, as well as the original forum layout, from up here, before delving in. From down inside the forums, you just don't get this sort of perspective; instead, you are dwarfed by the giant pillars and ruins of antiquity.

The modern street to the left of this vista is the **Via dei Fori Imperiali,** built by Benito Mussolini in 1932 as a convenient traffic thoroughfare and as a means to connect his famous **Palazzo Venezia balcony** (p. 57) to the Colosseum. Today, archaeologists are slowly digging out more artifacts and chipping away at the ruins without sacrificing the street, which would cripple the public transportation network of modern Rome. Do not let this street confuse you, and don't be distracted by the way the forums are divided by fences, entrance gates, sidewalks, and benches, which sit above still-unexcavated ruins. You have to overlook the suggestion that all these forums are separate entities, because in reality they were an intricate network of small streets and alleyways—much like the present city.

You should definitely come back up here another time to explore Piazza Venezia and the rest of the Campidoglio, but for now take the back steps down to the Via dei Fori Imperiali.

The Imperial Forums

Almost more complicated than figuring out what you are looking at is determining in what order to visit these forums. Start on the left-hand side of the Via dei Fori Imperiali (facing the Colosseum) with a brief sweep through the Imperial Forums of Trajan, Caesar, Nerva, and Augustus, which were built between 42 B.C. and A.D. 112. The best preserved is the semi-circular **Trajan's Market** (entrance Via IV Novembre, 94; €3.50; daily 9am–sunset), which gives you an idea of what an ancient 150-store Roman shopping mall looked like, though you wouldn't find Gucci and Prada here (these were primarily stores for grains, oils, spices, and supplies for the ancient Romans). It is not necessary to enter this site unless you are an archaeology buff; you can just as easily get the idea from the perimeter. From here you will also see the intricately carved **Torre delle Milizie (Tower of the Militia)** on top of the market. Many poets have written that Nero stood here to watch Rome burn, but historians differ and say he watched from the Colle Oppio (p. 54). Farther down the street is the **Colonna Traiana (Trajan's Column),** which is a white column carved with war scenes from Emperor Trajan's defeat of the Dacians (who occupied what is now Romania). The statue on top is St. Peter, which fills the spot where a golden statue of Trajan was pilfered in the Middle Ages.

The forums of Augustus, Nerva, and Vespasiano are below this street joined by a walkway, which you can reach from the Via dei Fori Imperiali or the Piazza del Grillo. The **Forum of Augustus** was inaugurated in 2 B.C. The main structure was the Temple of Mars, which the emperor Augustus (known then as Octavian) built to mark the victorious battle of Philippi in 42 B.C. Next is the **Forum of Nerva** which sits on both sides of the Via Fori Imperiali. This forum held the **Temple of Minerva,** of which there is still a frieze depicting Minerva, the goddess of home-making and weaving. The final forum here is the **Forum of Vespasiano.** It was dedicated to the emperor in A.D. 75, but most of it burned in 192. In A.D. 193, Septimius Severus placed a giant map of Rome on the walls here. The maps you now see on the wall opposite these forums were put there by Mussolini to show the rise of his own wannabe Roman empire-in-the-making.

At the time of this writing, you can only visit the **Imperial Forums** (Via dei Fori Imperiali; ☎ 06-6797786; €7; English for guided tours only at 3pm Wed and Sat–Sun) by guided tour 3 days a week. But again, it is not necessary to actually go down into the Imperial Forums to appreciate their significance. It's a much more rewarding journey to cross the street and visit the free Roman Forum.

The Roman Forum

You can spend an entire day at the **Roman Forum** ✪✪✪ (entrances at Largo Romolo e Remo, 5–6, or Piazza di Santa Maria Nova, 53, or Via di Monte Tarpeo; free admission; daily 9am to 1 hr. before dusk) and still come away wanting more. But a more practical way to visit the Roman Forum is with a detailed map from the visitor center on the Via dei Fori Imperiali before starting your expedition. The most central entrance is located in the middle, at Largo Romolo e Remo. You can also buy an integrated ticket here for the Colosseum and Palatine Hill for €8, which will allow you to bypass the line at the Colosseum. Rent a €4 audioguide here, which will save you from hearing others' often misguided explanations around you. The ruins here are among the worst labeled in the entire city, so without a detailed map, an audioguide, or a book dedicated entirely to the forum, you will be left with only half of the story.

From the entrance at Largo Romolo e Remo, you should first cover the area to the left heading to the Colosseum. Here you'll see the A.D. 141 **Temple of Antonino and Faustina,** which was reincarnated as a Catholic Church in the 8th century. Farther down the paved road is the backside of the **Basilica of Cosmas and Damian,** which houses a Franciscan monastery with a well-placed balcony overlooking the area. If you feel adventurous, go around the front of the church and ask if you can take a peek; there are many American Franciscans here on sabbatical or assignment who will happily take you up to see the view.

Along the path in the forum, you will then pass the barrel vaults of the ruined **Basilica of Costantino,** originally known as the Basilica of Massenzio. This was the largest structure in the entire Roman Forum and the last of the magnificent structures built before the decline of Rome. The giant vaults are said to have inspired Michelangelo, who came here often to study them before designing the dome for St. Peter's Basilica. At the end of this section of the forum is the **Arch of Titus,** depicting a carving of Titus's defeat of the Jews.

Heading back toward the entrance, you'll pass the **House of the Vestal Virgins,** where anatomically perfect, prepubescent girls tended Vesta's sacred fire.

They spent 10 years training, 10 years as dignitaries representing Vesta, and 10 years teaching all they knew to the younger generation. At 40, they could finally marry, and legend says that deflowering a vestal virgin was definitely something Roman men fought ardently to do. The vestal virgins who couldn't adhere to their vow of chastity until they reached 40 were buried alive. Not far away is the **Temple of Julius Caesar**—built on the site of his cremation—which is often adorned with fresh roses laid down by a Roman woman who believes she is a direct descendant.

Finally, you will come along to the **Sacred Way,** which leads in the direction of the Campidoglio. Here you'll pass by the **Basilica Aemilia,** which housed the administrative offices of ancient Rome, and finally the **Temple of Castor and Pollux,** whose statues flank the entrance to the Piazza del Campidoglio. The brothers are widely known as the saviors of Rome—they appeared out of nowhere to inspire the Roman military in a battle in 499 B.C. In this part of the forum are several standing columns that mark the sites of what were once important buildings. The eight similar granite columns outline what was once the **Temple of Saturn,** used as the city's treasury. The three white columns, attached by a broken slab of marble on top, make up what was once a corner of the **Temple of Vespasian.** The impressive display of 12 columns (though 5 are not original) is what's left of the **Portico degli dei Consenti,** and a tall lone column is the **Column of Phocus,** which was the very last monument erected in the forum in A.D. 608. Near this far end of the forum is the massive **Arch of Septimius Severus,** with its haunting carving in the center of the defeated Parthians (who occupied modern-day Iran) being led to their death in chains. See also the steps of the ruins of **Basilica Julia,** which was built by Julius Caesar to house the law courts. Note the carved squares on the remaining steps—these were board games used by those waiting for their day in court.

Also near here, look for the **Golden Milestone,** the point from which all roads leading from Rome were measured. And don't miss the Rostrum, where Shakespeare placed the delivery of Mark Antony's famous address, which began, "Friends, Romans, countrymen . . ." The nearby Curia is a replica of the Roman Senate, built in the 1930s. The original doors from the 3rd century A.D. now adorn the Basilica of San Giovanni (p. 79).

There is much, much more in the Forum than what's mentioned here. You could spend the whole day exploring it all, and you should if you have the time and a detailed map or a site guide. But if you just want to skim the surface, as we've done here, you can see the whole thing in about 1½ hours before heading next door to the Palatine Hill.

The Palatine Hill

The Forum may be from where Rome ruled the world, but the wonderfully green grounds of the **Palatine** ✭✭✭ (Via San Gregorio, 30, or Piazza di Santa Maria Nova, 53; €8 integrated ticket with Colosseum; daily 9am to 1 hr. before dusk) are whence it all began. According to legend, this is where the mythical she-wolf nursed Remus and Romulus, the latter of whom is said to have founded Rome. This is also the spot where the proof of 8th-century B.C. huts from the Iron Age can be seen, depicting the first known settlement in Rome. Emperors lived here, and you can easily see why—the views of Rome's seven hills are breathtaking.

The English word "palace" is believed to be derived from the lavish dwellings on the Palatine Hill. Most of the larger remains you see here are from the Emperor Domitian and this is another place worthy of a very detailed guide from the visitor center. The areas not to miss, though, are **Domus Augustana,** the living quarters, the **Stadio** (Stadium), and the **Baths of Settimio Severo,** which form the outer boundary of the Palatine Hill. These are the prominent, frequently photographed ruins you see from the Circus Maximus and really show the mass of these ancient dwellings.

Behind this wall of ruins, inward, are the stunning mosaic tile floors of the **Domus Flavia** and the Pompeian red frescoes of the 1st century B.C. **House of Livia.** The frescoes found in these ruins are on display at the National Roman Museum on Piazza della Repubblica. There are a handful of artifacts found in the excavations of the Palatine Hill in the large white **Palatine Museum,** which is included in your entrance ticket. Don't spend too much time here, though, because there are much better offerings at the ancient artifact museums in the city and the Vatican Museums.

From the edge of the Palatine Hill, you see the wide circular track of the **Circus Maximus,** which once held 200,000 spectators on the sidelines to watch gladiators race. Rent *Ben Hur* for a refresher of the history of this arena. Now it is a running track for Romans and a concert venue in the summer.

Arch of Constantine

Between the Palatine Hill and the Colosseum is the last triumphal arch that the Roman empire was able to build, erected by Constantine in A.D. 315. The decorations on this arch were pilfered from other monuments throughout the city. If you study the battle scenes, you may notice what art historians call a decline in artisan quality and detail—just one of the many precursors to the fall of the Roman empire. The ruins in front of the arch are those of the ancient *Meta sudans* fountain, which Mussolini bulldozed in the 1930s to make way for a road that has since been removed.

The Colosseum

No matter how many pictures you've seen, the first impression you'll have of the **Colosseum** ★★★ (Piazza del Colosseo, ☎ 06-39967700; €8; 9am to 1 hr. before sunset) is amazement at its sheer enormity. It is massive and looks as if it has been plopped down among the surrounding buildings, and not the other way around. The view of what was once called the Flavian Amphitheater is much different from that seen in pictures and postcards, which all seem to be shot from an angle you can never re-create when you're here. Nevertheless, the first way to visit the Colosseum is to walk completely around its 500m (1,640-ft.) circumference. It doesn't matter where you start, but do the circle and look at the various stages of ruin before delving in. Note the different column styles on each level (if you can make them out through the black soot from the passing cars). The structure is marked with movement devices now and is carefully monitored for cracks and structural weaknesses. The city's subway train runs nearby and it is an alarming sensation to stand at the foot of the giant theater and feel the vibrations below. There have been many attempts to reroute the subway to save the Colosseum, but so far none has been successful.

It's a huge time-saver to buy your ticket for the inside of the Colosseum at the Palatine Hill, where lines are generally much shorter. You can then bypass the long lines here, or at least get into a shorter line to go inside. Only a few years ago, the Colosseum was free to the public, but with the addition of museum space on the second floor (complete with a shiny new elevator), visitors now have to pay. Start by walking onto the wooden platform that partially covers the center and look back at the perimeter walls. The stadium could hold as many as 87,000 spectators, by some counts, and seats were sectioned on three levels, dividing the people by rank and gender. There were 80 entrances to the Colosseum and historians say the massive crowds could be seated within a few minutes. Most events were free, but all spectators had to hold a membership card to enter.

The Colosseum was built as a venue for gladiator fights against animals and slaves, but when the Roman empire fell it was abandoned and eventually overgrown with wild and exotic plants that are believed to have come from wild animals, imported from Africa for the gladiator fights. You'll notice on the top of the "good side," as locals call it, that there are a few remaining supports that once held the canvas awning that covered the stadium during rain or for the summer heat. During the Middle Ages it became a palace, and then a multihousing complex of sorts, with structures attached to its sides and top. Much of the ancient travertine that covered its outside was used for palaces like the nearby Palazzo Venezia and the Palazzo Cancelleria near the Campo de' Fiori.

Now the Colosseum is one of the most visited sights in Rome, and it has lately become a concert venue, with performers like Paul McCartney and Elton John setting up giant stages on the Via dei Fori Imperiali to perform free concerts for up to a million people. It is also a holy site, and the Pope generally delivers his Good Friday Mass here.

You can easily tour the whole of the Colosseum in less than an hour unless there is a particularly spectacular exhibit at the museum inside.

COLLE OPPIO

The gentle hill just behind the Colosseum known as the Colle Oppio holds one of Rome's most controversial treasures. Nero's **Domus Aurea (Golden House)** ✰✰ (Via della Domus Aurea; ☎ 06-39967700; €5 adults, €2.50 seniors and students, €1.50 mandatory booking fee; Wed–Mon 9am–7:45pm, reservations mandatory) was built on the singed site of ruins left over after the famous fire of A.D. 64, which the eccentric emperor allegedly set himself. Originally the villa was a three-story building dripping with gold on the outside and plastered with mother-of-pearl and precious gems on the inside. That which was not bejeweled was instead frescoed by famous artists of the day. The fountains on the grounds and inside the palace courtyards flowed with perfume, and one of the rooms had an enormous revolving ceiling painted with zodiac signs and stars. There were man-made lakes and forests surrounding a 35m (116-ft.) statue (in gold, of course) of Nero himself. It was as opulent as Rome ever was—nothing before it had been so expensively decorated. But Nero was despised by the Romans and when he died in A.D. 68, the next emperor, Vespasian, set to work destroying and burying the palace. The Colosseum was built on the spot where he drained Nero's largest lake. The ruins were visited by Renaissance artists like Raphael, who were inspired by the frescoes. The site you see today officially opened in 1999, after many years of excavation. There are still more than 30 rooms under the earth left to discover.

Cultural Events in Rome

Concerts at Rome's **Parco della Musica** (Via P de Coubertin, 15; box office ☎ 06-8082058; www.musicaperroma.it) and **Teatro dell'Opera** (Piazza B. Gigli, 1; ☎ 06-48160255; www.opera.roma.it) range in price from a few euros to several hundred for big name performers. The Italian president's office sponsors free concerts (www.quirinale.it) around the city, including a weekly Sunday morning concert inside the Quirinale Palace. Churches cannot charge admission for concerts and, therefore, host many events sponsored through advertising. *Romac'e* (www.romace.it) is a weekly guide, published each Wednesday, that tells what's going on in the city.

On the other side of the Colle Oppio is what would be an otherwise ordinary church by Roman standards, if not for its hidden masterpieces. **San Pietro in Vincoli (St. Peter in Chains;** Piazza di San Pietro in Vincoli, 4A; ☎ 06-4882865; daily 7:30am–noon and 3:30–6pm) has one of Michelangelo's greatest works, the statue of Moses. Its angry horns are a result of a mistranslation of a Hebrew text of the Old Testament in which the transcriber mistook the word for "radiant" to mean "horned." At the altar are the chains that the devoted believe were used to shackle St. Peter to his cross.

PIAZZA VENEZIA

Piazza Venezia is Rome's center square. This is where the city puts its Christmas tree, where parades generally culminate, where demonstrations usually start, and where the official New Year's Eve countdown is held. It is a square rich in historical significance and it would be a wonderful place to spend time if not for the screeching, screaming, maddening traffic that whirls around the center flower beds at lightning speed.

Il Vittoriano (Piazza Venezia; free admission; daily 9:30am–4pm), the Victor Emmanuel II Monument, is the centerpiece, but many Romans consider it to be an ugly eyesore polluting the antiquity park behind it. The most common complaint is that the marble is "too white" in contrast to the worn travertine of the surrounding buildings. It is often referred to as the typewriter or the wedding cake for its shape. The Vittoriano was built to commemorate Italy's unification under its first king, Victor Emmanuel II, in 1885, so it is a relatively new addition to this part of Rome. Inside is a war museum, and on the steps in front is the tomb and eternal flame for the unknown soldier. The best way to appreciate this monument is to climb to the top. Enter through the small opening in the wrought-iron fence in front and climb the steps, veering to your right (the guards will point you that way).

The terrace on top is generally quiet and empty, even though it offers some of the best views, free or otherwise, of the Colosseum, forums, and expanse of ancient Rome. From here take your binoculars and look out across the rooftops for an army of statues of angels, martyrs, saints, and Romans that line the church tops and private gardens all around, seemingly keeping watch over the city.

You will never see these statues from down below, and most of them are long forgotten.

Along the perimeter railing of the terrace are illustrations of the skyline, with multilanguage descriptions of what you are looking at. Before you leave, stop at the coffee bar. Table service is nearly triple the price, so stand at the bar or ask for your coffee *"da portare via"* and they'll give it to you in a plastic cup so you can sip it while you enjoy the view. Visiting the terrace takes about half an hour, coffee included.

If you are a war buff, swing through the **Risorgimento Museum,** inside the Vittoriano, on your way down. It's free, and it is entirely focused on war history, with weapons, battle plans, and uniforms used by the Italian military.

CAMPIDOGLIO

The first thing you'll likely notice about the two raised *piazze* behind the Vittoriano is the massive stairways used to reach the Campidoglio and the Basilica di Santa Maria in Aracoeli. You can reach both the church and the Vittoriano via the Piazza del Campidoglio, which is a much easier climb than the steep steps of the church.

The **Basilica di Santa Maria in Aracoeli** (daily 9am–5:30pm) is one of Rome's most celebrated Christmas churches when it becomes the stage for a live nativity scene during the 12 days of Christmas. The floor is a medieval patchwork of worn marble, and the glass chandeliers provide a dim light, giving it a positively eerie feel. Look down at the foot-worn tombs in the naves, where the babies and children of Italian royalty and aristocrats were laid to rest. Tubby cherubs line the walls, and there is a replica of a wooden statue of the baby Jesus which was carved out of an olive tree from the Garden of Gethsemane near Jerusalem.

Capitoline Museums

The Piazza del Campidoglio is enclosed by the world's oldest public museums, the **Capitoline Museums** ✪✪✪ (Piazza del Campidoglio, 1; ☎ 06-39967800; www.museicapitolini.org; €7.80 integrated; daily 9am–8pm, ticket booth closes at 7pm), housed in both the **Palazzo Nuovo** on the left (facing the forums) and **Palazzo dei Conservatori** on the right, where you will find the ticket booth. This square is also home to Rome's city hall; a notice board outside the Palazzo dei Conservatori lists couples who have been granted recent marriage certificates, giving a peek into the marital ages of the locals.

The masterpieces in the Capitoline Museum are considered Rome's most valuable (the Vatican Museums are not part of Rome's collection). Start your museum tour with **Palazzo dei Conservatori** by visiting the courtyard scattered with remnants of a massive 12m (39-ft.) statue of the Emperor Constantine, including his colossal head, hand, and foot. These are said to be the only pieces of the original statue made of marble; the rest was carved from wood. Go in through the side door beside the giant index finger.

The museum floor plan is straightforward, taking you through each of the rooms in a circle around the building's center courtyard. On the first floor, the major works are in the first rooms. In **Room 1,** the Sala degli Oraz e Curiazi, don't miss the 2nd-century bronze statue of Hercules. Room 3 holds a 1st-century statue of a young boy digging a splinter out of his foot, called *Spinario.* Room 4 is the Sala della Lupe, dedicated entirely to a bronze statue from 500 B.C. of the famous she-wolf that suckled Romulus and Remus, the mythical founders of Rome. The twins were not on the original Etruscan statue; they were added during the Renaissance period in the 15th century. **Room 5** has Bernini's famously pained portrait of *Medusa.* The rest of these rooms are less significant artistically, so you can skim them without regret until you reach the stairway to the second-floor picture gallery with several masterpieces, including Caravaggio's *John the Baptist,* as well as Titian's *Baptism of Christ,* Tintoretto's *Penitent Madgalene,* and Veronese's *Rape of Europa.*

At the end of the picture gallery, head down to the ground floor and the underground tunnel that will take you under the piazza to the **Palazzo Nuovo.** The vacant Tabularium, built to safely house Ancient Rome's city records, was later used as a salt mine, and then as a prison.

Once inside the Palazzo Nuovo, start your tour in the open courtyard with the statue of Marcus Aurelius, which stood for decades in the center of the Piazza del Campidoglio outside. This section of the museum is dedicated to statues that were excavated from the forums below and brought in from outlying areas like Hadrian's Villa in Tivoli (p. 85). These statues are well marked and the floor plan is very straightforward. The masterpieces here are the 1st-century Capitoline Venus, in **Room 3,** and a chronologically arranged row of busts of Roman emperors and their families. These rooms are often filled with students of art history who study the busts for changes in sculpting techniques. The collection is perhaps equally telling of changes in hairstyles and fashion during the Roman empire. When you wander through these elegant, airy rooms, make sure you look out the windows onto the city below. Here you get fresh views that are hard to come by.

These museums can be seen in a couple of hours, if you are pressed for time. Or you can easily break them up around lunchtime and grab a sandwich at the museum coffee bar. Your integrated ticket is good for multiple entrances for 3 days, so you can even revisit them.

Museo di Palazzo Venezia

There are a handful of significant exhibits at the **Museo di Palazzo Venezia** (Via del Plebiscito, 118; ☎ 06-69994243; €4 adults, €2 seniors and students; daily

Centrale Montemartini

Before the year 2000 Jubilee celebrations in Rome, the Culture Ministry relocated all the statues not displayed in the Capitoline museums to an abandoned electricity warehouse outside the city gates, on Via Ostiense. Few believed the project would take off, but the **Centrale Montemartini** ★ 🌟 (Via Ostiense, 106; ☎ 06-5748030; www.museicapitolini.org; €4.80 or free with Capitoline Museum integrated ticket; bus: 23 or 769) has become one of the most provocative venues in the city. The pristine statues, many of which had never been seen, were set against shiny black machinery and the spruced-up antique gasworks. This is inarguable proof of what Romans do best in the way of creating a visually stunning presentation out of abandoned ruins. This museum is a favorite of Italian school groups.

8:30am–7:30pm, last entrance 6:30pm), like rarely seen terra-cotta models that Bernini used as trials before digging into real marble. But the reason to visit this museum is more recent history: to see the offices of Benito Mussolini and gaze out from the famous balcony over Piazza Venezia below (on the eastern side past the temporary exhibit space). The view from here will give you an idea of what the dictator saw as he addressed the crowds. The postcard view of the Colosseum stands at the foot of the Via dei Fori Imperiali.

The Pantheon

For many residents of Rome, the area between Piazza Navona and the Pantheon is for lingering and strolling, especially on Sundays in the fall and early spring, when everyone in the city, it seems, is here.

The Pantheon ★★★ (Piazza della Rotonda; free admission; Mon–Sat 8:30am–7:30pm, Sun 9am–6pm, holidays 9am–1pm) is like an enormous elephant hiding in the middle of a crowded village. The structure is the best-preserved antiquity in the entire city, and holds an allure that is almost magical, especially if you happen to visit when it is raining and the drops form a cylinder from the opening in the dome to the marble drains below. Built under Hadrian's direction (many of the structure's bricks contain the emperor's seal) between A.D. 119 and 128, the Pantheon was a temple to 12 gods. It was saved from ruin only because the Catholic Church claimed it in 608, even though the Church used it primarily as a quarry for materials for other churches. It is an arguable theory that the Pantheon's once-bronze dome was removed and melted down by Bernini in 1626 to make the *baldacchino,* or canopy, in St. Peter's Basilica.

The best way to appreciate the Pantheon is first from across the piazza on which it sits, gazing at the sheer magnitude of the massive pillars and domed roof. As you walk closer to the building, the detail of the pillars (which do not match) becomes apparent. Many of these massive granite pillars have been replaced over the Pantheon's 2,000-year history, and you may notice the notches on which vegetable market stalls were affixed until the 18th century.

Once inside the massive doors, look up at the 9m (30-ft.) oculus, which is believed to be there to allow worshipers direct contact with the heavens. It is the only source of light in the building, and the sunbeam acts as a spotlight on various points around the building. The Emperor Hadrian would only enter the building when the sun shone on the door, around 11am, depending on the time of year.

The diameter of the dome is 44m (146 ft.), and the dome itself gets lighter and thinner toward the top, decreasing from 7m (23-ft.) thickness at the edges to a thin 1m (3¼ ft.) close to the apex. It would take a professional to notice, but the materials used to build the dome vary from a heavy concrete and travertine on the lower third of the dome, volcanic tufa in the middle section, and lightweight pumice in the upper reaches.

The dome's structure was unsurpassed in terms of size and architectural accomplishment until the 1500s, when other domes were built. The seven niches, which are now tombs of kings and artists (Raphael is buried in the glass-encased tomb), once held statues of gods and goddesses.

The Pantheon is a great place to sit on one of the wooden benches along the perimeter. In the summer it can be quite crowded during the day, but it is invariably empty when it opens at 8:30am.

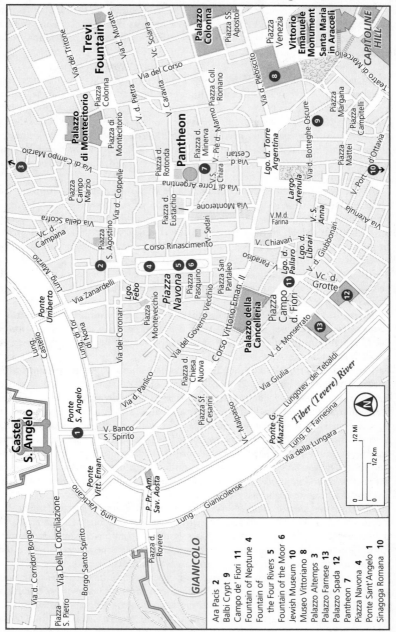

Trevi Fountain

Palazzo Colonna

Piazza SS. Apostoli

Piazza Venezia

Vittorio Emanuele Monument

Santa Maria in Aracoeli

CAPITOLINE HILL

Teatro di Marcello

Via del Tritone

Via delle Muratte

Vc. Sciarra

Via del Corso

Via del Plebiscito

Palazzo di Montecitorio

Piazza Colonna

Piazza di Montecitorio

V. d. Pietra

V. Caravita

Piazza Coll. Romano

V. Ple d. Marmo

Piazza Margana

Piazza Campitelli

Via di Campo Marzio

Via d. Coppelle

Piazza d. Rotonda

Piazza d. Minerva

V.S. Chiara

Via d. Cestari

Via d. Botteghe Oscure

Piazza Mattei

V. Port. d'Ottavia

Piazza Campo Marzio

Pantheon

Piazza d. Eustachio

Via di Torre Argentina

Lgo. d. Torre Argentina

⑦

⑧

⑨

⑩

Vc. d. Campana

Via della Scrofa

S. Agostino

Piazza S. Agostino

Corso Rinascimento

Via Monterone

⑫

Largo Arenula

V.M.d. Farina

V. S. Anna

Lung. Marzio

②

Via Zanardelli

Lgo. Febo

④

Piazza Navona

Piazza Pasquino

⑤

⑥

Piazza San Pantaleo

V. Chiavari

V. Paradiso

Lgo. d. Pallaro

Lgo. d. Librari

V. d. Giubbonari

Vc. d. Grotte

⑪

⑫

Ponte Umberto

Lung. Tor di Nona

Piazza Montevecchio

Via dei Coronari

Via del Governo Vecchio

Corso Vittorio Eman. II

Palazzo della Cancelleria

Piazza Campo d. Fiori

⑬

Lung. Castello

Via d. Panico

Piazza d. Chiesa Nuova

V. d. Monserrato

Via Giulia

Via Arenula

Castel S. Angelo

Ponte S. Angelo

①

Via d. Banco S. Spirito

Piazza Sf. Cesarini

Piazza d. Farnesina

Vc. Malpasso

Lungotev. dei Tebaldi

Tiber (Tevere) River

Ponte Vitt. Eman.

③

Ponte G. Mazzini

Lung. d. Farnesina

Lung. della Lungara

Lung. Vaticano

P. Pr. Am. Sav. Aosta

Via Gianicolense

Via d. Corridori Borgo

Via Della Conciliazione

Borgo Santo Spirito

Borgo Santo Pietro

Piazza S. Pietro

GIANICOLO

Piazza d. Rovere

0   1/2 Mi

0   1/2 Km

N

Ara Pacis **2**
Balbi Crypt **11**
Campo de' Fiori **9**
Fountain of Neptune **4**
Fountain of
  the Four Rivers **5**
Fountain of the Moor **6**
Jewish Museum **10**
Museo Vittoriano **8**
Palazzo Altemps **3**
Palazzo Farnese **13**
Palazzo Spada **12**
Pantheon **7**
Piazza Navona **4**
Ponte Sant'Angelo **1**
Sinagoga Romana **10**

Behind the Pantheon, in front of the Gothic Church of Santa Maria sopra Minerva, sits *Il Pulcino della Minerva*—also known as Bernini's elephant—which was symbolic in the Catholic Church for its wisdom and abstinence (elephants are notoriously monogamous).

PIAZZA NAVONA ✪✪✪

From the Pantheon it is less than a 10-minute walk west to Piazza Navona, which may be Rome's favorite square. It sits above an ancient stadium built by Emperor Domitian, which you can still see below the modern city from the Piazza di Tor Sanguigna, 16, on the northern end of the oval. The old stadium was often flooded for mock sea battles, which is said to be where Navona, which means boat in Roman dialect, is derived. Call ☎ 06-67103819 for guided tours of the old stadium Saturday and Sunday from 10am to 1pm.

In the center of the modern piazza above is Bernini's famous **Fontana dei Quattro Fiumi,** which represents the four rivers of paradise: the Nile, Ganges, Plate, and Danube. There is a false legend that Bernini designed one of the statues facing the church of Sant'Agnese to shield its eyes from the "horror of the church." If you look above the church of Sant'Agnese, you'll see what old timers say is the statue of a woman who is turned away from the fountain in disgust. But the legend, which is a delightful piece of trivia, is false—the fountain was built before the church. Bernini's statues, instead, are shielding their eyes from the unknown source of the rivers.

At the north end of Piazza Navona is the lovely **Fontana del Nettuno (Fountain of Neptune)** showing Neptune fighting a sea serpent. The **Fontana del Moro (Fountain of the Moor)** on the opposite end depicts another sea god and a dolphin designed by Bernini.

Just north of Piazza Navona, the **Museo Nazionale Romano: Palazzo Altemps** ✪✪ (Piazza Sant'Apollinare, 48; ☎ 06-6833566; adults €7, seniors and students €3.50; Tues–Sun 9am–7:45pm), tucked inside Palazzo Altemps, is one of Rome's most charming museums. It is rarely crowded and houses some of Rome's most famous private and public collections of art. This is the type of museum you visit as much for the venue as for the collections. The pieces here are not great in number, but they are individually superb. **Room 7,** in particular, has two 1st-century statues of *Apollo the Lyrist,* and in the south loggia do not miss the *Galatian Soldier and His Wife Committing Suicide* in **Room 26,** or the famous bust of the mother of Emperor Claudius in **Room 21.**

On the other side of Piazza Navona, the **Museo di Roma** (Palazzo Braschi, Via di San Pantaleo, 10; ☎ 06-67108346; www.museodiroma.comune.roma.it; adults €6.20, seniors and students €3.10; Tues–Sun 9am–7pm) is a wonderful respite from the summer heat, but it's not the best museum in Rome unless you are interested in recent history. There is an abundance of exhibits here depicting Rome in the 17th century and later, which does give perspective to the transition from ancient to modern Rome. There are many sculptures and drawings, but more interesting are the furnishings and clothing from wealthy Roman families.

There are also a handful of churches in this area worth ducking into. **Chiesa Nuova/Santa Maria in Vallicella** ✪ (Piazza della Chiesa Nuova; ☎ 06-6875289) houses stunning frescoes, including Neri's *Vision of the Virgin* and the *Assumption of the Virgin,* in the main apse by Pietro da Cortona. Down the street, **Santa Maria**

della Pace ★★ (Vicolo del Arco della Pace, 5; ☎ 06-6861156; officially but rarely open Tues–Fri 10am–12:45pm) is worth trying to get in, though it seems the posted hours mean nothing. But try to visit so you can see **Raphael's** *Sybils.* While you are here, duck into the **Cloister of Bramante** next door, which is primarily a modern venue for visiting art exhibits, though if you only want to see the heavenly cloister, you generally don't have to pay the admission for the exhibit. These cloisters are some of the best in Italy, and define precisely the meditative purpose these structures serve.

Back on the other side of the Pantheon is the glorious church of **Sant'Ignazio di Loyola** (Piazza Sant'Ignazio; ☎ 06-6794406; 7:30am–12:15pm and 3–7:15pm), which is the center of the Jesuit order of the Catholic Church. When this church was built in 1626, those living in a nearby monastery feared that a giant dome, which was in the original plans, would block their light. Instead, the artist Andrea Pozzo just painted the ceiling to mimic the inside of a dome—if you stand on the circular disk in the nave, you will be fooled into thinking the dome is genuine.

CAMPO DE' FIORI & THE JEWISH GHETTO

The sliver of city along the Tiber River stretching from the Jewish synagogue to the busy **Via Vittorio Emmanuel II** is very much the lifeblood of Rome's center. The streets here are tiny alleyways and, unlike Trastevere (p. 63) on the other side of the Tiber River, or the more posh Tridente close to the Spanish Steps, there is a better sense here of neighborhood and Roman culture. It is here you see the delicate balance between those who have always lived in Rome—mostly in this district—and those who come here to live for a few days or a few years. In the Jewish Ghetto, the matrons bring their kitchen chairs outside to sit together each evening before supper in a way more reminiscent of a tiny village than a sprawling European capital.

Campo de' Fiori is the core of this section of Rome. Starting about 6am, it offers a colorful display of regional pride as the market vendors make an art out of selling everything from rosemary plants to potatoes. It is a ridiculously expensive vegetable market, though, with prices per kilogram sometimes double those of other markets. But people don't necessarily come here for the produce—it is a piazza with energy and vibrancy—perfect for a visitor who wants to feel as if he or she is part of the community. It is very much *un*like Testaccio (p. 80), though, because there are many hotels and a very high concentration of foreign residents living in this part of Rome.

Mid-afternoon is the most dangerous time to be here; lately local police have pinpointed this area as an afternoon drug haven. But around 5pm, it becomes a mod locale to take an after-work drink, and those over 30 gather at the wine bars and beer joints around the perimeter. By mid-evening, though, the square transforms into an open-air mecca for the 20-something crowds whose stamina should be admired. There is a sense of unnerving chaos here come midnight, especially in the summer months when the piazza is filled with drinking, smoking, moped-driving kids.

It is never a mistake to take a walk through the **Galleria Spada** ★ (Piazza Capo di Ferro, 3; ☎ 06-6874896; www.galleriaborghese.it; adults €5, seniors and students €2.50; Tues–Sun 8:30am–7:30pm). This gorgeous *palazzo* houses the private art collection of Cardinal Bernardino Spada. Its most impressive aspect is the guided tour of the Borromini Perspective, which leaves when there are enough people gathered. This is a museum for those who don't like museums. The rooms, which were built as a private home for Cardinal Girolamo Capo di Ferro in 1540, are intriguing, with original frescoes and old uneven tile floors. The art here is literally plastered all over the walls, which makes it less assuming and somehow easier to enjoy than the showcase art at some of the more traditional museums. There is a very cozy feel here, and there are informative handouts with explanations in English.

The **Museo Barracco di Scultura Antica** (Corso Vittorio, 166; ☎ 06-68806848; adults €2.60, seniors and students €1.60; Tues–Sun 9am–7pm) is, unlike the Galleria Spada, a museum for people who do like museums. It has recently been restored and has a cold, almost institutional feel to it, though the exhibits of pre-Roman art are impressive. There are lots of vases, reliefs, and relics, but it's nothing compared to both the Capitoline and Vatican museums. Museo Barracco is definitely a worthy museum, even though a much more interesting stop is the very new **Crypta Balbi** ★★ (Via delle Botteghe Oscure, 31; ☎ 06-6780167; integrated ticket €7 adults, €3.50 children), which defines, in great detail, the layers of Rome and how they represent the city's evolution from the 5th to the 10th centuries. This museum is often empty, which is surprising because it is so well endowed with exhibits like the tools and objects from everyday life in ancient Rome. Down below the museum is the crypt and ruins of an old set of stores where grains were sold and distributed. This is the newest addition to Rome's National Museum and is still one of the city's best kept secrets.

The Ghetto

Between the Crypta Balbi and the Tiber River is what is known as the Ghetto, which is still home to Europe's oldest Jewish community, which has lived in this neighborhood for 2,000 years. The jewel of this area is the synagogue, which is accessible through the **Museo d'Arte Ebraica** ★★ (Lungotevere Cenci; ☎ 06-68400661; €6, includes admission to synagogue; Mon–Thurs 9am–4:30pm, until 6:30 during summer, Fri 9am–1:30pm, Sun 9am–noon). This museum has displays of some truly beautiful art—from crowns to Torah mantles—and it also tells the tragic history of the persecution of Rome's Jewish citizens over the course of history. There are papal edicts that surely make the modern-day Church cringe, as well as grim artifacts from concentration camps across Europe. Along the Via Lungara (p. 65) is a plaque commemorating October 16, 1943, the day that Rome's Jewish families were rounded up and deported from the Ghetto to concentration camps.

Behind the synagogue on the **Via Portico d'Ottavia** are the ruins of an ancient piazza and the remnants of great temples that date back to Emperor Augustus in the 1st century. You can walk behind the ruins through a small passage near the end of the street, and wind your way toward the **Fontana delle Tartarughe** (Piazza Mattei). This was built in the 1580s for the Duke of Mattei in 1 night to impress his fiancée (she lived in the large *palazzo,* which now houses the Center for American Studies). Hers is the window now walled in, but one can easily imagine her surprise when she woke to find the fountain built just for her.

TIBER ISLAND & BOCCA DELLA VERITÀ

Between the two similarly decaying districts of the Ghetto and Trastevere lies Tiber Island, which was said to be built on the site of a sunken ship in the 3rd century B.C. It was originally adorned with travertine marble in the shape of a giant ship, with an obelisk at the center for the mast. You can still see the remnants of the travertine siding on the east side of the island, below the police station, by walking down the narrow steps just below the Fate Bene Fratelli Hospital that occupies the entire northern end. The wide promenade on the bottom fills with Sunday strollers and springtime sunbathers, and is the location of Rome's annual open-air cinema for much of the summer. Up above the churches of St. Bartholomew on the southern side is a popular spot for weddings. Across the narrow street on the hospital side, the decadent marble-encrusted church and convent of San Giovanni Calibita Fate Bene Fratelli are dedicated to the hospital, but often host city-sponsored exhibits.

On the southern side of the island, you can stand below the remains of the **Ponte Rotto (Broken Bridge),** Rome's first stone bridge, built in 142 B.C. It connected the main city with the area across the Tiber, giving birth to *Tras tevere* which means "across the Tiber."

It's a short walk from the east side to one of the city's most-photographed sites. Inside the 6th-century church of **Santa Maria in Cosmedian** (Via della Bocca della Verità, 18; ☎ 06-6781419; free admission; daily 9am–5pm winter, until 6pm in summer) is the **Bocca della Verità (Mouth of Truth).** The legend states that anyone who tells a lie while his hand is in the mouth will have it bitten off, and locals like to say that it was Roman wives suspicious of cheating husbands who started requiring the test. The giant mask is actually thought to be an ancient drain cover.

TRASTEVERE

You need to spend but 5 minutes in Trastevere to appreciate its seductive allure. It has the most distinctive personality of all Rome's neighborhoods. It is at times unspoiled and unassuming, yet at other moments, it is darkly mysterious and wildly intriguing. The decaying facades of the tightly packed buildings give it an old-world feel. Sometimes Trastevere does not feel like Rome at all; at other times it is the only Rome there is.

It is a mistake to explore this area with a fixed agenda. This is the place where you should wander, as aimlessly as possible, like a mouse through the dizzying maze of alleyways. You should turn corners, walk into churches, sit on *piazze,* and simply gaze up at the rooftop gardens and down at the cobblestone streets. The time of day you visit Trastevere will dictate what you should do. Early mornings are glorious here, as the shutters are flung open and the Trasteverini start the day. You'll hear a chorus of *"oui"* and *"eh,"* as the locals greet each other from their windows and down in the streets. Old timers here tend to stick to their particular corner, and there are some locals who haven't been "to the other side" of the river for years. In the middle of the day, after the stores and churches close for the sacred siesta, stop and listen to the echo of footsteps and the whispers down the narrow cobblestone streets. Trastevere is like an a ghost town around 2pm, an ideal time to listen to the sounds that pour out of the open windows. It is truly a voyeur's paradise.

Trastevere is perhaps best in the late afternoons, when the children play soccer in the squares and the smell of the burning wood from the just-lit pizza ovens fills the air. At night, the restaurant scene is unimaginably vibrant, with people of every age, from tiny babies in buggies to elderly couples walking hand in hand, filling the streets. Even at midnight, especially in the summer, Trastevere is just springing to life. Because of that, don't stay in this part of town if you are fond of quiet nights.

To most people, **Piazza Santa Maria** in Trastevere is the proverbial heart and soul of this area. Any time of the day or night, this piazza is buzzing with the type of contagious activity that most visitors equate with life in Rome. The 17th-century fountain in the center is the meeting point for those who live here, and it typifies much of what Trastevere is all about, even though lately the residents on this piazza are mostly foreigners who have all but run out the locals with high rent prices. That said, there are still more than enough locals living in the back streets to keep this neighborhood genuine. The church on this square, **Santa Maria** ★★ (Piazza Santa Maria; ☎ 065814802; daily 7:30am–8pm), is famous for the 13th-century mosaics on the facade of Mary breastfeeding Jesus alongside 10 women with crowns and lanterns (often thought to represent the parable of the wise and foolish virgins). This is one of the oldest churches in Rome and it is by far one of its most captivating. It is a perfect place to light a candle or to sit in a pew, to take in the smell of burning incense, and to admire the 12th-century mosaics by Pietro Cavallini that cover the apse. On weekends in the spring, it's not uncommon to witness gorgeous weddings against a backdrop of fresh flowers, and on Saturday evenings, you can join the local faithful as they stream in for evening Mass.

Behind Piazza Santa Maria, the streets wind around and pour out into a number of interesting *piazze* with tiny museums. **Museo di Roma in Trastevere** (Piazza Sant'Egidio, 1B; ☎ 06-5816563; www.comune.roma.it/museodiroma.trastevere; €2.60; daily 10am–8pm, ticket booth closes 1 hr. earlier) hosts temporary exhibits in addition to the standing *Roma Sparita* (Vanished Rome) depictions by Ettore Roesler Frazz, the artist who captured views of Rome just as they disappeared. There is also another *bocca della verità*, but this one is without the tourists and long lines. It is by no means a museum you must see, but it is one that won't disappoint you if you feel intrigued.

Down the way from here are the lush **Botanical Gardens (Orto Botanico)** ★ (Largo Cristina di Svezia, 24; ☎ 06-49917106; adults €3, children €2; Nov–Mar 9:30am–5:30pm, 1 hr. later rest of the year), with over 3,500 species of plants, including a sight-and-scent garden for the visually impaired. These gardens once belonged to the controversial Queen Christina of Sweden, whose home was the adjacent **Palazzo Corsini, Galleria Nazionale d'Arte Antica** (Via della Lungara, 10; ☎ 06-6874845; www.galleriaborghese.it; adults €4, seniors and students €2; guided tours Tues–Fri at 9:30, 11:30am, and 12:30pm, Sat and holidays tours at 8:30am and 1:20pm). She moved to Rome when she abdicated the Swedish throne after converting to Catholicism, but her most famous epithet is "Queen without a realm, Christian without a faith, and a woman without shame." This stemmed from her blatant bisexuality, which in the 17th century was frowned upon—at least publicly. Several other big names stayed in this beautiful palace, including Michelangelo and Napoleon's mother, Letizia. Now it houses a moderately interesting museum with mostly the runoff from Italy's national art collection. There is a Caravaggio here worth note, the *Narcissus,* but otherwise the palace history and legend are more interesting than the museum itself.

Via Lungara, Back Street to the Vatican

The **Via Lungara** in Trastevere takes you up a winding path to Vatican City, past residential villas, glorious fountains, and captivating views of the center of Rome from various points on the side of the Gianicolo Hill. It's a walk worth doing if you have solid shoes and time to enjoy it. It is here that a plaque commemorates the fateful day of October 16, 1943, when the city's Jewish families were deported to concentration camps—it's a chillingly simple monument to commemorate such an unforgivable atrocity. Carry on this walk until you see the peak of St. Peter's Basilica, and follow the winding trail to the Vatican City gates.

A better museum is just across the street: the **Villa Farnesina** (Via della Lungara, 230; ☎ 06-68027268; www.lincei.it; adults €5, seniors and students €4; 9am–1pm, Mar 15–June 30, Sept 15–Oct 31, and Dec also open afternoons), which is one of the best places to see Raphael's works, from *The Triumph of Galatea* to *Cupid and Psyche.*

Continue your exploration of Trastevere from the Via Lungara, wind your way back to the busy Viale Trastevere, which bisects the district, and cross into the quieter side of this neighborhood. The heart of this part of the neighborhood is the charming **Piazza di Santa Cecilia** with its 9th-century **Basilica di Santa Cecilia** ★★ (daily 9:30am–12:30pm and 3:45–6:40pm). There is much to do in this tiny church, starting with the ruins of the house where St. Cecilia once lived. She was martyred for her strong faith and vow of chastity—even to her husband—first by a failed attempt at scalding her, and then by a slow decapitation that took 3 days to finish her off. The nuns inside the church, who charge €2 for entrance to the ruins of St. Cecilia's house below, say that she sang during the last days of her life, and as such was made the patron saint of music. Her body was allegedly found intact when her tomb was opened in 1599. Artist Stefano Maderno immediately captured this image and it was later sculpted in white marble. The nuns say the original is in the San Callisto catacombs (though the priests at the San Callisto catacombs say the original is here at the altar). You should also try to visit the 13th-century fresco of *The Last Judgment* by Pietro Cavallini (Tues and Thurs 10am–noon, Sun 11:30am–12:30pm) back in the choir, which is still used by the adjacent convent's cloistered nuns. If you are here when the frescoes are closed, you can almost certainly still see them if you pledge an offering to the sisters who tend the church. If you happen to be wandering in Trastevere around 6am, you will often hear the cloistered nuns of this church singing their morning prayers.

From here, you can easily visit the **Chiesa di San Francesco D'Assisi A Ripa** (Piazza San Francesco d'Assisi, 88) and its Bernini sculpture of the *Ecstasy of Beata Ludovica,* which may make you want to convert if her expression is any indication of what being a Catholic is really about. It also has the rock that St. Francis reportedly used as a pillow, but you'll have to twist the arm of the attendant to see it; it's not usually shown to the public.

You should definitely try to duck into the **Chiostro dei Genovesi** (Via Anicia, 12; Apr–Oct Tues and Thurs 3–6pm, Nov Tues and Thurs 2–4pm; ring SPOSITO on the intercom by the door) down the street. It makes up for the lack of cloisters in Rome. The green oasis is overflowing with gorgeous flowers and offers a tranquil respite from the chaos outside. It was once a hospice for sailors from Genoa, designed by Baccio Pontelli. Admission is free, but you should make a modest offering.

Gianicolo

Up above Trastevere is the Gianicolo, which runs all the way to Vatican City. At the top of the hill, a monument to Giuseppe Garibaldi stands in representation of the many battles fought for Rome, and nearby is a statue of his Brazilian wife, Anita, on a feisty horse, holding their baby in one hand and a pistol in the other. **Piazzale Giuseppe Garibaldi** is the best place to watch the sun set over Rome, as the orange hue of Trastevere below seems to wash to gray when night falls. It is ultraromantic, and you will see your fair share of public affection here. But it is also a nice diversion if you've got kids. There is a puppet theater (in Italian only) and merry-go-round and pony rides during the late afternoon.

VATICAN CITY

For many people, it is virtually impossible to separate Vatican City from Rome. The two entities seem to intertwine as one bustling metropolis, though, in reality, they are distinct places. Vatican City, called the Holy See, has been an independent state since 1929, when Mussolini and Pope Pius XII signed the Lateran Pact giving Vatican City sovereignty and giving the Pope ultimate control over this tiny parcel of land bordered by the Vatican walls. There are 800 mostly male residents in Vatican City, which has its own independent government, independent passports, embassies, and diplomatic status with nearly every country in the world. In addition, Vatican City has its own army, its own media outlets, its own well-stocked international pharmacy, and a postal system far more efficient than the regular Italian post.

Vatican City's most obvious gems, like St. Peter's Basilica, the Vatican Museums, and the Sistine Chapel, are really only a facet of this multi-dimensional country. Popes representing the Vatican have always had the ear of, or at least

---

The Swiss Guard

The Vatican army, or Swiss Guard, is made up of 100 Swiss men: 4 officers, 1 chaplain, 23 non-commissioned officers, 70 halberdiers (weapon carriers), and 2 drummers. In many ways they are a modern-day male version of the ancient Vestal Virgins (p. 51), though instead of the sacred flame of vestal, they are tasked with protecting the Pope when he travels, and with keeping harm from the Apostolic Palace within Vatican City. Their colorful formal uniforms were designed by Michelangelo in the colors of the Medici family. They live within the walls of Vatican City and must not marry until their duty is complete—they serve between 2 and 25 years. Recruits must be under 30 and at least 1.7m (5 ft. 8 in.) tall. And, of course, they must be upstanding Roman Catholics, as witnessed by their parish priests.

Bronze Door **4**	Sacristy & Treasury **10**
Excavations office **11**	Sistine Chapel **5**
Grotto Entrance **10**	Statue of St. Peter **7**
Hall of Audiences **13**	Vatican Gardens **2**
House of Pius IV **3**	Vatican Museums
Michelangelo's *Pietà* **6**	Entrance **1**
Palace of the	Vatican Post Office **12**
Governorship **8**	Vatican Radio **9**

been given royal treatment by, key world leaders. In theory, the Vatican is not supposed to meddle in Italian politics; the Church's influence is, however, often obvious in policy-making in Italy, which has recently adopted fertility laws backed by the Holy See and continues to hold conservative views on gay marriage.

St. Peter's Basilica

The most sensible place to start your visit to Vatican City is **St. Peter's Basilica** (Piazza San Pietro; ☎ 06-69881662; www.vatican.va; Oct–Mar 7am–6pm, until 7pm rest of year). Admission is free, though there are several collection boxes inside the church. You must enter the church via metal detectors on the right-hand side of the piazza (facing the church). At the time of this writing, there are two separate queues after the detectors, one for the *chiesa* (to go inside the basilica) and another for the crypt (to visit the papal tomb through a temporary entrance). (The second line may disappear when the crowds are no longer flocking to Rome just to see the tomb of Pope John Paul II, who died Apr 2, 2005.) Either way, there is a barricade near the foot of the steps into the church where your attire will be scrutinized by the Vatican's fashion police, who enforce the church's strict dress code. No one wearing shorts is allowed inside. (There are dressing rooms behind the main steps into the church to change into more appropriate clothing.) At the top of the steps into the church, the queue divides again between the *chiesa,* which leads to the inside of the church, and the Cupola, which takes you to the top of the dome. It makes the most sense to visit the church before the Cupola.

The current church took 120 years to build. It was completed in 1626 on the site of the original church that had been built 1,300 years earlier. A few remnants of the original basilica still exist, like the Giotto mosaic in the portico just opposite the main entrance door. Once inside, the natural tendency is to veer to your right to see Michelangelo's famous *Pietà* first, since that's the flow of the tour-group traffic. But you'll have a much better perspective of the sheer magnitude of this basilica if you walk down the center aisle from the back of the church all the way to the front (unless it is set up with chairs or otherwise closed for an event, which is common around Easter). Head toward Bernini's baroque *baldacchino,* or canopy, over the main altar, reserved for the Pope. The exquisitely detailed canopy is made from the bronze that may have once adorned the inside of the dome of the Pantheon. The design is inspired by a Mesopotamian tradition of draping woven silks made in Baghdad over a four-poster framework to mark a holy site. Bernini sculpted the face of a woman on each of the pillars, whose countenance is progressively contorted in childbirth pain starting with the first face on the left pillar (with your back to the entrance of the church). Circle the entire altar to see the progression until the fourth pillar, where the woman's face is replaced with a newborn's unmistakable mug.

While walking up the **middle aisle,** look for the various names of churches and brass lines inscribed into the marble floor—they identify the length of those churches compared to St. Peter's. Once you've reached the dark *baldacchino,* look up to the top of the giant dome above, where St. Peter is believed to have been

Pope-Spotting

Millions of devout Catholics come to Vatican City each year to make a religious pilgrimage and, more recently, to catch a glimpse of the new Pope, Benedict XVI, who blesses the faithful and curious alike in St. Peter's Square every Sunday at noon when he is in Rome. Go early if you want to see him in his apartment window above Bernini's colonnade. The best place to stand is near the obelisk in the center of the square, though these spots are generally taken by locals who arrive early. The Pope also holds a public audience each Wednesday, in St. Peter's Square on sunny days and in the Sala Navi auditorium when the weather is grim. You must apply for the free papal audience through the **Prefettura della Casa Pontificia** (☎ 06-69883114, 06-69883273; fax 06-69885863; Mon–Sat 9am–1:30pm), or, if you're a Catholic, through your local parish priest. Tickets must be picked up the morning of the audience at the bronze door to the left of St. Peter's Basilica on St. Peter's Square.

You can **write to the Pope** (which often results in an autographed photo) at **His Holiness Pope Benedict XVI, Apostolic Palace, Vatican City, EUROPE 00120.** He also has an e-mail address: benedictxvi@vatican.va.

Necropolis

With some planning, you can visit the excavations far below the church. Contact the **Uffizio degli Scavi** (☎ 06-69885318; fax 06-69885518; scavi@fsp.va; €10) in writing to reserve a much sought-after spot on a guided tour. That tour has lately become very exclusive and often you can only get in with a letter of recommendation from your parish priest or from a professor if you are a student of archaeology. It's worth at least applying to get in just in case, but you must keep in touch with the office yourself because they won't track you down. English-language tours must be booked 25 days in advance, and children under 12 are not allowed to take the tour.

crucified. Below the main altar in the enclave surrounded by steps is a tiny shrine with a modest 9th-century mosaic of Christ, again from the original church. Below that are what the devoted believe to be the bones of St. Peter.

From here, the top spot for pilgrims to the basilica tends to be the brass statue of St. Peter just behind the altar. There is usually a short queue to kiss his worn foot near the main altar.

From Bernini's *baldacchino,* head to the **right side of the church** to visit the important chapels here. In the first chapel near the entrance is the *Pietà,* Michelangelo's first major work, completed when he was 25 years old. Vandals attacked this statue, which is why it now stands behind bullet-proof glass. The crowds are thickest here, but they tend to move quickly, so it's easy to stand at the front for a few moments. From behind the baluster, it's difficult to spot Michelangelo's signature across the Virgin Mary's chest.

Other highlights include the only original painting left in this church, the *Trinity* by Pietro da Cortona, in the third chapel. The rest have been replaced with replicas made from mosaic tiles. At the very **back of the church,** pilgrims can attend Mass (check the sign at the entrance to the pews for times) under Bernini's *Throne to St. Peter.* Toward the papal altar, displayed on the pillars that support the giant dome, are several artifacts important to Catholics, including a fragment from the True Cross and a statue of St. Veronica holding a cloth she used to wipe Christ's face. All along the side aisles are chapels, shrines, altars, and monuments. These are generally not well marked, though they are worth exploring. The Vatican sells a guidebook that will give you more detail of these shrines.

The Crypt

Once you've finished exploring the inside of St. Peter's, head down to the grottoes below the current church, and above the necropolis of the ancient church. Since John Paul II's death in April 2005, visiting the papal tombs has become an ordeal. You must leave the church and re-enter the line where you almost have to nudge your way in to avoid starting back before the metal detectors. When the crowds cease to flock to pray at his tomb, you'll be able to reach the crypt from inside the church near the *baldacchino.*

The Cupola

Visiting the dome of St. Peter's is an essential way to connect the various entities of Vatican City that you can see from above. Follow signs on the right-hand side of the basilica for the **Cupola** ★★ (€4, €6 with elevator; Oct–Apr 8am–4:45pm, until 5:45 rest of year). The first "get off" point is the inner rim just under Michelangelo's dome, which allows you to appreciate both the detailed mosaics of the dome's interior and the intricate marble designs on the floor of the church. The mesh fence is to deter suicides, which were a common problem here in the 1980s. There is a gift shop outside on the rooftop, run by friendly nuns, but it's better to stop on your way back down so you don't have to carry your treasures up the remaining 320 steps. When you leave the inner dome, follow the tiny signs for the Cupola, which takes about 20 minutes to reach from here. It is well worth making this trek to get a view of the Vatican's walls and Rome from the city's highest point. But, do this only if you can physically manage. The passageway near the upper reaches is shoulder-width on an average person, and it is very crowded, with few options for resting, and absolutely no way to turn back until you've reached the top.

The Vatican Museums

There are many ways to visit the **Vatican Museums** ★★★ (Viale del Vaticano; ☎ 06-69883333; www.vatican.va; year-round, last Sun of month free 8:45am–12:20pm; €12 adults, €8 seniors and students, €21 reserved with guided tour; Mar–Oct Mon–Sat 8:45am–3:20pm, Sun until 12:20pm; Nov–Feb Mon–Sat 8:45am–12:20pm, closed Catholic holidays). If you are in Rome for only a day or two, consider the €21 guided tour with reserved ticket. The tour takes 2 hours to cover the highlights, and you save at least that much time by avoiding lines.

There are also four color-coded, self-guided itineraries through the massive museums which take between 2 and 5 hours, depending on the care with which you peruse the collections. The quickest way to see the museums, if you are among the first 100 in, is to head straight for the Sistine Chapel—following the often hidden signs—when you enter the main museum, and then make your way back around to the various rooms and galleries you want to see. If you are in the middle of thousands and thousands of visitors who are allowed to enter the museums at the same time, this shortcut won't make much difference because the Sistine Chapel will be jam-packed no matter how quickly you get there.

In 2000, the Vatican Museums installed metal detectors to deter both vandalism and terrorism, so the entrance to the museums is something like boarding an aircraft. Large monitors flash listings of closed exhibits and rooms under refurbishment, and there is a general sense of hasty movement, as tour leaders try to keep their groups close by and Vatican guards move the crowds quickly to let more inside. Do your best to weave through these groups and take the escalator to the mezzanine floor and the ticket booth. A separate booth rents audioguides, which are very useful. You don't have to listen to several hours of monotone descriptions; just punch in the number of the exhibit you are looking at (noted by tiny plaques near each exhibit displaying an earphone around the digits) for individual explanations.

If you can only spend a few hours here, narrow your tour to include only the **Sistine Chapel, Raphael Rooms, Pinacoteca,** and **Gallery of Maps.**

As with most museums, your own tastes should dictate where you focus your attention, but the following highlights should help you narrow down the choices.
Appartamento Borgia: The six rooms of these apartments are decorated with religious frescoes focused on biblical themes. They were originally designed for the Borgia Pope Alexander VI (1492–1503). **Museo Gregoriano Profano:** This small set of rooms houses sculptures found at the Baths of Caracalla (p. 79). The Greek statues are from the 4th and 5th centuries B.C.; the Roman statues are from the 1st, 2nd, and 3rd centuries A.D. **Galleria delle Carte Geografiche:** The 120m-long (394-ft.) Gallery of Maps was commissioned by Pope Gregory XIII. The frescoed maps were first drawn by Ignazio Danti of Perugia in 1580 to 1583 to represent each region, city, and island of Italy. **Museo Egiziano:** The collections in these rooms represent ancient Egyptian art from 3000 to 600 B.C., including mummies, a depiction of a baboon god, and marble statues of significant leaders like Trono di Rameses II. **Pinacoteca:** The picture galleries include many masterpieces collected by various popes and cardinals over the ages. You'll see the museums' most famous works here, including Giotto's *Stefaneschi Triptych,* Raphael's *The Transfiguration* (his last work), and Caravaggio's *Entombment.* **Stanze di Raffaello, Loggia di Raffaello, Cappella di Niccolo V:** The Raphael Rooms are among the finest museum offerings in the world. These rooms were originally used as the Papal Suite and designed by Raphael when he was only 26 years old. If you can, see these in the order in which they were painted, starting with the Study (Stanza della Segnatura), which was completed between 1508 and 1511 on the theme of the triumph of Truth, Good, and Beauty. Most notable here is the *School of Athens,* which features portraits of famous names of the day. Leonardo da Vinci is pointing up to the heavens a la Plato; Michelangelo (who was painting the nearby Sistine Chapel when Raphael did this work) is alone in front of the steps; and even a self-portrait of Raphael is on the right-hand corner.

Almost Hell

Down the Lungotevere, which borders the Tiber River from Vatican City, is Rome's smallest Gothic church, **Sacro Cuore del Suffragio (Sacred Heart of Suffrage;** Lungotevere, 12; ☎ 06-68806517; daily 7:30am–11am and 4pm–7pm), which holds the freakish **Museum of the Souls of Purgatory.** A chapel inside the original church was destroyed by fire in 1897 and in the singed remains the faithful congregation could see the outline of a face they believed was a soul caught in purgatory. The singed face prompted the local priest, Father Victor Jouet from Marseilles, to seek out other signs from the souls in purgatory, which he collected over the years. These haunting relics line the corridor to the church sacristy, and include fabrics, photos, writing materials, and other items that believers attest have been somehow touched by those waiting in purgatory. A book of devotion dated 1871 with the imprint of three fingers, and a photo of a deceased woman said to be asking for a holy Mass in her name are two of the relics on display. Followers are urged to come to this church to pray that the souls in purgatory be released.

January in Rome

There is no better time to be in Rome than January, when the museums are empty and the air is crisp and clean. In January, you can stand all alone in front of the Trevi Fountain and be one of a few dozen visitors in the Sistine Chapel. What you sacrifice in summer Mediterranean sunshine, you will more than make up for in the reward of having these great gems of Rome to yourself. The sales are in full swing and you can generally cash in on bargain "last minute" deals as hoteliers try desperately to fill their rooms. The restaurants light their fireplaces and you can linger longer over your warm meal. Savory soups replace pasta and the dark, warm *mirtillo* digestive is served instead of *limoncello*. The cafe-bars serve rich hot chocolate *con panna* and the cappuccinos seem extra frothy. The temperature is brisk, but almost never dips below freezing. Snow in Rome is a rare and celebrated event—one you can only hope you're here for. There is something very congenial about Rome in the dead of winter; it is still a place where you can have lunch outside most days, but it's also a place that seems to have come out of hiding.

The Sistine Chapel

The most famous frescoes in the world fill the massive ceiling of the Sistine Chapel, which is where the conclave to elect the Pope is held. Michelangelo completed the work over the period of 1508 to 1512; it is said he spent the entire 4 years on his feet, paint dripping into his eyes. Start your visual journey at the *Last Judgment* and move back through *Separation of Light and Darkness,* the *Creation of Sun, Moon and Planets,* the *Separation of Land and Sea,* the *Creation of Fishes and Birds,* the *Creation of Adam,* the *Creation of Eve,* the *Temptation* and *Expulsion from Paradise,* the *Sacrifice of Noah,* the *Flood,* and the *Drunkenness of Noah.*

At the age of 60, Michelangelo was summoned to finish the chapel decor 23 years after he finished the ceiling work. He was said to be saddened by the state of Rome and painted these dark moods in his *Last Judgment,* where he included his own self-portrait on a sagging human hide held by St. Bartholomew.

Along the chapel walls, starting on the left-hand side when facing the *Last Judgment,* are Perugino's *Journey of Moses,* Boticelli's *Events from the Life of Moses,* Cosimo Rosselli's *Crossing the Red Sea* and *Moses Receives the Tablets of the Law,* Luca Signorelli's *The Testament of Moses,* and Matteo da Lecce's *The Dispute over Moses' Body.* On the right-hand side facing the *Last Judgment* are Perugino's *The Baptism of Christ,* Botticelli's *The Temptations of Christ,* Ghirlandaio's *The Calling of the Apostles,* Perugino's *Handing over the Keys,* Cosimo Rosselli's *The Sermon on the Mount* and *The Last Supper,* and Hendrik van den Broeck's *The Resurrection.*

Castel Sant'Angelo

The rotund **Castel Sant'Angelo** (Lungotevere Castelo, 50; ☎ 06-6819111; €5 adults, €2.50 seniors and students; daily 9am–8pm) was built as Hadrian's family mausoleum and has been used as a fortress, papal residence, and military prison—remnants of which are still evident inside. This is a complex, multilayered site, so consider renting an audioguide at the ticket stand to help you fully understand the various entities. A wide stone ramp winds its way from the ground-floor entrance around the castle to the upper terraces, from which you can see the full facade of St. Peter's Basilica without the usual obstruction of neighboring buildings. From here you can wander through passageways and Renaissance apartments used by popes. Down below the apartments are ancient dungeons once used as torture chambers. Lower terraces house replica canons and travertine cannonballs. There are hidden stairways leading up to more rooms, and an abundance of lookout points. There is even a surprisingly inexpensive coffee bar with outdoor seating under the stone arches, selling fresh pastries in the mornings and sandwiches for lunch. The castle is connected to St. Peter's Basilica by **Il Passeto di Borgo** (free with museum entrance; guided tours Sat 3pm). This walled escape route was used by popes who needed to make a narrow escape to the fortress.

PIAZZA DEL POPOLO, SPANISH STEPS (TRIDENTE) & TREVI FOUNTAIN

The area immediately surrounding the Piazza del Popolo, bordered on one side by the Tiber River and on the other by the Spanish Steps, is the heart of historical central Rome. There is a balanced mix of museums, churches, antiquities, and modern amenities that makes many believe they have seen all of Rome if they've spent time here. While this is definitely the heart, Trastevere, the Jewish Ghetto, and Campo de' Fiori offer slightly more in the way of soul. Many of the restaurants here are expensive and ultratrendy, and the stores tend to be more upmarket than those in other parts of town.

Start your exploration of this area at **Piazza del Popolo,** which is joined in a straight line to the Piazza Venezia by the very narrow Via del Corso. At the far end of the piazza is the **Porta del Popolo,** which for centuries was the main gate into the city of Rome off the Via Flaminia (which extended all the way to the Adriatic Coast near Venice). The obelisk in the center of this piazza once graced the Circus Maximus, and the two churches leading into the city center create an optical illusion—they are not actually the same size, though they look identical from under the gates on the Porta del Popolo. The more interesting of the two churches is **Santa Maria del Popolo** ✦ (Piazza del Popolo, 12; ☎ 06-3610836), where you will find Raphael's frescoed Chigi chapel and a pair of Caravaggio masterpieces in the Cerasi Chapel on the left-hand side of the main altar.

There isn't much to do on Piazza del Popolo but spend money in expensive cafes, so head down the Via Ripetta toward the **Mausoleum of Augustus** (Piazza Augusto Imperatore, Via Ripetta)—which is spectacular in size, but not open to the public—and the newly renovated **Ara Pacis (Altar of Peace)** ✦✦ (Via Ripetta, Lungotevere in Augusta; ☎ 06-67106756), which has become the bane of existence for most Italians who are appalled by the modernity of this renovated showcase. This museum opened for special showings in September 2005, and should be open to the public by mid-2006 after an 11-year, multimillion-euro project. The Altar of Peace inside the boxy showcase was reconstructed from fragments found in museums across the country, and after a thorough excavation below a modern city block near Piazza San Lorenzo in Lucina. Until the 1990s the altar was housed in a rather shabby enclosure that the city fathers felt needed to be improved. Much to his credit, the American architect Richard Meier incorporated elements from the surrounding area, but to many Italians his "big box" is a far-too-modern addition to the area.

Following down the Via Ripetta from here will take you to Piazza Navona, so if you've already done that in conjunction with the Pantheon (p. 58), wind your way through this charming patchwork neighborhood and across to the Via del Corso to explore the rest of the area. There are several stops you can make along the Via del Corso and close to the Spanish Steps, though most are esoteric in nature, so pick and choose as your taste dictates.

For those interested in literature, your choices range from the **Casa di Goethe** (Via del Corso, 18; ☎ 06-32650412; www.casadigoethe.it; adults €3, seniors and students €2; Tues–Sun 10am–6pm), which has a collection of the German poet's diaries and letters, to the 18th-century **Keats-Shelley Memorial House** (Piazza di Spagna, 26; ☎ 06-6784235; www.keats-shelley-house.org; €3.50; Mon–Fri 9am–1pm and 3–6pm; Sat 11am–2pm and 3–6 pm), which is a treasure trove for fans of the two poets. Here you'll find Keats's death mask and an urn with some of Shelley's remains, as well as many volumes of letters and handwritten diaries.

If you are interested instead in modern art, visit the **Galleria Communale d'Arte Moderna e Contemporanea** (Via Francesco Crispi, 25; ☎ 06-4742848; €2.60; Tues–Sat 9am–7pm, Sun until 2pm), with some wonderful post-1950s works. Also farther down the Via del Corso is **Palazzo Doria Pamphilj** ✹ (Piazza del Collegio Romano, 2; ☎ 06-6797323; adults €8, seniors and students €7.50; gallery Fri–Wed 10am–5pm), which houses one of Italy's most impressive private art collections, owned by the Pamphilj family, including Caravaggio's *Rest on the Flight into Egypt* and *Mary Magdalene,* as well as Raphael's *Double Portrait* and scores more. This gallery is tucked in a small part of a 1,000-room *palazzo.* At the time of this writing, the gorgeous apartments are not open to the public, which makes this museum less interesting.

A third option in this area, whose exhibit schedule is worth checking, is the **Museo del Corso** (Via del Corso, 320; ☎ 06-6786209; www.museodelcorso.it; Tues–Sun 10am–8pm), a popular venue for big-name exhibits. It also has an Internet cafe in the coffee bar.

From the Via del Corso you can easily reach the **Spanish Steps** (Piazza di Spagna), which are, unfortunately, currently adorned with huge billboards hiding the seemingly never-ending work at the church of Trinita dei Monti at the top. Here you can sit and take in the spectacle of locals—primarily 20-somethings—socializing; it's packed with people year-round. The restaurants and wine bars in this area are trendy and the hotels here tend to be very pricey.

Just across the busy Via Tritone from here is the **Trevi Fountain** (Piazza di Trevi), which was built in the 1700s over the mouth of an aqueduct built in 19 B.C. to bring the famously therapeutic *Aqua Vergine* 25km (16 miles) from the hills outside of Rome. Bernini was originally given the job, but was redirected to Piazza Navona to sculpt the Fountain of the Four Rivers (p. 60) instead. The facade was designed by Nicolo Salvi, who many say died of a virus he contracted while overseeing the project before it was completed in 1762. Look specifically at the sculptures of Neptune and the angry horse, which are said to represent the angry sea. The origin of the name Trevi is disputed, believed either to be for a young girl named Trivia who showed the emperor Agrippa an original spring on the site, or from the phrase *"regio trevii,"* which may refer to the three streets surrounding the fountain. It is customary to throw a coin over your shoulder into the fountain (preferably in front of a camera) in order to ensure your return to Rome one day. The city collects these coins daily for the Red Cross.

If you've got kids in tow, or are obsessed with Italian cuisine, don't miss the **Museo Nazionale delle Pasta Alimentari** (kids) (Piazza Scanderbeg, 117; ☎ 06-6991120; www.pastainmuseum.it; €10 adults, €7 children; daily 9:30am–5:30pm), which is fondly called the "Spaghetti Museum" and offers much more information than you probably need about the art of making pasta by hand. Kids love it, though. And there is an excellent gift shop here with great Italian pasta souvenirs.

VIA VENETO & VILLA BORGHESE

Back behind the Spanish Steps and Trevi Fountain are several interesting *piazze* to savor and stops worth making. If you walk along the Via Tritone or any of the streets parallel, you will easily reach the bustling **Piazza Barberini,** with the playful **Fontana del Tritone** by Bernini in the center.

This glorified traffic circle is at the base of the **Via Vittorio Veneto,** the legendary hub of *la dolce vita,* which has now mostly relocated to the Tridente area below the Spanish Steps. Walking up the Via Veneto now is a mixed experience. There are expensive shops near the top, as well as the standards like Harry's Bar and Le Sans Souci restaurant. But there is also a Hard Rock Cafe (the Planet Hollywood down the street from here failed), which is great if you need a T-shirt for your collection, but the food is hardly comparable to regular Roman fare unless your children are dying for a "real" hamburger. Here you'll also find the heavily guarded American Embassy and a handful of luxe hotels, but mostly this street is a has-been and a mere silhouette of its former glory.

There are a few stops to make, namely the bizarre church of **Santa Maria della Concezione** ★ (kids) (Via Vittorio Veneto, 27; ☎ 06-48711857; donation requested; Fri–Wed), which is about as creepy as Rome gets. Downstairs, accessed around the back, is the **Cappuchin Crypt,** where the bones of over 4,000 monks are used as decorative art on the walls, urns, and chandeliers in the various chapels. There is a sign explaining the monk's take on mortality (YOU WILL BE WHAT WE NOW ARE) near the back. Kids, especially preteen boys, seem to love this spot, but it's also fascinating for adults. After about 5 minutes perusing the galleries, you won't even remember that you are looking at bones, until you see the inverted pelvic-bone hourglasses and delicate finger remnants shaped into religious art.

At the end of the Via Veneto lies the sprawling **Villa Borghese,** which is home to the city zoo, three magnificent museums, and the best green spot in the city complete with cultured gardens, a boating lake, and an equestrian stadium. Not to mention its fairly new free Wi-Fi capabilities (1-hr. limit per day) through 22 hot spots across the park (www.comune.roma.it).

Galleria Borghese ★★★ (Piazzale Borghese, 5; ☎ 06-32810; www.galleria borghese.it; adults €8.50, seniors and students €5.25; entrance by appointment only every 2 hr., 8:30am–7pm) has been reopened for several years after extensive renovations, but it is still considered the hot new spot on Rome's museum run. The art here is significant, from Bernini's *Apollo and Daphne* statue in **Room 3** to Raphael's *Deposition* on the second floor. Don't miss Canova's 1808 topless marble figure of Napoleon's sister *Pauline* in **Room 1,** and the collection of Roman copies of Greek original sculpture in **Room 5.** There are six Caravaggios in **Room 8,** including the much acclaimed *Boy with a Basket of Fruit* (1594) and *Sick Bacchus* (1593), which art historians believe is a self-portrait.

But an added advantage to this collection, over the much larger Vatican Museums collection, is that curators insist on a limited number of people in the museum at one time. You will never find yourself crowded here, and you are limited to a 2-hour visit, which is a perfect amount of time for sauntering through the masterpieces.

Within the Villa Borghese are two other museums. **Museo Nazionale di Villa Giulia** (Piazzale di Villa Giulia, 9; ☎ 06-3226571; €4; 8:30am–7:30pm) features Etruscan artifacts ranging from cooking utensils to jewelry in the central room of the museum to a more intricate form of jewelry in the Room of the Seven Hills. These collections have been exhumed from the graves of the Etruscans found in central Italy. There is a reconstructed temple next to the coffee bar in the courtyard.

The second museum within the boundaries of the Villa Borghese is the **Galleria Nazionale d'Arte Moderna e Contemporanea (National Gallery of Modern and Contemporary Art;** Viale delle Belle Arti, 131; ☎ 06-332981; www.gnam.arti.beniculturali.it/gnamco.htm; adults €6.50, seniors and students €3.25; Tues–Sun 8:30am–7:30pm). Its collections focus on the rarely noted 19th- and 20th-century Italian art. There are massive statues like *Hercules* by Canova in **Room 4,** and the plaster model used to make the bronze statue of Giordano Bruno, which stands in the center of Campo de' Fiori (p. 61). The museum is a great diversion from the Renaissance and ancient art most visitors to Rome see, and there is a delightful terrace coffee bar overlooking the lush green of the Villa Borghese on the main floor. If you don't feel like going to another museum, just come here for the coffee bar, which opens at 8am.

THE APPIAN WAY

To really enjoy the area immediately surrounding Ancient Rome's first major road, the Appian Way (bus: 118, 218, 660, or 664), built in the 4th century, start with the **Museo delle Mura** (Via di San Sebastiano, 18; ☎ 06-70475284; €2.60 adults; €1.60 seniors and students; Tues–Sun 9am–2pm), where you can amble down the top of a short expanse of the ancient fortification wall that surrounds the center of Rome. Here are mostly exhibits of old photos and diagrams of the wall's many gates and castles, but being inside the actual fortification wall gives you a sense of its purpose, which was to protect the ancient city from invaders, who mostly came via the Appian Way.

The Appian Way (Appia Antica on the street signs) originally extended well within the walls, but now it officially begins here, at the Porta San Sebastiano. Make your way down the busy first section until you reach the quiet lane where the road forks between Via Appia Antica and Via Ardeatina in the direction of **Catacombs of San Callisto.** You can rent bicycles on the weekends just before the fork from the **Centro Visite Parco Appia Antica** (Via Appia Antica, 42; ☎ 06-5126314; www.parcoappiaantica.org; €3 for 1 hr. or €10 for the day; Sat–Sun 9:30am–4:30pm). On this narrow lane that rises above both the Appia Antica on the left and the Via Ardeatina on the right, you'll see farm fields and wildflowers, and be less burdened by the traffic—though there are still taxis and tour buses that use the road, but nothing like the traffic on the Appia Antica below. You can also see the Castelli foothills outside of Rome and on clear days, you'll see much of the city around you.

Events Calendar

In spring, **Holy Week** is the official opening of tourist season in Rome. The week preceding Easter is a religious celebration for pilgrims, but it also marks the changing to summer hours for most stores and sites. **Culture Week,** whose dates are found at www.beniculturali.it (☎ **800-991199**) is when most of the major museums and paid exhibits like the Colosseum and Palatine Hill are free and offer extended hours.

In summer, jazz and outdoor cinema take over. At **Villa Celimontana** (www.villacelimontanajazz.com), the lush park of Celimontana hosts a nightly jazz festival from July to early September with food and wine booths. At **Estate Romana** (www.estateromana.it), each night from late June, the city of Rome sponsors a "Roman Summer" event that ranges from opera in the Baths of Caracalla and chamber concerts in the churchyards to rock concerts and outdoor festivals. At **Isola del Cinema** (www.isoladel cinema.com) throughout the summer, international movies are screened on the banks of the Tiber Island. This is becoming a showcase for avant-garde films and a launching pad for new directors' works.

In autumn, for one Saturday in September, **La Notte Bianca** (☎ 06-0606; www.lanottebianca.it) means that the city of Rome stays up all night. Museums, libraries, churches, stores, and restaurants stay open around the clock on that exciting occasion.

This lane meets up with the Appia Antica near the **Catacombs of San Callisto** ★★ (Via Appia Antica, 136; ☎ 06-5130151; www.catacombe.roma.it; guided tours €5 adults, €3 seniors and students; Thurs–Tues 8:30am–noon and 2:30–5pm). These are the largest of the entire network of underground tombs of Christians, extending 20km (13 miles). There are nine popes and thousands of Christians buried here, as well as the tomb of St. Cecilia (p. 65). Down the Appia Antica from these catacombs are the **Catacombs of San Sebastiano** ★ (Via Appia Antica, 136; ☎ 06-7850350; entrance only with a guided tour, €5 adults, €3 seniors and students; Mon–Sat 8:30am–noon and 2:30–5pm), which are very different from those of San Callisto. Here you'll visit the site of previously pagan mausoleums that have been converted into Christian tombs, and you will enter the tomb of St. Sebastian, for whom these catacombs are named. The word "catacomb" comes from this site, which means "near the quarry" or *kata kymbas* in Latin.

After visiting the catacombs, it is a short walk down what's left of the original Appian Way, which is lined with above-ground tombs of ancient Romans, who were not allowed to bury their dead within the city walls. The largest of these is the **Tomba di Cecilia Metella** (Via Appia Antica, 161; ☎ 06-7800093; €6 adults, €3 seniors and students; Tues–Sun 9am–4pm), which is a castle built on the site of the tomb of a woman who married into the Metella family in the 1st century B.C. The complex now serves as an example of the ritual of ancient Roman burials, and many of the funerary urns which once lined the Appian way are now housed here.

AVENTINO

The Aventino is by far the quietest of the seven hills of Rome. High above the bustling local neighborhood of Testaccio, the Aventino is mostly a lush residential area for Romans and expats who appreciate its secrets and frown on visitors. Ignore them and make the trek up from either the Testaccio side or from the Circus Maximus. At the top of the hill on Piazza dei Cavalieri di Malta is one of Rome's most famous keyholes at the door of the headquarters of the Priory of Malta (clearly marked). Lean close to the circular opening (which really isn't a keyhole anymore) to see a perfectly framed view of St. Peter's Basilica. Here you are also looking at three sovereign nations: Italy, Malta, and Vatican City.

Next door to the famous keyhole, past the 24-hour guards, is one of Rome's best preserved original churches, the 5th-century **Church of Santa Sabina** (Piazza Pietro d'Illiria, 1), which was built on the site of the original Titulus Sabinae, a private home used for worship in 442. The church has changed very little; the original wooden door (now with some replica panels) shows the life of Moses and a crucifixion scene that is believed to be one of the earliest artistic portrayals of the crucifixion of Christ. Notice the large windows that let in natural light.

A few meters from the church is one of this area's best kept secrets: **Orange Park.** In the springtime, when the grove of clementine trees is in bloom, the perfume is intoxicating. But the view from the overlook terrace is what you make this trek for; it is one you don't often see of the Roman skyline and Trastevere rooftops.

Down below the Aventino, you can't help but notice the massive and seemingly out-of-place pyramid at the edge of the **Cimitero Acattolico (Protestant Cemetery;** Via Caio Cestio, 6; ☎ 06-5741900; www.protestantcemetery.it; free admission; Mon–Sat 8:30am–4:30pm). Stop here to see the graves of both Keats and Shelley. The pyramid is the mausoleum of a Roman family.

MUSEUMS OFF THE BEATEN TRACK

Across the square from Termini Station at the edge of Piazza della Repubblica is the **Museo Nazionale Romano: Palazzo Massimo alla Terme** 🦘 (Largo di Villa Peretti, 1; ☎ 06-480201, bookings 06-39967700; integrated ticket €7 adults, €3.50 seniors and students; Tues–Sun 9am–7pm). The collections of this museum comprise a third of Rome's vast assortment of ancient art, represented by exhibits depicting Roman history and how the artistic demands of the Romans have been served over time.

On the ground floor is a vast coin collection alongside maps of trade routes and audio and visual exhibits on the network of traders over the centuries. The first floor has rooms of busts of emperors and their families. But the real draw to this museum is the second floor, where you can see some of the oldest of Rome's frescoes depicting scenes of ancient Roman life in lush gardens with wild animals, dating back to the house of Livia on the Palatine Hill (p. 53). The art on this level gives visitors an understanding of how wealthy Romans decorated their palaces through the centuries. This is a museum that caters as much to non-museum-goers as to those who can't get enough.

Across the Piazza della Repubblica is **Museo Nazionale Romano: Terme di Diocleziano** (Via Enrico de Nicola, 79; ☎ 06-399677000; www.archeorm.arti. beniculturali.it/sar2000/diocleziano; integrated ticket €7 adults, €3.50 seniors and students; Tues–Sat 9am–7:45pm). These were the largest of the hedonistic Roman baths, dating back to 298 A.D. and spread over 1 hectare (2½ acres) on what was then the city's edge. Visiting these baths should be done in conjunction with a stop at the church of Santa Maria degli Angeli (below), which sits inside the ruins. This is a great example of recycling old pagan ruins for Christian worship. In addition to the church, Michelangelo built a convent around the main section of the baths, which could hold 3,000 people at a time. The juxtaposition of Christianity, ancient ruins, and exhibit space makes this a compelling museum stop. You can see multiple phases of Rome's history in literally one spot. The collections of ancient art here make up the third part of a museum circuit consisting of the Museo Nazionale Romana: Palazzo Massimo alla Terme (p. 78) and Palazzo Altemps (p. 60).

The **Baths of Caracalla** (Viale delle Terme di Caracalla, 52; ☎ 06-5745748; €6 adults, €3.50 seniors and students; Mon 9am–1pm, Tues–Sun 9am–sunset) are a majestic set of ruins of some of ancient Rome's most popular thermal baths. Built in 213 A.D., the structure was basically a giant spa, where 1,600 Romans could come to play and relax. There was a gymnasium for games, a swimming pool, and a series of saunas and baths with varying temperatures and humidity levels. The baths were decorated with intricate mosaic tiles, which are still evident in some parts of the ruins. Others are preserved in the Vatican Museums (p. 70) and the National Archaeological Museum in Naples. The baths are a popular venue for operas during the summer (p. 77).

CHURCHES OFF THE BEATEN TRACK

A number of churches off the beaten track are still worthy stops, and not just for religious pilgrims. **Santa Maria degli Angeli** (Piazza della Repubblica; ☎ 06-4880812; www.santamariadegliangeliroma.it; 7am–6:30pm, Sun until 7:30pm) is an ingenious church, designed by Michelangelo, which sits snuggly inside the Baths of Diocletian. A giant 45m (148-ft.) bronze meridian runs across the main body of the church, which until 1870 was used to set Rome's clocks. On sunny days, beams of light shine through strategically placed holes in the walls, lighting up the points on the meridian and zodiac symbols. At the entrance of the church, the dome forms a prism that reflects rainbows of light on the statues below.

San Giovanni (Piazza San Giovanni in Laterano, 4; ☎ 06-69886433; metro San Giovanni or buses to Porta San Giovanni) is Rome's cathedral, making it the second-most significant church in the Catholic faith, after St. Peter's Basilica. Pilgrims visiting Rome can earn an Indulgence here, and this is the spot where the Pope washes the feet of ordinary (but carefully selected) people each Easter season. On the giant facade of the church are statues of Christ, John the Baptist, John the Evangelist, and the 12 Doctors of the church. There is a Giotto mosaic in the apse, and a 13th-century cloister around the back of the church that features some artifacts from the original church.

Across the street are the **Scala Santa (Holy Stairs;** Piazza di San Giovanni in Laterano; ☎ 06-7726641; daily 6:30am–noon, winter 3–6pm, summer until 6:30pm). These are said to be the steps that Jesus climbed before his crucifixion, and were relocated to Rome in the 4th century. Now they are covered with wooden planks, but are still as significant to the thousands of religious pilgrims who climb them on their knees each year, reciting the 28 different prayers, one for each step.

Santa Maria Maggiore (Piazza Santa Maria Maggiore; ☎ 06-483195; €4; 7am–7pm, museum 9am–6:30pm) is one of Rome's five patriarchal basilicas. Lately it has also been the site of protests because American Cardinal Bernard Law was assigned to this church after retiring from the Boston Diocese after the 2005 pedophile scandals. This church has the best collection of mosaics in the city. Start with the 5th-century mosaic depictions of the Old Testament above the columns in the nave, and work your way through the centuries along the length of the church. Thirteenth-century mosaics of Mary being crowned queen of heaven by Christ line the apse. Rome's baroque master Gian Lorenzo Bernini is buried here, marked by a plaque on the right side of the altar. On August 5, a celebration marking the miracle of a summer snowfall, which led to the building of this church, is celebrated with the release of thousands of flower petals from the church ceiling.

> **❝** *Rome was a poem pressed into service as a city.* **❞**
>
> —Anatole Broyard

Santa Maria della Vittoria (Via XX Settembre, 17; ☎ 06-42740571; daily 8:30am–noon and 3:30–6pm; Sun afternoons only) is home to one of Bernini's most famous and sensual sculptures, the *Ecstasy of St. Teresa,* inspired by a passage she wrote, "So intense was the pain I uttered several moans; so great was the sweetness caused by the pain that I never wanted to lose it." The statue of the angel and Teresa sits in the Cornaro chapel, which is decorated with frescoes of clouds from the heavens and hidden windows that light up the room differently throughout the day.

St. Clemente (Via San Giovanni in Laterano; ☎ 06-7740021; €3; 9am–12:30pm and 3–6pm, Sun opens 1 hr. later) offers one of the best examples of Rome's multilayered past. The main church, which is a relatively new 12th-century construction, is often covered with scaffolding, so skim this section and head straight to the first subterranean level for the 4th-century ruins of the original church and the chipped and faded frescoes of the life of St. Clemente, who was the fourth pope after St. Peter. Climb down another flight of dark steps to reach the pagan temple of the Persian god Mithras. Here, statues of testosterone-driven bullfighters, some actually holding testicles, indicate the types of meetings held here.

THE OTHER ROME

How about the life of the city that only the residents know? Try the working-class neighborhood of Testaccio, just across the Tiber River from Trastevere's Porta Portese. This is the neighborhood where many Romans come for dinner in the small *trattorie* and clamoring pizza joints. But it's great any time of day. It is one of the least pretentious spots in the city, and you never question the authenticity of what you see.

Early in the morning the locals crowd the market in the central square and haggle with vendors for their fresh produce. The fishmongers know well who caught the fish, and the vegetable sellers harvested most of the vegetables—just look at their hands. One stand is dedicated entirely to the many varieties of tomatoes in season, and the man who runs it will let you taste the difference. He's one

Rome with Children

If you bring your children to Rome, don't expect kids' menus or high chairs. There are few cities where children are more welcome (even at fancy restaurants), yet they are accommodated so poorly. Just bring with you almost all they need (if you make a reservation for dinner, you must also reserve the high chair, or *seggiolino,* since most restaurants only have one or two).

Children under 12 generally get in free to museums and sites in Rome. There are a handful of parks like the **Villa Borghese** and one in **Testaccio** with playground equipment, but they are laughable in comparison to what you find at home. Still, kids are always welcome in the city, and recently Rome has opened up a few venues just for them.

Explora (Via Flaminia, 82; ☎ 06-3613776; www.mdbr.it; children 3–12 €7, adults €6; reservations only Tues–Thurs at 9:30, 11:30am, 3, and 5pm, and Fri–Sat 10am, noon, 3, and 5pm) is a new concept in Rome: a museum for children. It was built out of an abandoned bus depot and has been a popular spot for Italian families since it opened in 2002. The pavilion generates 60% of its own light from an on-site solar-cell plant, and a sophisticated system of canopies utilizes the natural light to save even more energy. It is a hands-on museum with sections called "Me," "Society," "Environment," and "Communication." All the exhibits are in Italian, but English-speaking kids don't seem to mind—it's fascinating to watch how children can so easily communicate without a common language.

A little bit farther out of town, but well worth it for the kids, is the **Museo della Memoria Giocosa (Museum of the Playful Memory;** Via Vincenzo Coronelli, 24–26; ☎ 06-24407777; free admission). This is a private collection of toys assembled by Fritz Bilig, an Austrian who fled Europe during Nazism. The toys are those that children growing up in Europe between 1920 and 1960 played with, even during the height of World War II. It is a museum that the kids enjoy, and in which many parents feel nostalgic.

If you happen to be in Rome during the holidays, take the kids to the **Befana Christmas Toy Fair** (Piazza Navona). It is a Christmas fair stuck in time, with old-fashioned merry-go-round rides and a disturbingly thin Santa Claus (Babbo Natale), who poses with the kids. There are rows of stalls dripping with candies and Christmas goodies, in addition to Christmas stockings and the beloved Befana witch, who still brings toys to Italian children on January 6, the Feast of the Epiphany.

of the few green grocers in all of Rome who carries "real" orange pumpkins around Halloween for the expats, and he won't sell you anything that isn't fresh.

On the perimeter of the market, makeshift stands sell new shoes, interesting kitchen gadgets, and imported linens. The stores that circle the stands sell the kinds of housewares, wines, flowers, and food that Italians buy, and you can get some of the best deals in town here. You'll find no rainbow-colored pasta in pretty packages here.

Down the street from the market you'll pass by old-fashioned candy shops and seamstresses who barely look up from their needles as you pass by. You'll reach the Piazza Santa Maria della Liberatrice, which is a giant square with a children's park on one end and a line of park benches filled with elders on the other. Grandmothers push their grandchildren on swings in the morning and new moms stroll their babies in elaborate buggies after lunch. In the late afternoons in the summer, long lines form at the ice-cream shops that border the park and later in the evenings, local residents gather at the *enoteche* and fill the local *trattorie* out-door tables. You cannot find a parking spot here for Sunday lunch in the winter and, anyway, you'd better have made a reservation since most of the restaurants are filled with long tables of multi-generational families.

This is a classic Roman neighborhood that will always make you feel welcome, and the locals will never treat you like a tourist. If you make it to Testaccio, they'll assume you know why you came and they will treat you as one of their own.

SHOPPING

With so much to see, who has time to shop? If you do, here are some of the best choices. Note that many stores aren't open Sunday and Monday morning and adhere to the siesta, closing between 1 and 4pm, with the exception of those around the Spanish Steps.

ANTIQUES STORES

More than 40 antiques shops line the **Via dei Coronari,** selling everything from large pieces of furniture to such small treasures as crested silverware and divine candelabras.

BOOKSTORES

Many of the English-language bookstores in Rome have closed or downsized in recent years, as Italian megastores expand their inventory to include English books. **Feltrinelli** (Largo Torre Argentina, 11, and several locations throughout the city; ☎ 06-68663001; www.feltrinelli.it) is an American-style mega-bookstore complete with coffee bar. They have a large selection of music, books in English, and children's selections, in addition to stationery and calendars.

CLOTHING MARKETS

Even people who don't need to look for bargains shop at the sprawling **San Giovanni Clothing Market** (Via Sannio). The clothing here is all new and often you're better off not knowing where it came from, but the prices are exceptional. You can get very good quality leather shoes, belts, and purses at a fraction of the price you'd pay in stores.

Stalls are piled high with jeans, shirts, linens, and fabrics, but you'll have to hunt through the merchandise to find your size. *One warning:* Virtually no one here speaks English, and the international size charts are a mystery. There are no changing facilities and no returns on purchases.

DEPARTMENT STORES

Rome's three major department stores are Coin (shoes, undergarments, and midrange fashion); La Rinascente (sunglasses, cosmetics, mid- to upper-range fashion); and Upim (lower-end fashion, toys, cosmetics), all located throughout the city.

FASHION BOUTIQUES

The big names in Italian fashion like Gucci, Prada, Versace, Armani, and Valentino have boutiques in the Tridente, below the Spanish Steps. Mainstream shops selling more moderate fashions dot the city and it's not hard to find small boutiques with great deals.

FLEA MARKETS

The best known flea market in the city, and perhaps in all of Italy, is the Sunday-morning bonanza at the gates of Porta Portese between Trastevere and Testaccio. Stalls start setting up before 5am and you can start haggling shortly thereafter. If you have ever dreamed of owning it, you can find it here.

GIFT SHOPS

La Chiave (Largo delle Stimmate, 28; ☎ 06-68308848) sells imported crafts, interesting antique toys, and paper masks, in addition to lots of rugs, blankets, and handmade clothing. There is a small stationery shop in the back of the store selling journals and scrapbook albums.

If you are looking for a handmade memento, try the medieval-feeling **Polvere de Tempo** (Via del Moro, 59; ☎ 06-5880704). It specializes in handmade jewelry, antique-aspect globes, candles, and time-related gifts like hourglasses made from hand-blown glass or small used Campari bottles, which are calibrated to 3 minutes or 1 hour down to the last grain of sand. The items here are priced fairly and are one of a kind.

For the inner gladiator in you, go to **Archeo Roma** (Largo del Teatro Valle, 5; ☎ 06-6877590) for reproductions of statues, jewelry, and gladiator arms. You'll find costumes, capes, and realistic looking swords—perfect for your next costume party.

HOUSEHOLD GADGET STORES

One of the best souvenirs from Italy is a funky kitchen gadget or item of wine paraphernalia. Stores that cater to everyday Italians sell what's standard in an Italian kitchen, like pasta rollers, Parmesan-cheese graters, and mod-looking utensils, for much less than you'd pay for these imports at home. The best place to find these gadgets is in the Jewish Ghetto at **Leone Limentani** (Via del Portico d'Ottavia, 47; ☎ 06-68806686), though this is a true hunt-and-peck store resembling an abandoned warehouse that hasn't seen a duster in years. You can find Italian-designed crockery and gadgets for 20% less than their market value, and have your purchase shipped to your home. A source of household gadgets that's a little more expensive, but more straightforward in terms of the shopping experience, is **C.U.C.I.N.A.** (Via Mario de' Fiori, 65; ☎ 06-6791275; www.cucinastore.com), below the Spanish Steps. This is a perfect place to shop for things you don't actually need at prices you don't mind paying. And most of these gadgets are worthy gifts to bring back home.

OUTLET MALLS

If you are really set on getting good deals on Italian fashion, and have your own transportation, consider driving the 20 minutes or so south to the **Castelli Romana Outlet Mall** (Via Pontina, exit Castel Romano 15km; castelromano.mcarthurglen.it), which has 88 stores selling fashions for men, women, and children, as well as household goods and electronics. There is a restaurant and a play center for children.

SHOPPING STREETS

The expensive shopping streets (**Via Condotti** and **Via Frattina**) lie just below the Spanish Steps in the area called the Tridente. These streets are packed with top-end designer boutiques and expensive jewelry shops.

For more reasonably priced shopping try **Via Cola di Rienzo,** running from Piazza Risorgimento near Vatican City to the Tiber River. You'll find fashion, footwear, and funky gadget shops in this area, which is becoming more upscale by the minute. There is a Coin department store and several moderate fashion shops like Max Mara and Benetton here. Alternately, **Via Del Corso** which runs from Piazza Venezia to Piazza del Popolo is a narrow street packed with shops. (Up toward the Piazza del Popolo, the traffic is limited and you can shop more easily.) It's worth exploring the side streets in this area for tiny stores selling original fashions and jewelry and shoes. There are a number of bookstores and gift shops, too. Then try **Via Nazionale,** which runs from Piazza della Repubblica to just above Piazza Venezia. This street has always been the haven for leather shops selling handbags, belts, and wallets. You can find some names like Timberland as well. (But there is also a higher concentration of pickpockets here than on other streets, owing to the proximity to Termini, so watch your valuables.)

And finally, **Via Marconi** is somewhat off the beaten track, but it's one of the streets many Romans flock to. All the usual suspects are here, but the shopping experience is less touristy. This is an easy place in which to feel like a Roman—there aren't many tourists in this part of town.

TOILETRIES

No one sells simple soap like the Romans, and one of the oldest venders of perfumes and other essentials is **Antica Erboristeria Romana** (Via di Torre Argentina, 15; ☎ 06-6879493; www.anticaerboristeriaromana.com), where you can buy essential oils, tinctures, and other herbal remedies, in addition to more mainstream cures.

VINTAGE STORES

People (Piazza Teatro di Pompeo, 4A; ☎ 06-6874040) is an innovative store where the designers Germana and Sara use material from vintage clothing to create updated fashions. You can find some great club wear here, as well as interesting scarves, jackets, and gloves. No two items are alike, so whatever you buy will be unique.

NIGHTLIFE

Rome's nightlife centers primarily around two diverse spots. First, the nightclubs and discos around Monte Testaccio set the standard for the city, and this area is literally jumping from 10pm onward. The three big clubs are all on the Via di Monte Testaccio, but there are many more to choose from along the street. **Fake**

(Via di Monte Testaccio, 64; ☎ 06-45447627; cover €10 includes 1st drink) plays hip-hop, R&B, and electronica. **Jungle** (Via di Monte Testaccio, 95; ☎ 333-720-8694; www.jungleclubroma.com; cover €5 Fri, Sat until 11pm, then €10 plus annual membership of €2) is Goth heaven, and one of the most popular clubs in the city for vinyl (not the kind you listen to). **Metaverso** (Via di Monte Testaccio, 38A; ☎ 06-5744712; www.metaverso.com; €5 or more if live band) is the least pretentious of all the clubs on this street. It brings in international DJs and offers theme nights like reggae, '60s, and electronica.

The **Big Mama** (Vicolo San Francesco a Ripa, 18; ☎ 06-5812551; www.big mama.it) is the primary spot for live blues in Rome. Check the website for concerts and schedules. Booking is recommended if you want a table. Light dinner is also available.

SIDE TRIPS FROM ROME

After a few days of trolling museums and breathing exhaust fumes, it's understandable that you'd want to change your perspective. Rome's comprehensive train and bus networks make it easy to take a day or half-day trip to the hinterland.

VITERBO This is a classic fortified town where you can amble around with the locals who live there and feel as if you're witnessing the village culture firsthand. It was an important Etruscan enclave and was used in the 8th century by King Desiderius as a base for carrying out the sacking of Rome. The center of the tiny town is a walled medieval quarter on the southern edge. Highlights include the 16th-century **Palazzo Communale,** which still serves as the city's town hall. Walk in and tour the building on your own; there is no ticket booth or information desk. On the upper floors are frescoes and canvas paintings by Sebastiano del Piombo and Bartolomeo Cavarozzi. Outside the city walls, visit the Gothic chapel in the church of **Santa Maria della Verità,** made famous by a young boy named Lorenzo di Viterbo, whose wall scribbles are some of the most detailed frescoes in this part of Italy. You'll need a car to get to the natural sulphur springs, used by Julius Caesar, that dot the countryside. Local Cotral buses (p. 20) from Rome to Viterbo cost just €1. Trains (p. 16) cost €6.70 return trip.

TIVOLI One of the most enjoyable day trips from Rome is also one of the easiest. Tivoli is just 36km (22 miles) from the city center, and easily accessible by Cotral buses (p. 20). Once there, visit the **Villa Adriana (Hadrian's Villa)** ★★★ 🄺🄸🄳🄢 (Via di Villa Adriana; ☎ 0774-382733; adults €6.50, seniors and students €3.50; Nov–Jan 9am–5pm, Feb until 6pm, Mar and Oct until 6:30pm, Apr and Sept until 7pm, May–Aug until 7:30pm). You get hard-to-find views of Rome, and you can meander the expanse of ruins of what is believed to be the largest villa ever built in ancient-Roman times. This is a relaxing site, one that you should explore slowly and carefully. Inside the museum is a miniature replica of the villa, which is worth locating first (after picking up a map at the ticket booth) so that you have a better idea of what you are looking at. Also, be sure to check out the underground tunnels, which were built to move supplies throughout the villa without obstructing the views and the columns and statues that surround the fountains. Hadrian designed the rooms personally and incorporated influences of his vast travels.

Before you leave Tivoli, stop by the **Villa d'Este** (Piazza Trento, 1; ☎ 0774-312070; €6.50 adults, €3.50 seniors and students; Nov–Feb 9am–5:30pm, Mar

Side Trips from Rome

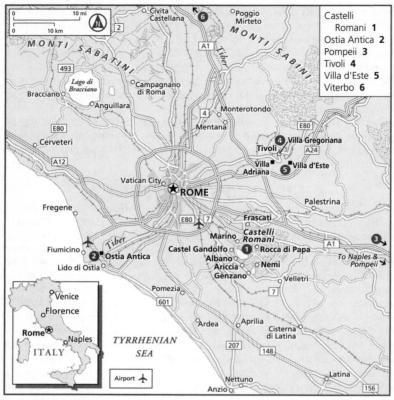

Castelli Romani **1**
Ostia Antica **2**
Pompeii **3**
Tivoli **4**
Villa d'Este **5**
Viterbo **6**

until 6:15pm, Apr until 7:30pm, May–Aug 8:30am–7:45pm, Sept 9am–7:15pm, Oct 9am–6:30pm). This was once a Benedictine convent but in 1550 the Cardinal Ippolito II d'Este decided to turn it into a country home. You're not here for the actual villa, though, but for the landscaped gardens that are adorned with fountains, like the **Viale delle Cento Fontane,** which spouts water out of 100 nozzles among the greenery. Bernini designed and built a collection of fountains that produced the sounds of organs and owls.

OSTIA ANTICA   Ostia Antica 🧒 (Viale dei Romagnoli, 717; ☎ 06-56358099; €4.20; Feb–Oct 9am–7pm, Nov–Jan until 5pm) is one of the most educational day trips you can make from Rome. The metro B (blue) line runs to station Magliana, where you change for the train in the direction of Ostia. You can make the whole trip with a €1 ticket. Get off at the Scavi stop.

   Ostia Antica is supposed to have served as Rome's main seaport as early as the 7th century B.C., although the earliest excavations are only from 330 B.C. After the sacking of Rome, the port town was abandoned and, over the centuries, covered with river mud as the coastline receded to where it is today, 3.2km (2 miles) away. These ruins are much like Pompeii's—without the lava—and many remain intact. There is an ancient amphitheater (where pop stars perform during the summer), a comprehensive set of mosaics from the floors of the port town's many stores, thermal baths, and what is believed to be an old Roman bar, complete with an advertising fresco on the back wall. These ruins are best visited with a site map, available at the ticket booth.

After Ostia Antica, continue on the metro to Ostia Lido, the last stop on the blue line and the closest beach to Rome. From the station you can easily walk to free beaches or paid establishments that rent chairs and umbrellas.

POMPEII   If you're not planning to visit Southern Italy, consider a day trip to the ruins of Pompeii. Trains (www.trenitalia.it) run every couple of hours and take just over 2 hours to get to Scavi di Pompeii. Cost: €44 round trip. See p. 508 for more information.

The ABCs of Rome

American Express The main offices in Rome are at **Piazza di Spagna, 38** (☎ 06-67641). Travel services are open Monday to Friday 9am to 5pm, Saturday until 12:30pm. Financial and mail services operate Monday to Friday 9am to 5pm. The tour information office is open Monday to Saturday 9am to 12:30pm during summer.

Area Code **06** in Rome. Numbers beginning with 3 are cellphone numbers.

Business Hours & Siesta Banks are open Monday to Friday from 8:30am to 1:30pm and 3 to 4pm; stores generally open at 9:30 or 10am and many close at 1 or 1:30pm for the afternoon siesta, reopening between 4 and 4:30pm until 7:30pm. It is difficult to eat lunch before 12:30pm or dinner before 8pm unless you go to a *tavola calda* self-service style restaurant or *pizza taglio* (pizza-by-the-slice venue). Kitchens often stay open until midnight.

Car & Bike Rental Major car-rental kiosks are at both airports and in the Villa Borghese parking lot, entrance Metro Spagna, where you can also rent bicycles, three-wheel peddlers, and 50cc mopeds.

Currency Exchange Exchange bureaus are called CAMBIO and are well located throughout the city. There is generally a service charge of 1½% imposed by both banks and cambio outlets.

Doctors The U.S. Embassy (☎ 06-46741) has a list of English-speaking doctors. For emergencies, go to a *pronto soccorso* emergency room at any hospital. The **Aventino Medical Group** (Via della Fonte di Fauno, 22; ☎ 06-5780738; www.aventinomedicalgroup.com) is a consortium of English-speaking specialists who cater to the large expat community in Rome.

Emergencies For an ambulance, call ☎ **118** or **113.**

Hospitals If you take a car or taxi, ask to be driven to the *pronto soccorso* at **Policlinico Gemelli, Policlinico Umberto I,** or **Bambino Gesù.** The ambulance will take you to the nearest hospital, which is not always the best.

Internet Cafes Internet cafes now dot the city and many hotels offer free Wi-Fi, as do some city parks like Villa Borghese. In general, Internet cafes charge €3 a half-hour, €5 an hour. New anti-terrorism laws require users to provide an ID, which is photocopied.

Newspapers & Magazines The *Herald Tribune, New York Times, USA Today,* and the major American newsweeklies are all available at newsstands throughout the city. Rome does not have an English-language newspaper, but a twice monthly magazine *Wanted in Rome* has interesting English articles on local events.

Pharmacies There is an international pharmacy open 23 hours a day on **Piazza Barberini, 49** (☎ 06-6879098); it is closed 7 to 8pm. Most pharmacies are open weekdays from 8:30am to 1pm and 4 to 7:30pm and Saturday mornings. Pharmacies in each area rotate Saturday afternoon and Sunday openings; check the notice by each pharmacy for the rotation schedule.

Police For police, call ☎ **113.**

Post Office The city's main post office is at **Piazza San Silverstro** near the Spanish Steps, but you can buy stamps *(francobolli)* at tobacco shops and from most hotels. Vatican City has its own postal service, run through Switzerland, with offices in Vatican City near the metal detectors at the entrance to the basilica. It is open 8:30am to 7pm Monday to Friday and 8:30am to 6pm Saturday.

Public Transportation For information: public transportation in the city, **ATAC** (☎ 800/431-784; www.atac.roma.it); regional public transportation, **COTRAL** (☎ 800/150-008; www.cotralspa.it); regional and local trains, www.trenitalia.it.

Restrooms Public restrooms in Rome are frightening by most standards. The best bet is to check for facilities at museums, coffee bars, and department stores.

Safety Pickpockets remain the biggest nuisance in Rome, especially around tourist areas like the Colosseum and Trevi Fountain. Table-snatching (where someone lifts your purse or valuables from a cafe table) is increasingly a problem, and there is a growing concern with nighttime arsonists setting fire to cars and mopeds, including rentals, making it vital that your car insurance cover fire.

Tourism Information Rome has an impressive website (www.romaturismo. com) that features itineraries, suggestions for accommodations, and one of the best interactive maps around. You can take a virtual tour of the city before you come or use this site at computers found at the many information kiosks in the city. The site has a particularly detailed list of local legends, and some great recipes for classic Roman fare.

3 Florence: Great City of the Renaissance

It was here that humankind cast off the shackles of the Middle Ages.

by Bill Fink

A THIRD OF ALL UNESCO WORLD HERITAGE SITES ARE IN ITALY. AND A THIRD of these are right here in relatively small, compact Florence, making it one of the most historically important cities in the world.

Those who are familiar with Florence's history know that the designation makes a strange sort of sense: After all, this is exactly the status that Florence enjoyed in the minds of most Europeans back in the 15th and 16th centuries, when its achievements in art, architecture, science, and literature were unmatched. As the center of the Renaissance movement, and the hometown of its leaders—Michelangelo, Brunelleschi, da Vinci, Giotto, Galileo, and others—it built up a store of riches that still dazzles today: the masterpiece-packed Uffizi Gallery, the ingenious domed cathedral, Michelangelo's *David,* and the city's stunningly decorated halls, palaces, and chapels. These treasures are still representative of the best mankind can achieve. And because of this, Florence remains a must-visit destination for every first-time traveler to Italy, and a must-return destination for anyone who cares about art and architecture.

DON'T LEAVE FLORENCE WITHOUT . . .

SEEING MICHELANGELO'S *DAVID* IN THE ACCADEMIA   Rarely does a work of art live up to its reputation as this one does. Note that the outdoor *David,* in the city's main plaza, is a copy of the original, which is preserved in the Accademia.

TOURING THE UFFIZI   Yes, everyone does it, but for good reason: The Uffizi has one of the best art collections on Earth.

GETTING INTO LEATHER   Florence is a mecca for leather goods, attracting hundreds of jacket-, boot-, and bag-makers. Tour the street stalls of San Lorenzo Market or the higher-end shops of Santa Croce for good deals and/or fine craftsmanship.

ROAMING THE DOME   Check out the Duomo, Florence's cathedral, and Brunelleschi's massive dome from the inside, the outside, and up on top.

TASTING BISTECCA ALLA FIORENTINA AT TRATTORIA LE FONTICINE   Yum. Order the city's specialty: a thick juicy steak prepared in an open wood-fired oven. The aroma and smoke waft around this famous family restaurant. Wash your steak down with some Chianti and finish off with gelato.

ENJOYING THE MEALTIME THEATER AT TEATRO DEL SALE   The chef announces the upcoming entrees by screaming from a window in the kitchen. Diners jockey for spots near the huge buffet-style serving table. After dinner, sit back and enjoy the onstage entertainment at this superb supper club.

VISITING THE SHOPS OF OLTRARNO   See fifth-generation artisans practicing their craft in family workshops on the south side of the historic Ponte Vecchio.

CHEERING ON ACF FIORENTINA   Join the people of Florence as they root for the ACF Fiorentina, which competes for the championship of Italy's elite Serie A soccer league.

A BRIEF HISTORY OF FLORENCE

Julius Caesar founded the city of Florentia as an encampment by the Arno river in 59 B.C. Veterans of his Roman legions later decided that the flat plain by the river would be a good place to settle (and, notwithstanding a few thousand years of floods, it was).

Florence grew to prominence in the early Middle Ages, as guilds evolved into textile businesses. It gained independence in 1125, electing a council of 100 of the richest merchants to rule the city. The most powerful families then branched out to create the world's first private banking industry, amassing incredible wealth along the way. By the late Middle Ages, Florence was *the* city in Europe, supporting a population of well over 100,000. Their loans and investments financed kings and popes alike, and attracted the top artistic talent money could buy.

The same outlays brought in a huge amount of international trade, and by the mid-1300s this crowded and unsanitary medieval city was an epicenter of commerce. Shipments of spices, silks, and slaves arrived daily from the Orient via the ports of Pisa, Mantua, and Venice. Among these imports in 1348 was the bacillus responsible for the Black Death (buried in the bellies of fleas riding the backs of black rats). What soon became known as the Florentine Plague swept like a tsunami through the city, then the region, then all of Europe, killing nearly a third of the continent's population. In Florence and Tuscany, the plague hit hardest, wiping out half the citizens in the first year, and then flaring up again over the next 3 decades.

The Florentine Renaissance, meaning "rebirth," was certainly in full bloom by the year 1400, a date that coincides with Ghiberti's commission to create the doors of the Baptistery outside the Duomo. Not only did the city experience a reawakening following the devastation of the plague, but the artists and intellectuals of the day began to take an interest in the ancient Greeks and Romans, reviving their humanistic ideals and reverence for nature. You can still see the influence of this movement in the realistic carvings on Ghiberti's doors, and in the engineering feats (some of them derived from close study of the Pantheon in Rome) that allowed Brunelleschi to create Florence's Duomo. The late 15th and early 16th centuries saw the continued flowering of this movement in the works of Michelangelo, Leonardo da Vinci, Raphael, and Botticelli.

But beyond these artists and architects, it can be said that the history of Renaissance Florence is also the story of the powerful Medici clan. Originally clothing suppliers, the family created a dominant banking conglomerate, and eventually became city rulers, princes, popes, and cultural leaders who not only created history but also often rewrote it to properly extol their efforts. Many of the buildings and statues—even the layout of the city—resulted from the wealth and will of this important family. Without their money, Florence would not have achieved the prominence and grandeur that it did.

Florence boasted military power to match its economic and artistic leadership in the Renaissance. Its armies conquered Pisa, Arezzo, Siena, and a host of other Tuscan cities during its expansionary period. But infighting among Florence's families weakened the city, and by 1600, with the Medici fortunes having faded, Florence began its gradual transformation into a tourist town. The creation of the Uffizi Gallery, in 1581, and thus the replacement of living history with a museum, was perhaps the signal that Florence's best days were in the past.

Florence tried for another rebirth in the 1860s, following Italian unification. It was named capital of the new Republic of Italy, and, to celebrate, constructed the neoclassical Piazza della Repubblica from old medieval neighborhoods. In 1865, the capital moved to Rome, and Florence was on the back burner again.

During World War II, Florence was as divided as in the heyday of the internecine Renaissance battles between the Guelph and Ghibelline clans. Nazis and fascist collaborators fought Partisans in street battles even after the end of the war. The Germans destroyed all but one of the bridges over the Arno to slow down the Allied advance, but they left the Ponte Vecchio standing in a nod to its historical significance. Allied aerial bombers also avoided hitting monuments, using the reflection of the sun off the Duomo as a beacon.

Today Florence remains a vibrant, living city. Vespe buzz through the streets like the wasps for which they are named. Steel garage doors between old stone villas discharge Italian sports cars. The Ferragamos, akin to the Medicis, rule their own mercantile empire from a castle on the Arno. And Florence's hosting of important fashion fairs recalls the initial rise of the fortunes of the city, and shows, too, that some Florentines continue to amass fortunes.

> " To be sure, anyone who has seen Michelangelo's David has no need to see anything else by any other sculptor, living or dead. "
>
> —Giorgio Varasi, *Lives of the Artists*, 1579

LAY OF THE LAND

The first order of business is to get oriented. The **Santa Maria Novella district,** anchored by the eponymous church and the main train station, is at the far west side of the tourist's world, with the Arno river to the south. This area has spawned a tourists' ghetto of cheap lodging, Internet cafes, and souvenir stands centered on Via Faenza centered on Via Nazionale and Via Del Giglio. Moving toward the city

When Should You Visit?

Summer can be awfully hot, and the locals usually flee town en masse in August, when many shops and hotels close. Weather-wise, spring and fall are the best times in Florence, as well as in the Tuscan countryside. If you're traveling on a budget, however, you may want to consider a winter visit, when prices are at their lowest. Yes, the city will be cold and wet, but not unbearably so, and you'll be able to see all of Florence's top sights without battling crowds.

---

center on Via Faenza, you'll pass the stall-filled streets around **Mercato Centrale and San Lorenzo Church,** which are claustrophobic but good spots to shop for leather deals.

All roads lead to the **Duomo.** Piazza del Duomo, the site of Florence's massive domed cathedral, the Baptistery, and 10 million tourists, is centrally located at the end point of over a dozen streets. So it's easy to find, but hard to exit in the right direction. Remember, the Baptistery, the smaller building with the doors everyone is staring at, stands on the western end of the piazza.

Go **north from the Duomo** on vias Ricasoli, Cavour, or Servi to find the **Accademia** (which houses Michelangelo's *David*), the **Piazza San Marco,** and **Piazza Santa Annunziata** respectively. These large attractions create the northern borders of your tourist world.

The **western edge** of the historical center focuses around the cavernous **Santa Croce** church, as well as the many leather stores nearby. The streets are a little more residential, the feeling a bit more local than in the central part of the district.

South from the Duomo, Via Roma will lead you to the neoclassical **Piazza della Repubblica** and its huge arch. Via dei Tornabuoni, the high-end shopping street with the Ferragamo and Prada stores, is a few blocks west of Piazza della Repubblica. A couple of blocks east of Piazza della Repubblica, Via dei Calzaiuoli brings visitors to the statue-filled medieval **Piazza Signoria** and **Palazzo Vecchio** (the fortress with the pokey tower). Piazza Signoria connects on the south end to the **Uffizi Gallery,** which is just east of the shop-filled Ponte Vecchio, the landmark bridge crossing the **Arno River.**

South of the Arno, across Ponte Vecchio, or Ponte S. Trinità, is the **Oltrarno** district, more of a laid-back, locals-focused part of town, with winding streets filled with artisans' workshops and small stores. But it's still tourist friendly, with hotels, restaurants, and the massive **Pitti Palace,** along with several other churches and **Piazzale Michelangelo** and **San Miniato Church** up high in the hills above the Oltrarno.

A growing number of international and European discount airlines fly into both Florence's **Amerigo Vespucci Airport** (☎ 055-3061302; www.aeroporto. firenze.it) and Pisa's nearby **Galileo Galilei Airport.** Florence's airport is only about 4.8km (3 miles) from the city center, making it a reasonable €15 to €20 cab ride, or a €4, 20-minute bus ride into town via the direct Ataf-Sita buses that leave the airport every 30 minutes. Regular city buses make the connection for about €1.50. The Pisa airport is about an hour from Florence. Low-cost airlines

Touring Florence

A number of companies offer walking tours of Florence. Because the historical district is very walkable, this is a good way to see, and learn about, the city. The streets are filled with many historical buildings and sites that would otherwise escape your attention. Quality of the tours varies widely, though. Many local tour guides, while knowledgeable, lack English-language skills or the ability to entertain. One of the best tour companies, which combines native English speakers with interesting stories, is **Walking Tours of Florence** (Piazza San Stefano, 2, near Ponte Vecchio; ☎ 055-2645033; www.italy.artviva.com). Its owners have a theater background and choose guides who are natural performers—their spirited tours aren't just dry presentations of names and dates. The group offers half- and full-day tours of the major sights in town, as well as an assortment of custom tours, including out-of-town trips and a fascinating walk through the artisans' shops south of the Arno. Prices range from €25 for a 3-hour tour of the city center to €94 for a full-day tour, including museum admissions. **Mercurio Tours** (Via Cavour 36R; ☎ 055-213355; www.mercurio-italy. org) runs a similar selection of town and regional tours.

A less recommended way to get oriented is to take a bus tour through the area. The **City Sightseeing Firenze** (Piazza Stazione, 1; ☎ 055-290451; www.city-sightseeing.it) has two lines of open-air, double-decker bus tours on which you can sit back and get a tan while you see the town. Its €20 ticket is a bit pricey, but if you're jet-lagged or just don't want to deal with walking through the heat or traffic, it may make sense. (The elevated perspective is nice, as is the ability to take in Florence without the fear of getting run over by, say, a bus.) City Sightseeing Firenze permits you to hop off the bus, tour a sight, and catch the next coach when it comes around again. The tour even goes up to the hill town of Fiesole. *Note:* The recorded headphone tour has all the basic town info, but the company promos get a little tiresome, and the narration is often corny.

have a dedicated bus service running a dozen shuttles from the airport to Florence each day for €7.50. From other airlines, you buy a train ticket for €5.10, and walk to the nearby airport train station. Both airports have a full selection of rental-car services—but you won't want a car if you're staying in Florence.

Florence sits on the main rail line between Milan (3 hr. away) and Rome (about a 2-hr. ride). **Stazione Santa Maria Novella** (**SMN;** ☎ 800-888088 in Italy, or 055-288765; www.trenitalia.it) is the main Florence station, across the street from the bus station, and a short walk away from dozens of hotels and restaurants. A tourist information office is in the station, but it's really a hotel booking service—go across the street toward the Santa Maria church to find the main tourist office. Florence's other two stations, **Campo di Marte** and **Refredi,** are much farther from the tourist districts, and should be avoided.

Florence Accommodations & Dining

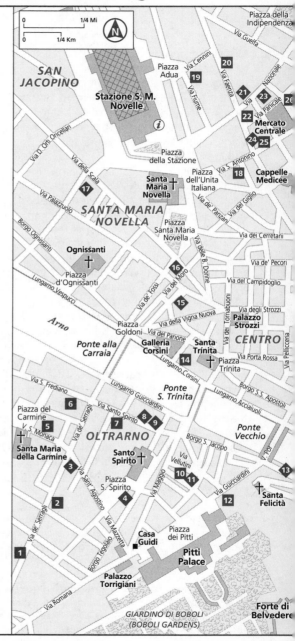

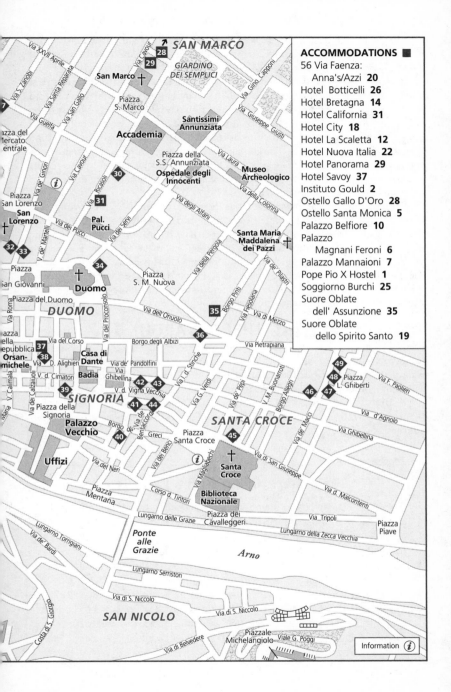

ACCOMMODATIONS ■
56 Via Faenza:
  Anna's/Azzi **20**
Hotel Botticelli **26**
Hotel Bretagna **14**
Hotel California **31**
Hotel City **18**
Hotel La Scaletta **12**
Hotel Nuova Italia **22**
Hotel Panorama **29**
Hotel Savoy **37**
Instituto Gould **2**
Ostello Gallo D'Oro **28**
Ostello Santa Monica **5**
Palazzo Belfiore **10**
Palazzo
  Magnani Feroni **6**
Palazzo Mannaioni **7**
Pope Pio X Hostel **1**
Soggiorno Burchi **25**
Suore Oblate
  dell' Assunzione **35**
Suore Oblate
  dello Spirito Santo **19**

Almost all regional and city **buses** arrive at the station right outside SMN. But since Florence is such a rail hub, there's usually no need to hassle with longer bus rides, unless you're traveling to Florentine suburbs off the rail network.

It's fairly easy to reach the outskirts of Florence **by car,** via the A1 autostrada cutting down the center of Italy. Then all hell breaks loose. Assuming you can find the historical center among the tangled collection of one-way streets, you won't be able to enter it: Only cars with special permits are allowed. Even if police don't stop you, cameras can take a picture of the car's plates, and you'll get hit with a whopping fine months later. The good news is that hotels have arrangements with the city to permit guests to at least stop by to drop off luggage. But this means you need to have made arrangements with your hotel prior to arrival; don't expect to simply drive around and find a place.

For **parking,** you can make it as far as the garage under SMN for parking rates of about €2 per hour. Most hotels offer some sort of parking option, but prices vary widely, from €10 to more than €30 per day. If you're far enough from the historical center, free street parking is available, but make very sure it's legal or you're going to have a nightmare of a time getting your towed car returned. About the cheapest overnight parking option is at Piazza della Libertà at €15 per day. Best of all would be to rent a car before and/or after your Florence stay, and not deal with any of the hassle and expense.

GETTING THERE & AROUND

Despite the uneven cobblestone streets, the crazy high-speed Vespe, and an unnerving number of large, fast buses, the best way to get around Florence is by walking. The central historical district takes only about 25 minutes to cross— assuming you don't get lost. Avoid the city buses, which will bring you to outlying districts before you can say "there goes the Duomo!" and then you'll have to figure out how to find your way back. So bring some comfortable shoes, and keep your eyes on traffic.

Deal Alert: Going with a Package

Like Rome, Florence has a bounty of hotels, meaning that those who want to save (and who are willing to stay in somewhat dull hotels) may want to look into air/hotel packages. Certain companies work closely with Florentine hotels and get discounts that the individual traveler can almost never match. I've seen off-season packages to Florence for as little as $569 for airfare from the U.S. and 4 nights' lodging.

The best packages to Florence are offered by **Go-Today** (☎ 800/227-3235; www.gotoday.com), **Virgin Vacations** (☎ 888/937-8474; virgin vacations.com), **Gate 1 Travel** (☎ 800/682-3333; www.gate1travel. com), and **Europe ASAP** (☎ 415/750-5499; www.europeasap.com). For more about travel packages, see p. 578.

ACCOMMODATIONS, BOTH STANDARD & NOT

Florence has over 1,000 registered places to stay, not including an equal number of unofficial apartment and room rentals, so there really is something for everyone here. Recently, many of the semi-legal private-room rentals and bed-and-breakfasts have been forced to register with authorities, creating a visible glut of rooms. All the hoteliers I interviewed have complained of a slow tourism market and high vacancy rates. Such market factors should give you increased bargaining power for rooms, though standard offered rates have not dropped to date. Many owners have been upgrading their facilities to justify keeping the same level of rates, giving visitors a better experience than in years past.

Christmas, Easter, and occasional trade shows make for tighter times in booking rooms. A number of smaller hotels and B&Bs close for a couple of weeks in August as well, making it a little tougher to find lodging during this period.

Accommodations Index

€   Rooms €50 or less a night

Azzi ★ (near Santa Maria Novella, p. 100)

Hotel Anna's ★ (near Santa Maria Novella, p. 100)

Hotel Panorama (North of the Center, p. 104)

The Instituto Gould ★ (Oltrarno, p. 99)

Ostello Gallo D'Oro ★ (North of the Center, p. 104)

Ostello Santa Monica ★ (Oltrarno, p. 103)

Palazzo Mannaioni (Oltrarno, p. 103)

Pope Pio X Hostel (Oltrarno, p. 99)

Soggiorno Burchi (near Santa Maria Novella, p. 100)

Suore Oblate dell'Assunzione (Central District, p. 99)

Suore Oblate dello Spirit (Central District, p. 99)

€€   Rooms €51 to €100 a night

Hotel Abaco ★★ kids (Central District, p. 101)

Hotel Botticelli ★ (near Santa Maria Novella, p. 101)

Hotel Bretagna ★★ (Central District, p. 102)

Hotel City ★ (near Santa Maria Novella, p. 100)

Hotel La Scaletta ★★ kids (Oltrarno, p. 103)

Hotel Nuova Italia ★★★ (near Santa Maria Novella, p. 100)

Maria Luisa de'Medici ★★ (Central District, p. 101)

€€€   Rooms €101 to €150 a night

Hotel California (Central District, p. 102)

€€€€   **Rooms more than €150 a night**

Boscolo Astoria ★★★ (Central District, p. 102)

Palazzo Magnani Feroni ★★★ (Oltrarno, p. 104)

Hotel Savoy ★★ (Central District, p. 102)

APARTMENTS FOR RENT

As I've said, Florence currently has a glut of housing, particularly for those planning to rent an apartment, with the lowest prices going to those who rent for a week or longer. It's a winning situation for travelers; renting an apartment can dramatically cut lodging costs, given that a decent, centrally located two-bedroom flat with kitchen and sitting room averages about €600 to €800 a week, a much lower price than a similar level hotel would entail. Plus, you can stock a fridge with breakfast and snacks, cutting down on food expenses, though you'll certainly want to get out for dinner to sample the local cuisine. An apartment also offers a relaxing home base, and can give you a real flavor of local Italian living.

A variety of agencies in Florence offer furnished apartment rentals to tourists for weekly or monthly periods. Independent locals also sublet their apartments directly, by advertising on the Internet, in school bulletin boards, or through fliers on laundromat walls (though these can be iffy, as you never know what you're getting). Instead, I'd opt for an agency that vets the properties it rents. There's something for everyone, from the palatial to the monastically simple. One thing to keep in mind: A number of Internet-based companies consolidate listings from private owners, so you'll often find the same apartments advertised on multiple sites. Research carefully before you book.

Rentals Florence (☎ 055-2347206; www.rentalsflorence.com) offers a dozen different apartments for rent across the city, including three recently renovated models literally a stone's throw away from the Duomo. The furnishings are basic, but perfectly functional, and the location is unparalleled—you'll be able to climb to the roof patio to enjoy sunset over the city. One of these two-bedroom apartments rents for €820 a week or €2,200 a month, and can sleep up to six people. Gabriela, the rental manager, speaks English well and works hard to make sure people enjoy their stays. She also can give recommendations for rentals elsewhere in Tuscany.

For a wider selection of centrally located apartments in all price ranges, look to **Lodging in Florence** (Vicolo degli Adimari, 2; ☎ 055-280007; www.lodging inflorence.com). Lorenzo Clemente, its manager, and his team are hard workers and know the options in Florence well. You can trust them to find an apartment that matches your tastes and needs. The cheapest rentals are about €400 a week for tiny (but centrally located) "bed-sits." These small studio apartments have bathroom and kitchen, and are clean and functional—but don't expect to do any entertaining. On the higher end are cushy two-bedroom, two-bathroom refurbished apartments with views across the Arno to the Uffizi, for €1,450 a week. The group also has a bed-and-breakfast option permitting you to rent a room in a local's apartment (a cheap and sometimes fun option), and they can find you out-of-town lodging as well.

I've also found that the American-based agency **Travel Italy** (www.travel-italy. com) has a good, if slightly pricier, selection of apartments in the center of Florence. These range from cozy, antique-laden one-bedrooms in the Santa Croce area (from €490 per week; with fold-out couch, bedrooms can sleep four) to more modern studios off the Piazza Pitti (from €490 per week for two people) to larger spaces that can house up to six people. The Travel Italy staff is friendly and knows its properties well.

Because you came all the way to Florence to experience a Renaissance town, perhaps you should stay at a period apartment. **Palazzo Belfiore** ★ (Via dei Velluti 8, Oltrarno; ☎ 055-611115) offers seven unique apartments in a 15th-century palace. The rooms boast frescoes and antique furniture, and are restored to their original glory, but with the addition of satellite TV, modern kitchens, and central heating and air-conditioning. (The nobles never had it so good.) Apartments rent for €850 to €1,600 per week, and sleep up to six people.

RELIGIOUS HOUSING

€–€€€   While Florence doesn't have the same meditative atmosphere as, say, Assisi or a smaller town in the countryside, you can still save a bit of money, and enjoy a spiritual interlude, at a religious house in the city. Two excellent options are **Suore Oblate dello Spirito Santo** (Via Nazionale, 8; ☎ 055-2398129), which seems a bit out of place close to the chaos of the train station, and **Suore Oblate dell'Assunzione** (Via Borgo Pinti, 15; ☎ 055-2480583) near the Duomo. Run by nuns, they are both pretty basic. Spirito Santo admits only married couples, families, and single women, and requires a minimum 2-night stay at €44 for a double. Dell'Assunzione is more flexible about who can stay, charging €52 for a double with private bathroom. Aside from the need to act respectfully, the only rule travelers should be aware of in these two hostels is an 11:30pm curfew (though you may be able to come in a little later).

€   My preference is for a *semi*-religious stay. Despite the severe appearance of the **Pope Pio X Hostel** (Via dei Serragli 106, Oltrarno; ☎ 055-225044), with photos of the Pope and religious paraphernalia everywhere, it's really a relaxed hostel popular with Italian students, as it should be at €17 a night, about the cheapest option in town. Get there early to claim one of the 58 beds.

€–€€€   Finally, **The Instituto Gould** ★ 🧒 (Via dei Serragli 49, Oltrarno; ☎ 055-212576; gould.reception@dada.it) is more upscale than a regular hostel, charging €58 for a courtyard double with bathroom (or €21 per person in a quad without bathroom). But the building, an old palace, has been modernized to provide clean, basic dorm rooms, and boasts an attractive courtyard. A portion of your room rate goes to help the disadvantaged children whom the Institute supports.

HOTELS OF THE SANTA MARIA NOVELLA DISTRICT

It's not the most glamorous area of town, but for budget lodgings this tourist district has the greatest number of affordable accommodations. It's also brimming with Internet cafes, bars, laundromats, shops, and the train station—in short, everything needed for a convenient stay. It's a good place for meeting other travelers, too, especially backpackers who can afford something better than basic hostel accommodations. There are also a handful of classier hotels, of which I'll recommend a few. The Santa Maria Novella District is centered on the Via Faenza–Via Nazionale intersection.

€–€€   The one-stop shop for budget lodging in this area is **56 Via Faenza.** That four-story building contains no fewer than six hotels/hostels. The most surprising perhaps is **Hotel Anna's** ★ (Via Faenza, 56; ☎ 055-2302714; hotelannas. com), an extremely pleasant place tucked into the third floor of what appears from the street to be only a low-end backpacker flophouse (it's not). The newly refurbished rooms here are spotlessly clean, with the type of classy, functional furniture you'd expect to see at a three-star business hotel. It's also a friendly place with a helpful staff. Continental breakfast is served in a little frescoed alcove, or in your room upon request, adding €5 to the €70-to-€90 room rate. The ground floor is home to **Azzi** ★ (☎ 055-213806; www.hotelazzi.it), a quirky, bohemian hotel comprising 16 rooms, which range in price from €70 for a smallish double with fan, to €130 for a suite during high season. Most doubles cost between €70 and €110. Rooms are brightly decorated, and most feature an antique piece here and a colorfully painted wall there to add a bit of ambience. The manager, Valentino, and his partners run a number of hotels, apartments, and B&Bs in town, offering what he calls "a total housing solution"; they'll find something for you even if the Azzi is booked.

€   The friendly, older Italian couple who own and run **Soggiorno Burchi** (Via Faenza, 20; ☎ 055-268481; www.soggiornoburchi.com) don't speak much English, but they'll cheerfully yell at you until you get your luggage and room sorted. They have about the cheapest decent private rooms in town, at €45 for a clean, extremely plain but spotless double without bathroom. Plus, they offer a great deal on parking at €10 per day in a hidden garage next door. The 13 rooms on three separate floors offer a mishmash of furnishings and views of the neighbors through interior courtyards.

€€   The proud motto of the service-oriented **Hotel Nuova Italia** ★★★ (Via Faenza, 26; ☎ 055-268430; www.hotel-nuovaitalia.com) is "just ask." And they mean it. Owned by Luciano Vito and his affable Canadian wife, Eileen (they met 3 decades ago when she was a tourist, and his family's hotel was recommended in Arthur Frommer's *Europe on $5 a Day*), it's a labor of love and the hotel has been steadily improving over the years. Recently, the couple added double-paned glass, air-conditioning, new carpeting, and re-tiled bathrooms (and even more changes are in the works). In addition, Luciano and Eileen will do anything they can to help you out during your stay in Florence, with honest recommendations for sightseeing, shopping, and area travel. High-season rates are €119, but if that's too pricey for you, you may be able to bargain them down. As they say, "just ask."

€€–€€€   From the outside, **Hotel City** ★ (Via Sant'Antonino, 18; ☎ 055-295451; www.hotelcity.net) looks like all the other undistinguished offerings in this part of town. Inside, however, this highly recommended place is another story: The rooms are newly renovated and quiet despite the central location; plus the staff is eager to please. (They even have a reserve air-conditioning system in case the primary one breaks down.) With half-timbered arched rooms and white-washed interiors, this is a beautifully maintained hotel—especially when compared with others in the immediate vicinity, which seem to be operated chiefly as tax write-offs by their absentee owners.

€€–€€€€   Tucked away on a small side street, the tastefully refurbished **Hotel Botticelli** ✖ (Via Taddea, 8; ☎ 055-290905; www.hotelbotticelli.it) has a resort feel to it, thanks to the downright pretty rooms of this restored 16th-century villa. Many are done in the same wash of gentle colors that the artist Botticelli himself used, and each features a nice framed print of the artist's work, along with satellite TV, air-conditioning, and a minibar. It's located not too far from the central market and the crowded street stalls of San Lorenzo. The breakfast room is large and airy (as is the balcony patio), and the buffet breakfast is good (so, too, is the blessed, blessed silence of the hotel on this small side alley). Rooms go for €125 to €180, but you can sometimes get lodgings for below €100 when business is slow. Check the website for seasonal deals; they often reward longer stays with a 5th night free.

HOTELS IN THE CENTRAL DISTRICT, AROUND THE DUOMO & PIAZZA DELLA SIGNORIA

This, of course, is the ideal place to stay, especially if you can get the fabled "Room with a View," allowing you to wake up each morning to the beauty of the Duomo and its nearby buildings. Consequently, lodgings here tend to be pricier than those around the train station, but if you can afford to splurge, this is one of the places in Italy where price will make a difference in the quality of your stay (and if you can't afford a splurge, see below for two good budget options).

€€   The first of these is a gem, one of my favorite *pensioni* in Italy. That's because the **Maria Luisa de'Medici** ✖✖ (Via del Corso, 1; ☎ 055-2800058) has all the creature comforts you could want—firm beds, thick walls, a hearty complimentary breakfast—in a setting that's delightfully imaginative, quirky, and, in an odd way, stylish. In fact, the decor here is a mishmash of many styles: You have the wonderful bones of the place, a 1650s *palazzo* filled with funky 1960s high-design furniture, exquisite baroque paintings on the walls, and fun modern murals of the Medicis on guest-room walls (the place is named for the last Medici princess). The five rooms are oversize and thus terrific for families, and the hosts as friendly and helpful as can be. The drawbacks? Well, the cheaper rooms share a bathroom (these cost €67 for a double, €93 for a triple, and €118 for a quad; expect to pay €13–€20 more for rooms with private bathroom facilities), and to reach the *pensione* you'll need to walk up three flights of steps. Finally, rooms do not have phones. But aside from those minor quibbles, the place is a delight.

€€–€€€   Halfway between the train station and the Duomo, the **Hotel Abaco** ✖✖ 🐱 (Via dei Banchi, 1; ☎ 055-2381919; www.abaco-hotel.it) is a budget charmer boasting nine rooms, each named for a different artist and done up in the colors that artist tended to use (you can compare the color of the drapes with the framed print of "your" artist that will be hanging on the wall). Because some rooms share a WC (all have private showers) the prices are reasonable, especially for the toilet-less rooms where a double will range from just €72 to €82 (€85–€95 with private bathroom facilities). There are also nice triples and quads, good for families, that cost between €95 and €125 for a triple (varying by seasons and bathroom facilities) and €135 to €155 for a quad. All rooms have air-conditioning, TV, and a nice bit of ambience thanks to the high wood ceilings and stone floors of this 15th-century *palazzo*.

€€–€€€   In a prime location overlooking the Arno River, this 1880s palace, now the **Hotel Bretagna** ★★ (Lungarno Corsini, 6; ☎ 055-289618; www.hotel bretagna.net), has swallowed up several surrounding offices to create a warren of widely varied rooms. Some are quite nice, with a classic Victorian look; others, unfortunately, resemble converted closets. But even the small rooms, with interior-facing windows, are a good option, given the location of the hotel and the fine breakfast and common rooms. The prices are also quite fair for what you get, and vary widely from room to room. For example, a single with shared bathroom can cost as little as €35 (going up to €60 in high season); a double with shared bath-room ranges from €45 to €85, while doubles with private bathroom facilities are €55 to €115. Renovations in 2006 will create some triples (with or without private bathroom) and family rooms with frescoed ceilings and chandeliers, with bal-conies overlooking the river—making these rooms truly a choice pick of Florence (especially at a reasonable €110–€160). Be sure to check the website for last-minute specials, which can often shave €10 off the price of a room.

€€€   Though it looks seedy from the outside, and the entrance isn't much bet-ter, the **Hotel California** (Via Ricasoli, 30, near the Duomo; ☎ 055-282753; www. californiaflorence.it) is actually quite nice once you make it up to the second-floor lobby. Its recently remodeled rooms are spacious and comfortable, particularly the triples and quads which are perfect for families. Some rooms have a terrace over-looking the Duomo; all have air-conditioning, satellite TV, and positively swank bathrooms (some with Jacuzzi). The rear terrace, bedecked with flowers in spring and summer, is the perfect place to kick back with a bottle of Chianti and write postcards. A double room runs about €120, but, as everywhere, prices vary widely by season.

€€€€   Worth a splurge for its unique historical rooms, some with a view of the Duomo, **The Boscolo Astoria** ★★★ (Via Giglio, 9; ☎ 055-2398095; www.boscolo hotels.com) will make you feel as if you're staying in a palace because, well, you are. This 16th-century mansion has museum-quality furnishings, frescoed walls, and the unmistakable air of nobility. Add to that a rooftop bar with a spectacular Duomo view and a secret entrance into a cozy alley wine bar, and you have all the fixings for a romantic getaway. Prices vary widely by season, but average €250 for a night.

€€€€   Our second Florence splurge, the **Hotel Savoy** ★★ (Piazza della Repubblica, 7; ☎ 055-27351; www.roccofortehotels.com), while not as special as the Boscolo Astoria, has much to recommend it: It's a full-service property, in a renovated palace, located right on Piazza della Repubblica, with luxurious rooms and original art lining the hallways. Unlike the Boscolo, however, there's much less of the traditional Florentine decor here: Appearance is of that same Art Deco style that you'll see at plush hotels around the world, which is a disappointment. However, many rooms, including the well-equipped fitness room, are graced by views of the Duomo. Plus the massive suites are fit for a Medici, and usually booked by the most affluent Italian business families. In winter, double-room rates can drop to €270 on the hotel's website; in summer they're listed at an unaffordable €375, but deals can be had through travel agencies both online and off (and the hotel is recommended only if you can snare such a discounted deal).

HOTELS IN OLTRARNO

More of a residential area than the one immediately surrounding the Duomo, Oltrarno has a lively mix of restaurants and bars, as well as some of the most charming shops in the city: the workplaces of jewelers, leather craftsmen, and woodcarvers who have toiled on the side streets of this district for decades. This is also Florence's most bohemian area, somewhat similar to Paris's Left Bank, though escalating rents have been driving some of the artists out. In short, it's a fun area within walking distance of all the major sights.

€   **Ostello Santa Monica** ★ (Via S. Monaca, 6; ☎ 055-268338; www.ostello.it) is my first pick, though it has little charm and too many rules. But the youthful clientele here know a value when they see it and are delighted with the top location and the prices. It's a good place to connect with other backpackers, and the bulletin boards are usually packed with budget tour options, bars, restaurants, and other hookups around town. For €17 a night, and a good Oltrarno location, it's probably the top shoestring-budget choice in town. Lockout times are 10am to 2pm and 2 to 6am.

€–€€   For those who'd like the convenience of having a kitchen, but can't commit to a full-week rental, the **Palazzo Mannaioni** (Via Maffia, 9, near Piazza Santo Spirito; ☎ 055-271741; www.florenceresidence.it) offers an affordable solution. It's a 15th-century building that's been subdivided into a number of small apartments, each with its own efficiency kitchen. While these digs are nothing special decor-wise, the location is terrific and the prices can't be beat for studios that can comfortably house two for as little as €70 a day. In all, there are 19 little apartments, some with balcony terrace and some that can house up to eight in four double beds (€157 per night for these, while rooms with two beds go for €120 per night). To reduce costs even further, you can rent for a week. Do that and a double-bedded apartment costs just €800, with an extra bed an additional €150.

€€–€€€   The views are why you want to stay at the **Hotel La Scaletta** ★★ 🄺🄸🄳🅂 (Via Guicciardini, 13; ☎ 055-283028; www.lascaletta.com). Located right next to the Pitti Palace, it has spectacular patios overlooking both the Boboli Gardens and the city (you're going to want to spend your entire vacation just gazing at the sight). New management has also extensively renovated the rooms and the common areas, creating a cheery, colorful atmosphere throughout the 13 rooms and winding hallways. One quadruple room is a good family choice at €110 to €180 a night, while a double ranges from €85 to €130, depending on season. The only downside here, I think, are the small bathrooms, but those can't be helped: The hotel, like many others in this city, is set in a 15th-century *palazzo* with real character and thick walls.

€€€€   For that once-in-a-lifetime vacation—say, a 50th anniversary—the place to pick is the **Palazzo Magnani Feroni** ★★★ (Borgo San Frediano, 5; ☎ 055-2608908; www.florencepalace.com). An actual palace, owned by one family for the past 250 years, its suites are all super lavish, with the same antiques the family installed in the 19th century. They'll have shirt-makers, hairdressers, and local restaurateurs visit your suite for in-room service. You'll be paying top dollar for every benefit (€210–€320 for the very cheapest suites), but go crazy—this is as nice as it gets in Florence. There's a rooftop bar, a billiards room, 9m (30-ft.) bedroom ceilings in the rooms, and everything you could want to play Italian noble for a day or two.

HOTELS NORTH OF CENTRAL FLORENCE

€   One of the cleanest, most efficient hostels I've ever seen is the **Ostello Gallo D'Oro** ★ (kids) (Via Covour, 104; ☎ 055-5522984; www.ostellogallodoro.com). It's a 15-minute walk north of the historical center, but the walk is worth it because you'll enjoy crisp, shiny rooms, a friendly staff, and a brand-new interior at budget prices. The lobby has two free Internet terminals, the kitchen is free for use by all, and the friendly manager may very well offer to cook something up for you (it's been known to happen). There are also nice private rooms—with TV, phone, and private bathroom—available at reasonable rates.

€€   As you can tell from the name, **Hotel Panorama** (Via Cavour, 60; ☎ 055-2382043; www.hotelpanorama.fi.it) has an excellent view of the city from its third-floor breakfast room and the bulk of its guest rooms. They do get some large groups staying here, so reserve ahead to snare one of the 32 rooms. Rooms and facilities aren't anything special, but they're serviceable and definitely affordable—€70 to €94 per double. And anyway, you're here for the scenery, right?

DINING FOR ALL TASTES

In general, *cucina rustica* (rustic cuisine) is what you'll find in Florence's restaurants. This is food that's meant to stick to the ribs and leave you sated, so it's no accident that the great specialty of the city is a huge slab of steak dripping with juices *(bistecca alla fiorentina)*. But this is not peasant fare by any means; there's a balance to these bold flavors that makes eating out in Florence a special occasion, even when you're just catching a quick lunch.

And if you need to catch a quick lunch, it's always best to arrive at a *ristorante* or trattoria at the beginning of the lunch hour, which is from noon to 2:30pm and is the biggest meal of the day. Otherwise, you may have to wait for a table. Italians tend to eat dinner between 7 and 9:30pm—you can assume that those are the hours of operation for the following eateries (with the exception of the *gelaterie*) unless it's indicated otherwise. For a **map of Florence's restaurants,** see p. 94.

Dining Index

Price for a *primo* course: € = €7 or less; €€ = €8–€14; €€€ = €15–€19; €€€€ = €20 or more

RESTAURANTS NEAR SANTA MARIA NOVELLA

€   If you wanted to design a quaint Italian restaurant for a movie, it would look something like **I'tozzo . . . di Pane Osteria** ★ (Via Guelfa 94R; ☎ 055-475753; Tues–Sat). Outside: a brick-terraced patio under a vine-covered trellis tucked into a quiet garden. Inside: a cluttered, lively room with faded paint on the walls and a little nook of a door on an untrafficked street. Yeah, this is the place. Go for *orecchiette con speck* (light pasta with ham) for €7, or maybe a panino sandwich with portobello mushrooms, fresh greens, and tomato for €6, and then sit back with a glass of wine and enjoy the day.

€€–€€€   A surprisingly good meal amid the Internet cafes and cut-rate shops of Via Faenza can be had at **Trattoria da Guido** (Via Faenze 34R; ☎ 055-289746; Thurs–Tues). Quick and friendly service and a relaxed setting make this trattoria a way to escape the chaos outside. The €6 prosciutto sampler appetizer is well recommended, as is the strong-tasting veal *tonnato* ensemble with capers and anchovies for €12. The restaurant prepares a hearty and delicious *bistecca alla fiorentina* as well, running in the €20 to €25 range (depending on weight).

€€–€€€   For the quintessential Florentine dining experience, have a *bistecca alla fiorentina* at **Ristorante le Fonticine** ★★★ (Via Nazionale 79R; ☎ 055-282106; www.lefonticine.com; Tues–Sun). Waiters bring steaks from the open-air oven to be carved at a central table and then distributed to guests packed into the two large rooms of Gianna and Silvano Bruci's family restaurant, where diners have been going home happy since 1959. Their son Gian Piero helped with a 2004 updating of the restaurant, refreshing the facilities, adding air-conditioning, and a few menu items, but leaving the colorful cluttered collection of original artwork covering the walls. Start with the Tuscan salami appetizer or a bowl of minestrone soup for around €5, continue with the *tagliarini 'fonticine*—thin homemade noodles in a truffles-and-mushroom sauce for €8—and then move on to the mouth-watering steaks, €24 per person but well spent. The dessert ice cream comes direct from Vivoli's, perhaps the top *gelateria* in Florence.

€€€   Set in a 14th-century *palazzo*, **Trattoria Garga** ★ (Via del Moro 48r; ☎ 055-211396; www.garga.it) has to be one of the most original spots in town, utterly infused with the personality of its owners, the husband-and-wife team of Giuliano Gargani ("Garga") and Sharon Oddson. They cook the food, an updated, slightly experimental, and always delicious version of traditional Tuscan fare; painted all of the colorful walls themselves; and put on quite a show during mealtime, bellowing out orders, singing opera, and generally making sure everyone has a good time. Sharon also runs cooking classes out of the trattoria kitchen during the week for €155 for a daylong session (you cook and then feast). Recommended menu items include spaghetti with shrimp, tomatoes, orange, and chiles; and tortellini with orange and mint.

RESTAURANTS IN THE CENTRAL DISTRICT

€   **Caffè Duomo** (Piazza Duomo, 29/30R; ☎ 055-211348; daily 9am–midnight) serves a darn good pizza for only €6, set quickly on the plate and with no *coperto*. This is a great place to hang out and people-watch, with only shrubbery separating you from the crowds around the Duomo, 6m (20 ft.) away. Sure, it's touristy, but you're a tourist—get over it.

€   The best of the best: **Gelateria Carabe** ★★★ (Via Ricasoli, 60R; ☎ 055-289476) is regarded as equal in artistic merit to Michelangelo's *David* down the street. The caramel gelato is reason enough to immigrate to Italy. Be sure to order it: €1.70 for a small, up to €7.30 for a mongo scoop; and don't forget to specify the size before your order or you may be eating more than you planned.

€   If you're tired of Italian food—hey, it happens!—I have three suggestions. First, there's **Eby's Latin Bar** (Via dell'Oriulo, 5R; ☎ 055-240027), where you'll

The Cibreo Empire of Food & Fun

Chef Fabio Picchi, and his wife, Maria Cassi, have created a small empire of food and fun at the corners of Via Verrocchio and Via de'Macci in the Santa Croce area.

€€€€   Want great food in an elegant setting? Put on a tie and make reservations at **Cibreo Ristorante** ★★ (Via A. Del Verrocchio, 8R; ☎ 055-2341100; www.cibreo.com; Tues–Sat), where there's no pasta on the menu, but the fare is refined (if a bit spicy).

€€   Would you rather take advantage of a good deal on tasty dishes in a casual trattoria? **Trattoria Cibreo** (Via de'Macci, 122R) on the other side of the kitchen has the identical menu at nearly half the price.

€   Perhaps you'd prefer to relax in a cafe for a while? **Cibreo Caffè** (Via A. Del Verrocchio, 5R; ☎ 055-2345853), across from the restaurant, has a small patio and a stylish interior—and it's even cheaper than the trattoria.

€€–€€€€   The real fun starts at the couple's latest venture, the **Teatro del Sale** ★★★ (Via de'Macci, 111R; ☎ 055-2001492; www.teatrodelsale.com) supper club. "Dinner and entertainment 6 nights a week," doesn't really sum it up. The entertainment varies from Italian experimental theater to jazz and gospel bands to Elvis Costello, who recently played a 5-night set.

The dishes, served buffet-style, are created in a glassed-off kitchen to the side of the theater area. Chef Picchi announces each order as it emerges from the kitchen, shouting them out like a ship's captain: "Women and children take care! The penne is powerfully hot and spicy." Diners jockey for position around the table to grab helpings from the surprise dishes as they arrive. Wine is dispensed freely from two large casks, and desserts arrive in big servings.

And Teatro del Sale really is a club. Non-Italians pay €5 (€8 for locals) to join, and there are rules designed to preserve the spirit of the club. One command is "ethical listening"; another requirement is to share the latest cultural information with other members. "Any member discovered in the act of non-communication" (not being chatty) can get their membership revoked.

Buffet dinners at the Teatro are €24, including the entertainment, which comes on at 9:30pm after the plates are cleared and diners grab a seat for the show. Buffet breakfasts are available for €5, lunches for €14, but without the shows. The front part of the building is a store selling local olive oils, wines, and ingredients used in the cooking, as well as souvenir glasses made from recycled wine bottles.

enjoy an assortment of burritos and wraps at €3.50 each, including a made-to-order shrimp burrito with fresh salsa. Grab a €3 sangria, kick back to some Latin music, and watch the traffic go by from the second floor of this colorful bohemian hangout. Across the street is a vegetarian favorite, **Kooclikoo** (Via Borgo Pinti, 2/r; ☎ 055-234220), where you can make a sandwich to order with any one of a number of vegetarian patties and toppings, including tofu, seitan, sun-dried tomatoes, and eggplant. A sandwich, cookie, and a Coke cost just €5. Or, for the genuine American burger, you can drop by **Ari's Diner** ★ 🧒 (Via Giraldi, 4A, crossing of Via Ghibellina), which serves all the Yankee specialties—pancakes, Philly cheese steaks, steak and eggs, beer, milkshakes—from 9am to 3am in a brightly lit, Americana-decorated diner. It's a place to take kids who just won't eat another truffle, and most of the dishes run in the €7-to-€9 range, service and cover charge included.

€€   Just around the corner from Piazza Signoria, a good spot to stop for lunch after a morning tour or shopping expedition, is **Caffè Italiano** (Via della Condotta, 56r; ☎ 055-291082; www.caffeitaliano.it; Mon–Sat; no credit cards), a pastry-and-sandwich bar with an early-20th-century feel. It serves a good selection of soups, salads, and sandwiches to a full house. Morning visitors can enjoy custom coffee blends and fresh pastries made on the premises. And you can relax at a window table to people-watch, or dine in the large upstairs room.

€€   Another good snack stop is **Antica Pizzeria–Ristorante Nuti** (Borgo S. Lorenzo, 39; ☎ 055-210410), where they've been cranking out pizzas in an open wood-fired stone oven since 1955. The Napoletana cuisine is a fun change from Tuscan fare. You'll find the pizzas here to be thinner and heavier on the veggies, creating a meal for only €5 to €8, and €4 for a beer.

€€   With its frescoed ceilings, antique fixtures, and tuxedoed waiters, **Ristorante Paoli** (Via dei Tavolini, 12R; ☎ 055-216215; Wed–Mon) is the type of place you'd imagine late-19th-century visitors on "the grand tour" frequented. Yes, it's a bit touristy, with a standard spaghetti-and-meatball-type menu, but the food is actually quite good, if expensive for what you get (pastas range €7–€14). One highlight of the menu: the light and fresh sea bass, at €14, with lemon, olive oil, and peppercorn. And you have to like the "no service charge, no *coperto*" policy.

€€€   Hidden on a lightly trafficked side street close to the Arno, the **Belcore Ristorante** ★★ (Via dell'Albero, 28/30R; ☎ 055-211198; www.ristorantebelcore. it) features Middle Eastern–influenced Tuscan dishes in a cool minimalist white restaurant. A friendly and well-informed waitstaff will guide you through menu choices that include seared tuna with peppercorn and shallots, stuffed tortellini with ricotta cheese, and lamb with sweet onions. Artistic presentations on Polish ceramic dishes complete the international flavor of the restaurant. Every Friday is "fish night," with a €30 set menu featuring the catch of the day and three additional courses. Reservations are highly recommended.

€€€   It doesn't look like much from the outside, but the expansive (and expensive) **Ristorante Buca Mario** ★ (Piazza Ottaviani, 16R; ☎ 055-2647336;

www.bucamario.it) has been packing 'em in since 1886. A large underground warren of rooms with white walls, red-and-white tablecloths, and Italian folk art on the walls, its classic appearance is one that scores of Italian-American restaurants have tried to evoke for years. Here, it's the genuine article, despite the fact that most of its clientele nowadays are tourists. Still, the food is excellent and the old-school waiters lend an air of authority (though they'll also joke with guests in perfect English). You won't go wrong if you order the *tagliarini* pasta with salmon (€14), or the classic *bistecca alla fiorentina* done perfectly (€26). A €3 cover charge per person will be added to the final bill.

€€€   If Ristorante Buca Mario (see above) looks like the quintessential Florentine restaurant, **Il Latini** ★★ (Via Dei Palchetti, 6R; ☎ 055-210916; www.illatini.com; Tues–Sun) is its country cousin, a place where strangers and friends jam together at long communal tables under a canopy of hanging sausages and make like they're dining at a bucolic tavern on some saint's feast day. Though it sounds hokey, it's a chaotic, spirited experience that truly does feel Italian. And the food is first rate, not to mention the wines, which come directly from the Latini family's estate in Chianti. It's doubtful that you'll get a look at the printed menu. Most patrons simply order the €35-to-€40 family-style sampler, a stomach-busting mound of meats, soups, and pastas with unlimited wine. This is a fun, fun experience, and reservations are recommended.

RESTAURANTS IN THE SANTA CROCE AREA

€   Competing with Gelateria Carabe for the title of best gelato in town, **Vivoli** (Via Isole delle Stinche, 7R, a block west of Piazza Santa Croce; ☎ 055-239334) is conveniently open from 9am to 1am, so you can come by nearly any time to taste the wide selection of freshly made flavors. Creative combinations vary by the season, but have included black currant and amaretto, along with every variety of almond and vanilla. Pay first at the register, and then take your receipt to the counter for your treat.

€€   Chef Gino began his restaurant with only a couple of items on the menu, hence the name, **I'Che' ce' ce'** ★ (Via Magalotti, 11R; ☎ 055-216589), which means "there is what there is." But over the years he's catered to customer requests in his intimate trattoria, and slowly expanded his offerings. Dinner begins with fried bread balls, courtesy of the house. Pastas range from €4 to €7, and the London-trained chef (he came home to start this restaurant) is a master of pasta: Try the spaghetti *alla brigante*—brigand-style pasta with some extra spice to it. The €11 set menu is a good pasta-and-mixed-grill combo with a small salad. These are generally cheap eats, but don't forget the €2 *coperto* and 10% service charge. The restaurant is a little tricky to find: Look for the alleyway sign on Borgo de Greci street en route to Santa Croce.

€€   If you have difficulty choosing just one dish, you're going to love **Acqua al Due** ★★ (Via della Vigna Vecchia, 40R; ☎ 055-284170; www.acquaal2.it), which has made a name for itself with its tasting plates—small dishes of lightly experimental Tuscan cuisine that give you the chance to graze through the entire menu. The best way to begin is with the €8 *assaggio di primi,* a selection of five mixed pasta dishes, including those with eggplant, broccoli, mixed veggies, and a

---

After-Hours Eats

€ The "Best Drunk Food" in town, according to a student poll, is found at **Turkuaz** (Via dei Servi, 65R, 2 blocks from the Duomo; ☎ 055-2399959), which fires up mouthwatering kabobs, fries, wraps, and baklava until 6am. Elsewhere in town, late-night pizza joints along Via dei Servi dish out slices by weight. And, finally, **Ari's Diner** (open until 2am; see p. 108) is another good option for late-night meals meant to soak up the alcohol.

---

yummy risotto with pesto. For a unique *secondo,* try the beef with the surprisingly complementary toppings of blueberry sauce and balsamic vinegar for €18. Acqua al Due's new sister restaurant, **La Via Dell'Acqua** (Via Dell'Acqua, 23; ☎ 055-290748), has more of an alternative menu heavy on California cuisine; a modern-jazz soundtrack and hipster artwork are part of the ambience. The €11 spaghetti and fresh clams is particularly tasty. (If you happen to live in San Diego, you may recognize the name of this place—its owners recently hopped the pond to open an offshoot there.)

€€€ Don't be fooled by the graffiti on the cement walls outside, or the faded PIZZACHERIA sign above the door; this is no place for pizza. **Il Francescano Trattoria** ✪ (Largo Bargellini, 16, next to Santa Croce; ☎ 055-241605; www.ilfrancescano.com; Wed–Mon) serves excellent traditional Tuscan cuisine in its chandelier-lit interior rooms (romance personified) and on its well-situated outdoor patio against the wall of Santa Croce church. Its gnocchi with pears and Gorgonzola (€8) is outstanding, as are the grilled dishes, including *tagliata di manzo*—lightly breaded slices of beef (€15). The restaurant offers a variety of huge salads for €7, but save room for dessert; the crème caramel or *cantuccini* can top off an excellent meal. With €1.50 *coperto,* 10% service charge, and a half-liter of house wine (€5), a complete dinner will run about €45.

RESTAURANTS IN OLTRARNO

€ Catering to the hostelers at the nearby Santa Monica, **Bar Trattoria da Ginone** (Via dei Serragli, 35R; ☎ 055-218758; Mon–Sat 7am–3pm and 7–10pm) offers a decent quick bite, featuring a €9.80 dinner of bread, pasta, veggies, and a meat dish. Breakfast and lunch specials ensure backpackers won't have to survive on instant noodles in hostel kitchens.

€–€€ For a more upscale option, try **Il Cantione Ristorante** ✪ (Via della Condotta, 7/9R; ☎ 055-218898; daily noon–4:30pm and 7–10:30pm), a charming hidden cave of a restaurant beneath busy Via Santo Spirito. It's always crowded—with both locals and visitors—and its offerings are always delicious. The €9 set lunch with macaroni and grill is a great deal, but be careful of ordering a half-liter of the house wine, which could double the price of the meal. Besides the special, *primi* run €5 to €7.50, with *secondi* ranging from €6 to €15 for a steak.

€€   For a quick bite, try **Olio & Convivium** (Via Santo Spirito, 4; ☎ 055-2658198; www.conviviumfirenze.it; Tues–Sat, Mon lunch only), a combination shop, bakery, classroom, and restaurant—spawned by a catering company—which has a huge selection of wines, olive oils, and sandwiches to match. In fact, you can assemble a gourmet picnic here out of such ingredients as *prosciutto di cinta senese* (made from pork bred on chestnuts); *pecorino Toscana,* a tangy cheese created from the milk of the sheep in Italy's Maremna region; and *schiacciate con l'uva,* a scrumptious flatbread in which juicy sangiovese grapes are embedded. Sandwiches average about €7, the ultratasty ravioli with meat sauce €6.50. In addition to serving meals, the restaurant hosts cooking classes, wine seminars, and, of course, olive-oil tastings (the coat of arms in the awning comes from a 14th-c. guild of oil sellers).

€€   The folks at **Le Volpi e L' Uve** (Piazza de'Rossi, 1; ☎ 055-2398132; www.levolpieluva.com) boast that no shop in town carries their selection of wines from small Tuscan vineyards—and they may just be right. This is an excellent place for wine lovers. Waiters will recommend cheese and meat platters to match any type of wine, which you can enjoy on a small outdoor patio or in a room with windows overlooking the Arno. Have a hot ham-and-cheese focaccia and then you can sample some more wines! Owners found the right name to capture the essence of this wine bar, being clever like a fox *(volpi)* to find the right grapes *(uve)* to make the best wines.

€€   There used to be statues of four lions at each corner of Piazza della Passera, but now only the restaurant, founded in 1550, bears that motif: **Trattoria 4 Leoni** ★★ (Via dei Vellutini, 1R; ☎ 055-218562; www.4leoni.com; closed Wed for lunch, otherwise noon–2:30pm and 7–11pm). The menu is in Italian, of course, but the waiters all speak English and are generous with recommendations for the authentic Tuscan cuisine featured here. Try the *pappa al pomodoro,* a Florentine specialty for a *primo* (only €4), the €9 veal *vitello tonnato,* or any of the other juicy grilled meats. For dessert, the freshly made cheesecake is excellent, and €4 well spent. Patio seating enables you to enjoy the neighborhood feel of Oltrarno.

WHY YOU'RE HERE: THE TOP SIGHTS & ATTRACTIONS

The best method for planning your time here is to scan all the possibilities below and then confine yourself to a limited number of sights that interest you. You may, of course, want to organize your itinerary geographically, as I've done in the following pages; each sight is listed according to the nearest piazza. But do know that in this open-air museum of a city, you'll find delights around most every corner, so a day of aimless wandering is also highly recommended (after you've already hit the Duomo, the Uffizi, and the other top attractions).

THE SIGHTS ON & NEAR THE PIAZZA DELLA SIGNORIA

A logical starting point is the giant **Piazza della Signoria** ★★, filled with massive sculptures and surrounded by cafes, palaces, and museums. This has been Florence's political center since the 1400s, when the Signoria group of noblemen

Florence Attractions

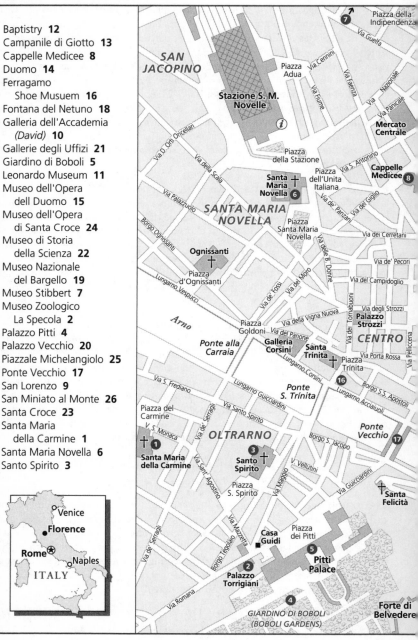

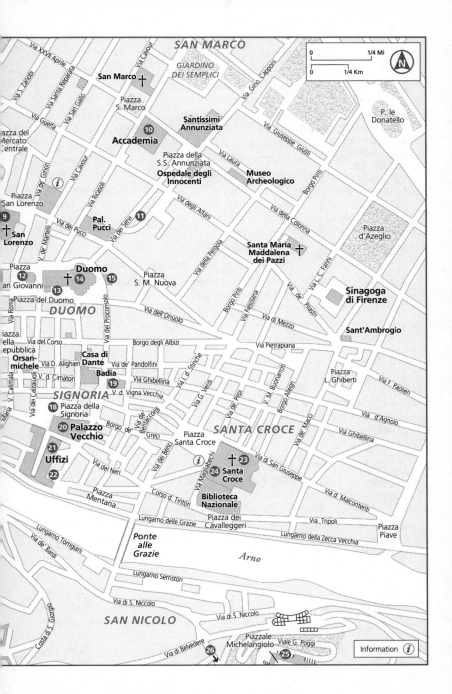

Florence Itineraries

If you have only 1 day in Florence
I feel bad for you. But that's still enough time to do a quick run north to south: Visit Michelangelo's *David* in the **Accademia,** and then walk to see the outside and inside of the massive **Duomo** and **Baptistery** in Piazza Duomo. Continue south via Piazza della Repubblica to the medieval center of the city, the statue-filled **Piazza della Signoria,** and then to the **Uffizi Gallery** for its unparalleled art collection. Cross the historic **Ponte Vecchio** to the **Oltrarno** district and make the climb to **Piazzale Michelangelo** or **San Miniato Church** for a panoramic sunset over the town—or you could skip the walk up the hill and, instead, shop at the designer stores of **Via Tornabuoni** or haggle at the **leather shops** around **San Lorenzo.**

If you have only 2 days in Florence
Follow the above itinerary, but add visits to **Santa Maria Novella** church, at the east end of the historical district, and to **Santa Croce,** on the western side. Also visit the **Bargello** sculpture gallery, north of Piazza della Signoria, and enter the **Palazzo Vecchio** in the central piazza. Don't forget to stop for gelato, which will fuel you for a **climb to the top of the Duomo** or **Giotto's Tower** next door.

If you have only 3 or 4 days in Florence
You'll be able to add a leisurely tour of the shops of the **Oltrarno** district, the **Pitti Palace, Santo Spirito church** and its peaceful piazza, and the disturbing **Museo Specola.** In the central district, you can also visit **San Lorenzo church** and the connected **Medici chapels.** Stop by the **Central Market** to sample local produce, and escape the art world with a visit to the **Science Museum.**

If you have 1 week in Florence
Add a half-day excursion to the hills of **Fiesole** and its Roman ruins. Take a bus to see the armored knights at **Museo Stibbert.** And if you're in town over a weekend from September to May, go see ACF Fiorentina play a **soccer game** at the stadium. Take a **cooking class,** go **wine tasting,** and linger in those sights that you would have rushed through if you were trying to pack them all into 1 day.

ruled the city. Today, the statues may seem like museum pieces, but they brilliantly reveal the dynamic political nature of the square. The immediately recognizable *David* (it's a copy of Michelangelo's original, which can be found in the Accademia) wasn't just placed near Palazzo Vecchio's walls because of its beauty; it was meant as a reproof to the deposed Medici family in 1504. The naked youth represents the classical Greek ideal of democracy: David's slaying the giant symbolizes the stand taken by Florentines against oppressive rulers. Similarly, in 1495, city magistrates had moved Donatello's *Judith and Holofernes* from the former Medici palace to the piazza to remind all residents of the virtuous woman about to slay her brutal assailant.

But the Medicis eventually came back to town and proved they could play the symbolic-statue game as well. They placed Cellini's *Perseus,* done in 1545, directly across from *David.* The work, depicting a battle-clad Perseus who has just severed Medusa's head, symbolizes the military might that had defeated small, competing governments, which are represented by the now-dead snakes in Medusa's hair.

As the Medici leader Cosimo I consolidated power through the 16th century, he envisioned himself as a new Roman emperor. So he filled the square with massive Roman-influenced statues of himself. One of them portrays the warrior on horseback, with reliefs at the base depicting his land-based military triumphs, while the flamboyant *Neptune Fountain* is meant to show his mastery in naval battles.

Near the fountain you'll see a small plaque commemorating the "Bonfire of the Vanities." In the 1490s, the famed rabble-rousing monk named Savanarola briefly became leader of Florence, on a fire-and-brimstone platform of piety and anti-materialism. He convinced citizens to bring their "vanities"—paintings, silks, and books—to Piazza della Signoria, and torched them in a huge bonfire. Eventually, Savanarola crossed the Pope and soon after he was branded as a heretic, excommunicated, and burned at the stake at the spot of the plaque, in the area of his original bonfires. It was an ironic and yet another symbolic moment in the history of the Piazza della Signoria.

It's worth a visit to stroll through the beautiful central courtyard and chambers of the **Palazzo Vecchio** ✪ (☎ 055-2768224; www.comune.fi.it; €6; 9am–7pm daily, Thurs closes at 2pm), directly on the Piazza. The Gothic building looms over the east side of the square with protruding battlements and a 90m-tall (300-ft.) tower jutting up "like a stone hypodermic," as author Mary McCarthy described it. The multifunctional structure, built during the late 13th century and modified over the years, has been home to the city hall, a residence for the Medicis, and even the chamber of deputies for the Republic of Italy before becoming again city offices. The museum portion of the building includes the Salanoe dei Cinquecento (The Hall of Five Hundred), the historic gathering place for Florence's 500-man ruling congress. Tour the rooms to see Vasari's frescoes and Michelangelo's *Genius of Victory.* The second floor presents an interesting contrast because it was converted into lavish living quarters for Cosimo I and his family during the 1540s.

You'll also want to stop by **Orsanmichele** ✪ (Via Arte della Lana, 1; ☎ 055-284944; free admission), a 14th-century church and the last trace of high-Gothic architecture in the city. Its hours and the hours of its attached museum are sporadic (call first), but you'll enjoy simply touring the exterior where you'll see reproductions of the saint's images by such fabled names as Ghiberti, Donatello, and Giambologna. To see the originals of these statues, you'll have to visit the small museum (across Via dell'Arte della Lana from the church's main entrance) to the **Palazzo dell'Arte della Lana.** Here you'll find such masterpieces as Ghiberti's *St. John the Baptist* (1413–16), which was the first life-size bronze to be cast during the Renaissance, and Donatello's *St. Mark* (1411–13).

THE UFFIZI GALLERY

The south side of the square exits into the Piazzale degli Uffizi. There you'll find one of the world's greatest museums, the **Gallerie degli Uffizi (Uffizi Gallery)** ✮✮✮ (Piazza degli Uffizi, 6; ☎ 055-2388651; www.uffizi.firenze.it; €6.50, free for children under 18, €3 booking fee; Tues–Sun 8:15am–6:50pm; ticket office closes 6:05pm). Long lines, erratic open hours, occasionally surly staff, and galleries closed for never-revealed reasons make the Uffizi a sometimes frustrating place to visit. But the Uffizi's 45 rooms and marble corridors are absolutely jam-packed with famous paintings—among them Botticelli's *Birth of Venus,* Leonardo da Vinci's *Annunciation,* Michelangelo's *Holy Family,* and many more. So for all its potential inconveniences, the Uffizi is a must-see.

Be sure to plan your visit to the Uffizi wisely or you'll waste a valuable day in Florence standing in a 2-hour line, miss the top paintings, or find the museum to be closed altogether. The first thing to do: **Make reservations.** Call ☎ 055-294883 Monday through Friday 8:30am to 6:30pm or Saturday 8:30am to 12:30pm up to a couple of weeks in advance. You can also order tickets over the Internet at www.selectitaly.com. By paying the €3 booking fee, you'll bypass the long lines and cross the velvet rope like a Hollywood celebrity gaining entrance to a hip club. If you do come to town without a reservation, lines will be shorter toward the end of the day (which means you have to do the museum at a slow jog, but that's better than skipping it).

Giorgio Vasari designed the building for Cosimo Medici in 1560 as a combination office and art gallery. The last of the Medicis, Anna Maria Lodovica, donated the family's art collection to the city of Florence in the 1730s, and the pieces have been in the Uffizi since. The building itself is a work of art. Once you enter and climb the dramatic staircase to the second floor galleries, look down at the multicolored marble floors and up to the ceiling. The elaborate ceiling frescoes start with scenes from antiquity in the east corridor, transition into the "grotesque" style in the south corridor toward the river, and glorify the Medicis in the west corridor.

The Uffizi's rooms are grouped by schools and presented in chronological order. Below are a few noteworthy items. Keep in mind that the museum randomly closes rooms, or changes the order of certain paintings for restoration or remodeling.

Start with **Room 2** for an early look at the Renaissance. First, compare teacher and student as you examine Cimabue's 1285 *Maesta* and Giotto's version, done in 1310. The similar subject and setting for the two paintings allows the viewer to see how Giotto transformed Cimabue's iconic Byzantine style into something more human. Giotto's Madonna actually looks like she's sitting on a throne, her clothes emphasizing the curves of her body, whereas Cimabue's Madonna and angels look like portraits on coins, or maybe an Egyptian pyramid painting, with flattened positioning and stiff angles.

Room 7 contains your next don't-miss sight, the world's most famous mug shots: the unflattering profiles of the Duke and Duchess of Urbino, done by Piero della Francesca in 1472. The subjects are portrayed in an unflinchingly realistic way. The Duke, in particular, exposes his warts and his crooked nose, broken in a martial tournament. This focus on the earthly, rather than on the Christian, elements harkens back to the teachings of classical Greek and Roman times, and is made all the more vivid by depiction of the couple riding chariots driven by the humanistic virtues of faith, charity, hope, and modesty (for her), and prudence, temperance, fortitude, and justice (for him).

In **Room 8,** highlights are the works of Filippo Lippi from the 1440s. After you examine the *Novitiate Altarpiece* (important for its use of perspective) and the *Coronation of the Virgin* (to me, the bright colors look a lot like a 1970s "Love" stamp), spend some time in front of his most famous work, *Madonna with Child and Two Angels,* from 1465. In the celebrity scandal of the time, the woman who modeled for the picture was said to be Filippo's lover—a nun—and the child looking toward the viewer the product of their union. The background, with distant mountains on one side and water on the other, frames the portrait of a woman's face, was shamelessly stolen by Leonardo da Vinci 40 years later for his *Mona Lisa.*

Rooms 10 to 14 are devoted to Botticelli and are among the most popular in the museum. His *Birth of Venus* (also known as *Venus on the Half Shell*), from 1484, hangs in Room 10 like a highway billboard you've seen a thousand times. In its original, the colors seem lighter than they do in reproductions, and, in fact, look more like a pastel-chalk interpretation of the classical theme (though the painting was actually done with tempera mixed with egg yolk). Venus' pose is taken from classical statues of the time, while the zephyr wind blowing her to shore, and the muse welcoming her, are from Ovid's *Metamorphosis.* On the opposite wall is Botticelli's 1482 *Primavera* and its bold colors are a stark contrast to the filmy *Venus.* Also be sure to look at his *Adoration of the Magi,* which contains a self-portrait of the artist (he's the one in yellow) on the far right side of the canvas.

Leonardo da Vinci's *Annunciation* anchors **Room 15.** In this painting, his ability to orchestrate the viewer's focus is masterful: The line down the middle of the brick corner of the house draws your glance to Mary's delicate fingers, which themselves point along the top of a stone wall to the angel's two raised fingers. Those, in turn, draw attention to the mountain in the center of the two parallel trees dividing Mary from the angel, representing the gulf between the worldly and the spiritual.

Crossing from the east to the west side of the Uffizi, don't be in such a rush that you fail to appreciate the view of the Arno River to the south side, and the plaza to your right. The columns and roadway between the buildings look like a study in perspective of one of the early-Renaissance paintings.

Once on the west side, stop and look at Michelangelo's 1507 *Holy Family* in **Room 25.** The twisting shapes of Mary, Joseph, and Jesus recall those in the Sistine Chapel in Rome for their sculpted nature and the bright colors of their folded, hanging clothes.

Room 26 has a number of Raphaels, including the often-copied *Madonna of the Goldfinch,* again with the da Vinci/Botticelli landscape in the background. The reds in the recently restored *Pope Leo X* portrait are particularly vibrant.

Titian's *Venus of Urbino* is found in **Room 28.** It's no coincidence that the edge of the curtain, the angle of her hand and leg, and the line splitting floor and bed all intersect in the forbidden part of her body. The domestic scene on the right half of the painting, with the sleeping dog, and the little girl gathering clothes, provides an interesting contrast to the open sexuality of the left.

In stark contrast to the clean lines (and dirty mind) of Titian, seek out an El Greco masterpiece from 1600, the nearly hidden *St. John and St. Francis* (on the wall behind you when you walk into **Room 33** from 32). It shows the two saints stretched and blurred, with a gathering storm behind them. The minidragon poking its head out of St. John's goblet alludes to his miracle of turning a poison into this creature. El Greco's characteristic elongated forms and surreal landscape provided inspiration to many 20th-century artists, including Salvador Dalí and Modigliani.

By the time most visitors reach the rooms numbered in the **40s,** they run out of gas. But do check out the Rubens and Rembrandts in this section for a feeling of Flemish versus Italian styles of painting. The detail of the hair, skin, and cloth of the Rembrandt portraits from the 1630s, in **Room 44,** are amazing—just look at the contrast between the faces of the young and old men.

On your way down from the second floor, you'll be strolling through the recently added first-floor gallery rooms—created after a bombing in 1993—which include plenty of Carvaggio, and the 17th- to 18th-century artists who copied his "bright light among dark shadows" style of painting. Here a rare female artist in the Uffizi, Artemisia Gentileschi, has one of the more brutal paintings in the gallery, *Judith and Holophernes.*

A short stroll behind the Uffizi is the **Ponte Vecchio (Old Bridge)** ✯✯✯ , one of the most potent symbols of Florence. Here you'll find a rich collection of jewelry shops housed in crammed-together, multicolored buildings from the 1600s; many of the shops are owned by descendants of the original 41 artisans whom Cosimi di Medici invited here at that time. The open spot in the middle of the bridge is where butchers used to slaughter and section their animals, dumping the offal off the edge. Cosimo wanted less smelly tenants, so he replaced the butchers with the jewelers (and increased the rent!). The large metal ring at the wall was for tying up horses. Now small padlocks cover the ring—symbols left by lovers to celebrate their mutual connection.

The bridge itself has survived since 1345, despite floods, wars, and the German bombing near the end of World War II. In 1944, the local commander, sympathetic to the Ponte Vecchio's historical importance, blew up all the buildings around the bridge in order to preserve it while still hampering advancing Allied troops.

Balancing on top of the bridge like a big white log is "Vasari's Corridor," a Medici-commissioned addition from the 1560s. The Medicis didn't like mixing with the commoners much, so they had the corridor built to connect their Palazzo Vecchio to Palazzo Pitti, enabling them to move from home to home without setting their feet on the ground. During World War II, Mussolini walked the visiting Hitler through the bridge. Hitler complained it was too dark, so the ever-accommodating Benito opened up the walls to add the three large windows.

If you're following a geographical itinerary, you're going to want to walk north next, through the Piazza della Signoria and past it to our next sight, which is one of the most important museums anywhere for Renaissance sculpture. In a far cry from its original use as the city's prison, torture chamber, and execution site, the **Museo Nazionale del Bargello** ✯✯ (Via del Proconsolo, 4; ☎ 055-2388606; www.sbas.firenze.it; €4; 8:30am–1:50pm) now stands as a peaceful sculpture garden and three-story art museum containing some of the best works of Michelangelo, Donatello, and Ghiberti.

In the ground-floor Michelangelo room, you'll witness the awesome variety of his craft, from the whimsical 1497 *Bacchus* to the severe *Brutus* of 1540. *Bacchus,* created when Michelangelo was just 22, really looks like he's drunk, leaning back a little too far, his head off kilter, and the cupid is about to bump him over. Also note Giamobologna's twisting *Mercury,* who looks like he's about to take off from the ground.

Be sure to climb the stairs to Donatello Hall to see some of his famous works. Notable among them is his *David,* done in 1440, the first free-standing nude sculpture since Roman times. Donatello's 1417 *St. George* statue, which originally stood in the niche of the armorers' guild at the Orsanmichele church, has the same boyish features as his *David.* The classical detail of these sculptures, as well as their naturalistic poses and reflective mood, is the essence of the Renaissance style.

On the right wall, note the contest entries submitted by Ghiberti and Brunelleschi for the commission to do the Baptistery doors in 1401. Both had *Abraham's Sacrifice* as their biblical theme, and both displayed an innovative use of perspective. Ghiberti won the contest, perhaps because his scene was more thematically unified. Brunelleschi was so upset by the outcome that he left town, not to return until he created the plans for the Duomo dome, perhaps as a means of getting back at Ghiberti (see "Engineering the Duomo," below).

The second floor also has a small but elaborate chapel in which condemned prisoners prayed, and guilty magistrates atoned for their sins.

The top floor is worth a quick walk-through for the statuary of the Verrocchio Room (including yet another effeminate *David*) and the decorative helmets of the Armory, but the many small bronzes and medals can be skipped if you're short on time.

THE INCOMPARABLE DUOMO
& THE PIAZZA DEL DUOMO

The undisputed, preeminent, free-standing stone dome in the world is Florence's cathedral, whose roof is wider than the U.S. Capitol, greater than St. Paul's in England, bigger than the Pantheon in Rome, and a scientific marvel of its time. The **Duomo (Cathedral) of Santa Maria del Fiore** ✪✪✪ (Piazza del Duomo; ☎ 055-2302885; www.operaduomo.firenze.it; free admission; daily 10am–5pm) is the symbol of Florence and the city's biggest attraction, both in size and popularity.

The Piazza del Duomo really contains five sights in one: the central church area, the climb to the top of the dome, the climb up Giotto's Bell Tower, the Museum of the Duomo, and the Baptistery outside. In choosing which to visit, I'd say the cathedral, the museum, and the Baptistery doors are must-sees, while a climb up one of the towers is purely optional and should be done only if you have the time.

The cathedral, like Florence, has evolved over the years. It began as a Romanesque church whose foundations date to the 5th century, and expanded through the 13th century before it reached its present dimensions. The top of the dome wasn't completed, though, until Brunelleschi capped it off in 1434 (see "Engineering the Duomo," below). And it took until the late 1800s for the tri-color marble exterior to be added in honor of the new Italian Republic.

The inside of the Duomo is surprisingly empty, aside from the mobs of visitors. So like everyone else, you'll want to walk to the altar to look up at the dome soaring above you. From 1575 to 1580, Giorgio Vasari and his student Federico Zuccari painted the bulk of *The Last Judgment* fresco covering the interior of the dome. It's no Sistine Chapel, but, still, imagine the challenges involved in painting with quick-drying materials on a curved surface more than 45m (150 ft.) above the ground.

For a closer look at both the painting and the dome, take a walk up the 463 steps to the **cupola** ✪ (€6; Mon–Fri 8:30am–7pm, Sat 8:30am–5:40pm). The line for this climb can sometimes wind around the corner, but there's no better way to appreciate the engineering marvel of the dome. The steps can be exhausting, crowded, smelly, and claustrophobic, but that just makes the view on top that much more appreciated. Interestingly, when seen up close, the figures painted on the dome look almost impressionistic, with vague features and skewed proportions. Vasari wasn't lazy when he drew the figures this way, he planned them to be viewed from the perspective of people on the church floor.

For fewer steps and crowds, and for an actual view *of* the dome instead of *from* it, climb **Giotto's Bell Tower** (Campanile di Giotto; €6; daily 8:30am–7:30pm). This nearly became Florence's version of the Leaning Tower of Pisa because Giotto couldn't quite transfer his painting talent into architecture. He created the plans and finished the first level of the structure by his death, in 1337. When the next level was added, the tower nearly collapsed under its own weight, and had to be redesigned. Now standing a sturdy 75m (250 ft.) tall, the tower offers great views over the city of Florence, and excellent photo-ops of the dome.

The **Baptistery** ✪✪✪ (€3; Mon–Sat noon–7pm, Sun 8:30am–2pm), across from the front of the Duomo, has the doors that opened the way to the Renaissance. Here was one of the first major works to incorporate the period's naturalism and semi-realistic perspective. (Ghiberti also began the era of unreliable contractors—it took him 27 years to finish a commission that was supposed to take 5.) For an instant comparison between periods, go to the south (entry) doors and view Andrea Pisano's far less dynamic 1336 Gothic work.

Ghiberti, who won the commission in a contest between himself, Donatello, and Brunelleschi, created the north doors first. The panels, all scenes from the New Testament, are actually reproductions. To protect them from the elements, the originals have been moved inside the Museum of the Duomo (see below). After his brilliant success with the first panels, Ghiberti didn't have to compete for the right to create those on the east side of the Baptistry, and many feel that these are his real masterpiece: 10 panels of Old Testament scenes that flow splendidly one to the next, and are among the most exquisite creations of the Renaissance. When he first saw them, Michelangelo is said to have exclaimed, "These doors are fit to stand at the gates of Paradise," and ever since they've been nicknamed "the Gates of Paradise." Amid the splendor of the doors, you may forget to enter the Baptistery, but the interior boasts some spectacular Byzantine mosaics from the 1200s.

The **Museum of the Duomo,** called **Museo dell'Opera del Duomo** ✪ (Piazza del Duomo, 9; ☎ 055-2302885; €6; Mon–Sat 9am–7:30pm, Sun 8:30am–1:30 pm), is a must for persons interested in the development of the church (and many contemporary travelers may have read the best-selling *Brunelleschi's Dome* by Ross King, a highly recommended read for anyone visiting Florence). Here you'll see the original panel doors of the Baptistery (for reasons of preservation, those outside are copies), models of the Duomo, and even the death mask of architect Brunelleschi.

Engineering the Duomo

The dome crowning Florence's cathedral is impressive, but to appreciate just how amazing an accomplishment it was in the 15th century, consider that nothing even remotely its size had been constructed since the Pantheon in Rome 1,300 years before.

Because massive construction projects like the Duomo typically took over 100 years to complete, city planners assumed somebody would figure out how to cover the church by the time they finished construction in the late 1380s. That didn't happen, though, and the church remained open to the elements for two generations.

Enter frustrated sculptor Filippo Brunelleschi. After losing to Ghiberti in the contest to design the church's Baptistery doors in 1401 (p. 120), Brunelleschi took his tools and went to Rome to study classical architecture. He knew of the construction challenges of the dome, so he measured, poked, and peered at the Pantheon, studying it for several years, trying to figure out the mysteries of its design.

The challenge of the dome was this: For hundreds of years, arches had been constructed by placing stones on wooden frames, and then removing the frame when the stones were able to support each other. For larger constructions (Gothic cathedrals in France, for example), "flying buttresses" were added for support.

The Duomo in Florence did not have the space around it to allow for buttresses. And even if that problem had been solved, nobody could imagine building a wood frame tall enough to support the dome-in-progress. The wood would have sagged under the pressure even if the heights could have been reached.

Brunelleschi came up with a three-part solution. First: He made the dome with two concentric shells that supported each other, each thinner than would have been necessary for a single dome. Second, he created a puzzle-piece set of bricks, thicker at the bottom of the dome, hollow at the top, fitting them all together in a self-supporting matrix. And, finally, he added giant hoops around each level, like a barrel, to deal with the outward pressure of the bricks.

It worked, and many years after the humiliation of the Baptistery contest, Brunelleschi had his hometown victory. The Pope came to consecrate the capping of the dome in 1436. To this day, nobody has built a bigger dome out of stone.

Not bad for a second-place sculptor.

The museum is also notable for its magnificent sculptures, including three standouts: a disturbing but beautiful wooden sculpture of the Virgin Mary by Donatello (depicting her torn with grief); Donatello's and Luca della Robia's marble choirs from the 1430s; and the final *Pietà* that an 80-year-old Michelangelo was to create. Early on in the process he had told students that he wanted this *Pietà* to stand at his tomb, but when the work didn't go well, he took a chisel to it. He would have destroyed the beautiful sculpture had his apprentices not intervened and finished some of the minor characters (the figure of Nicodemus was untouched, legend has it, because this was a self-portrait of the artist).

PIAZZA SANTA CROCE & NEARBY

Basilica di Santa Croce ✪✪ (Piazza Santa Croce; ☎ 055-2466105; €4; Mon–Sat 9:30am–5:30pm, Sun 1–5:30pm; Opera di Santa Croce Mon–Sat 9am–7:30pm, Sun 9am–2pm) contains the elaborate, status-symbol tombs of the brightest and the best (or at least the richest) of the Renaissance, including Michelangelo, Machiavelli, and Galileo. Dante has a tomb, but he didn't make the trip (see "Who is Buried in Dante's Tomb?" below). Over 250 others are interred above and below visiting tourists. (It's said the expression "stinking rich" came from commoners holding their noses with disdain as they walked on top of these expensive graves in churches.)

The church looks large but shabby from the outside, and massive and majestic inside. Rent the comprehensive audio-tour headphones from the stand outside the side doors for a nearly 2-hour explanation of over 200 locations in the church.

Who is Buried in Dante's Tomb?

Not Dante. Actually, Dante's tomb in Santa Croce is more properly called a "cenotaph," a memorial tribute when the body is elsewhere. Dante Alighieri, author of the sublime *Divine Comedy,* is credited with popularizing (if not creating) the modern Italian language. He was born in Florence in 1265, and from the cenotaph, the statue outside Santa Croce, and the various shrines around town, you'd think he had always been a hometown hero.

But Dante became involved in politics and chose the wrong side during one of Florence's incessant civil wars. He took the side of the pro-imperial bankers of the White Party versus the Black Party of noble families who supported the Pope's financial and political interests. In 1302, the Black Party was on top, and Dante was exiled from the city for 2 years. Angered by his expulsion, he wandered the northern Italian landscape for the rest of his life, refusing all offers to return to his hometown. Instead, he wrote his three-part poetic saga of heaven, hell, and purgatory, being sure to populate the lowest depths with his former opponents in Florentine politics.

Dante died in Ravenna in 1321, and the town claimed him as its own, denying Florence's continued requests for the body.

Florence had better luck with Michelangelo's corpse. Despite the fact that the artist did the bulk of his work in Rome, the Medicis decided he belonged to their city. Ten years after his death, agents stole his body and brought it to Florence in 1574, ensuring only one cenotaph among the many tombs in Santa Croce.

The Floodwaters Are Rising!

I am now in the Third Circle of the Rain
Eternal, cold, accurst, and charged with woe.
Its law and quality ever the same remain.
Big hail, and clots of muddied water, and snow
Pour downward through the darkness of the air:
The ground they beat stinks with the overflow.

—Dante's Inferno, Canto VI

On the morning of November 4, 1966, early risers would have seen shopkeepers on the Ponte Vecchio hurriedly emptying their stores of valuables and rushing to higher ground. This is never a good sign. The jewelers were the only persons in town notified that, up river, a dam had been opened after a month of rain, and torrents of floodwaters were rushing toward the city.

The streets were submerged by some 6m (20 ft.) of water, with toxic home heating oils spilling out to mix with the muck of the river. Thirty-five people were killed in flooded underpasses or drowned in basements.

The floodwaters and mud damaged or destroyed numerous works of art, many of which had been stored in underground rooms despite the city's history of flooding. An army of experts and volunteers quickly gathered to help dig out relics from the refuse. Some art was lost forever, some is still being restored, but thanks to innovative restoration techniques, thousands of pieces are back on display.

Nowadays the dam upriver is much stronger, but the flood is not forgotten. Plaques across town mark the high level of the floodwaters. In the Piazza del Limbo, north of Ponte Trinità, a sign indicating the high-water mark is affixed about 7.5m (25 ft.) above street level. And in many older restaurants and hotels, you can see photos of a manager shoveling slime out of his lower rooms.

Among the notable sights in the church is Michelangelo's grave, designed by Vasari; it's close to the front door, allegedly because Michelangelo said if he ever came to life again, he wanted to awake to see Brunelleschi's Duomo. Also walk over to Machiavelli's tomb farther along the wall to see his majestic resting place, along with his pithy epitaph: TANTO NOMINI NULLUM PAR ELOGIUM, of which a liberal translation might be, "What can you say about this guy?"

It took 90 years after his death before Galileo received the honor of having a tomb in Santa Croce because, as the audioguide delicately states, of the "complicated relationship" between the scientist and the Church (authorities originally had the heretical body unceremoniously dumped outside city walls). The grand tomb now stands near the church's front doors.

Aside from the tombs, visitors should seek out the Giotto frescoes near the front altar. The 14th-century works have faded from their original glory, but reflect the Franciscan nature of the church much more than the self-important tombs along the aisles.

Outside the main church, visit the peaceful Pazzi Chapel. Brunelleschi (of Duomo fame) designed this structure for the Pazzi family just before their unsuccessful coup/murder plot against the Medicis. The Pazzi name was erased from the chapel for hundreds of years, and no Pazzis were ever buried here, but the chapel retains its simple, symmetrical Renaissance beauty.

Keep walking through the enclosed garden to reach the refectory. This quiet area contains many Renaissance artworks including the famous Cimabue *Crucifixion,* restored after it was covered by water in the 1966 floods (see "The Floodwaters Are Rising!" above). The cross now hangs from retractable wires so that it can be yanked up should water fill the building again.

For fans of Michelangelo (and who isn't?), the other worthy sight in the area is the small house that he inhabited in Florence. It's now a museum: **Casa Buonarroti** (Via Ghibellina, 70; ☎ 055-241752; €6.50; Wed–Mon 9:30am–2pm). Inside you'll view some of Michelangelo's bas-relief sculptures, done when he was a teenager, as well as a number of his sketches.

PIAZZA SANTA MARIA NOVELLA, PIAZZA SAN LORENZO & PIAZZA MADONNA DEGLI ALDOBRANDINI

Just across the street from Florence's main Santa Maria Novella train station stands perhaps the most conveniently located historic site in Italy, the **Santa Maria Novella Church** ✯✯ (Piazza Santa Maria Novella; ☎ 055-215918; €2.50; Mon–Thurs 9am–5pm, Fri–Sun 1–5pm). Even if you only have a 30-minute train layover in town, pop across the street to see this church which contains some of the finest frescoes in Florence—no small feat. Construction began in the 1240s, prior to the Renaissance, and the main part was completed in 1360. The artwork inside traces this journey of pre-Renaissance styles through the dawning of the new age, and the top three treasures include Ghirlandaio's frescoes behind the altar, Giotto's *Crucifix,* and Masaccio's *Trinità* fresco.

Giotto's *Crucifix* is an early example of naturalistic depiction of the human body. Painted in 1289, Christ's body appears to hang heavily on the cross, with the twists of the limbs and curves of the torso adding to the emotional weight of the composition. Compare this piece with the church's other crucifixion scenes, done in a Byzantine, iconic style. Masaccio's *Holy Trinity* fresco, midway along the left wall of the church, is the epitome of Renaissance-style perspective. The 1428 composition incorporates mathematical principles that give the work a certain realism.

Domenico Ghirlandaio and his assistants (including a 16-year-old Michelangelo) created the series of frescoes behind the main altar. While formally known as *Lives of the Virgin and St. John the Baptist,* the series of religious scenes is more about Florence of the 1480s. Note how characters in the scenes wear contemporary clothes, and note especially the prominent appearance of random folks (actually the sponsors of the painting, members of the Tornabuoni clan) next to various saints. And before you leave be sure to stop for a moment in front of

Brunelleschi's 15th-century pulpit. It was on this spot that Galileo was first denounced as a heretic for declaring that the earth revolved around the sun.

And if you think commercialism has only recently come to churches in Italy, look at the facade for proof otherwise. The mosaic inscription near the top has a 600-year-old advertisement that says, "This church brought to you by Giovanni Rucellai," the nobleman who funded renovation of the church in 1458.

Now, from the Rucellais to the much more important Medicis, who ruled Florence and Tuscany for generations, fought popes, became popes, and wanted a church and memorial worthy of their ambitions. So they had themselves entombed in great glory in their home parish, in the **Basilica di San Lorenzo** and in the **Medici chapels** ★ (Piazza Madonna degli Aldobrandini, enter behind the Basilica di San Lorenzo; ☎ 055-2388602; www.firenzemusei.it; €6; Tue–Sat 8:15am–5pm and 1st, 3rd, and 5th Mon of every month and the 2nd and 4th Sun). The first room of the latter, the extravagant Chapel of the Princes, displays gaudy but entertaining marble decorations of all shapes and sizes. For a more artistic and restrained setting, continue inside to the New Sacristy. Michelangelo designed the tombs here, as well as his famous foursome of statues, *Dawn, Dusk, Night,* and *Day.* Compare and contrast Michelangelo's figures: There's not much difference between the bulk and musculature of the massive female and male bodies, sort of a Renaissance version of the old East German swim teams.

The **Basilica di San Lorenzo** (Piazza San Lorenzo; ☎ 055-216634; €2.50; Basilica Mon–Sat 10am–5pm, Biblioteca Medicea-Laurenziana Mon–Sat 9am–1pm), a very short stroll west of the Medici chapels, offers a peaceful respite from the mass of vendors outside. Brunelleschi, of Duomo fame, designed the structure in the 1440s. Donatello's final works, the bronze pulpits, display dramatic crucifixion scenes. For his effort, the artist earned a tomb in the church. Depending on your other options and interests, this church may not be worth your time or the admission charge.

The **Biblioteca Medicea-Laurenziana,** attached to the church, is notable not only for its historic collection of manuscripts but for the Michelangelo-designed architecture and stone staircase. Go through the gateway to the left of the church entrance, walk up the stairs, and take a peek; it's free, unless they've closed it for an exhibition.

The final notable sight in this area is another Medici chapel, this time at the **Palazzo Medici-Riccardi** ★ (Via Camillo Cavour, 1; ☎ 055-2760340; €4; Thurs–Tues 9am–7pm). Once the home of Lorenzo the Magnificent (before Cosimo de Medici moved the family to the Palazzo Vecchio), it boasts splendid frescoes by Benozzo Gozzoli, who took as his theme the journey of the Magi and filled this lighthearted, color-rich fresco with dozens of portraits of the notables of the day. If you have time, stop by to see this lovely chapel; if not, save it for your next visit to Florence.

NEAR OR ON PIAZZA SAN MARCO

Rarely does a famous piece of art live up to the hype. Michelangelo's *David,* in the **Galleria dell'Accademia (Academia Gallery)** ★★★ (Via Ricasoli, 58–60; ☎ 055-2388609; www.polomuseale.firenze.it; €6.50; Tues–Sun 8:30am–7pm), does. The statue is much larger than most people imagine, looming 4.8m (16 ft.) on top of

The Strange Symbols of the Medicis

Walk anywhere around Florence and you'll see the symbol plastered on walls like the Nike swoosh. A set of 6 to 12 small circles, red on a gold background, these make up the family crest of the mighty Medicis. Members would put it on any of their own buildings, or those they sponsored, renovated, or conquered over the years.

But what is the origin of these circles? Some say they represent pillboxes, symbolizing the medical derivation of the Medici name. Or, they could be coins, representing the banking foundations of the family's wealth. One story says the circles are really dents on the shield of an old knight of the family who fought and defeated a giant on behalf of Charlemagne.

Regardless of the true explanation, this coat of arms remains a recognized trademark hundreds of years after the end of the Medici clan.

---

a 1.8m (6-ft.) pedestal. *David* hasn't faded with time, either, and a 2004 cleaning makes the marble gleam as if it were opening day, 1504. Viewing the statue is a pleasure in the bright and spacious room custom-designed for *David* after the statue was moved here in 1873, following 300 years of pigeons perched on his head in the Piazza della Signoria. Replicas now take the abuse in the Piazza della Signoria and the Piazzale Michelangelo.

One should not forget the Accademia museum built around *David*. It's at least worth a stroll through the five or six rooms to see some of the Renaissance paintings, if only for the pleasure of turning around and being surprised by the statue again. Michelangelo's unfinished *Prisoners* statues are a superb contrast to *David*, with the rough forms struggling to free themselves from the raw stone (they also provide a unique glimpse into how Michelangelo worked a piece of stone; he famously said that he tried to free the sculpture within from the block and you can see this quite clearly here). Be sure also to visit the back room leading to the Academy part of the Accademia, where you'll see a veritable warehouse of old replica carvings, the work of hundreds of years of students. It's almost as if a Roman assembly line has just stopped for lunch. And continue through this back room, to the student section, to see some modern interpretations of the classical work.

Along with the Uffizi, the Accademia is a sight where it's essential to make reservations. Be sure to **book ahead** by calling ☎ **055-294-883;** it'll be €3 well spent.

Travelers who enjoy the serene, jewel-toned works of Fra Angelico will want to add the small **Museo di San Marco** ★ (Piazzo San Marco, 3; ☎ 055-2388608; €4; Mon–Fri 8:30am–1:50pm, Sat–Sun 8:15am–7pm, closed 1st, 3rd, and 5th Sun and 2nd and 4th Mon of each month) to their itineraries. It's here in this former 13th-century monastery that you'll find the largest collection in Florence of the master's altarpieces and painted panels. But perhaps the most moving and unusual work is his *Annunciation* and a fresco of the life of Jesus painted not on one giant wall but, scene by scene, on the individual walls of small monks' cells that honeycomb the second floor. The idea was that these scenes, painted by Fra Angelico and his assistants, would aid in the monks' prayer and contemplation; the paintings are entrancing (especially in cells 1, 3, and 9). The final cell on the corridor belonged to the fundamentalist monk Savanarola, who briefly incited the populace of the most art-filled city in the world to burn paintings, illuminated manuscripts, and anything else he felt was a worldly betrayal of Jesus' ideals. Ultimately, he ran afoul of the Pope and was hanged and burned at the stake. You'll see his notebooks, rosary, and what's left of the clothes he wore that day in his cell.

THE OLTRARNO DISTRICT

Don't try to visit the **Pitti Palace** ★ (Piazza Pitta, a few blocks south of the Ponte Vecchio; ☎ 055-2388614; www.firenzemusei.it; cumulative ticket €11; see below for hours) and the Uffizi on the same day. Both are astoundingly, almost exhaustively, rich museums, the Pitti offering up the largest and best collections of paintings by Raphael in the world. And no gallery comes closer to Mark Twain's description of "weary miles" in *Innocents Abroad* than the 26 art-crammed rooms of the **Pitti's Galleria Palatina** (separate admission €6.50, €8.50 in summer; Tues–Sun 8:15am–6:50pm). Paintings are displayed like cars in a parking garage, stacked on walls above each other in what the museum explains is the "Enlightenment" method of exhibition. Rooms are alternately dimly lit, or garishly bright; rugs are mildewed, restoration projects endless. And the high admission fees are unspeakably vulgar (just my own opinion; many visitors to the Pitti also go the Palatina on the Pitti's first floor).

And like when touring Roman ruins, visitors will find important historical treasures amid the Palatina's haphazard collection. Some of the best efforts of Titian, Raphael, and Rubens line the walls. Raphael's *Portrait of a Young Woman* and *Madonna with Child* are a couple of my favorites, along with Fra Bartolomeo's dramatically colored *Pietà*. (I also think Caravaggio's creepy *Sleeping Cupid* recalls that weird dancing computer baby of the '90s.) You'll also see wonderful examples of the Northern European Flemish style of art, such as the intricate *Cardinal Bentivoglio* by van Dyck. Titian's 1536 painting of the demure *La Bella* is a good example of a proper Italian noblewoman. But if you want to see the other side of this young lady, check out the *Venus of Urbino* painting in the Uffizi, where the same model lies provocatively naked.

The **Galleria D'Arte Moderna** (☎ 055-2388601; €5 or as part of cumulative ticket; Tues–Sat 8:15am–1:50pm, also some Sun and Mon), also within the Pitti Palace, actually has a pretty good collection of 19th-century Italian paintings with a focus on Impressionism. But if you have limited time, a visit here really shouldn't take precedence over the Renaissance treasures of Florence.

If you want to get a feeling for the conspicuous consumption of the Medicis and their ilk, visit the Pitti Palace's **Apartamenti Reali** (☎ 055-2388614; Tues–Sun 8:15am–3:50pm), where you can see some notable paintings in their original ostentatious setting. The **Galleria Del Costume & Museo Degli Argenti** (☎ 055-2388709; €4; hours are the same as those for Galleria D'Arte Moderna) shows that wealth and taste do not always go hand in hand (be sure to spend some time among the Medicis' over-the-top gold and jewel-encrusted household items). The **Boboli Gardens** (☎ 055-2651816; €4, free for kids under 18; daily Nov–Feb 8:15am–4:30pm, Mar 8:15am–5:30pm, Apr–May and Sept–Oct 8:15am–6:30pm, June–Aug 8:15am–7:30pm, closed 1st and last Sun of the month) and the grounds of the palace, with well-manicured shrubbery and fine views of the city from the fortress, are quite pleasant. However, I'd advise spending that €4 admission fee on a panino and Coke, and then walking up to Piazzale Michelangelo to enjoy a spectacular view of the city for free.

And before you leave the Pitti Palace complex, be sure to stop by the grotto in the central courtyard. This covered area—with its grotesque statues, its fountain, and dripping water—suggests a Renaissance version of the grotto at the Playboy mansion. One can imagine the Medicis were up to some high jinks here after their upper-class fiestas.

And as long as you've gone to the "other" side of the river, seek out the non-touristy **Santo Spirito** ★ (Piazza Santo Spirito, Oltrarno; Mon–Tues and Thurs–Fri 8:30am–noon and 4–6pm, Wed 8:30am–noon, Sat–Sun 4–6pm). Brunelleschi's last project, the simple yet elegant structure was erected in the mid-1400s. Inside, it's dark and usually empty, a stark contrast to the overvisited Duomo. Many of its original works were destroyed in a 1471 fire, so most of the replacements came from the same era just afterward, creating a unified feel to the many side chapels.

One of the notable works in the left transept of the church, in the second chapel, is a severe *St. Monica and Augustine Nuns.* The 1472 Francesco Botticini painting shows serious nuns in black and gray gathered around the saint. A couple of sisters glare at the viewer, and you almost want to apologize for interrupting them. On the right transept seek out Filippo Lippi's *Madonna and Child* for the detail of the figures, as well as for the background. Many of the other fine works throughout the church have English descriptions.

In order to visit the morgues beneath the church's hospital, Michelangelo used to sneak through the side door to the left of the main entrance. With the permission of the church director, Michelangelo studied the corpses for help in his painting and sculpting of the human form. As a thank you, Michelangelo carved a wooden crucifix and donated it to the church; pass through a door on the north wall, and you'll find it in the sacristy. The crucifix's thin, delicate body is a sharp contrast to most of Michelangelo's muscular figures, leading some to question the attribution. But written documentation seems to verify the authenticity of the piece.

In the 18th century, a massive fire destroyed much of the nearby **Santa Maria della Carmine Church.** Miraculously, its **Brancacci Chapel** ★★ (Piazza Santa Maria della Carmine; ☎ 055-2382195; €5.50; Wed–Sat and Mon 10am–5pm, Sun 1–5pm) survived intact, as did the masterpiece it contained within, a 1425 fresco cycle by painters Masaccio and Fra Filippo Lippi that is arguably one of the most influential of the Renaissance. Michelangelo and Leonardo da Vinci, among others, came to study and sketch the colorful biblical scenes with their contemporary Florentine background. One of the most famous scenes is that of Adam and Eve's expulsion from Eden.

While I'm not pleased by the €5.50 viewing fee, which was added in 1980 after a highly successful restoration of the piece (during which they removed the prudish fig leaves painted onto Adam and Eve), this is an important work, really a watershed in the rediscovery of perspective painting. Just try to ignore the signs that command DO NOT LINGER—you've paid, so enjoy the fresco, which is as much a testament to friendship as to anything else. After Masaccio's untimely death, at the age of 27, Fra Filippo Lippi faithfully continued to work on the piece, using his colleague's ideas and techniques.

You shouldn't leave Florence without getting a bird's-eye view of town from **Piazzale Michelangelo** ★. While buses and hordes of tourists don't exactly make this a reflective spot, it is quite accessible, and the vantage point over the cityscape is phenomenal, particularly at sunset. If you're walking, take Via del Monte alle Croci from Porta San Miniato, or the slightly less steep Via di San Salvatore al Monte to reach the piazza. For a quieter setting, climb the extra 10 minutes to the front steps of the Romanesque **San Miniato church** ★, which is the second-oldest religious building in Florence (after the Baptistery). If you make it there before 7:30pm, enter for a look at the funky 13th-century mosaic floor, with the signs of the zodiac and the spare furnishings, frescoes, and 11th-century crypt (with additional frescoes by Taddeo Gaddi, better known as the architect of the Ponte Vecchio).

FLORENCE FOR KIDS

You'll need a bus (no. 4) or a taxi to get to the site, but the kids will thank you for a visit to **Museo Stibbert** ★ 🧒 (Via Stibbert, 26; ☎ 055-475520; €5; Mon–Wed 10am–2pm, Fri–Sat 10am–6pm). It's essentially the giant toy box of an eccentric Scottish-Italian arms-and-armor collector, which was made into a museum in 1906. Enter into the "Hall of the Cavalcade" to see a scene from King Arthur and Camelot, with gangs of life-size knights sitting fully armed on horseback. Dozens of their compatriots are geared-up through the Salone della Cupola, sort of a United Nations of medieval mayhem, with every variety of weapon, armor, and shield imaginable. Even the samurai warriors have made the trip, as the museum boasts the biggest collection of Japanese armor outside of Tokyo.

Amazingly enough, the **Museo di Storia della Scienza** ★ 🧒 (Piazza dei Giudici, 1; €5; Mon–Wed 10am–5pm, Fri–Sun 10am–6pm) actually displays a bone from Galileo's middle finger. It also has a wide collection of scientific instruments from early-Arab scientists, as well as Galileo's telescopes, including the one he used to discover the moons of Jupiter. Kids (and inquisitive adults) will appreciate the old maps and globes, scary doctors' instruments, and a medieval pharmacy, all of which are a nice change from the religious art of Florence.

Another group of attractions good for kids, and for those interested in engineering, are the dueling Leonardo museums. Two independent companies have set up nearly identical exhibits of life-size versions of Leonardo's inventions based on his codex drawings. Visitors can see wooden models of everything from a medieval tank to a machine gun, parachute, glider, and hydraulic press. **The Leonardo Museum** ★ 🧒 (Il Genio di Leonardo, Via dei Servi, 66R; ☎ 055-282966; www.mostredileonardo.com; €7, €5 for kids; daily 10am–7pm) is the better of the two because it actually encourages visitors to touch and play with the 33 interactive models: Spin the drill and push the flying machine while you read the English description. The **Macchine di Leonardo da Vinci** 🧒 (Via Cavour, 21; ☎ 055-295264; www.macchinedileonardo.com; €5, €4 for kids; daily 9:30am–7:30pm) is nearly identical, but newer, with a better presentation of the models and more info on the inventor. But the spoilsports added DON'T TOUCH signs on most of the items, and since that's the most fun thing to do, I'd choose the first museum for my visit. This museum also has identical franchises in Arezzo and Lucca, while the Leonardo Museum has another exhibit in San Gimignano, so you may get another chance to see them if you've overbooked yourself with Florence sights.

A sad damsel with pale skin, half-closed eyes, and delicate lips lies on her back as if she had just fainted. Also, her torso has exploded and her intestines are spattered around her case. The wax anatomical models are one reason the **Museo Zoologico La Specola** ★★ 🧒 (Via Romana, 17, follow signs to the museum entrance on 2nd floor of Università degli Studi di Firenze; ☎ 055-2288251; €4; Sun–Tues and Thurs–Fri 9am–1pm, Sat 9am–5pm) is the only museum I've visited in Italy where kids eagerly pull their parents from room to room. Creepy collections of threadbare stuffed-animal specimens transition into rooms filled with incredibly lifelike human bodies suffering from horrible dismemberments, flayings, and eviscerations—all in the name of science. The wax models served as illustrations for medical students studying at this scientific institute in the 1770s. But there's no real reason for the gruesome wax plague dioramas in Room 33, except that apparently the original curator liked gross stuff.

THE OTHER FLORENCE

Nothing says the "other Florence" like the **Oltrarno** section of town, literally the "other" side of the Arno River from the main section of the city. This district has fewer tourists, and more local students and residents. While the Oltrarno has many traditional sights such as churches, museums, and hotels, it also has dozens of small artisans' shops, neighborhood stores, and neglected attractions that seem a world away from the mobbed *piazze* Duomo and Signoria.

The best way to experience the Oltrarno is to allow serendipity to be your guide as you walk the narrow streets south of the river between Ponte Vecchio and Ponte Alla Carraia. Wander into small shops to see craftsmen using techniques hundreds of years old. Metalworkers, engravers, bookbinders, woodcarvers, and jewelers operate their businesses almost clandestinely, without any sign above the shop entrances, without regular working hours, marked prices, or promotions of any sort. Don't try to drop by in August, however—that's when the artisans all go on vacation.

While some of the shop owners speak English, many don't, so you'll need a little help to learn about the various crafts. The city of Florence runs free workshop tours in the Oltrarno, during which local guides take visitors to three randomly selected shops each Monday and Thursday afternoon. I highly recommend these. For booking information, contact **Centro Prenotazioni** at ☎ 055-3036108 or at itinerary.turistici@siwebsrl.com.

Another good option is to book a tour through **Walking Tours of Florence** ★ (Piazzo Santo Stefano, 2; ☎ 055-2645033; www.italy.artviva.com). This well-run company coordinates custom tours on which bilingual guides take visitors to meet, and learn from, a half-dozen artisans in their workshops.

For information on some of the more accessible artisans' shops south of the Arno, see p. 133.

To see Florentines at their most passionate, beyond even the most heartfelt bridge embrace, attend a local **soccer match.** The ACF Fiorentina team has arisen from both a spectacular 2002 bankruptcy and burial in the lowest division, returning to fight for the championship of the prestigious Italian Serie A league. The renovated Artemio Franchi stadium, southeast of the city center, is packed with up to 47,000 fans for weekend matches from September to May. And these aren't like, say, baseball fans in the U.S.—expect singing, chanting, screaming masses of locals who live and die with each shot on goal. Tickets begin at €20, and you need to select a "home" or "away" team section. Choose your outfit carefully. (*Hint:* The home team color is violet.) You can order online at www.acf fiorentina.it, at the stadium box office, or from a variety of bars in town a few days before the match. Resellers also have tickets and can be reached at ☎ 055-503261 or 055-583300. The stadium is about 400m (¼ mile) from the Firenze Campo di Marte train station on Via Largo Gennarelli. Or take bus no. 17 or 20 from Santa Maria Novella station.

Nothing is more valued by Fiorentinos (or Tuscans, or Umbrians, or . . .) than the art and passion that goes into the preparation of their regional cuisine. And what better way to become part of this local culture than to get into the kitchen and learn how to make a meal? Florence offers a variety of options for taking a **cooking class,** ranging from formal courses at the **Cordon Bleu Academy** (Via di Mezzo, 55r; ☎ 055-2345468; www.cordonbleu-it.com) to exchange-school type instruction at the **Apicius Institute** (Via Guelfa, 85; ☎ 055-2658135; www.apicius.it) to lunchtime seminars at local restaurants. But probably the best option for a short-term tourist is to take a daylong class from **The Accidental Tourist** (☎ 055-699376; www.accidentaltourist.com). For €80, guests participate in an all-day trip to the Tuscan countryside that includes sightseeing, wine-tasting, and cooking lessons. In a home kitchen, instructors teach the making of a well-rounded Tuscan meal, from appetizer to dessert, using local ingredients. Then they turn theory into practice by walking the group through a hands-on creation of their own dinner. It's a great activity for families—members compete to roll the tightest pasta or present the prettiest pizza. And when the creations are finally ready to eat, everyone's a winner.

If you want to interact with the locals, a good first step would be to learn how to speak with them. When a simple *"Como estai?"* is enough to open doors of friendship, imagine what an **Italian language class** could do for you! In Florence, dozens of programs offer Italian instruction ranging from 1-week intros to multi-year degree courses. A highly recommended option for those interested in a mini study-abroad program is to take a part-time class at the well-respected **Centro Linguistico Italiano Dante Alighieri** (Piazza della Repubblica, 5; ☎ 055-210808; www.clida.it), whose 2-week Italian course combines 4-hour morning lessons with afternoon cultural seminars and field trips, all for €540. The **Centro Lorenzo de'Medici** (Via Faenza, 43; ☎ 055-287360; www.lorenzodemedici.it) is another good source for short- and long-term courses in language and culture. And the Florence tourist offices have additional listings of local learning centers for people looking for a refresher class.

Next, have your kids mix with the locals at the **Museo dei Ragazzi (Museum of Children)** ★ 🧒 (Palazzo Vecchio; ☎ 055-2768224; €6.90; daily 9am–1pm and 3–7pm). The museum's courses are mainly in the Italian language, but highly entertaining and interactive classes on such subjects as architecture for kids (building and destroying an arch), clothing (an actor portrays a Renaissance noble getting dressed), and optics (assembling a replica of Galileo's telescope) can often be understood by youthful visitors. And while it can be fun to try to figure out what's going on in Italian and joining Florentine families, the museum also offers some English performances, usually on weekends. Contact them via phone or at info@museoragazzi.it to learn about special workshops and their latest opening hours—which change often.

Many locals do their **food shopping** at the central market, **Mercato Centrale,** near the San Lorenzo church. They've cleaned it up for tourists, and the Japanese exchange students serving as store clerks are a signal that this isn't quite the locals-only destination it used to be. But still, neighborhood restaurateurs come here for fresh meat, produce, and olive oils from the Tuscan-area farms. You can pick up ingredients for a picnic in the park, or just ogle the amazing colors, shapes, and sizes of the fruits and vegetables on display. Get advice from vendors about a gift bottle of olive oil or essence of truffles, or snack on some sample sausages from the butcher. On the opposite side of town, the smaller Sant'Ambrogio market also offers a "super" market experience. The city of Florence has free guided tours of these markets, with food explanations and tastings on Tuesday and Wednesday mornings at 9:30am. For more information, contact ☎ 055-3036108 or itinerary.turistici@ siwebsrl.com.

After Romans beheaded St. Minias in the 3rd century, he supposedly picked up his head and rushed up the hill to the spot of his future church. Visitors don't need to make such a sacrifice to join the locals for **afternoon vespers at San Miniato church.** Just leave your camera in the hotel, dress conservatively, and climb to the church behind Piazza Michelangelo in time for the 4:30pm ceremonies. Monks begin with Gregorian chants in the same way they did almost 1,000 years ago.

If you can't make it to the evocative services at San Miniato, try to attend Mass at any one of a number of other central Florence churches during those times when "tourists are forbidden." Times vary by church, but there are often daily services around 7:30am and 5:30pm, while on Sundays, Masses happen at 8, 10am, noon, and 5pm at selected churches. Again, so long as you act like a parishioner, with bowed head and whispered tones, you'll be treated like one.

Florence's early fortune was built with the textile trade, and today the city is still a leader in the fashion world. There's no better way to glimpse this vibrant modern side of the Florence than to go to one of its major **fashion fairs.** The Pitti Immagine fairs are held in winter, spring, and fall in the Fortessa da Basso. Admission is €20 for the official events, and they're technically for "the trade" only, but you can probably fudge some info on the registration forms. For more information, go to www.pittimmagine.com. Accommodations in town can be tight during the fairs, but Florence is alive with official and unofficial events, including fashion shows, product displays, and corporate promotions. Even passing on the periphery of one of these fairs is a good way to get an insider perspective on the modern business of the Italian fashion industry.

SHOPPING

As I've noted more than once, Florence built its medieval riches from the textile and clothing trade, and it continues to be a mecca for shopping as well as a center for fashion and design. Ferragamo makes its headquarters here in a riverside castle, and the high-rent Tournabuoni street features showrooms of all the top **designer brands,** including Armani, Gucci, and Prada. But Florence is equally well known for its many **artisans** carrying on their family craft traditions in jewelry, furniture-making, engraving, and bookbinding. Their small workshops can be found south of the Arno River, primarily in the Oltrarno district. **Leather** is one of the major products of the city, with high-end stores selling jackets, purses, and bags in the Santa Croce district, and dozens of street-side stalls selling cheaper versions in the San Lorenzo area.

A note about hours: In general, Florence's stores are open between 4 and 7:30pm on Mondays; and from 9 or 10am to 1pm and again from 3:30 or 4 until 7pm Tuesdays through Saturdays (though in the summer many shops also open on Mon mornings). If you're big on shopping, you won't want to visit in August, when many shopkeepers draw their shutters and take a week or even the entire month off for vacation.

BOOKS & PAPER GOODS

Enrico Giannini does bookbinding and creates handmade artistic papers at his shop, **Giulio Giannini & Figlio** (Via Dei Velluit, 29; ☎ 055-2399657; enrico giannini@inwind.it), in the same way that his family did for 150 years before him. He speaks English well, and can be persuaded to give a near magical demonstration on how he creates the swirling colors on his book jackets and wrapping papers. He not only does custom bookbinding but also sells reasonably priced boxes, papers, and journals for unique souvenirs. This is the leading shop in Florence for paper goods, but you may also want to visit close competitor **J Pineider** (Via Cavour, 55R; ☎ 055-215262), the oldest *paperie* in the city, founded in 1774 and still turning out exquisitely crafted paper and paper goods, from diaries and photo albums to engraved stationery.

One of the larger bookstores with English-language guidebooks, art tomes, and history texts is **Libreria Feltrinelli** (Via Cerretani, 30/r, near the Duomo, and Via Cavour, 12R; ☎ 055-2382652; www.lafeltrinelli.it). Used English-language books can be found at **Paperback Exchange** (Via Fiesolana, 31R, southeast of city center; ☎ 055-2478154; www.papex.it), an excellent and cheap place for books and an unofficial gathering place for expat English-speakers in Florence.

CHEAP NECESSITIES

A good place to stock up on necessities, like forgotten toothbrush, soap, paper, pen, a rubber duck, or purple tableware, is the **Nine T Nine Cent Paradise,** where, you guessed it, everything is €.99. Sweet! You can find its bright yellow sign at the intersection of Via Guelfa and Nazionale, as well as at about six other locations in the city.

ENGRAVING & WOODCARVING

A cluttered cuckoo-clock of a shop, packed with every variety of woodcarving, is **Bartolucci,** which has two centrally located branches (Via Condotta, 12R; ☎ 055-211773; and Via Borgo dei Greci, 11A/R; ☎ 055-211773; www.bartolucci.com). Since 1936, the family has been carving wood versions of everything from Tuscany's own Pinnochio, to half-size motorcycles, model airplanes, picture frames, and clocks. These make wonderfully unique keepsakes.

An Oltrarno shop where you can see the engravers in action is **L'Ippogrifo Stampe d'Arte** (Via S. Spirito, 5R; ☎ 055-213255; www.stampeippogrifo.com). Examine the cityscapes and still lifes on the walls, and then step back into the workshop to witness the copperplate pressing technique, the same one that has been used in Florence for 500 years. For antique engravings, stop by **Giovanni Baccani** (Via della Vigna Nuova, 75R; ☎ 055-214467), which has a grand collection of prints and engravings.

FASHION

For chic Italian clothes at last season's prices (generally because you're getting last season's styles), I have two suggestions: **Guardaroba/Stock House Grandge Firme** (Borgo degli Albizi, 87r; ☎ 055-234-0271) and **Stock House Il Giglio** (Via Borgo Ognissanti, 86; no phone). Both carry overstock clothing in perfect condition from some of the biggest names in Italian fashions—at discounts of as much as 60%.

If you need to be more au courant than that, you can find affordable clothes at the department store **Coin** (Via dei Calzaiuoli, 56r; ☎ 055-280531; www.coin.it) or at **La Rinascente** (Piazza della Repubblica, 1; ☎ 055-219113; www.rinascente.it). Both are members of national chains. And for the fashionistas among you, head directly to the **Via dei Tornabuoni, Via Nuova,** or **Via degli Strozzi,** where Pucci, Gucci, and other big names in Italian fashion have their chic shops.

JEWELRY

Florence doesn't offer the same buys on jewelry that it once did. Prices tend to be high and there are some shops that will pass off inferior stones, so choose carefully. I can, however, heartily recommend the following two shops, not just for their craftsmanship but also for their honest service. First up is the **Alessandro Dari Museum Shop** ★ (Via S. Niccolo, 115R, eastern Oltrarno; ☎ 055-244747; www.alessandrodari.com), where the jewelry is truly unique. Goldsmith/craftsman/musician Alessandro Dari is always busy at his bench in this combination showcase, lounge, and workshop. Prices range from €120 for a simple "love ring" to €30,000 for what looks like an actual-size jeweled golden village for your finger. For a wider variety of jewelry, go to **Gioielleria Manetti** (Via dei Calzaiuoli, 92r, near the Duomo; ☎ 055-214401; www.gioielleriamanetti.it), a popular family-run craft shop with jewelry, watches, and silver.

LEATHER SHOPS & STALLS

A decent leather jacket can be found for not much more than €100 in the stalls around San Lorenzo, but don't expect it to be an heirloom. Indeed, it's not uncommon to experience fraying stitches and broken zippers after only a few weeks' use of the cheaper leather goods, so check the craftsmanship closely before purchasing. Generally, the fewer number of pieces used for construction, the higher the quality: A jacket that looks like a quilt has a greater chance of falling apart. Feel free to haggle: You have buyer's power because of the number of stalls in the area. You can usually get the seller to drop the initial price by half, more if you buy multiple items.

A better option is to go into one of the nearby stores, whose permanent location makes them more likely to be accountable for quality. Also, these stores will

Festive Florence

Florence has a number of annual festivals and events, some focused on the modern business of textiles and fashion. But the more entertaining ones have history as their theme.

The games of the **Calcio Storico** are held in connection with the celebrations related to St. John the Baptist, Florence's patron saint, on his feast day of June 24.

After parading through town in 16th-century costumes, teams from each of Florence's four city quarters assemble in a dirt-filled Piazza Signoria and/or Santa Croce. They then play a set of games said to have originated during a siege of Florence in 1530. If the Renaissance soldiers were as brutal as their modern descendants, the siege was probably broken quickly.

The games are a combination of rugby and soccer, as well as general mayhem, with teams—consisting of 26 people—beating the daylights out of each other while trying to advance from one end of the square to the other. Qualifying matches are played in the 2 weeks prior to the 24th, with the final on feast day. The winning team, assuming they have any teeth left, enjoy a roasted calf as their prize, and then they watch that night's fireworks with the rest of Florence. Tickets can be hard to come by for the bleachers in the squares, but the processions through town during the weeks approaching the finals are free.

Scoppio del Caro is Florence's Easter festival, in which the descent of the Holy Spirit to earth is celebrated by blowing up a cart filled with fireworks. This creative interpretation of heaven meeting earth is said to have begun with a burning wagon pulled around town by returning crusaders, to bring the flame of Holy Saturday to Easter Sunday. The modern buggy is hauled by six nervous bulls from Porta a Prato to the Duomo. In the Piazza, a mechanical dove on a wire descends from up high to set the wagon (minus the relieved oxen) ablaze for a resulting explosion of holy spirits.

Moving to the secular, Florence's notable multimonth music festival is the **Maggio Musicale Fiorentino** (www.maggiofiorentino.com). It features opera, dance theater, and orchestra performances at venues across town, including the Teatro Comunale, Teatro Verdi, the Palazzo dei Congressi, and several outdoor performances. The season usually runs from May to early June. Tickets begin at €10 for the cheap seats to €100 or more for the best seats at the marquee events. A semi-related opera season runs from September through January under the auspices of the same organization.

usually alter a jacket at no extra cost (be sure to allow at least a day, though, if you need any work done). **Gherardini** (Via della Vigna Nuova, 57R; ☎ 055-215678; www.gherardini.it) and **Cesar Elater Factory** (Piazza San Croce; ☎ 055-2340315; caesarleatherfactory@libero.it) are two recommended stores for quality and service in this area. **Beltrami** (Via della Vigna Nuova, 70R; ☎ 055-287779) is another top name for leather and one you may recognize—its goods are also sold in the United States. You'll find them for less here than in Venice, especially if you make the trek to **Beltrami Spa** (Via del Panzani, 11R; ☎ 055-212661), which offers discounts of 20% to 50% off last season's fashions.

High-quality jackets can be found in the shops around Santa Croce, or in a few Oltrarno stores. **Suola del Cuio** (Piazza Santa Croce, 16; ☎ 055-244534) initially began as a leather-crafts school for Franciscan monks, and has expanded its partnership over the years with a major Florentine trading house to develop into a well-known and full-service leather shop (with prices to match). A good cheaper option is **Lorenz Leather** (Piazza San Lorenzo, 10R; ☎ 055-213348), with a wide selection and quick turnaround on alteration. Bags and purses can be found in these same stores, and both get good reviews. The high-end Prada and Gucci stores also offer finely crafted products, but you'll be paying a lot for the name and their high-rent location. Moreover, if you've come all the way to Florence, you should probably buy something more unique than a name brand you can pick up in your hometown. South of the Arno, **John F.** (Lungarno Corsini, 2; ☎ 055-2398985; www.johnf.it) and **Anna's** (Piazza Pitti, 40R; ☎ 055-283787; www.annapitti.it) both have soft-as-a-baby's-fanny leather jackets for both men and women.

NIGHTLIFE

Florence isn't especially known for its nightlife. Live-music venues are few, clubs are scattered around town, and there really isn't any particular neighborhood that lights up at night.

That being said, the influx of tourists and exchange students ensures there's always going to be an Irish pub within a couple of blocks. Additionally, the younger set has its four or five requisite dance clubs; the cultured have opera; and the too-cheap-to-buy-a-ticket can enjoy free evening concerts in historic squares during the summer. And open-container laws are lax, so if all else fails you can always kick back with a drink on the steps of a historic building and watch the evening promenade of locals and visitors (possibly the best nightlife option of all).

PERFORMING ARTS

While it's not Milan or Roma, Florence has a respectable arts scene boasting two well-regarded symphony orchestras and a large concert hall, **Teatro Comunale** (Corso Italia, 12; ☎ 055-213535), which presents seasons of ballet and classical music (it's also the venue for the annual Maggio Musicale; see "Festive Florence," above). Prices can vary widely by show (up to €150 for headliners), but in general it's possible to get a ticket here for as little as €15 to €20 if you're willing to accept a seat in the second gallery.

A secondary theater, the **Teatro Verdi** (Via Ghibellina, 99; ☎ 055-212320; www.teatroverdifirenze.it), is where you go to see touring shows. Major international stars of opera, ballet, and classical and pop music play this venue. Ticket prices are all over the map, but it's usually possible to snag a seat for between €10 and €30.

Going to church might not be your idea of a night out on the town, but it often is in Florence, where *le notti* are filled with the sounds of Vivaldi, Bach, and Mozart, and church concerts are a staple. The majority of concerts take place in the autumn months, but rarely does a week go by without some house of worship sponsoring one of these events. To find out which churches are having concerts, or to book tickets to the Verdi or Comunale, visit the agency **Box Office** (Via Alamanni, 39; ☎ 055-210804; www.boxol.it). It's also a good source for the Maggio Musicale fest, local soccer games, and other events.

MUSIC CLUBS

For some (literally) underground live music, try **BeBop** ✸ (Via dei Servi, 76; ☎ 055-490397), a surprisingly cavernous warren of basement rooms. This is the sort of place into which local college students take their guitars, with the hopes of jamming with whoever happens to be on stage. Bands vary from awful Beatles cover groups, to great funk/folk/rock combos; you just have to try your luck and see who's playing that night. On weekends the place can get quite crowded, but on a weekday it could just be you and the family of the band in the audience.

Popular with locals, the cavelike **Chiodo Fisso Vini Club** (Via Dell'Anguillara, 70R, just behind Palazzo Vecchio; ☎ 055-2381290) features Italian folk singers, jazz artists, and a variety of other small acts on a tiny stage surrounded by a dozen or so tables. Performers begin around 10pm, and the bar gets crowded about an hour later. It's a good peek at a local scene.

Caruso Jazz Café (Via Lambertesca, 14/16R; ☎ 055-281940; www.carusojazz cafe.com) is the most sophisticated choice. Its live jazz combos play most nights of the week, beginning at around 10pm. The stone arched stage area is an atmospheric setting for music. You can sit in the front section at the bar for drinks, or enjoy the tunes with your dinner. A side room has couches for relaxing and a closed-circuit TV so you don't miss any of the onstage action. They also have an expensive Internet cafe, just in case you need to look up some jazz scores.

BARS & TAVERNS

About the hippest place in town in recent summers has been **Capocaccia** ✸ (Lugarno Corsini, 12R; ☎ 055-210751), which attracts a young and beautiful crowd drawn by the free buffet treats and the superlative views. Really what could be cooler than sitting on a beanbag chair, drink in hand, with a view of Ponte Vecchio on one side and the sunset on the other? A couple of other good *aperitivo* choices in a chic setting are the loungey **Angels** (Via del Proconsolo, 29/31R; ☎ 055-2398762; www.ristoranteangels.it) and the happening cafe **Dolce Vita** (Piazza del Carmine; ☎ 055-284595). At the **Nova Bar** (Via Martelli, 14R; ☎ 055-289880), for the price of a drink, you can snag a free buffet of Tuscan treats (6–10pm) in a Los Angeles–meets–the Duomo setting.

Among the dozen or so near-identical Irish pubs in Florence (think dark woods and lots of Celtic bric-a-brac), I've returned a number of times to the **Dublin Pub** (Via Faenza, 27R; ☎ 055-293049) for its well-pulled pints and calm ambience—quite a contrast to the busy Via Faenza/Via Nazionale area outside.

Doubling as Firenze's favorite frat house, **The Fish Pub** (Piazza del Mercato Centrale, 44R; ☎ 055-2654029) certainly can't be recommended for any cultural reason. But you can get five shots for €5, a pizza for another €5, and between the patio and the upper floor, not to mention the main bar, there's always some sort of silliness going on.

The clientele have sworn they'd tan my hide for sharing the location of **The Joshua Tree Pub** ✖ (Via Della Scala, 37R; www.thejoshuatreepub.com), but it's such a fun place, I'm doing so anyway. A quirky neighborhood bar popular among international students, gray-haired neighborhood characters, and pink-mohawked local punks, it's certainly one of the friendliest spots in town thanks to manager Max and his spirited staff. They welcome everyone equally, and offer cheap drink specials (including nine beers on tap) and amateur DJs. The neighborhood near the station gets a little sketchy, so bring a friend if you're planning a late night.

DANCE CLUBS

Central Park (Via Fosse Macinate, 2, Parco delle Cascine; ☎ 055-353505) attracts over a thousand partiers on a good night, including both locals and tourists. It boasts four large dance areas, with all types of high-energy music. Drinks are pricey, as is the admission (€16), and it's best to go late at night; the place doesn't really get hopping until about 1am. You'll want to take a cab to and from the club, however, because the neighborhood is a bit dicey.

Club Yab (Via Sassetti, 5; ☎ 055-215160; www.yab.it) probably qualifies as Central Park's biggest competitor (you may remember its earlier incarnation as Yab Yum), with three dance floors, house and dance music, and an enthusiastic crowd of 20-somethings. It opens at 11:30pm; there is a bouncer at the front to keep out the unstylish, so be sure to wear your club clothes.

For an alternative to typical hip-hop clubs, **Club Meccano** (Viale degli Olmi, 1; ☎ 055-352143) features Latin, salsa, and some '70s retro music nights. You'll pay €10 cover charge, which includes a drink.

Gay/lesbian nightlife centers in a neighborhood a little west of Santa Croce church, where you'll find **Crisco** (Via Sant'Egidio, 43/r; ☎ 055-2480580), a swinging nightspot popular with men, while **Piccolo Café** (Borgo Santa Croce, 23/R; ☎ 055-241704) and **Flamingo** (Via dei Pandolfini, 26/R; ☎ 055-243356) are co-ed. **Tabasco Bar** (Piazza di Santa Cecilia, 3/r; ☎ 055-213000) is Italy's oldest gay disco but still going strong, and the **YAG b@r** (Via de Macci, 8R; ☎ 055-2469022; www.yagbar.com) is a colorful new cafe/bar/DJ space.

The ABCs of Florence

American Express There's a currency-exchange office (**Via Dante Alighieri**, 22R; ☎ 055-50981; Mon–Fri 9am–5:30pm), which also provides free mail pickup and other services for cardholders (non-cardholders pay a fee).

Area Code The country code for Italy is **39**. The Florence area code used to be

055, but this has now been incorporated into the regular numbers, so dial it if you see it.

Business Hours Shops are usually open from about 9:30am to noon or 1pm, then from 3 or 3:30 to 7:30pm. Or 5pm . . . or 6pm. Or maybe the weather's nice, so they're closed for the day. In short, hours are erratic. The town comes close to shutting down in August as everyone leaves the sweltering heat for the mountains or beaches. Many museums are closed on Mondays. It can be pretty tough to find an open restaurant any time from 3 to 6pm, though many do stay open past midnight, particularly in tourist-heavy areas.

Consulate The U.S. Consulate in Florence is in the big pink Palazzo Canevaro (**Lungarno Vespucci**, 38; ☎ 055-266951; www.usembassy.it/florence;9:30am–1:30 pm for non-emergencies). It has a list of English-speaking attorneys and doctors on its website. Generally not your first point of contact for anything except a lost passport.

Currency Exchange All over the place in the Santa Maria Novella district, but banks are safer, albeit confusing and rarely open. ATMs are probably the best option for getting your hands on euros. More machines are clustered around the high-end shopping district of Tournabuoni Street.

Doctors The U.S. Consulate has a listing of local English-speaking doctors (see consulate info above). You can also call a 24-hour English-speaking medical service line (☎ 055-475411), or the "tourist" medical-service (☎ 055-212221).

Emergencies Dial ☎ **113** for general emergencies, ☎ **112** for police, ☎ **115** for fire, or ☎ **118** for medical emergencies.

Hospitals Italy has socialized medicine, so you can get treated without insurance or payment problems. Try **Arcispedale di Santa Maria Nuova** (☎ 055-27581) in the Santa Maria Nuova Piazza, north of the Duomo, or for more pressing emergencies, the **Misericordia Ambulance Service** (☎ 055-212222), which is actually in Piazza del Duomo, on the south side by Giotto's Bell Tower. A volunteer group, AVO, offers phone translation services for medical issues (☎ 055-2344567) from 10am to noon, Tuesday and Thursday,

and from 4 to 6pm Monday, Wednesday, and Friday, so it's best to get sick during these times.

Information & Tourist Offices Florence has three tourist offices in town. One is across from the Santa Maria Novella train station at **Piazza della Stazione, 4** (☎ 055-212245). The "tourist office" in the station is just a commercial hotel-booking service. The **main city tourist office** is at Via Cavour, 1R (☎ 055-2760383). The latter has standard city maps as well as information on hotels, restaurants, local classes, and area trips. It does charge for some of the materials. There is also a **newer tourist office** a block south of Santa Croce (**Borgo Santa Croce, 29;** ☎ 055-212245). Florence tourism's comprehensive website is www.firenzeturismo.it.

Internet Access Many hotels offer a free "Internet point," although sometimes it can be a hassle waiting for other guests to get off the machine. Besides a few hot spots, wireless Internet hasn't really made it to Florence, although some high-end hotels offer wireless access for a fee. Internet cafes, which usually charge about €2.50 to €3 per hour, are easy to find in most districts of the city. Many Internet cafes line Via Faenza, including **Caironet** at no. 49, open 9:30am to midnight; rates start at €2 per hour, with the same rates at the Via De Ginori shop. **Internettrain** is a large chain with 12 shops across Florence (www.internettrain.it).

Laundry The **Wash & Dry Lavarapido** chain has eight laundromats in town, all open from 8am to 10pm; most offer Internet access for €.50 per 10 minutes. Laundry costs €3.50 to have a large load washed and dried. Soap is available in vending machines. Locations: Via Dei Servi, 105; Via Della Scala, 52; Via Del Sole, 29; Borgo S. Frediano, 39; Via Dei Serragli, 87; Via Nazionale, 129; Via Ghibellina, 143; Via Dell'Agnolo, 21.

Newspapers & Magazines Every major international newspaper or magazine is available at kiosks or bookstores around town. The tourist office publishes a weekly English-language newspaper, *The Florentine,* with extensive events listings, articles about tourist sites, and important headlines like "Topless in Tuscany Not Tolerated." Many advertising-driven "information" brochures are available at the tourist office and hotels, including the decent *Vivi Firenze,* targeted at foreigners living in Florence.

Pharmacies Twenty-four-hour pharmacies are available at **Santa Maria Novella train station** (☎ 055-289435)—ring the bell if it looks closed; Farmacia Molteni (**Via dei Calzaiuoli, 7r;** ☎ 055-289490); and Farmacia All'Insegna del Moro (**Piazza San Giovanni, 20R;** ☎ 055-211343).

Police In an emergency, call ☎ **112.** For filing a report, contact the Questura Centrale (Via Zara, 2; ☎ 055-20391); English-speaking personnel are on hand there from 9am to 2pm, as well as at the main Carabinieri Station (Borgo Ognissanti, 48; ☎ 055-24811).

Post Office The main post office (**Via Pellicceria, 3,** by Piazza della Repubblica; ☎ 160 or 055-218156) sells stamps and sends packages—but if they're over 5 pounds you must go to the package office on Via dei Sassetti 4, in Piazza Davanzati behind the regular office. Stamps can be bought at any tobacco store, and for shipping a package probably the best option is to go with **UPS** (**Via Pratignone, 56a;** ☎ 055-8825501), **DHL** (**Via della Cupola, 243;** ☎ 055-3080877), or **Mailboxes Etc.** (**Via San Gallo, 55R;** ☎ 055-4630129; www.mbe.com), which have all the packing materials you'll need, but charge a hefty service fee.

Restrooms Florence has recently instituted the "Courtesy Point" system where 82 bars and cafes were assigned to put a yellow sticker in their windows to welcome guests to use their toilets. If you can't find the yellow sticker, stop in at a high-end hotel or a local McDonald's. In addition, Florence has 10 public restrooms

scattered around town (cost to use one is €.60), but it's unlikely you'll be near one when you need it.

Safety The tourist district is very safe, but it can get a little dicey around the edges (the Arno side of Santa Maria Novella station late at night, as well as some of the southern parks). There's no longer the gypsy pickpocket situation of previous years, though crowds and tourists will always attract some thieves, so stay aware of your possessions.

Transit Info City **buses** leave from the Santa Maria Novella train station on dozens of routes going across town and out to the suburbs. You most likely won't need one to tour the historical center. The cost is €1 for a 1-hour ticket, €4.50 for a full-day ticket, with various other options available. You're supposed to validate your own ticket by sticking it in the machine in the bus. They rarely check tickets, but if they do, you'll pay a hefty fine if you're ticketless or unvalidated. The "I'm a tourist, I didn't know" excuse doesn't work; believe me, they've heard that one before.

Taxis are available at the train station, and line up around major *piazze.* You can order one to come fetch you by calling ☎ 055-4390, 055-4242, or 055-4798. Flag-fall is over €2.50, double that late at night or on weekends; add extra for pickups and for luggage. Drivers expect about a 10% tip. Again, you most likely won't need one to get around town, unless you're trying to ferry luggage from the train station to your hotel.

If you like hills, you might enjoy **renting a bicycle** and riding around south of the Arno, up to San Miniato and Piazzale Michelangelo. Given the tight traffic in town, I wouldn't recommend using a bike as a way to see the city. But rentals are available at several locations for about €2.70 an hour, including Alinari (Via Guelfa, 85r; ☎ 055-280500; www.alinari rental.com). If you're going to be in Florence for a while, Florence by Bike (Via

S. Zanobi, 120/122r; ☎ 055-488992; www. florencebybike.it) has an interesting rental option whereby you actually purchase a bike for €125 and then sell it back to them at the end of a month for €60.

If you want to zoom around on a Vespa like a local, it is possible to **rent a motor scooter,** but you *really* need to know how to handle one. Florence is definitely not the place to learn to ride, and even experts have trouble in the traffic chaos—think bike messenger in Manhattan. That being said, it's a fun way to zip up nearby hills, pop over to Fiesole, or visit 20 sites in a single day. Prices start at about €50 per day for 125cc scooters, the largest size for which you won't need a license. The bike-rental places also rent scooters, as does Dueruote (Via Borgo Ognissanti, 153R; ☎ 055-2399696; www.dueruoterent. com).

Because of the small size of the historical district, and the traffic and parking hassles, it's not worth renting a car if you're staying in town. However, **renting a car** is a great idea if you want to get out of Florence, especially if you intend to get off the beaten track in Chianti country. Rental agencies in town include Europcar (Borgo Ognissanti, 55R; ☎ 055-290438; www.eurocar.com), Avis (Borgo Ognissanti, 128R; ☎ 055-213629; www. avis.com), and Hertz (Via Fininguerra, 33R; ☎ 055-2398205; www.hertz.com).

4 Tuscany

On winding roads through famous wine country, and in awesome cities, visitors lose themselves in masterworks of the past.

by Bill Fink

THIS IS THE ITALIAN COUNTRYSIDE OF PEOPLE'S DREAMS: ROLLING HILLS covered with vineyards and castles; and fortified hill towns punctuated with medieval stone towers and Gothic church spires. In its cities are Renaissance *palazzi,* and on its farms are houses and manors transformed into charming bed-and-breakfasts.

There are plenty of visitors in this ultrapopular part of Italy. But the fame continues to be deserved, and the legions of tourists haven't diminished Tuscany's character. Pisa and Siena are historical rivals to Florence, both containing some of the most famous monuments in the world. Little Lucca, with its massive stone walls now topped by green parks, is proud of its long tradition of music, art, and architecture. San Gimignano, a "medieval Manhattan" with its many stone towers, stands as a reminder of the vibrant centers of trade that these cities once were.

Take the famed Chianti road, winding like a string of spaghetti past dozens of wineries in the hills between Florence and Siena. Stop in Siena for its churches, palaces, art museums, and the famed Piazza del Campo, site of the Palio horse races. Continue south to enjoy the festivals of Arezzo, the gateway to the Umbria region.

In planning a Tuscan holiday, it makes sense to base yourself at one, maybe two, locations, and do day trips to the various towns. It's much easier to make the commute (either by bus, train, or car) than to change hotels every day. The cities are surprisingly close to one another. For trips to Lucca, Pisa, and San Gimignano, I would either base myself in some countryside lodging or in Florence. Siena is worth several days' stay, both as a destination and as a base to visit Chianti and nearby hill towns.

LUCCA

Lucca is a bite-size city of churches, shops, and gardens, surrounded by a thick circle of walls. And it's free of the throngs that can make even the most beautiful attractions of nearby Florence or Pisa feel like a chore to tour at times. Though no place in Tuscany could be called "undiscovered," Lucca has somehow managed to retain its historic aura.

The main attractions of Lucca are the walls themselves, arguably the best preserved Renaissance ramparts in the world. Twelve meters (40 ft.) high, 15m (50 ft.) across, and with a 4km (2½ miles) circumference, the walls, which once offered protection, are now a recreation area. Topped by trees, walking paths, parks, and playgrounds, this is where locals and visitors come to unwind; you'll see elderly women gossiping, men playing cards on benches, and grandchildren picnicking in the shade.

The sight from the walls is nearly as striking: a grid-patterned town, laid out by the methodical ancient Romans, with a soaring cathedral at its heart. Off to one side is the Anfiteatro Romano, an oval-shaped enclosure of medieval buildings surrounding the original foundation of a Roman amphitheater. It makes a certain kind of sense that Lucca's famous son, opera legend Giacomo Puccini, was sired here, amid all this beauty and drama.

DON'T LEAVE LUCCA WITHOUT . . .

WALKING OR BIKING ALONG THE TOP OF THE CITY WALLS   These are Italy's premier *passeggiate* (promenades).

VISITING THE CATTEDRALE DI SAN MARTINO   Its exterior has an interesting mix of styles and carvings, and the interior features the famous Volto Santo woodcarving of Jesus, said to have been done at the time of his crucifixion.

SAVORING ZUPPA LUCCHESE   Try some of this Luccan specialty, a layered custard dessert made from liqueur-soaked ladyfingers, custard, and fresh berries.

HAVING A MEAL AT BUCA DI SAN ANTONIO   A city favorite for years, this 18th-century roadhouse-turned-country-kitchen offers the best of Luccan regional cuisine.

ATTENDING THE OPERA   Since Lucca is the home of Puccini, the Lucchese love to catch the latest incarnation of their hometown hero's operas in the open air during summer around Torre del Lago, or in autumn at the Teatro del Giglio.

A BRIEF HISTORY OF LUCCA

Lucca has been a significant city since Roman times, when Caesar, Pompey, and Crassus met here to create their Triumvirate government in 56 B.C. At that time, Lucca had already been a Roman colony for 200 years. In the 2nd century A.D., the Romans added the amphitheater, whose arches and columns still form the supports of the medieval buildings surrounding Lucca's oval Teatro Romano piazza.

Lucca's history was also touched by the early days of Christianity. St. Paolino, one of St. Peter's deacons, is said to have brought the faith to the city in A.D. 47, making Lucca the first Tuscan city to be converted. In 588, a wandering Irish abbot settled in town

> *Lucca . . . that compact and admirable little city, overflowing with everything that makes for ease, for plenty, for beauty, for interest and good example.*
>
> —Henry James, *Italian Hours*, 1909

Tuscany & Umbria

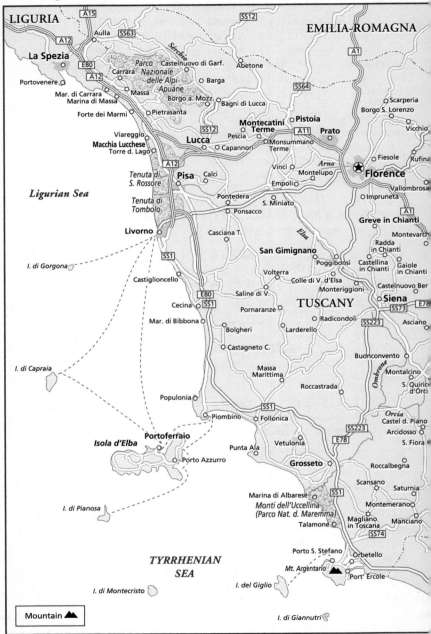

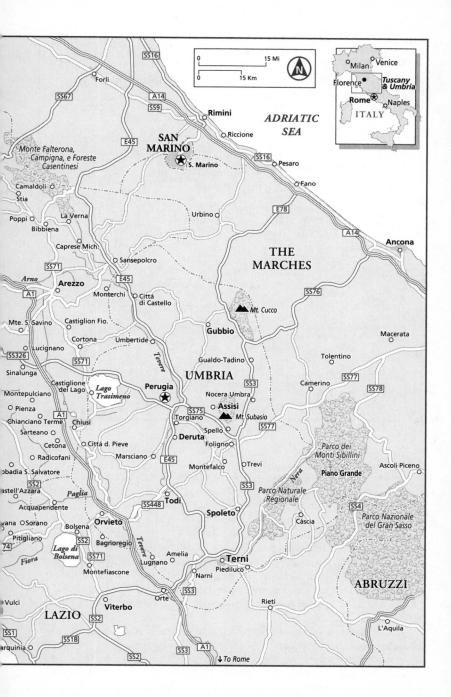

Lucca

to become Bishop (and later St.) Frediano, for whom the church in the northern part of Lucca is named.

Following the fall of Rome, Lucca spent centuries changing hands between various warlords. It wasn't until the 12th century that Lucca emerged as a free commune, erecting another set of city walls, palaces, and churches as trade brought prosperity to the city. The bulk of the city's Romanesque churches, including San Martino, Frediano, and Michele, were raised, improved, and expanded over the next 100 years.

The 1300s saw Lucca get involved in the Guelph versus Ghibelline civil wars wracking Tuscany. Internal city divisions allowed external invaders, including the city states of Pisa and Florence, to conquer Lucca. But Lucca reemerged as a small and independent state, maintaining its freedom over the next 200 years through skillful diplomacy.

Peace enabled Lucca to construct increasingly solid walls, until the present boundary took form between 1544 and 1645. One hundred twenty-six cannons lined these fortifications, and the adjacent parklands were cleared to give the gunners an open line of fire. But the walls never faced the test of invaders. By the time Austrian armies overran Northern Italy in the 18th century, improvements in artillery technology had made such battlements irrelevant, and Lucca surrendered, along with its cannons, without a fight. When Napoleon became King of Italy in 1805, he put his sister, Elia Baciocchi, in charge of Lucca. She freshened up the town, adding gardens and the appropriately named Piazza Napoleone.

Today, Lucca has a vibrant small-city feel amid its historical monuments, palaces, and gardens. Regional food (especially local olive oils) fills its shops and restaurants, opera fills its theaters, and local Lucchese fill its wide avenues on their evening promenades through town.

LAY OF THE LAND

Reaching Lucca **by train** is pretty easy from Florence. Over 20 trains a day connect the cities on an 80-minute ride costing just €5. The **Lucca train station** (Piazza Ricasoli; ticket office ☎ 0583-467013) is just a couple of blocks from the historic south edge of the wall. Trains go to Pisa with similar regularity, and cost only €2.50 for the half-hour ride. While it's a snap to walk into town, if you're traveling with heavy luggage, take city bus no. 1, 2, or 3, all of which go to the center of Lucca. There are also plenty of taxis at the train station.

Hourly **buses** connect Lucca to Florence via the **Lazzi line** (☎ 0583-584876; www.lazzi.it). The ride takes about 75 minutes, costs about €5, and stops at Piazzale Verdi on the west side of Lucca.

It's less than an hour's drive to Lucca from Florence, about 64 km (40 miles) away on the A11 expressway.

> ❝A few of the churches are justly famous . . . but with Florence nearby and Pisa around the corner and Siena not too far away, these don't call for studious attention, and that can be great relief and Lucca's greatest asset.❞
>
> —Kate Simon, *Italy: The Places in Between,* 1970

The commute to Pisa is even shorter, just 24 km (15 miles) to the south on SS12. Traffic and parking are restricted inside the city, though free parking can be found on city streets outside the walls.

Lucca's main **tourist office** (Piazza Santa Maria, 35; ☎ 0583-919931; www.luccaturismo.it; May–Oct daily 9am–8pm, Nov–Apr daily 9am–1pm and 3pm–6pm) is located on the south side of the piazza, just inside Porta Santa Maria. It has the usual collection of maps and brochures, and also a bookstore selling the useful English-language *Grapevine* magazine of events and listings for €2, as well as Internet access (€3 for 30 min.). For an entertaining and informative audio tour of the city, rent headphones from the tourist office for €6. At a leisurely pace, the tour takes about 2 hours. Lucca has **another tourist office** with similar services in Cortile Carrara, off Palazzo Ducale, facing Piazza Napoleone (☎ 0583-919941).

If you want to do as the Lucchese do, you may feel inspired to travel around the city—especially the city walls—by bike. **Bikes** are available for rent at two shops next to the main tourist office: **Antonio Poli** (Piazza Santa Maria, 42; ☎ 0583-493787; www.biciclettepoli.com; Tues–Sun 8:30am–7:30pm) and **Cicli Bizzarri** (Piazza Santa Maria, 32; ☎ 0583-496031; 8:30am–1pm and 2:30–7:30pm). Just about every place in town charges the same €2.10 per hour, or €11 per day for basic bicycles.

ACCOMMODATIONS, BOTH STANDARD & NOT

€   A choice hostelling option is **Ostello San Frediano** ★ 🎒 (Via della Cavallerizza, 12; ☎ 0583-469957; www.ostellolucca.it). This large 140-bed hostel was, at varying times, a convent, a library, and a school before its 2002 renovation and transformation into this clean, character-filled hostel. The wide, tiled hallways and large common rooms echo with footsteps, while the rear garden offers a nice place to relax. Rooms are institutional but ultraclean with new furnishings, and are priced from €17 per person in an eight-bed dorm to €43 for a double with private bathroom. They have a decent breakfast buffet for €3.80, and a passable lunch and dinner for €9. Plus, they have beer in the vending machines!

€–€€   Because of the small number of hotels inside the city walls, Lucca is also a good place to look into B&Bs or private rooms. Among the best choices are **Affittacamere Centro Storico** 🎒 (Corte Portici, 16; ☎ 0583-490748; www. affittacamerecentrostorico.com), a collection of tidy rental rooms, with decent beds, that go for €60 to €130 for a double with bathroom, fan, and fridge (the rate varies by season). Centrally located near Piazza San Michele, six rooms are for rent here, including a triple and a large suite perfect for families. **La Camelia** (Piazza San Francesco, 35; ☎ 0583-463481; www.affittacamerelacamelia.com) is another centrally located option, with rooms that are cheap and clean but more basic at €75 for a triple and €65 for a double.

€–€€   If you'd rather stay in a more standard lodging, **Casa Alba** ★ (Via Fillungo, 142, just north of Piazza Anfiteatro; ☎ 0583-312800; www.casa-alba. com) is a small but pleasant guesthouse, and one of the best lodging deals inside town. Its two doubles with bathroom cost just €50 to €80 per night (varying by season), while the three rooms that share the other bathroom go for a mere €35 to €60. Decorated with a hodgepodge of furnishings, which are nonetheless clean and well maintained, each room has satellite TV, air-conditioning, and a small fridge. A free breakfast is served in the room. Alba, the multilingual energetic manager, can offer good tips for Luccan dining, shopping, and area attractions. The only downside here: Rooms are on the third floor, up 53 very steep steps.

€€   The six rooms of the **San Frediano** ★ (Via degli Angeli, 19; ☎ 0583-469630; www.sanfrediano.com) offer much of the authentic, local flavor of a B&B and are sometimes cheaper at €80 for a double. The rooms are somewhat basic, but the building maintains the feel of its 1600 origins.

€€€   A couple of "residence" style lodging options give you the chance to experience a more traditional setting inside the walls of Lucca. **Albergo San Martino** (Via Della Dogana, 9; ☎ 0583-991940) has a quaint B&B feel to it, with a friendly English-speaking staff, and when I last visited had plans to freshen up the rooms. A double goes for €130, which includes a large buffet breakfast.

€€€   In one of the odder modern-meets-traditional hotels you'll ever see, the **Hotel Universo** ★ (Piazza del Giglio, 1; ☎ 0583-493678; www.universolucca. com) combines a classic 19th-century decor in some of the rooms (and the lobby) with futuristic *Jetsons*-like decorating in others. The €120-to-€140 standard rooms are a little worn around the edges, and some lack air-conditioning, though the hotel says they're upgrading soon. The superior rooms (€140–€160) are really superior, with slick, 21st-century wood paneling and minimalist furniture. Each of the 60 rooms has a grand view either of the cathedral, the tree-lined Piazza Napoleone, or Piazza del Giglio.

€€€   A definite step up, the **Alla Corte degli Angeli** ★★ (Via degli Angeli, 23; ☎ 0583-469204) has flatscreen TVs to go with the stylishly decorated but still traditional rooms with wood-beam ceilings; rooms run about €150 for a double.

DINING FOR ALL TASTES

€–€€   A prime location in front of the cathedral—a lively scene of locals and tourists—and fresh salads and appetizers make **Giro Vita** ★ 🧒 (Piazza Antelminelli, 2; ☎ 0583-469412) a great spot for lunch or an evening *aperitivo* (7:30–9:30pm). Children enjoy the snack menu and fruit slurpees, and if they kick up a fuss, their parents can relax—it's noisy enough here to cover all but the loudest tantrums. Entrees are in the €6-to-€8 range, including the large seafood salad (recommended) at €7 and a light veggie pasta for €6.50. Because the place is open 8am to 1am, you can always depend on getting a decent quick bite here. Simple dinners are served Tuesday to Thursday nights.

€€€   If you're looking for a more substantial meal, a popular spot for dinner since 1782 is **Buca di Sant Antonio** ★ (Via della Cervia, 1/3, near Piazza S. Michele; ☎ 0583-55881; www.bucadisantantonio.com; Tues–Sun; reservations recommended for dinner). It's a homey restaurant serving characteristic Luccan cuisine, with hanging hams, pots and pans, a fireplace, and assorted antiques clutter. Tops on the menu is a tummy-warming flat pasta with stewed hare in wine sauce *pappardelle alla leper,* for €14; and breast of guinea fowl with grapes, *petto di faraona all'uva moscato,* for €17. On a cold evening, order the traditional pudding, *castagnaccio,* a rich combination of chestnut flour and ricotta cheese. Most main courses cost between €13 and €17.

€€–€€€   For a change of pace, you can try the seafood at **Osteria del Neni** (Via Pescheria, 3, between Piazze San Michele and Napoleone; ☎ 0583-492681; www.leosteriedilucca.com; Tues–Sun). The menu changes by the season, but usually offers a variety of fresh fish combined with homemade pastas. The sea bass with pesto is a good combo for €13, as is the seafood *(frutti di mare)* linguini at €11. Pastas cost from €9 to €13, and *secondi* are slightly higher. Summers offer the chance to dine at the restaurant's street-front patios. Even with reservations, expect to do some waiting for your meal at this very popular restaurant.

€€–€€€   My final choice is a trendy, ultramodern bunker of an eatery that serves as a cafeteria/restaurant/jazz bar, its personality shifting depending on the time of day. Early on, **San Colombo** ★ 🧒 (Via Baldeschi, 9; ☎ 0583-464641; www.caffetteriasancolombano.it) is a snack shop/*gelateria,* at dinner it's a nice restaurant, and later in the evenings it becomes a hopping nightspot, especially on Wednesdays and Fridays, when you can listen to the DJ or live jazz until about 1am. If you stop by for dinner, try the traditional set menu (€28), with such regional specialties as pasta with wild hare, grilled boar, and zuppa Lucchese. (Pastas run €6–€8, *secondi* €8–€12. A large beer is €4.)

WHY YOU'RE HERE: THE TOP SIGHTS & ATTRACTIONS

If you go to Lucca, you are *required* to walk or bike along the **Walls of Lucca** ★★★. It's one of the highlights of a trip to Tuscany. As you saunter along the 4km-wide (2½-mile) green pathway 12m (40 ft.) above the city, you'll become a voyeur par extraordinaire, peeking over villa walls into elaborate private gardens filled with statuary, watching as the lucky citizens of this town stroll its broad avenues. Join the locals in enjoying a picnic under plentiful shade trees, or let your kids frolic in one of the many playgrounds lining the walls.

Although the only original remaining parts are a few arches and empty space, the **Anfiteatro Romano (Roman Amphitheater)** is another impressive site, the symmetrical oval of its shell surrounded by a crowd of medieval buildings. In 1830, city rulers cleared out the slums that stood in the middle of the piazza, creating the current scenic photo setting. The best way to see the amphitheater's outline is from the **Torre Guinigi** ★ (Via S. Andrea and Via Chiave d'Oro; ☎ 0583-48524; €3.50; Mar–Sept 9am–7:30pm, Oct–Feb 10am–5:30pm), an odd 45m (150-ft.) tree-topped tower sprouting up in the middle of town. The shade trees on top were planted for the benefit of soldiers standing watch on hot summer days. In addition to offering views of the amphitheater, the tower is a good vantage point from which to view the walls and the surrounding landscape.

If anything in town deserves studious attention, it is the **Cattedrale di San Martino** ★★ (Piazza San Martino; ☎ 0583-957068; free admission; daily 9:30am–5:45pm). Start with the facade, a perfect example of Pisan-Lucchese Romanesque architecture, with its repeating dwarf rows of columns. The exterior columns and atrium have interesting bas-relief carvings, including a labyrinth symbolic of the difficult journey to salvation and scenes from the Bible. Those over the doors, created in 1205, detail the life of St. Martin, a 4th-century saint famous for sharing his cloak with a beggar (as well as the usual miracles of curing lepers, and raising the dead, all recounted on the panels). The interior of the church is a mishmash of styles, ranging from Gothic arches to Renaissance paintings (including a *Last Supper* by Tintoretto) and 19th-century stained glass.

The cathedral's holiest relic is the caged wooden Volto Santo crucifix, said to have been miraculously created by Nicodemus, an eyewitness to Jesus on the cross. The crucifix reportedly arrived in Lucca in 782 by similarly miraculous means: Set adrift on a raft to escape Muslim marauders, the statue beached near a small Italian village, where the local bishop, following a vision, put the crucifix on a cart and let oxen take it wherever God meant it to rest. Since its arrival in Lucca, the Volto Santo has been a source of pride for the city, culminating in the September 13 festival in which the crucifix is paraded through town. Art historians think the carving, with its Byzantine and Indian influences, may have been a 12th-century copy of an 11th-century copy of a Syrian statue from the 8th century (whew!).

The cathedral's other highlight is the 1407 tomb of Ilaria Carretto Guinigi, a stunning 26-year-old woman whose beauty was immortalized in an unusually naturalistic manner (note the graceful flow of her robes) by sculptor Jacopo della

Nature's Cathedral

The Grotta del Vento (Cave of the Winds) ★ 🦘 (Loc. Fornovolasco; ☎ 0583-722053; www.grottadelvento.com; €6.50 for 1-hr. tour, €11 for 2 hr., and €15 for 3 hr., 20% discount for kids; Apr 1–Sept 30 daily 10am–6pm; Oct–Nov Sat–Sun; Dec–Apr Sun and public holidays), an hour's drive north from Lucca, will add a nice dash of variety to any Tuscan vacation (your kids especially will enjoy this set of caves). The stalactites and stalagmites are equal to any Gothic church spire, and the open caverns are as voluminous as the interior of a cathedral. In fact, ceilings of some rooms tower over 60m (200 ft.) above visitors, with every imaginable shape of protruding rock formations. For more wonders, there are winding underground rivers and reflective lakes and rooms with such appropriate names as "Giant's Abyss" and "The Hall of Wonders."

The caves drop about 135m (450 ft.) underground through more than 8km (5 miles) of passageways. But you don't have to be an experienced spelunker to enjoy a trip through them; the park has created tourist-friendly concrete pathways with guide rails along well-lit passages. Exploration is by guided tour only.

To get there, take the SSN12 Abetone/Brennero as far as Ponte a Moriano (8.5km/5¼ miles). Then cross the Serchio River and proceed along the main road, through the valley, as far as Gallicano (another 28km/17 miles). After passing Lake Trombacco, take the road for Fornovolasco at the 44km mark. Continuing uphill, cross another three valleys, and you've reached it.

Quercia. The small dog at her feet symbolizes fidelity. Unfortunately, the famous tomb has now been placed in a side room, where, like a peep show, you need to pay €2 to see her marble figure.

On the northern edge of the city is the **Church of San Frediano** ★ (Piazza S. Frediano; ☎ 0583-493627; free admission; 8:30am–noon and 3–5pm, opens 10:30am Sun and holidays) with a glittering 13th-century mosaic on its facade. An elaborate baptismal font (dismantled and hidden away in the 18th c. and only reassembled a few decades ago), and a magnificent fresco cycle by Amico Aspertini (1508–09) of the history of Lucca, are the other highlights of the church. But most fascinating to me is the mummified body of St. Zita inside a glass case in a side chapel. This 13th-century maid was caught smuggling bread out of her employer's house to feed beggars. To escape punishment for stealing, she told guards that she only had flowers hidden in her apron, and when the guards pulled her apron aside, the bread had miraculously turned into roses. (It's unclear whether the beggars then got stuck eating the plants, but in any case Zita was sainted for her lifetime of effort on behalf of the poor.) The body of this patron saint of maids and ladies-in-waiting is paraded through town on her feast day of April 26. The church itself gets its name from the wandering Irish abbot who helped to develop Christianity in Lucca in the 6th century. Frediano is buried beneath the altar.

The archangel Michael stands in winged glory on top of the spectacular facade of **San Michele in Foro** ★ (Piazza S. Michele; ☎ 0583-48459; free admission; daily 7:30am–noon and 3–6pm). Exquisitely detailed columns of every size, shape, and color bedeck the four-tiered facade in a composition that echoes that of the Duomo in Pisa (this "column-mania" was characteristic of the area in the 12th–13th c.). Note how the facade extends beyond the church's roof, a result of ambition outstripping funding. The interior can't quite match the outside, but it does have a fancy organ decorated with fleur-de-lis, and a nice Filippo Lippi painting at the far end of the right side of the church. The "Foro" part of the church's name comes from the fact that it was built on the original site of a Roman forum. The square outside is a prime spot for people-watching at all hours of the day.

SHOPPING

The purchases you'll make here are arguably as good as those in Florence. Lucca offers a wealth of shopping opportunities along Via Fallungo and Via Santa Lucia: Olive oil, jewelry, chocolates, perfumes, and wines are among the Luccan treats. A few worth mentioning:

- A branch of the historical **Officina Profumo di Santa Maria Novella** (Via Vittorio Veneto, 29; ☎ 0583-490850; www.smnovella.it) sells soaps, colognes, and "Vinegar of the Seven Thieves," a cure for "fainting-fits."
- Visit **Cioccolateria Canoparoli** (Via San Paolino, 96; ☎ 0583-53456) for some of the best chocolate in the region.
- **Lucca in Tavola** (Via San Paolino, 130; ☎ 0583-581002) has a wide selection of famous regional olive oils.
- **Carli Pietro** (Via Fillungo, 95; ☎ 0583-491119) is a jewelry store-cum-museum, with fresco-covered walls and jewel-filled display cases. You may not be able to afford anything here, but it offers exquisite window-shopping.
- The **English Bookshop** (Borgo Giannotti, 493; ☎ 0583-4696446) can be a good spot to buy detailed area guides, or to pick up some summer reading.

NIGHTLIFE

A city that was home to Paganini, Puccini, Boccherini, and Catalani and others would obviously be a good place to hear some classical music or attend the opera. The **Teatro Del Giglio** (Piazza del Giglio, 13/15; ☎ 0583-467521; www.teatrodel giglio.it) is where Rossini premiered *William Tell* in 1831. Today it has a full opera season running from October to April. Tickets range from €25 to €40. Aside from opera, the theater also hosts plays and dance performances.

For more music, the University of Cincinnati College Conservatory of Music, of all places, coordinates the Opera Theater and Music Festival of Lucca in tandem with its study-abroad program. Visitors can watch rehearsals and outdoor performances around town from June to July. Check www.ccmoperalucca.org or the tourist office for details.

PISA

Even a lifetime of seeing images of the famous Leaning Tower of Pisa doesn't quite prepare you for your first sight of this tourist icon. Up close it looks like a giant white cylinder of a spaceship that has crash-landed at an awkward angle in a green field and discharged an army of mimes. People of all sizes, ages, and races, stand in front of the tower in goofy positions. Some attempt the "Look, ma, I'm holding up the tower" pose, with outstretched arms "catching" the leaning tower in the background. Others go for the "push," the "foot save," or the "Ow, it just fell on my head" pantomime.

The mob of tourists, the hot dog stands, the aggressive souvenir peddlers—these all point to the fact that Pisa is one of Italy's oldest tourist traps. But you should still go here, not only to see the Leaning Tower but also to tour the four lesser known, though equally impressive, monuments in the appropriately named Campo di Miracoli, the Field of Miracles.

That being said, the city doesn't hold much beyond this central area to attract visitors. I'd advise a day trip here while staying in Florence (about 1 hr. away) or Lucca (30 min. away), or just passing through on a Tuscan excursion. But on your way out, try to stop at the Passigia factory, birthplace of the Vespa, just for proof that Italians really can design stuff the right way.

A BRIEF HISTORY OF PISA

Pisa was once a major economic, political, cultural, and sea-faring power. And then it experienced a string of disasters: Its harbor and river silted up, it lost a couple of wars, the economy tanked, and all it had left was a tower that couldn't stand straight and a few major churches. (One of those churches was firebombed in World War II, so you really have to feel a little sorry for this faded empire.) Nowadays Pisa is a lively university town and industrial center, with an international airport and transport hubs, but it's still just a shadow of its former self.

In its heyday in the 1100s, Pisa was the terror of Tuscany. It conquered large areas of the region, including Lucca, in a series of brutal wars. Pisa was a major naval power as well, controlling Mediterranean sea lanes and expanding its empire to Corsica and Sardinia. But following a disastrous naval battle with Genoa in 1284, its sea power began to wane, and with it much of its military might.

However, Pisa's years of prosperity lasted long enough to fund the construction of the major edifices in the city during the 12th and 13th centuries, including the Leaning Tower, the Camposanto, the Baptistery, and the Duomo. The Pisan Romanesque style of architecture, with its colorful columns, striped decor, and repeating arches, permeates Tuscany, and can be seen in Lucca's St. Michele Church, as well as in churches in Siena and even those in archrival Florence.

> ❝The group of buildings clustered on and about this verdant carpet comprising the Tower, the Baptistery, the Cathedral and the Church of the Campo Santo is perhaps the most remarkable and beautiful in the whole world.❞
>
> —Charles Dickens, *Pictures from Italy*, 1846

Florentine armies conquered Pisa in 1406 and turned it into a tribute state. Once the rivers became silted, Pisa literally became a backwater town, losing what remaining significance it had as a port to supply mighty Florence with goods.

Pisa

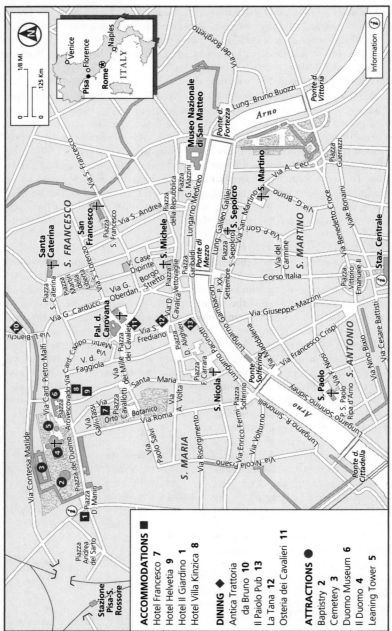

ACCOMMODATIONS ■
Hotel Francesco **7**
Hotel Helvetia **9**
Hotel Il Giardino **1**
Hotel Villa Kinzica **8**

DINING ◆
Antica Trattoria
da Bruno **10**
Il Paiolo Pub **13**
La Tana **12**
Osteria dei Cavalieri **11**

ATTRACTIONS ●
Baptistry **2**
Cemetery **3**
Duomo Museum **6**
Il Duomo **4**
Leaning Tower **5**

By the time of the first wave of tourists to Italy in the 1800s, Pisa was a desolate, half-empty city teeming with beggars camped around its monuments. But the city's university, founded in 1343, remained open during all those years, and has maintained Pisa's reputation as a progressive, activist city. Native son Galileo Galilei was one of those over-educated troublemakers; at the Leaning Tower and the Duomo, he conducted experiments disproving Church-endorsed "science," and, in turn, got in trouble with the authorities.

LAY OF THE LAND

Pisa's nearby **Galileo Galilei Airport** (☎ 050-500707; www.pisa-airport.com) receives many international as well as regional flights. A 5-minute, €1 train trip or an €8 cab ride is all you need to get to the center of the city.

Pisa is a convenient 90-minute **train** ride from Florence. Over 40 trains a day connect the two cities on a high-speed rail line. Rome is a 3-hour train journey. Lucca is a half-hour commute, with trains on that line stopping at the San Rossore station, closer to the Campo di Miracole than Pisa's Centrale station, where most of the inter-city trains stop. The Centrale station is nearly a mile away from the Campo, so consider a taxi (about €6) or a bus (no. 1, 3, or 11).

It's about a 1-hour **drive** (depending on traffic) to Pisa from Florence via the autostrada. Lucca is a half-hour trip via the ASS12. Parking in the historical district is restricted, but meters can be found just outside the walls for €.50 to €1 per hour, or at nearby lots for the same rates. Hotels will often let visitors use (either free or for a charge) an overnight permit which allows for street parking in the historical district.

Pisa's **main tourist office** (Piazza Duomo, 1; ☎ 050-560464; www.pisa.turismo. toscana.it; daily 9:30am–5pm) is on the north side of the Campo, next to the Leaning Tower ticket office. It has some limited information and pamphlets, but on the whole it isn't too helpful. The lockers for the Tower (no bags allowed) are behind the ticket counter, so the place can get pretty packed with people either waiting for their tour, or coming back to grab their stuff. Another tourist office with similar brochures is at the train station.

ACCOMMODATIONS IN PISA

It's unlikely that you'll spend the night here, but if you do, consider the following places.

€–€€   If you must lodge in Pisa, a good cheap option is the **Hotel Helvetica** ★ (Via Don G. Boschi, 31; ☎ 050-553084). Its very simple rooms begin at a mere €35 for a single with shared bathroom, €62 for a double with bathroom, and €100 for a four-person room; all rooms contain overhead fans and TVs. For an additional €5, you can enjoy breakfast in a colorfully painted side room, and then check out the hotel's small interior garden, which has a Thai temple.

€€–€€€   Just outside the walls, behind the Baptistery, is the pleasant **Hotel Il Giardino** ★ 🅺 (Via della Cavallerizza, 12; ☎ 050-562101; www.pisaonline.it/ Giardino). This conveniently located three-story building contains 16 basic but clean rooms; doubles range from €80 to €115, while one four-bed room can be had for €110 most times of the year. The hotel has a nice terrace for breakfasting in summer.

€€€   A flurry of midrange hotels line the streets around the Campo. A couple of the nicer ones are **Hotel Francesco** ★ (Via Santa Maria, 129; ☎ 050-554109; www.hotelfrancesco.com) and **Hotel Villa Kinzica** ★ (Piazza Arcivescovado, 2; ☎ 050-560419; www.hotelvillakinzica.it). Both have air-conditioning in all rooms, with doubles averaging €100. The Francesco features a terrace with lovely views, a good lounge with Internet access, and an airy breakfast area. The Kinzica has more upscale rooms and offers free street parking (a €5 charge at the Francesco).

DINING FOR ALL TASTES
It's doubtful you'll stay here for dinner, but if you do, consider the following options.

€   Enjoy a high-quality meal at **La Tana** ★ 🈁 (Via San Frediano, 6; ☎ 050-580540; closed Aug). This locals' dominated pizzeria serves tasty *primi* averaging about €3.50, *secondi* at €5, and pizzas from €4.50 to €8. Large booths around long wooden tables encourage family dining in this friendly, noisy establishment.

€   For some late-night eats and a beer, try **Il Paiolo Pub** ★ (Via Curtatone e Montanara, 9; ☎ 050-42528). A popular student hangout, it stays open until 2am, with the kitchen serving until midnight. Simple but fresh *primi* average €5; *secondi* are in the €7.25 range. Beer is a reasonable €3.60 for a large glass.

€€   A homey restaurant featuring tasty Pisan specialties, the **Antica Trattoria da Bruno** ★ (Via Luigi Bianchi, 12, at the Porta a Lucca gate; ☎ 050-560818; www.pisaonline.it/trattoriadabruno; closed Tues; reservations required) is always packed. Pots and pans hang from the ceiling, the walls are cluttered with family pictures, and the atmosphere is chaotic and friendly. Try the excellent Pisan pasta with garbanzo beans *(ceci)* or the *baccalà con porri*, a salt cod with tomatoes and leeks, which tastes much better than it sounds. *Primi* run from €8 to €10, *secondi* from €10 to €15.

€€–€€€   The kitchen caters to people of all tastes at **Osteria dei Cavalieri** (Via San Frediano, 16, near Piazza dei Cavalieri; ☎ 050-580858; Mon–Sat, closed Aug). Three set menus are offered here, starting at €17. The vegetarian meals are highly recommended, as are the fish and game dishes. They do try to move people in and out quickly, but that means the service is fairly swift. English-speaking waiters can help with the menu. *Primi* cost from €7 to €11, *secondi* from €11 to €15.

WHY YOU'RE HERE: THE TOP SIGHTS & ATTRACTIONS
The **Campo di Miracoli** is where you want to be: This geometrically perfect, bright green "field of dreams" has the big four attractions of the Leaning Tower, the Baptistery, the Camposanto, and the Cathedral. Locals refer to the area more prosaically as Piazza del Duomo. The park is easy to find, what with that leaning tower in the middle of it.

Obviously, you've come here primarily to see the **Campanile (Leaning Tower)** ★★★ (☎ 050-560547; www.opapisa.it; €15, €2 reservation fee; Apr to early June 9:30am–8:30pm, mid-June to Sept 9:30am–11pm, Oct 9:30am–7pm, Nov–Feb 9:30am–5pm, Mar 9:30am–6pm). The experience of climbing the 300 skewed steps to the 56m-tall (185-ft.) summit is slightly claustrophobic and tiring, but not undoable. Millions of tourists have created curved grooves in the middle of each step, making the marble stairs smooth and slippery—flip-flops are not recommended. Walking up the stairs gives you the feeling of being on a listing ship at sea. You almost hesitate to touch the downward-facing wall for fear of helping topple the tower.

Guards strictly enforce the 30-minute limit of the site, herding visitors up the steps and allowing them only a couple of intermediate stops on balconies for views. Once you're on top, the countdown begins: When your time is up, you'll be brought down again. To be fair, the time allotted is more than enough for everyone but die-hard engineering or architectural students.

The views from the top of the tower—taking in the old city and the mountains in the distance—are spectacular. Given the 4.5m (15-ft.) slant from the perpendicular, it's hard to believe this massive tower is secure as you peek over the edge. But it's actually more solid than ever (see "She Leans Me, She Leans Me Not—the Tipping Tower," below).

So is it worth the €15 to €17? I'd say just barely. It's fun to think of hundreds of years of tourists climbing the same steps, fascinated to lean over the same balcony from which Galileo allegedly dropped his experimental weights to prove his principles of gravity. And you'll be able to look at pictures of the Leaning Tower for the rest of your life and say, "Yeah, I was up there." But if you're on a tight budget, you shouldn't skip a meal (or a couple of meals) to get to the top. The most impressive part of the Tower is really just seeing the giant thing stuck into the ground at its goofy angle.

If you want to make the climb, it's best to reserve in advance. Tickets need to be ordered at least 15 days ahead, at www.opapisa.it, which adds a €2 fee to the €15 ticket price. If you're not able to plan that far in advance, it's often possible to show up and purchase a ticket on the same day, but arrive before 9am or else

---

Buying Tickets to the Sites of the Campo di Miracoli

If you plan to enter more than two sites, you'll save money by purchasing a single ticket that covers every major tourist attraction except the biggie, the Leaning Tower. Unfortunately, the way the tickets are priced is needlessly complicated. For entry to either the Baptistery, the Camposanto, or the Museo Dell'Opera, the price is €5 each. For entry to two of the above sites, the charge is €6, for three sites €8, and all four (adding in the Cathedral) €10. Tickets can be purchased at the office at the north end of the piazza. For more information, see **www.opapisa.it**.

Note: As of early 2006, the Sinopie Museum (with sketches of the Camposanto murals) is closed indefinitely; in the future it will be linked in some typically convoluted fashion to the rest of the group.

most (if not all) of the tour times will be sold out. The 11pm closing time does allow for increased tour times for last-minute planners, but obviously your views won't be as spectacular.

Bags are absolutely not allowed on the climb up the tower, and must be left at the hectic tourist office north of the tower. Children under 8 also aren't allowed up the tower (though it is not recommended to leave them in the lockers). Arrive at the ticket office an hour before your reserved tour time to pick up your ticket. And woe betide you if you've forgotten your receipt, as it nearly takes a papal decree to get the thing reissued.

The Leaning Tower overshadows (literally) the other fine sites in the Campo. But you should visit the **Cathedral** ★★ (☎ 050-560547; www.opapisa.it; €2 or as part of cumulative campo ticket; Apr–Sept 10am–8pm, Mar and Oct 10am–7pm, Nov–Feb 10am–1pm and 3–7pm), a construction (completed 1064–1275) that displays all the famous characteristics of Pisan architecture, from the multicolored, multishaped columns of the facade to the Moorish-influenced marble tiling (black and white stripes around the building). The cavernous interior is nearly 120m (400 ft.) from end to end, with over 60 columns supporting the building's weight. Notable attractions are Giovanni Pisano's pulpit (a 20th-c. reconstruction of the fire-damaged original), Cimabue's 13th-century Christ mosaic, and the 16th-century lamp hanging by the altar. This is the light that supposedly intrigued Galileo during a boring sermon one day. The lamp was bumped and began to swing side to side, and Mr. Galilei came up with his formulas describing pendulum movement.

The north side of the piazza has the giant **Camposanto (Cemetery)** ★★ (☎ 050-560547; www.opapisa.it; €5 or as part of cumulative ticket; Apr–Sept 8am–8pm; Mar and Oct 9am–6pm; Nov–Feb 10am–5pm). Designed by Giovanni di Simone in 1278 to contain soil brought back by crusaders from Cavalry, the site of Jesus' crucifixion, it was the chic place for noble burials. To make their final resting places even more impressive, locals appropriated the sarcophagi of ancient Romans. Now the long hallways are filled with rows of these tombs, while dozens of skull-and-crossbones memorial blocks line the floors. The walls of the building were covered in extensive frescoes until 1944, when a massive fire (from either Allied bombing or an unattributed "grenade") torched the structure. Photos from that time are on display in a northern room. Thankfully, one set of frescoes survived, including the series *Triumph of Death, Last Judgment,* and the *Inferno.* These soaring pieces depict aerial battles between flying angels and devils, a giant Godzilla-like devil in hell, and tough angels at the Last Judgment knocking people into line. Also note the nobles on horseback holding their noses in the *Triumph of Death* as they confront three rotting corpses in the ground—the fresco was done in 1398, only months after the Black Death had run rampant through Tuscany.

The giant orange-squeezer-shaped **Baptistery** ★ (admission and hours same as for Camposanto) dominates the eastern side of the piazza. Its exterior matches that of the Cathedral, with blank arches topped by myriad columns supporting further levels with their own decoration and statuary. The structure, at nearly 105m (350 ft.) around, is the largest of its kind in Italy. Construction began in 1152, and improvements continued through the 1300s. Inside, the Baptistery is

She Leans Me, She Leans Me Not— the Tipping Tower

It seemed like a good idea at the time. Construction began on a perfectly straight tower in 1173. For a dozen years, as three levels were completed, you can imagine the conversations: "Call me crazy, but I think the thing is leaning . . ." By 1185, people had concluded that the tower was definitely tilting, and they halted construction to ponder the matter.

In 1275, after nearly a century of pondering, architects decided that rather than try to correct the tilt, they would build the next levels tilted in the opposite direction. This goofy solution now gives the tower a slight banana shape. By 1284, construction was halted again. In 1360, the belfry was added, of course leaning in yet another direction.

The 14,500-ton marble structure continued to tilt about a millimeter a year, sinking into the soft soil around it. In 1838, engineers dug a basin around the entrance because the doors had completely settled underground. They also poked around the foundations, pumping out groundwater (which only served to accelerate the tilt).

By 1990, following the fatal collapse of a nearby church tower, authorities decided to close the Leaning Tower and deal with the issue. The top was leaning 4.5m (15 ft.) from the vertical, and with nearly a million visitors a year, they didn't want a disaster. So engineers placed 900 tons of lead weights at the base, opposite the tilt, to even out the pressures. They then wrapped huge steel hoops around the lower level to support the stressed marble. Then engineers drilled the northern grounds to remove silt and earth to counteract the tilt and solidify the earth below. Locals worried that the engineers would do too much, and fix the tilt altogether, killing their tourist industry.

Pisa reopened its tower at the end of 2001 after 11 years and over $30 million of investment. The result? The tower only leans as much as it did in 1838, but it should remain that way for the next 300 years.

sparely decorated, with the waiflike St. John statue in the center of the room. A carved wooden Jesus, in an odd pose, hangs from the altar. The other notable quality of the Baptistery is its echoing acoustics, which you can test with an "accidental" cough or two while standing in the center of the room.

Unknown to most visitors is the fact that most of the outdoor statues on the piazza buildings are reproductions. You can see the originals up close and personal at the **Museo Dell'Opera** ★ 🧒 (admission and hours same as for Camposanto). The museum has a kid-friendly video kiosk with interactive displays about the statues and monuments outside. You can zoom in and out, and spin the displays for 360-degree views—a cheap way to duplicate the tower-top perspective. Each room also has English descriptions of the works of art and artifacts. The items include relics and tapestries from the piazza's monuments, as well as trophies brought back from the Crusades. The building also has a good "poor man's" view of the piazza from its upper balcony.

THE OTHER PISA

Ancient Italy may have been obsessed with art and architecture, but as anyone who's driven its highways knows, modern Italians are obsessed with speed. That yen for everything shiny, metallic, and turbo-charged is on display at **Museo Piaggio** (Viale Rinaldo Piaggio, 7, Pontedera; ☎ 0587-27171; www.museopiaggio. it; free admission; Wed–Sat 10am–6pm). Here you have a factory museum that tells the story of Rinaldo Piaggio, who launched his engineering business in 1888, at the age of 20, and soon rose to the forefront of Italian industry, going from ship fittings to railway cars and steam ships, and finally in 1941 to that most-Italian form of transportation, the Vespa. (Be sure to check out the Vespa Alpha designed for a 1960s spy movie. In the film at least, it could be converted into a submarine and a helicopter, which are pretty good dealer options for a scooter.) Along with the many Vespe, there's an impressive collection of Gilera motorcycles and Piaggio ships and planes.

SAN GIMIGNANO

San Gimignano once had a skyline that boasted over 70 towers, with competing business, military, and family interests controlling trade routes through the Tuscan plains. Only 14 towers remain, but they still give this small town a unique and ancient urban character.

You can easily cover the city in a day trip from Florence or Siena. And since so many tourists do so, San Gimignano has become perhaps Tuscany's greatest tourist trap—each day hundreds of visitors are stuck for hours within the town walls waiting for the call back to their bus in a remote parking lot. The church has an electric turnstile for reading tickets, the main square hosts a tasteless torture museum, and streets are jammed with shops filled with every mass-produced trinket imaginable.

And yet San Gimignano keeps some of its 1,000-year-old character despite the tourist influx (especially for those who overnight here and see the city without its throngs of visitors). Many family-run restaurants in town serve traditional Tuscan specialties with San Gimignano–area wines. The summit of Torre Grossa offers views of Tuscan farmlands unchanged for centuries. The less-touristed Sant'Agostino allows visitors to examine its frescoes without a prepaid ticket. And old men still assemble in the shade of the arches of Piazza del Duomo to have their breakfast and share their opinions on the state of the world.

A BRIEF HISTORY OF SAN GIMIGNANO

San Gimignano takes its name from the bishop who is said to have saved the town from Attila the Hun in the 5th century by clever diplomacy. By the 10th century, San Gimignano (the town) consisted of a fortified castle surrounded by a small village. It wasn't until the 12th and 13th centuries that the towers and town walls began to appear in great height and quantity.

As with many Italian hill towns, warring factions within San Gimignano battled each other through the 12th and 13th centuries in continuous power struggles. The towers served not only as defense fortifications but as symbols of prestige—and even as a means for drying the dyed textiles from which many of the families built their wealth. The Black Death of 1348 not only cut the town's population in half, but it also wiped out the pilgrim and merchant trade from which San Gimignano made much of its money. Florence conquered the weakened city in 1353 so easily that the conquerors didn't bother destroying the defensive towers as they did in many other cities. A couple of more visits by the Black Death, in 1464 and 1631, ensured that San Gimignano never quite got on its feet again, leaving it a backwater city of crumbling towers and poor villagers for hundreds of years.

It wasn't until the mid–20th century that tourism revitalized the town. Today, San Gimignano has leveraged its lively tourist trade into a city filled with sightseeing, dining, and festivals throughout the year. It's definitely worth at least an afternoon visit to walk the winding medieval streets under the watch of the last of the towers.

LAY OF THE LAND

Probably the easiest way to reach San Gimignano is by an **organized tour** from Florence or Siena. You won't have to deal with parking (which is impossible), and you can drink as much as you want with your meals. Virtually every tour operator in Florence has some kind of San Gimignano trip, and you should be able to easily book one at your hotel or a travel agency near your hotel.

If you decide to **drive** here for an overnight visit (highly recommended), you'll find San Gimignano is just 13km (8 miles) from the Poggibonsi exit on the autostrada/SS2 between Florence and Siena, about 48km (30 miles) from Florence, 32km (20 miles) from Siena. Parking is not allowed within San Gimignano's city walls, but if you have a hotel in town, you can drive your car to the door (very carefully—the city has some of the narrowest streets in Tuscany) to unload your luggage. Parking is available at a number of pay lots outside of town, or for free along the roads approaching the walls.

While San Gimignano isn't on a **train** line, many buses make the 10-minute trip from the station in Poggibonsi into town. Trains take from 30 to 45 minutes from Siena, and about an hour from Florence.

San Gimignano has an extremely helpful **tourist office** (Piazza Duomo, 1; ☎ 0577-940008; www.sangimignano.com; Mar–Oct 9am–1pm and 3–7pm, Nov–Feb 9am–1pm and 2–6pm), which carries lists of local apartment rentals, wine tours, and events. It also offers a worthwhile audioguide city tour for €5. The self-paced program gives visitors an extensive historical and architectural guide of the city from more than 40 viewpoints, covering everything from the usual tourist spots to deserted alleyways. The whole program takes about 2 hours.

ACCOMMODATIONS, BOTH STANDARD & NOT

€€–€€€€ Renting an apartment gives you a terrific base from which to explore both the town and the surrounding countryside. Apartment rentals, some weekly, are available at the tourist information center, or you can book one of the spiffy apartments managed by a local woman, who is known simply as Carla, and her English-speaking son Francesco. Through **Busini Rossi Carla** ★★ 🧒 (Via Cellole, 81; ☎ 0577-941268; www.rossicarla.it), Carla offers four apartments, starting at €70 per night (€450 per week). My favorite is the Tortoli Palace Apartment on the upper level of an old tower with an eye-popping view of the Piazza della Cisterna. It offers a full kitchen, dining room, comfortable bedrooms (containing up to five beds), and views of the countryside and main square (€160 per day, or €1,040 per week). They also have a newly restored farmhouse called Podere Ponte a Nappo, just outside San Gimignano, with two apartments, two bedrooms, free parking, and even a barbecue pit. Prices range from €450 to €650 per week for two people in an apartment, up to €1,010 for six jammed into the one-bedroom apartment with loft. Daily rentals are also available. Part of the fun of staying here is meeting Carla, who will often treat guests to a glass of *vino* on the square after they settle into their temporary homes. Book far in advance, as these apartments get many return renters, year after year.

€   For those on a tight budget, a good deal can be had with the friendly nuns at the **Foresteria del Monastero San Girolamo** ★ 🧒 (Via Folgore, 32, just behind Porta San Jacobo; ☎ 0577-940573). For €27, you'll get breakfast and a bed in one of the nine basic but clean rooms. Most rooms have from three to four beds. They generally don't place random people together, so a family has a good chance of snagging an empty four-bed room. Free parking is available in a dirt lot across the street.

€€   My second choice for hotel digs would be the **Hotel Bel Soggiorno** (Via San Giovanni, 91; ☎ 0577-940375; www.hotelbelsoggiorno.it), perched at the top of the southern walls of the city. The junior suites (€120 per night) with balcony views of the countryside are the top choices here, but there are also nice standard doubles with a street view for €95, and doubles with a terrace and country view for €110. Rooms are modern and spotless, if somewhat lacking in character. The restaurant serves dinner and boasts fine panoramic views as well.

€€–€€€   The choice hotel in the central Piazza della Cisterna is the **Hotel Leon Bianco** ★ (Piazza della Cisterna; ☎ 0577-941294; www.leonbianco.com). This crisp and clean refurbished 11th-century *palazzo* has 25 inviting rooms with modern fixtures combined with stone arches, wood-beamed ceilings, and terra-cotta tiles. Doubles with a view run from €105 to €135 in the high season, while a single without a view can be had for €60. The hotel even has a mini fitness center, a pleasant deck for breakfast, and a Jacuzzi in a random niche. The helpful staff can offer tourism tips for the area.

DINING FOR ALL TASTES

€–€€€   A brasserie, set in an actual castle, complete with rib-vaulted ceilings and a terrace with great countryside view, the **Ristorante La Griglia** ★ (Via San Matteo, 34/36; ☎ 0577-940005; www.sangimignano.com/lagriglia) is a lovely place to dine. Its lively bar is about the only thing going for nightlife in this quiet town, so dine late and then stay to socialize. If you want to avoid the *coperto* charge, start and end your evening at the tables around the bar, ordering from the brasserie menu: Pizzas and pastas are €6 to €8; a half chicken, roasted, at €10 is the most expensive item on the *secondi* menu. The interior restaurant offers more gourmet fare with wild boar and truffle-covered pastas (*primi* €10–€17, *secondi* about €15, plus service charge).

€€ Very traditional Tuscan fare, in a medieval-barrel vaulted room, is paired with '80s pop music and contemporary paintings at the confused but still charming **Osteria delle Catene** ★ (Via Mainardi, 18; ☎ 0577-941966; closed Wed). Try the sausage with stewed tomatoes and beans *(salsicce con fagioli all'uccelletto)* or penne covered in a cheese and cream sauce *(penne al porro);* both are delightful. Or go for a prix-fixe meal for €12, €20, or €32 (not including wine). Even the lower-priced fixed-price option will give you a good combination of flavors, accompanied by local cheeses, a light pasta, and a pastry dessert. If you choose to go a la carte, *primi* range from €8 to €10, *secondi* from €12 to €14.

€€€ A traditional Tuscan meal and setting can be found at **Ristorante il Pino** ★ (Via Cellolese, 4; ☎ 0577-940415; closed Thurs). Since 1929, this friendly restaurant has been serving regional specialties at candlelit tables underneath brick-arched rooms tucked into a medieval building. *Primi* range from €10 to €13, *secondi* from €14 to €16. Try the cannelloni with goat milk cheese and pepper sauce (€13) or the roasted duck with truffles and potato cake (€14). Happily, *coperto* and service charge are included in the prices. Upstairs are rooms at €55 a night. (The rooms are actually quite nice for the price, with whitewashed walls and wood-beamed ceilings.)

WHY YOU'RE HERE: THE TOP SIGHTS & ATTRACTIONS

The main attraction is the town itself, and especially the towers poking above the winding medieval streets of this hilltop city. The Piazza della Cisterna, in particular, is a lovely place in which to linger, its central 13th-century well framed by imposing stone buildings unchanged since the Renaissance. You'll also want to walk through the gardens around the Rocca, the old fortress from the 1350s, and climb the ramparts for a free view of the countryside to the west.

The **Torre Grossa** ★★ (Piazza del Duomo; ☎ 0577-990312; €5 joint admission to Torre and Museo Civico; 9:30am–7pm, Nov–Feb open until 9:30pm), as the name implies, is the biggest tower left standing in San Gimignano (35m/115 ft. tall) and the only one you can climb. The view over the countryside is stunning, as is the bird's-eye perspective over the town—you'll see into private gardens usually hidden by compound walls, and far off into the distant countryside blanketed with vineyards. The 220 steps to the top of the tower are split at several wide landings, to allow climbers a spot to rest. Connected to the tower is the city art gallery **Museo Civico/Pinacoteca** ★★, which has a small but interesting collection of artwork in its four rooms, including the emblematic 14th-century painting of San Gimignano holding the eponymous city in his arms. The most entertaining part of the museum is the faded series of wedding frescoes on the walls of the small room off the side of the stairway; they depict a hapless husband first being ridden and whipped by his wife, then sitting naked (aside from his hat) in a bath with her, and finally in bed with her. She's turned away from him in full "I have a headache" mode while he sulks on the other edge of bed, still wearing his red hat.

You'll want to visit the amazing frescoes of **The Collegiata** ★★ (Piazza Duomo; ☎ 0577-940316; €3.50; Apr–Oct 9:30am–7:10pm, in winter closes 4:40pm, Sun and holidays opens 12:30pm) as early or as late in the day as possible because the combination of surly guards, mobs of visitors, and a general carnival sideshow atmosphere can make the experience less than enjoyable if you hit it at the wrong time. (I never thought I'd visit a church with automated turnstiles and magnetic tickets!) The church itself (formerly a cathedral, but no bishop resides here now) was begun in the 11th century, and took its present form in the 15th century. Among the many great masters who added frescoes to its densely decorated walls were Lippo Memmi (the 22 New Testament scenes along the right wall, including the moving crucifixion); Taddeo Di Bartolo, who added the frightening *Last Judgment* (look for the gluttons and the lustful suffering diabolical tortures); and Bartolo di Freddi (the 26 Old Testament scenes). Pop €1 into the AV kiosk toward the entrance to hear a decent summary of the scenes depicted on the panels. Best of all is the elaborate Cappella di Santa Fina (at the far end of the right aisle) with exquisite frescoes from Renaissance superstar Domenico Ghirlandiao. He tells the story of Santa Fina, San Gimignano's other patron saint, a young 13th-century woman who lay for 6 years on a plank in one position to better understand the sufferings of Jesus. St. Gregory eventually came to claim her and bring her to heaven, and as she died the plank filled with flowers (a yearly festival for the saint takes place here on Mar 12, a time when the towers of San Gimignano are blooming with pansies).

The serene, undervisited **Sant'Agostino Church** ★ (free admission; 7am–noon and 3–7pm, Jan–Mar closes 6pm), at the north edge of San Gimignano, has a spare exterior but an elaborate interior combining over-the-top 18th-century rococo decor with a series of 15th-century frescoes. The best of the bunch is near the high altar. Benozzo Gozzoli painted this 17-panel depiction of the life of St. Augustine in the 1460s. Note the panel toward the lower left, which shows the 4th-century saint having a bad day at school and getting whacked by the teacher. The background in most of the scenes vividly illustrates typical daily life and city scenes in Renaissance Tuscany. Also check out the Chapel of San Bartolo near the side door of the church. The chapel contains the remains of this 13th-century saint. Reliefs on the altar depict the miracles of his life, including the re-attaching of his toes, which had fallen off as a result of the leprosy he contracted while ministering to the poor.

Privately run museums in town include a **Leonardo Museum** 🧒 (Mostre di Leonardo, Via Quercecchio, 26; ☎ 0577-907015; www.mostredileonardo.com; €6; 11am–7pm), which is identical to the one in Florence (p. 128) with models of da Vinci's inventions. It's a much more worthwhile stop than the repugnant Torture Museum on the Piazza della Cisterna, which (like the Leonardo museums) has lately been franchised into most tourist cities in Tuscany. While the display of exotic torture devices does make an important point about the savagery of medieval and Renaissance rulers, the displays are designed more to titillate than to educate, and are about as classy as porno movies at a memorial to rape victims.

> ## Pros & Cons of San Gimignano's Combination Tickets
>
> The Civic Combo of San Gimignano offers a €7.50 combination ticket good for admission to the following city-managed sites:
>
> * Torre Grosso
> * Pinacoteca Art Gallery in the Palazzo Pubblico
> * Archaeological museum (Museo Archeologico)
> * Spezeria Santa Fina (a refurbished Renaissance pharmacy)
> * Museo Ornitologico (museum of stuffed birds)
> * Modern Art Gallery "Raffaele De Grada"
>
> Unless you have a specialized interest in archaeology, pharmacies, or birds, the last four museums aren't likely to excite you. Better to spend your time exploring the streets, the walls, or the surrounding countryside.

Give it a pass. If you need a torture fix, the art museum displays dozens of paintings of bloody martyrdoms.

CHIANTI COUNTRY

When people envision typical Italian countryside, they usually conjure up visions of Chianti: vine-covered rolling hills dotted with castles and Renaissance villas, and populated by family-owned wineries, rustic *agriturismo* vacation spots, and hill tops frozen in time. Although busloads of tourists and wealthy transplants from Milan, Rome, and overseas have been slowly transforming—some would say destroying—the character of the region for the past few decades, the spirit of Chianti has not been entirely diluted. Smaller towns still have traditional market days and family-run restaurants offering local specialties, and not every winery has been incorporated into an international conglomerate. You'll want to see this region sooner rather than later, though; in certain ways it's being loved to death, and you want to visit before much more changes.

The 168 sq. km (65 sq. miles) of Chianti Country fill the area between Florence and Siena, sandwiched between the A1 autostrada and the SS2. The famed "Chianti Road" (SP222) winds and weaves through the middle of Chianti. You can explore the region on day trips from Florence and Siena, or stay around one of the smaller Chianti towns, such as Greve in Chianti, Castellina, Radda, or Gaiole in Chianti. You can casually drop in on smaller wineries you discover on the road, or make reservations for visits to some of the larger ones, paying upward of €30 for a tour, tasting, and snacks.

A BRIEF HISTORY OF CHIANTI

As usual, the Etruscans got here first. Legions of conquering Romans, Lombards, and Goths passed through the hilly region until it stabilized under the alternating control of Florence and Siena, beginning in the 1200s.

Chianti Country

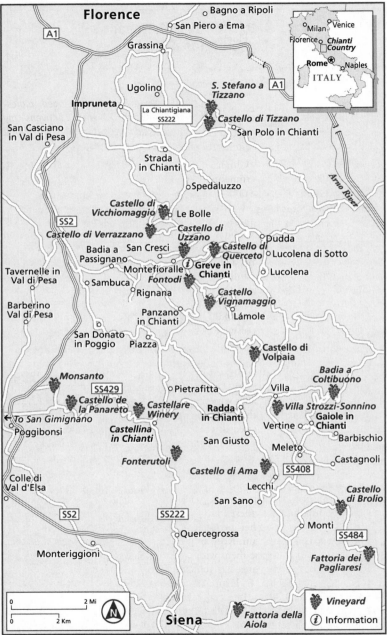

Florence

Bagno a Ripoli
San Piero a Ema

A1

Grassina

Ugolino

S. Stefano a Tizzano

Impruneta

La Chiantigiana SS222

A1

Castello di Tizzano
San Polo in Chianti

San Casciano in Val di Pesa

Strada in Chianti

Arno River

Spedaluzzo

Castello di Vicchiomaggio

Le Bolle

SS2

Castello di Verrazzano

Castello di Uzzano

Badia a Passignano

San Cresci

Dudda

Castello di Querceto

Lucolena di Sotto

Tavernelle in Val di Pesa

Montefioralle

Greve in Chianti

Lucolena

Fontodi

Sambuca

Rignana

Castello Vignamaggio

Barberino Val di Pesa

Panzano in Chianti

Lámole

San Donato in Poggio

Piazza

Castello di Volpaia

Monsanto

SS429

Pietrafitta

Villa

Badia a Coltibuono

Castello de la Panareto

Castellare Winery

Radda in Chianti

Villa Strozzi-Sonnino

To San Gimignano

Poggibonsi

Castellina in Chianti

Vertine

Gaiole in Chianti

Barbischio

San Giusto

Meleto

Castagnoli

Fonterutoli

Castello di Ama

SS408

Colle di Val d'Elsa

Lecchi

Castello di Brolio

San Sano

SS2

SS222

Monti

SS484

Quercegrossa

Monteriggioni

Fattoria dei Pagliaresi

0   2 Mi

0   2 Km

N

Siena

Fattoria della Aiola

Vineyard

i Information

Italy inset:
Milan   Venice
Florence   Chianti Country
Rome   Naples
ITALY

166

Florence and Siena fought for dominance of the Chianti area from the 13th through the 15th centuries, each of the city-states building castles in the area to protect its interests. Under Florentine organization, the military "Lega del Chianti" (Chianti League) was formed in 1255 by the cities of Radda, Castellina, and Gaiole. They chose the "Gallo Nero" as their symbol, the same black rooster silhouette which serves as the symbol of Chianti Classico wine today.

Wine from the region took on the Chianti name by the early 15th century. In the early 1700s, Chianti became the first official government-designated wine area in the world. In the 1830s, Bettino Ricasoli, "The Iron Baron," brought professional processing techniques to wineries on his estates. He experimented with different combinations of grapes until he created the standard blend that has been known as Chianti ever since.

> **❝** *Good Chianti, that aged, majestic and proud wine, enlivens my heart, and frees it painlessly from all fatigue and sadness.* **❞**
> —Grancesco Redi, *Bacco in Toscana,* 1685

To protect the Chianti name, a group of winegrowers in the region formed the Chianti Classico Consortium in 1924. They then adopted a set of regulations regarding the blend of the wine, the production techniques, and, of course, the area from which the grapes must come. Today, nearly 104 sq. km (40 sq. miles) of Chianti are covered with over 6,800 hectares (17,000 acres) of grapevines producing some 90 million liters of wine per year.

LAY OF THE LAND

You have two choices for touring the region: **Drive** your own car, or join an organized tour from a nearby city. Driving obviously gives you more freedom to explore the less-touristed, smaller wineries and wander back roads to your heart's content. The drawbacks are that you won't be able to sample as many wines as you'd like if you're the designated driver, and it's very easy to get lost. If you do decide on driving yourself (and I'd recommend it), take the scenic N2 highway between Florence and Siena, exiting on some of the smaller side routes to reach the central S222. To see the best of Chianti in a single day, cruise the S222, and stop in Greve and Rada.

With an **organized tour,** you can sit back and let others do the work, and not worry about getting lost. But these tours only go to the places that can accommodate hordes of visitors, have their own fixed schedules, and eliminate some of the adventure that makes travel fun. Keep in mind that wine-tasting tours aren't the only option; you can combine them with cooking classes, biking or hiking trips, and shopping. The Chianti area has **tourist offices** in **Greve** (Via Giovanni da Verrazzano, 59, and Piazza F. Mori; ☎ 055-8546287; www.comune.greve-in-chianti.fi.it; Mon–Sat 9:30am–1pm and 2:30–7pm), in **Castellina** (Via Ferruccio, 40; ☎ 0577-7741392; 10am–1pm and 3:30–7:30pm, Sun closes 1pm), and in **Radda** (Piazza del Castello, 6; ☎ 057-7738494; 10am–1pm and 3:30–7:30pm). For general area information visit www.chianti.it/turismo and www.terresiena.it.

Why Is a Chianti a Chianti?

There are strict rules that govern what can and cannot be called "Chianti Classico." With that designation, the grapes must come from 1 of 12 municipalities between Siena and Florence. The sangiovese grape must compose at least 80% of the blend, and from 2006 on, no white grapes will be allowed in the mixture. Also, only a certain density of vines are allowed per acre, and the end product cannot be sold until October 1 in the year following the harvest.

ACCOMMODATIONS, BOTH STANDARD & NOT

€€   I think one of the best ways to experience the life of the area is to actually bed down at a winery for the night, and perhaps the loveliest place to do that is the **Casali Della Aiola** ★★ (North of Vagliagi on sp 102; ☎ 0577-322797; www. aiola.net). Once a famous Siennese stronghold (the Florentines razed it in 1544, after which it was rebuilt with a moat), this estate is today a 100-hectare (250-acre) working farm operated by the extended family of Senator Giovanni Malagodi. His daughter runs the vineyards and winery, and his granddaughter, the charming Federica, and her husband, Enrico, have turned one of the farmhouses on the property into a B&B, polishing the terra-cotta floors to a shine, restoring the wood-beam ceilings, and preserving the farmhouse look. As is appropriate for this winery/lodging, the small reading room contains an honor bar where you can partake of the farm's bounty. Doubles go for €90, including breakfast. There's also a family-size junior suite. For those not staying here, there are cellar tours and tastings.

€€   Another solid B&B option, the **Albergo Il Colombaio** ★ 🧒 (Castellina in Chianti, Via Chiantigiana, 29; ☎ 0577-740402; www.albergoilcolombaio.it) has 14 rooms (doubles for €103) behind the thick stone and wood walls of a 16th-century house that once sheltered shepherds and their sheep. For a reasonably priced place, it has some very nice amenities like good-quality bed linens, fluffy towels, and a pool with countryside views. Ask for an upstairs room—they're bigger with better views; downstairs was where the sheep used to sleep! The Albergo's sister property, the Villa Casalta, sits about a mile outside of Castellina, and has 13 homey rooms in the main manor house and six in another farmhouselike structure, with a pool between them. You can reserve a room with a kitchen, or stay B&B-style and eat in the large breakfast room. Doubles go for €90, including breakfast. Be sure to check out the Etruscan Tomb at the end of the dirt road next to the hotel. You'll see a huge green mound topped with a ring of trees. Below are the empty vaults, lit by button-operated lights. It's quite spooky to visit at night.

€€€-€€€€   As its name implies, it sometimes gets windy at **Borgo Casa al Vento** (Gaioloe in Chianti; ☎ 0577-749068; www.borgocasaalvento.com), but the stone buildings on the ridge's top location are as solid on the outside as they are soft on the inside, with cushy beds and couches, some canopied beds, and calming decor. They offer a number of lodging options, from apartments and bedroom suites to a huge vacation villa. Weekly apartment rental for a double is €1,000 in high season, or €150 a night (down to €800 a week when business is slow). There are also suites for €140 to €160 a night. The high-end villa (€5,000 per week) has its own heated pool, huge second-floor terrace, and can comfortably sleep six people it its three bedrooms, plus a couple of others on pull-out beds.

€€€–€€€€   **Palazzo Leopoldo** ★ (Radda in Chianti, Via Roma, 33; ☎ 0577-735606; www.palazzoleopoldo.it) in the center of Radda, has been hosting rich and famous visitors for 300 years. This former nobleman's villa, with original frescoes still on the walls and ancient wooden beams holding up the ceilings, is the epitome of elegance and a worthy splurge, its rooms starting at €150 for a double, €220 for a superior room (you're paying for the view), and about €300 for one of the huge suites. Another lure: a heated "hydromassage" pool in a hidden underground cave.

DINING FOR ALL TASTES

€   For simple, flavorful meals, with little fuss, **Tre Porte** ★ 🧒 (Via Trento e Trieste, 4, Castellina in Chianti; ☎ 0577-741163; closed Tues) is the best stop in the area, and everyone knows it—it's packed day and night with local families and large groups. I particularly enjoy the pesto linguini and the grilled pork, but I don't think you'll be disappointed with anything on the menu. In the evenings, pizza is added to the choices (try the wonderful mushroom pizza). *Primi* cost €6 to €8, *secondi* €8 to €18.

€€   If you're looking for a genuine countryside trattoria, try **La Cantinetta di Rignana** ★★ (exit from Badia a Passignano near Montefioralle; ☎ 055-852065; www.lacantinettadirignana.it). Set in a farmhouse at the end of a long dirt road, it has a folksy decor (red tablecloths and family photos) and a lovely outdoor dining patio. Tops here are sausage ravioli, or the beef-and-vegetable combination known as *involtini di manzo*. *Primi* range from €7 to €9, *secondi* from €9 to €12. Reservations are highly recommended for dinner.

€€€   The meals aren't cheap at **Albergaccio** ★★★ (Via Fiorentina, 63, outside of Castellina; ☎ 0577-741042; www.albergacciocast.com). Tasting menus are a whopping €45 (for five courses), *primi* average €13, and *secondi* €20, but the food is outstanding, and the ambience is everything you could hope for—with a view-heavy outdoor dining area. For those chillier nights, there is an elegant, white-tablecloth-robed room within. I still dream about the stuffed pigeon (*piccione*) and the ricotta-truffle-thyme gnocchi combo I had on my last visit. A top dining experience.

THE LURE OF BACCHUS—VISITS TO THE WINERIES

Consistency is a virtue when it comes to Chianti. For several thousand years, the people here have been primarily doing just one thing: lovingly tending the local grapes and producing, in vineyards that now spread across nearly 6,800 hectares (17,000 acres) of the region, one of the most prized wines in the world. My favorites of the many wonderful wineries here are:

Castello Monsanto winery ★ (☎ 055-8059000; www.castellodimonsanto.it; €16), with 72 hectares (178 acres) of vineyards, produces about 400,000 bottles a year of chardonnay, Chianti Classico, and sangiovese wines. They export the bulk of their production to the U.S., so if you like what you drink, you can probably get it at home. One of the most innovative of the region's vineyards, it was one of the first to substitute steel tanks for wooden wine casks, and to play around with the number of days for maceration. You'll learn all about this fascinating history on the tour, which takes you on a stroll through the grounds, with a visit to the original 1742 cellars. It's a little tricky to find the place because it doesn't have any signs (call for directions), but it's close to the SS2, two exits north of Poggibonsi on an SS429 side route.

Castello de la Panaretto (☎ 055-8059003; reservations required; €17 for a tour plus 2–3 wines, with hors d'oeuvres, €20 for 3–4 wines plus some more local produce, or you can make a quick visit to taste a wine or two at no cost) is a smaller castle with exquisite gardens and an expansive view, from which you're going to want to bring a bottle or two home. The winery is located about 1km (⅔ mile) north of Monsanto.

Just how beautiful is **Vicchiomaggio** (Via Vicchiomaggio, 4, Le Bolle exit south of Strada; ☎ 055-854079; www.vicchiomaggio.it), a centuries-old castle? I can only assume that Leonardo da Vinci took some inspiration from its surroundings: It was here that he painted his famous *Mona Lisa* (she grew up in the castle). Though the castle, which looms over the Greve Valley, was originally built in the 5th century A.D., what you see today is the Renaissance reconstruction (approximately 1450), still one of the best-preserved castles in the region. Now British-owned, the vineyards here produce a number of delightful wines, particularly the Ripa Delle More, an award-winning sangiovese/cabernet. Free tastings are available at the San Jacope shop (daily 9:30am–12:30pm and 2:30–6:30pm; on the SSS222 right at the turnoff for the castle). You can arrange a tour of the cellars and castle if you reserve in advance. If you really like it here, you can rent rooms, stay for a few days, and take one of their cooking or wine appreciation classes (€100 a night is the starting price for rooms).

Formed from the merger of five vineyards in 1968, **Castellare Winery** (Poceri Castellare di Castellina, about 2.4km/1½ miles from Castellina; ☎ 0577-742903; www.castellare.it; a brief tour and tastings for €9) proudly puts out a much lower yield than neighboring wineries because it eschews the use of any pesticides or herbicides and never mixes its local grapes with French or international strains. I think you'll taste the difference—these wines are quite prized and difficult to get outside the region.

One of Italy's top vineyards for the past 300 years, **Castello di Brolio** ★ (☎ 0577-7301; www.ricasoli.it; €3 to tour the grounds, bottling room tours and tasting for €21; daily 9am–noon and 3–6pm; reservations required), a handsome 15th-century castle, was once owned by Chianti creator Baron Ricasoli (see above). The tour, while pricey, is fascinating, and the wines here are exquisite, particularly the Casalferro, which has won just about ever prize there is. The wine tastes even better with a meal at their **Osteria del Castello restaurant** (☎ 0577-747277; €18 for an entree) on the driveway to the castle.

Le Cantine di Greve in Chianti ★ (Piazza delle Cantine, in the historical center across the river from the parking lot; ☎ 055-8546404; www.lecantine.it; daily 10am–7pm) is the region's best wine store, where you can taste some 140 different wines at a single sitting (well, you wouldn't be able to walk if you did that, but you do have a choice of that many wines). You can also buy small samples of olive oil, salami, and sandwiches. For information on each wine, check out the computer terminals in the shop. They have tasting seminars, plus an interesting corkscrew museum (no really, it's interesting).

SIENA

Founded by the Etruscans, and colonized by Rome, Siena rose to power in the early Middle Ages as a center of banking and the textile trade, a rival to Florence in art, commerce, culture, and military might. In 1348, however, the Black Death dealt Siena a deathblow from which it never fully recovered. Estimates of those who perished range as high as 75% of the town's population. Given sanitary habits at the time, and some 70,000 corpses in the city, it's a wonder that Siena wasn't completely abandoned.

With its art and architecture frozen in time, Siena today offers visitors a wealth of museums and churches. The town also supports a small university, a fair amount of shopping, a number of first-rate restaurants, and two pro sports teams, bringing just enough of a cosmopolitan breeze to freshen up the atmosphere of the medieval streets and buildings. The town is accessible but has never become as oversaturated with tourism as Florence, San Gimignano, or Pisa.

> ❝Siena was a flawless gift of the Middle Ages to the modern imagination. No other Italian city could have been more interesting to an observer . . . ❞
>
> —Henry James, *Confidence,* 1879

Unlike cramped and crowded Florence, Siena is a pedestrian city, its hilly streets largely free from the mopeds that menace its Tuscan rival. The Duomo and the famous Piazza del Campo, with the grand tower of Palazzo Pubblico, are among the notable architectural achievements of the region. Art galleries, including the Museo Civico, the Pinacoteca Nazionale, and the Museo dell'Opera del Duomo, offer you a chance to enjoy many early-Renaissance masterpieces.

DON'T LEAVE SIENA WITHOUT . . .
GOING TO THE DUOMO   Siena's cathedral is a storehouse of art, and a work of art in itself.

TOURING THE MUSEO DELL'OPERA METROPOLITANA   The statues, the paintings, and the view are all spectacular.

RELAXING IN THE PIAZZA DEL CAMPO   This central plaza is among Italy's finest. Sit with a gelato and watch mobs of tourists, street musicians, and locals enjoying the scene.

ENJOYING THE ART IN THE MUSEO CIVICO   The huge murals here reflect the peak of Siena's military and artistic power.

CHECKING OUT A SPORTING EVENT   The Sienese love their pro basketball and up-and-coming soccer team.

JOINING THE MOBS IN THE PALIO   Siena hosts famous midsummer horse races. The weeks around the event are alive with many neighborhood *contrada* street parties.

LAY OF THE LAND

Siena is one of the few major tourist towns where it's more convenient to arrive **by bus** than by train, as the train station is nearly 3.2km (2 miles) north of the city center. If you do arrive by train (about a 2-hr. ride from Florence), most city buses (nos. 3, 4, 7–9, 14, and 17) will take you to Piazza Matteotti, just north of the walls. Long-haul bus line **Tra-in** (☎ 0577-204228; www.trainspa.it) goes from Florence to Siena in 75 to 95 minutes for €6.50. The buses arrive in Piazze San Domenico or Gramsci.

Siena is a fairly simple **drive** from Florence (64km/40 miles via the SS2), or from Rome (193km/120 miles via the A1-326). Free parking can be had in the lots north of the fortress, or on the city streets around it, but be sure to check signs for street-cleaning days. It's about a 15-minute walk to central Siena from this area. Parking on streets in the historical center is virtually impossible, although some hotels have discounted rates at the closer pay lots.

Siena has a famously unhelpful **tourist office** (Piazza Duomo, 1; ☎ 050-560464; www.pisa.turismo.toscana.it; daily 9:30am–5pm). What, you want a map? Yeah, right. They sell some tourist guides, but the selection is half that of any bookshop in town. For what it's worth, the office is on the north side of the piazza next to the Tower ticket office. The privately run **"Info Casato Viaggi"** office (Via Casato di Sotto, 12, to the right of the palace; ☎ 0577-46091; www.sienaholiday.com), southeast of the Piazza del Campo, has better free information and a helpful staff. They can also book tours, help you find a room, and sell you a daily discount card for €5. The private **hotel booking office, Hotel Siena,** on the north edge of town (Piazza Madre Teresa di Calcutta, 2; ☎ 0577-288084; www.hotelsiena.com), is also helpful and good for a free map. A company called Ecco Siena runs a good set of guided city tours at 3pm daily (except Sun), meeting outside the San Domenico church. The 90-minute tour is only €5 if you have a coupon from one of the hotels in town that provide them; otherwise, it's €15.

ACCOMMODATIONS, BOTH STANDARD & NOT

€€   The key word is "simple" when it comes to the central and cheap **Albergo Hotel La Perla** (Via delle Terme, 25; ☎ 0577-226280; info@albergolaperla.191. it). The building (a former palace, though you wouldn't know it to look at it) is somewhat somber, and the rooms are very standard, with flowered bedspreads and tile floors. But it's only half a block from the Piazza del Campo, so the location is great and prices start at just €70 for a double in high season for air-conditioned rooms with private bathroom. Expect a few minor downsides to staying here—no phones in the rooms and no elevator (meaning you've got to climb the 32 steep steps to the third floor). But on the whole I think it's quite a good deal.

€€   Another of the better options in central Siena is the **Hotel Bernini** ✯ (Via della Sapienza, 15; ☎ 0577-289047; www.albergobernini.com), a friendly family-run operation that boasts excellent views of the Duomo from the hallway and a small terrace (a great place to relax). Other pluses: new bathrooms, clean rooms, and an extremely quiet setting above a convent. Double rooms with private bathroom go for €82, €62 without one. You can also rent one of a couple of well-appointed apartments, with useable kitchens, around the corner, through their **Bernini Apartments** ✯, beginning at €100 per night.

€-€€   Slightly more stylish digs can be found at the **Hotel Chiusarelli** ✯ (Viale Curtatone, 15; ☎ 0577-271177; www.chiusarelli.com), a colonnaded neoclassical villa just 1 block from the bus station. Rooms are light and airy, with modern decor and comfortable beds, many with good-size verandas. Double-room prices are €122, including breakfast. As a bonus, on weekends you get balcony views of Siena's soccer team playing in the stadium behind the hotel. The hotel has a small parking lot, a large restaurant, and an Internet terminal for guests.

€€-€€€   **Casolare la Vigna** (near Belcaro Castle; ☎ 0577-283311) is a friendly family-run *agriturismo*/apartment 4km (2½ miles) south of town, and a good choice for those seeking a peaceful hideaway near the city. Their recently refurbished two-bedroom apartment (converted from an old stable) includes a full kitchen, antique furnishings, satellite TV, and a washer/dryer, and costs about €150 a night—more during festival time, less in winter. The family also rents a bedroom with bathroom in their house for €80 to €90 a night. Though it's obviously not a full-service hotel, there are many extras. Your hosts, gourmet chefs, will cook meals on request, and also give cooking lessons using ingredients from an organic garden behind the house. Daughter Cinzia Mariotti is a licensed guide who leads city tours and treks into the countryside. This may be one of the few *agriturismi* accessible to those traveling by train and bus, as there is regular bus service from the house into Siena proper.

DINING FOR ALL TASTES

€-€€   A very popular pizzeria tucked in a winding street beneath San Domenico, **Ristorante La Pizzeria di Nonno Mede** ✯ (Camporegio, 21; ☎ 0577-247966) is a good choice for a quick but extremely pleasant meal. You may need reservations, however, because this scenic patio spot (with views of the Duomo) is packed until almost midnight. Pizzas begin at only €5, and toppings range from the usual sausages and mushrooms to seafood and artichokes.

€€   You'll be spending your days among the medieval marvels of Siena, so why not dine medieval as well? At the **Gallo Nero** ✯ 🧒 (Via del Porrione, 65/67; ☎ 0577/284-356; www.gallonero.it), the chefs have consulted with professors at the local university to create an authentic medieval menu, and they don't shy away from the unusual, such as braised peacock or pork cold cuts with "aromatic lard." Kids will enjoy the Dungeons and Dragons setting (a 14th-c. castle with thick stone walls, stained glass, and medieval art) and costumed waitstaff, and I think you'll enjoy the food. Set menus for €23 include spiced wine, salted onion tart, and bittersweet duck with cheese ravioli. The more common *primi* run from €5 to €10, while main courses are €8.50 to €13. It's a trip, but a colorful, historical one.

€€   The touristy but good **La Vecchia Taverna di Bacco** (Via Beccheria, 9, near the Campo; ☎ 0577-41299) has *primi* averaging €8, *secondi* from €10 to €12, served in a crowded set of rooms below a wood-beamed ceiling. The patio dining is popular. Try a Tuscan pasta dish with garlic sauce.

€€€€   The high-end **Cane & Gato** ✪✪✪ (Via Pagliaresi, 6; ☎ 057-333879) is Siena's finest restaurant. The interior is peaceful and intimate, with candlelit tables and modern art on the walls. Chef/owner Paolo Senni's menu changes with the seasons but if *tagliata di fesa di vitella* with zucchini is being offered, be sure to order it; simpler but still delicious is his homemade spaghetti with fresh tomato-and-basil sauce with local olive oil and greens from their garden. Set menus approach €50 per person, so it's not cheap, but if you want a night on the town, this is where to go. Reservations are necessary.

WHY YOU'RE HERE: THE TOP SIGHTS & ATTRACTIONS

Siena boasts some of the finest art and architecture in Italy. Ideally, you should have 2 days to tour the sights, and even that will be a busy time. With a single day, treat yourself to the Duomo, the Duomo Museum, and the Museo Civico. On the second day, be sure to add the Ospedale di Santa Maria, the Pinacoteca, and San Domenico Church on the north edge of town.

You should start your visit, as people have been doing for centuries, at the breathtakingly beautiful **Piazza del Campo** ✪✪✪. This large square is a logical gathering place, the site of the Palio race, and a perfect spot to sit, have a gelato, and watch mobs of tourists, street musicians, and locals enjoying the scene. Siena's ruling Council of Nine had the piazza constructed in its present form from 1290 to 1349. The council divided the area into nine segments as a tribute to themselves. The nine white dividing lines actually serve as gutters to funnel water into the grate at the bottom of the sloped area. Fonte Gaia, the "Happy Fountain" at the peak of the piazza, is topped with a goddess of the seas, and framed with the Virgin Mary flanked by the Virtues. It's a 19th-century reproduction of the 15th-century original.

The **Palazzo Pubblico (Town Hall),** at the base of the piazza, is an expression of Siena's civic power and pride, constructed in the early 14th century. The 95m (315-ft.) **Torre del Mangi** (€6; Mar–Oct 10am–7pm, in winter closes 4pm) jutting up from the structure is climbable and offers spectacular views over the city and surroundings. The view from the tower on top of the Museo dell'Opera is nearly as good, and admission to an art gallery is included in the €6 fee. The clunky structure sticking out from the front of the Palazzo is the Cappella di Piazza, meant as a religious offering following the end of the Black Death in the late

1300s. The city ran out of funding, and the chapel wasn't topped off for another century.

Inside the Palazzo Pubblico is the **Museo Civico** ★★★ (Palazzo Pubblico, Piazza del Campo; ☎ 0577-292226; www.comune.siena.it/museocivico; €7; Mar–Oct 10am–7pm, Nov–Feb 10am–5:30pm), home to countless huge murals and paintings created when Siena was at the peak of her military and artistic power. In the Sala del Mappamondo is Simone Martini's first known work: His *Maesta* (1315) is an extraordinary debut for any artist. Even in this early work you'll see Martini's mastery of color and texture in the Madonna's elaborately patterned gown; his later work, *Guidoriccio da Fogliano* on horseback, is also here. Note how Peter (with key) and other saints are on tent-post-holding duty. The knight on horseback across the room is a Sienese army captain riding by conquered Montemassi. The message to the town officials who would gather in the room: Govern not only with power but with justice.

The art continues to teach lessons for rulers in the Sala di Pace next door. In these allegorical works, we see the results of Good Government—people dancing, prosperous fields, and so on—and Bad Government. In the latter, a devil rules over post-plague Siena, where muggers attack villagers and thieves roam the countryside attacking travelers. The artist Ambrogio Lorenzetti himself died of plague in the epidemic 10 years after he completed the frescoes.

Siena's **Duomo** or **Cathedral of Santa Maria dell'Assunta** ★★★ (☎ 0577-283048; www.operaduomo.siena.it; €3; 10:30am–7:30pm, Sat opens 1:30pm, in winter closes 3:30pm) is one of Italy's—and, I think, the world's—most handsome Gothic churches. It was begun in 1196, at a time when the Pisan proclivity for incorporating black and white marble stripes into their great church building was at its height, and these striking bands define both the exterior and interior spaces. You'll see one of the church's greatest treasures just as you enter: the 56 exquisite mosaic marble panels created by artists from the 14th to 16th centuries (a few were unfinished until the 19th c.). They're roped off, some covered with cardboard for protection (if these mosaics are the reason for your visit, come in Aug when they're fully uncovered). The famous **Pulpit,** carved by Nicola Pisano in 1265, dramatizes the story of Christ's life on its panels. The **northern transept** has a set of tombs, including Donatello's 1415 bronze of Bishop Pecci. The Piccolomini altarpiece features four statues of saints done by a young Michelangelo. He had signed on to do another 11 statues, but skipped town for a better gig—the *David* in Florence. Don't overlook the **Libreria Piccolomini,** halfway down the left nave near Michelangelo's saints, noteworthy for its beautiful frescoes. Pope Pius II is the subject of 10 of the large frescoes, while Siena's St. Catherine gets her own piece on the left side of the room.

Money problems plagued the construction of the Duomo, and plans to make it the largest in the world never panned out. The unfinished area now houses the **Museo dell'Opera Metropolitana** ★★ (Piazza del Duomo, 8; ☎ 0577-283048; €6; Apr–Oct 9am–7:30pm, Nov–Mar 9am–1:30pm), home to many of the artworks that once graced the Duomo, inside and out. If you climb the highest tower of the museum, you'll end up at about the same height as Siena's main tower. The view is, to my mind, even better (partially because you get to see that tower!). Of the many highlights here, the statues in the first room by Giovanni Pisano, with their craning necks—they were taken from the exterior and meant to be viewed

Siena's Cumulative Ticket Prices

Siena's multiuse tickets can be a good deal, but only if you're planning on being in town for a few days. The tickets come in four flavors:

- Tower + Museo Civico   €10
- "Musei Comunali": Museo Civico + Palazzo delle Papesse + Santa Maria della Scala   €10 (good for 2 days)
- "SIA Inverno": Museo Civico + Palazzo delle Papesse + Santa Maria della Scala + Museo dell'Opera + Battistero S. Giovanni + Libreria Piccolomini   €13 (good for 7 days)
- "SIA Estate": Museo Civico + Palazzo delle Papesse + Santa Maria della Scala + Museo dell'Opera + Battistero S. Giovanni + Libreria Piccolomini + Oratario di San Bernardino e Museo Diocesano   €16 (good for 7 days)

Here's what attractions cost if you pay separately:

	Regular	Reduced
Museo Civico	€7	€4.50
Santa Maria della Scala	€6	€3.50
Palazzo delle Papesse	€5	€3.50
Museo dell'Opera	€6	€5
Battistero S. Giovanni	€3	€2.50
Oratorio di San Bernardino e Museo Diocesano	€3	€2.50
Total	€30	€21.50

from below—are my favorites; they look as though they're coming to life and peering around the dimly lit hall. *The Maesta,* the former Duomo's altarpiece created by Duccio in 1311, is the museum's star attraction. It even has its own room. The colors, composition, and realistic (for that time) feel of the subject exhibit the characteristics of what is known as the Siena style of painting and make it one of the most famous medieval paintings in Italy.

Across from the Duomo is the **Ospedale di Santa Maria della Scala** ✫✫ (Piazza Del Duomo, 2; ☎ 0577-224811; www.santamaria.comune.siena.it; €6; 10am–6pm, Nov–Mar closes 4:30pm), an erstwhile hospital, now a museum containing original sick-room frescoes, winding hallways with chapels, and recently created archaeological and contemporary art exhibits. It was a combined pilgrims' hostel and hospital back in the 800s, staffed by nuns caring for the sick. The city of Siena ran it as a hospital until the 1990s, funding both patient care and the artwork now displayed within. The most notable feature is the frescoed walls of the Sala del Pellegrino, where Domenico di Bartolo (among other artists) created a telling visual history of the hospital in the 1440s, giving insights into Sienese life at the time and extolling the good works of the hospital itself. The left wall shows the founding of the hospital, with divine intervention, city officials monitoring construction, and a Pope's blessing. Note the busy Siena street scenes with Middle Eastern merchants, arguing workers, and posturing politicians. The far wall's frescoes are late-16th-century additions that illustrate the role of wet nurses at the hospital—as they took in many orphans, women were needed to feed them. The right wall has a portrait of workers tending to the sick and distributing charity. Note the unappealing conditions of the hospital, with cats and dogs fighting on the floor, scary-looking instruments, and general chaos (in the next panel, don't miss the helpful baby in his mother's arms who kindly aims her breast at the beggar children). The next-to-last panel shows the hospital as a school at which the orphans were raised and educated—a somewhat grim process from the looks of the menacing teacher with a switch in his hand.

The on-site **Cappella del Sacro Chiodo** is worthwhile for Vecchietta's frescoes of the Last Judgment. The chapel once held a nail said to be from Jesus' crucifixion, purchased at great cost by the city of Siena in the 1300s. Hallways continue in mazelike fashion to the Fienile, which displays the original panels of the fountain in Piazza del Campo. From the Fienile level, another stairway leads to the occasionally interesting Museo Archeologico and rotating modern exhibits.

Around the back side of the Duomo is the **Battistero (Baptistery;** Piazza San Giovanni; ☎ 0577-238048; €3), which is often overlooked by tourists, but has a baptismal font worth seeing, surrounded by elaborately frescoed vaulted ceilings. The early-15th-century hexagonal font allows you to play art critic as you walk around the panels designed by competing artists. For your scorecard, Jacopo della Quercia sculpted the *Annunciation* panel facing the altar. The *Birth and Preaching of the Baptist* panels were done by Giovanni di Turino. Florence Baptistery veteran Ghiberti is responsible for the panels of the *Baptism of Christ* and the *Arrest of St. John.* For my money, the best of the bunch is Donatello's *Feast of Herod,* which uses new and improved perspective techniques in a dramatic scene with natural figures. But you make your own call.

The **Pinacoteca Nazionale (National Picture Gallery)** ✹✹ (Via San Pietro, 29; ☎ 0577-281161; €4) has nearly 40 rooms jam-packed with over 500 paintings covering 400 years of art history. You could easily spend a full day here. The Sienese school obviously represents itself well, with rooms full of Duccio and Simone Martini on the **second floor**—go to this floor first if you're short on time. And be sure to check out Martini's entertaining *Il Beato Agostino Novello* in **Room 5:** St. Augustine appears to be the patron saint of clumsy people as he flies from scene to scene saving babies and fallen horsemen. **Room 30** has large-scale "cartoon" (charcoal and ink on paper) drawings made by Beccafumi as diagrams for the marble flooring in Siena's Duomo. From the Sala di Scultura **(Room 26),** you get a lovely view of the city. The third floor has a surprisingly good selection of Flemish works, including those by Dürer, and a Bruegel-esque *Tower of Babel.*

It's worth the trek to see the interior of **San Domenico Church** ✹ (Piazza San Domenico; free admission; Apr–Oct 7am–1pm and 3–6:30pm, Nov–Mar 9am–1pm and 3–6pm), at the northern edge of the city—the exterior is less memorable. The church celebrates Siena's St. Catherine with a 1414 portrait (in the raised chapel

The Palio Festival

Somehow, this 700-year-old horse race is both the most touristy and the most local event in Italy. Ten of the neighborhoods of Siena have horses that compete in the three-lap race around the Piazza. If the barebacked horse finishes with the rider on top, great; if not, that's good, too. Rules are few, crashes are many, conspiracy theories are common. In short, every July 2 and August 16 the town goes nuts. (Ten neighborhoods compete in the first race; the top three compete with seven other Siennese 'hoods in Aug.)

The 17 neighborhoods that take part in the race on a rotating basis treat the event as a combination Super Bowl, Mardi Gras, and World War III. Parties begin weeks before the races and continue for the month after. Booster clubs spend huge amounts of money to hire the best riders and horses in Italy, and betting reaches astronomical heights. Rumors of drugged horses, mugged riders, and general thuggish behavior color the events.

But for a visitor, the races offer a glimpse into the medieval spectacles of Italy, with all of the pageantry and the generally harmless chaos. The neighborhood *contrade* parties are a welcoming blend of street fair, frat party, and Fellini movie, with free-flowing wine mixing with rock bands, gossiping elders, carnival booths, and family parties.

The grandstand and bleacher seats around the square go for hundreds of euros and are sold out months before the event. If you have plenty of cash and planning skills, contact **Palio Viaggi** (☎ 0577-289114) for tickets. Otherwise, join the masses in the center of the square for the race. To see anything, you need to arrive hours ahead of time and fight to hold your ground. From the center of the square, the race doesn't make much sense. It's over in less than 2 minutes, and chances are you'll miss the whole thing. But who cares? You're part of the scene.

at the rear), paintings of her miracles (at the Chapel of St. Catherine midway along the right wall), and relics of the poor woman's severed head and thumb. The thumb is in a case to the right of the chapel, while her head (original skull, skin redone) is in a case next to the high altar. Among the paintings of the church, look for St. Catherine's three symbols, the white lily, cross, and book. St. Catherine was born in 1347 and spent her life in spiritual contemplation, in ministering to the poor in post-plague Siena, and in diplomacy. She spent many years trying to reunite papal and anti-papal factions in Italy before retiring from the world, receiving the stigmata in this very church and eventual sainthood.

Toward the south side of the city stands the neglected **Sant 'Agostino** (Via Pier Andrea Mattioli, south of Pinacoteca; €2; 7am–noon and 3–7pm), a rarely visited church far from the madding tourist crowds. If you've purchased a cumulative ticket, it's worth a visit. A small park outside the church with a playground can give the kids a break during their cultural march around town. Artwork here includes an excellent *Crucifixion* by Perugino (1506); a 1338 Lorenzetti fresco with Virgin, saints, and a really surprised-looking Jesus; and a number of chapels dating from the 1400s to the 1700s. A helpful English-language handout describing the art and artists is available to visitors.

THE OTHER SIENA

Of course, there's no better place to meet locals and witness the best of Sienese life than at one of the annual neighborhood *contrade* parties. They are part traditional festival, part frat party, and part carnival—with everything from rock bands to weathered accordion players. Booths and local shops sell wine and food; games, gossip, and gambling on the upcoming Palio races are popular nighttime activities. These are not tourist-oriented events, but the locals are very welcoming—just don't be carrying the flag of a competing neighborhood! You can find out about these events by asking your concierge or a waiter at a restaurant, or just by hearing some noise and walking to it. The parties take place in various neighborhoods during the month before and after the races, from late June to late August.

Or go to a local game. Siena's up-and-coming **AC Siena** soccer team (Via dei Montanini, 87; ☎ 0577-281084; www.acsiena.it) has risen to the top Serie A division after years of barely maintaining Serie B status. Tickets begin at €20, and can be purchased at most tobacco shops. The team plays in black-and-white striped shirts in tribute to the striped Duomo and other sites in town. A spirited crowd fills the 16,000-seat Stadio Comunale on the north side of town every other Sunday from September through May.

If you're tired of soccer, choose basketball—Siena is hoops crazy! Their **Montepaschi Mens Sana** pro basketball team (Via Sclavo, 8; ☎ 0577-38071) won the Italian league title in 2003–04, and claims to be Italy's oldest club. If you're there during the fall-winter season, check out a game—it's fun to join the raucous, singing, chanting, soccer-style crowd. You can purchase tickets (€6–€48) at most tobacco shops, including the one next to the bus terminal at Piazza Gramsci. Games are played at the Palazzo Dello Sport, a few miles north of town.

To check out the local English-speaking literary scene, drop by the **Book Shop** (Galleria S. Pietro, 19; ☎ 0577-226594; www.bookshopsiena.com). You can attend readings or just hang out in the comfy chairs; sample English-language books; and meet some British, American, and Australian expats.

SHOPPING

Siena doesn't have nearly the depth and breath of shopping opportunities as nearby Florence, but it does offer more than most Tuscan cities. In summer 2005, the city encouraged all shops to stay open until midnight; as this book goes to press, I can't say whether the experiment will be repeated, but I think it will (allowing you to satisfy a late-night Gucci fix).

Books

Libreria Senese (Via di Citta, 64; ☎ 0577-280845) has a wide selection of specialty art and travel books in English, in addition to local guides, maps, and souvenirs.

Clothing

For a great selection of Armani, Gucci, and all the usual suspects, stop at **Cortecci** (Via Banchi di Sopra, 27, and Il Campo, 30; ☎ 0577-280984), which has a friendly staff and a large inventory.

If you're in the mood for something more unique, drop by **Tesutto a Mano** (Via San Pietra, 7; ☎ 0577-282200), where the owner weaves luxurious sweaters, scarves, and shawls—you may see her hard at work on her loom.

Curios

An interesting glass workshop/souvenir shop is **Vetrate Artistiche** (Via della Galluzza, 5; ☎ 0577-48033), where you can watch workers complete their stained-glass projects. If you're not building a church, you can still buy their jewelry, picture frames, and mosaic household items. They also offer apprenticeships if you're planning on sticking around for a few months.

Wine

Part museum, part wine shop, part bar, the government-run **Enoteca Italiana** (Fortezza Medicea Via Camollia, 72; ☎ 0577-227187; www.enoteca-italiana.it; Tues–Sat noon–1am) is meant to promote Italian wines, with a focus on Tuscany. The 750-label, multithousand-bottle collection represents the best the region has to offer. Stop by in the early evening to enjoy some snacks with the tastings.

The **Enoteca San Domenico** (Via del Paradiso, 56; ☎ 0577-271181; www.enotecasandomenico.it) is a good place to shop for area wines and gourmet products, including olive oils, dried herbs, pastas, and sweets.

NIGHTLIFE

In 1765, Scotsman James Boswell wrote of the after-hours pleasures of Siena: "I found that people lived there in a completely natural fashion, making love as their inclinations suggested . . . Intoxicated by that sweet delirium, I gave myself up, without self-reproach and in complete serenity, to the charms of irregular love." While Siena is not the hotbed of free love that it apparently was in the 1760s, a good time can still be had at night in a variety of stylish, smaller nightspots, as well as in the requisite Irish pubs. For larger clubs, locals head down the road to Poggibonsi.

I particularly like the artsy, ever-so-hip **Corte del Miracoli** (Via Roma, 56; ☎ 0577-48596), a student/hippie hangout with live shows, avant-garde theater, and music. The shows can be odd, but always amusing, and the crowd is quite friendly. For a more adult night on the town, catch occasional live music in the swank jazz bar, **The Tea Room** (Porta Giustizia, 11; ☎ 0577-222753).

Or try what seems to be Siena's unofficial drink—sangria!—at **Buena Vista Social Pub** (Via San Martino, 31; ☎ 0577-221423). It offers a Spanish/Caribbean flair and is a popular place to hang out. It also has limited pub grub. Sangria, Guinness, and general foolishness can be had at **Barone Rosso** (Via dei Termini, 9; ☎ 0577-286686; www.barone-rosso.com), which also features DJs and live music.

AREZZO

Arezzo is most famous for its medieval square, scene of a yearly jousting festival; its massive Duomo; and Piero della Francesca's *Legend of the True Cross* fresco. But take a walk through the evocative old town and you can't help but notice you have entered the land of Vasari. Giorgio Vasari, architect, painter, sculptor, writer, and general busybody was born in Arezzo in 1512 and appears to have designed, built, or painted everything in town aside from the Roman amphitheater (he was probably on the renovation committee for that, too).

You can stand on Via Vasari in the Loggia di Vasari in Arezzo's Piazza Grande, and admire the Vasari-designed bell tower at the top of the palace. Walk uphill to the Duomo to see Vasari's *cantoria* (choir gallery), as well as his paintings in the museum there. On your way to the city museum to admire more Vasari paintings, you can stop at his self-consciously elegant house. Vasari did the altar and frescoes at the Badia church, and a work in the Santissima Annunziata. He doesn't have any frescoes in San Domenio, but sure enough, his dad does. No matter how much you love Vasari, by the time you leave Arezzo, you may be feeling like Mark Twain after a tour of Michelangelo's work: "I never felt so fervently thankful, so soothed, so tranquil, so filled with a blessed peace, as I did yesterday when I learned that the man was dead."

While Vasari's achievements are worth a look, the real artistic treat in town is Francesca's fresco in San Francesco (just try saying that 10 times fast . . .). The 15th-century masterwork illustrating everything from original sin to redemption has been recently restored and is a must-see, along with the Duomo and the main square. But don't make the mistake of thinking Arezzo is as dead as Vasari: The first Sunday of every September, the city holds its Giostra del Saraceno jousting competition, and in late June Arezzo turns into techno-paradise with the Arezzo Wave music fest.

DON'T LEAVE AREZZO WITHOUT . . .

VIEWING FRANCESCA'S *LEGEND OF THE TRUE CROSS* One of the greatest works of Italian art, it's in San Francesco Church.

STROLLING AROUND PIAZZA GRANDE View the Palazzo della Fraternità and Vasari's Loggia, and then peek into antiques shops in the area.

VISITING THE DUOMO Savor its notable stained glass, chapels, and frescoes.

A BRIEF HISTORY OF AREZZO

Arezzo began as an Etruscan city-state about 500 B.C., controlling trade routes through the central Apennine mountains until Roman legions colonized the area. Visitors can still see remnants of Arezzo's Roman amphitheater, built in the 1st and 2nd century A.D. Its 9,000 seats point to the vitality of the city at that time. The control of trade routes enabled Arezzo to become a prosperous state in the 10th century, allowing the good times to continue until Florentine armies destroyed Arezzo forces in 1289. While it lost its independence, Arezzo maintained its artistic vitality, giving birth to the careers of the poet Petrarch in the

Arezzo

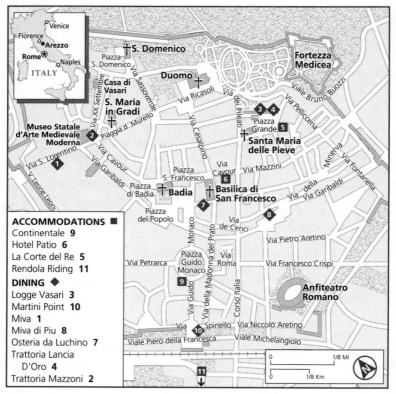

ACCOMMODATIONS ■
Continentale 9
Hotel Patio 6
La Corte del Re 5
Rendola Riding 11

DINING ◆
Logge Vasari 3
Martini Point 10
Miva 1
Miva di Piu 8
Osteria da Luchino 7
Trattoria Lancia
   D'Oro 4
Trattoria Mazzoni 2

1300s and Vasari in the 1500s. Music has also played a part in Arezzo's history, as can be seen in the "do-re-mi-fa . . ." plaque (at the corner of Via De Montetini and Via Desalpino) commemorating the birthplace of Guido Monaco, who created the diatonic musical scale.

LAY OF THE LAND

Arezzo is conveniently reached **by train** on the Rome-Florence line, with almost hourly departures from Rome (a 2- to 3-hr. trip) or nearly half-hour schedules from Florence (a 45- to 90-min. trip). The Arezzo train station is next to a tourist office, and only a few blocks from most city hotels.

If you're **driving,** you'll find that Arezzo is centrally located just off the A1 autostrada, 75km (45 miles) from Florence, 200km (120 miles) from Rome. Free parking is available in the lots north of the city walls. Amazingly enough, a set of escalators will take you from the lot into the city, where you'll pop out of a tunnel right next to the Duomo.

Arezzo has three different **tourist offices,** each with English speakers and a wealth of pamphlet info. The main tourist office is in front of the train station in

Piazza della Repubblica, 28 (☎ 0575-20839); the regional office is a couple of blocks into the city in **Piazza Risorgimento, 116** (☎ 0575-23952); and a supplemental office is at the north end of the city next to Palazzo Comunale. The tourist board website at www.apt.arezzo.it is useful as well.

ACCOMMODATIONS, BOTH STANDARD & NOT

I have three hotels and one farm stay to recommend.

€€€ If you're simply seeking a normal night's lodging in a standard hotel, the **Continentale** (Piazza Guido Monaco, 7; ☎ 0575-20251; www.hotelcontinentale. com) is a good call. With 73 rooms, you'll probably find space, and the rooms themselves are decent, though a little tired and noisy on the street side. Request an "old style" room for a little more character, a garden room for more quiet. The rooftop garden offers nice views of the city, and the lobby has a couple of free high-speed Internet terminals. The staff is professional, and the location, while not in the heart of the old town, is an easy walk from there. Prices are a reasonable €108 for a double.

€€€ If I were to build my ideal apartment in a historical Italian town, it would resemble a room at **La Corte del Re** ★★ (Via Borgunto, 5; ☎ 0575-401603; www.lacortedelre.com). A perfect combination of old and new, the nine apartments at La Corte have stylish and functional modern furniture and full kitchens blending coolly into the arched wood beams and stone walls of a 14th-century building. Five of the rooms look directly over Piazza Grande, the best view in town. Room rates are €750 to €1,000 for a week, or €130 a night in high season. Energetic manager Franca Gianetti will do what it takes to make sure your stay is a good one.

€€€€ Just down the street from St. Francesco church is the lavish **Hotel Patio** ★ (Via Cavour, 23; ☎ 055-401962; www.hotelpatio.it), perfect for those looking for a blowout stay in the city. Each of its seven rooms and suites are designed from the theme of a Bruce Chatwin travel book, from the Wu-Ti Chinese suite to the Fillide Moroccan room. And who wouldn't want to spend a night in the Ouidah Trophies' Room, named for a story of "tropical madness and cruelty"? Just be sure to turn on the light when you get up at night, or you'll be gored by one of the antlers sticking out of the walls. The beds and bathrooms are top-notch; the rooms are super quiet—and just a touch bizarre. Room rates for 2006: about €170 to €220 for a double. Stay a night and enjoy a journey within your journey.

€€ Unlike most *agriturismi* (farm stay accommodations), **Rendola Riding** ★ (Rendola, 66, Montevarchi, about 24km/15 miles northeast from Arezzo; ☎ 055-9707045; www.rendolariding.freeweb.org) is an actual working ranch, with a dozen horses for lessons and multiday treks. Rendola Riding also raises barnyard animals and vegetables for the dinner table. Jenny Bawtree, an Englishwoman, founded Rendola in 1970 before *agriturismo* became hip. Guests come for the riding, but are not required to be experts at the English technique used here. The place has the feel of summer camp, partially owing to the youth classes taking place in summer, but mostly from the communal dining, and the "scrape the dung off your own shoes" spirit of the place. Several detached apartments down the hill offer a good option for families, or couples looking for privacy. Double rooms and breakfast are €80, and riding is €15 per hour. The weeklong advanced trail-riding program with lodging and half-board runs €600.

DINING FOR ALL TASTES

€   For the best food deal in town, drop by the **Martini Point** ✫ (Corso Italia, 285; ☎ 347-6221586) cocktail bar from about 6 to 9pm any night. For the price of a drink, you can down a buffet's worth of appetizers, and people-watch at the south gate of town. The couscous, mushrooms, and minipizzas are actually pretty good, and the olives are everything you could hope for in a bar called Martini. Light dishes cost about €5 to €8, but why pay when you get 'em for free during happy hour?

€   Toward the north end of town is **Trattoria Mazzoni** (Canto all Croce, 1; ☎ 0575-26857; closed Tues), a charming family restaurant/food shop easy to find (it's next to the sign with the pink pig face advertising its specialty: *porchetta* cooked over a wood fire). Open only for lunch, it gets crowded with locals and a few passing tourists. Of course, you'll be ordering the smoked *porchetta* for €6.50, but those who feel sorry for the piggy out front can order an equally good pesto gnocchi for €5.50. A liter of house wine goes for a reasonable €5.

€–€€   As a reproof to the restaurants that achieve economy by concentrating on pizza, the **Osteria da Luchino** (Via Deccheria, 3; ☎ 0575-333388) has a NO PIZZA sign in the window. Instead, the *osteria* offers a tasty selection of homemade pastas, including my fave: tagliolini in a tomato and basil sauce for only €6. Most other pastas range from €6 to €10, with grilled *secondi* in the €8 to €12 range. In summer, you can dine alfresco until 11pm every day but Tuesday.

€€–€€€€   Or try either of two local institutions on the Piazza Grande: **Trattoria Lancia D'Oro** (Logge Vasari, Piazza Grande, 18–19; ☎ 0575-399124; www.loggevasari.it) and **Ristorante "Logge Vasari"** (Via Vasari, 19; ☎ 0575-300333), which are both under the same ownership, and under the same arcade at the north end of Piazza Grande. Logge Vasari is the more upscale of the two, with candelabras and antique furniture. Here, you'll sit back and enjoy a multi-hour Italian-style meal with perhaps an assorted prosciutto starter, followed by homemade ravioli with truffles, and a *secondi* of Chianini steak with a side of fresh vegetables. Pasta dishes cost from €11 all the way up to €20 for a truffled selection, while grilled second platters are €16 to €22. Be sure to save room for a cheese platter or chocolate cake for dessert. The cheaper option, Lancia D'Oro, is not quite as swank in looks but its food is darn good, especially its grilled lamb with rosemary and homemade tagliatelle with regional herbs. Their *primi* are €8 to €15, their *secondi* €10 to €15.

WHY YOU'RE HERE: THE TOP SIGHTS & ATTRACTIONS
Your first stop should be the **Basilica di San Francesco,** which houses one of Italy's masterworks, Piero della Francesca's *Legend of the True Cross* ✫✫ (Piazza San Francesco; ☎ 0575-352727; www.pierodellafrancesca.it; free admission to

The *Legend of the True Cross*

Almost from the start of Christianity, the cross upon which Jesus was crucified was thought to possess mystic powers, as if sanctified by the spirit of God. Crusaders sought it out almost as fiercely as the Holy Grail, and enough alleged pieces of the True Cross appeared throughout Europe to create not only a few crosses, but Noah's ark, the tower of Babel, and a boardwalk around Jerusalem.

The legend, as detailed in della Francesca's fresco, goes like this—top to bottom, right to left:

1. Seth, the son of Adam, plants a sprig of the tree of knowledge in his dead father's mouth.
2. (diagonally from the top) Workmen for King Solomon take part of the tree to use for a bridge.
3. King Solomon constructs the bridge, which the Queen of Sheba recognizes as holy and prophesies that the wood will be used to crucify Jesus.
4. (diagonally from 3) Constantine has a vision of the cross. Constantine holds out a minicross while leading his troops in battle.
5. (across from 4) The Annunciation, in which an angel tells Mary she will bear the son of God. Doesn't really have anything to do with the cross legend, but an Annunciation painting is always nice.
6. Judas is tortured by being lowered into a well until he tells where the cross is.
7. (to the left of 6) St. Helena (and her trusty dwarf) directs her people to dig up the cross, and it promptly causes the miracle of resurrecting a man.
8. (below 7) A dramatic battle scene shows Heraclius defeating the Persian king Chosroes, who stole the cross and will be beheaded on the right.
9. (above 8) Heraclius returns the cross with great acclaim to Jerusalem, where people wear clothes oddly similar to those of 15th-century Tuscany.

church, €6 for entry to chapel; 9am–7pm, Nov–Mar and weekends closes 6pm). The fresco, painted on 12 panels in the 1450s, details the long story of the wood of the cross that crucified Jesus (see "The *Legend of the True Cross*," above). Its fame derives from its vivid colors, the use of perspective, and the realistic (for that time) setting of the scenes. The tourist board recommends calling the above number or using the website to make ticket reservations to view the fresco, but on my last visit there were few tourists, and I was able to enter easily. There is an official 30-minute time limit for viewing the fresco.

Arezzo's **Duomo** ★ (Piazza del Duomo; ☎ 0575-23991; daily 7am–12:30pm and 3–6:30pm) gets short shrift in the shadow of Francesca's mural, but it's worth a trip up to see its ornate interior. It took 250 years to complete from its start in 1278, and even then residents had to wait until 1859 for the bell tower, and until the 20th century for the facade to be completed. The 16th-century stained-glass windows by Guillame de Marcillat (a Frenchman!) are beautiful, but they don't let in enough light to see much of the other works here, including the masterful *Santa Maria Maddalena* fresco by Piero della Francesca to the right side of the tomb of Bishop Tarlati. Past the fresco is a large *cantoria* designed by Vasari in 1535.

Vasari's architecture can also be seen in the main square, the tilted **Piazza Grande** ✮ in the center of the old town. The square is used for antique fairs the first Sunday of every month and for jousting on the first Sunday in September. It was a setting for the movie *Life is Beautiful* in 1999. Vasari's loggia, built in 1573 (looking pretty similar to "Vasari's corridor" in Florence), is now filled with shops and restaurants on the north end of the square. In 1550, Vasari designed the bell tower, which tops off the **Palazzo della Fraternità dei Laici.** Dominicans sponsored the construction of the Gothic and early Renaissance Palazzo in the 1370s. The portal is worth a look, as is the Madonna relief above the door.

For a glimpse into the lifestyle and mind of Vasari, you can stop by his house, **Casa di Vasari** (Via XX Settembre, 55; ☎ 0575-409040; €2; Wed–Mon 8am–7:30pm, Sun and holidays closes 1pm). Ring the bell outside for admission, as the door will be locked. On a recent visit, I could tell the place doesn't get many visitors, as the one employee followed me around giving me an impromptu tour, in Italian. Vasari bought the house in 1350, and decorated it as a monument to himself. You can see his wall paintings featuring his portrait enshrined among the greats of art (he places himself right next to Michelangelo), and a ceiling painting of a battle between Virtue, Envy, and Fortune, perhaps Vasari's three main concerns in life. And just to show he had some humility, there's a small bare chapel off the living room, still with some original floor tiles, and a wooden altar for his prayers.

A more serene location for prayers would be the **San Domenico church** ✮ (Piazza San Domenico; ☎ 0575-22906; 8:30am–7pm) in the far northern part of town. The tree-lined piazza doesn't see many visitors, and the church interior is

The Joys of Jousting

The most famous festival of Arezzo is the **Giostra del Saracino (Saracen Joust)** ✮. Competitive jousting took place in Arezzo at least as far back as 1400, and this particular festival commemorates battles against invading Saracens. On the first Sunday in September, the Piazza Grande is filled with dirt and packed with people. Horsemen arrive in medieval garb to take their oath of combat in front of a decked-out town hall. Historical parades of flag-wavers and jugglers tour through town during the day. The event itself features horsemen competing with horse and lance to nail the metal "Saracen" figure propped up in the middle of the square. The catch is that the Saracen gets to fight back: If his shield is hit, the figure spins around, swinging the whip propped in his other arm.

silent under its huge wooden arches. The church was constructed in
features an appropriately dark and somber crucifix by Cimabue, painted 1
and only recently restored to its original glory. Remnants of frescoes covei
walls, beyond hope of full restoration, but the fragments are compelling.

THE OTHER AREZZO

About a mile outside of town, on Via Fiorentina, 550, is one of the world's largest
gold jewelry manufacturing companies, **Uno A Erre,** which sold 41 *tons* of gold
jewelry and accessories in a recent year. Arezzo has historically been a center for
gold and jewelry, and Uno A Erre certainly continues that tradition in a big way.
You can visit the fairly interesting museum to see production machinery, jewel
designs, and historic collections of jewelry styles that the company has produced
since its inception in the 1920s. Call ☎ 0575-925862 or 0575-925953 to make
an appointment. Naturally, it has a factory outlet store (Mon–Fri 9am–6pm, Sat
9am–1pm), where you can sometimes get decent deals on midrange jewelry. For
unique or high-end items, it's more fun, and just as expensive, to go to local artisans' shops in Arezzo or Florence.

Umbria

A logical next step after visiting Rome is to · drive through the remarkable hill towns that make up this important region.

by Bill Fink

THE SMALL BUT VITAL REGION OF UMBRIA, WHICH LIES NORTHEAST OF Rome, is made famous by St. Francis' hometown of Assisi and the Basilica there. But despite that major attraction, Umbria has always played second fiddle to its northern neighbor, Tuscany. And that's a darn shame because the region has much more to offer than a single side trip on the road between Rome and Florence.

Umbria has at least a half-dozen remarkable cities of unique charm and historical significance: Perugia, the capital, with a major university, jazz festival, and Umbria's best art museum; Assisi of St. Francis fame; Gubbio, a medieval town frozen in time with art-filled fortresses and churches along the slopes of a scenic mountain; Spoleto, with its own famous festival, Duomo, and shop-lined squares; Todi, a picturesque hilltop village with a maze of attractive streets; and Orvieto, with its famous wines, its underground caves, and famous cathedral.

Seeing all the major sights of Umbria in a single trip is a reasonable proposition. Umbria is just over half the size of Connecticut, measuring about 97km (60 miles) north to south and 64km (40 miles) east to west (though winding mountain roads can easily double the distance). The ideal way to explore the area is to base yourself in an apartment or country cottage for a week, and drive a rented car on day trips to various cities. Don't waste valuable vacation time changing hotel and home city every day. Rail and bus lines connect the cities as well, but not quite as conveniently as a rental car does.

The Umbrians are a festive people whom you'll greatly enjoy mixing with, particularly in their nightly ritual, the festive "see and be seen" *passeggiata,* as they stroll up and down the streets of their historic towns.

PERUGIA

Perugia is a spirited city of 150,000 that seems at first glance to be a sprawling confusion of railroad tracks and minimarts, a spaghetti of highways, tunnels, and roundabouts. But reach the center of Perugia and you'll find one of Italy's most vibrant historical districts, with a wealth of both traditional sites and eating and entertainment options, culminating in the October Chocolate Festival and July's world-class Umbrian Jazz Fest.

Perugia

Escalator ····
Parking Ⓟ
Train ┠━━━━┨

Arco Etrusco

San Francesco
Piazza S. Francesco
Piazza S. Paolo
Muro Urbico Etrusco
Via dell'Aquilone
Via Cesare Battisti
Via U. Rocchi
Acquedotto

Oratorio di San Bernardino
Via S. Francesco
Via Francolina
Via dei Priori
Piazza Cavallotti
Piazza Ansidei
Via Bartolo
Piazza Piccinino
Piazza Danti
Via Bontempi
Piazza Raffaello

Via della Sposa
Pellini Ⓟ
Via della Cupa
Via Ritorta
Cattedrale
Piazza IV Novembre
Fontana Maggiore
Via Cartolari
Via G. Alessi

Viale Pompeo Pellini
Cupa Ⓟ

Palazzo dei Priori
Via Boncambi
Via della Cupa
Galleria Kennedy
Via G. Mazzini
Corso Vannucci
Piazza Matteotti
Via XIV Settembre
Mercato Coperto

GIARDINI DEL CAMPACCIO

Piazza della Repubblica

Via C. Caporali
Corso Vannucci
Via Baglioni
Via Oberdan
Via Tancredi Ripa di Meana
PARCO S. MARGHERITA

Via Bonazzi
Piazza Italia Ⓟ
Porta Marzia
Viale Indipendenza
Via XIV Settembre

Viale Indipendenza
Piazza del Corso
Via Masi
Corso Cavour
Via Marconi
Piazza G. Bruno
Stazione S. Anna
San Domenico
Museo Archeolgico Nazionale

Via Fiorenzo di Lorenzo
Piazza Partigiani Ⓟ
GIARDINI DI S. GIULIANA
Via Fiume

Stadio di Atletica Leggera
Piazzale Europa
Porta S. Pietro

ITALY
Venice
Florence
Perugia
Rome
Naples

ACCOMMODATIONS ■
Hotel Brufani Palace **9**
Hotel Priori **7**
La Rosetta **8**

DINING ◆
Contrapunto Jazz Club **3**
Corso Garibaldi eateries **2**
Kadinsky's Pub **10**
La Lanterna **5**
Osteria del Gambero **4**
Rob Roy **1**
Trattoria di Borgo **6**

0 — 1/4 Mi
0 — .125 Km

Perugia, the capital, also makes a sensible headquarters from which to explore the region. Convenient highway, rail, and bus links connect it to Assisi in the east, Todi to the south, Gubbio to the north, and Cortona to the west. Once you start exploring Perugia's historical center, with the National Gallery, the Guild Halls, and its winding, stone streets linking medieval churches and museums, you won't be in any hurry to leave.

DON'T LEAVE PERUGIA WITHOUT . . .

POKING YOUR HEAD INTO THE GUILD HALLS See where the Donald Trumps of the 1400s met in the lavishly decorated and well-preserved Exchange, Merchant, and Lawyers' Guild Halls.

GOING FOR AN EVENING PROMENADE   The *passeggiata* along central Corso Vanucci lets you see and be seen, culminating in a mass chill-out on the steps of the Duomo in front of the impressive Maggiore Fountain.

VISITING THE NATIONAL GALLERY   Perugia's famed museum has recently been renovated to better show off its medieval and Renaissance art collection, including a display of hometown hero Perugino's greatest works.

ENJOYING THE TOP MEALS   At Trattoria Di Borgo, you'll savor a multi-course Umbrian banquet in the backyard garden. At Osteria del Gambero, you'll find an excellent menu with all manner of truffle dishes and seafood.

MEETING THE PEOPLE   At Perugia's Umbrian Jazz Fest or at the city's Eurochocolate Festival, you'll mingle with Perugians. At an AC Perugia soccer match, you'll look on as the Perugians seek to regain their ancient glory through sports.

A BRIEF HISTORY OF PERUGIA

Perugia has been an Umbrian capital since Etruscan times (around 700 B.C.). Roman legions conquered the city and its trade routes in 309 B.C. Hoping to regain its former power, Perugia backed Mark Antony in his battles against soon-to-be-emperor Octavian. Bad bet: Perugia was burned to the ground in 40 B.C. In what came across as a kind of early urban-renewal project, Octavian, after he became the Emperor Augustus, rebuilt the city and called it Augustus Perusia. Many of the city's walls, Roman aqueducts, and even Etruscan foundations are still visible in the city today.

Perugia didn't rise to eminence again until the early Middle Ages, when it became a free commune, then a city-state astride the same trade routes it dominated in Etruscan times. The mid-13th to late 14th century saw the construction of most of its significant landmarks, including the Duomo, the Fontana Maggiore, the central Palazzo, and the Guild Halls. Perugia added military conquests to its economic prowess, seizing land as far north as Siena in 1358.

Like Florence, Perugia coupled this time of economic, military, and artistic achievement with a morally bereft ruling family, the Baglionis, who made the Medicis look like altar boys. The Baglioni men married their sisters and murdered their brothers. As they began to spend most of their time fighting each other and other families in town, they fell prey to an outside invader. Pope Paul III's forces entered the city in 1538, destroyed the Baglioni palaces, and built a fortress above the rubble (the streets and houses that the Pope's forces buried can still be seen today in tunnels beneath the city). When Paul III came to Perugia for his post-conquest victory parade, he took a page out of the Baglioni playbook and forced the nuns of the city to line up and kiss his feet.

Perugia remained subdued under papal control until citizens began to revolt during the Italian Unification campaign of the 1860s. The Pope sent the quaint Swiss Guard from the Vatican to Perugia, where they massacred citizens and looted the town.

The 20th century has seen Perugia rise again to a position of economic and cultural significance. A variety of important industries now surround the town, and several major universities are active within it, including the Università per

Stranieri (University for Foreigners), a major Italian-language and culture school. Today's festivals and lively food, music, and business scenes continue to keep the hills of Perugia alive with activity.

LAY OF THE LAND

Perugia is at the center of regional **rail** connections, an easy trip from Rome (2¼ hr.; try for the five daily direct trains, not those that transfer at Foligno) and from Florence (transferring at Cortona, taking about 2½ hr.). Trains also run almost hourly to Todi (a 45-min. trip) and twice an hour to nearby Assisi, a 20-minute ride.

Perugia's **bus** terminal at Piazza Partigiani also connects Perugia to Assisi, Gubbio, and Todi (about a 1-hr. ride to each); to Florence (a 2-hr. ride, once daily); and to Rome about six times a day for the 2½ hour trip.

The **drive** to Perugia is about 185km (115 miles) from Rome, 145km (90 miles) from Florence. From Rome, take the A1 to Orte and connect to the A3. From Florence, take the A1 south and connect to the A75. The roads around central Perugia can be maddeningly confusing, so it may be easiest to park in the first parking garage you see, and take an escalator to the historical district. Garages cost €7.75 for a day, if you pay upfront. Free parking can be had at a lot at Piazza del Cupa, where you can walk to the series of long escalators bringing you to the center.

Perugia's **tourist office** (☎ 075-5736458) is found in the southwest corner of Piazza IV Novembre, and has a ton of pamphlets on both the city of Perugia and the region of Umbria. It's open 8:30am to 1:30pm and 3:30 to 6:30pm daily, Sundays from 9am to 1pm. The regional Umbrian tourist office located a couple of blocks away is just an administrative headquarters, so don't bother going there. Look for a copy of *Living Perugia,* a free monthly guide with restaurant, event, and activity listings.

If you're planning to visit several of the museums in town, for a savings, purchase the **Perugia Museo Card.** It comes in various denominations, from €7 to €35 depending on number of museums covered, people admitted, and length of validity. Even if you're just planning on seeing the National Gallery and one or two others, the €7 card is a good deal. The cards are sold at each attraction for which they give entry.

Many Perugia hotels offer an Internet terminal in the lobby or a lounge. But if you're stuck for Internet or business services in Perugia, try the **Internet Corner** (Via Ulisse Rocchi, 4, 1F; ☎ 075-5720901; daily 9:30am–midnight, Sun opens at noon). It has 30 computers, a phone center, fax, copying, and other services. Internet costs €2.70 per hour here or €1.80 an hour at the shop around the corner from the University for Foreigners on Via Fabretti.

ACCOMMODATIONS, BOTH STANDARD & NOT

Long-stay visitors should turn to **Atena Service** (Via del Bulagaio, 38; ☎ 075-5730821; www.atenaservice.com; no credit cards), a booking agency used by many foreign university students and some travelers for monthly-and-longer lodgings. The apartments are basic but clean and well maintained, and rates are cheap (€200 for a month for a double room in a shared apartment, €600 a month for a one-bedroom apartment). The downsides: A service charge raises the bill, and none of the lodgings will accept credit cards. Apartments are generally in the university area north of the historical center, some a bus ride away. If you're planning to be in the area for a while, and are on a tight budget, this could be a good call.

€–€€   **Hotel Priori** (Via dei Priori, 40; ☎ 075-5723378; www.hotelpriori.it) is a good deal in the historical center featuring simply decorated but fairly spacious rooms with terra-cotta floors. They aren't exactly high end, but they'll do for a decent night's sleep. And the prices can't be beat: as little as €40 in the off season (up to €66 in high season), €60 to €95 for doubles. I'd recommend in particular rooms 355 and 353, which are nicely refurbished doubles with air-conditioning, though these can cost up to €115 in high season. The hotel also has three huge suites with kitchenettes, period decor, and space for a family of four. These, however, are available only for long-term stays: €500 a week or €1,100 a month. The Priori's balcony is a pleasant place for breakfast, but beware of the ravenous pigeons. Internet access is available in the basement meeting room.

€€–€€€   An even better choice is the well-located **La Rosetta** ★ (Piazza Italia, 19; ☎ 075-5720841; www.perugiaonline.com/larosetta), which offers a wide range of choices for all budgets. The hotel has refurbished its first-floor rooms to resemble those of an 18th-century palace, with frescoes, vaulted ceilings, and chandeliers in the large superior doubles. Above are less pricey digs, with lower ceilings and more modest furnishings, but all rooms come with satellite TV, minibars, safes, and air-conditioning. Doubles start at €65 per person. The hotel itself has a restaurant on-site (which provides room service) and a concierge. It's quite nice and, with 90 rooms varying in price, size, and view, most visitors will be able to find something to meet their needs and budget.

€€€€   For a splurge in the center of town (honeymoon, anyone?) the **Hotel Brufani Palace** ★ (Piazza Italia, 12; ☎ 075-5720210; www.brufanipalace.com) lives up to the "palace" part of its name. Rooms are traditionally decorated, with a lavish 19th-century feel (the hotel opened in 1884, so think velvets and silks and patterned wallpapers), but fully modernized with large bathrooms. Prices are over the top in high season (€320 a night), but at quieter times of the year, I've seen this hotel go for as little as €130 on Expedia.com. The Brufani has spectacular views over the valley from its enviable position on a hilltop in the historical center of the city (at the end of Corso Vanucci at Piazza Italia). It even has a subterranean stone chamber with a small swimming pool and exercise equipment, a rarity in Italian hotels.

DINING FOR ALL TASTES

For the cheapest eats, follow the students. Go north of the city walls and into the smaller alleys around the Università per Stranieri for a variety of affordable dining options. **Corso Garabaldi,** due north of the Etruscan Arch, has four cheap *pizzerie,* a kabob shop, a *creperia,* and two bars in the space of 2 blocks. You can fill yourself for under €10 at most of these spots (just don't expect health food). You'll also want to stop off at one of the city's many chocolate shops, as the city is rightly famous for its sweets (the chocolate gelato here is the best in Umbria).

€€   For a creative approach to the popular Umbrian dishes, walk behind the Duomo to **La Lanterna** ★ (Via C. Monti, 33/H, and Via U. Rocchi, 6; ☎ 0743-44592; closed Wed), which features such novelties as *ravioli all'arancia* (orange ravioli with rose petals) and gnocchi *alla lanterna* with truffles and spinach topped by a cheese crust. Pasta dishes range from a reasonable €7.50 to about €10 for anything with truffles (less without); a half-liter of the house wine is just €3.50 and the food is scrumptious. The setting is also quite charming: You'll have the choice of dining in the medieval subterranean restaurant, or in the hidden, wisteria-draped alleyway garden lunch area (both are lovely). My only quibble? You'll give back some of the savings with the €2 *coperto* (cover charge).

€€   For a true multicourse, multihour Italian feast in a traditional setting, go to **Trattoria Di Borgo** ★ <kids> (Via della Sposa, 23/a–27; ☎ 075-5720390; Mon–Sat, sometimes closed Mon). Here both the restaurant and garden backyard dining area are packed until well past 11pm nightly, with a mostly local crowd devouring Umbrian specialties. Pastas range from €6.50 to €10, *secondi* (second plates) from €8 to €16. I especially enjoy the *tagliatelli al tartufo* (homemade pasta with truffles) for €7 and the mixed meat appetizer (*misto di salumi*, €4.50), though some may find the "mystery meats" on the plate a bit off-putting (but do try them, they're delicious). For *secondi*, order the juicy *maialino all perugino*, a pot-roast-type ensemble with veggies and mushrooms for €8.

€€   If you're looking for a little more elegance with your meal, as well as a wide variety of local tastes, order the €19 *degustazione* (tasting) menu at **Osteria del Gambero** (Via Baldeschi, 9; ☎ 075-5735461; www.osteriadelgambero.it). It's a sophisticated, simple place that's simply crazy for truffles. In season, you'll find truffle-enhanced sauces for its pasta courses, truffles on the meats, even truffles mixed into the seafood dishes. For a strong-tasting alternative to pasta and grilled meats, try the sea bass (*spigola*) with greens, capers, and olives, for €11. Other *primi* cost €7.50, and *secondi* are all priced at €11. Wine-lovers will appreciate the wide, thoughtful collection.

WHY YOU'RE HERE: THE TOP SIGHTS & ATTRACTIONS

For Umbria's best collection of medieval and Renaissance art, displayed in a renovated museum, visit the **National Gallery** ★★ (Palazzo dei Priori, 4F, entrance at Corso Vannucci, 19; ☎ 075-5741247; €6.50 or as part of the Perugia museum pass; Tues–Sun 8:30am–7:30pm). Its paintings, altarpieces, and stained-glass displays are spread through well-lit rooms, and are explained by bilingual inscriptions. It seems as though three-quarters of the works depict the Madonna and Child, so don't come expecting a variety of subjects; but you'll be able to explore in depth the variations on the Madonna theme from Byzantine times to the early Renaissance (see "Mamma Mia, Another Madonna & Child!" below).

The gallery culminates in **Room 23** with favorite son Perugino's greatest works. He taught painting to Raphael, collaborated with Pinturicchio, and earned consideration by art historian Vasari and others as a worthy peer to Michelangelo and da Vinci. Look at the innovative colors, poses, and landscapes he brought to traditional themes like *The Adoration of the Magi*, the *Pietà*, and his *Madonna della Consolazione*.

Mamma Mia, Another Madonna & Child!

Spend even a few hours in any Italian city, and you'll see dozens of Madonna-and-Child pictures, paintings, and statues on restaurant walls, car windows, street corner shrines, and church entrances. Enter a cathedral and museum, and you'll see dozens more, with Mary and Jesus in every possible pose and period of life, paired with saints, angels, and local patrons. After a day or two, you may have Madonna overload, and give them no more than a passing glance.

But look closer. As Perugia's Madonna-heavy National Gallery demonstrates, the dominant Mary-and-baby-Jesus theme in Italian art is a window through which you can understand Italian culture and history. The closer you look, the more will be revealed about the time and place of the art, and the people who made it.

A few things to look for:

1. **What are they wearing?** You can see a Madonna and Child in every type of garment, from royal robes to contemporary regional fashions to richly decorated Byzantine costumes. Mary usually wears a blue robe atop a red dress, the blue symbolizing fidelity and purity, the red standing for the blood of Christ. Jesus is either naked, or wearing a regional costume of the time. The nudity suggests the vulnerability of the sacrificed son, while contemporary robes link Jesus closer to contemporary life.

For an interesting perspective (literally) on the Annunciation, go to **Room 11** to see Piero della Francesca's Madonna polyptych, and note the sci-fi look of the arches and hallway between the Angel and Mary.

A taste of the wealth and prominence of the medieval guilds that ran the economy of Perugia is found at **The Guild Halls** ★★★, near Piazza IV Novembre. (You can see the **Exchange Guild Hall** at Corso Vanucci, 25; the **Merchants' Guild Hall** at Corso Vanucci, 15; and the **Lawyers/Notaries Hall** in the Palazzo. A combined €3.10 admits you to all 3, or pay €2.60 at the Exchange Guild Hall, €1 at the Merchants Guild Hall; Lawyers/Notaries Hall is free). Though the rooms here are small, and all three of the guilds can be toured in less than 45 minutes, you should not pass up the opportunity to see what are arguably the best preserved guilds in Italy, organizations that in their day had far more power and prestige than modern unions do today. This might is embodied by these halls, which were decorated by the best artists of the day. The highlight is the Exchange Hall, with its frescoes by Perugino created in the early 1500s. The gods of classical antiquity along with handsome men and women personifying the various virtues are the subject here, though, tellingly, Perugino also included a self-portrait in this pantheon (on the left-hand wall, look for the chubby fellow in the red cap up there among the great gods). Most art historians think that Perugino's protégé, Raphael, assisted with the

If you find the standard blue robe and red dress next to a haloed naked baby, the artist or the original owner of the work may have had a strict interpretation of the Bible and the role of the church. If Jesus has a Florentine robe, and Mary a stylish belt, then you can guess that the painter or patron wanted to more directly address the spirituality of contemporary life, and make the teachings more "modern" and accessible.

2. **What are their expressions? Their gestures?** The Baby Jesus may be pointing to the heavens, or to an unfurled banner. A bent thumb and two small fingers signify the trinity of the Father, Son, and Holy Ghost, with the first two fingers extended in benediction. Jesus could be holding an apple, pear, or grape, the seeds symbolizing rebirth. Mary and child can look at each other with love and caring, or directly at the viewer with a "God is watching you" type message. A sad or downcast Mary communicates her awareness that her child is doomed for crucifixion.

3. **And what's this? A pelican?** On many crucifixion scenes of the suffering Jesus and the weeping Mary, you'll see what seems to be a random sea bird hanging out at the top of the cross. The pelican, in times of need, will cut its own throat with its beak in order to feed its children with its blood. This natural symbol parallels Christ allowing his own blood to be spilled to atone for the sins of mankind.

work, possibly painting *Fortitude* himself (the figure on the cloud on the second bay of the left wall). At the Collegio della Mercanzia, you'll see very beautiful but unusual-for-Italy wood-inlaid walls (it's thought that Northern European artisans were imported in the 15th c. to do the work).

You should also spend some time in **Piazza IV Novembre** ★ (named for Italy's National Unity day), a picturesque medieval square built directly atop a Roman reservoir. In the center of the square is the notable **Fontana Maggiore,** a massive fountain designed by a local monk named Bevignate in 1278. Peek through the protective iron fence to see the carved marble scenes from daily life of the Middle Ages, plus figures from Aesop's Fables, signs of the zodiac, and even local government officials. On the north side of the square, climb the steps to spend a few minutes touring the **Duomo.** It's by no means the best in the region, but the dark, baroque interior provides a striking contrast to the fashionable shops lining Corso Vanucci outside. The massive **Palazzo,** on the south side of the square, houses the National Gallery and the Guild Halls. Built from about 1300 to 1450, this government palace still has some city offices in addition to the museums.

To appreciate the ingenuity of the Etruscans who founded Perugia, climb down into the **Pozzo Etrusco (Etruscan Well)** ★ 🧒. Over 2,200 years ago, Etruscans dug this 38m-deep (125-ft.), 5.4m-wide (18-ft.) well to provide water for the city. Nowadays, visitors can walk down the slippery steps, past dripping walls, and cross a walkway at the bottom. Admission is included with the €2.50 ticket for entrance to the moderately interesting **Capella di San Severo** (Piazza Raffaello; summer daily 10am–1:30pm and 2:30–6:30pm, Nov–Mar closed 5pm), which features a Raphael fresco.

A good spot for weekend visits with the kids is the **POST (Perugia Officina per la Scienza e la Tecnologia) science museum** <kids> (Via del Melo, 34; ☎ 075-5736501; www.perugiapost.it; €3; Fri–Sat 4–7:30pm, Sun 10:30am–1pm and 4–7:30pm, Nov–Mar opens 30 min. earlier). It's a hands-on museum of the button-pushing, interactive-display type, although most of the explanations are in Italian only. Regardless, parents and kids can figure out what's going on together, and it makes a nice break from Duomos and Roman ruins.

THE OTHER PERUGIA

For insight into the people of Perugia, you'll want to delve more deeply into their daily pleasures: chocolate, soccer, and leisurely strolls in the evenings.

In particular, the **passeggiata** ★★, an evening promenade along Corso Vanucci, is a must-do while in Perugia. Join the many locals every evening (until past midnight on weekends) as they stroll from Piazza Italia to Piazza IV Novembre. Along the way, do some window-shopping, stop at a bar or cafe, and just be part of the scene. Finish up by gazing over the countryside from the balcony at Piazza Italia, or sit with half the town at the steps in the medieval Piazza IV Novembre. It sounds like a simple activity, but it is truly at the heart of the life of this city.

Continue your walk underneath Piazza Italia through the refurbished exhibit spaces and streets of **Underground Perugia.** In the 1530s, the Pope's forces razed the southern part of rebellious Perugia and built the Rocca on top of it. Many of the streets and stone houses remained forgotten under the fortress for hundreds of years. Now, escalators lead people through the area on the way to lower town parking garages. Get off one of the escalators and tour the hidden streets, some with art galleries.

The Foreign University

The oldest and largest university in Italy for foreigners is the **Università per Stranieri di Perugia** (Piazza Forteraccio, 4; ☎ 075-57461; www.unistrapg.it/english). Since 1921 it has been teaching the language, culture, and arts of Italy. The school offers 3-month intensive language courses for all levels of students, as well as monthlong cultural classes for non-Italian speakers. Fees run €230 to €300 per month, and classes are taught all year long. Also of note is the university's free Wednesday lecture series, which sometimes features English-speaking guest speakers on all aspects of Italian art, culture, and history. Finally, the University hosts music, sports, and performing groups for foreigners—hang around the lobby and you may be able to sneak into a few.

The Perugia Jazz Fest

Virtually every major jazz musician has played the Perugia Fest, from Dizzy Gillespie to Herbie Hancock to Miles Davis. The event remains one of the most electric in the world of jazz as dozens of performances occur all over town, virtually 24 hours a day. It's not unusual to see staggering fest-goers exit late-night jam sessions as the morning's entertainment is being set up in the *piazze*. Tickets range from €10 for late-night bar performances, to €100+ for front row seats to the big-name events. The most popular events do sell out, but you can still arrive sans tickets and see a lot of jazz. What you can't do, though, is show up in town without hotel reservations and expect to get a room; it's absolutely mobbed during the festival, so make travel arrangements far in advance (and expect to pay higher rates). Even if you can't book something in the center, it's worth commuting for a day to Perugia if you're anywhere in Umbria during the festival.

For more information, see www.umbriajazz.com, or contact the box office (a couple of months before the festival) at ☎ **039-800462311.**

You'll also want to visit that mecca for chocoholics, the **Perugina Chocolate Factory** 🧒 (E45 Hwy. Madonna Alta exit, end of San Sito Rd.; ☎ 075-5276796; free admission; Mon–Fri 8:30am–1pm and 2–5:30pm), about 20 minutes outside of Perugia. It's a Willy Wonka–like experience as you take a guided tour around a huge plant processing tons of chocolate in every size and shape that pours off dozens of assembly lines. (The only downer: The pre-tour instructional video in English is a long corporate advertisement; watch the animated presentation for kids in Italian—it's much more entertaining.) The factory museum boasts a hollow replica of the world's largest piece of chocolate (2.1m/7 ft. tall, weighing 6 tons) wrapped in foil. It also has photos of famous Perugina spokespeople, from Joe DiMaggio to Frank Sinatra, and an odd picture of Mussolini visiting the factory about a year before it was bombed to the ground in World War II. The tour is free (and so are the samples!) but phone ahead for reservations, especially as the workforce is prone to 1-day strikes. *Note:* The staff gets quite testy if you take pictures during the tour. Perugina also has a shop at 101 Corso Vannucci in town.

If you'd really like to dip into the world of chocolate, **The Eurochocolate Festival** (www.eurochocolate.com) is a yearly bacchanalia devoted to all things brown and sugary. Organizers say they attracted a mind-boggling 900,000 visitors to a recent 10-day festival. The event has featured over 100 booths of international chocolate makers, exhibits on "crucial periods in chocolate history," chef demonstrations, and a "choco-reality" show. (I swear I'm not making this up.) Local producer Perugina plays a big role in the happenings.

Dropped to the third division of **Italian soccer** (Serie C) following a bankruptcy, AC Perugia is still a team with a glorious history and strong fan base. Going to a game is a way to experience the Italian passion for soccer. And with the team's recent weakening, it may be easier to get a ticket than for one of the big-city Serie A games. The season runs from about September to June, and home games are played at the 28,000-capacity Curi stadium south of the city center. Tickets can be purchased online at www.ticketone.it.

A DAY TRIP FROM PERUGIA: IN SEARCH OF CERAMICS

If you've been admiring the colorful ceramics in Italy, hold off on making any purchases and make a special side trip to **Deruta** (20 km/13 miles south of Perugia by car; you can also take a €3 30-min. bus ride from Perugia). Since the 12th century it has served as a center for the creation of glazed terra cotta. Today there are over 300 ceramic manufacturers in town whose bowls, plates, ladles, and other goods are shaped and glazed here and then shipped to all parts of Italy (in fact, it's a pretty good bet that that bowl you admired in Venice, Milan, or Rome was actually created here). Consequently, you'll find a greater variety in Deruta than anywhere else in Italy, at a much lower cost. You can simply walk from store to store along the Via Tiberina, or go to one of the big players, like the family of **Ubaldo Grazia** (Via Tiberna, 16; ☎ 075-9710201), which sells both traditional Deruta patterns (with the dragon motif, a design popular since the Renaissance) as well as quirkier contemporary offerings.

NIGHTLIFE

With its large university population and a world-famous jazz festival, Perugia has the critical mass to support a lively entertainment scene of pubs, discos, and live music venues for people of all tastes. Check out www.perugiabynight.com for a good listing of current entertainment options.

The **Contrapunto Jazz Club** ★ (Via Scortici, 4; ☎ 075-5733667) not only features regular live entertainment but also boasts an outstanding view of the countryside north of Perugia. The terraced patios are a good place to grab a beer at the end of a day, or to gather with friends to hear some music. The club is located across Piazza Fortebraccio and around the corner from the Foreigner's University, so it attracts an international crowd.

If you're just looking for a beer, check out one of Perugia's Irish pubs: **Rob Roy** (Via Fabretti, 95; ☎ 075-5724682), **Shamrock Pub** (Piazza Danti, 18; ☎ 075-5736625), or **Sullivan's Pub** (Via Bovaro, 2; ☎ 075-5720207). Rob Roy is often jammed with students (especially during happy hours), because the university is just around the corner.

Kadinsky's Pub (Via dal Pozzo, 22; ☎ 075-5728130) is a more sophisticated scene, with local art showings, parties, and music events. It has some good drink specials, and you can order pub grub from its always open kitchen. Kadinsky's is usually open 9pm to 2am.

ORVIETO

To the average traveler, Orvieto is a wine. To the connoisseur of art, it's the site of a great painting: Signorelli's *Last Judgment*. An almost perfectly preserved medieval hilltop town, Orvieto contains more than enough attractions to merit the status of "must see" on even the most hurried tour of Umbria.

Signorelli's soaring fresco (seen on the walls and ceiling of the city's Duomo) has something of the up-and-down quality of Orvieto itself. In it, you witness the turbulent life of people on earth, accompanied by the rise of some (to heaven) and the descent of others (to hell).

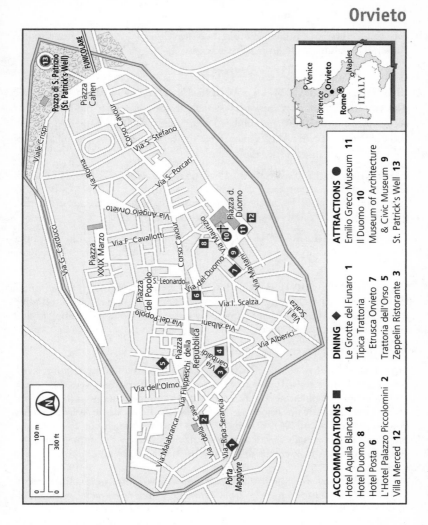

Orvieto

ATTRACTIONS ●
Emilio Greco Museum 11
Il Duomo 10
Museum of Architecture
& Civic Museum 9
St. Patrick's Well 13

DINING ◆
Le Grotte del Funaro 1
Tipica Trattoria
Etrusca Orvieto 7
Trattoria dell'Orso 5
Zeppelin Ristorante 3

ACCOMMODATIONS ■
Hotel Aquila Blanca 4
Hotel Duomo 8
Hotel Posta 6
L'Hotel Palazzo Piccolomini 2
Villa Merced 12

Visitors to hilltop Orvieto can't help but follow some of the same pattern. You will first rise a thousand feet above the plains to the plateau containing this walled city. But to escape the blazing sun, you will then descend to the vaulted wine cellars and restaurants dug into the lava rock of the city's foundation. To reach the heights, you won't confront Signorelli's armed guardian angels but only a ticket-taker for the steps up Torre del Morro, the town's bell tower. To descend to the depths, an inexpensive pass (the Carta Orvieto Unica; see below) lets you explore the underground caves that Etruscans dug into the mesa some 2,500 years ago.

After going up and down all day, you'll be ready to join the citizens of the town for a promenade back and forth along the mercifully flat street of Via Cavour, to see and be seen, just another soul passing through a city of history, mystery, and verticality. Though the stair-climbing may leave you panting, I count Orvieto among the highlights of all my trips to Italy.

DON'T LEAVE ORVIETO WITHOUT . . .

VIEWING THE DUOMO'S FACADE IN THE AFTERNOON LIGHT
The golden-tiled mosaics shimmering in the setting sun turn the front of the church into a 46m (150-ft.) illuminated text, with Gothic spires standing as massive exclamation points. Walk closer to see the carved figures on the pillars grow even more frightening in the fading light.

CHECKING OUT SIGNORELLI'S *LAST JUDGMENT* FRESCO   The recently restored masterpiece, in the Duomo's San Brizio Chapel, was greatly admired (and copied) by Michelangelo himself. It is one of the most colorful, graphic, and entertaining artworks in Italy.

TAKING AN UNDERGROUND TOUR   Both a city and a private tour offer chances for visitors to experience history as they walk through some of Orvieto's 1,200 caves.

TRYING SOME ORVIETO CLASSICO   Orvieto is rightly famous for its Orvieto D.O.C., white wines produced from grapes grown in the surrounding hills and valleys. They've been endorsed by everyone from ancient Romans and Gothic marauders to the trendiest wine critics of today.

A BRIEF HISTORY OF ORVIETO

Orvieto (*urbs vetus,* or "old city") sits on a plateau of tufa and clay left from a volcano rising from a seabed millions of years ago. The Etruscans were the first to build a major settlement here, about 600 B.C., choosing the location for its seemingly perfect defensive position (see "Who Are the Etruscans & Why Are They Following Me?" on p. 206). But the Romans flattened the city in 254 B.C., and there followed an equally devastating series of conquests by Byzantine, Lombard, and papal invaders (so perhaps the plateau method of defense had some kinks to work out).

Most of the towers, churches, and buildings that you'll see were constructed in a period of prosperity from the 12th to the 14th century. The solid stone buildings have thick walls for a reason: Incessant battles between the Guelph and Ghibelline factions (think the Hatfields and McCoys, but with poison, torture, and excommunication) kept the town in a mini civil war for over a hundred years.

In 1348, the "smallest" invaders had the most lasting impact on the city. Fleas carrying the bubonic plague killed over half the population of Orvieto in 5 months—including six of the Council of Seven leaders of the town. The labor force was decimated, commerce crumbled, and construction of new buildings came to a halt, leaving the same medieval tourist town you see today. Beginning in the 1400s, a number of popes used this now backwater fortress as a hide-out whenever things got too dangerous in Rome. The papal connection sponsored the creation of several more tourist favorites, including the magnificent Signorelli frescoes in the Duomo.

Present-day Orvieto has had a rebirth of sorts, hosting the Umbria winter jazz festival, as well as a quorum of ceramic makers, wine producers, and fine-dining

A Helpful Museum Card

If you're planning on seeing most of Orvieto's central sights, save some cash by purchasing the **Carta Orvieto Unica:** The tourist office and participating museums sell this comprehensive ticket for €13. It covers admission to the Cappella, Torre Del Moro, the Museo Claudio Faina, the city's Orvieto Underground tour, and a round-trip funicular ride. It also gives small discounts at some restaurants and shops. The museums alone cost €17.

chefs. Seasonal dance, theater, and academic conferences breathe life into a city that has seen its share of both figurative and literal ups and downs.

LAY OF THE LAND

The best way to reach Orvieto is either **by car,** a convenient stop on the Rome-Florence autostrada, or by train, about midway on the rail line connecting the two cities.

Orvieto is 150km (90 miles) south of Florence, 120km (75 miles) north of Rome on the A1 autostrada. You can park in pay-lots near the town center, in underground lots connected to the city center by escalator and elevator, or park for free by the train station below the city, and take the cheap funicular cable car to the top.

Trains stop almost hourly on the Florence-Rome line, and take 1¾ hours from Florence, or 80 minutes from Rome.

Once you reach the city, you can obtain sightseeing and lodging information at the **tourist office** (Piazza Duomo, 14, across from the Duomo; ☎ 0763-341772; www.umbria2000.it; Mon–Fri 8:30am–1:50pm and 4–7pm; Sat 10am–1pm and 3:30–7pm, Sun 10am–noon and 4–6pm).

ACCOMMODATIONS, BOTH STANDARD & NOT

The facilities maintained for tourists in Orvieto are among the best in Umbria.

€   Along with Villa Merced (see below), the cheapest option is the **Hotel Posta** (Via Luca Signorelli, 18; ☎/fax 0763-341909; www.orvietohotels.it; no credit cards), which offers small but decent rooms with new beds, thick walls, and a friendly but frantic staff (they're overworked). The shared bathrooms are clean; those connected to rooms are small but workable. Rates range from €26 for a single without a bathroom to €56 for a double with bathroom in high season. The old building is a little decrepit, but in a personable sort of way; the central "garden" doubles as a storage area, contributing to the "squatting in a noble's villa" feeling of the place. There's no air-conditioning, but the thick walls keep the rooms pretty cool in summer.

€-€€   My favorite choice here is a monastery stay, but one with a twist—a monastery with its own tennis courts, soccer field, private parking spaces, rooms with private bathroom facilities, and none of the elaborate curfews and rules that usually accompany these types of accommodations. That's what you get at **Villa Merced "Religious Guest House"** (Via Soliana, 2; ☎ 0763-341766; www. argoweb.it/casareligiosa_villamercede/villamercede.uk.html), just around the corner from the Duomo. If you've ever wanted to do this type of stay and get a small peek into monastic life, but have been worried about all the sacrifices you'd have to make, this is the one to try. As usual rooms are spartan, whitewashed, and filled with religious paraphernalia, but the prices are the lowest in town: 12 rooms, all with bathroom, €56 for a double, and €35 for a single. Book far in advance, as Merced tends to fill with student and religious groups. Send requests to villamercede@orvienet.it.

€€-€€€   Rates are refreshingly reasonable at the high-class **Hotel Aquila Blanca** ★ (Via Garabaldi, 13; ☎ 0763-341246; www.hotelaquilabianca.it), a 250-year-old palace that has served as a hotel for over 100 of those years. A royal-looking lobby stuffed with antiques (and a random rickshaw) gives it an imperial feel. Rooms are bright and cheerful, with a surprisingly homey flowered bed-and-breakfast ambience. Double rooms range from €80 to €105, depending on the season; singles are €20 cheaper.

€-€€   The pick of the three-star hotel group in Orvieto is the **Hotel Duomo** ★★ (Vicolo di Maurizio, 7; ☎ 0763-341887; www.orvietohotelduomo. com). Completely renovated in 2001, the family-run Hotel Duomo has a bright, fresh decor, with modern art, new furniture, spacious bathrooms, and a street front garden. It's also perfectly located just around the corner from the Duomo. In an odd move, one "Internet point" is set up for guest use at the front desk . . . but there is no chair (the manager Giovanni likes to keep things moving). Doubles run from €85 to €105, and five suites range from €120 to €150 for up to five people (although five would be cramped).

€€-€€€€   The luxe hotel choice in town is **L'Hotel Palazzo Piccolomini** ★★ (Piazza Ranieri, 36; ☎ 0763-341743; www.hotelpiccolomini.it), set in a 16th-century family *palazzo*. It's a beaut, with whitewashed walls and exposed stone masonry in the rooms, tasteful furniture, and terrific views over the rooftops of the city (though the windows do tend to be on the small side, as do the showers, which are coffin-cramped). The hotel has 22 double rooms (€106–€116), seven single rooms (€75–€85), and three suites (€186–€205). A helpful, friendly staff and free valet parking add to the appeal, as does the vaulted basement breakfast room—a cool place to eat, both architecturally and temperature-wise. In the lobby is a free Internet point for guest use.

Farm Stays
€€-€€€   Kids and starry-eyed adults alike will enjoy staying at a country apartment at the **L'Uva e le Stelle** ★ 🧒 (Localita Boccetta, III, 05010, Porano; ☎ 0763-374781; www.uvaelestelle.com), about 20 minutes northeast of Orvieto. The name means "Grape and the Wine," and guests can actually sign up for astronomy classes at the home observatory, which are, of course, accompanied by food and *vino*. A dozen cats prowl the grounds, and there's a swimming pool, full bocce-ball court, table tennis, and hilly gardens near woodlands. The six unique,

antiques-filled apartments are named for constellations, and decorated in warm, rustic tones. An indoor Jacuzzi offers yet another method for relaxation. Rooms range from €98 to €138 a night, €180 to €250 for a weekend, and €510 to €695 for a week.

€€€ It's worth lodging outside the city to stay at the lovely and terrifically family-friendly **Villa Ciconia** 🧒 (Via dei Tigli, 69, Loc. Ciconia; ☎ 0763-3055823; www.hotelvillaciconia.com). Kids will enjoy the swimming pool, and the twisting hallways, hidden alcoves, and old-fortress feel of this 16th-century villa. Parents will like the secluded peace of the gardens and the wood-beamed ambience, with colorful tiled floors and elaborate tapestries on some of the walls. The standard rooms (€130) are large, with iron fixtures, whitewashed walls, tiled floors, and a combination of antique and more modern furniture. The superior rooms (€155) are even bigger, and have the best garden views of the lot. Both varieties have space to add a cot for children. The Villa's restaurant is open to the public, and features a truffle-oriented pasta and grill menu, with *primi* ranging from €6.50 to €10, and main dishes going for €10 to €14.

Vacation Home & Apartment Rentals

If you're looking for a vacation home or apartment rental, the company to choose is **Galli Immobiliare** (Via del Duomo, 19A; ☎ 0763-343933; www.galliimmobiliare. com), a local real-estate agency, with a staff that knows the area and local properties inside and out. As usual, rentals are available by the week, month, or season, as are all levels of lodgings from a basic one-bedroom apartment, in the heart of Orvieto, to five-bedroom villas with swimming pool, barbecue, and modern kitchens out in the countryside. Rentals usually have a 1-week minimum and some are seasonal. The rental office (and the website) has photos of the rentals with details of features, and they tend to be fairly accurate. I'd be wary, however, of renting an apartment that only has an exterior shot accompanying the listing. Apartments begin at €80 per night for a small room, while out-of-town villas begin at €1,100 a week. Note that the tourist office in town also has an extensive rotating list of local and regional apartment properties, though these are probably not as carefully vetted as Galli Immobiliare's will be.

DINING FOR ALL TASTES

€€ For the quintessential Orvietan dining experience, combining the modern and the medieval, try first the **Tipica Trattoria Etrusca Orvieto** ★ (Via L Maitani, 10; ☎ 0763-344016; www.argoweb.it/trattoria_etrusca; Tues–Sun). Dishes in this crisp, clean restaurant focus on local specialties that include handmade *umbrichelli* pasta (€7–€9), rabbit dishes (€12), fresh bread with olives and rosemary, and an outstanding minestrone soup with fennel (€4). Normal pasta plates average €7 to €9, *secondi* €10 to €15. Salads are mixed at the table, and the dessert cart features the *tarta estruscana,* a sweet cake of lemon and almond. Also try the local Passito sweet wine. The manager greets diners at their tables, and will show off the medieval well and the old cellars, which are 20m (66 ft.) underground, complete with a long dining table (which can be reserved for tastings), dusty bottles of wine, hanging bananas, and a general feel of a secret gastronomical cult hideaway.

€€   Three stars for ambience go to **Le Grotte del Funaro** ★ 🛦 (Via Ripa Serancia, 41; ☎ 0763-343276; www.ristoranti-orvieto.it; Tues–Sun), where you'll descend a long stairway into this "cave of the rope maker," walking under stone arches through the extensive wine storage/tasting area and past the open wood-fire stoves to the long room containing a dozen dining tables. Kids will like the hidden bat-cave feel of the place, as well as the pizzas (listed only in Italian), which cost around €7. I like the local mixed grill for about €12, and the *funaro* version of local *umbrichelli* pasta at €10. Overall, pastas range from €9 to €14, and grilled *secondi* meat dishes go from €10 to about €18. Service is on the border-line between relaxed and just plain slow, but most waiters speak English.

€€   For a rather basic but friendly restaurant popular with both locals and tourists, you may want to try **Trattoria dell'Orso** (Via della Misericordia, 16–18; ☎ 0763-341642; Wed–Sun), where chef Gabriele di Giandomenico serves fresh country-style meals, including a delicious vegetable-and-mushroom tagliatelle for €7 (€9.50 with local truffles). The game hen in a bed of polenta is mouthwater-ing. *Primi* run €7 to €11, *secondi* €10 to €15.

€€   An interesting (but slightly pricey) Art Deco take on an Umbrian restau-rant is the **Zeppelin Ristorante** (Via Garabaldi, 28; ☎ 0763-341447). The name comes from the fact that this converted warehouse is long and narrow with a rounded ceiling and windows on the side, sort of like a . . . zeppelin. The grilled wild boar with sage and tomatoes is delicious (€15), as is the spaghetti *alla norcina,* with truffles, garlic, and anchovies (€12). A first course will run you from €11 to €15, grilled second dishes from €12 to €18. Lorenzo Polegri also presents very popular cooking courses, lasting from a day to a week (www.cooking initaly.it).

WHY YOU'RE HERE: THE TOP SIGHTS & ATTRACTIONS

Orvieto's Cathedral, the **Duomo** ★★★ (free admission, €1 for brief history recording; 7am–1pm and 2:30–7pm, sometimes closes 1 hr. earlier or later), both inside and out, deserves its status as one of the indispensable attractions of Italy. Even from kilometers outside the city, you can see its spires reaching above the plateau like the control towers of a massive ship. Up close, the square can hardly contain the massive structure (and unless your camera has a wide-angle lens, your photos won't either).

The front of the Duomo is awe-inspiring. The afternoon sun reflects off a dozen golden mosaics as if a holy light were shining down on you. (The original tiles, moved to Rome, were replaced in the 1800s with the equally shiny ones seen today.) In medieval times, the sick and the lame would have assembled at the church doors to beg for alms.

The Duomo's famed attraction is **Luca Signorelli's** *Last Judgment* **fresco** painted from 1499 to 1504 on the walls and ceiling of the **Cappella San Brizio** (**Chapel of San Brizio;** €4 or free with Carta Unica; Jan–Feb and Nov–Dec week-days 10am–12:45pm and 2:30–5:15pm, Mar and Oct weekdays closes 6:15pm, Apr–Sept weekdays closes at 7:15pm, Oct–June Sun and holidays 2:30–5:45pm, July–Sept Sun and holidays closes at 6:45pm). It has recently been restored to its original state, and visitors are required to pay a €4 admission fee. It's well worth

Dueling Underground Tours: Which Is Better?

For more of an archaeological perspective, join the city-organized **Orvieto Underground** (begins at tourist office; ☎ 0763-344891; www.orvieto underground.it; tours daily at 11am, 12:15, 4, and 5:15pm). Coordinated by the Speleological Society, this tour has a feature-rich bent to it: Background is given on an Etruscan well, an olive press, an underground stable, workshops, and the pigeon farms. Admission is included with the Carta Unica; otherwise it is €5.50.

If you're looking for the personal touch, try a tour with the same name but which is actually quite different from the one above: The **Orvieto Underground** (begins at Bar Hescanas, Piazza Duomo, 31; ☎ 335-1806205; www.orvietounderground.com; †5; daily hourly from 10:30am) starts at a stairway underneath a nearby restaurant. It has more of an "exploration feel." Caves are a little cramped; one passageway is quite claustrophobic (you can opt out of cistern-viewing). The bonus is that these are private caves under a restaurant, so you get to sample some of the owner's wines, with tasty snacks.

You can follow your descent into the caves with a climb up toward heaven when you visit the **Torre Del Moro** (Via Duomo and Via Cavour; ☎ 0763-306414; €2.80, €2 students and seniors; May–Aug 10am–8pm; Mar–Apr and Sept–Oct 10am–7pm; Jan–Feb and Nov–Dec 10am–1:30pm and 2:30–5pm). Climb 162 steps on a wide, well-lit stairway to stand on top of this 45m-tall (150-ft.) 13th-century tower. You'll feel like you're on top of the mast of sailing ship Orvieto, gliding through a sea of farms, watching waves of wine fields undulating on the horizon. It has particularly nice sunset views during the extended summer hours. Also check out the rear of the clock face (added in 1876) on the way to the two bells on the peak. Admission included with the Carta Unica.

it. What is most memorable about Signorelli's work is his ability to vividly transfer the feeling of contorted bodies, like those carved on the pillars outside, to the two-dimensional world of painting. Even Michelangelo came here to study how it was done, applying the lesson to the Sistine Chapel. And if the overly stretched bodies and surreal landscape in the *Resurrection of the Dead* (the segment on the right upon entering) seem familiar, check some Salvador Dalí paintings to see what he lifted.

Note Signorelli's self-portrait, the man dressed in black, at the left edge of the wall to the left of the entry. He looks annoyed perhaps because his mistress dumped him while he was painting the fresco. She is now forever immortalized (1) as the blonde prostitute in the blue skirt, standing nearly in front of him, taking money for her services; (2) riding naked on the back of a devil, about to be plunged into hell (top center of the right front fresco); and (3) in the pits of hell, being groped by a blue devil whose face looks suspiciously like Signorelli's.

The chapel across from Cappella San Brizio is almost forgotten today, but it's worth a brief visit to see the religious relic for which the church began to be constructed in 1290: a cloth said to be stained with the blood of Christ. The jeweled case containing the relic and the surrounding paintings illustrate this "Miracle of Bolsena." Every visitor to Orvieto should take the opportunity to descend into the depths and explore some of the caves hidden beneath the city. **Organized cave tours** (see "Dueling Underground Tours: Which Is Better?" on

Who Are the Etruscans & Why Are They Following Me?

Across Umbria the signs are always the same: 'x' BUILDING IS THE RECENTLY REFURBISHED VILLA OF A RENAISSANCE NOBLEMAN WHO EXPANDED A MEDIEVAL HOME BUILT FROM A ROMAN WATCHTOWER BASED ON AN ETRUSCAN FOUNDATION. NOTE THE ORIGINAL ETRUSCAN WALLS IN ROOM 'y'. Or THE TOWN WELL WAS DEVELOPED IN THE 14TH CENTURY FROM THE ETRUSCAN ORIGINAL.

Who were these people whose apparent mission in life was to bake pottery, stack stones, and bury their dead all over Tuscany and Umbria?

It is known that the Etruscans settled widely across northern and central Italy in the 9th century B.C., and reached the peak of their power and influence across the western Mediterranean between 700 and 600 B.C. Their presence was felt in trade, war, culture, and shipping, until they were defeated in the Greek naval wars in the 4th century B.C. Later, they were absorbed into the Roman empire. Beyond that, things get fuzzy. Even as far back as 500 B.C., the Greek historian Herodotus was trying to figure out where the Etruscans came from. Were they indigenous peoples of Italy? Had they emigrated from Asia Minor?

Secondhand Greek and Roman histories, combined with archaeological evidence gleaned from Etruscan ruins and tombs, suggest that the Etruscans developed a unique culture native to Tuscany and Umbria. They consolidated local tribal groups into a collection of city-states centered in what are now Orvieto, Perugia, and Arezzo, among others. The Etruscans are credited with the creation of much of the art, language, and architecture commonly associated with the Roman empire, including arches, aqueducts, and, yes, the first paving of an ancient autostrada. Their downfall came after they developed the art of internecine warfare.

What is exciting today is to stare at stacked 2-ton stones, a 90m (300-ft.) well shaft, or a thousand symmetrical, decorated urns and think, "How in the world did they *do* that?" Imagine the effort, the ingenuity, and the communal spirit that was necessary not to re-create, not to improve upon, but to build all these major structures with little more than tools of bone and bronze, and brute strength. On the other hand, there's plenty of evidence that the Etruscans themselves built on top of the Villanovans, who were influenced by the Phoenicians, who studied the . . . .

p. 205) offer a chance to experience some of Orvieto's history while escaping either the hot summer sun or cold winter winds.

The Etruscans were the first to burrow into the soft stone for building materials and wells more than 2,500 years ago. Now there are over 1,200 caves underneath Orvieto, essentially turning the plateau into a huge black chunk of Swiss cheese.

The bulk of Orvieto's caves are small private basements dug to store wine or other food to go with cheese. The caves on the city tour have also been used as a stable, an olive-oil workshop, a World War II bomb shelter (no bombs hit), and a pigeon farm.

During extended sieges of this fortified city, townspeople discovered that pigeons were an almost magical source of food. Hundreds of pigeon coops were dug into square holes in the cave walls, creating a kind of giant shoe rack. Pigeons nested in the holes, and flew out gaps in the walls to the countryside to feed themselves. As pigeons reproduce every 20 days, Orvietans could alternate between feasting on eggs and birds, without jeopardizing their food source.

Even if you miss Orvieto's many performance events at the **Teatro Mancinelli** (Corso Cavour, 122; ☎ 0763-340493; www.teatromancinelli.it; €2; 9:30am–1:30pm and 3–6:30pm), take the opportunity to visit the building, a show in and of itself. For only €2, you can wander through the building built in the 1860s. The 560-seat theater was refurbished to all its neoclassical, neo-Renaissance splendor in the 1990s. The decor certainly isn't subtle, but it does give you a feeling for the rock-star status of opera in the late 19th century.

For some interesting Umbrian historical artifacts (and a great view of the Duomo facade), go to the **Museo Claudio Faina e Museo Civico** (Piazza del Duomo, 29; ☎ 0763-341216; www.museofaina.it; €4.20 adults, €2.50 seniors and students; summer 10am–1pm and 2–6pm, Oct–Mar 10am–1pm and 2:30–5pm). This museum houses an extensive and eclectic collection of Etruscan and Roman artifacts, coins, art—basically anything spoiled rich kid/grave robber Claudio and his father could seize in the 1800s. Museum management has tried to liven up the displays with interactive signs, as well as buttons to rotate the coin trays. And if you don't think pottery can be lively, check out the pornographic penis procession on the urn in the upper-right case in Room 7. Also note the three-legged candle holder from 300 B.C. on the third floor, in Room 16. As a bonus, the museum's second- and third-story windows offer the city's best views of the Duomo's facade directly across the piazza.

SHOPPING

It's a worthwhile stroll to check out "Artists Alley" (Via Dei Magoni off of Via della Duomo) for a representative selection of ceramics, leather, and embroidery. Even if you don't want to buy, it's interesting to watch the artisans at work. You can find variations on the yellow-and-green theme at **Mastro Paolo's** (Piazza Duomo, 36, ☎ 0763-343667). The 70-year-old Paolo says that when he retires, the store will, too, so don't delay. Most pieces run €20 to €40.

A quality, family-run wine shop in town is the Vinari cantina at Corso Cavour, 5, with only a green flag in front with their name and a jug on it. On sale: reasonably priced whites and reds (starting at €7) from their local estates.

ASSISI

Assisi is a typical Umbrian village that happens to be the hometown of St. Francis. Don't be put off by the busloads of visitors. St. Francis's Basilica isn't a standard tourist attraction; it's home to some of the finest art in Italy, and remains a deeply spiritual pilgrimage site. And beyond the Basilica and the souvenir stands lies a peaceful medieval town full of natural retreats in stark contrast to the flag-waving group tours. Every visitor should explore it: from the peaceful Erme delle Carceri to the panoramic views from the ruined fortress standing above Assisi.

DON'T LEAVE ASSISI WITHOUT . . .

VISITING THE BASILICA   One of the top sites in all of Italy, the massive church is notable not only for its magnificent artwork (including Giotto's frescoes), but also because it's a major pilgrimage destination.

GOING TO ST. FRANCIS'S RETREAT ON MOUNT SUBASIO   Take some time to enjoy the calming Erme delle Carceri, the spiritual retreat of St. Francis, far from the commercialism of central Assisi.

CLIMBING THE ROCCA TOWER   Take in spectacular 360-degree views of Assisi and the wilderness on the other side of the hills.

A BRIEF HISTORY OF ASSISI

Assisi had the usual history of an Umbrian hill town: Umbrian tribal origins, Etruscan influence, Roman colonization, barbarian invasions, a sacking by Barbarossa. The usual history, that is, until St. Francis and his female counterpart St. Clare were born at the end of the 12th century (see "The Life and Times of St. Francis" on p. 213). And then Assisi took off, becoming one of Italy's major centers for religious pilgrimages. Following papal approval of Francis's new sect in 1210, and the increasing popularity of his preaching, Assisi began to attract its first hordes of followers. After Francis died in 1226, the massive Basilica project began. Contrary to Francis's teachings of poverty and simplicity, the Pope and some of Francis's followers directed the construction of the epic structure over the next 20 years. The Basilica has been a steady pilgrim and tourist attraction ever since.

After the time of Francis, Assisi suffered from continuous attacks—as much from within as without. For nearly 200 years, Assisi's Parte de Sotto (lower part) fought the Parte de Sopra (upper part) in almost continuous factional battles for control of the city, which then left Assisi open to be sacked and looted by invading forces no fewer than four times. It is no wonder that in 1578, the writer Cipriano Piccolpasso found Assisi to be "a poorly arranged city where one sees many abandoned and ruined houses . . . they are unpleasant people, not very courteous to foreigners nor even to each other." For good measure, Napoleonic troops invaded and looted the city (was there anything left?) in 1808.

Times have changed. The city is now quite prosperous and well maintained, owing to the continuous tourist and pilgrim trade. The many religious seminaries, workshops, and festivals create an atmosphere of spirituality, while the now-courteous residents make a good living serving an army of visitors. The only danger comes from the earthquakes that continue to shake the city. The most recent major quake, in 1997, resulted in five deaths and damage to the older buildings, from which they have just recovered.

LAY OF THE LAND

Assisi isn't the simplest town to reach **by train,** but it's definitely doable. Assisi's station is 4.8km (3 miles) from town, requiring you to wait for the half-hourly bus, or take a €12+ cab ride. A walk to town up the steep roads amid heavy bus traffic isn't recommended.

Trains from Rome connect through Foligno, a journey of close to 3 hours. It takes about the same time from Florence, transferring at Cortona. Perugia is only a 30-minute train ride from Assisi's station. **Buses** also connect Assisi to Perugia and Gubbio and parts beyond via the bus terminal at Piazza Matteotti.

The **drive** to Assisi is about 193km (120 miles) from Rome, 177km (110 miles) from Florence. Take SS3 from Perugia, then the SS75 in the direction of Foligno. The Assisi exit drops you in the modern lower town (Santa Maria degli Angeli), where you have to keep your eyes open for signposts to Assisi.

Parking is pretty much impossible in town, but it's available in a variety of pay lots for about €11 per day, €1.50 per hour. If you're willing to walk a few extra blocks, free parking can be had below the pay lots at Porta Nuova, in the road or in the dirt lot across from the hospital. The Porta Nuova lot has a covered escalator reaching town level. You can also drive around the city to reach free street parking on the approach to the Rocca, thus avoiding the steep hike up there.

Assisi's **tourist office** (☎ 075-812534) is on the west side of **Piazza del Comune.** It has the usual maps of the city, as well as a good collection of "Franciscan Itinerary" hiking and site guides for the area around Assisi. The office is open from 8am to 6:30pm during summer months, and closed 2 to 3pm weekdays and at 1pm on Sundays from November to March. The official website (www.umbria2000.it) is weak; try the independent **www.assisionline.com** for better information in English.

ACCOMMODATIONS, BOTH STANDARD & NOT

Assisi is the place to try a stay at a **monastery, convent,** or **religious retreat.** There are over a dozen in town and an equal number scattered in the general area. Staying in this type of accommodations, you'll absorb more of the religious spirit of Assisi. As always, these lodgings tend to be much cheaper than standard accommodations. *Note:* It's very important to reserve well ahead when you're visiting Assisi—rooms fill up, particularly during Easter and other religious holidays.

€ Catholic-school flashbacks aside, there's no reason whatsoever to be intimidated by the French nuns at the **Monastery of St. Colette** ★ (Borgo San Pietro, 3; ☎ 075-812345; Apr–Oct; no credit cards). They're a friendly bunch (just take a peek at the bulletin-board photos of them partying on their retreats) who love welcoming travelers to Assisi. The sisters offer 19 basic but recently refurbished rooms with one to three beds for €26 per person. Even better, they throw in free parking, impose no curfews, and offer great suggestions for low-cost places to eat in the neighborhood. There's also a lovely garden and several lounges where guests can relax.

€   If St. Collette is booked up, turn to **La Cittadella** (Via Ancajani, 3; ☎ 075-813231; www.cittadella.org), a huge religious institution housed in an extended complex of buildings. On-site are 70 guest rooms, a dining hall for 500, a conference center, a library, an art gallery, and a church. Not surprisingly, the place has a rather bureaucratic flavor, and it can be a hike to reach the rooms spread around the campus. On the positive side, with so much activity in the area, you'll feel part of the pilgrim community. Lodging is of the college-dorm-room variety, but with private bathrooms. Rooms with breakfast range downward from €38 for a single, to €25 per person in a room with four people (bring all four—they don't mix and match). This is a popular group destination, so reserve in advance.

€   For a one-stop shop for lodging, go a quarter-mile east of Porta Cappuccini to the **Complesso Turistico Fontemaggio** (Via Eremo delle Carceri, 7; ☎ 075-813636), which comprises a hotel, a youth hostel, campgrounds, bungalows, and a house for rent. There are endless lodging options, but a **camping** spot is €5.50 (with shower, plus €4.50 per tent, and €2.50 per car), a bed in the **youth hostel** is €20, a double with breakfast in the **hotel** is €52, and the first floor of "**Papi House**" is €130 for two suites and a kitchen. There's also a very nice attached restaurant (see below), trattoria, and convenience store. This turns into quite the community, especially at holiday times, when the 250-site campground gets rowdy with late-night guitar-led hymns.

€€€   Two quite decent and centrally located hotels under the same ownership are the **Priori** (Corso Mazzini, 15; ☎ 075-812237) and the **Alexander** 🎒 (Piazza Chiesa Nuova, 6; ☎ 075-816190; both at www.assisi-hotel.com). The Priori fills three floors of a 16th-century *palazzo* with 34 rooms and antique furniture, frescoed ceilings, and small but modern bathrooms. A double is €150 in high season, but can drop closer to €110 the rest of the year. The Alexander lacks air-conditioning, elevators, and meal service, but has a nice roof terrace, and most rooms have extra beds, which make it a good spot for families. It's also cheaper than the Priori, at about €110 for a double in high season.

€€€€   **Hotel Subasio** ★ (Via Frate Elia, 2; ☎ 075-812206; www.hotelsubasio. com) has been the high-end choice in town since Assisi became a tourist destination in the 1860s. With lavish period rooms (twins cost around €180, including breakfast for two), awesome countryside views, an excellent restaurant, and good service, it's no wonder the hotel register is filled with the names of Italy's rich and famous. Request a room with a view of either the country or of the Basilica of St. Francis, which is just down the street.

Rural Accommodations

€€   For an out-of-town treat, make your Assisi-area headquarters **Le Silve Hotel** ★★ (Loc. Armenzano; 075-8019000; www.lesilve.it), a remote hideaway in the hills beyond Assisi. Rooms in the main old converted farmhouse have a rustic elegance, while those in the detached building have patios with panoramic views for a reasonable €91. Le Silve has a swimming pool, tennis court, and even miniature golf. Apartments and villas are also available for rent on the extensive property. The apartments have fireplaces, kitchenettes, an outdoor barbecue, and their own swimming pools, and rent for about €520 per week during summer. The Silve estate is at the end of a long gravel hill road, about a 20-minute drive east of Assisi.

DINING FOR ALL TASTES

€   For cheap eats, you can first try **Foro Romano** 👶 (Via Portica, 23; ☎ 075-815370; www.selfservicefororomano.com), a very popular cafeteria-style eatery. Order one of the varied pasta selections for €5 to €6, or hit the salad bar for a very reasonable €3.50. Foro Romano is just down the street from Piazza del Comune. It claims to serve over 60,000 dishes a year, so they must be doing something right.

€€   While it's close to Piazza del Comune, **Restaurant Pallotta** ★ (Via San Rufino, 4; ☎ 075-812649; www.assisionline.com/trattoriapallotta; closed Tues) isn't your typical tourist trap. Through an arch and at the end of an alleyway off the piazza, this traditional Umbrian restaurant features such specialties as *strangozzi* with mushroom sauce, homemade tagliatelle, gnocchi of potatoes, and cacciatore-style rabbit. The tasting menu (without wine) is €24, and offers a great selection of local delicacies.

€   Connected with the Fontemaggio campground/hostel complex a mile south of town, **La Stalla** ★ 👶 (Via Eremo delle Carceri, 8; ☎ 075-812317) is about as genuine a country trattoria as you're going to find. When they say the place is a "refurbished" barn, they mean they've moved the sheep out of the stalls. The walls are blackened with smoke from the open fire that cooks sizzling sausages and local game dishes, and long benches encourage fun communal dining with the mobs from the campground. Excellent homemade gnocchi and Umbrian pastas are only about €5 a dish.

WHY YOU'RE HERE: THE TOP SIGHTS & ATTRACTIONS

La Basilica di San Francesco (Basilica of St. Francis) ★★★ (www.sanfrancesco assisi.org; free admission; upper church 8:30am–6:50pm, lower church opens at 6am, Nov–Mar both closed noon–2pm and at 5:50pm) is among the must-see sights of Europe, not only because of its magnificent Giotto frescoes but also because it is still the second-most-important pilgrimage site in Italy (after Rome), and third in the world (after Bethlehem). Unlike many of Italy's churches, which have more snapshot-taking tourists than worshippers, the Basilica and Francis's teachings attract devout pilgrims. Busloads of religious groups fill the Basilica, celebrating Mass in side chapels, kneeling at Franciscan relics, and praying silently at altars around the church. And if there's too much talking, be prepared to hear a voice from the heavens as *"Silencio!"* booms from the security guards' PA system.

To be sure, there are plenty of people visiting just to see the works of art. And this, too, is a worthwhile pilgrimage. Seeing these frescoes, paintings, and altars in the context of the Basilica is a much more rewarding experience than seeing dozens of Madonna-and-Childs stacked in a museum.

The massive Basilica is split between an upper and a lower church. To first appreciate the artistic, and then the religious, nature of the structure, I'd recommend going in reverse chronological order, from the top down. Start with Giotto's frescoes and the traditional upper church, then descend to the darker, meditative lower church, and finally enter the almost mystical crypt of St. Francis.

Begin with the 28 panels, **Giotto's *Life of St. Francis* frescoes,** which will give you the perfect overview of the life of the saint, as well as the story of medieval Italian art as it breaks away from Byzantine tradition. Giotto's work, done about 1296, is significant not only for its accessible cartoon-strip method of communicating the life of St. Francis, and its delightfully bright colors, but for its "form follows function" philosophy. Traditional Byzantine art, which dominated church decoration for a thousand years, outlined stiff wooden figures, draped in gold, a symbolic representation of the glory of God. Giotto chose to paint the life of St. Francis with the simplicity and attention to nature that Francis himself espoused in his teachings. Although the perspective is askew and detail rudimentary, the robes flow; the expressions of surprise, pain, and fear seem genuine; and St. Francis seems humble, even as he ascends to the heavens on a big pink cloud **(panel 12).**

From the front of the right aisle of the church, going clockwise, you'll follow Francis as he renounces his worldly goods in **panel 5,** expels demons from multicolored Arezzo in **panel 10,** gives his sermon to the birds in **panel 15,** and receives the stigmata in **panel 19,** about a quarter of the way down the left wall.

Don't leave the upper church until you take a look at Cimabue's *Crucifixion,* which, though damaged in the quakes (and faded by time), still retains some of its former radiance.

Exit the airy Gothic upper church for the **lower church** to see another series of astonishing frescoes you could spend an entire day examining. You'll see pre-Giotto Byzantine works lining the walls, and masterpieces like the Simone Martini frescoes in the Capella di San Martino, and Cimabue's famous *Madonna with St. Francis,* the portrait that is reproduced all over town, on the right wall.

Take the stairs in the middle of the lower church to visit St. Francis's **crypt.** This formerly secret room contains the body of St. Francis in a humble stone tomb, more fitting to his wishes than the huge church above it. Pilgrims kneel, touch the stone, pray, and radiate joy as they come close to the object of their worship.

On your way out, check out the side Chapter Hall to see the **relics of St. Francis,** his robe, sandals, prayer book, and other personal items.

As you leave the Basilica, you'll pass dozens of souvenir stands selling every imaginable item emblazoned with the saint's name. The rampant commercialism is a stark contrast to St. Francis's teachings of poverty, personal reflection, and

---

Free Tours with the Brothers

The Franciscans affiliated with the Basilica offer free English-language tours every Monday through Saturday. Though the tours don't go into the Basilica itself, they discuss the church in detail and visit a number of other sites associated with St. Francis and his teachings. Meet at the visitor center (the office just to the left of the lower church entrance) between 9am and noon; and 2:30pm and 5:30pm. You may wish to call in advance (☎ **075-8190084**) for more information.

The Life & Times of St. Francis

Francis of Assisi was born in 1182, the son of a wealthy cloth merchant. As a teen, he enjoyed all the passing pleasures of life—drinking, partying with other rich kids—and then joined a military expedition to Perugia, probably for the glory of it. He was taken prisoner, and, following his release, became more spiritual, committing himself to a life of poverty and self-sacrifice. After extended meditation he began to have visions. In 1209, the crucifix of St. Damiano is said to have spoken to him and told him to "rebuild the Church." Francis first took this literally to mean that he should find some stones to support the building's walls. In Giotto's Basilica fresco, St. Francis can be seen lifting the church, superhero style.

Francis's father criticized him for squandering his company's profits on church stones, and for preferring the company of lepers to nobles. In protest, Francis stripped naked in the main square in Assisi, and gave away all his material possessions. In Giotto's fresco, Assisi's father is being restrained from smacking his son.

It would seem that Francis's philosophy of poverty was in direct conflict with the jewel-encrusted, power-hungry, institutional Church of the day. But his humility and obedience to Church rule (per the scene of the monks kneeling in front of the Pope) made his order more attractive to Rome than other splinter sects of the day. So Rome approved the Franciscan Order in about 1211.

Francis spent the remaining 17 years of his life ministering to the poor and communing with nature and all of God's creatures, which helped earn him the title of "patron saint of animals."

In 1224, Francis was said to have received the stigmata of Christ, when bleeding wounds appeared on his hands, feet, and sides. He was canonized in 1228, only 2 years after his death.

The Roman church, and some of Francis's followers, promptly co-opted the Franciscan Order by funding the building of the ornate Basilica in the 1230s, in part by selling indulgences to visitors, pardoning their sins on behalf of St. Francis for a few gold coins. Nevertheless, the Franciscan Order has kept its philosophy intact, as can be seen by the many Franciscan Brothers still walking the streets of Assisi dressed in their brown sackcloth robes tied with a simple rope belt.

God's message communicated through the purity of nature. You can almost hear the whirring as St. Francis spins in his grave below.

For a more serene experience, head to **San Pietro** (Piazza San Pietro at end of Borgo San Pietro; €3.50 admission to crypt; 9am–noon and 2–6pm), a neglected church on the southwest edge of town, reopened after years of earthquake retrofitting. The plaza outside offers lovely views of the countryside, and a peaceful rest

The "Poor Clares" & the Patron Saint of TV

In a life that paralleled that of St. Francis, Clare was born in Assisi in 1194, and walked away from her family fortune to preach a life of poverty. From age 17, she was a close follower of Francis, cutting off her long blond hair as a symbol of her rejection of the material world. Locks of her hair are said to be on display at Assisi's **Church of St. Chiara** (Piazza Santa Chiara; free admission; 7am–noon and 2–6:45pm), alongside other relics in the Oratorio Del Crocifisso room, including the crucifix that talked to St. Francis. The church also houses her body in its garishly decorated crypt. The upper church is decorated sparingly, not so much at the behest of Clare but because a later bishop erased most of the frescoes to keep tourists away.

St. Clare founded the order of the Poor Clares for women whose lives were to be occupied with work and prayer, penance, and contemplation. The Pope, in 1215, approved the right of the Poor Clares to live solely on alms, without any personal property.

Despite Clare's rejection of the material world, and her commitment to a quiet life of spiritual contemplation, Pope Pius XII declared her the patron saint of television in 1958. Apparently when St. Clare was on her death bed, too sick to attend Mass, the performance of the last rites were projected on a wall in front of her, complete with live audio. And thus, every August 11, on St. Clare's feast day, TV writers, workers, and watchers are to send a prayer her way.

away from the tourist hordes. The crypt is what you'll want to visit here, particularly the side room that features the best Franciscan diorama in all Christendom. See a miniature electric fisherman cast his reel, and the wood-chopper chop, in a 7.5m-long (25-ft.) medieval town filled with plastic sheep. Other rooms in the crypt museum include a random assortment of rotating modern-art exhibits, Roman artifacts, and a Salvador Dalí lithograph.

Towering above the town is **Rocca Maggiore** ★★ (☎ 075-815292; daily 10am–sunset), the fortress built by Cardinal Albornaz to extend his control over Umbrian towns in the 1360s. While most of the Rocca still remains shut due to earthquake damage, for €2 you can enter and climb two of its towers. Between the thick stone walls in a hallway lit only by narrow slits, try imagining how terrifying it must have been to defend the castle during a siege from this claustrophobic room. Then ascend to the roof for an unmatched 360-degree view of the majesty of the Umbrian countryside and the town of Assisi.

When the famed German writer Goethe visited Assisi in the 1780s, he passed up the Basilica "with great distaste," and focused instead on the **Temple of Minerva** ★ (daily 7:15am–noon and 2–7pm) in the main Piazza del Comune. The 1st-century Roman temple is well preserved, with its Corinthian columns and original paving stones, and provides a window into Assisi's ancient past. However, the best of the temple is outside, as the interior was transformed in the 17th century into a lackluster baroque church.

Above the town, and well worth the journey, is **Erme delle Carceri** ★ (free admission; 6:30am–7pm), the prison; it's really a hermitage where St. Francis retreated to pray, meditate, and preach to his disciples. A ramshackle collection of rooms cut into the stones many centuries before Francis lived, this rustic friary seems much more in line with St. Francis's teachings than the massive Basilica that looms over the town. You can visit the cell where Francis prayed, and follow the path outside to the woods where he must have experienced a close connection with nature. At the door is a 1,000-year-old oak, where, according to legend, Francis blessed birds that then flew off in four directions—a symbol of how Francis's teachings would eventually reach all four corners of the globe. Along the path is an amusing statue of St. Francis lying on the ground with his sandals off, hands behind his head, peacefully pondering the clouds in the sky. Friars still live in these simple caves and will guide you, though be sure to give a donation as the monks live entirely on alms.

The hermitage is a tough 2-mile uphill walk from Porta Cappuccini, but is on the main road, so it's easy to drive and pay a couple of euros for parking, or to take a cab.

THE OTHER ASSISI
Tourists are not permitted to visit the Basilica of St. Francis during Mass on Sundays, and gawkers are discouraged from entering chapels during a daily Mass. But if you want to experience the spiritual and ceremonial side of the Basilica, leave your camera in the hotel, dress conservatively, keep silent, and join the elderly and the young, both local and international pilgrims, as they celebrate Mass. Holy Masses are given at 7 and 11am, and 6pm daily in summer; November to March 6pm only. At 7:15pm, you can see daily vespers and meditations at the tomb. Sundays and holidays, Mass is celebrated at noon in the upper church.

TODI
Todi is a classic Umbrian hilltop village with winding cobblestone streets, stone towers, and spectacular views of the countryside. Although much of the city has been refurbished and taken over by Rome weekenders, it maintains its medieval charm. It doesn't boast enough sights to merit an extended stay, but is worth at least a day trip if you're based in nearby Assisi, Perugia, or Spoleto.

The best experience in Todi comes from wandering the streets and enjoying the views of the countryside, and from the buildings themselves. Four churches in town merit a visit. The main **Duomo** on the town square has colorful stained glass, a fresco modeled after one in the Sistine Chapel, and an odd "Pope in a boat" modern bronze statue jutting from one wall. You can climb the tower of **San Fortunato,** above the main square, for impressive views. The interior, unlike the crumbling facade, has a cool whitewashed solidity that is worth a peek.

On a side street, as you come back down to the road, is the **Santa Maria in Camuccia,** housing a curious (and twice-stolen) 12th-century wood Madonna-and-Child statue in a protective plastic box. Just off the main road is the Romanesque **Temple of Santa Maria della Consolazione,** which is scenically framed with the countryside behind it, and more impressive outside than within.

You can get maps and information from the tourist office below the steps in the main square, Piazza del Popolo; it's open from 9:30am to 1pm and 3:30 to 7pm Monday through Saturday, opening at 10am on Sundays.

ACCOMMODATIONS IN TODI

If you decide to spend a night in town, you have three good options.

€€   You need to cut down a side street from the main square, and then climb three flights of dark stairs to find **San Lorenzo Tre** ✦ (Via San Lorenzo, 3; ☎ 075-8944555; lorenzotre@tin.it), a "Residenza d'Epoca" consisting of six old-style villa apartments turned into charmingly cluttered lodgings with spectacular views of distant plains. Double rooms are €100; a single with shared bathroom is €70.

€€€–€€€€   The **Hotel Fonte Cesia** ✦ (Via Lorenzo Leonj, 3; ☎ 075-8943737; www.fontecesia.it) is a full-service hotel in a 600-year-old building with views, a high-end restaurant, and modern, comfortable rooms. The junior suites with patios are particularly nice. Doubles are €135 to €155 a night; a junior suite is €200.

€€€–€€€€   Near Todi on the road to Orvieto is the **Tenuta di Canonica** ✦✦ (Loc. Canonica, 75-06059 Todi; ☎ 075-8947545; www.tenutadicanonica.com), a great base from which to explore central Umbria. The complex, with a swimming pool and stellar views, includes three handsome stone structures—one medieval, one Victorian, and one that actually boasts ancient Roman foundations. The buildings are plush and comfortable, filled with antique furniture and offering dozens of nooks and crannies filled with Italian art and history books hoarded by co-manager Maria Fano, a former art-history teacher. She and her husband, Daniele, both English-speakers, can help arrange local activities, including horse-back riding, language classes, and hikes. A superlative chef from the *cordon bleu* Perugia, Daniele also offers cooking classes on-site. The standard rooms, with oversize modern bathrooms, rich fabrics, and comfortable beds cost €130—or up to €170 in season.

DINING FOR ALL TASTES

€€   Todi offers the usual tourist fare of pizza and set-menu tourist specials. One better option is the **Il Donatello** ✦ (Via della Storta, 29; ☎ 075-8942366), run by a former apprentice to one of Italy's top chefs. The small alley restaurant has a country charm, with bright colors livening up its stone interior. The menu features only a handful of items, but it changes every few weeks to feature the best seasonal dishes. On my last visit I enjoyed the "Tower of Tomatoes" *(piccola torre di pomodoro e mozzarella),* excellent mixed bruschetta, and an herbed lamb steak. *Primi* average €6 to €8, *secondi* €7.50 to €10.

€–€€€   The **Umbria** restaurant ✦ (Via S. Bonaventura, 13; ☎ 075-8942737) is justly famous for its 15th-century interior and the views from the patio over the countryside. The food is special, with steak or boar grilled over an open fire, and rich spaghetti dishes. However, given its popularity, the place can be packed (make reservations), and the staff indifferent. Pasta dishes range from a basic €8 spaghetti to a €18 truffle-based delicacy. *Secondi* range from a smaller mixed grill for €9.50 to a big steak for over €20.

THE OTHER TODI

A local language and culture school, **La Lingua La Vita** (Via Mazzini, 18; ☎ 075-8948364; www.lalingualavita.com), offers classes for foreigners ranging from 1 to 24 weeks. Students of all ages and nationalities have the opportunity to rent school apartments, or to stay with a local family for the duration of the program. The school coordinates area tours and art, cooking, and Italian-language classes for all levels. Even if you're not in the program, you can stop by their offices in front of the theater for information on tours or day courses. Price for a 2-week course, including apartment, is €822 (1-week classes without lodging are available for €250).

SPOLETO

Spoleto is known for its music festival, as well as for its ancient bridge, its fortress, and its Duomo, all of which have been renovated and restored over the centuries.

The towering Ponte delle Torri bridge south of the city is built on top of a Roman aqueduct using recycled stones from Roman ruins, Etruscan walls, and wrecked town towers. Walking through the medieval streets of the old town, you can see a Roman amphitheater converted into a jazz stage, and a monastery refurbished into a hotel and restaurant. The Duomo rose from the rubble of a Spoleto destroyed in 1155, using scavenged stones, the foundation of an early Christian temple, and the marble flooring of a previous church. The Rocca fortress above town has been recycled many times; it began

> ❝ We came to Spoleto . . . I never saw a more impressive picture; in which the shapes of nature are of the grandest order, but over which the creations of man, sublime from their antiquity and greatness, seem to predominate. ❞
>
> —Percy Bysshe Shelley, *Letters from Italy*, 1840

as a Roman watchtower, was converted into a papal castle, then into a garrison headquarters, and finally into a modern high-security prison. It's now a combination gallery, museum, performance space, and civic office building.

The greatest example of recycling in Spoleto has been the city itself. This once proud town became a central Italian non-entity for 500 years, before leaping back into the world spotlight with the "Festival of Two Worlds" (now the Spoleto Festival) in 1958. Spoleto is now home to year-round schools for world-class opera, music, and theater performance, highlighted by the yearly summer event. But any time of year, the medieval streets and connected series of squares provide a colorful setting in which to experience the best of Umbrian food, wine, and entertainment.

DON'T LEAVE SPOLETO WITHOUT . . .

TAKING A STROLL ACROSS THE PONTE DELLE TORRI BRIDGE
The 700-year-old stone bridge is a marvel to observe from afar, and even better to walk across. Check out the gorge below.

Spoleto

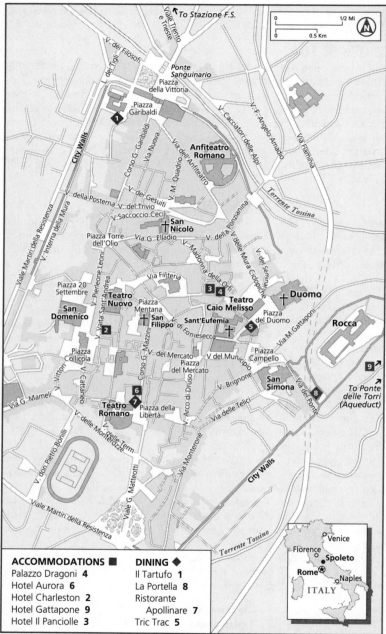

To Stazione F.S.

Viale Trento e Trieste

V. dei Filosofi

L. dei Tigli

Ponte
Sanguinario

Piazza
della Vittoria

Piazza
Garibaldi

1

V...F. Angelo Amadio

Via Flaminia

Corso G. Garibaldi

Via Nuova

V...M. Quadrio

Via dell'Anfiteatro

**Anfiteatro
Romano**

V. Cacciatori delle Alpi

City Walls

Viale Martiri della Resistenza

V...della Posterna

V...del Trivio

V...Saccoccio Cecil

V. dei Gesuiti

Torrente Tossino

V...Interna della Mura

† **San
Nicolò**

Via G. Elladio

V...della Ponzianina

Piazza Torre
dell'Olio

Via Filiteria

V. della Mura Ciclopiche

V. del Seminario

Piazza 20
Settembre

V...a Pierleone Leoni

**Teatro
Nuovo**

Piazza
Mentana

3 **4**

Via Madonna della Griti

**Teatro
Caio Melisso**

† **Duomo**

**San
Domenico**

V...a ta Sant'Andrea

2

† **San
Filippo**

Piazza
di Foniesecca

Sant'Eufemia
†

5

Piazza
del Duomo

Via M. Gattaponi

Rocca

Piazza
Collicola

V...Vittori

V...Cattaneo

Corso G. Mazzini

V...del Mercato

Piazza
del Mercato

V. del Municipio

Piazza
Campello

V. del Ponte

9 ↗

To Ponte
delle Torri
(Aqueduct)

Via G. Mameli

V...delle Montefiozze

6
7

**Teatro
Romano**

Piazza della
Libertà

Arco di Druso

V. Brignone

Via delle Telici

**San
Simona**

8

V...don Pietro Bonilli

Via G. Matteotti

City Walls

Viale Martiri della Resistenza

Via Monterone

Torrente Tossino

0   1/2 Mi
0   0.5 Km

Venice

Florence

Spoleto

Rome ⊛

Naples

ITALY

ACCOMMODATIONS ■	DINING ◆
Palazzo Dragoni **4**	Il Tartufo **1**
Hotel Aurora **6**	La Portella **8**
Hotel Charleston **2**	Ristorante
Hotel Gattapone **9**	Apollinare **7**
Hotel Il Panciolle **3**	Tric Trac **5**

LOOKING AT FILIPPO LIPPI'S FRESCO IN THE DUOMO   Gaze up at the *Life of the Virgin*, with its rainbow colors, and then look down to examine the original marble floors.

CHECKING OUT THE ROCCA   See the latest incarnation of this historic fortress, with its art museum, medieval rooms, and recently used "dungeons."

GOING TO THE FESTIVAL   Try to make it to town for the yearly Spoleto Festival, a world-class music and performance extravaganza in June and July.

A BRIEF HISTORY OF SPOLETO

Like many Umbrian cities, Spoleto's history cycles through Etruscan origins, Roman colonization, Italian infighting, and papal misrule. In 217 B.C., a well-defended Spoleto stopped Hannibal's invading armies from marching toward Rome. The city then flourished as a Roman colony, and to this day is replete with remains of Roman buildings and walls. Thanks in part to its strategic position astride the Rome-Ravenna route, the city developed into the powerful city-state of the Duchy of Spoleto, dominating central-Italian politics and commerce. This caught the attention of the warlord Emperor Barbarossa, who didn't like the fact that the Duchy wasn't paying him tribute. Barbarossa invaded Spoleto in 1155, and literally flattened the city, destroying every one of its famed 100 towers.

Spoleto was rebuilt from the rubble. Most of the city's current landmarks were constructed in the 13th century, including the Duomo and the Ponte delle Torri bridge. As Pope Innocent VI consolidated his rule over central Italy in the 14th

---

The Spoleto Festival

For Spoleto, the dawn of a new age came in 1958. It was then that Gian Carlo Menotti, an Italian-American composer, settled on this small medieval town after an extensive search for the perfect spot for a festival that would, in his words, "match and exchange American and European artistic cultures." From the very beginning, he recruited top names in the arts, both mainstream artists and experimental: Louis Armstrong, Al Pacino, Twyla Tharp, Pablo Neruda, Franco Zeffirelli, and Andy Warhol, to name but a few. From the very beginning, the festival was a powerhouse in the worlds of opera, music, dance, and theater. Today, over 200 official events take place during the festival each summer, and just as many side activities are sponsored by restaurants, hotels, and shops.

Menotti chose Spoleto to take advantage of its superb historical performance venues, including the ancient Roman amphitheater, the 17th-century Caio Melisso theater, and the Duomo square, where over 15,000 fest-goers jam for the yearly finale. The town, restaurants, and hotels are absolutely packed for the duration, so plan ahead.

For more information, check out **www.spoletofestival.it**.

century, papal armies constructed the Rocca fortress, which still occupies a commanding position over the city. Vatican forces kept the city subjugated under the intimidating watch of the Rocca fortress, and Spoleto faded from significance—until Italian-American Gian Carlo Menotti dreamed up the Spoleto Festival and gave the city a new burst of life.

LAY OF THE LAND

Over a dozen **trains** reach Spoleto daily from Rome (1½ hr.) and Perugia (45 min.). The Spoleto train station is about a mile outside the old town, so you'll probably want to catch the C bus to the historic center or take a cab.

If you're **driving,** Spoleto is easy to reach, directly on the SS3, about 80 miles from Rome, 120 miles from Florence. Parking in the old town is nearly impossible, but you can park for free on the streets just outside the old city walls, on Viale Martiri Della Resistenza, or Via DonBonilli, next to the soccer stadium.

Spoleto's **tourist office** is located on Piazza della Libertà, 7 (☎ 0743-238920). It has a good selection of fliers about events in town, and brochures on dozens of farmhouse stays outside town. It's open Monday through Friday 9am to 1pm and 4 to 7pm; Saturday and Sunday the office opens at 10am.

Note: The **Spoleto Festival** usually extends over 3 weeks from the end of June to mid-July. During this time, accommodations need to be booked far in advance. After the festival concludes, most of the city takes a 2-week holiday, so expect to see many restaurants, shops, and hotels closed at that time.

ACCOMMODATIONS

Except during the time of its world-renowned festival, Spoleto's hotel rates are reasonable.

€€   The centrally located **Hotel Aurora** (Via Apollinare, 3; ☎ 0743-220315; www.hotelauroraspoleto.it) is a steal, with pleasant rooms for €70 to €80 in summer, and only €50 in low season. Bathrooms are a little on the small side but functional; rooms are clean, with hardwood floors and air-conditioning. The breakfast room is especially cheery, with tiled floor and wood-beamed ceiling. And guests get a 10% discount at the Ristorante Apollinare, with which the hotel shares its original Roman walls.

€€   Hotel **Il Panciolle** (Via del Duomo, 3–5; ☎ 0743-45677; no credit cards) is an even cheaper but satisfactory, and centrally located, option. It's €60 for a double for each of the seven rooms, though only two have air-conditioning. The friendly manager doesn't speak much English, but can wrangle his grandkids to help with local recommendations.

€€€   **Hotel Charleston** (Piazza Collicola, 10; ☎ 0743-220052; www.hotel charleston.it) is tucked away in a square next to the modern-art museum. Like the museum, the hotel is an interesting combination of old and new, with the original tiled floors and wood beams. The rooms of this 17th-century villa are now filled with contemporary art and furniture. The junior suites (€150) are very nice, and the double rooms are a decent deal at €100. The Charleston also rents out apartments in an adjacent building for €450 per week.

Elegant Hilltop B&Bs near Spoleto

North of Spoleto, two excellent hilltop bed-and-breakfasts offer alternative options for your stay. Both B&Bs are close to the highway, but be sure to call for directions, as they're hard to locate.

€€€€ **Le Logge di Silvignano** ★ (Franzione Silvignano, 14; ☎ 0743-270518; www.leloggedisivignano.it) is a meticulously restored and decorated collection of houses in a tiny hilltop village. Rooms range from the three-room Loggiato "honeymoon suite," with raised bedroom behind a medieval romance screen, to the Elia Room, built into an old dungeon of the keep. Owners and co-hosts Alberto and Danielle are fluent English-speakers, full of stories and local recommendations, and glad to share a glass of wine with guests. By early 2007, they plan to have added a dining room, swimming pool, and entertainment clubhouse to their ever-expanding complex. Suites run from €190 to €250 a night.

€€€ That's the luxury rooming option. Nearby **Il Castello di Poreta** ★ (Localita Poreta; 0743-275810; www.seeumbria.com) has the better historical setting, in a fortified keep and 15th-century church, with a high-end restaurant on the premises, but basic rooms. In a crazy arrangement typical of Italy, the province owns the site, the walls are owned by the state of Italy, the olive groves are privately owned, and the Vatican still has the deed to the church. The restaurant has been rated one of the top 50 in Italy, and has hosted the prime minister for lunch. Rooms are serviceable, but nothing special, aside from the old priest's quarters, which are decorated in a traditional style. Doubles run €110 to €115 a night.

€€€ **The Palazzo Dragoni** ★ (Via del Duomo, 13; ☎ 0743-222220; www.palazzo dragoni.it) is my choice for best value in town. Most rooms have views over the valley, and a great period feel with antique furniture and decor. The superior rooms at €145 are *really* superior, with canopy beds and super views, while the standard rooms are still quite nice at €119. The breakfast room is an elegant nook with arched windows and a view of the Duomo. As a special bonus the Dragoni has free wireless Internet access in all rooms.

€€€-€€€€ Worth a splurge just for its jaw-dropping views of the bridge and the river gorge, the **Hotel Gattapone** ★ (Via del Ponte, 6; ☎ 0743-223447; hgattapone@tin.it) has sharp modern rooms with glossy wood floors, split levels, and comfy beds. The older rooms still have good views but aren't quite as nicely furnished. The hotel is on an isolated street south of town, but road traffic can be annoying in some rooms. The older, standard, and inner-facing rooms cost €140 in summer, the superior rooms €190.

DINING FOR ALL TASTES

€   A nice place in which to hang out, grab a small meal, and look over the bridge and the gorge is bar/*gelateria* **La Portella** 🧒 (Via Del Ponte, after Piazza Campello and before Hotel Gattapone). Walk up the stairway to the left of the entrance to reach a terrace half-hidden by greenery. Sit on a swinging chair, have some gelato (or a beer when the upstairs taps are open), and enjoy a sunset over the valley. The gelato and snacks can be had for under €5.

€€   In the same building as Hotel Aurora, tucked behind the walls of a 12th-century Franciscan convent and St. Apollinare's Church, is **Ristorante Apollinare** ★ (Via S. Agata, 14; ☎ 0743-45863; www.ristoranteapollinare.it). It's long on atmosphere, both in its timbered ceiling and stone walls. The food is tasty and creative. I particularly liked the chef's renowned pumpkin gnocchi with pigeon (€12). Also recommended is the tomato ravioli stuffed with apples and nuts (€11). Most *primi* run €10 to €14; *secondi* are €9 to €16.

€€€   You can eat in front of the cathedral at a restaurant named for a card game. The **Tric Trac** ★ (Via Arlingo, 10; ☎ 0743-44592; www.trictrac.it), in Piazza del Duomo, is an old artists' hangout that is jam-packed at festival time. The menu changes weekly, but you can usually find a grilled guinea hen for €15 or a kitchen salad piled with the freshest ingredients for €11, or in winter, a thick lamb stew for about €15. In late 2006, keep your eyes open for a medieval grill opening next door.

€€€   Known as *the* place to go for truffles, **Il Tartufo** ★ (Piazza Garibaldi, 24; ☎ 0743-40236) is considered by many to be the finest restaurant in town. Even if you're not a truffle connoisseur, once you try an Umbrian pasta or risotto with fresh grated local truffle (€15–€17) you're likely to be converted. Truffled meat dishes go for €15 to €22. The location in the lower town is a bit inconvenient for those staying in the historical center, but if you want to try the best, it's worth the trip.

WHY YOU'RE HERE: THE TOP SIGHTS & ATTRACTIONS

The three main attractions of Spoleto's **Duomo** ★★ (Piazza del Duomo; ☎ 0575-23991; free admission; 8:30am–12:30pm and 3:30–7pm) are (1) the glowing mosaics on the facade, (2) Filippo Lippi's *Life of the Virgin* fresco, and (3) the original marble floors. The Duomo is a reconstruction of the original structure destroyed in 1155 by Barbarossa. The facade features late-12th-century Romanesque stained-glass windows and mosaics that glow in the late-afternoon sun. The portico was a late-Renaissance add-on meant to bring the church into the "modern age."

Filippo Lippi painted the *Life of the Virgin* fresco in the 1460s. Visitors can view the recently restored work in the dome above the altar for no charge, a rarity in Italian church restoration projects. The circular rainbow and the bright gold sun in the *Coronation of the Virgin* in the center of the work give the fresco a New Age feel; I always expect, on seeing it, to find a unicorn and a dolphin frolicking in the background. The colors and texture of the clothes, and the vivid figures, practically leap off the walls. Take a close look at the scene of the Virgin's death: The painter's self-portrait and a portrait of his son are in that panel.

Be sure also to look down at the geometric designs of the marble floor, said to be the original of the Christian temple built in the 7th century. Then walk to the chapel at the left of the altar to see a genuine St. Francis autograph, at the bottom of a letter he wrote to one of his followers, now preserved behind glass in an ornate frame. On the right side of the altar is a chapel containing a spooky black-and-silver Virgin Mary icon. Barbarossa stole the icon from Constantinople, and then donated it to the newly constructed Duomo in a "sorry I destroyed your town" gesture.

Walk the steps to the top of Piazza Duomo, and then follow Via Saffi to Via del Ponte to reach Spoleto's famous **Ponte delle Torri bridge** ★★ 🄺. This awe-inspiring arched stone structure towers 75m (250 ft.) above the Tessino gorge and 225m (750 ft.) across the river, from Spoleto to Monteluco. The architect Gattapone designed the bridge in the 14th century on top of an ancient Roman aqueduct, the still-visible structure serving as the medieval bridge's base. A number of shaded mountain paths begin at the far side of the bridge. Maps are available in the tourist office.

Viewed from the bridge, or from anywhere else in town, the **Rocca fortress** (☎ 0743-43707; €5) stands in intimidating watch over Spoleto, and was designed to look that way. Pope Innocent VI had his "pit bull," the Cardinal Albornoz, supervise construction of this castle in the 1360s, and populated it with troops to keep Spoleto under Vatican control. As the need to subjugate the city faded, the fortress served as a prison for hundreds of years. It went through renovations the reverse of those seen in many Italian hotels: medieval walls stripped bare of frescoes, rooms made *less* hospitable, windows bricked shut. It has housed enemies of the state, including Slavic political prisoners, Red Brigade terrorists, and the man who tried to assassinate Pope John Paul II.

Nowadays, the Rocca has been converted once again, this time into an art gallery, performance space, and medieval museum showing off restored frescoes and original gardens. Admission is only by guided tour, and English-language tours are offered only twice daily, at 11am and 3pm. But because the guides don't really add much beyond the info pamphlet, consider joining one of the hourly Italian tours and simply admiring the views. Tickets can be bought at the wood shed at the gate of the castle drive at the end of Via Saffi, where a minibus will take you to the fortress. Tours (in Italian) run from 10am to 6pm in summer, but are more limited in winter months. Call for more information on their ever-changing schedule.

To gain an appreciation of ancient *Spoletium,* visit the **Teatro Romano** ★ and the connected **Museo Archeologico** (Via San Agata, 18, just below Piazza della Libertà; ☎ 0743-223277; €2.50). You can enter through the doors and peek through the railing for a free view of the Roman theater, or pay the €2.50 for the combination visit. The theater, constructed in the 1st century A.D., sank into the ground and had to be rebuilt at that time, sort of an ancient Leaning Tower of Pisa. It lay buried over the years, and was only excavated and restored in the 1950s. Today it's used as part of the Spoleto Festival. The museum has some noteworthy artifacts, including a set of stone tablets outlining local Roman laws, and a shield and weapons recovered from a Bronze Age tomb.

Another view into the distant past can be seen in the crypt of the usually ignored **Sant'Ansano Church** (next to Piazza del Mercato; free admission; 7:30am–noon and

3–6:30pm, Nov–Mar closes 5:30pm). Stairs to the left of the altar lead to the underground chambers of the crypt. The rough Byzantine fresco fragments on the walls (possibly dating to the 8th c. or earlier), the darkened room, and the funereal nature of the altar all open a window into the early days of the Church.

THE OTHER SPOLETO

Sure, the Spoleto Festival is the town's big draw, but culture doesn't begin and end there. If you arrive before the festival in June you can visit a number of competitions in which aspiring artists studying in the city strut their stuff, hoping to earn a spot in the main festival. The European Community Competition for Young Opera Singers is in March, the International Dance Competition is in April, and a biannual Competition for New Chamber Opera debuts its winner in the off season. For information about specific show times and locations, pick up a copy of the bilingual *Nuovo Spoleto,* a free monthly magazine, or stop by the tourist office, which will have listings of upcoming performances.

After the festival, both novices and near-professionals can join a course at the **Spoleto Arts Symposia** that takes place in late July to early August. They offer workshops in music, cooking, and writing. Wondering what to do with the kids? No problem, the arts group also offers the **Spoleto Kids Camp** with arts and crafts, drama, music, sports, and field trips. Enrollment can be from 5 days to 3 weeks. Many attendees stay together at the Istituto Bambin' Gesù convent. See **www.spoletoarts.com** for more information.

GUBBIO

Geography saved Gubbio. Because it's so far off the beaten path, and so difficult to get to by any means other than private car, this classic medieval hill town survived the 20th century with much of its historic soul intact. At night, when the streets are largely deserted, the medieval stone walls loom in the darkness and eerie lights illuminate the ruins of the amphitheater outside the town walls. You'd almost expect to see toga-clad Romans rushing to catch the latest entertainments. Walking around a corner and gazing at the ethereal silhouette of the ruined medieval watchtower, you wouldn't be surprised to have to dodge a 10th-century horseman, or the contents of a chamber pot tossed from a window above. Instead, the next day, screaming kids kick soccer balls around the same squares and locals gather for lively discussions over thimbles of espresso at street-front bars.

DON'T LEAVE GUBBIO WITHOUT . . .

VISITING THE TOP OF THE MOUNTAIN BY CABLE CAR Not for those scared of heights, the slightly rickety gondola delivers visitors near the summit. But get up there by any means necessary to see the church, and climb to the tower on the peak to enjoy views of the city and the wilderness to the rear.

SEEING A FESTIVAL If at all possible, plan to see Gubbio during one of its many lively festivals. The Corsa dei Ceri race on May 15 is the biggest event, but a dozen others are worth seeing to get a flavor of traditional Gubbio.

GOING TO THE PIAZZA GRANDE AND THE PALAZZO DEI CONSOLI
The central medieval plaza of Gubbio boasts memorable views of the countryside. It's also home to a worthwhile museum inside the Palazzo dei Consoli.

A BRIEF HISTORY OF GUBBIO

The Romans declared an alliance with the city of Iguvium at present-day Gubbio in the 1st century B.C. The empire's print can be seen in the still-extant amphitheater, and in the relics in the local museums. With the fall of Rome, the citizens of Gubbio retreated up the hill to a more fortified city to fend off barbarian attacks, but this didn't stop the marauding armies. Not until the 12th century did Gubbio develop into a stable city, with walls and leadership strong enough to fend off invaders. In 1155, Bishop (later to be St.) Ubaldo negotiated peace with the warlord Barbarossa, preserving the city from destruction.

By the 13th century, Gubbio had developed into a prosperous city-state, enjoying its important commercial location on the road from Rome to Ravenna. Peace and prosperity through the mid-1300s fueled the construction of most of the palaces, walls, and churches still standing today. But then Gubbio succumbed to the 1348 plague, to generations of mismanagement by the dukes of Urbino, and to 100 years of neglect by the papal states. Discarded as an unimportant backwater, Gubbio was able to preserve its medieval traditions, architecture, and spirit.

Gubbio's spirit was particularly evident during World War II, when it hosted a number of anti-Nazi Partisan groups. The Germans retaliated with a massacre in 1944, memorialized in the Mausoleum of 40 Martyrs below town. Post-war Gubbio has seen a rebirth of artisans' workshops, traditional festivals, and an epically ugly cement factory north of town.

LAY OF THE LAND

Reaching Gubbio can be a bit of a challenge because it's not on any of the main highways or rail lines. Probably **the best option is by car,** taking the winding SS298 north about 39km (25 miles) from Perugia or the No. 3 to the 219 coming south 90km (60km) from Arezzo. Free parking is available at the lot next to the Roman amphitheater.

If you're **train-bound,** stop at Fossato di Vico, about a half-hour bus-shuttle away from town on the Rome-Ancona line, itself about a 2¼ hour ride from Rome. Buses also go from Perugia to Gubbio 11 times daily, taking over an hour.

The Gubbio **tourist office** (Piazza Oderisi, 6, above Corso Garibaldi; ☎ 075-9220693) distributes tons of maps and brochures, but not advice.

ACCOMMODATIONS, BOTH STANDARD & NOT

€€   For the feel of a hidden apartment in the medieval city, try the **Residenza Le Logge** ★ (Via Piccardi, 7–9; ☎ 075-9277574; www.paginegialle.it/residenza lelogge). This small building on a side street off Via Baldassini offers six smallish but homey rooms, and a quiet backyard garden area where guests can enjoy morning coffee or a picnic lunch while they gaze at the palaces above. Along with three additional mini-apartments in the next building, Le Logge's rooms can be rented for €400 a week (or €80 per day in the high season).

€€-€€€   Rodolfo Mencarelli has built a bit of an empire in town with his three hotels, the Gattapone, the Bosone Palace, and the Relais Ducale (www.mencarelligroup.com). The **Relais Ducale Hotel** ★ (Via Galeotti, 19; ☎ 075-9220159), as the name implies, is built from a duke's palace, and even has its own secret tunnel. Each of the 30 rooms is unique, ranging from the smaller, cheaper, but still atmospheric stone-walled, wooden-arched rooms on the lower level, to larger rooms with city-wide views above. Doubles average €150. The junior suites originally made for the duke's pals and courtesans are particularly lavish, including Jacuzzis, which the duke could only have dreamed of. Guests can also relax and enjoy the views from the large rooftop garden.

The **Bosone Palace** ★ (Via XX Settembre, 22; ☎ 075-92-0552) has a real claim to fame: Dante himself stayed here as a guest of the Rafaelli family in the 14th century soon after the palace was built. The rooms are a little weathered compared to the Relais Ducale, but still comfortable; the hotel decor gives you the feel of coming to the Continent on a grand tour. Doubles average €100 a night.

The **Gattapone** (Via Ansidei, 6; ☎ 075-9272489) is the best deal of the bunch (doubles for around €90), but with its generic refurbishing in 1999, it lacks the charming ambience of its sister hotels. It's on a quiet street (the church bells notwithstanding) and has perfectly decent rooms, albeit with small bathrooms.

€–€€   A good out-of-town base for trips in the area is the **Cinciallegre Bed & Breakfast** ★ (☎ 075-9255957; www.leciniciallegre.it). About a 20-minute drive northwest of Gubbio, this secluded hideaway consists of seven converted farm buildings perched on top of a ridge overlooking dense Umbrian forests. Each room has the characteristics of the bird for which it's named: Depending on your preferences, you can choose the "robin" room, with its bright spring theme; the "titmouse," with its small windows; or the "sparrow," a small single. Price per person is €48 for bed and breakfast, €65 including dinner. Maria Christina, co-owner and chef, prepares excellent meals using ingredients from her organic gardens; the rabbits, geese, and ducks are also raised on the property. Her husband, Fabrizio, can give tips for peaceful hiking treks on local trails, and the two even rent ATVs. Cinciallegre can be reached on SS219, signposted from Mocaiana, on tricky winding gravel mountain roads, so try arriving during the day.

DINING FOR ALL TASTES

€€   The **Rosati group** (www.rosatihotels.com) competes with the Mencarellis (see above and below) for control of the Gubbio hospitality industry, with three hotels, two restaurants, and an *enoteca* (wine bar). Their **La Fornace di Mastro Giorgio** (Via Mastro Giorgio, 2, just off of Via XX Settembre; ☎ 075-9221836) is slightly less expensive and stuffy than the Lupo (below), and has atmosphere to spare in a converted 15th-century ceramics workshop. The restaurant features characteristic Umbrian cuisine with a creative twist, including *filetto alle prugne* (steak with prune sauce), and roasted duck with oranges. *Primi* pasta dishes cost around €10, while *secondi* range from €12 to €20.

€€€   The Mencarelli empire stretches to restaurants, featuring the excellent (but pricey) **Taverna Del Lupo** ★ (Via Ansidei, 21, under the Bosone Palace; ☎ 075-9274368). Its set menu, at €23, changes by the season, but has featured excellent local pastas, including *Srangozzi all'ortolana,* with fresh vegetables and a grilled meat assortment with mouthwatering boar, rabbit, and chicken morsels. A light tagliatelle works well for hot days on their patio, while the minestrone soup warms diners inside when it's cold. Older waiters in bow ties and tuxedoes lend the restaurant a feeling of upscale propriety, as does the book-length wine list. The medieval restaurant has five rooms with stone arches, giving it the feeling of a nobleman's banquet hall.

€€€   While it looks like a small bar from the Piazza Boscone, the **Osteria de Re** ★ (Via Cavour, 15/B; ☎ 075-9222504) has two large underground vaulted chambers full of happy eaters munching away on the restaurant's specialty, a €22 sampler platter of fried breads, olives, bruschetta, veggies, and baked cheeses—a good feast for two. In summer, you can sit at tables in the piazza while locals shout from windows above and kids play soccer.

WHY YOU'RE HERE: THE TOP SIGHTS & ATTRACTIONS

Every visit to Gubbio should include a walk to the **Piazza Grande.** This wide, stone-covered plaza borders the medieval city halls on either side. Backed by the neoclassical Palazzo Ranghiasci, it opens to a panoramic view of the city and the Umbrian countryside around it. Travelers can stop to visit the restaurants and shops surrounding the piazza or sit on the steps and watch the steady stream of tourists and locals.

The tower of the Palazzo stands almost 60m (200 ft.) above the plaza, which is itself supported by columns and arches soaring 30m (100 ft.) above the lower city. Bell-ringers pull the ropes of 2-ton "Il Camanone" ("The Big Bell") with their feet—perhaps to avoid becoming hunchbacked?

To learn about the city, walk to the right of the plaza up the fanned steps and pay €5 to enter the **Palazzo dei Consoli (Palace of Consuls)** ★ (☎ 075-9274298; €5; winter daily 10am–1pm and 3–5pm, Apr–Oct to 6pm). The same ticket offers entry to all exhibits in the Civic Museum, which is inside the palace, and allows re-entry after the 1 to 3pm lunch break. Originally constructed in the 1330s as the headquarters for the city assembly, the Palace now serves as a multilevel museum exhibiting art and history of the region. The archaeological exhibit features the famed "Eugubian tablets," discovered in the 15th century, upon which are carved some of the world's oldest and most detailed descriptions of religious rites, from at least 200 B.C.

The **upper floors** of the palace **contain an art museum** with works by local son Giorgio Andreoli, who used innovative ceramic techniques in the early 1500s. His *Circe* and *Fall of the Phaeton* can be seen in the Sala della Loggetta. Also check out the "secret corridor" for bonus views of the city, as well as some of the hidden workings of the Palace.

Walking from the Piazza Grande, take one of the city's public elevators (!) off Via XX Settembre to reach the street outside the 13th-century **Duomo** ★ (9am–6pm). Inside, note the Gubbian-characteristic "wagon vaulted" arches supporting the roof. The bent, curved beams are meant to represent praying hands. The cool silent interior has pleasant stained-glass windows and frescoes, which are overshadowed, I think, by the gaudy baroque chapels.

Around the corner from the Duomo is the **Museo Diocesano** ★ (Via Federico da Montefeltro; ☎ 075-9220904; www.museogubbio.it; €5), a well-presented collection of art and antique relics in three stories of vaulted stone rooms of a 12th-century palace. If you want to save the €5 admission fee, at least walk into the lower-level bookshop entrance, and poke your head into the side room to see a

Gubbio's Festivals

While Gubbio's art and architecture remain locked in medieval times, the **festivals** ★★★ live vividly in the modern age and are tremendous fun:

Procession of the Dead Christ: Good Friday.

Corsa dei Ceri (Race of the Ceri): May 15. This is the most important of the yearly events. The town becomes feet-can't-touch-the-ground crowded, with people watching three teams sprint 300m (1,000 ft.) up Mt. Ingino with the "candles" (really 6.6m/22-ft. carved wooden logs on platforms) representing three saints: Ubaldo, Anthony, and George. *Hint:* Bet on Ubaldo—he's the patron saint of Gubbio, and his team hasn't lost in about 700 years.

Palio della Balestra (Crossbow Festival): Last Sunday in May.

Spettacoli Classici (Roman Theater Festival): July to August.

Toreo dei Quartieri (Tournament of the Quarters of Gubbio): August 14.

Gubbio Festival: September.

Mostra Mercato Nazionale del Tartufo Bianco (White Truffle Fair): End of October.

El Mucho Grando Christmastio (World's Biggest Christmas Tree): December 7 to January 10. The city attaches lights in the shape of a giant Christmas tree in the forest on the slopes of Mt. Ingino. Guinness has declared that this is indeed the world's biggest Christmas tree at 800m (2,624 ft.) tall and 400m (1,312 ft.) wide.

must for any party, a 20,000-liter, 3.6m-tall (12-ft.) wine barrel from the 15th century.

No visit to Gubbio is complete without a visit to the **top of Mt. Ingino,** towering 750m (2,500 ft.) above the town. The peak boasts 360-degree views over Gubbio and Umbria to the west, and the wilderness of the Marches to the east. You can reach the top via a quad-burning hike up the path from Porta Sant'Ubaldo, east of the Duomo, or by driving the dizzying road up the mountain.

But the most fun way to ascend Mt. Ingino is to take the **cable car** ★ (€5 round-trip) from its origin at the south edge of town. You'll ride in a rickety coffin-size metal basket hanging from a cable slung 45m (150 ft.) or so over the ground. It's definitely not for those scared of heights, but it's a cool way to fly up a mountain. The cars run in summer from 8:30am to 7:30pm, but times vary widely by season, so note the occasional lunch closing times or you may be spending an extra hour on top.

Once up Mt. Ingino, go to the **Basilica di Sant'Ubaldo** (8am–6pm) to see the mummified remains of St. Ubaldo himself (minus a few fingers snipped off by one of his servants eager to sell saintly remains) in a glass box on top of an altar.

You can also see the three pagoda-like "candles" carried in the Corsa dei Ceri race from the city to this church.

Walk up the road across the street from the Basilica to reach the remains of the **Rocca** ★★ on the mountain peak. The 12th-century fortress and tower is in ruins, and unremarkable, but the views are spectacular, broken only by the spectacularly ugly framework used for the famed Christmas lighting.

THE OTHER GUBBIO

To get the very best feel for Gubbio, don't just walk by and look at the ceramics—take a class and make some! The city of Gubbio, in cooperation with Centro Servizi Santo Spirito (www.inumbriadanordest.com), runs a dozen **single-day classes,** including ceramics, mosaic- and fresco-making, cooking, and, for the adventurous, truffle-hunting, hang-gliding, and mountain biking. Costs range from €15 to €25 for a 2- to 4-hour crafts course, to €65 for a 15-minute hang-gliding ride. Reservations are required at least a day in advance: Call ☎ **075-9220066,** or e-mail info@inumbriadanordest.com.

SHOPPING

Gubbio became famous in the 14th century for its ceramics, and keeps up the tradition today. One shop I recommend is **Rampini** (Via dei Consoli, 52; 075-9274408; www.rampiniceramiche.com), which also has a workshop on Via Leonardo da Vinci, 92, where you can stop by to watch the craftspeople at work. The second-generation family owner spent years in Brazil, and now gives a bit of a tropical spin to traditional works. Also recommended is **Mastri Vasai Gubbio** (Via Leonardo da Vinci, 66; ☎ 075-9274580), which has created a unique, antique-looking style using local materials and a traditional process.

Bologna & Emilia-Romagna

You'll find plenty of great art and architecture here—but not many tourists.

by Reid Bramblett

MANY TRAVELERS WHIZ THROUGH THE EMILIA-ROMAGNA REGION, OF which Bologna is the capital, en route to and from Florence, Milan, Venice, or Rome. Which is a terrible shame because they not only are bypassing some of Italy's finest art and architecture but are also missing the opportunity to experience a way of life that has been largely unaffected by those two great demons of the 20th century: mass tourism and massive industrialization.

Those ills are largely absent in Emilia-Romagna, a region comprising two ancient lands: Emilia, named for the Via Emilia, the ancient Roman road that bisects its plains and art cities; and Romagna, named for its prominence in the Roman empire. History has left its mark here on some of Italy's most beautiful, yet lesser-known, cities—Ravenna, last capital of the empire and later the stronghold of the Byzantines and the Visigoths (the former leaving behind spectacular mosaics); Ferrara, a center of art and culture during the Renaissance; and Parma, one of the most powerful duchies in Europe under the Farnese family.

Bologna, the regional capital, is home not only to great pasta (spaghetti bolognese anyone?) and cured meats but also to the oldest university in Europe. This venerable institution accounts for much of Bologna's great sights—from frescoed and sculpture-adorned churches to rich museum collections—and for the liveliness and active cultural scene of this student-filled city.

DON'T LEAVE BOLOGNA WITHOUT . . .

SEEING A TEENAGED MICHELANGELO'S SCULPTURES They adorn the revered tomb of San Domenico.

STUFFING YOURSELF WITH SOME OF THE BEST FOOD IN ITALY Even the non-Bolognese agree: Emilia-Romagna is the culinary heart of the country.

CLIMBING TO THE TOP OF TORRE DEGLI ASINELLI From the top, you'll get a panoramic view of the city.

HANGING OUT WITH THE COLLEGE KIDS You'll find them in the wine bars, pubs, and *osterie* lining Via del Pratello and Via Zamboni.

A BRIEF HISTORY OF BOLOGNA

Starting in the 13th century, scholars began descending upon Bologna in droves, and the growing city took shape to accommodate them. The burgeoning community built *palazzi* and churches, and artists came from throughout Italy to decorate them.

These treasures remain amid a handsome cityscape of ocher-colored buildings, red-tile rooftops, and the occasional tower constructed by powerful medieval families to display their wealth and power. Bologna's famous 40km (25 miles) of *loggie* have turned this into a city of covered sidewalks, allowing students and locals alike to stroll and discourse even in bad weather. The students remain a vibrant presence in Bologna, giving the city a youthful exuberance.

LAY OF THE LAND

Bologna is 105km (65 miles) north of Florence and 210km (130 miles) both south of Venice and southeast of Milan.

Flights, including **eurofly**'s (www.eurofly.it) new summertime **direct flights** from New York, land at **Aeroporto G. Marconi** (☎ 051-6479615; www.bologna-airport.it), 8km (5 miles) north of the city. The **bus to the train station** (☎ 051-290290; www.atc.bo.it), a 15-minute ride, runs about every quarter-hour from 6:05am to 11:45pm.

Trains arrive from and depart for the following major Italian cities almost hourly: Florence (60–90 min.), Rome (3–4 hr.), Milan (1½–2½ hr.), and Venice (1¾–2¼ hr.).

The center of Bologna is Piazza Maggiore, about a 15-minute walk down Via dell'Indipendenza from the train station (or take bus no. 25 or 30). Since old Bologna is densely concentrated within the ring roads that follow the lines of its old walls, most everything of interest lies within a 10- to 15-minute walk from this central square.

Following Via Rizzoli, which skirts the north end of the piazza, you come to Bologna's famous leaning towers, and from there Via Zamboni leads northeast toward the university and the Pinacoteca Nazionale; Via Ugo Bassi runs west from the piazza to Via del Pratello and its antiques shops and *osterie;* and Via degli Orefici takes you southeast into the midst of Bologna's colorful food markets and toward the San Stefano church complex.

The **main tourist office** (Piazza Maggiore, 1, in the Palazzo Comunale; ☎ 051-246541; www.bolognaturismo.info; daily 9am–8pm) has two annexes. The branch office in the train station will book rooms Monday through Saturday 8:30am to 7:30pm. The airport office is open Monday through Saturday 8am to 8pm, Sunday 9am to 3pm, and can not only book rooms but also advise travelers about how to get into the heart of Bologna. For **information on museums and such,** visit **www.comune.bologna.it/bolognadeimusei** and **www.provincia.bologna.it/cultura.** For tourism information on the region, visit **www.emilia romagnaturismo.it.**

ACCOMMODATIONS, BOTH STANDARD & NOT

In a city devoted to students and their needs, you can be sure that there are many non-standard accommodations. I'll give three cheers to the **tourist office,** which has posted on **www.bolognaturismo.info** the complete, searchable database, not just of hotels but of B&Bs, residences, *affittacamere* (rooms for rent), and apartments in Bologna—as well as *agriturismi* (farm stays) in the surrounding area. Unlike most local websites, this one includes all the details you need to make an informed decision: phone numbers, number of rooms, amenities, prices, and, where available, websites.

And what will you find here? Everything from modest folk charging €20 to €40 per person, to hosts who feel their accommodation's size, beauty, or location is good enough to charge €100 per person. In a very, very general sense, I'd say rental rooms and B&Bs tend to go for €30 to €50 per person in this region, though, again, it depends on the place. Regarding style, there is no norm. I've stayed in B&Bs and rental rooms that were just the spare bedroom in a modern apartment, others that were a cluster of bedrooms in an old-world apartment full of creaky antiques and doilies (like staying with your Italian great-aunt Maria), and still others that were like having my own little loft.

As for apartments, there is no formula. Price varies depending on size, location, number of bedrooms, number of guests, length of stay, type of apartment, time of year, and mood of the owner. Honestly, you could spend €400 per week or €4,000 per night. So study the site carefully because you could get a gem, as I did on my last trip to neighboring Parma when I stumbled upon a gorgeous and huge studio apartment, with a wood-beamed ceiling, a full kitchen, two double beds with a fold-out sofa, an entertainment center featuring a flatscreen TV, and a washing machine in the large bathroom. I mean, it was a real apartment, and a comfortable one at that. And I kept pinching myself that it only cost €35 a night—for me that is; had I been two people, it would have been €70—still a great deal, and wonderful that she charged precisely half the price for a single lodger, which hotels rarely do.

€–€€€   Bologna boasts more than 280 B&Bs and rental rooms. Because winnowing that list will take a while, here are some surefire choices in the historical center. Perhaps the best option is the boutique-ish **Bologna nel Cuore** (Via Cesare Batisti, 29, west of Piazza Maggiore; ☎ 051-269442 or 329-2193354; www. bolognanelcuore.it), in which you can rent two stylish rooms with a pleasingly odd assemblage of designer furnishings and antique touches—bang in the center of town—for €80 to €180, depending on period and length of stay. **Casa Ilaria** (Largo Respighi, 8, just off Via Zamboni in the university district; ☎ 051-270512 or 335-5336613; www.casailaria.com) rents a pair of rooms with frilly curtains and Jacuzzi tubs or showers for €80 for two people, or for €120 during trade fairs.

€   **La Mansarda** (Strada Maggiore, 29, just southwest of Piazza di Porta Ravegnana; ☎ 339-1228884 or 339-3508148; www.lamansarda.net) means "the attic," and this lovely, €160 one-room nook, which sleeps up to four, is crisscrossed with heavy wood beams and sports views over the rooftops to one of Bologna's famous towers, Torre degli Asinelli.

€   Halfway between the train station and Piazza Maggiore, **Beatrice Bed & Breakfast** (Via dell'Indipendenza, 56, near Piazza dell'VIII Agosto; ☎ 051-246016 or 338-9203407; www.bb-beatrice.com) offers two rooms—elegant "Patrizia" and plain "Elizabetta," costing €70 to €75 per night, up to €95 on Saturdays, holidays, or trade fairs—with twin beds, a shared bathroom, and Internet access in the fifth-floor apartment of a young couple and their cat.

€–€€   Though the *palazzo* is late 18th century, the two rooms (€65–€130) are modern at **Fine '700** (Via Galleria, 12, 1 block south of Via Riva di Reno; ☎ 051-238565; www.fine700.com); definitely try for the huge "Master Bedroom" rather than for the plainer twin-bedded room. At the southern edge of the historical center, **B&B Miramonte** (Via Miramonte, 11; ☎ 339-5697513; www.miramonte-bologna.it) is nice because it is made up of a pair of modern two-room apartments—the one on the second floor has wood ceilings—and you can choose

Beware the Trade Fairs & Watch the Seasons

Bologna is a city of *fiere* (trade fairs) that frequently leave the city booked solid—and cause every hotel to jack up rates to the maximum allowed by law. Following are the 2006 dates of the major trade fairs; although they'll vary slightly from one year to the next, count on having to book far in advance for these general periods (such as the middle 2 weeks of Feb and the second half of Apr): April 5 to 11 and 18 to 22; May 9 to 13 and 24 to 28; September 7 to 10 and 25 to 30; October 10 to 14 and 24 to 29; November 15 to 19; December 7 to 17.

You'll find the cheapest hotel rates in summer, especially in August, when the Bolognese flee the city for cooler climes.

whether to rent just one of the rooms (with private bathroom, TV, and Internet for €70–€75) and share the living room/kitchenette with the other room on that floor, or you can rent the entire two-room apartment on either floor for €145. The contemporary **B&B Anna** (Via Orfeo, 24; ☎ 349-9011981; www.bebanna.it), in the southeast corner of the historical center, offers a single (€50) and a double (€80), as well as optional shiatsu massages.

The tourist office also has a list of 29 local **religious institutions that provide housing** for students during the academic year, and will often rent the rooms to tourists during the summer.

€   There's also a university-run student dorm in which you can snag a room—which includes a bathroom, telephone, and Internet connection for €45 per single, €50 per double—from the end of the school year (which varies) to July 19: **Collegio Erasmus** (Via de' Chiari, 8; ☎ 051-276711; www.ceur.it/collegio-erasmus).

Another resource is the local merchants' association, **CST** (☎ 051-234735 or 800-856065 toll-free in Italy; www.prenotabologna.it or www.bolognareservation.com), which maintains a desk inside the main tourist office and will **book you a room for free** at any of dozens of hotels in town, including most of those listed here.

ACCOMMODATIONS NEAR PIAZZA MAGGIORE

€   I'm delighted whenever I discover another charming, old-fashioned *pensione* like the **Panorama** ★ 🄺 (Via Livraghi, 1, off Via Ugo Bassi 3 blocks west of Piazza Maggiore; ☎ 051-221802; www.hotelpanoramabologna.it; no credit cards) still in business. In fact, if you don't mind rooms without bathrooms, and a lack of breakfast service, you may want to consider staying in one of these €70 doubles even if your budget allows for more luxurious accommodations. The location near Piazza Maggiore is excellent, and the women who own/manage the hotel, which occupies the top floor of an old apartment house, make guests feel like family. The rooms are very large and high-ceilinged, with creaky old parquet floors in a herringbone pattern, and most look through large windows over a pleasant courtyard to the hills above the city (avoid rooms 6–10, whose double-paned windows can't keep out the traffic noise). The furnishings are functional but modern and include enough wooden armoires and other homey touches to make them cozy. Some rooms even sleep four (€95) or five (€105) people.

€–€€   The attractive **Centrale** ★ kids (Via delle Zecca, 2, off Via Ugo Bassi 2 blocks west of Piazza Maggiore; ☎ 05l-225114; werterg@tin.it) offers one of Bologna's best values: It's cheap, central, and clean, and has all the amenities you need plus the occasional touch of class in the form of a chandelier hanging from decorative ceiling moldings. An ancient cage elevator deposits you at the door on the third floor of an old apartment house in the amiable company of an interesting mix of travelers from all over the world. The rooms—€78 for a double without bathroom, €96 with; skip the overpriced €8 extra for breakfast—have been redone with crisp modern furnishings and either pleasant pastel or brocaded deep blue fabrics. The bathrooms can be small but are newly tiled with large sinks and showers. Most rooms are unusually spacious for Italy, and several have three and four beds or futon-chairs, making this an especially affordable stopover for families. (I like room 18, with a big window overlooking a brick tower and church dome.)

€€€   If you prefer your hotels a bit less creaky and more modern, the gracious **Roma** ★ (Via d'Azeglio, 9, just a few steps south of Piazza Maggiore; ☎ 051-226322; www.hotelroma.biz) offers many of the amenities you'd expect in larger hotels. Those include a cozy lobby bar, adequate though not outstanding in-house restaurant, efficient English-speaking staff, porters to carry your bags, and a garage—all for €150 per double. What really makes this hotel worth seeking out, though, are its unusually comfortable rooms. They're large and bright (albeit dominated by overwrought floral patterns), with brass beds that are often king-size, roomy armchairs, long tables, and most with dressing-room foyers between the bathrooms and bedrooms. The green-tiled bathrooms were redone several years ago and tend to be huge, with bidets and luxuriously deep tubs—though you'll have to hold the shower nozzle yourself, and there's rarely a curtain. Ask for one of the top-floor rooms with terrace (rooms 301–303, 306–309, 422–425, and 428–429).

ACCOMMODATIONS NEAR THE UNIVERISTY

€–€€   The plain but comfortable **Rossini** (Via Bibiena, 11, off Piazza G. Verdi, between Via Zamboni and Via San Vitale; ☎ 051-237716; www.albergorossini.com) will fill the bill, if not thrill, for basic comfort at a good price. Its location in the heart of the university district is what draws many guests and visiting academics. The rooms aren't much more than functional, right down to the no-nonsense small bathrooms, but at least they tend to be large, with very firm beds, and they're cheap: Doubles without bathroom cost €45 to €75, with bathroom €80 to €110; breakfast is an extra €3. Regular renovations have kept the place up-to-date, with TVs in all but one room, and air-conditioning in the eight top-floor rooms. The lobby bar is a fun place to sip wine and listen to intellectual chatter.

€–€€   If you're looking for a high level of comfort and service, don't even consider the **Accademia** (Via delle Belle Arti, 6; ☎ 051-232318; www.hotel accademia.com; no credit cards). On the other hand, it's cheap—€65 to €100 for a double without a bathroom, €80 to €130 with bathroom—the location on a lively street near the university is superb, and the centuries-old *palazzo* is full of character. The lobby and staircase, with well-worn stone flooring and vaulted ceilings, are deceivingly grand; the bright, no-frills, functional rooms are far simpler. The bathrooms don't seem to have been updated for a couple of decades, so the worn fixtures and half-size bathtubs can pose a bit of a challenge.

ACCOMMODATIONS NEAR SAN DOMENICO

€€–€€€   Quiet **Hotel Touring** ★ (Via de' Mattuiani, 1–2, off Via Garibaldi; ☎ 051-584305; www.hoteltouring.it) lies on the edge of the *centro storico* near San Domenico. The stylish rooms are nicely fitted out with shiny hardwood or faux-marble ceramic floors, sleek contemporary furnishings, rich upholstery, and (in almost all) air-conditioning (a few have ceiling fans). Most bathrooms are striking, many with gilt-framed mirrors on the white tile walls, deep sinks (double sinks in a few units), and roomy showers. Some rooms are quite large indeed, and many on the third and fourth floors have large balconies. The eight nonsmoking rooms come with minibars. The roof terrace affords wonderful 360-degree views, and in 2004 they added a small Jacuzzi up there so you can better enjoy them. Double rooms start around €99 (jumping up to €235 during trade fairs). They also rent an apartment starting at €150.

ACCOMMODATIONS WORTH THE SPLURGE

Dottor Mauro Orsi, an elegant man of bow ties and a toothy smile, runs a small local hotel empire of ultrarefined inns at surprisingly reasonable rates: **Bologna Art Hotels** (☎ 051-7457335; www.bolognahotels.it). A premium is placed on service at each hotel, from free bikes and Internet access to free 2-hour city walking tours for guests every Sunday (as well as a private guide on call the rest of the week who will craft thematic tours to your specifications)—all of which make the slightly high prices more reasonable than they first appear.

€€€–€€€€   A loyal cadre of travelers have come to love the cheapest of the quartet, the 34-room **Orologio** ★ (Via IV Novembre, 10; ☎ 051-7457411), which overlooks a small pedestrian street off Piazza Maggiore on the clock-tower side of the town hall (*orologio* means "clock"—hence the name). Aside from this wonderful location, two of the attractions are the lounge, with its comfy couches, free snacks, and free Internet terminal, and the adjacent breakfast room with its generous morning buffet. The rooms—doubles for €170 to €212 (up to €320 during trade fairs)—are often small but nicely done, with patterned silk walls and old photos of Bologna, wrought-iron bed frames or inlaid wood headboards, handsome contemporary furnishings, and well-equipped marble-clad modern bathrooms. The suites, while not very large, have two rooms with extra touches like ceiling stuccoes in the bathrooms or marble column capitals serving as end tables.

€€€€   Rates start just €10 higher—doubles for €180 to €212 (up to €320 during trade fairs)—at the **Dei Commercianti** ★★★ (Via Pignattari, 11; ☎ 051-7457511). The lovely structure facing the flank of San Petronius was built in the 12th century as the city's first seat of government, and a recent renovation took full advantage of this antiquity, showing off original beams and flooring in cutaway views through protective glass, and, in places, even a bit of fresco. Antique pieces and Oriental carpets fill the lobby, vaulting and columns the breakfast room. The polished woodwork and rustic touches extend down the twisting halls into the stunning rooms, which have been carved out of the centuries-old structure and vary widely in size and shape. Even the smallest, though, are welcoming. Most of the beds are canopied or have iron frames; the fabrics are rich red, gold, and blue; the TVs are flatscreens; and lots of rooms have beamed ceilings and inlaid marble tables. "Deluxe" rooms (€190–€231) have small terraces overlooking San Petronius.

€€€€   Charging the same rates as the Dei Commercianti is the relatively new (it opened in 2003) **Novecento** ✪ (Piazza Galileo, 4; ☎ 051-7457311), which from the outside looks a bit like a turn-of-the-20th-century theater house on its own quiet square a few blocks southwest of the main piazza. Inside, however, is a sleek boutique hotel done in a full-bore repro of Secession style (the Viennese version of Art Nouveau—very modernist, with lots of straight lines, simple curves, and a restrained color palette).

DINING FOR ALL TASTES

There's a good reason it's called "Bologna the Fat." Chubby tortellini are filled with cheese and meat and topped with cream sauces. Heaping platters of grilled meats are served without a care for cholesterol. Yes, you can eat very well in Bologna—what is surprising is that you need not spend a fortune doing so.

RESTAURANTS NEAR THE UNIVERSITY

€   At the **Enoteca Italiana** ✪✪ (Via Marsala, 2b; ☎ 051-235989), an inviting and award-winning shop–cum–wine bar on a side street just north of Piazza Maggiore, you can stand at the bar and sip on a local wine while enjoying a sandwich or platter of cheese and mortadella. Simple, family-run **Trattoria Da Danio** (Via San Felice, 50; ☎ 051-555202) consists of one brightly lit tiled room, usually filled with the clamor of families who live in this old neighborhood just east of Piazza Maggiore (follow Via Ugo Bassi its length to Via San Felice). The kitchen sends out good, substantial servings of traditional Bolognese fare: heaping bowls of tortellini topped with bolognese sauce, delicious gnocchi stuffed with spinach and ricotta, homey chicken and pork dishes, and the like. The weekday €7.50 *menu turistico* (single course with wine and water), and €12 *menu prezzo fisso* (pasta, main course, side dish, wine, water, and cover), are great deals.

> ❝ First thing at Bologna: tried Bologna sausage on the principle that at Rome you go first to St. Peter's. ❞
>
> —Herman Melville,
> *Journal of a Visit to Europe and the Levant,* 1857

€–€€   **Trattoria Belfiore** (Via Marsala, 11a; ☎ 051-226641; Wed–Mon) is a series of narrow, high-ceilinged rooms on one of the old streets between Via dell'Indipendenza and the university area, and as a result it attracts an incongruous group of students and businesspeople who chatter noisily as friendly waiters run to and from the kitchen. This is not the place for a romantic conversation or a foray into haute cuisine—simple is the rule. Dishes don't get much more elaborate than tortellini or a platter of *salsiccia al ferri* (grilled sausages; €6) or *pollo arrosto* (roast chicken; €7). But like much of the fare, including the pizzas (€2.60–€6), they're prepared over an open fire and are delicious and very fairly priced.

€-€€   Why do theatergoers flock to the **Trattoria-Pizzeria Belle Arti** (Via delle Belle Arti, 14; ☎ 051-225581; www.belleartitrattoriapizzeria.com; closed Wed) after performances at the nearby Teatro Comunale? Because the food is excellent and the kitchen keeps later hours than most in Bologna. Even on weeknights you may have to wait to get a table in the handsome brick-and-panel dining room, but once the *tortellini neri tartufati* (homemade tortellini in a truffle sauce; €8.50) or *tagliatelli con funghi porcini* (flat noodles with porcini mushrooms; €8.50) starts arriving at the table, you'll be glad you waited. Or choose from a stupendous selection of pizzas (€3.80–€9) that emerge from a wood-burning oven.

€€-€€€   At **Trattoria Anna Maria** ★ (Via delle Belle Arti, 17a; ☎ 051-266894; Wed–Sun lunch and dinner, Tues dinner only), Anna Maria herself always seems to be on hand at her animated trattoria, serving some of the finest food in Bologna in a big room wallpapered with the head shots of hundreds of actors and opera stars who've dined here following performances at the nearby Teatro Comunale. All the pasta is freshly made and appears in some unusual variations, including wonderful tortellini, prepared in a soup, *al ragù, al Gorgonzola, al pomodoro* (tomato sauce), or *al burro e salvia* (butter and sage) for €9 to €12. While any of these pasta dishes is a meal in itself, you may be tempted to try one of the substantial second courses, most of which are simple, deliciously prepared dishes from the region: *trippa con fagioli* (tripe and beans; €11), *fegato alla Veneta* (liver and onions; €10), or roasted rabbit, guinea fowl, or duck (€9–€9.50).

RESTAURANTS AROUND VIA PRATELLO

€€   Of the many *osterie* lining Via del Pratello, the tavern **L'Osteria del Montesino** ★ (Via del Pratello, 74b; ☎ 051-523426; Tues–Sun, dinner only) would be my choice for a light meal. It has a huge selection of *crostini* (toasted bread with a variety of toppings), and you can get a heaping sampler platter of *crostini misti* (€6.20). A daily trio of pastas costs €6 for one, €6.50 to sample two, or €7 for all three (or for the ricotta-and-spinach *tortellacci*, available weekends only). These *primi*—along with most wines and the mixed meat-and-cheese platters—ignore the famed local cuisine and are proudly Sardegnan.

€-€€   The down-to-earth **Trattoria Fantoni** ★ (Via del Pratello, 11a; ☎ 051-236358; no credit cards; Tues–Sat lunch and dinner, Mon lunch only), on the other hand, is my fave for a full meal. The two simple dining rooms are almost always jammed with people who work in the neighborhood, and the menu reflects their culinary tastes. You can sample horse meat, which appears on many traditional Bolognese menus, prepared here several ways, including *bistecca cavallo* and *cavallo alla tartara* (horse steak and horse-meat tartare; €9–€10). Or you can opt for nicely prepared versions of more familiar fare, such as *salsiccia* (grilled sausage; €8) or *tacchino* (grilled turkey breast; €8). The food is so good and the prices so low—especially at lunch—that you can expect to wait for a table just about any evening.

RESTAURANTS NEAR PIAZZA MAGGIORE

€€   Wander into inconspicuous **Olindo Faccioli** ✪✪ (Via Altabella, 15b; ☎ 051-223171; Mon–Sat, dinner only) for a glass of wine and you may end up spending the entire evening. Just a few tables are wedged into two tiny rooms behind a bar lined with the more than 400 vintages and manned by Carlo Faccioli (grandson of founder Olindo). There's no menu, but the daily fare is posted on a chalkboard—or, when Carlo forgets to do that, recited orally. A carpaccio of tuna or a selection of bruschetta or *crostini misti* are perfect openers, followed by zucchini flowers stuffed with mozzarella, spaghetti *al ragù* (€8), and the almost too-rich *involtini di melanzane alla mortadella* (a cheesy mess of eggplant and bologna; €12). While 2am is the official closing time, Carlo often stays open later.

RESTAURANTS WORTH A SPLURGE

€€–€€€€   Just watching the whirl in the clamorous, cavernous dining rooms of **Ristorante al Montegrappa da Nello** ✪✪ (Via Montegrappa, 2; ☎ 051-236331; Tues–Sun) is part of the experience at this venerable Bologna institution. You can get by with a simple and relatively inexpensive meal here, but you'll probably want to splurge on a full meal. Truffles and porcini, the hallmarks of the house, appear in salads, atop rich pastas, and accompanying grilled meats, which range into wild boar and venison in season. There's a menu, but because the chef only prepares what's fresh at the market that day, it's best just to let the waiters tell you what they're serving.

WHY YOU'RE HERE: THE TOP SIGHTS & ATTRACTIONS

AROUND PIAZZA MAGGIORE

The central **Piazza Maggiore** is the heart of Bologna, and it's flanked by the city's finest buildings: the medieval **Palazzo di Rei Enzo,** named for Enzo, king of Sardinia, who died here in 1272 after languishing in captivity for 23 years; the Romanesque **Palazzo del Podestà;** and the **Palazzo Comunale,** seat of the local government. The square is dominated, though, by a relative newcomer: an immodestly virile 16th-century bronze state of Neptune, who presides over the ornate **Fontana del Nettuno** ✪✪, inhabited by sensual sirens.

Massive as the **Basilica di San Petronio** ✪✪ (Piazza Maggiore; ☎ 051-225442; daily 7:30am–1pm and 2:30–6pm) is, it's not nearly as big as its 14th-century architects intended it to be. Rome got wind of the Bolognese scheme to build a church bigger than St. Peter's and cut off funding. Even so, the structure that was erected over the next 3 centuries is impressively grand. Its facade is partially striped in white and red (the city's heraldic colors) and punctuated by one of the

> ❝ *Bologna is to the Middle Ages what Pompeii has been to antiquity—a monument of the manner of their domestic existence.* ❞
>
> —Lady Morgan, *Italy,* 1820

Bologna Itinerary

If you have only 1 day in Bologna
Start in the heart of the action—the lovely **Piazza Maggiore**—with an early (around 8:30am) peek inside the **Basilica di San Petronio.** Head east on Via Orefici to plunge into the city's lively **morning street market** (see "The Other Bologna" on p. 244), making your way back to Piazza Maggiore and down Via dell'Archiginnasio to pop in and see the fascinatingly grue-some **Teatro Anatomico.**

Continue south to pay your respects to St. Dominic (and some early Michelangelos) at **San Domenico,** and then make your way back north into the university district. Lunch at Trattoria Anna Maria, and then work it off by wandering the galleries of Old Masters at the **Pinacoteca Nazionale.** Next, climb the **Torre degli Asinelli** before popping into the frescoed oratory of **Santa Cecilia** and its attached church of **San Giacomo Maggiore.** Finally, spend some time at **San Stefano** making sense of the seven churchlets, built willy-nilly against one another, from the 5th through 13th centuries.

Depending on how speedy you are, you may even have time to fit in the medieval or archaeological museums before they close at 6:30pm. For dinner and late-night gallivanting, head to hopping Via del Pratello.

great works of the Italian Renaissance: a marble doorway surrounded by bas-reliefs depicting the Madonna and Child and other biblical scenes carved by Jacopo della Quercia, which are now sadly weather-worn.

Several of the chapels in the cavernous interior, where Charles V was crowned Holy Roman Emperor in 1530, are richly decorated with frescoes, the best of which are in the chapels to the left as you enter. One contains Lorenzo Costa's *Madonna and Child with Saints,* and the other (fourth on the left) is enlivened with colorful depictions of heaven and hell, the life of St. Petronius, and *Stories of the Magi* by Giovanni da Modena (who also did the frescoes in and around the left aisle's first chapel).

Embedded in the floor of the left aisle is an enchanting curiosity—**Italy's largest sundial,** a 66m (216-ft.) astronomical clock installed by the astronomer Cassini in 1655. The two-room "museum" (free admission; Mon–Sat 9:30am–12:30pm and 2:30–5:30pm, Sun 2:30–5:30pm) at the end of the left aisle contains drawings and wooden models of the church and various plans for its facade; some fine illuminated choir books; and the usual gilt and silver reliquaries, robes, and chalices.

THE LEANING TOWERS OF BOLGONA?

Only a few of the more than 200 towers that once rose above Bologna, built by noble families as symbols of their wealth and prestige, are still standing—and just barely. The two most famous lean alarmingly toward one another on Piazza di Porta Ravegna, where the seven main streets of medieval Bologna converge. The

50m (165-ft.) Torre Garisenda tilts a precarious 3m (10 ft.) off the perpendicular, while Torre degli Asinelli, which is nearly twice as tall, is 2.3m (7½ ft.) out of plumb. Best of all, you can climb the **Torre degli Asinelli** ★ (Piazza di Porta Ravegna; €3; May–Sept daily 9am–6pm, Oct–Apr daily 9am–5pm), 500 steps to the reward of a stunning view over Bologna's red-tile rooftops and the surrounding hills.

TOP MUSEUMS

Though a Roman wall runs through the courtyard of the **Museo Civico Medioevale** ★ (Via Manzoni, 4; ☎ 051-203930; www.comune.bologna.it/iperbole/MuseiCivici; €4; Tues–Sat 9am–6:30pm, Sun 10am–6:30pm), the collection itself is devoted to depicting life in medieval Bologna. During the Middle Ages, the city revolved around its university, and the most enchanting treasures are the sepulchers of professors, surrounded for eternity by carvings of dozing and mocking students. Also on view are fascinating cooking utensils from daily life in medieval Bologna, illuminated manuscripts, and a sizable collection of arms and armor. It also has a healthy handful of medieval objects from cultures around the world (collections left over from previous incarnations of the museum), and the museum's name hasn't kept it from squirreling away a few small Renaissance and baroque bronzes by the likes of Giambologna, Bernini, and Algardi.

Many of the galleries at the **Pinacoteca Nazionale** ★ (Via delle Belle Arti, 56; ☎ 051-4209411; www.pinacotecabologna.it; €4; Tues–Sun 9am–6:30pm) are devoted to either Bolognese painters or painters from elsewhere who worked in Bologna, including Italy's largest collection by the city's most illustrious artist, Guido Reni (1575–1642). Perhaps his best-known work is the *Ritratto della*

Europe's First University

Bologna's university is Europe's oldest, rooted in a Roman law school from A.D. 425 and officially founded in the 10th century. By the 13th century, more than 10,000 students from all over Europe were descending on this center of learning. Their scholarly numbers have included Thomas à Becket, Copernicus, Dante, Petrarch, and, much more recently, Federico Fellini. Always forward-thinking, even in the unenlightened Middle Ages, the university employed female professors, and the political leanings of today's student body are displayed in leftist slogans that emblazon the 15th- to 19th-century buildings.

While most of the university is now housed up Via Zamboni, the most interesting bit to visit is in one of its oldest buildings just south of Piazza Maggiore: the Teatro Anatomico inside the baroque **Palazzo di Archiginnasio** ★ (Piazza Galvani, 1; ☎ 051-276811; www.archiginnasio.it; free admission; Mon–Fri 9am–6:45pm, Sat 9am–1:30pm). In this quite theatrical anatomical theater, ancient wooden benches surround a marble slab used for the continent's first (legal) gross anatomy classes, and carved skinless human pillars support the lectern.

Cumulative Ticket

A cumulative ticket for all the city's civic museums—including the archaeological and medieval ones—is available for 6€ for 1 day or 8€ for 3 days.

Madre, a portrait of his mother, hanging in a Reni room that also includes *Samson the Victorious.* More striking, however, is the *St. George and the Dragon,* an early work (1335) by one of Emilia-Romagna's first great masters, Vitale da Bologna. The contorted figures and sense of movement evoked by George's fluttering cloak and wind-whipped hair show an expressive side to early Gothic painting every bit as impressive as that being practiced by the followers of Giotto south of the Apennines.

The museum's most sought-out work is not by a native son but by Raphael, whose *Ecstasy of St. Cecilia* is one of the great achievements of Renaissance painting.

The Etruscan and Roman finds from the surrounding region and many fine Egyptian antiquities make Bologna's **Museo Civico Archeologico** ✪ (Via dell' Archiginnasio, 2; ☎ 051-2757211; www.comune.bologna.it/museoarcheologico; €4; Tues–Sat 9am–6:30pm, Sun 10am–6:30pm), one of Italy's most well-rounded collections of antiquities. The Egyptian holdings include a portion of the Book of the Dead and bas-reliefs from the tomb of Horemheb, followed by replicas of well-known Greek and Roman statues, plus a peaceful central courtyard littered with ancient milestones from Via Emilia. The next floor is filled with the museum's impressive Etruscan collection (crowded into glass cases a la the 19th c.), including remnants from Bologna's own beginnings as the Etruscan outpost Felsina. Among the burial items and other artifacts is a bronze urn from the 5th century B.C., the Situla di Certosa, decorated with a depiction of a ceremonial procession.

MORE CHURCHES

The remarkable assemblage of hallowed buildings known as **Basilica di Santo Stefano** ✪✪ (Via Santo Stefano, 24; ☎ 051-223256; daily 9am–noon and 3:30–6pm) actually incorporates seven separate churches and chapels dating variously from the 5th to the 13th centuries. A walk through the complex provides a remarkable overview of the history of Bologna. The first church you enter is the Crocifisso, begun in the 11th century (as you enter, notice the pulpit built into the facade). San Petronio, Bologna's patron saint, lies in the church to the left—the most charming in the group—the 12th-century San Sepolcro, a polygon modeled after the church of the Holy Sepulcher in Jerusalem. According to legend, the basin in the courtyard is the one in which Pontius Pilate absolved himself after condemning Christ to death (in truth, it's an 8th-c. Lombard piece). The oldest church is the 5th-century Santi Vitale e Agricola, incorporating fragments of a Roman temple to Isis; Charlemagne allegedly worshiped here in the 8th century. Just beyond is the 13th-century Trinità and the complex's 11th-century cloisters, where plaques honor Bologna's war dead. A small museum/gift shop opens off the back, containing some unmemorable paintings and frescoes spanning the 13th to the 18th centuries. And out here you'll find yet another church: the tiny Cappella della Benda.

In the sixth chapel on the right inside **San Domenico** ✪ (Piazza San Domenico, 13; ☎ 051-6400411; Mon–Sat 9:30am–12:15pm and 3–6:30pm, Sun 3–5:30pm) is one of the great treasures of Bologna, the beautifully crafted **tomb of San Domenico** ✪✪. St. Dominic, founder of the teaching order that bears his name, died in Bologna in 1221, and his venerated modern X-ray decorates the chapel wall (it's an actual X-ray of his bones; I've seen pilgrims kiss their fingers and touch it before turning to pray at the tomb). These saints and angels are a joint effort of Michelangelo, Pisano, and, most notably, Nicolo di Bari, who was so proud of his work on the cover of the tomb *(arca)* that he dropped his last name and is better known as Nicolo dell'Arca. Postcards near the entrance to the chapel show you who carved what. A 20-year-old Michelangelo did the candle-bearing angel at the lower right as well as the statue of San Petronius bearing a tiny model of Bologna up on the tomb toward the left. He also carved San Proculus—his cloak slung over one shoulder—on the tomb's backside. The chapel's apse fresco is by Guido Reni, who's buried in the baroque chapel across the nave. The two striking stilt-tombs on the piazza out front date from 1298 and 1300.

The masterpiece of the 13th-century **San Giacomo Maggiore** (Piazza Rossini; ☎ 051-225970; daily 7am–12:30pm and 3:30–6:30pm) is the chapel/burial chamber of the Bentivoglio family, who ruled Bologna through the 15th century. Among the masterpieces here are a *Madonna and Child* by Francesco Francia, along with the frescoes the Bentivoglios commissioned from Ferrarese master Lorenzo Costa to depict life in a Renaissance court—an apt decoration for Bologna's most influential (and tyrannical) clan.

Guided Walks & Bike Tours

Looking for a guided intro to Bologna? Take a €13, **2-hour walking tour**, in Italian or English, that hits most of the sights around Piazza Castello and the Two Towers, plus the creepy Teatro Anatomico in the Palazzo Archiginnasio, and the septet of churches making up San Stefano.

Reservations are not necessary, but because the virtually identical tours are run by different companies on different days, where you meet changes slightly. Those on Wednesday, Saturday, or Sunday at 10:30am (☎ 051-2950005; www.guidebologna.com), and on Saturday at 3pm (☎ 051-2750254; www.guidedarte.com) all meet at the tourist office on Piazza Maggiore. The tours on Monday and Friday at 11am, and on Tuesday and Thursday at 3pm (4pm July–Aug), meet nearby at the Fontana del Nettuno (☎ 051-524274 or 340-2207699).

If wheels are more your style, Wednesday at 10am, weather permitting, you can take a €18, **2-hour guided bike tour** (☎ 051-524274 or 340-2207699) on one of several itineraries; call for details and to book.

Toward the back of the left flank of the church, with a separate entrance, is the **Oratorio di Santa Cecilia** ✹ (Via Zamboni, 15; ☎ 051-225970; daily 9:30am–1pm and 2–6pm). This oratory was frescoed with scenes from the lives of St. Cecilia and her husband, St. Valerian, by the best artists working in Bologna in the 16th century. These included Il Francia (who painted the best of the bunch: the *Marriage of St. Cecilia* to the left of the altar and the *Burial of St. Cecilia* to the altar's right), Lorenzo Costa (the two panels abutting Il Francia's), and Amico Aspertini (the two scenes closest to the entry door on either side; he may have had a hand in the four middle panels as well).

THE OTHER BOLOGNA

The Bolognese people just love to eat—and eat well. Life in Bologna revolves around the kitchen, so to get under the skin of this city, forget the museums and monuments. Take a morning to explore the gastronomic side of Bologna. Start early, around 8am, to mingle with the market workers, professional trattoria chefs, and home-kitchen master chefs out doing their morning shopping.

Bologna's **main-street market** lines Via Drapperie and Via delle Pescherie Vecchie with fishmongers and fourth-generation grocers. **A. F. Tamburini** ✹ (Via Caprarie, 1, at Via Drapperie; ☎ 051-234726; www.tamburini.com) has stacks of salami, pendulums of prosciutto, and cheap cafeteria-like *tavola calda* (pasta and simple meat dishes, €3.50–€5.50) in the back, and **Drogheria Gilberto** (Via Drapperie, 5; ☎ 051-223925), maintains shelves stacked to the ceiling with chocolates, candies, liqueurs, marmalades, and preserves, and always offers free samples (I scored brownies on my last visit). Also nip down Via Caprarie to **Paolo Atti & Figli** ✹✹ (Via Caprarie, 7; ☎ 051-220425; www.paoloatti.com), purveyors of Bologna's finest baked goods since 1880 under high frescoed ceilings.

My favorite stands, though, are the numerous **fruit-and-vegetable stalls** groaning under the weight of purple-fringed artichokes, crinkly bunches of arugula, sleek indigo eggplant, pink pomegranates, orange zucchini flowers,

---

Ragù Straight from the Source

Don't just describe those fantastic meals to your friends back home; learn to make them at a Bologna cooking school. **Gli Amici di Babette** (Via San Felice, 116, scala G; ☎ 051-6493627 or 339-7011003; www.lacucinadi babette.com) offers more than a dozen 3-hour courses on breads, pastas, pastries, and desserts for all skill levels for €65 to €80 per lesson (there are also double-session lessons on historical cooking—ancient Roman, medieval, Renaissance, and 19th c.—for €150).

La Vecchia Scuola Bolognese (Via Malvasia, 49; ☎ 051-6491576; www.lavecchiascuola.com) does 4-hour courses on making fresh pastas at €70 a pop (or a 5-day course for €220). **Cookitaly** (☎ 051-6448612; www.cookitaly.com) costs more, at €250 for one or €350 for two, but you get a 6-hour lesson and learn to cook a three-course meal—*primo, secondo,* and dessert.

Bologna's Music Festivals

If you're in Bologna April to October, you can spend your evenings at the classical and jazz concerts and other events that are part of the **Bologna Festival** (Via delle Lame, 58; ☎ 051-6493397; www.bolognafestival.it; tickets start around €10–€20). The performances are held in church cloisters and other scenic settings throughout the city center. Performances can range from Mozart to the Academy of St. Martin in the Fields, from the Dee Dee Bridgewater & Trio to the Tokyo Quartet.

A far less tame event is the **Made in Bo festival** (☎ 051-533880; www.madeinbo.it), a series of late-night outdoor rock concerts held in summer (June–July or July–Aug) in Parco Nord (bus no. 25 serves the area from the train station; free buses from Piazza Maggiore are provided for some events). Get tickets at CD Mania (Piazza Sacrati, 33; ☎ 0532-210292). Ask the tourist office for details on both of these festivals, as well as the many concerts, dance and theater performances, and other events the city stages throughout the year.

---

pungent mushrooms, tiny *susine* plums, pointy San Marzano tomatoes, mounds of grapes, trays of chestnuts, garlands of fiery red pepperoncini, and ropes of garlic.

In a city this devoted to food, there are also two **covered markets**—though the **Mercato Clavature,** in the midst of that street market, has definitely seen better days (word is that the owners are trying to run out the few remaining traditional stall owners with high rent and dilapidated conditions in order to turn the place into a more upscale cafe-and-shops joint).

Far more of a going concern is bustling **Mercato delle Erbe** ✸, with a blink-and-you'll-miss-it entrance on Via Ugo Bassi, 2 blocks west of its intersection with Via G. Marconi. This covered market houses 36 specialty food shops and 72 fruit and vegetable stands; make sure you get here before they close up shop for the lunch break around 1pm.

Exit the market from the back onto Via Belvedere, where you can still see the market's original 1910 facade in all its orange-and-yellow neoclassical grandeur. Across the street is **Le Sflogline** (Via Belvedere 7B), a traditional *sfoglini* shop run by a trio of smiling ladies who spend their days making fresh pasta and pastries, as well as lasagna in tiny takeout foil containers. (*Sfoglini* are Bolognese pasta makers who roll out fresh pasta in great sheets, and then cut it into strips using rolling pins set with rows of plastic discs.) There's another such shop, **La Braseria Sfoglia**, at Via A. Tostoni 9A.

End your gastronomic journey with a pilgrimage to **Majani** ✸✸ (Via Carbonesi, 5; ☎ 051-6562209; www.majani.com), chocolatiers extraordinaire since 1796. About €4.50 will buy you a sampler baggie filled with their greatest hits—one each of the chocolate "tortellini" (in milk, dark, and white, each filled with a chocolate cream), a selection of the famous *cremini Fiat* (chocolate napoleons), and a few *scroza* (thin sheets of dark chocolate, roughly accordioned up into a bar).

Bologna the Fat, indeed.

NIGHTLIFE

A good way to keep up with performances in Bologna—whether a poetry reading in the back of a bar or a pop concert at the Stadio Comunale—is to scan the posters plastered on walls around the university. Just troll Via Zamboni, and ignore all the notices looking for roommates or selling "slightly used" couches and TVs.

The **Teatro Comunale** (Largo Respighi, 1; ☎ 051-6174299; www.comunale bologna.it) hosts Bologna's lively opera, orchestra, and ballet seasons, as well as intriguing shows, such as homages to Frank Zappa or Charlie Chaplin. The box office (☎ 051-529995) is open Tuesday to Saturday 11am to 6:30pm.

BARS & PUBS

Because of its young and restless student population, Bologna stays up later than most Italian cities. The main night-owl haunts are Via del Pratello and, near the university, Via Zamboni and Via delle Belle Arti. You can usually find a place for a drink, a shot of espresso, or a light meal as late as 2am.

There's Guinness and Harp on tap and an attendant Anglophone following at the **Irish Times Pub** (Via Paradiso, 1; ☎ 051-261648), though a well-dressed, but not always so well-behaved, young Italian crowd predominates in the noisy, smoky, publike rooms; happy hour lasts until 9pm (10:30pm Tues). More popular these days is the **Cluricaune Irish Pub** (Via Zamboni, 18b; ☎ 051-263419; www.cluricaune.com), a raucous joint near the university with quite good live music some nights (no cover), and where the party spills out under the street's arcade. Happy hour lasts until 8:30pm (10:30pm on Wed).

The **Osteria de Poeti** (Via Poeti, 1; ☎ 051-236166; www.osteriadepoeti.com; closed Mon), is Bologna's oldest *osteria* and has been in operation since the 16th century—the brick-vaulted ceilings, stone walls, and ancient wine barrels provide just the sort of ambience you would expect in such a historic establishment. Stop in to enjoy the live jazz and folk music. (This place is also open for lunch Tues–Fri.)

You'll want to retire at 10:30pm to the cellars of a 16th-century *palazzo* near the university at **Cantina Bentivoglio** (Via Mascarella, 4b; ☎ 051-265416;

Bologna's Thriving Gay Scene

Bologna is the seat of Italy's Arcigay movement, and that plus the large student population make it rather more open to same-sex couples than most Italian cities.

Cassero/Salara (Via Don Minzoni, 18; ☎ 051-6494416, "phone friend" help line 051-555661; www.cassero.it), is a combination of the main gay/lesbian organization's offices, help center, and meeting point that happens to turn into the hottest gay/lesbian disco Saturday nights. The downstairs disco also hosts a variety of shows, cabaret, movies, and concerts throughout the week, especially Friday and Sunday. During the day (Mon–Fri 10am–1pm, 3–7pm, and 9pm–midnight), they offer gay-friendly services, including a library and a help line. Though Italians need to be members of Arcigay to use the facilities, the bar is more than happy to welcome foreign tourists free of charge.

---

www.cantinabentivoglio.it). That's when you'll hear some of the best jazz in Bologna. It's also a popular spot for filmgoers, who stop in for some food (most dishes €6–€12) and tunes after catching one of the first-run movies at the Odeon 2 across the street.

SIDE TRIPS FROM BOLOGNA

I recommend taking at least one of these three side trips from Bologna.

FERRARA

One family, the Estes, accounts for much of what you'll find in Ferrara, an enchanting city on the plains of Romagna. From 1200 to 1600, the Estes ruled and ranted from their imposing castle that's still the centerpiece of Ferrara. They endowed the city with palaces, gardens, and avenues, as well as intrigues, including those of their most famous duchess, Lucrezia Borgia.

After the Estes left (when Rome refused to recognize the last heir of the clan as duke), Ferrara fell victim to neglect and finally, during World War II, to bombs. Despite the bombing, much of the Renaissance town remains and has been restored. In fact, this city of rose-colored brick is one of the most beautiful in Italy and, shrouded in a gentle mist from the surrounding plains as it often is, one of the most romantic.

Lay of the Land

Ferrara is 45km (27 miles) north of Bologna. **Trains** arrive from and depart for Bologna (25–60 min.) and Venice (1¼–2 hr.) every half-hour. There are one to two trains per hour to Ravenna (1–1¼ hr.) and Padua (45–85 min.).

The train station is a 15-minute walk from the center (or take bus no. 1 or 9); just follow Viale Costituzione through the small park in front of the station to Viale Cavour, which leads directly into the center of town.

The extremely helpful tourist office is in the Castello Estense (☎ 0532-299303; www.ferraraterraeacqua.it or www.comune.fe.it).

Accommodations, Both Standard & Not

€–€€   For basic budget lodgings, choose **Pensione Artisti** (Via Vittoria, 66; ☎ 0532-761038; no credit cards), in the atmospheric medieval Jewish quarter a few blocks from the Duomo. It's utterly utilitarian, but excellently priced at €43 for a double without bathroom, €60 with. The simple rooms are big, bright, and clean; the heavy 1950s-era furnishings are a nice change from the banal furnishings in most cheap hotels; and the shared bathroom facilities are plentiful and clean. Rooms have orthopedic mattresses, sinks, and bidets. Plus, there are some pleasant and unusual amenities here—a few rooms have vine-covered balconies, guests have use of kitchen facilities on each floor, and there's a shared roof terrace.

€€   A step-up in amenities and price, the **San Paolo** (Via Baluardi, 9; ☎ 0532-762040; www.hotelsanpaolo.it) faces the old city walls at the southern edge of the Jewish ghetto with its warren of lanes and small shops. Add to this atmospheric location the attentive service of the proprietors, who rent bikes (€5 per day), dispense advice on sightseeing and restaurants, and serve coffee from the little lobby bar. The €85 doubles are pretty bland but comfortable, with inoffensive contemporary blond furnishings and small but functional bathrooms. They're always taking small

Bike Like a Ferrarese

To get around like a true Ferrarese—especially for that Sunday tool along the park that rings the city atop its massive walls—you need a bike. Several of the recommended hotels provide free bikes (Borgonuovo, Europa) or cheap rentals (San Paolo). Otherwise, you can **rent a set of wheels** just outside the train station from **Pirani e Bagni** (Piazzale Stazione, 2; ☎ 0532-772190). In the center, rent just west of Piazza Castello from **Romanelli** (Via della Luna, 10, at Via Frizzi; ☎ 0532-206017; www.ferraracicli.it). At the town's main southern gate, Porta Paula, east of the bus station are two outfits: **Ceragioli** (Piazza Travaglio, 4; ☎ 339-4056853) and **Itinerando** (Via Kennedy, 2; ☎ 0532-202003; www. itinerando.it). Rates tend to be the same at all: €2 to €2.50 per hour, €5 to €5.50 for 2 hours, €9 to €9.50 for 3 hours, and €10 to €11 per day.

steps to invigorate the place—in 2004, they added air-conditioning to more than half the rooms.

€€–€€€   The elegant **Borgonuovo Bed & Breakfast** ✦✦✦ (Via Cairoli, 29; ☎ 0532-211100 or 0532-248000; www.borgonuovo.com) is the most charming hostelry in Ferrara. The gracious owner, Signora Adele Orlandini, has spruced up an apartment that once housed her father's law offices in a medieval *palazzo* on a pedestrian street around the corner from the *castello*. The four large, stylish rooms are a tasteful mix of rustic and Art Deco antiques with posh new bathrooms (one large double also has a kitchenette), and rent for €85 to €105. She serves a hearty breakfast (in the lovely garden, weather permitting), and offers bicycles, discount coupons for museums and nearby shops, and plenty of advice on how to enjoy her native city. Book well in advance—Signora's rooms and hospitality are much in demand.

Fortunately, she has recently added two elegant new apartments with antique furnishings in the building next door. One is a mansard apartment with rooftop views, the other has higher ceilings and a large living room. Both come with two double bedrooms and a kitchenette, and can comfortably sleep up to five (but cost no more than a regular double for two). Services in the apartments are the same as in the main *locanda* itself (you take your breakfast there), but get your own key to a separate entrance. Signora also offers an 8-day Italian-language course for adults (in conjunction with a nearby language school), consisting of 3-hour lessons each day in the hotel garden.

€€€   Built in 1700, the elegant **Europa** (Corso Giovecca, 49, between Via Palestro and Via Teatini; ☎ 0532-205456; www.hoteleuropaferrara.com), 1 block from the Castello Estense, has served as a hotel since 1880. Multiple renovations have left it with a somewhat contemporary look, though enough of the original architecture remains to render the premises atmospheric. Several of the enormous guest rooms—including most along the main street—were converted from grand salons and have frescoed ceilings, the original checkerboard terra-cotta tile floors, Art Nouveau furnishings, and Murano chandeliers. Unfortunately, you pay the same price (€115) even if you end up in one of the less-grand rooms—though even those are gracious and large, with a nice mix of contemporary furnishings and reproduction Venetian antiques. There's a free Internet terminal, and free bikes for guest use.

Dining for All Tastes

The walls and Ferrara's other green spaces are ideal for a **picnic.** Buy what you need on narrow brick Via Cortevecchia, near the cathedral, lined with *salumerie,* cheese shops, and bakeries. The nearby Mercato Comunale, at the corner of Via Santo Stefano and Via del Mercato, is crowded with food stalls open Monday to Saturday 7:30am to 1pm (Fri also 3:30–7:30pm). At Negozio Moccia, Via degli Spadari, 9, you can indulge in a chunk of *panpeteto,* Ferrara's hallmark chocolate-covered fruitcake.

€-€€   **Al Brindisi** ★★ (Via Adelardi, 11; ☎ 0532-209142; www.albrindisi. com; closed Mon and July 10–Aug 10) claims to be the oldest wine bar in the world (established 1435), with a roster of famous artists (Titian, Cellini) and poets (Tasso, Ariosto) who used to get sloshed here. It serves a staggering selection of wines by the glass (from €2.50) and a wonderful selection of panini and other light fare. I like the *torte salate,* a selection of flatbread wedges topped with an assortment of vegetables (€6). The *cappellaci di zucca* (pumpkin ravioli; €7.50) is also sublime. When the weather is nice, you can sit at boothlike tables on a little lane facing a flank of the Duomo.

€-€€   Dozens of beers and an extensive selection of local wines are available at the cozy **Antica Osteria Al Postiglione** ★ (Vicolo Chiuso del Teatro, 4; ☎ 0532-241509) wine bar/*osteria* on a narrow lane off Piazza Castello. You can also eat very well. The family members who cook and wait tables make the pastas fresh each day, and pride themselves on such simple home-cooked dishes as grilled *salsiccia* (sweet sausages), *mozzarella al forno* (baked mozzarella), and *pasta e fagioli* (a substantial soup of beans and pasta)—all for €6 to €7. Come here for lunch for a bargain bonanza of fixed-price menus ranging from €8.50 (*primo or secondo,* side dish, and drink) to €20 (two courses, side dish, dessert, drinks, coffee).

€€   Just south of the city walls, a block from the traditional market square, **Antica Trattoria Volano** ★★ (Viale Volano, 20; ☎ 0532-761421; www.antica trattoriavolano.com; closed Fri) is a roadside trattoria that has been satisfying hungry travelers since the 1700s. The decor is unassuming (and a tad staid), and the traffic noise detracts, but the cooking is superb. The menu is a veritable study in traditional Ferrara specialties. To sample the best of them all, order a €9 *tris di primi:* a trio of *cappellaci di zucca* (squash-stuffed ravioli), *taglioline al prosciutto,* and *tortelloni di ricotta.* Or warm yourself up with their delicious *cappelletti in brodo* (pasta soup; €7). Stay in the sampler category with the *misto di bolliti* (a selection of hand-carved boiled meats; €12), or try the ultratraditional *salama da sugo* (salty salami diced, cooked in red wine and cognac, and dolloped over mashed potatoes; €10).

€€-€€€   One of the pleasures of dining at **La Provvidenza** ★ (Corso Ercole I d'Este, 92, at Vicolo Parchetto; ☎ 0532-205187; closed Sun dinner and Mon) is the walk here along a stone-paved road leading past the Palazzo dei Diamanti and many of the city's most lovely old mansions and brick-walled gardens. Once inside the dining room, with its cream-colored walls and attractively rustic furnishings, you'll feel you're in the country; there's even an arbor-shaded, partially enclosed garden for dining in good weather. The pastas are excellent and include *cappellaci* (pasta pillows stuffed with squash in a butter and sage sauce; €8) and tortellini stuffed with Gorgonzola and walnuts (€8). The *salama da sugo* (giant sausage stewed in tomato sauce; €14) comes with mashed potatoes. They make their own pastries; try the Ferrarese specialty *torta di tagliatelle* (€5).

Why You're Here: The Top Sights & Attractions

The imposing, moat-encircled **Castello Estense** ✸ (Via Cavour and Corso Ercole I d'Este; ☎ 0532-299233; www.castelloestense.it; €6, or €10 when there's a temporary exhibit; June–Mar 2 Tues–Sun 9:30am–5:30pm, Mar 3–May 31 daily 9:30am–5:30pm) dominates the city center as it did much of Ferrara's Renaissance history. It was built in 1385, and it was here in 1435 that Nicolo III d'Este, with a contrivance of window mirrors, caught his young wife, Parisina Maletesta, *in flagrante delicto* with his son Ugo and had them beheaded in the dank dungeons below. Robert Browning recounted the deed in his poem "My Last Duchess," and today's visitors clamber down a dark staircase to visit the damp cells where the lovers, and others who fell out of favor with the Este clan, once languished. Not to be overlooked is the fact that the Estes also made Ferrara a center of art and learning, and the infamous (and unjustly maligned) Lucrezia Borgia entertained poets and artists beneath the fragrant bowers of the *orangerie.*

Most of the palace is now used as offices for the province, but you can still catch a glimpse of the Estes' enlightenment in what remains of their grand salons—the **Sala dell'Aurora** and **Sala dei Giochi (Game Room),** both ornately festooned with frescoes. Another remnant of court life is the marble **chapel** built for Renta di Francia, the daughter of Louis XII. Those fond of views and stout of heart can climb the 122 steps to the top of the **Torre dei Leoni** (which predates the castle) Tuesday through Sunday from 9:30am to 4:45pm; admission is an extra €1.

With its pink-marble facade highlighted by layers of arches, Ferrara's handsome 12th-century **Duomo** ✸✸ (Corso Libertà and Piazza Cattedrale; ☎ 0532-207449; Mon–Sat 7:30am–noon and 3–6:30pm, Sun 7:30am–12:30pm and 3:30–7:30pm) reflects a heady mix of the Gothic and the Romanesque. The glory of the otherwise austere structure is its marble portal, where carvings by an unknown artist depict a fearsome *Last Judgment.*

An 18th-century renovation relegated many of the paintings, sculptures, and other works that noble families commissioned for the cathedral over the centuries to the **Museo della Cattedrale** (☎ 0532-244949; €5; Tues–Sun 9am–1pm and 3–6pm), installed in the former Church of San Romano around the right side of the Duomo, at the corner with Via San Romano. The pride of the collection is a painting depicting St. George slaying the dragon by Cosmè Tura, Ferrara's 15th-century master. Another masterpiece here is Jacopo della Quercia's *Madonna of the Pomegranate,* in which Mary seems to balance the fruit in one hand and the Christ Child in the other. A nearby relief showing the 12 months of the year once graced the cathedral's exterior, where it served prosaically as a calendar for the largely illiterate citizenry.

Cumulative Tickets

Ferrara has lots of museums. Luckily, it also sells two kinds of *biglietto cumulativo* to help ease the burden on your wallet. The €8 **"Arte Antica"** covers the Palazzo Schifanoia, Museo della Cattedrale, Museo Marfisa, and Museo Civico Lapadario.

The less useful (only because its museums are generally less interesting to a wide audience) €8 **"Arte Moderna"** covers the modern-art collections contained together in the Palazzo Massari: Museo d'Arte Moderna e Contemporanea Filippo de Pisis, Museo Giovanni Boldini, Museo M. Antonioni, and the Arte Contemporanea pavilion. Purchase either at the ticket offices of any of the participating museums.

Don't bother with the €14 **Card Musei (Museums Card),** which merely gets you reduced admission to the Palazzo dei Diamanti and the Palazzo Bonacossi.

The **Loggia dei Mercanti (Loggia of the Merchants),** a line of shops flanking one side of the church, is still the scene of active secular trade, as it has been since the 18th century, and the surrounding streets and *piazze* are filled with lively cafes.

Ferrara is loaded with elaborate old *palazzi,* many containing one or several small museums, while others are simply frescoed and elaborately bedecked monuments to the grandeur of centuries past.

Borso d'Este, who made Ferrara one of the Renaissance's leading centers of art, commissioned the Salone dei Mesi frescoes in the **Palazzo Schifanoia** (Via Scandiana, 23; ☎ 0532-244949; €5; Tues–Sun 9am–6pm). It's a fascinating cycle of the months that's both a Renaissance wall calendar and a rich portrayal of life and leisure in the 15th-century Este court. Each of the 12 sections shows Ferrara's aristocrats going about their daily business; looming above them, though, are gods from classical mythology. The work is a composite of the geniuses of Ferrara's heyday—Francesco del Cossa painted the March, April, and May scenes; Ercole de'Roberti and other court painters executed the rest; and Cosmè Tura, the official painter of the Este court, oversaw the project. The *palazzo* also houses the **Museo Civico d'Arte Antica,** a small collection of coins, bronzes, and other artifacts unearthed from the plains around Ferrara, 14th- and 15th-century ivories, and some medieval and Renaissance ceramics (including a pair of Andrea della Robbia saints).

A recent restoration has returned the 16th-century **Palazzina Marfisa d'Este** (Corso Giovecca, 170; ☎ 0532-244949; €3; Tues–Sun 9am–1pm and 3–6pm) to its former splendor. Marfisa was an ardent patron of the arts, and period furniture and ceiling frescoes (most retouched in the early 1900s) bespeak the glory of the Este dynasty. The little theater in the garden is a reminder that drama, onstage as well as off, was one of the family's great passions.

You'll have no problem figuring out where the **Palazzo dei Diamanti (Palace of Diamonds;** Corso Ercole I d'Este, 21; ☎ 0532-205844; €4; Tues–Wed and

In the Garden of the Finzi-Continis

Ferrara's **Jewish Cemetery** ✖ (Via della Vigna, near the walls off Corso Porta Mare; Sun–Fri 9am–6pm, in winter to 4:30pm), with its ancient tumble of overgrown tombstones, is the most haunting place in Ferrara. A monument to the Ferrarese murdered at Auschwitz is a reminder of the fate of the city's once sizeable Jewish community, whose last days are recounted in the book (and film) *The Garden of the Finzi-Continis,* evocatively set in the gardens and palaces of Ferrara and required viewing for anyone planning to visit the city. The book is semiautobiographical, and its author, Gorgio Bassani, died in 2000. He is buried here, in a tomb designed by famed modern sculptor—and Romagna native—Arnaldo Pomodoro. Nearby, the gorgeous **Cimitero di Certosa** (Via Borsa, 1; ☎ 0532-230175; daily 7:30am–7:30pm) is centered on the long, graceful *loggie* sweeping out from the church of San Cristoforo, designed by Biagio Rossetti.

To learn more about Jewish Ferrara, take a guided tour—in Italian only—at the **Museo Ebraico** (Via Mazzini, 95; ☎ 0532-210228; €4; Sun–Thurs tours at 10, 11am, or noon, closed Aug).

Fri–Sat 9am–2pm, Thurs 9am–7pm, Sun 9am–1pm) gets its name: Nine thousand pointed marble blocks cover the facade. Less interesting are the collections in the museums clustered within. The most deserving of a visit is the **Pinacoteca Nazionale,** containing some notable works by Cosmè Tura, Il Garofalo, and other painters of the Ferrara school, as well as Carpaccio's *Death of the Virgin.* By and large, though, the holdings aren't spectacular. The ground-floor galleries often house temporary exhibits and charge separate admission; check with the ticket office here or with the tourist office to see what's on view.

Ludovico il Moro, famed duke of Milan who married Beatrice d'Este, commissioned the lovely little **Palazzo Costabili** (Via XX Settembre, 124; ☎ 0532-66299; €4; Tues–Sun 9am–2pm) as a place to retire from his courtly duties. Unfortunately, Beatrice died young, and the duke spent his last years as a prisoner of the French. The couple's 15th-century palace, built around a lovely rose garden, contains their furniture and paintings, and provides a lovely view of life in Ferrara during its Renaissance heyday. Part of the *palazzo* houses the small but fascinating collections of the **Museo Archeologico.** The bulk of the treasures are Etruscan and Greek finds unearthed near Ferrara at Spina.

The quartet of museums housed in the exquisite late-15th-century **Palazzo Massari** (Corso Porto Mare, 9; ☎ 0532-244949; €8 to visit all four museums, see below for individual admissions; 9am–1pm and 3–6pm) contain Ferrara's modern-art holdings. The Museo Giovanni Boldini (€5) has works by the 19th-century Italian painter. A Museo d'Arte Moderna e Contemporanea (€3) is largely devoted to the output of Filippo de Pisis—who studied the *metafisica* school of Giorgio de Chirico—plus works by contemporary regional artists. The Museo dell'Ottocento (€4.20) of 19th-century art is skippable. There's also a Padiglione d'Arte Contemporanea in the former stables, open only for special exhibits.

RAVENNA & ITS AMAZING MOSAICS

Few cities in Europe are so firmly entrenched in such a distant past. This flat little city on the edge of the marshes that creep inland from the Adriatic was witness to the last days of the waning ancient Western Civilization. Strong connections with the Eastern Byzantine empire kept the ideals of ancient Rome alive a bit longer while the rest of the west fell to barbarian hordes and dissolved into 1,000 bickering feudal fiefdoms. Ravenna is where the final emperors of the west ended their reign, gilding churches and tombs with glittering mosaics.

Though Ravenna has been an off-the-beaten-track backwater since the 6th century, it continues to dazzle visitors with its mosaics and other artistic vestiges of the Romans, the Byzantines, and the Visigoths. Aside from its horde of treasures, Ravenna is also a fine place to pass the time in sun-drenched *piazze* and pleasant cafes.

Lay of the Land

Ravenna is 75km (47 miles) east of Bologna, with hourly **trains** (70–90 min. trip), and 75km (47 miles) southeast of Ferrara, from which there are 12 trains daily (1–1¼ hr. trip). Ravenna's train station is only about a 15-minute walk down Viale Farini (which becomes Via Diaz) from the central Piazza del Popolo.

The **tourist office** is just off Piazza del Popolo at Via Salara, 8 (☎ 0544-35404; www.turismo.ravenna.it and www.racine.ra.it/ravennaintorno). The office now gives visitors **free bikes** to use for the day. You might also want to check out the private website www.ravennablu.it for info on the city.

Accommodations, Mostly Standard

With the notable exception of Cappello, the lodging scene in Ravenna is pretty dismal. Few of its largely bland hotels are in the historical center. The tourist office has a general lodging booklet listing 35 tiny (two- and three-room) **B&Bs** scattered throughout the city. Double rooms go for €45 to €90—though, again, only a handful are in the center.

€€   True to its name, the **Centrale Byron** (Via IV Novembre, 14; ☎ 0544-33479 or 0544-212225; www.hotelbyron.com) couldn't be more central: right off Piazza del Popolo. The second part of the name is a tribute to Lord Byron, who shared a nearby *palazzo* with his mistress and her husband. Despite these colorful associations (and an elegant marble lobby and chandeliered bar), this hotel is no-nonsense and serviceable. Upstairs, the narrow halls are harshly lit, but the modern-style furnishings in the immaculate rooms, while fairly run-of-the-mill, are pleasant, and most were replaced in 1999 or 2002. Lone travelers make out well with unusually large and sunny single accommodations, many of which are equipped with "French beds" (wider than a single bed but a little narrower than a double). The handful of smaller *"economica"* rooms cost €80 to €92 rather than the standard €95 to €108.

€-€€   There are also two perfectly serviceable, if terribly boring, joints just to the right as you exit the train station. The **Ravenna** (Viale Maroncelli, 12; ☎ 0544-212204), with €60 doubles without private bathroom and €73 with, and the slightly nicer **Minerva** (Viale Maroncelli, 1; ☎ 0544-213711; www.minerva-hotel.com), selling doubles with bathroom for €65 to €90.

Ravenna

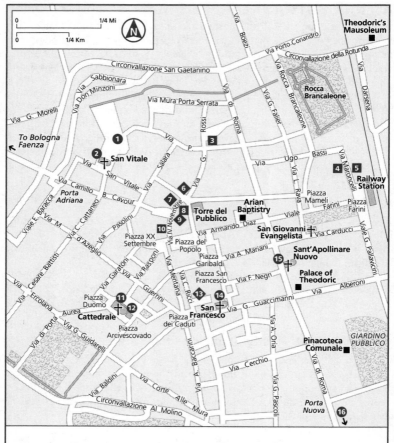

€€–€€€   Though the stylish **Diana** ★ (Via G. Rossi, 47; ☎ 0544-39164; www.hoteldiana.ra.it) occupies an old *palazzo* just north of the city center, it has the feel of a pleasant country hotel. The surrounding streets are residential and quiet, and the bright lobby and bar open onto a lovely garden. The rooms, no two of which are the same, are handsomely decorated with an innovative flair—with pretty striped wallpaper and mahogany headboards and armories. Those on the top floor are the most charming, with sloped ceilings and large skylights. Rates depend on the room category: €83 "standard" (slightly smaller with blander, but new, furnishings), €100 "superior" (larger, with nicer stuff and minibars), €115 "deluxe" (superior plus ADSL Internet), and €125 "executive" (deluxe with a canopy bed).

€€€   Now about that one exciting option: The boutique inn **Cappello** ★★ (Via IV Novembre, 41; ☎ 0544-219813; www.albergocappello.it) has been a hotel since 1885—though the current, seven-room version only opened in 1998—occupying a beautifully restored, 14th-century *palazzo* in the city center. The four suite-category rooms (€160–€180) have been carved out of the grand salons and are enormous, while smaller doubles (€110) occupy less grand, but no less stylish, quarters of the old *palazzo*. Fifteenth-century frescoes grace the corridor, lounge, sitting room, and two junior suites (no. 106, "Towards Blue," and no. 103, "Amaranthine Dream"), while throughout the rest of the hotel, terra-cotta floors, painted beamed ceilings, and other architectural features have been restored when possible. The furnishings are either reproduction or contemporary design. Because the Cappello is operated as an annex of the Diana (see above), services are minimal—the front desk is staffed only during the day—but there are two restaurants on the premises (for the cheaper, cozier *osteria,* see Cantina Cappello, below). The hotel is up two short flights of stairs from a hallway often used to exhibit work by a local artist. Reserve well in advance.

Whatever you do, stay away from the nearby Al Giaciglio, recommended in some guides—unless, of course, you don't mind sharing your room with bedbugs.

Dining for All Tastes

For picnic pickings, take a stroll through Ravenna's lively **food market,** the Mercato Coperto, near the center on Piazza Andrea Costa, open Monday to Saturday 7am to 2pm.

€   The most atmospheric *osteria* in Ravenna, **Ca de Ven** ★★ (Via C. Ricci, 24; ☎ 0544-30163; Tues–Sat), is tucked away under massive brick vaults on the ground floor of a 16th-century building next to Dante's tomb. In fact, Dante is said to have lived here when the premises served as a lodging house. The ornate shelves that line most of the walls come from a later reincarnation and were installed to outfit a 19th-century spice shop; they now display hundreds of Emilia-Romagna wines, many of which are available by the glass (from €1.50). *Piadine,* the delicious local flatbread, is a specialty here, topped with cheeses, meat, or vegetables—or served plain as a perfect accompaniment to cheese and assorted salamis (€3.50–€6). The *osteria* offers three to four pasta and meat courses daily. If there are two of you, you can share a *bis di primi* (pick any two pastas) for €8 each, or a *tris di primi* (sample three) for €9.

€€   The high-shuttered windows, timbered ceiling, and ocher-colored walls render **Cantina Cappello** ★ (Via IV Novembre, 41; ☎ 0544-219876; Tues–Sun lunch and dinner, Sun lunch only) as chic and inviting as the hotel above. Add friendly service, excellent grub, garden courtyard seating at lunch, and a handy location, just off Piazza del Popolo, and this becomes my first choice for a meal in Ravenna. You can order just about any wine from Emilia-Romagna by the glass (from €1.50) or carafe (from €6). Accompany it with a *tavolozza* (mixed platter of cheeses, *crostini,* salami, and salad) or choose from the daily pasta (€10) or seafood (€17–€18) specials.

€€€   The plain but elegant **La Gardela** (Via Ponte Marino, 3; ☎ 0544-217147; closed Thurs) is a good place to satisfy your appetite after wandering through the food stalls of the Mercato Coperto across the street—if you don't mind glacially slow (albeit friendly) service. Daily specials often include seafood from the nearby Adriatic, and there's a killer "piccolo menu" that includes a pasta (tortelli stuffed with pumpkin and spinach in a butter and sage sauce), meat (grilled shish kabob with rosemary potatoes), mineral water, glass of wine, and coffee, all for €15.

Why You're Here: The Top Sights & Attractions

Ravenna's most dazzling display of mosaics adorns the dome of the 6th-century octagonal and exotically Byzantine **Basilica di San Vitale** ★★ (Via San Vitale, 17; for all details, see "Ravenna's Cumulative Ticket & Open Hours," below) commissioned by Emperor Justinian. The emperor and his court appear in splendidly detailed mosaics of deep greens and golds on one side of the church. Theodora, his empress (a courtesan born into the circus whose ambition, intelligence, and beauty brought her to these lofty heights), and her ladies-in-waiting appear on the other; and above and between them looms Christ, clean-shaven in this early representation.

Perhaps the most striking of Ravenna's monuments lies on a lawn behind the Basilica: the small and simple **Mausoleum of Galla Placidia** ★★, lit only by small alabaster windows. This early Christian was the sister of Honorius, last emperor of Rome and wife of Ataulf, king of the Visigoths. Upon his death, she became regent to her 6-year-old son, Valentinian III—meaning she was, in effect, ruler of the Western world. The three sarcophagi beneath a canopy of blue-and-gold mosaics—a firmament of deep blue lit by hundreds of bright gold stars—are meant to contain Galla Placidia's remains and those of her son and husband, but it is more likely that she lies unadorned in Rome, where she died in A.D. 450.

The enchanting 4th-century octagonal **Battistero Neoniano** (Via Battistero; for all details, see "Ravenna's Cumulative Ticket & Open Hours," below) was built

A Summertime Music Festival

The **Ravenna Festival International** (☎ 0544-249244; www.ravennafestival. org)—6 or 7 weeks between June and August—has become world renowned, drawing a top list of classical musicians and opera stars in concert in *palazzi* and on *piazze.*

Ravenna's Cumulative Ticket & Open Hours

They keep changing the way this works, but currently a single €7.50 cumulative ticket, valid for 7 days, covers admission to the Basilica di San Vitale, the Mausoleum of Galla Placidia, the Battistero Neoniano, the Cappella di San Andrea/ Museo Arcivescovile, and the Basilica di Sant'Apollinare Nuovo.

All sights are open daily as follows: November to February 10am to 4:30pm; March and October 9:30am to 5:30pm; and April to September 9:30am to 7pm (exception: Mar–Oct, San Vitale and Galla Placidia open at 9am). For more information, call ☎ 0544-541688, or visit www.ravennamosaici.it.

as the baptistery of a cathedral that no longer stands; it's now behind Ravenna's banal present-day Duomo, built in the 19th century. Fittingly for the structure's purpose, the blue-and-gold mosaics on the dome depict the baptism of Christ by St. John the Baptist, surrounded by the Twelve Apostles.

Nearby is the tiny **Museo Arcivescovile & Cappella di San Andrea** (Piazza Arcivescovado; for all details, see "Ravenna's Cumulative Ticket & Open Hours," above), housed in the 6th-century Archbishop's Palace. The highlight of the one-room collection is the stupefyingly intricate ivory throne of Emperor Maximilian. Adjoining the museum is a small chapel built in the shape of a cross and dedicated to St. Andrea, every inch of which is emblazoned with dazzling mosaics. Sadly, this is currently closed for renovations and may remain so for years.

The famous mosaics in the 6th-century **Basilica di Sant'Apollinare Nuovo** ★ (Via di Roma; for all details, see "Ravenna's Cumulative Ticket & Open Hours," above), punctuated by Greek columns taken from a temple, are clearly delineated by gender. On one side of the church, the side traditionally reserved for women, a procession of 22 crown-carrying virgins makes its way toward the Madonna; on the other, 26 male martyrs march toward Christ. The mosaics near the door provide a fascinating look at the 6th-century city and its environs—one on the right shows the monuments of the city, including Emperor Theodoric's royal palace, and one on the left shows the port city of Classe.

Silt covered that ancient port long ago, but Ravenna's final grand 6th-century sight remains there, a 15-minute bus ride south of town, looming above farm fields and pine woods: the early-Christian basilica and campanile of **Sant'Apollinare in Classe** ★★ (Via Romeo Sud, 224, Classe; ☎ 0544-473569; €2; Tues–Sat 8:30am–7:30pm, Sun 1–7:30pm; bus: 4 or 44 from Piazza Farini in front of the train station, every 20 min.). The plain exterior belies a splendor within, a long sparse nave punctuated by Greek columns, capped by an apse dome slathered with lustrous gold mosaics. Imagine how transporting the effect was when the floor, too, was tiled in gold mosaic. The dominating figure depicted here, flanked by 12 lambs representing the apostles, is St. Apollinare, bishop of Ravenna.

PARMA

Its prosciutto di Parma hams and Parmigiano-Reggiano cheeses are justly famous, as they have been since Roman times, but the pleasures of this exquisite little city

Et Tu, Dante?

Exiled from his native Florence on trumped-up political charges, the poet Dante Alighieri ended up making Ravenna his home. It is here that he finished his epic *Divine Comedy*, of which the famed *Inferno* is but the first third. It is here that he died in 1321. And—despite efforts by the Florentines to reclaim their famous son—it is here that he resides for eternity, in an elaborate **tomb** behind the Basilica di San Francesco. The tomb's inscription reads: HERE IN THIS CORNER LIES DANTE, EXILED FROM HIS NATIVE LAND, BORN TO FLORENCE, AN UNLOVING MOTHER. The adjoining **Museo Dantesco** (Via Dante Alighieri, 4; ☎ 0544-30252; www.centrodantesco.it; €2; daily 9am–noon, Apr–Sept also 3–6pm) contains a small collection of Dante memorabilia.

extend far beyond the gastronomic. The Farnese, who made their duchy one of the art centers of the Renaissance, were succeeded by Marie-Louise, a Hapsburg and the wife of Emperor Napoleon. Her interest in everything cultural ensured that Parma never languished as a once-glorious backwater, as was the case with nearby Ferrara and Ravenna. As a result, today's residents of Parma live in one of Italy's most prosperous cities and are surrounded by palaces, churches, and artwork.

Parma is also a city of music, a favorite of Verdi's and the hometown of the great 20th-century conductor Arturo Toscanini. If you're here for the late October through mid-April season, be sure to catch a concert at the glorious **Teatro Regio** (Via Garibaldi, 16A; ☎ 0521-039399; www.teatroregioparma.org; from €20 for decent seats, €5 for nosebleeds).

Lay of the Land

Parma is 95km (59 miles) northwest of Bologna and 122km (76 miles) southeast of Milan. Because it lies on the busy north-south rail lines, connections are excellent. There are two to four **trains** per hour to and from Bologna (50–77 min.), many of which continue all the way to Milan (1½–1¾ hr.). About six high-speed trains a day connect with Florence (1¾–2¼ hr.).

The train station is about a 20-minute walk from the city center; from the front of the station, follow Viale Bottego east for 1 block to Via Garibaldi, which leads past the grassy lawns of Piazza della Pace, backed by the massive and museum-filled Palazzo della Pilotta, and then continue on to the central Piazza Garibaldi.

The **tourist office** (Via Melloni, 1A; ☎ 0521-218889; turismo.comune.parma.it) is closed Sunday afternoons.

Accommodations in the Heart of Town

€€–€€€   The charming **Hotel Torino** ★★ (Via A. Mazza, 7, just off Strada Garibaldi; ☎ 0521-281046; www.hotel-torino.it) is my top choice for moderately priced accommodations in Parma, with doubles going for €90 to €125. The location—in the pedestrian zone between the Teatro Reggio and the Duomo—is only half the allure. The elegant proprietor has fitted out her modern hotel with a careful eye to style and comfort. There are fresh-cut flowers and a collection of antique porcelains in the pretty lobby, with Liberty-style accents like a chandelier and lots of curves, and antiques gracing the breakfast room and bar. Breakfast, by the way, is something of an occasion, served on china and including fresh pastries, excellent coffee, and a selection of teas and juices; in summer, you can take it in the pretty little terra-cotta courtyard. The tile-floored rooms are comfortably modern with modular furnishings but natty grace notes, including in some dramatic headboards emblazoned with reproductions of Correggio frescoes. The bathrooms are clean, if cramped, and fitted with box showers.

€€   Tucked into the quiet warren of little streets and squares just off the southeast corner of Piazza Garibaldi, the pleasant **Button** ★ (Borgo Salina, 7; ☎ 0521-208039) is usually filled with European tourists. The rooms cost €97 (€6 extra for breakfast) and are large and serviceable, though a little somber, with dark floral wallpaper and spartan modern furnishings. The bathrooms are nicely tiled and have stall showers. Single travelers enjoy quarters much larger than the ones to which they are usually relegated, with "French beds" that are quite a bit wider than standard single beds. A few of the doubles have small balconies overlooking a *piazzetta* behind the hotel. The Cortesi, who run the place, are most accommodating, and you're always welcome to join them in the lobby lounge to watch a soccer match.

Accommodations near the Station

€€   The **Brenta** (Via G. B. Borghesi, 12; ☎ 0521-208093; www.hotelbrenta.it) is a perfectly decent fallback if the more atmospheric places in town are full. The lobby is a little drab, but don't let that put you off. The English-speaking management is very helpful and eager to point visitors to sights and nearby restaurants. Surroundings brighten considerably as you go upstairs. Guest rooms—€75 to €85 per double, plus €5 for breakfast—are large and quite up-to-date, with functional modern furniture and new bathrooms with stall showers. Most face side streets and are extremely quiet.

€€€€   No-nonsense and businesslike are the terms that come to mind to describe the **Astoria Executive** (Via Trento, 9; ☎ 0521-272717; www.piuhotels. com), down the street to the left as you exit the station. The facade is sheeted in blue-tinted glass, and everything inside sports a contemporary decor (doubles go for €180). This doesn't mean the Astoria isn't welcoming—if you don't mind the complete absence of old-world charm. It's an excellent choice for wood-veneer cabinetry, firm low-slung beds, and efficient bathrooms. Double sets of double-glazed windows ensure a good night's sleep, even on the side facing the railroad tracks. (Honest: There's barely a whisper when a train passes.)

€€€   Around the corner and 2 blocks away, the hotel maintains a residence, **Liberty** (Piazza Salvo d'Acquisto, 15; ☎ 0521-227100), intended mainly for long-term stays—but the studios (€115 for two), lofts (€135 for two), and two-room apartments (€170 for two), each with TV, telephone, and kitchenette, can also be rented by the night. It's called "Liberty" after the building's Art Nouveau architectural styling—which sadly doesn't extend into the blandly modernized, functional rooms.

A Riverside Hotel Splurge

€€€€   Service is notably gracious at the thoroughly modern **Park Hotel Toscanini** ✸ (Viale Toscanini, 4; ☎ 0521-289141; www.hoteltoscanini.com) near the center along Parma's lovely riverfront. The rooms are large (even singles, which enjoy those extra-wide "French" beds). Reproductions of works by Renaissance and modern masters enliven the otherwise nondescript, soothingly pastel-shaded contemporary decor. Ask for a room in front to enjoy the river views (double-glazed windows keep noise from the busy riverfront avenue to a minimum). Because the hotel caters mostly to businesspeople, the management is usually willing to lower the rack rate of €195 considerably during August and other slow periods. And hey: free bikes.

Dining for All Tastes

If there's one thing that has brought the name of Parma to the attention of the wider world, it's the food. This is, after all, where they cure that **prosciutto di Parma** ham that costs twice as much as the domestic kind in your local deli, not to mention that aged "cheese of parma" (in Italian: *parmigiano*) that people from Boise to Bangkok grate over their pasta.

Speaking of pasta, the favored *primi* in Parma are tagliatelle noodles and tortellini (look for the kind stuffed with *zucca,* or pumpkin), which come to the table with some wonderfully creative sauces—from simple butter and sage to *arrabiata,* a "hopping mad" mix of tomatoes, onions, bits of meat, and spicy pepperoncino. Main courses lean heavily toward meat, including the *filletto di cavallo* (filet of horse meat), which is a staple on most menus. Parma's hallmark wine is **Lambrusco,** a rich, sparking red that goes great with pizza.

For picnics, there's a **food market** on Piazza Ghiaia, near the Palazzo della Pilotta, open Monday to Saturday 8am to 1pm and 3 to 7pm.

€   Parma is blessed with many excellent wine bars, but the best just may be **Enoteca Fontana** ✸ (Via Farina, 24/a; ☎ 0521-286037; Tues–Sat). Belly up to

Hamming It Up in Parma

For a true taste of Parma, in addition to visiting the outdoor food market at Piazza Ghiaia, you should also sniff out **Salumeria Specialità di Parma** (Via Farini, 9C; ☎ 0521-233591; www.specialitadiparma.it) for a huge selection of prosciutto and other meats. Aficionados can tour the factories of the **Consorzio del Parmigiano Reggiano** (Via Gramsci, 26C; ☎ 0521-292700; www.parmigiano-reggiano.it)— check out the Quicktime movies detailing how parmigiano is made, with free 2-hour tours Monday through Friday at 8am (book ahead at least 3 weeks); and **Consorzio del Prosciutto di Parma** (Via M. dell'Arpa, 8b; (☎ 0521-243987; www. ProsciuttodiParma.it), with visits arranged when you call ahead.

Parma Violets

Pasticceria Torino, with branches at Via Garibaldi, 61 (☎ 0521-235689), and Via Farini, 60 (☎ 0521-282796), is an elegant, century-old shop-cum-coffeehouse, where you can enjoy Parma violets—a prissy delicacy of violets coated in sugar that you've probably encountered affixed to wedding cakes. Here, they come plain or topping an assortment of cakes and tarts (and they make a great gift for pastry-chef friends back home).

the ancient bar, take a seat at one of the long communal tables, or snag one of the crowded little tables out on the flagstones of the street and settle in for an evening of sampling any of hundreds of wines from Emilia-Romagna and beyond. There are a couple of dozen available by the glass (€1.20–€3), though even a whole bottle won't break the bank, as they start at €6.50, and there are a whopping 58 choices that cost €10 or less. For a truly special experience, though, flip to the back of the wine list and the hand-scrawled page devoted to *"ottimo rapporto prezzo-qualità"* (excellent value): 15 bottles of amazing quality that ring in under €16. To accompany your tasting, pick from among a dizzying 55 varieties of panini (€2.10–€5) or a platter of local salamis and prosciutto (€6.50) or of cheeses (€6). At lunch you can also get a simple plate of pasta like *farfalle piccanti* (€5), or a heaping salad (€6.50).

€   **Pizzeria La Duchessa** (Piazza Garibaldi, 1b; ☎ 0521-235962; Tues–Sat) is the most popular pizzeria in Parma—open late and almost always crowded. You'll probably have to wait for a table, especially if you want one outdoors, but there's a lot of activity to watch in the piazza while you're waiting. Although you can eat a full meal here, you're best off with the exquisite pizzas (€4.20–€11) and meals-in-themselves plates of pasta (€5–€8), washed down with a carafe of the house Sangiovese or a bottle of Lambrusco, Italy's best pizza wine.

€€   Diners are wedged in among an odd assortment of antique toys, movie posters, and casks of the wonderful house Lambrusco in the maze of rooms inside **Gallo d'Oro** ★ (Borgo Salina, 3A; ☎ 0521-208846; www.gallodororistorante.it; daily, Sun only lunch), a lively trattoria 1 block south of Piazza Garibaldi. The huge antipasto platters of prosciutto di Parma and assorted salamis (€8) make a satisfying late-night supper. The sublime *tris di tortelli* (€8) is a sampler platter of homemade tortellini stuffed variously with cheese, herbs, or pumpkin. The lamb with artichokes (€8) is nice, or take your cue from the Parmigiani in the room and dig into a delectable *stracotto di asinina* (tender, braised donkey served with sticky polenta; €7.50)—though I'd steer clear of the *pesto di cavallo* (basically, horse hamburger patties served raw and cold; €6.50).

€€–€€€   The lunchtime crowd at boisterous **Trattoria Lazzaro** (Via XX Marzo, 14; ☎ 0521-208944; closed Thurs) is mostly neighborhood businessmen,

---

Splurge on a Memorable Feast

€€€-€€€€ One of Parma's true temples of gastronomy, **La Greppia** ★★ (Strada Garibaldi, 39A, at Via Bodoni; ☎ 0521-233686; reservations required; closed Mon–Tues and July) manages to be unpretentious while at the same time making you feel as though you're experiencing the meal of a lifetime. This is because the wife-and-husband team, Paola Cavassini and Maurizio Rossi, preside over the plain dining room with grace and ease. While you can enjoy many traditional Parmigiana favorites—their *stracotto* (braised beef) is the city's best—the menu also offers dozens of exciting dishes that rely on Parma's famous hams and cheeses as well as fresh vegetables. Parmigiano-dusted tortelli stuffed with fresh herbs is a perfect starter. My favorite main course is veal kidneys with truffle shavings, though a very close second is the veal scaloppini with lemon and a light sauce of white wine and herbs. Or you can splurge on a steak (beef this time) *filetto* for €24—the only thing on the menu that costs more than €16 (most *primi* go for €12). The dessert chef prepares many kinds of fruit tarts, including one made with green tomatoes (€6), and the chocolate cake with zabaglione cream (€6) will convince you that you have indeed enjoyed the meal of a lifetime.

---

replaced at dinner by neighborhood families out for a night of fun and good food. The largely carnivorous menu begins with a tray of prosciutto and other cured meats (€7.50), followed by grilled veal (€10) or succulent lamb chops (€11)—though the locals really come for a traditional *filleto di cavallo* (horse-meat steak; €12) like grandma used to make. The homemade pastas are wonderful and served in copious portions; try the *strozzapreti* (pasta so rich it'd "strangle a priest") with zucchini and saffron (€7.50).

Why You're Here: The Top Sights & Attractions

When the abbess of the convent containing the **Camera di San Paolo** ★ (Via Melloni, 3, just off Piazza Pilotta, down a little gated, shade-lined street; ☎ 0521-233309; www.gallerianazionaleparma.it; €2; Tues–Sun 8:30am–1:45pm) sought to commission an artist to fresco her dining room, she went to Correggio, a High Renaissance master who lived and worked in Parma in the early 16th century. He rose to the occasion by turning the room's late-Gothic umbrella vaulting into a magnificent deep green pergola framing colorful, muscular *putti* (cherubs). His portrait of the abbess as Diana, goddess of the hunt and—more to the point in a convent—of chastity is painted above the fireplace. These intimate rooms are an excellent place to begin a tour of Parma—you'll encounter Correggio again in the city's churches and its museum, but nowhere else are you able to observe his work so closely. The ceiling of the adjacent room (which you actually pass through first) was frescoed in 1514 by Alessandro Araldi.

Parma's **Duomo** ★ (Piazza del Duomo; ☎ 0521-235886; daily 9am–12:30pm and 3–7pm), made of soft pink marble (very dirty, though in 2005 they were in the process of cleaning it), and embellished with three rows of *loggie* and flanked by a graceful campanile, was built in the 12th century; it's one of the great achievements of Italian Romanesque architecture. Once inside, all eyes are lifted to celestial realms, as every inch of the nave walls and ceilings is slathered in mid-16th-century frescoes. They culminate in Correggio's great masterpiece, his dramatic *Assumption of the Virgin,* swirling up inside the octagonal cupola. The Virgin and her entourage of *putti* seem to be floating right through the roof into a golden heaven. Correggio captured them in what seems to be three-dimensional depth—long before this technique became prominent during the baroque period. Even before Correggio added his crowning embellishment, between 1522 and 1534, the Duomo shone with another masterpiece—a bas-relief of *The Deposition* by the 12th-century sculptor Antelami. Look for it in the right transept.

In front of the Duomo stands the pink-and-white marble octagon of the 1196 **Battistero (Baptistery)** ★★ (Piazza del Duomo; ☎ 0521-235886; €4; daily 9am–12:30pm and 3–6:45pm), a tribute to the work of Benedetto Antelami, one of the most important sculptors of the Italian Romanesque. His friezes of allegorical animals encircle the base of the structure, which rises in five graceful tiers. Inside is his famous 14-statue cycle depicting the 12 months as well as winter and spring, now stuck way up in the lower colonnade above the tall niches that once held them. Those niches and the ceiling are covered in 13th-century frescoes (by an unknown artist) that portray the lives of the apostles, Jesus, and other biblical figures in a stunning display of visual storytelling and color.

Behind the baroque facade of **San Giovanni Evangelista** (Piazzale San Giovanni, just behind the Duomo; ☎ 0521-235511; daily 6:30am–noon and 3:30–8pm) are works by the two masters of Parma, Correggio and Il Parmigianino. Il Parmigianino frescoed the first two chapels on the left aisle, as well as the fourth one. Drop €1 in the box at the end of the left aisle to light up, in sequence, Correggio's fresco of *Saint John the Evangelist* writing down his vision (accompanied by his iconic eagle, preening its feathers) in the lunette above the sacristy door in the left transept, followed by the artist's *Transfiguration of St. John* in the dome, infused with golden light and widely considered to be one of the great achievements of the High Renaissance. (After that light snaps off, the apse fresco of the *Incarnation of the Virgin* lights up, if for no other reason than to show us how much better an artist Correggio was than the hack who slapped that one on the walls.) Correggio also did the narrow frieze surrounding the nave of prophets, sibyls, *putti,* and pagan altars. Off the cloisters in the adjoining monastery (entrance just left of the church doors) is a *biblioteca* (library) frescoed with grotesques, maps, and battle scenes.

A Hidden Fresco

For an added treat, exit the Camera di San Paolo gate and take two rights to get onto Borgo Giordani, which runs along the back side of the convent's garden. Enter those gardens to peek through the window of the hutlike Cella di Santa Caterina, named for its marvelous Araldi fresco of *The Mystical Marriage of St. Catherine.*

Around the corner is the entrance to the **Spezeria** (Borgo Pipa, 1; ☎ 0521-233309; €2; Tues–Sun 8:30am–2pm), the pharmacy from which the good monks have supplied Parma with potions and poultices (today, honeys, *ptisans*—an herbal tea infusion—and beauty products at the cloister entrance) for nearly 700 years. An array of medieval-looking mortars and jars continues to line the shelves.

The grim-looking massive fortress, which the Farnese put up near the banks of the river Parma in 1603, would be an empty shell if it weren't for Marie-Louise, the Hapsburg wife of Emperor Napoleon and niece of Marie Antoinette, who ruled the duchy in the early 19th century. Marie-Louise shared her aunt's passion for art and, under her guidance, paintings from throughout her domain were brought here to fill the rooms the Farnese had left empty when Isabella Farnese assumed the throne of Spain in the 18th century and the clan left Parma for good. Though Allied bombings came close to flattening the palace in May 1944, much of it has been rebuilt and continues to house Parma's **Galleria Nazionale** ★★ (Palazzo della Pilotta, Piazzale Marconi; ☎ 0521-233309 or 0521-133617; www.gallerianazionaleparma.it; €6, or €2 for just the theater; daily 9am–2pm).

You enter the museum through the Teatro Farnese, a wooden jewel box of a theater that Giambattista Aleotti, a student of Palladio, built for the Farnese in 1618, modeling it after the master's Palladian theater in Vicenza. This was the first theater in Europe to accommodate moving scenery. Its elegant proportions provide a warm, intimate atmosphere, and the stage floor slopes, er, dramatically up and away from the audience. That's to help achieve the illusion of great depth, helping the set builders force a sense of long perspectives and the actors seem to bestride the distances like giants. If it looks in too good a shape to be that old, it is. American bombs destroyed it in 1944, and the current version is a faithful, painstaking reconstruction carried out from 1956 to 1965.

Though one of the prizes of the museum's outstanding collections is a Leonardo da Vinci sketch, *La Scapigliata,* the real stars are the works by Parma's great masters, including Correggio's *Madonna of St. Jerome* and *Rest on the Flight from Egypt,* and Il Parmigianino's pink-cheeked *Schiava Turca,* along with good stuff from lesser-known local talents Il Temperelli, Filippo Mazzola, Josaphat and

---

A Night at the Theater

Parma's opera house, the **Teatro di Regio,** is not too far down the scale of high regard from Milan's La Scala. After all, Verdi was born nearby and Arturo Toscanini, who often conducted at the theater, is a native son. Tickets can be hard to come by because they're swallowed up for the entire October-to-March season well in advance by opera buffs from across the region. However, the tourist office sometimes sells standing-room-only tickets. You should also check the **box office** (☎ 0521-039399; www.teatroregioparma.org) at Via Garibaldi, 16A, near Piazza della Pace, for last-minute cancellations.

Alessandro Araldi, Del Grano, and Michelangelo Anselmi, who moved to Parma from Siena and worked alongside Correggio and fellow Mannerist Parmigianino.

Every room has little signs, translated into English, that do a great job explaining and contextualizing the works and artists, so I can just list some of the other great names you'll run into: Fra Angelico, Spinello Aretino, Sebastiano del Piombo, Tintoretto, Il Guercino, El Greco, Tiepolo, Canaletto, and several members of the Carracci clan (Agostino even contrived to die here in Parma). Marie-Louise's tastes were worldly, and she collected works from north of the Alps as well, including one of Hans Holbein the Younger's most famous portraits, *Erasmus,* along with a small collection of canvases by Jan and Pieter Brueghel the Younger, Paul Brill, and van Dyck. There's also a long hallway at the end that helps contextualize Parma itself, with 19th-century street scenes and lots of reproductions of old maps and portraits of the Farnese dukes.

7 Venice

Though threatened by the ravages of time and tourism, Venezia continues to enthrall its visitors.

by Keith Bain

VENICE WAS ONCE THE RULER OF A GIANT MARITIME AREA, A VIRTUAL empire whose army and navy dominated what is today Turkey, the Greek Isles, and Crete (as well as the inland areas of Italy that immediately surround the city). And as befits that position, it created *palazzi* and churches as grand and impressive as any in the world. The military, commercial, and political power of Venice have long since vanished, but its artistic impact is undiminished. Its monuments, its facades, its paintings and sculpture, its graceful docks and mooring poles, its fanciful gondolas—all reach across the ages and never fail to enchant.

The city is a testament to human creativity. As you wander the streets that no motor vehicle has ever seen, you encounter genius at every turn. Titian, Tiepolo, Tintoretto, and Bellini are among the painters whose frescoes and canvases fill churches and museum galleries. Vivaldi's *Four Seasons* stirs hearts at church recitals and in hotel lobbies. The designs of Palladio and Longhena grace the waterfronts. Even the contemporary, mostly foreign art collection assembled by Peggy Guggenheim seems perfectly at home here.

Sadly, the city faces many dangers. Its squares flood nearly every year, and its buildings are deteriorating under the weight of time. The city's very uniqueness makes it an expensive, difficult place to live. Everything takes longer to get done, and even the simplest items—like bread—seem overpriced. The city's population has dropped as low as 70,000, and the average resident is on the brink of retirement.

Venice is sinking into the sea, but Italy, and the world, will never permit Venice to disappear. People have always written about it, painted it, photographed it. For as long as Venice remains afloat, people will continue to be seduced by La Serenissima.

DON'T LEAVE VENICE WITHOUT . . .

GETTING LOST   Venture deeper into the maze of streets and canals. So sublime is Venice's lineup of architectural eye-candy that the city simply forces one to venture forth. And believe me, if you stick to the areas thick with tourists, you'll never discover the real Venice.

SAILING THE WATERS OF THE GRAND CANAL   If snuggling up with your beloved in the hull of a lacquer-black gondola is in your list of fantasies, don't pass up the costly opportunity, and be sure to budget accordingly. Even if you're taking a more modest approach to holiday expenditures, you'll have no excuse for passing up at least one complete circuit of the Canal Grande by water bus. Hop aboard *vaporetto* no. 1 for a complete lap of Venice's main highway, adorned with views of the city's most jewel-like *palazzi.*

VISITING ST. MARK'S BASILICA   In the city's pigeon-covered main piazza, it's free and fun simply to spend a part of 1 day watching other tourists at play in the square. On it, the basilica is one of the greatest examples of architectural overkill, but is no less worthy because of that.

SNACKING ON *CICCHETTI* (APPETIZERS) AT A *BACARO*   Tapas-style snacking is all the rage in Venice; order your late-morning spritz along with reasonably priced *tramazzini* or panini, or order a plate of pickled sardines.

DANCING TO THE MUSIC OF A LIVE QUINTET IN PIAZZA SAN MARCO (ST. MARK'S SQUARE)   When the open-air, cafe-sponsored bands strike up, the moment becomes magical and the square seems lifted from a film of the '20s. Avoid sitting at Florian's famous but ultraexpensive cafe, but be carried away by the free music it offers.

EXPERIENCING ART, ART & MORE ART!   The Accademia Gallery has the greatest collection of classic Venetian art on earth, while the nearby Peggy Guggenheim Collection displays some of the best of Western Modernism. All around the city are churches and *scuole* stuffed with compelling masterpieces, while every 2 years the International Biennale fills the city with cutting-edge modern art from around the globe.

A BRIEF HISTORY OF VENICE

Over the centuries, Venice thumbed its nose at those who tried to undermine its independence, and survived against the odds. Once a group of muddy islands set in a lagoon on the Adriatic Sea, Venice was settled by farmers retreating from the onslaught of the Huns and other violent conquerors. The city later became a part of the Byzantine empire, but over time asserted its independence and became a self-sustaining republic and a major world power. The city's central monument—the Basilica of St. Mark—is devoted to another act of defiance; in 828, a group of merchants stole the body of St. Mark from Alexandria, so that the evangelist could be installed as Venice's patron saint. You'll spot St. Mark's symbol—the winged lion—everywhere, a constant reminder of the city's sovereign past. In later years, the bodies of St. Nicholas and St. Isidore were also snatched and re-interred here, as spiritual protectors of Venice.

The Venetian city-state next established dominance over the Adriatic and its eastern shores. Not only was its naval and merchant might secured with the construction of the famous Arsenale (or naval dockyard) at the start of the 12th century, but it controlled the Brenner Pass and several mainland territories. Motivated primarily by commercial prospects, Venice continued to grow as an imperial power, contributing to the defeat of Constantinople during the Fourth Crusade and once again, Venice got its fair share of the spoils of war.

The aristocrats of Venice elected their first Doge (the Venetian word for "duke") back in 697, taking power away from the tribunes who had represented the various lagoon settlements, and putting it in the hands of a single authority. Over time, Venice developed a complicated governmental structure combining Byzantine and Islamic elements, under the authority of the Doge. The system included all manner of checks and balances, mostly in the form of councils and noble bodies, like the much-feared Council of Ten, which had the power to try and convict anyone in the state. While there was much bureaucratic wheeling and dealing, the system contributed to a thriving economy, boosting the city's position as a trade center, and creating a lucrative taxation system. With its port abuzz, and with Venice the principal connection between the East and West, the government worked industriously to sustain the economic might of the city-state; international trade and diplomacy were prioritized to the extent that Venice functioned much like a well-oiled corporation.

Venice was much esteemed by other major powers, drawing diplomats and travelers from around the world. It was here, in a spirit of economic expansion, that East truly met West. As fortunes grew, Venetian life developed a reputation for licentiousness—so much so that the author Thomas Coryate (1577–1617) compared Venice to Sodom and Gomorrah, and feared a downpouring of fire and brimstone. Venice became Europe's playground, attracting yearlong revelers smitten with its beauty and the voluptuous pleasures offered by its libertine citizenry.

With the focus on play rather than work, Venice eventually went into decline, its foreign influence undermined by the opening of new trade routes by competing powers, and the rise of newer monopolies of markets that Venice had begun to take for granted. By the 18th century, the empire was waning. Napoleon Bonaparte arrived in 1797, at the end of Venice's final fling; the Doge and his administration quickly conceded to his military power. Venice was given to the Austrians in 1798, only to become part of Napoleon's Kingdom of Italy between 1805 and 1814, when it again became an Austrian territory. Finally, in 1866, Venice became part of Italy. Its popularity as a destination for foreign visitors has never abated.

LAY OF THE LAND

What you are seeing is a collection of 118 islands, most of them separated from each other by narrow canals but linked by hundreds of small bridges. Cutting an "S" through that checkerboard is the relatively wide Canal Grande, which on maps seems to cut the city in two. Venice is located in a shallow lagoon, protected from the Adriatic by a narrow strip of land known as the Lido.

In modern times, Venice has grown a tail, a man-made causeway linking the historic city to the urban sprawl of mainland Mestre. The railway linking Venice to the mainland was built in the 19th century, the motor causeway in the 20th century. Europe's largest parking garage stands at the Venetian end of this causeway, and there's a major bus terminal—the Piazzale Roma—just steps away from the Grand Canal.

Venice Orientation

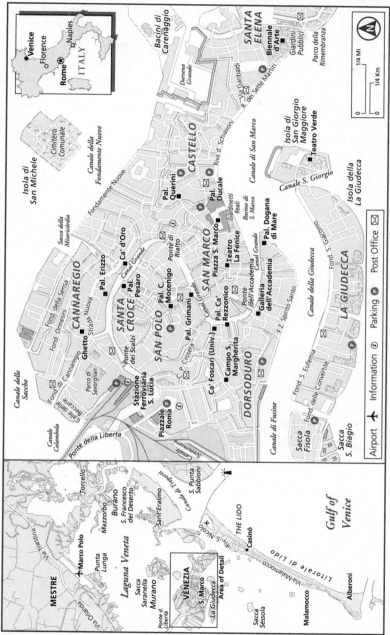

Generally, walking will be your principal mode of transportation, and certainly your only means of getting to many hotels, sights, and restaurants that lie a distance from the water buses or taxis. Walking can be hellishly (and delightfully) confusing, making a mockery of even the most exquisitely crafted map. You also won't have much fun carrying heavy luggage up and down the steps.

San Marco is always the busiest area, and many visitors never venture far beyond its souvenir-infested epicenter.

West of San Marco is the traditional working-class neighborhood of **Castello,** still inhabited by the old-time Venetians. Venture far enough west, possibly strolling along the broad lagoon-side promenade of Riva degli Schiavoni, and

---

Acqua Alta & Sirocco

The pessimists will claim that Venice is drowning. Much of the lagoon is a shallow, muddy area that is susceptible to oceanic tides, and in certain seasons, the water level rises to flood parts of Venice. When *acqua alta* (high water) hits—generally late September through April—it is usually the result of a combination of a very high tide, low atmospheric pressure, and the onset of the sultry sirocco, a wind that blows from the Adriatic, forcing water into the lagoon. (To get a sense of the sirocco, watch Visconti's film version of Thomas Mann's *Death in Venice,* shot principally in the Lido's famous Hotel Des Bains.)

Freak *acqua alta* floods leave their mark. On October 31, 2004, the water rose 135 centimeters (53 in.) to put 80% of the city under water. Areas in the low-lying historical center are more susceptible to flooding, and elevated boardwalks are set in place here for foot traffic (you'll find route maps at some of the *vaporetto* stops). Rubber boots are never in short supply. A siren will begin to sound several hours before the arrival of any particularly high tide, but there's no real need to panic. The high water has long been a part of Venetian culture and there are numerous tales of pleasure-loving locals refusing to leave parties even as the floor beneath them begins to flood. There has been increasing cause for concern, however; whereas tidal flooding occurred roughly 8 times a year a century ago, that figure rose to 108 in 2002.

The Italian government has already taken action. A system of 79 hinged flood barriers is currently being installed at the edge of the lagoon; these will function with compressed air, rising from the seabed during *acqua alta* to form a wall against the threat of floods. Despite warnings from some environmental agencies that the plans will turn the lagoon into a dank swamp, it seems that the city, at least for a while, will remain afloat.

you'll come upon Castello's hushed, tree-shaded public parks and gardens, undiscovered by the visiting masses. Castello is also where Venice's world-renowned maritime dockyard, the Arsenale, is situated. To the extreme east are the islands of Sant'Elena and San Pietro.

To the north of Castello is **Cannaregio,** another residential neighborhood that stretches eastward toward the train station. This is a wonderfully varied part of Venice, with busy markets and forgotten corners; it's also home to the world's first Jewish ghetto. From the Fondamente Nuove promenade along Cannaregio's northern shore, you can see the cemetery island of San Michele. **San Polo** is linked to San Marco by the famous Ponte di Rialto (Rialto Bridge), named for the islands (Riva Altus) upon which Venice was originally settled. San Polo is the densest part of Venice, home to some of its narrowest streets and alleys, and of course the ancient Rialto markets that still are abuzz today. Bordering **Santa Croce** and San Polo, and across the lovely Ponte dell'Accademia (Accademia Bridge) from San Marco, is **Dorsoduro,** an area defined by its lively student culture, and a predominance of art galleries. Dorsoduro's southern border is lined by another popular promenade, the Fondamenta Zattere, where you can enjoy views across the Giudecca Canal toward the island of Giudecca.

Giudecca was once a refuge for victims of the plague; today it's a refuge for locals wanting to escape the endless stream of tourists in Venice proper; it's also where people like Elton John and Madonna have their little piece of Venice. The island at the eastern tip of Giudecca is San Giorgio Maggiore.

Elsewhere in the lagoon are a number of smaller islands, most with tiny fishing populations. The most popular of these are **Murano,** famous for its glassware; **Burano,** famous for its lace; and **Torcello,** increasingly famous for its almost total loss of population (down to less than 100).

Sheltering Venice and the lagoon from the Adriatic, is a long, narrow strip of land known as the **Lido,** one of the world's most famous beach resorts, which began attracting well-to-do Europeans during the 19th century; today it's also home to one of the great international film festivals, and a good place to escape crowded Venice on a bicycle.

GETTING TO & FROM THE AIRPORT

The cheapest way to get from Marco Polo Airport to Venice is **by bus** (as little as €2 on the no. 5, which stops outside the arrivals door and takes you all the way to Venice's Piazzale Roma), but this will rob you of one of the biggest thrills for the first-time visitor—coming upon Venice by water. For €10, you can catch the half-hourly **water shuttle** from the airport (there is a free bus that will take you from the airport building to the departure point) to one of several important *vaporetto* (water-bus) stops around Venice. The transfer between the airport and the city is operated by **Alilaguna** (San Marco 4267/A; ☎ 041-5235775; www. alilaguna.it).

GETTING AROUND

If, like me, you have a penchant for getting lost, you're best off navigating by prominent landmarks, such as a bridge, a palace *(palazzo),* or one of the many public squares, known as *campi.* The latter are meeting points for locals because many are lined with cafes, bars, and restaurants, and are home to the obligatory church with an attached campanile (bell tower).

There are signs posted—in yellow—with arrows indicating the (general) direction of major sights, important areas, Grand Canal bridges, and *vaporetto* launches, but using these signs as a means of navigation is an art unto itself; you simply have to go with the direction of the arrow as far as humanly possible. Venetian addresses do not make any sense; each building is simply numbered according to an unfathomable system, supplying it with an arbitrary three- or four-digit code.

As convoluted and confusing as Venice's footpath network is, the city planners have provided names for the plethora of streets *(calli)*, be they canal-side boulevards *(fondamenta)*, major streets *(salizzada)*, larger streets *(lista)*, wide lagoon-side streets *(riva)*, streets formed by filling in canals *(rio terrà)*, or streets lined with shops *(ruga)*, canals *(rio)*, courtyards *(corte)*, or passageways *(sotoportego)*. To increase the muddle, at the intersection of certain bridges and streets are a number of seemingly conflicting signs painted on the buildings; I've stood for ages on a bridge trying to figure out which of the signs refers to the *calle* I'm looking for.

There are only three bridges traversing the Grand Canal. The Rialto Bridge is considered to be the geographical center of the city, and sees an almost endless stream of tourists passing over it, often on their way to or from the popular Rialto markets.

There are several tourist offices scattered around Venice, though none of these is overwhelmingly helpful; they are best at dishing out maps and advertising materials, and selling dated guidebooks. For a full list of contacts, see "The ABCs of Venice," at the end of this chapter, or visit www.turismovenezia.it.

PUBLIC TRANSPORTATION

As I've already mentioned, you'll be relying chiefly on your feet to get around; there are no cars, buses, rickshaws, bicycles, carts, or horses. The only public transport is waterborne.

Venice's public water buses are known as **vaporetti,** which run through the Grand Canal and also circle the entire city, stopping at strategic points. There is, as well, water transport to some of the islands of the lagoon. As with any metro transport service, *vaporetti* services follow a number of lines (color-coded on maps), and run in both directions; lines are numbered, but nevertheless require some analytical skill if you don't want to find yourself heading off to some island when you're simply trying to get back to your hotel. The lines running along the Grand Canal are 1 and 82, the latter being the faster as it does not stop at every landing stage; both lines continue on to the Lido (where there are buses and bicycles). Many of the other *vaporetto* lines circle the city (known as a Giracittà route), also connecting various islands around the lagoon.

The *vaporetti* are operated by the **ACTV** (☎ 041-5287886; www.actv.it). You can purchase a variety of tickets at the booths found at most *vaporetto* stops. A single-direction journey along the Grand Canal is a hefty €5; non–Grand Canal trips are €3.50. If you're planning to make fairly regular use of the water buses, it's a far better idea to buy a travel card. One type, which costs €11, allows unlimited public transport for a 24-hour period. A 72-hour ticket is €22. These cards also cover bus services on the Lido and to the airport.

More Than a Striped Shirt & Straw Hat

Venice has some 400 gondoliers, and advertisements for new ones are posted every 3 years. For those Venetians who don't inherit a gondolier license, there's a 6-year training period, followed by a rigorous examination. If you haven't inherited the badge, and you've gotten through the training and examination period, you'll need to buy a license from an existing gondolier, which will cost around €250,000; fortunately, getting a loan from a local bank is easy—financiers know that gondoliers easily make enough cash to pay back the loan. If you don't manage to get a license, you can always work as a substitute, filling in for a principal gondolier and earning a percentage of his income. Venetians will tell you that a gondolier earns around €2,000 per day.

Although some of the busier stops are patrolled by ticket inspectors, passengers are seldom checked once aboard. The fine for being caught traveling without a valid ticket is €23; I must admit to once traveling with an expired ticket, and my sense of impending doom seriously undercut my ability to enjoy the ride. You should get your ticket before boarding, and ensure that it is validated at one of the time-stamp machines at the stops. If you happen to get on board without a ticket (a few stops don't have ticket booths), ask the conductor for one immediately.

The **cheapest gondola ride** you'll get in Venice is aboard a *traghetto,* a ferry that transports passengers across the Grand Canal between two fixed points; you'll pay a mere €.40 for the short trip, but at least you'll be able to say you tried a gondola if the real thing is too expensive—and you'll cut down on a considerable amount of walking and getting lost trying to find one of the three bridges across the Canal (although there's another in the planning).

Should you, the visitor, ever hire a gondola? If romance is what you're after, throw budgetary caution to the wind and cough up for this enchanting experience. Technically, there are fixed prices in place, but most gondoliers will make at least some attempt to "take you for a ride" when negotiating the price; it's a good idea to know how much you're meant to be paying (the current rate is €62 per 50 min., with a €15 surcharge after 8pm and before 8am), but even this union barometer may not protect you from a rip-off. Bear in mind that you're paying for up to six passengers, so it may be worth sharing your fare with fellow hotel guests (although it's worth getting to know them before you hop on a gondola with just anyone).

ACCOMMODATIONS, BOTH STANDARD & NOT

Finding the right lodging in Venice can be daunting, despite the fact that in some popular areas there are dozens of hotels. The problem is that in a city this small, space comes at a premium. A budget that might afford you a degree of luxury elsewhere will get you a simple room in Venice; and we're talking about scraping your knees between the bed and the door!

Venice Accommodations & Dining

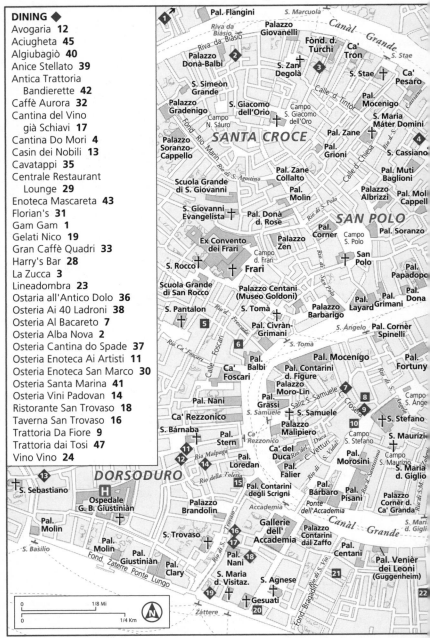

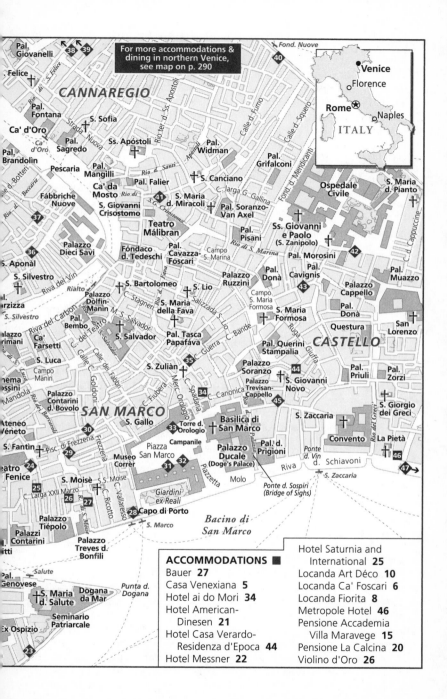

CANNAREGIO

Pal. Giovanelli

Felice

For more accommodations & dining in northern Venice, see map on p. 290

Fond. Nuove

Pal. Fontana

S. Sofia

Ca' d'Oro

Ss. Apóstoli

Pal. Sagredo

Pal. Widman

Pal. Brandolin

Pescaria

Pal. Mangilli

Pal. Grifalconi

Ospedale Civile

S. Maria d. Pianto

Fábbriche Nuove

Ca' da Mosto

Pal. Falier

S. Canciano

S. Giovanni Crisostomo

S. Maria d. Miracoli

Pal. Soranzo-Van Axel

Ss. Giovanni e Paolo (S. Zanipolo)

Teatro Málibran

Fóndaco d. Tedeschi

Pal. Cavazza-Foscari

Pal. Pisani

Campo S. Marina

Pal. Morosini

S. Aponàl

Palazzo Dieci Savi

Pal. Donà

Pal. Cavignis

Palazzo Cappello

Pal. Muazzo

S. Silvestro

Riva del Vin

S. Bartolomeo

S. Lio

Palazzo Ruzzini

Campo S. Maria Formosa

S. Maria Formosa

Pal. Donà

rzizza

S. Silvestro

Rialto

Palazzo Dolfin-Manin

S. Maria della Fava

Questura

San Lorenzo

alazzo rimani

Pal. Bembo

Ca' Farsetti

S. Salvador

Pal. Tasca Papafáva

Pal. Querini Stampalia

CASTELLO

S. Luca

Campo Manin

Palazzo Contarini d. Bovolo

S. Zuliàn

Palazzo Soranzo

S. Giovanni Novo

Pal. Priuli

Pal. Zorzi

nema ossini

Ateneo Véneto

SAN MARCO

S. Gallo

Torre d. Orologio

Palazzo Trevisan-Cappello

S. Zaccaria

S. Giorgio dei Greci

S. Fantin

Piazza San Marco

Basilica di San Marco

Convento

La Pietà

eatro Fenice

Museo Corrèr

Campanile

Palazzo Ducale (Doge's Palace)

Pal. d. Prigioni

Ponte d. Vin

Riva d. Schiavoni

S. Moisè

Piazzetta

Molo

S. Zaccaria

Palazzo Tiépolo

C. Larga XXII Marzo

Capo di Porto

S. Marco

Ponte d. Sospiri (Bridge of Sighs)

Palazzi Contarini itti

Palazzo Treves d. Bonfili

Bacino di San Marco

Pal. Genovese

Salute

S. Maria d. Salute

Dogana da Mar

Punta d. Dogana

Seminario Patriarcale

Ex Ospízio

ITALY

Venice

Florence

Rome

Naples

ACCOMMODATIONS ■

Bauer **27**
Casa Venexiana **5**
Hotel ai do Mori **34**
Hotel American-
 Dinesen **21**
Hotel Casa Verardo-
 Residenza d'Epoca **44**
Hotel Messner **22**

Hotel Saturnia and
 International **25**
Locanda Art Déco **10**
Locanda Ca' Foscari **6**
Locanda Fiorita **8**
Metropole Hotel **46**
Pensione Accademia
 Villa Maravege **15**
Pensione La Calcina **20**
Violino d'Oro **26**

Seasonal Fluctuations

Venetian hotels have one of the most convoluted seasonal pricing systems in the world, all because of the nearly endless popularity of the city. Generally speaking, high season runs for as long as business permits, stretching over the Christmas-to-New-Year's period, then from February 13 to 24 (or whenever Carnevale is scheduled), April 1 to July 21, and August 28 to October 31. Low season runs from January 4 to the end of March, excluding the busy Carnevale period, and again from November through Christmas. There's a quiet "middle season" when many Venetians pack up and go on holiday themselves, from July 22 through August 27.

You can generally expect room prices to follow these seasonal patterns, often doubling when there's an important festival. Venice's low seasons are generally coupled with soggy, chilly weather and the inconvenience of the *acqua alta* (see "*Acqua Alta* & Sirocco," above). Bear in mind that these are also the times when tourist numbers are down, meaning you'll be paying less to have more of the city to yourself.

Fortunately, a room in Venice doesn't need to be more than a place to lay your head after an exhausting day of rewarding experiences; there's just too much out there for you to worry about the state of your hotel. Venice does have some affordable rooms, however, as well as a number of hostels and a fairly extensive range of apartments for rent. It also has a selection of bed-and-breakfasts, where you'll not only save cash but have an opportunity to schmooze with locals, and take advantage of their insider tips and recommendations. I've included a number of these B&Bs below.

In general, all hotel rooms have air-conditioning, a television (usually tiny and sometimes only capable of receiving Italian broadcasts), and bathrooms that range in size from tiny to small. If you find yourself in a room that feels like the smallest space on earth, well . . . that's pretty much the norm in Venice. Breakfast is included in the rate, unless I've noted otherwise.

LIVING LIKE A VENETIAN: FINDING A SELF-CATERING APARTMENT

The best way to get a sense of Venetian life is to stay in an apartment where you can prepare your own meals and occasionally share an elevator or stairway with "locals" rather than with other foreign guests. Start out by contacting **Venetian Apartments** (☎ 041-5226441; www.venice-rentals.com). This well-established operation has around 85 very different apartments on its books. Operated by a London office, it provides a relatively hassle-free method of finding a place that's right for you. The price? You're looking at paying anything upwards of €900 per week for a fairly simple place, while a midrange flat with a view and perhaps a terrace will cost around €1,300. It sounds like a lot, but it breaks down to as little as €130 a night per apartment—not bad in a city this pricey. What has impressed me over the years has been the level of cleanliness and the obvious pride that has gone into the styling of the apartments. Even the simpler flats are well furnished, and usually reflect some stylistic preference of the owner; most have air-conditioning in summer and heating in winter. You could even land one with a view of St. Mark's.

The key to using a booking service like this is to supply them with detailed specifications about the type of place you're seeking. Some are modern, complete with brushed steel and designer trim, while others are more relaxed and filled with family heirlooms (or cast-offs). Ask a lot of questions before booking. Also bear in mind that, for example, not all Venetians have a kettle in the home (they're not tea drinkers), so if you must have any specific appliances or kitchen ware, be sure to request them in advance (this goes for microwaves, televisions, and anything else you might require). And remember, if you want to stay in a palace with all-original artwork and antique pieces, this can also be arranged—at a price!

If you'd like to have a good look at a selection of apartments on the Internet before settling on a choice, navigate toward **Venexia home** (☎ 041-5208575; www.venexiahome.it), which also offers a fair range of private accommodations, from comfortable two-room suites (for as little as €80; see their "comfort" range for the cheapest options) to luxurious three-story apartments and elegant penthouses with panoramic views of the city. Some have private gardens, and many are large enough to accommodate family groups. You'll also have a wide choice in terms of decor and design; whether you've got a taste for contemporary style, or prefer the '80s look, there's something that will suit you and won't sting your pocket too badly (the average price for an apartment sleeping four people is around €150).

You're encouraged to rent the apartment for at least a week, but a daily rate can occasionally be had if you're on a short stay (note that it will be slightly costlier). These apartments are all fully furnished, with toasters and coffee machines in the kitchens; and they're usually well maintained, immaculately clean, and serviced regularly. If you call on arrival at the airport, a representative will meet you at your boat or taxi, and then personally show you to your apartment. You will also have round-the-clock access to an assistant assigned to take care of your local travel needs, including the booking of shows, restaurant recommendations and reservations, sightseeing guides, and general city information. And if that's not enough, you can even have meals prepared for you by an in-house chef. If you're planning to be in Venice for Carnevale or during the Film Festival, I recommend that you book 3 months in advance.

Flats in Venice (☎ 041-2413875; www.flatsinvenice.net) is a smaller operation that rents out five different apartments, its daily rentals starting at €80. Most of these are very basic one-room spaces, and not my first choice for a comfortable self-catering stay. Their so-called "Family Apartment," however, is a decent enough choice for a couple with children, especially if you'd like to be in the heart of San Marco—it's right near La Fenice. The flat has two upstairs bedrooms (one of which has two single beds, making it ideal for the kids), a bathroom with bathtub, kitchen, and living room. Flats are serviced, but the cost goes up with each additional person in your party.

If you're planning to be in Venice for a full week, you might want to consider either of two self-catering apartments owned by Jonathan Hollow and Alasdair Wight, who let their properties out privately (so you won't be paying an agency markup). They only do Saturday-to-Saturday rentals, but offer an excellent deal if you're traveling as a family or in a group. Both **Casa Tre Archi** ★★ and **Casa Battello** ★ (www.visitvenice.co.uk) are in Cannaregio, close to the fresh produce markets of Rio Terà San Leonardo, and also a nearby supermarket. Battello is the smaller of the two; although it doesn't have a major canal view, it's more affordable. The week costs €800 in the low season (Jan 7–Feb 18 and Nov 4–Dec 23) and €1,019 during peak periods (Feb 18–Mar 4, Apr 1–Sept 30, and Dec 23–30). Built in the early 19th century, the house occupies two floors off a narrow side street *(sottoportego);* it has one bedroom and two living rooms, each with a double sofa bed (meaning that you can squeeze five people in here at a stretch).

Situated on the top floor of a 17th-century merchant's building, the larger and wonderfully renovated Tre Archi has a charming view of Cannaregio Canal; it's a little more expensive ($1,215 in low season; $1,580 in peak periods), but still a good value. The apartment has two air-conditioned bedrooms (one double, one twin), and a living room with sofa bed; the kitchen is well equipped. There's plenty of wardrobe space, and I also like that you can hang your washing across the courtyard the way most Venetian households do. Unlike Battello, Tre Archi has a dishwasher and telephone. The owners have made an effort to provide guests with information and tips that will improve their stay in Venice, and there are always a handful of useful recipe books to help spice things up in the kitchen.

It may sound logical to want to stay near the tourist epicenter around St. Mark's Square, but I prefer to escape the constant bustle and soaring inflation of this densely crowded area. When it comes to lodging, my favorite areas in Venice are Cannaregio, Dorsoduro, and Castello's Riva degli Schiavoni, the broad lagoonside promenade that runs from the Palazzo Ducale to the Arsenale and beyond. Of course, the latter is wall-to-wall with high-end luxury accommodations, such as the prestigious Danieli, long considered one of the finest hotels in Europe.

Accommodations Index

€   **Rooms €50 or less a night**

Alloggi Gerotto Calderan
(Cannaregio, p. 285)

Domus Civica (San Polo & Santa Croce, p. 291)

Foresteria Valdese (Castello, p. 288)

Hotel Bernardi-Semenzato ★★★
(Cannaregio, p. 283)

Ostella Santa Fosca (Cannaregio, p. 285)

Ostello di Venezia (Giudecca, p. 292)

Room in Venice (San Marco, p. 281)

€€ **Rooms €51 to €100 a night**

Albergo Adua (Cannaregio, p. 282)

Albergo Casa Peron (San Polo
& Santa Croce, p. 289)

Apostoli Palace (Cannaregio,
p. 284)

B&B San Marco ✹ 🧒 (Castello,
p. 282)

Ca' Pozzo (San Marco, p. 281)

Ca' San Giorgio ✹✹ (San Polo
& Santa Croce, p. 291)

Casa Venexiana ✹ (Dorsoduro,
p. 287)

Hotel ai do Mori (San Marco,
below)

Hotel American-Dinesen ✹
(Dorsoduro, p. 286)

**Hotel Casa Verardo—Residenza
d'Epoca** ✹✹ (Castello, p. 288)

Hotel Falier (San Polo & Santa
Croce, p. 289)

Hotel Fontana (Castello, p. 287)

Hotel La Residenza ✹ (Castello,
p. 287)

Hotel Locanda Salieri (San Polo
& Santa Croce, p. 289)

Hotel Messner (Dorsoduro, p. 286)

Hotel San Geremia ✹ (Cannaregio,
p. 283)

Locanda Art Déco ✹ (San Marco,
p. 280)

Locanda Ca' Foscari (Dorsoduro,
p. 285)

Locanda del Ghetto ✹
(Cannaregio, p. 283)

Pensione La Calcina (Dorsoduro,
p. 286)

Sant' Agostin ✹ (San Polo &
Santa Croce, p. 289)

Hotel Tre Archi (Cannaregio,
p. 283)

Violino d'Oro (San Marco, p. 280)

€€€ **Rooms €101 to €150 a night**

Locanda Cà San Marcuola ✹
(Cannaregio, p. 284)

Locanda Fiorita (San Marco, p. 280)

Locanda SS. Giovanni e Paolo ✹
(Castello, p. 288)

Metropole Hotel ✹✹✹
(San Marco, p. 281)

**Pensione Accademia Villa
Maravege** ✹ (Dorsoduro, p. 286)

Villa Igea ✹ (Castello, p. 288)

€€€€ **Rooms more than €150 a night**

Ca' Dogaressa (Cannaregio, p. 284)

Hotel Giorgione (Cannaregio,
p. 284)

Hotel Saturnia and International
(San Marco, p. 281)

ACCOMMODATIONS IN SAN MARCO

San Marco is the most expensive of the city's hotel areas, with only an occasional property offering near-budget rates.

€€-€€€   If you're determined to be in the heart of the city, then by all means get a room at the friendly **Hotel ai do Mori** (Calle Larga San Marco, San Marco 658; ☎ 041-5204817; www.hotelaidomori.com), a budget option right off St. Mark's Square (it really is 10m/33 ft. away). Rooms can be quite cramped, in both the main hotel and the nearby Annex, but bright walls, wooden floors, exposed beam ceilings, and an air of recent renovation help keep spirits up (the decor here is modern rather than antique Venetian). Some top-floor rooms have views of the Basilica (ask for room 6, if it's available, for a particularly spectacular view). Your biggest concerns here will be the steep stairways (no elevator) and cramped rooms (not unusual for Venice), although rooms on the lowest (second) floor are slightly more spacious. Doubles with bathroom are €80 to €135, without bathroom €60 to €90.

€€–€€€€   Campo San Stefano is wonderfully located, within easy walking distance of both Piazza San Marco and the Accademia. This is where you'll find **Locanda Art Déco** ★ (Calle delle Botteghe, San Marco 2966; ☎ 041-2770558; www.locandaartdeco.com), with ordinary rooms that stand out thanks to their complete lack of faux-antique styling so typical of Venice's moderately priced hotels. Decor and furnishings are minimalist, and bathrooms quite small, but the rooms are immaculate, with spectacularly comfortable orthopedic mattresses, as insisted on by the hotel's charming French proprietor, Judith. You can connect to the Internet in your room, and take breakfast on the tiny midfloor landing, while the friendly receptionist is eager to provide advice on dining and nightlife. Double rooms start at €75 per night, including a simple continental breakfast, but you may pay as much as €190 during peak periods. It's a good idea to check the hotel's website for a discounted rate; there are regular package deals for stays of 2 days or more. A bonus here: You can order a private in-room massage at a reasonable rate.

€€€   Also near Campo San Stefano, on a quiet *campiello*, is **Locanda Fiorita** (Campiello Novo, San Marco 3457; ☎ 041-5234754; www.locandafiorita.com), which occupies a salmon-colored building topped by a profusion of chimneys. White garden chairs are clustered around the entrance, which is easily mistaken for the entrance to someone's private home. You arrive in a small, neat lobby with timbered ceilings and mountains of brochures; there are only 10 rooms, and things are very low-key. Guest rooms are pleasant, not too tiny (room 8 is a good twin), with standard antique styling and the usual amenities; mattresses are firm, and the bathrooms small and tiled. You'll find towels on the bed and windows looking onto a neighborhood side street; rooms 1 and 10 have tiny private terraces overlooking the square. Doubles here go for no more than €145 with private bathroom; €110 without, but you'll pay much less than this out of peak season; breakfast is included. **Ca' Morosini-Dependance** (Calle San Stefano, San Marco 3465; ☎ 041-2413800; www.camorosini.com) is the Fiorita's more expensive annex, where double en suite rooms cost €180.

€€–€€€€   One of Venice's most fabulous and fabled hotels is the **Bauer** ★★ (www.bauerhotels.com), with its vast Soviet-style lobby, beautiful guest rooms, tradition of hosting international celebrities, and award-winning restaurant. Because it's strictly for the well-heeled, I mention the Bauer simply as a reference: Right next door is the far less ostentatious, but far more affordable, **Violino d'Oro** (Campiello Barozzi, San Marco 2091; ☎ 041-2770841; www.violinodoro.com), occupying the Palazzo Barozzi. Small and smart, rates here are quite flexible: There are times when you'll pay as little as €80 for a double room, if you're able to score a last-minute booking (although this is more likely to be €190). Be aware that this hotel charges more for early reservations, so planning a stay here too far in advance will mean you'll end up paying too much. If you like watching gondolas, you'll love the location; it's right at the edge of what can only be described as a busy gondolier highway (it's right at the San Moisè gondola stop), and "Sole mio" can be heard regularly in the early evening. The 26 guest rooms (all nonsmoking) are white-glove clean, and done out in standard faux-Venetian antique style.

€€€€   Nearby, at **Hotel Saturnia and International** (Via XXII Marzo, San Marco 2398; ☎ 041-5208377; fax 041-5207131; www.spacehotels.it), the best (or worst) part of one's stay is the free entertainment provided by musicians busking on the street below your room. The hotel opened in 1908, and is still operated by the Serandrei family; they've assembled a wide range of rooms, some with a decidedly dated ambience, and others given a bold Modernist makeover. Double rooms start at €153 per night.

€€€-€€€€   Before moving on to San Marco's B&Bs, I must tell you about one of the classiest lodging options in the vicinity of St. Mark's Square. Not only is it an excellent blend of historic charm and genteel service, but also its sense of intimacy makes the **Metropole Hotel** ★★★ (Riva Schiavoni, Castello 4149; ☎ 041-5205044; www.hotelmetropole.com) a standout among all of Venice's top accommodations. Filled with antiques, the comfortable public areas are decorated with shelves displaying unusual collections, laid out like an irreverent museum; among the displays of fans, Belle Epoque evening bags, and corkscrews is a fine collection of crucifixes. Every guest room is unique, combining elements that preserve a strong sense of Venice as it might have been in its heyday, with modern conveniences thrown into the mix. Best is room 403, with its own terrace looking onto the lagoon; inside, it's all carved wood, velvet bedding, and Fortuny lamps. The Metropole is expensive, and some rooms are smaller than you might expect; doubles start at €150, though they can go to €495 when the city gets crowded; add €100 for a lagoon view. The hotel's website occasionally offers room upgrades and discounts, so surf there before booking.

Bed & Breakfasts

€-€€   Not far from the Rialto bridge and *vaporetto* launches is the extremely well-priced B&B **Room in Venice** (Calle San Antonio, San Marco 4114/a; ☎ 041-5229510; www.roominvenice.com). Claudette and Andrea rent out three bedrooms in their apartment situated in a lovely neighborhood taken up mainly by municipal offices. Rooms are bright, simple, and functional, with basic antique furniture. There are no televisions or telephones, but accommodations are spotless, and represent great value. Claudette prepares breakfast for guests, and this is served in your room. She and her husband are also a wonderful source for advice and keep a small cabinet of books on Venice for their guests' use. Rates start at €50 per night for a room with shared bathroom. The maximum charge for the guest room with private bathroom facilities in high season is €95; you can ask for a discount if you stay for several days. Note that the apartment is reached via several sets of marble stairs, so it may not be practical for everyone.

€€-€€€   Operated by Flats in Venice, **Ca' Pozzo** (☎ 041-2413875; www.flatsinvenice.net) is a recent addition to Venice's B&B lineup, favorably situated on Campo San Maurizio, near Teatro la Fenice. Rooms vary somewhat, each with a rather idiosyncratic color scheme, but they all have private bathrooms (choose between a tub or shower), and amenities include air-conditioning, a minibar, safe, and Internet port. Rates start at €80 for two guests, and the maximum price you'll pay is €120, depending on the season.

€€–€€€   A lovely, modestly priced bed-and-breakfast near the heart of Venice is **B&B San Marco** ★ (kids) (Castello 3385/L; ☎ 041-5227589 or 335-7566555; info@realvenice.it). It's just 3 years old, but word of mouth has made it a favorite with travelers who prefer to avoid hotel banality and inflated prices. Guest rooms are in the family home of Marco Scurati, on the third floor of a century-old apartment building; the location is superb, close to the San Zaccaria *vaporetto* launch, and an easy 6-minute walk to Piazza San Marco. All three rooms are spacious, but fork out a little extra to have the largest room, with its terrace and views toward the Scuole San Giorgio. Rooms have wooden floors, rugs, desks, antique chairs, and wrought-iron beds; expect to pay between €70 and €110 per night, depending on the season. Guest rooms share a bathroom, but unless you keep precisely the same schedule as your fellow guests, this shouldn't be a huge problem. Marco will go out of his way to help you with sightseeing and useful recommendations, many of which will allow you to escape the tourist crowds. A basic breakfast (tea, coffee, croissants, and toast) is served in the kitchen; there's also an extra fridge for your own drinks and snacks.

Also available at B&B San Marco is a fully furnished self-catering apartment, ideal for families or two couples traveling together (daily rate €100–€180; weekly rate €600–€950); this has two bedrooms, a living room, a bathroom, a dining nook, a kitchen, and its own balcony. Decor is faintly 1970s, and here you have your own television, DVD player, and library of information. There's a grocery store just moments away, so you can stock up and put the kitchen to good use, just like a real Venetian. The apartment shares a main entrance with the B&B; contact details are the same.

ACCOMMODATIONS IN CANNAREGIO

Occupying the northernmost swath of Venice, Cannaregio stretches from the train station, which is where many budget travelers prefer to stay because it saves them from lugging their backpacks around. For me, the area around the station and along tourist-intensive Lista di Spagna is without much appeal, while the rest of Cannaregio—particularly west of Canale di Cannaregio—is lovely; this is where many Venetians choose to live. Behind many of those weathered facades, there's a great deal of restoration going on, testament to people's commitment to maintaining Venice's historic charm.

Hotels near the Train Station

€€   If being right near the station is a priority, the **Albergo Adua** (Lista di Spagna, Cannaregio 233/A; ☎ 041-716184; www.aduahotel.com) offers a reasonable deal; rooms here with shared bathroom go for around €70, depending on the season. Don't expect anything to write home about, but accommodations are relatively large and have air-conditioning; breakfast (€6) is not included.

€€   On Campo San Geremia, just 270m (900 ft.) from the station, is the good-value **Hotel San Geremia** ★ (Campo San Geremia, Cannaregio 290/A; ☎ 041-716245 or toll-free 800-391992; www.sangeremiahotel.com), one of the most pleasant budget hotels in town. I was once drawn here by the cool music playing in the small lobby, and then shown upstairs by a welcoming manager; guest rooms are charmingly bright and cheerful, and those on the top floors have terraces. If you get one overlooking the square, you'll have views of the church, and can keep track of one of the artists busily sketching or painting it. Rooms with private bathroom cost between €95 and €115 during the high season, or you can shave off €30 by opting for a room with shared bathroom facilities. Either way, the San Geremia is a sound deal.

Hotels in the Heart of Cannaregio

€–€€   Two people who have made me feel right at home in Venice are Maria Teresa and Leonardo Pepoli, a marvelously outgoing couple who have owned and run **Hotel Bernardi-Semenzato** ★★★ (Calle dell'Oca, Cannaregio 4363–4366; ☎ 041-5222424; www.hotelbernardi.com) for the last quarter of a century. The good value offered here is combined with a relaxed, friendly atmosphere, generated by people intent on going out of their way to make guests happy. Also impressive (especially for a budget hotel) is the endless array of genuine antiques and artwork scattered throughout the main hotel and—even more so—its nearby annex, where rooms are generally much larger and more attractive, and feature newer amenities. Maria Teresa (who reminds me of Giulietta Masina, the beautiful star of films by Federico Fellini, her husband) is a seasoned purveyor of antiques and shamelessly worships art and places of architectural beauty; her enthusiasm for Venice is intoxicating, and has left its mark on the design of the rooms, all of which have something special to offer. Ask her to point you toward a restaurant or special church, and she'll put you on to a good thing. I recently stayed in a huge room in the annex (which will soon become a hotel in its own right) with splendid views over the neighborhood. The Pepolis offer the best lodging deal in Cannaregio (and one of the best in the city); you'll pay on average between €75 and €100 for a room, with off-season specials starting as low as €28 per person. The cheapest rooms have shared bathroom facilities (from €50 double), and there are units for up to four people sharing.

€€–€€€€   During quieter periods, you can get a double room at the crimson-colored **Hotel Tre Archi** (Fondamenta di Cannaregio, Cannaregio 923; ☎ 041-5244356; www.hoteltrearchi.com) for as little as €55 (at other times that amount can triple). Like Ca' Dogaressa (see below), the styling here is Venetian "antique," but this is a larger hotel, with a less intimate atmosphere and more public space, including a small courtyard garden where you can enjoy breakfast in summer.

€€–€€€€   Situated on the edge of Ghetto Nuovo, **Locanda del Ghetto** ★ (Campo del Ghetto Nuovo, Cannaregio 2892/2893; ☎ 041-2759292; www.venezia hotels.com) may not look like much from the outside, but it has pleasant accommodations in a 15th-century building that is also a former synagogue. Guest rooms are all on the first floor and feature parquet floors, modern and antique furnishings, and neutral-toned fabrics; two of the rooms have small terraces from where you can observe the Ghetto below. Double rooms go for €80 to €220, depending on season, but an extra bed is only slightly more, making this a fine choice for groups. Breakfast is included, and is served in a smart little room with views onto the canal at the back of the hotel.

€€€   When it comes to getting your luggage to your hotel, an excellent choice is the good-value **Locanda Cà San Marcuola** ★ (Campo San Marcuola, Cannaregio 1763; ☎ 041-716048; www.casanmarcuola.com). Its lion-flanked entrance is just a few steps from the San Marcuola *vaporetto* stop on the Grand Canal; this seriously cuts down the time you spend getting lost while dragging your luggage along every possible wrong alley. Guest rooms are unexpectedly spacious for Venice, with quaint, comfortable furnishings. Remarkably, you can get a double room here for €120 during high season (breakfast is not included), although—as with all Venetian hotels—rates jump up and down like a volatile stock exchange; always check the website for specials. Because the hotel backs onto a small canal, you'll also have access to a private boat, although it's only available after 3pm. Guests can now order in-room Ayurvedic massage.

€€-€€€€   Opened in 2003, the **Apostoli Palace** (Calle del Padiglion, Cannaregio 4702; ☎ 041-5203177; www.apostolipalace.com) is an unexpected gem hidden down an inconspicuous lane with eight guest rooms at the top of a narrow, steep stairway. After the tiny reception area, the bedrooms are fabulously spacious (by Venetian standards, they're exceptional), with handmade Venetian floors, timbered ceilings and antique-styled furniture; the bathrooms are particularly bright, and there's Wi-Fi reception in every room. Two rooms have balconies, while the unit named "San Andrea" has its own terrace. Far from the crowds and the madness of the tourist areas, this tiny hotel—in an old house renovated by its original owners—is quiet and friendly. There are future plans to add four guest rooms, which may diminish the wonderful intimacy. Double rooms here can range from as little as €77 in November up to €200 in the summer months.

€€€€   All the rooms at **Ca' Dogaressa** (Fondamenta di Cannaregio, Cannaregio 1018; ☎ 041-2759441; www.cadogaressa.com) are named for the wives of the doges and have furnishings these pampered ladies would appreciate. In fact, the hotel is a mecca of 18th-century lavishness, including all the standard Venetian "antique" trimmings such as Murano chandeliers, reproduction furniture, silk-covered walls, and elaborately carved headboards (first-floor units are in shades of green, while on the second floor there's lots of yellow). Ca' Dogaressa is owned by Giampaolo and Graziella Antenori, who lived here before turning to the hospitality industry; you'll feel as if you're visiting a modestly wealthy Venetian uncle, rather than staying in a hotel. There's a terrace on the roof, and you can also take drinks at one of the tables at the edge of the Cannaregio Canal. Standard doubles cost €180 in high season; Internet specials on the website can lop 35% off that rate, so be sure to check online first.

€€€€   One of Cannaregio's most interesting hotels, packed full of historic ambience and occupying a former confectionary warehouse, is **Hotel Giorgione**

(SS. Apostoli, Cannaregio 4587; ☎ 041-5225810; www.hotelgiorgione.com). I call it interesting because the shape and size of every room is unique; there's simply no way to be certain of what to expect. Giorgione may look small, but there are 76 rooms, including some rather small standard rooms, and wonderful units with private terraces (my favorite is room 308), from which the rooftop views are magical. Whichever room you end up with, you'll enjoy the service here; its staff maintains a sharp sense of what four-star service is all about, and there are plenty of welcome touches and facilities like all-day tea-and-coffee service, a billiards room, and an enclosed fountain courtyard. Expect to pay between €150 and €265, but off-season Internet specials can often drop the price even lower (always check the website before booking). During slower periods, lunch may be included in the competitive room rate. Just like the more affordable Hotel Bernardi Semenzato nearby, Giorgione is a short walk from the Rialto, and just 10 minutes from St. Mark's Square.

Hostels in Cannaregio

€–€€   If you book well enough in advance (I suggest 2 weeks) you can get a bed in a dorm at **Alloggi Gerotto Calderan** (☎ 041-715562; no credit cards) for €21. En suite rooms range from €46 to €62 per night. Guest rooms (singles, doubles, and triples) are toothpaste-white and spartan, with faux-antique headboards and eclectically dressed beds (some have floral linen, others feature shocking pink covers). Ask for a room overlooking the square, as these have views of the Palazzo Labia.

€   **Ostella Santa Fosca** (Fondamenta Canale, Cannaregio 2372; ☎ 041-715733; www.santafosca.it) occupies a former nunnery, and is now run by students. Dorm beds start at €19, and there's a small discount for holders of various youth concession cards, including the ISIC and Rolling Venice. A bed in a double room is only marginally more expensive. The old convent includes a garden, which is a great spot to stroll. In summer you have access to a self-catering kitchen. Reservations are accepted only a week in advance.

ACCOMMODATIONS IN DORSODURO

Dorsoduro is a vibrant neighborhood with a number of lively student hangouts and affordable restaurants. In the early evening, residents come to Dorsoduro's long south-facing Zattere promenade to relax, jog, or walk their dogs. Many of its lodgings are discreetly disguised as private residences, as though they'd rather not cause offense, but inside, there's nearly always a warm welcome and a degree of hospitality not always matched by more expensive options in San Marco.

€€–€€€   Dorsoduro's last word in standard budget hotels has got to be **Locanda Ca' Foscari** (Calle della Frescada, Dorsoduro 3887/B; ☎ 041-710401; www.locandacafoscari.com), where a double with private bathroom costs just €93. A word of warning, however: The rooms are exceptionally plain, with bland floral bedspreads, and a genuine lack of space. Sure, this is a viable option when other plans fall apart, but I for one would rather fork out a tiny bit extra for a night at **Hotel Messner** (Fondamenta Ca' Balà, Dorsoduro 216–217; ☎ 041-5227443; www.hotelmessner.it), which offers three tiers of accommodations: The cheapest are heavy on linoleum but comfortable (and cost a reasonable €115 per double), while midrange options border on budget-plush (with an uptick in price of €30).

€€-€€€€   Call me sentimental, but there's something of the aura of writer John Ruskin that still hangs in the air at **Pensione La Calcina** (Zattere, Dorsoduro 780; ☎ 041-5206466; www.lacalcina.com), a classic Venetian hotel owned and run by Debora and Alesandro Szemere. A typewriter displayed on the stairway is a reminder that the famous Ruskin wrote most of his novel, *The Stones of Venice*, in room 2, a lovely corner unit looking onto the Giudecca Canal; it's spacious, with parquet flooring, a Murano chandelier, and a good-size bathroom. These days, most of the rooms (recently refurbished, but retaining a sense of tradition) have something special to offer, but those with views toward Giudecca's Redentore church are the most popular; the price of a double with bathroom ranges from €99 to €186, varying according to season and view. I once stayed in what is almost certainly the smallest room in Venice (a single unit about the size of a bathroom at the Cipriani), but even this had a tiny balcony overlooking rooftops, the adjacent canal, and the lagoon (single rooms cost €55–€75 without bathroom; or €75–€106 en suite, with or without a view). There's a lovely rooftop terrace, and the restaurant, La Piscina, which floats on the Giudecca Canal, is a very special breakfast spot. The Szemeres also rent apartments in a block near the hotel; these are immaculate and average around €200 per night.

€€-€€€€   I really enjoyed my recent stay at **Hotel American-Dinesen** ★ (San Vio, Accademia 628; ☎ 041-5204733; www.hotelamerican.com), primarily because I'm a sucker for friendly, welcoming service. From the very helpful porter to the useful recommendations made by the desk clerk, everybody here makes a concerted effort. Accommodations occupy two adjoining buildings facing a small canal. It's ideal for art-lovers; not only is it close to Venice's two best galleries, but the walls are crammed with all manner of paintings, giving the public spaces the feel of someone's home. Guest rooms are neat and functional, with patterned silk-covered walls, reproduction antiques, and gold-lacquered fittings; the automatic blinds over the windows ensure complete blackout and are good for noise control. Bathrooms are cramped, in the manner of most Venetian hotels. Rooms 102 and 101 have lively views; the latter is more spacious than many of the other units. Double rooms start at €90 in low season, but soar to €260 over peak periods; expect to pay even more if you want a view.

€€€-€€€€   Hotel gardens are scarce in Venice, and few are as pretty as the leafy grounds at **Pensione Accademia Villa Maravege** ★ (Fondamenta Bollani, Dorsoduro 1058; ☎ 041-5210188; www.pensioneaccademia.it). This 17th-century villa was formerly occupied by the Russian Embassy and now has a distinctive, elegant feel, enhanced by Victorian relics and no-nonsense antique styling. Operating since the 1950s, and last refurbished in 2003, the *pensione* has an atmosphere of sophistication; staff members try to maintain a purse-lipped composure for a posh clientele, but a social and congenial breakfast in the garden overcomes any such pretensions. Last-minute deals are regularly offered on the website, but even the regular rates are excellent for Venice, ranging between €130 and €193 for a double room with private bathroom.

A Choice Bed & Breakfast

€€ **Casa Venexiana** ★ (Fondamenta del Gaffaro, Dorsoduro 3515; ☎ 041-5242637) offers one of the best lodging deals in Dorsoduro, with three simple, comfortable en suite guest rooms; they're themed according to color schemes; rooms come in pink, blue, and green. Each room has a double bed or two singles, as well as a day bed. The blue room has a private entrance off a small square, or *campiello*. Owner Tiziana Magoni herself prepares breakfast for guests, and you dine with views over the Gaffaro canal. A bonus here is Franco, who seems to take infinite pleasure in guiding guests through the city and introducing them to off-the-beaten-track experiences and sights.

ACCOMMODATIONS IN CASTELLO

Castello can be a fine place to stay in Venice; many of its hotels are close to St. Mark's and yet feel miles away from the crowds. Rates are also considerably better than in neighboring San Marco.

€€-€€€€ On bustling, lively Campo San Provolo is one of Castello's lovely surprises: **Hotel Fontana** (Castello 4701; ☎ 041-5220579; www.hotelfontana.it), owned and operated by the Austro-Italian Stainer family since 1968. The best rooms in the main hotel are on the third floor; these are spacious but spartan and a little dark, but during the day, light streams in through the open windows from which you have a lovely view of the street below. Rooms are furnished with some Art Deco–type pieces, while walls are left stark white; bathrooms vary in size and have tub-shower combos. You'll pay a little more for one of the rooms with a private terrace, and you must specifically request one of these when booking. Downstairs, there's a bar, lounge, and dining area with walls strewn with photographs—mostly old blown-up images of Venice, circa 1970. Most rooms have an extra fold-out bed, making them useful for small families. Double rooms cost €85 to €170—a wide range that reflects the size of the rooms as well as seasonal fluctuations. Diego, who operates the business, also offers guest rooms in a five-unit palace across the *campo;* rates are slightly lower simply because you're not in the main building.

€€-€€€€ In terms of value and ambience, one of the most alluring lodging choices in Venice is **Hotel La Residenza** ★ (Campo Bandiera e Moro, Castello 3608; ☎ 041-5285315; www.venicelaresidenza.com), occupying the first floor of the 15th-century Palazzo Gritti-Badoer. The large lobby-lounge-dining area is filled with antiques, Oriental rugs, and Murano chandeliers; there's even a grand piano and lovely terrace overlooking the square below. Guest rooms, which were entirely renovated in 2001, aren't quite as spectacular as the public area, but they're spacious and uncluttered; in fact, the Venetian antique styling really stands out against the stark white walls, reminding you exactly which city you're in. All rooms have en suite showers, and the usual amenities. Rates range from €80 to €160 double.

€€–€€€€   Here's a really special option occupying a restored 16th-century palace, just 3 minutes from St. Mark's Square. **Hotel Casa Verardo—Residenza d'Epoca** ★★ (Campo SS. Filippo e Giacomo, Castello 4765; ☎ 041-5286138 or 041-5286127; www.casaverardo.it) is a rare combination of good taste, spaciousness, and excellent rates (a "classic" double goes for €90–€220). It's not exactly budget, but you could score a last minute deal, paying considerably less than the seasonal rate (check the hotel's website for "last minute" offers). Owners Daniela and Francesco acquired the property in 2000, and since then have been hard at work transforming it into a romantic combination of historic ambience and understated luxury, offering a touch of class and sophistication that you won't find elsewhere at this price. Each room is done in a different color; expect good-quality furniture, Murano chandeliers, and stucco wall pieces. Some ceilings feature bits of original frescoes. My favorite space here is the large, sun-drenched terrace overlooking the canal, where long, casual breakfasts are a great way to start the day in summer; there's also a gorgeous courtyard.

€€€   A surprisingly good value in the heart of Castello is **Locanda SS. Giovanni e Paolo** ★ (Barbaria de le Tole, Castello 6401; ☎ 041-5222767; www.locandass giovannipaolo.it), a relatively new hotel situated a short distance from the popular church and *campo* of the same name. Breakfast is served in your room, and is included in the relatively reasonable rate (you'll pay €120–€135 for a double room during the high season). The air-conditioned guest rooms are clean and well kept, and are done in typical faux-antique Venetian style, with pale shades and white walls.

€€€–€€€€   Looking onto a wide, open square and facing the San Zaccaria church, **Villa Igea** ★ (Campo San Zaccaria, Castello 4684; ☎ 041-2410956; info@hotelsavoiajolanda.com) makes you think you're in the lap of luxury without feeling the sting in your wallet. This plush hotel has recently received a thorough makeover, retaining the Venetian antique styling against pleasant pastels. When I last visited, breakfasts were being served at the Igea's upmarket sister establishment, Savoia e Jolanda, right on the Riva degli Schiavoni. With breakfast included, you can expect to pay between €144 and €218 for a standard double room, and just €20 more for a superior room.

Castello's Popular Hostel

€–€€   Protestant-run **Foresteria Valdese** (Calle Lunga Santa Maria Formosa, Castello 5170; ☎ 041-5286797; www.diaconiavaldese.org/venezia) is another cheap place to park your backpack. Accommodations occupy the recently renovated 16th-century Palazzo Cavagnis, which still has some 18th-century frescoes (these "historical" rooms cost a bit more). Take your pick of a few double rooms (€57 without bathroom; €75 with bathroom), a bed in a dorm (€22 per bed), a family-size room (€104 for four people with a private bathroom), or a miniapartment that sleeps four or five people (€104–€116). Unless you're in an apartment, a simple breakfast is included. Things are a tad spartan, but if you keep in mind that this is a church-affiliated budget establishment for pilgrims, you'll find that the welcoming atmosphere, canal-side balconies, and excellent rates more than make up for any lack of sophistication. Note that Valdese is quite popular and often fully booked by groups, so reserve well in advance (the Catch-22 is that single travelers can't book); if you want a private room or apartment, you'll most likely be subjected to a 2-night minimum stay. One downside: Check-in times are limited; don't arrive before 9am or after 8pm, or between 1 and 6pm. On Sundays, reception closes at 1pm.

ACCOMMODATIONS IN SAN POLO & SANTA CROCE

Santa Croce and San Polo are central and relatively close to Piazzale Roma, making accommodations here particularly convenient if you're arriving by bus or car.

€€   For absolute bottom-of-the-barrel room rates in this area, there's no place much cheaper than **Albergo Casa Peron** (Salizzada San Pantalon, Santa Croce 85; ☎ 045-710021; www.casaperon.com), which has clean, spartan bedrooms with private bathroom for under €100 in peak season. The main problem here may be the quality of the mattress, but the backache won't hurt your budget. The hotel has a somewhat ramshackle feel, with tawdry lace wall-hangings in the lobby, and you might find the live-in house parrot sleeping on the office door, but such oddities—surprisingly—add character.

€€-€€€€   **Hotel Locanda Salieri** (Fondamenta Minotto, Santa Croce 160; ☎ 041-710035; www.hotelsalieri.com) is a refurbished one-star property which may have two-star prices by the time you read this guide. Situated on the lovely Rio del Gaffaro, a canal-side promenade, the hotel offers a choice of views from otherwise ordinary, smallish modern rooms. Units overlooking the Gaffaro Canal are slightly more expensive, while those looking onto the garden at the back are considerably quieter. The new rates start at €70 for a double room in the low season, and reach as high as €140 during peak periods; but keep an eye out for specials on the regularly updated website. The hotel is right next door to Ristorante Ribò, a pricey but classy Michelin-rated restaurant with a garden, which is where Salieri's guests enjoy breakfast.

€€-€€€€   Venturing up the carpeted, marble stairway toward **Sant' Agostin** ★ (Campo S. Agostin, San Polo 2344; ☎ 041-2759414; www.locandasantagostin. com), you'll usually hear the strains of Vivaldi's *Four Seasons,* which seems permanently featured in the spacious lobby. Occupying the first floor of a recently restored 16th-century *palazzo,* right next to the university, this quiet (Vivaldi notwithstanding), relatively new hotel exudes a welcoming but restrained atmosphere. With wooden floors and antique styling, guest rooms are fairly smart and comfortably proportioned; bedrooms have small, immaculately clean marble bathrooms. I love the way the windows admit so much light on bright days, and I love the rooms that have their own tiny terraces. Besides all the standard amenities, there's in-room Internet access. Sant' Agostin is close to the Frari Church. Its location also makes for easy nighttime excursions into Dorsoduro. A double costs €90 in low season, rising to €120 in midseason, and as much as €178 during peak periods; weekends may be more expensive.

€€-€€€€   Another low-key charmer, not too far from the station, is **Hotel Falier** (Salizzada San Pantalon, Santa Croce 130; ☎ 041-710882; www.hotelfalier. com), which also has a small enclosed garden. Guest rooms are somewhat cluttered (the bed, tiny cupboard, and small writing desk taking up nearly all the

Northern Venice

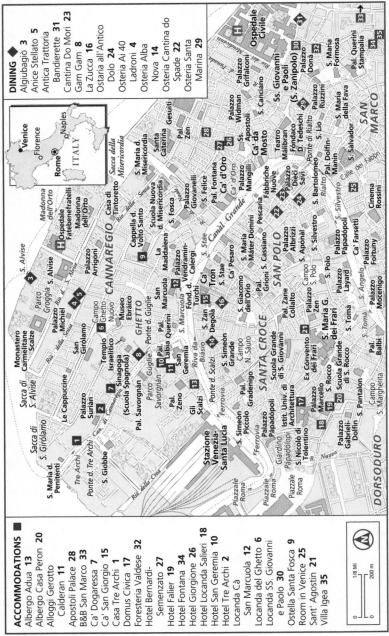

space) and you'll instantly note that the faux-antique look is in full force here, with rooms done out in green and sunflower yellow. Definitely reserve the one room on the top floor with a private terrace. Falier has a pleasant atmosphere and the helpful staff go out of their way to please; the owners have also worked diligently to keep things neat and clean. It's also well situated, near the Frari church and the Scuole Grand San Rocco. Note, however, that while the starting rate for a double room is €90, it's certainly not worth forking out the top price of €210, so check the website for special deals.

A Bed & Breakfast Gem

€€–€€€€   Tucked into one of those few parts of the city that really feel undiscovered by the crowds, **Ca' San Giorgio** ★★ (Salizzada del Fontego dei Turchi, Santa Croce 1725; ☎ 041-2759177; www.casangiorgio.com) is a real find in a recently restored 18th-century building. Although it's way off the beaten track, it's just short steps from the Grand Canal, and within easy reach of the Riva de Biasio *vaporetto* stop. Guest rooms here are luxurious, spacious, and special, benefiting immensely from a contemporary makeover. With classy Venetian styling and such thoughtful modern conveniences as flatscreen televisions, wireless Internet, and hi-fi systems, the look is fresh and inspired. Bathrooms? They're tiled, with good showers. The best accommodations have their own terraces and are more expensive (you pay according to size); expect to pay anywhere between €90 and €200 per night for a double room, depending on the season. If you're traveling alone, this is a real treat, with single use of a double room from €60. Search the website for spectacular specials during quieter months; I once found a weekday special of €80 for a double in April.

A Hostel

€   It may sound overbearingly institutional, but the **Domus Civica** (Campiello Chiovere, San Polo 3082; ☎/fax 041-5227139; www.domuscivica.com) is not a bad option at all; it's a great value, and just a few minutes' walk from both the train and bus stations. Also not far from the Frari church, this seasonal hostel operates from June through September in a gorgeous centuries-old building with spiraling staircase and ancient central elevator. You can get a single room (€29), or share a bed in a double or triple room (€26 per person); these all have metal cots, a desk, bookshelf, and cupboard, with shuttered windows overlooking the *campiello* below. Some rooms even have small balconies. Bathroom facilities are shared but clean, with individual shower cubicles. There's no lockout during the day (but you'll have to observe a 12:30am curfew), and there's free Internet access, a TV lounge, a room to store your luggage, and two cafes right outside, either for people-watching or an affordable meal.

ACCOMMODATIONS ON GIUDECCA

€   Steadily, the island of Giudecca is drawing Venetians who wish to be out of the web of tourists in Venice proper. Elton John has a house on the island, and rumor has it that Madonna is also looking to purchase property here. But a good reason for you to consider staying on Giudecca—despite the *vaporetto* trip to get here at the end of a day of sightseeing—is the prospect of sleeping in one of the cheapest beds in Venice. Right near the Zitelle *vaporetto* launch, **Ostello di Venezia** (☎ 041-5238211; www.hostelbooking.com) benefits from its shore-front location right on the Fondamenta, facing Dorsoduro. Breakfast is included in the ultralow €17 you'll pay for a bed in a unisex dorm. *Note:* This hostel isn't church-operated, but the management here believes that cleanliness is next to godliness. Book through the Internet, and coordinate your arrival to coincide with reception times (7–9:30am and 1:30–11:30pm). Dorm access is restricted during the day, and there's an 11:30pm curfew. If you don't already have one, you can purchase your HI (hostelling) card upon arrival.

DINING FOR ALL TASTES

Venice has absorbed a remarkable variety of **culinary influences,** resulting from centuries of occupation, borrowing, and assimilation. Naturally, the ocean is responsible for many of the more expensive dishes on the city's menus; fish and a range of exotic-sounding shellfish are taken from nearby waters and sold at the *pescheria* (fish market) in Rialto. You'll be able to order everything from spider-crab *(granseola)* to carpet-shell clams *(caparozzolli)* to the very unusual *cappelunghe,* a long, pencil-shaped shell creature. One Venetian oddity you have got to try is *sarde in saor,* a cold sour-sweet dish of sardines in vinegar and onions, which is great as a starter (available city-wide) or as a snack at a bar.

Sarde in saor is one of the many varieties of *cicchetti,* Venice's version of tapas-style snacking, which usually takes place at any of the myriad wine bars, or *bacari,* and tends to be dominated by a smorgasbord of panini and *tramazzini.* Other local specialties are *baccalà montecato* (dried, salted stockfish whipped into a mousse), cuttlefish prepared in its own ink, *fegato* (calf's liver with onions), and—less regularly—*anquilla* (eel). *Bigoli* is a variety of large Venetian pasta you'll see on most menus.

Venice's range of influences makes it an excellent place to experiment with new tastes, but if you do have a conservative palate, there's always pizza, pasta, and even steak to fall back on. Every menu in town has something for vegetarians. Don't expect to get away with anything too cheap, because for the most part Venetian restaurants are aimed squarely at the tourist buck. I've met a number of

Don't Let Them Eat Cake

Venice has long had a love affair with fine dining, so much so that in times gone by, the city fathers passed laws to curb the tide of conspicuous over-consumption of decadent, expensive foods. In 1514, a body of "Luxury Commissioners" known as *Provveditori alle Pompe* was set up to tone down the reportedly depraved tastes of the citizenry. It became illegal to serve oysters at large dinner parties, and there were serious limitations on the type of confection that could be served for dessert.

waiters who've worked in reputable establishments that literally operate three pricing systems: one for Venetians, one for Italian tourists, and one (the highest) for foreign tourists. Unfortunately, there's not much you can do about this economic discrimination, but eating where locals tend to congregate, and avoiding the most markedly "tourist-hungry" places, will make a big difference; another general rule is to avoid most restaurants directly around St. Mark's Square, those near the Rialto lining the Grand Canal, and places advertising "tourist menus" *(menu turistico)*. For **maps of Venice's restaurants,** see p. 274 and 290.

Dining Index

Aciugheta (Castello, €–€€, p. 297)

Algiubagiò ★★★ (Cannaregio, €€, p. 299)

Anice Stellato ★ (Cannaregio, €€, p. 299)

Antica Trattoria Bandierette (Castello, €–€€€, p. 298)

Cantina do Mori ★ (San Polo & Santa Croce, €, p. 295)

Casin dei Nobili (Dorsoduro, €–€€, p. 301)

Cavatappi ★ (San Marco, €–€€, p. 294)

Centrale Restaurant Lounge (San Marco, €€–€€€, p. 295)

Enoteca Mascareta ★ (Castello, €€, p. 298)

Gam Gam (Cannaregio, €–€€, p. 299)

La Zucca ★ 🧒 (San Polo & Santa Croce, €–€€, p. 296)

Mistrà (Giudecca, €€, p. 302)

Osteria ai 40 Ladroni (Cannaregio, €€, p. 299)

Osteria Al Bacareto ★ (San Marco, €–€€, below)

Osteria Alba Nova ★ (San Polo & Santa Croce, €, p. 296)

Osteria all'Antico Dolo (San Polo & Santa Croce, €€–€€€, p. 297)

Osteria Cantina do Spade ★ (San Polo & Santa Croce, €–€€, p. 296)

Osteria Enoteca Ai Artisti ★ (Dorsoduro, €€, p. 301)

Osteria Enoteca San Marco ★★ (San Marco, €€–€€€, p. 295)

Osteria Santa Marina ★★ (Castello, €€€, p. 298)

Osteria Vini Padovani (Dorsoduro, €–€€, p. 301)

Ristorante San Trovaso ★ (Dorsoduro, €–€€, p. 301)

Trattoria Da Fiore (San Marco, €–€€€, p. 294)

Trattoria dai Tosi (Castello, €–€€, p. 297)

Vino Vino ★ (San Marco, €–€€, p. 294)

Price for a *primo* course: € = €7 or less; €€ = €8–€14; €€€ = €15–€19; €€€€ = €20 or more

---

RESTAURANTS IN SAN MARCO

€–€€   My recommendation for San Marco's warmest service, coupled with good-value food, is **Osteria Al Bacareto** ★ (San Samuele, San Marco 3447;

☎ 041-5289336). When you're presented with your bill, you're given a nip of sherry. The family-run restaurant is just out of reach of the tourist chaos, not too far from Campo San Stefano. Decorated with black-and-white photographs of Venice, it's filled with simple, pleasant charm, and is the type of place where you can trust your waiter to make a selection for you. For dinner, the handful of tables outside are very pleasant, but you can always stand at the counter and order a simple panini (from €2.50). Sit-down meals will cost you quite a bit more (*primi* courses will run you around €13, and there's a €1.60 cover and 12% service charge). Local dishes include *pasta e fagioli* (pasta and bean soup), *bigoli in salsa* (spaghetti with anchovies and onion), and Venetian fish soup to start, while *fegato alla veneziana* (fried liver and onions) and *baccalà* are served alongside roast rabbit and veal.

€-€€   During intermission at La Fenice (p. 333), I usually race back to **Vino Vino** ★ (Calle del Cafetier, Calle delle Vesta, San Marco 2007/A; ☎ 041-5237027; www.vinovino.co.it; Wed–Mon 10:30am–midnight) for a replenishing spritz or—depending on my mood—a glass of red wine. This small *bacaro,* staffed by a handful of gracious women, offers a formidable selection of local wines to accompany its good-value, wholesome food. Although dishes change from day to day, expect to choose from such diverse options as *sarde in saor,* sautéed calf's kidneys, quail served with polenta, baked guinea-fowl, braised beef in Barolo wine, and loin of pork prepared in milk sauce. All pasta dishes cost €5.50, while main courses are €9 (fish) or €11 (meat). Starters are all €7, and you can get a side order of vegetables for €3.50. Owned by Emilio Baldi, who also operates Antico Martini, one of Venice's classiest (and priciest) restaurants, Vino Vino maintains reliable quality in every dish. Be sure to check out its website before visiting, as there are regular special discounts that require the presentations of a computer-generated printout when settling your bill. Cover charge is €1.

€-€€   Sommelier-couple Francesca and Marco decided to put their love of wine to good use, so they opened a contemporary-styled wine bar called **Cavatappi** ★ (San Marco 525/526; ☎ 041-2960252; Tues–Sun 9am–midnight). To go with the 40 varieties of Italian wines in stock at any one time (the wine menu changes bimonthly), there's a small kitchen where Marco prepares simple, wholesome dishes of fresh seasonal ingredients. The small menu changes daily, and is also different for lunch or dinner; there's an emphasis on value, so you'll be able to afford that extra glass of wine. Pastas are always a good choice; look for tagliatelle with shrimp and pumpkin flowers, or penne with artichoke hearts and blue cheese. At lunch, main courses (from €11) come with a glass of wine, and may include such filling offerings as filleted pork with red chicory, or roast beef. Most *primi* courses cost between €7 and €10, and dinner is a little pricier.

€-€€€   At **Trattoria Da Fiore** (Calle delle Botteghe, San Marco 3461; ☎ 041-5235310; www.trattoriadafiore.com; Wed–Mon) you have a choice of either traditional *bacaro*-style snacking or a real Venetian seafood feast in the sit-down restaurant. Either way, you'll be under the careful watch of Sergio Boschian, who has been satisfying locals and tourists for over 20 years. Stick your head inside, and you'll have no doubt about what's on the menu—fish, fish, and more fish.

What makes the *bacaro* special is that you can have calamari as a snack rather than the usual ham-and-cheese panino you'll find everywhere else in the city. In the restaurant, your best bet is to ask Sergio (or his son David) about the day's specials, or order the famous "fish in a bag," which is mixed seafood spaghetti. I can also recommend the raw tuna (prepared with a lemon sauce) and the filleted turbot. If you've had it with seafood, you can always find a version of the local specialty, *fegato* (calf's liver). And you can order the lovely house wine by the carafe.

€€–€€€   It may be pricey, but in the vicinity of Piazza San Marco you won't find a classier, more quality-conscious restaurant than the chic **Osteria Enoteca San Marco** ★★ (Frezzeria, San Marco 1610; ☎ 041-5285242; Mon–Sat 12:30–11pm). Serving local specialties as well as several international dishes, San Marco is part of a wave of young businesses in Venice operated by locals who want to move away from the tourist exploitation that preoccupies so much of the service industry. Quality control begins with above-average prices, including a €2.60 cover charge, but the sexy, contemporary wine-cellar ambience, in proximity to St. Mark's Square, just about justifies a one-time splurge (and you certainly won't be among the tourist throngs). Expect to pay from €16 for a starter, from €14 for a *primo* dish, and between €23 and €26 for a *secondo*. You might start with a light salad of goat cheese, walnut, and apple, and then dive straight into the filleted red mullet, Mediterranean-style sea bream filet, or squid stuffed with mussel sauce. If you're in a romantic mood, chefs Ivan and Giorgio can whip up a cold seafood salad for two, served with champagne.

€€–€€€   Another worthwhile flirtation with contemporary chic is **Centrale Restaurant Lounge** (Piscina Frezzaria, San Marco 1659; ☎ 041-2960664; www.centrale-lounge.com; 6:30pm–2am), now all the rage with the trendy crowd. Combining glass and brushed metal in a cavernous room of exposed brick and ambient lighting, the focus at Centrale is on Mediterranean dishes and contemporary twists on traditional Venetian cuisine. *Primi* dishes are simple, tasty experiments: *carnaroli* rice with pumpkin and almonds (€14) or fettuccine prepared with seasonal vegetables (€16) are two vegetarian-friendly examples. *Secondi* are pricier, and might include steamed lobster with an avocado sauce (€32) and filets of roasted sea bass wrapped in a potato tart (€26). The kitchen stays open later than most, making full meals available after a show at nearby Teatro la Fenice (p. 333). Live music often accompanies the classy, laid-back ambience; check the website for upcoming events.

RESTAURANTS IN SAN POLO & SANTA CROCE

€   **Cantina Do Mori** ★ (San Polo 429; ☎ 041-5225401; Mon–Sat 8:30am–9:30pm), not far from the Rialto markets, is something of a Venetian institution. This tiny tavernlike wine bar offers not only tasty *cicchetti*—such as chunks of pecorino cheese, *banchio*, or fishy *baccalà*, spread thickly over slices of wholesome bread—but also wine in abundance (most of it on tap), which is what attracts most of the locals who traipse in and out. If the standard *cicchetti* don't look like they're going to fill the gap, the helpful mensch behind the bar will also whip up a freshly made panino with ham sliced from a huge leg stashed behind the counter. You come in from either of two entrances (one is on Calle Galiazza, another on parallel-running Calle Do Mori), and immediately feel working-class tradition hanging in the air, just like the copper pots dangling from the ceiling; there's plenty of history here, including bar licenses from the 17th century. Note that just because you're snacking, you needn't be caught off guard when it comes to racking up a hefty bill; I recently had seven (or perhaps eight) *cicchetti* items (I really couldn't help myself), and at around €1.50 a piece, I could just as easily have enjoyed a large plate of pasta at a sit-down trattoria.

€   Having run a restaurant in her native Paris for 15 years, Maria Lacombe came to Venice several years ago to be in the city she adores; she decided to carry on doing what she does best, and established **Osteria Alba Nova** ★ (Lista Vecchia dei Bari, Santa Croce 1252; ☎ 041-5241353; Mon–Sat 9am–11pm), a small, family-run eatery far off the beaten track. It's all very unassuming; dishes are chalked up on the board, but at lunchtime you can get any *primo* dish plus a glass of wine and coffee for €6.60; for €2 more, you'll get a *secondo* dish instead. Maria also prepares some really extravagant-sounding dishes made from ancient recipes that you won't find anywhere else; only available in winter are her pasta with crab and strawberry sauce, or—even more decadent—pasta with chocolate and mixed seafood sauce. Portions are generous and filling, and well worth the detour.

€–€€   Walking through San Polo's crowds of tourists, I once came upon **Osteria Cantina do Spade** ★ (Calle Do Spade, San Polo 860; ☎ 041-5210574; www.dospadevenezia.it; 9am–3pm and 5–11pm). I was desperate for a really wholesome meal, and quite unaware of the fact that this homey cantina is renowned for hosting Casanova, who apparently enjoyed some lively parties here. The interior of this ancient place is divided into various alcoves and dining rooms, and comfortably crammed full of all manner of decoration, from Burano lace over the *cicchetti* display, to plastic kitsch novelties along the walls. Seated at a long table, you'll be served by a cheerful, upbeat pair of Venetians who, despite their years, are full of vitality; at one point, you may get an arm around your shoulder, and without understanding your English, the manager will know you are enjoying his pasta immensely. Cuisine is real Venetian, so expect to find a full range of local specialties like cuttlefish in ink sauce, and *baccalà fagioli*. If you're keen on a range of tastes, ask for the mixed *cicchetti*, a huge serving for €10. *Primi* courses cost a perfectly acceptable €7 to €14, while *secondi* are quite reasonable at €12 to €19.

€–€€   With Sting's melancholic strains often setting the mood, **La Zucca** ★ (kids) (Santa Croce 1762; ☎ 041-5241570; www.lazucca.it; Mon–Sat 12:30–2:30pm and 7–10:30pm) is an understandably popular venue of casual ambience and whole-some food. The menu adapts to the whims of the kitchen. There are new dishes every day, but there's a careful nod to the health-conscious, and vegetarians are particularly well looked after. If you turn up in summer, you probably won't get a seat outside (or anywhere for that matter); you may have to return twice before finally getting an unreserved table at lunch. This is a good place to patronize if you're tired of Venetian fish dishes, or really feel in the mood for a fresh salad (chicken and avocado, or *caprese* made with freshly shaved buffalo mozzarella). Casual and child-friendly, La Zucca buzzes at night and serves up simple, nour-ishing fare such as lasagna with zucchini and almonds, pumpkin flan, and even

English roast beef served with guacamole, or tagliatelle with puttanesca and olive sauce. Pasta dishes are well priced at €7 to €8.50, while meat and chicken dishes cost €13 to €14; the cover charge is €1.50.

€€-€€€   Tucked into a cheerful corner in busy Ruga Rialto is **Osteria all'Antico Dolo** (Ruga Rialto, San Polo 778; ☎ 041-5226546; www.anticodolo.it), which occupies a location that has not only been a restaurant since 1434, but is also a former brothel. Either splurge on a meal, opting for one of the day's specials, or simply snack on *cicchetti,* from €1.50 per portion. Under ownership of Bruno Ruffini since 1989, Antico Dolo's roots have remained resolutely Venetian. Served with polenta, the *baccalà mantecato,* prepared with top-quality *ragno* stockfish, boiled and flavored with olive oil and black pepper, is legendary. If you're not scared to taste a true Rialto working class favorite, ask for the *rissa* tripe, which has to be accompanied by a glass of Chardonnay.

RESTAURANTS IN CASTELLO

€-€€   For a truly "local" night out, and some of the best pizzas in town, I must let you in on a discovery I made as I strolled through Castello one Sunday evening. Drawn by the roar of garrulous locals, I ventured into **Trattoria dai Tosi** (Secco Marina, Castello 738; ☎ 041-5237102), not to be confused with the similarly named pizzeria down the road. Outside, most of the tables had merged into one big fiesta, while inside, pizza after pizza was being thrust into the two-door oven behind the busy serving counter. On return visits I found it just as raucous; it's a great place to try if you prefer the cackling of Venetian gossips to the restrained ambience of recorded versions of Vivaldi's *Four Seasons.* Operated by a husband-and-wife team (he's local, but she's from Cornwall in the south of England), this generous and popular eatery has been packing 'em in for more than a decade. Start with one of the house aperitifs (a deadly combination of vodka and fruit juice) while you study the extensive menu and enjoy the crowd. Pizza is always top-notch (and splendidly priced from €3.50 to €9); I recently had the "Squeraiola," a winning combination of Nameko "nail" mushrooms, eggplant, and rocket, but the variations are endless. Pasta dishes (€5–€9) are prepared to order; try the seafood house pasta, or the simpler, cheesier *zucchini e gorgonzola.* Fish dishes cost around €12. Other options range from the simple to the extraordinary; you can even get a massive platter to share for €37.

€-€€   The name means "little anchovy" but that shouldn't dissuade you from visiting **Aciugheta** (Campo SS. Filippo e Giacomo, Castello 4357/4359; ☎ 041-5224292; www.aciugheta-hotelrio.it; 8am–midnight, Nov–Mar closed Wed), one of those long-reliable eateries that is excellent despite its proximity to Piazza San Marco (often a formula for high prices and questionable quality). This was originally a wine bar, so there's always an abundance of freshly prepared *cicchetti;* try the meatballs, or sample the marinated anchovies that gave this place its name (you'll be able to sample a range of different tastes for just a few euros). Having been expanded into a full trattoria, the Aciugheta now offers good, affordable pizza (from around €6); your best bet is to call affable Gianni over to your table and have him make the recommendations.

€–€€€   Not far from the church of SS. Giovanni e Paolo, is **Antica Trattoria Bandierette** (Barbaria delle Tole, Castello 6671; ☎ 041-5220619; www.bandierette.com; Wed–Sun, Mon lunch only), popular with locals from Castello and Cannaregio, and frequented by those who really don't want to overspend (all the dishes here cost €6–€15) but demand quality. Run by a husband-and-wife team, this low-key spot doesn't look like much, but the seafood served here is wonderful. Start with *schie con polenta* (shrimp served with creamed polenta; €7.50), and, if they're available, get a serving of baked scallops for the table—these are done either in garlic or a variety of sauces. A delicious main course is *filetti di branzino con crema di carciofi* (€11), a filet of fish with a fragrant artichoke sauce. If you're after something simple and affordable, have one of the seafood pastas; I recently had spaghetti *con calamaretti e zucchini* (mainly because this is the only restaurant in Venice where the unusual calamaretti squid is served), all for a pleasing €8.50. Give dessert a skip, and move straight on to grappa; there's a fine selection of top-grade stuff that will ensure a good night's sleep.

€€   **Enoteca Mascareta** ★ (Calle Lunga S. Maria Formosa, Castello 5183; ☎ 041-5230744; Fri–Tues 7pm–2am) is, strictly speaking, a wine bar, and has grown famous for the cozy atmosphere that makes people want to settle in for a long night. It's owned by wine expert Mauro Lorenzon, who always wears a bow tie and a smile; he is so fond of wine and so keen to see his customers enjoying his vast selection of vintages, that he'll gladly open any bottle, even to let you try a single glass. His cheerful, cantina-style eatery has a limited menu, but the freshly prepared dishes include excellent snack platters including seafood morsels or deli cuts with a variety of cheeses and cured meats (€15 per plate). There are also individual dishes such as soup, vegetable ravioli, homemade meat lasagna, roast duck, traditional Venetian cuttlefish in black ink sauce, and *baccalà*. Food is only served from 8pm, and a *primo* dish is €12.

€€€   Finally, I must tell you that Castello is also home to one of the city's finest restaurants and one of its best kept secrets: **Osteria Santa Marina** ★★ (Campo Santa Marina, Castello 5911; ☎ 041-5285239; www.osteriadisantamarina.it; Tues–Sat 12:30–2:30pm and 7:30–10pm, Mon 7:30–10pm), situated in a quiet neighborhood, far from the attention of most tourists. Here, dishes combine tradition with class, with great attention to detail. Starters include a selection of seafood items: carpaccio of tuna (€14); Venetian-style scampi, flavored with ginger and leek (€11); or octopus, boiled and flavored with onion, orange peel, and balsamic vinegar (€12). As a first course, you may like to try the crepe-style lasagna stuffed with shrimp and red radicchio (€14) or baby dumplings with a *ragù* of baby squid, monkfish, and tomato (€14). *Secondi* include both seafood (€18–€25) and meat (€19–€23) dishes; for my money, the fragrant tuna steak is a winner (€18). Reservations are strongly recommended.

RESTAURANTS IN CANNAREGIO & ALONG THE FONDAMENTE NUOVE

€€   You can either walk through the quiet back streets of Cannaregio or catch a *vaporetto* to the Fondamente Nuove, a short walk from two worthwhile eateries, one of which—**Algiubagiò** ★★★ (Fondamente Nuove, Cannaregio 5039; ☎ 041-5236084; www.algiubagio.com; 6:30am–late)—is among my favorites in Venice. Here, the jovial young entrepreneurs who opened this relaxed deli-style restaurant sometimes crowd around your table while going into loving detail about the dishes. If you don't feel like eating a full meal, you can join the locals at the bar for *prosecco,* or red wine (€1.30–€2.50 per glass), with your *cicchetti;* a real treat is the *prosciutto di Parma* (€5), ham seasoned for 20 months and served with homemade bread. Also excellent is the pecorino cheese (made from sheep's milk), strong and flavorful, and served with fig and balsamic vinegar. Angus beef filet is the specialty, served with delicious sauces, like chocolate and crab apple. Angus beef dishes cost €17 to €25, depending on the topping, or you can order *chianina* steaks by weight (€4–€4.60 per 100 grams). There are a few vegetarian options (€6.50–€14), and some unusual and innovative pizzas (€4–€14). Save room for a taste of Algiubagiò's homemade, out-of-this-world ice cream. Note that there's a sit-down service charge of 12%, over and above the €2 cover.

€€   It's pronounced *quaranta ladroni,* and the name means "40 thieves," but you'll never feel robbed at this pleasant little find, **Osteria Ai 40 Ladroni** (Fondamenta della Sensa, Cannaregio 3253; ☎ 041-715736; closed Mon), where the food surpasses expectations even if service is ho-hum and you're relying on the buzz of other patrons for atmosphere. Luckily, locals from the area (the "real" Venice) tend to come here in a celebratory frame of mind. During lunch (which is quieter), old men from the neighborhood gather to gossip and greet passersby. You should definitely book a canal-side table if you're planning dinner here. Try their excellent *sarde in saor* (€7) to start, and then choose either a *primo* or *secondo* dish. Most of the *primi* are pastas costing around €8; their spaghetti bolognese is excellent, as is spaghetti with *seppie,* which is cuttlefish in black ink sauce (remember to add heaps of the excellent, fresh Parmesan). *Secondi* comprise a good selection of grilled and fried fish (€10–€13).

€€   Practically next door to 40 Ladroni is another favorite spot, **Anice Stellato** ★ (Fondamenta della Sensa, Cannaregio 3272; ☎ 041-720744; Wed–Sun), which is nearly always full, but is certainly worth reserving. If you can't get a table along the canal, you'll find the booths inside are just as cozy. Here, it's the unusual use of spices—recalling Venice's ancient links with Eastern trade—that adds character and flavor to traditional Venetian dishes. The menu is small and changes weekly, but is always reliable; there's usually a *cicchetti* platter with various fish items, including eel marinated in two different ways (a small platter costs about €7; a larger portion is €13). If, like me, you're fond of Japanese sashimi, you'll probably enjoy the *carpacci di pesci*—thin slices of raw fish (I'm particularly fond of the tuna and the swordfish). While the selection of seafood dishes is always first-rate, the traditional calf's liver (*fegato alla veneziana,* €12) is also excellent. *Primi* dishes cost €7 to €12; *secondi* are also reasonable at €12 to €17.

€-€€   If you keep kosher, you may become a regular at **Gam Gam** (Canal di Cannaregio, Cannaregio 1122; ☎ 041-715284; Mon–Thurs noon–10pm, Sun noon–5pm), which serves much the same fare as numerous other Venetian restaurants, but also offers falafel (€9) and homemade potato latkes with apple sauce

Make Mine a Double

If, like me, you need a stiff **espresso** to get you going in the morning, you'll be interested to know that in 1763, Venice already had over 200 coffee shops. Coffee first became known in Venice in the 1600s, when it was served as a type of medicine. The first "cafe," where coffee was served recreationally, opened in 1683, somewhere in the vicinity of the famous Caffè Florian, and it seems that the popularity of sipping the bitter liquid has never quite diminished. In the 19th century, Adolphus Trollope noted that the *caffè* played a greater part in Venetian life than in any other city. He further remarked that this was the only city in Italy where female aristocrats frequented the *caffè*. Originally called "Venice Triumphant," Florian was opened in 1720 by Floriano Francesconi, and immediately earned a powerful reputation that has kept it at the center of fashionable Venetian life ever since.

Getting your caffeine fix at either **Caffè Florian** or its archrival, **Gran Caffè Quadri,** can be expensive; you're looking at paying around €7 for a cappuccino. If you have the dough, feel free to grab a table, but know that you're really paying to join the ranks of famous and notable people who've whiled away their afternoons here. If it's simply a pick-me-up you're after, follow my lead and head to **Caffè Aurora** (right next door to Florian), being sure to stand at the bar counter while you order and drink your beverage (a shot of espresso is an acceptable €.80). I've stood at that counter with gondoliers, local policemen, and even lower-paid workers who've popped into the piazza to see what the tourists are up to, but certainly aren't keen on courting bankruptcy.

Most of Venice's more affordable cafes are far removed from the tourist chaos of St. Mark's. A favorite stop-off of mine is **Caffè Costa Rica** (☎ 041-716371), dedicated to rich and rewarding coffee beans; here the air is fragrant with coffee that's been brewing at this spot since 1930, and most of the clientele is from the neighborhood. You'll find the small cafe along Cannaregio's busy market-centered Rio Terrà San Leonardo, not far from the Ponte Guglie. Sidle up to the orange linoleum counter where rows of cups on saucers let you know that your hosts mean business; you sip (or down) your double espresso surrounded by sacks of beans imported from (among other bean-growing nations) Costa Rica. All the while, locals drift in to adjust their own caffeine levels, stopping for a spirited conversation with the friendly staff. You can also buy coffee beans, which you'll pay for by weight.

(€5.50). The fried artichokes are particularly good, and every meal should be followed by a stiff shot of Israeli grappa. Seafood dishes will set you back €13 to €17, which makes this a good value option. On Friday evenings, a Shabbat service is held, followed by a special meal, offering an opportunity to mingle with local Jews.

RESTAURANTS IN DORSODURO

€€   **Osteria Enoteca Ai Artisti** ✦ (Fondamenta della Toletta, Dorsoduro 1169/A; ☎ 041-5238944; www.enotecaartisti.com) has a handful of canal-side tables that are enormously popular in summer. Owners Vincenzo and Francesca opened this small wine bar in 2004, and it's easily the best place in Venice for a fresh, massive salad. Over and above the extensive wine menu, there's a pizza and panino selection. The daily-changing lunch menu includes such light meals as crepes with prawn and tomato salsa, or buffalo mozzarella with seasonal vegetables; each day, five *primi* dishes are on offer, which will set you back an affordable €9 to €12. *Secondi,* which are always accompanied by a side dish, cost €12 to €15. Dinner is only served on Wednesday and Saturday; other nights it's strictly *cicchetti* (€1.20–€4.50), with plenty of panini, vegetables, marinated fish, and slices of baked aubergine. You can also try the assortment of cured meats and cheeses—platters range in price from €10 to €18. Wine by the glass costs anything from €1.50 to €8, while more budget-friendly bottles of wine sell for as little as €9.

€–€€   Fortunately, there's a great deal of wine to keep you busy while you ponder the extensive menu at the large and lively **Ristorante San Trovaso** ✦ (Fondamenta Priuli, Dorsoduro 1016; ☎ 041-5230835; www.tavernasantrovaso. com; Fri–Wed noon–2:30pm and 7–9:50pm), where a bevy of young waiters carry platefuls of fish and liters of wine to an appreciative clientele. On summer evenings, grab a table outside, where you'll be rewarded with a cool breeze; don't come if you've got anything against large portions of fresh, simply prepared seafood (€10–€20)—I usually begin by ordering *cozze e vongole* (a mussel and clam antipasta), served as a veritable mountain of shellfish. *Primi* dishes cost between €5 and €11, while the meat and chicken dishes among the selection of *secondi* are slightly more expensive (€8.50–€18). All vegetarian options cost €4. House wine is served by the glass for €2.50. Note that there's a cover charge of €2.

€–€€   **Osteria Vini Padovani** (Calle dei Cerchieri, Dorsoduro 1280; ☎ 041-5236370; Mon–Fri 9am–10pm) is a superbly relaxed place for trying out traditional Venetian dishes. Owned by an ex–tennis star named Mirko, who often greets and speaks with guests while his wife, Christina, is busy behind the counter, this small restaurant with sidewalk tables attracts mainly local people who come for wine and *cicchetti* or a full-blown meal. A favorite is *fegato alla veneziana* (liver with onions), made here just the way Venetians like it. You can also sample three different preparations of swordfish. Other specialties include *baccalà* (also made with swordfish) with polenta, *sarde e saor,* and *bigoli* in salsa.

€–€€   Those two supple, naked, Barbarella-type temptresses on the place mats at **Casin dei Nobili** (Dorsoduro 2765; ☎ 041-2411841; Tues–Sun) are meant to represent the atmosphere of this fun place. Amid the bohemian drama at large animated tables, waiters prance about in burgundy aprons delivering armloads of good-value pizzas (usually with an armada of toppings) and more exotic fare to a clientele of all ages and incomes. The menu regularly includes special recommendations by the chef, such as oven-baked rabbit with rosemary, gnocchi with Gorgonzola cheese, and filleted turbot prepared with saffron and zucchini flowers. When it's busy—which it usually is—be prepared to wait up to 30 minutes or more for your pizza.

€€   Across the canal from Dorsoduro is the island of Giudecca. On its south side, amid the boatyards, is a pleasant, low-key restaurant in the upstairs portion of a warehouse, called **Mistrà** (Fondamenta Ponte Lungo, Giudecca 212/A; ☎ 041-5220743; Wed–Mon noon–3:30pm, Wed–Sun 7:30–10:30pm), which is valued as much for its views over the lagoon as for its seafood, including *sarde in saor* and *baccalà mantecato.* Generally unknown to tourists, this is a place for dining among the locals, many of them shipbuilders and gondola makers.

WHY YOU'RE HERE: THE TOP SIGHTS & ATTRACTIONS

The major problem on a visit to Venice is running out of time. Even long-time residents will claim that there is always something more to see that they have

---

Venice Itineraries

If you have only 1 day in Venice

The quickest, cheapest, and most convenient way to see a lot of Venice is to hop on a *vaporetto* and do the entire stretch of the **Grand Canal;** you'll see most of the city's finest *palazzi* and get a sense of life along the arterial highway. Start your day by boarding the boat at the train or bus station and heading in the direction of St. Mark's Square. Jump off at Rialto, and cross the bridge to visit the early-morning **fish markets.** You should still have enough time on your ticket to continue with the *vaporetto* as far as **St. Mark's Square.** Take the elevator to the top of the Campanile to scan the city, before heading back to terra firma and taking in the **Basilica** and the **Palazzo Ducale.** If possible, you should book in advance one of the Secret Itineraries tours, which is the best way to see the Doge's Palace and learn a great deal about the city (see "The Secret Life of the Doges" below). Then venture over to **Dorsoduro,** picking your way past the Teatro la Fenice and heading over the Accademia Bridge. Explore the Accademia Gallery for an overview of Venetian art. If you've got enough time, head back to St. Mark's Square and wander along Riva degli Schiavoni, stopping to admire the **Bridge of Sighs,** and enjoying the non-stop activity on the lagoon.

If you have only 2 days in Venice

If you don't have to rush through the city in a single day, try to schedule a performance at **Teatro la Fenice** on your 1 night in town, and save the Accademia for a combined tour to the nearby **Peggy Guggenheim Collection** on the second day. Then, since it's nearby, pop into the **Salute** church. From here you can catch a *vaporetto* to the San Tomà stop, getting off to visit the Scuole Grand San Rocco and nearby Santa Maria Gloriosa dei Frari. Try to leave time for simply wandering through the streets and idling in the campi; Santa Margherita Square is particularly lively, often busy with antiques markets and impromptu street performances.

somehow missed. See "Venice Itineraries" (below) for the indispensable sights for a visit of varying lengths.

EXPLORING THE GRAND CANAL

In 1498, a French envoy to Venice declared the Canal to be "the most beautiful street . . . that exists in all the world." His observation remains valid, despite the addition of motor-propelled boats, water taxis, tourist-laden gondolas, floating fruit stalls, police boats, and floating ambulances speeding up and down the privileged highway. The Grand Canal is just that—a grand watery cruise-way for observing the ceaseless activities of a floating city. Like an endlessly changing film reel, a trip along the Canal provides non-stop views of the most spectacular facades, on magnificent buildings carved from marble and stone. Some are frescoed and some are simply extraordinary in their designs; much of the architecture

If you have only 3 days in Venice

Cannaregio and Castello are refreshingly laid-back, once you get away from the main areas. Use your third day to see beautiful Carpaccios in Castello's **Scuola Dalmata di San Giorgio degli Schiavoni** and wander through its relaxed public gardens (Giardini Pubblici) for a completely different sense of the city; then head toward Cannaregio's ancient **Jewish Ghetto.** En route, explore the massive church of SS. Giovanni e Paolo and the comparatively miniscule Santa Maria dei Miracoli. While venturing along Cannaregio's **Strada Nuova,** visit Venice's Golden Palace, the Ca' d'Oro, with its important art collection, and try to time your visit for a meal at Algiubagiò, along the Fondamente Nuove.

If you have only 4 days in Venice

Use one of your days to experience **lagoon island life;** there are regular *vaporetti* to Murano, Burano, and Tortello. You'll notice the tourist numbers dropping off as you get farther away from Venice.

If you have 1 week in Venice

Rather than cram all the major sights into a shorter time, divide them up, and take time to walk through the different neighborhoods, perhaps venturing into the occasional church or low-key museum along the way. Being in Venice with enough time to savor just a fraction of its sweet, melancholic charms is a unique privilege; the trick is not to feel the constant need to rush from attraction to attraction. Explore the **Giudecca,** and visit **less touristy museums** and galleries like the Querini Stampalia, Ca' Pesaro, Ca' Rezzonica, Palazzo Mocenigo, and the Correr Museum at one end of St. Mark's Square.

Venice Attractions

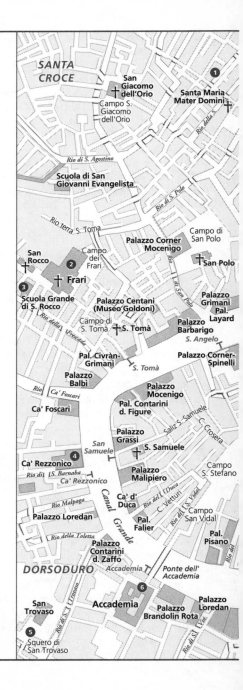

Castello & Riva degli Schiavoni

Carnevale!

Venice may not be throbbing with nightclubs and discothèques, but it has festivals and special events galore. Most famous of these is Carnival ("Carnevale di Venezia"), which in its very earliest days earned Venice a reputation as a city of outrageous hedonism. In a pagan-style inversion of social order, the Carnevale was a period of non-stop partying leading up to Lent (today it runs for the 7 days leading to Shrove Tuesday, the day before Ash Wednesday). Technically, Carnevale is derived from the Latin term for "Farewell, meat!," referring to the need to clear the pantry before the start of the Christian fast. Celebrations were first held in 1162, when a military ritual ended with the slaying of a bull and 12 pigs in Piazza San Marco. Annual festivities caught on, and the revelries soon grew into full-on bacchanalia.

Carnevale has long been associated with the wearing of masks, first documented in 1268. By the 14th century, laws were being decreed to prevent licentious behavior associated with those concealments, as gangs of masqueraders were going around town at night performing all manner of undesirable acts. In 1458, a law had to be passed to prevent men from dressing up as women in order to gain access to convents. By 1608, the Council of Ten so feared the moral decline of the Republic that it banned mask-wearing, with the exception of the days of Carnevale. It was also the only time when dancing was permitted.

Carnevale was a time of fancy-dress balls and excessive parties. In its heyday, so called Forze d'Ercole (Feats of Hercules) were enacted in St. Mark's Square, and a bullfight there culminated in the beast's decapitation before the Doge and his Dogaressa. During the "Volo," an acrobat

you'll witness today is the same that greeted that French envoy 5 centuries ago. I never cease to be impressed by the sinking, crumbling palaces made of brick and mortar but fashioned by hands that seem to have stitched lace and floating tapestries from the hard, rough materials of the building trade.

The Canal curves its way between the train and bus stations in the northwest and spills into the Bacino di San Marco (St. Mark's Basin) right in front of the Piazza San Marco. There are regular *vaporetto* stops all along it, many of them close to important palaces, museums, and other attractions; look especially for the facade of Ca' d'Oro, once the most opulent canal-side *palazzo,* and the squat, single-story *palazzo* that houses the Peggy Guggenheim Collection. The famous Rialto Bridge lies approximately halfway along the Canal, and is probably the most distinguishable feature along its length.

PIAZZA SAN MARCO, AT THE HEART OF IT ALL

Piazza San Marco (St. Mark's Square) ✪✪✪ is Venice's photographic hot spot, permanently mobbed by camera-clicking visitors drawn to the thrill of seeing the would slide along a rope strung from the top of the Bell Tower to the Palazzo Ducale's Scala dei Giganti, and present the Doge with a bouquet of flowers.

During the 18th century, Carnevale reached its pinnacle, and was deeply entrenched in the city's spirit of decadence and moral decline; the world's wealthy revelers came here to taste its infamous pleasures. Part of the allure was the sense of anonymity granted by the masks. Whether you were dressed as a character from the commedia dell'arte or something far more extravagant, no one could identify you or assess your social status; wanton flirtation and open debauchery became permissible. You can get a sense of what the streets were like during Carnevale in the film version of Henry James's *The Wings of the Dove*.

The popularity of Carnevale waned consistently until the 1930s, when it was banned outright by Mussolini. Only in 1979 did the annual event start up again. Certainly, Carnevale is not the same as it was in the 1700s; today, there's a great deal of sponsorship and marketing and expensive parties and events, not to mention hordes of perplexed tourists afraid to participate. If you want to get the best out of the experience, you'd do well to actually don a costume and mask and get out in the streets. (Be warned that for many, Carnevale is just an excuse to get drunk and misbehave—usually in and around St. Mark's Square.) Get your mask and costume from **Nicolao Atelier** (Calle del Magazin, Cannaregio 5590/a; ☎ 041-5209749), the city's largest costume-supplier. If you make a prior appointment, you can also visit the workshop, where you can see costumes being sewn.

city's most celebrated attractions: the whimsical Basilica San Marco and the urbane Palazzo Ducale, which stand side by side like some testament to the yin and yang of Venice.

I'll assume you've arrived here by boat and thus approached St. Mark's Square the way foreign dignitaries would have during the heyday of the Venetian Republic. Once you climb off the vessel (at San Marco Giardinetti *vaporetto* stop), turn right and walk just a few meters until you are standing between the two statue-capped columns that once represented the entrance to the city. These are the Columns of San Marco (topped by the winged lion of St. Mark in bronze) and San Teodoro (topped by a marble statue of the city's original patron saint standing on the sacred crocodile of Egypt).

In less civilized times (when capital punishment still prevailed in Europe; it has since been abolished throughout), open-air executions were carried out between these two columns. Public humiliations and other extreme punishments were also

Piazza San Marco

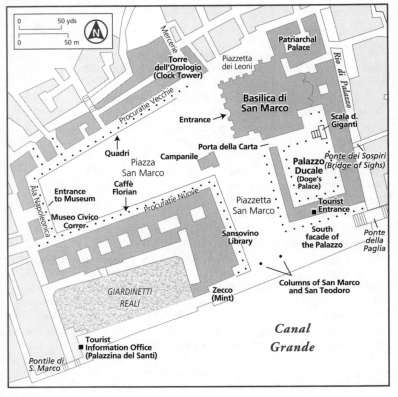

meted out here; even today, locals superstitiously refuse to walk between the two columns.

As you stand between these columns with your back to the lagoon, you'll be looking along the length of the Piazzetta dei Leoncini, with the Doge's Palace on its right, and the Biblioteca Marciana (Libreria Sansoviniana)—capped by a series of statues of gods from antiquity—on its left. Head straight through the Piazzetta, toward the Basilica, until you pass the tall Bell Tower, or Campanile. The Piazza is the pigeon-and-tourist-covered concourse that stretches out on your left.

To best appreciate the Basilica, head for the middle of the square, which is actually trapezoidal and enclosed on three sides by arcaded wings. As you stand and face the Basilica, you will have the Procuratie Vecchie on your left, the Procuratie Nuove on your right. Behind you is the Ala Napoleonica, built by Bonaparte to house a ballroom; today it forms part of the Museo Correr, which includes an impressive picture gallery. The ground floors of these buildings are mostly occupied by shops and expensive cafes.

During the Occupation of Venice, Austrian officers gathered at Grand Caffè Quadri in the Vecchie, while Venetians favored Caffè Florian across the way;

today, such political rivalry has been replaced by a more melodic battle in which the quartets and quintets of the rival cafes play competing renditions of stirring classics and Andrew Lloyd Webber favorites.

At one end of the **Procuratie Vecchie** (towards the Basilica) is the 15th-century Torre dell'Orologio (Clock Tower), which has been under repair for years but is due for public unveiling any day now. Once the scaffolding has come down, visitors will again be able to witness the hourly bell-striking performed by two large bronze Moors.

Basilica di San Marco (St. Mark's Basilica) ★★★ (☎ 041-5225205; go to www.alata.it for preferential entrance through St. Peter's Door; free admission; Apr–Sept Mon–Sat 9:30am–5pm, Sun 2–4pm, the rest of the year Mon–Sat

---

Rolling Along, Saving a Lot . . . or Not

The **Rolling Venice Card** costs only €3 and can save you a great deal; unfortunately, it's only for visitors ages 14 to 29. Besides offering considerable discounts on dining, lodging, and shopping at numerous participating businesses, the card also allows you to pay lower prices on entry to various museums, events such as the Art Biennale, and public transport. The card is valid for an entire year. It can be bought at any tourist office, as well as at certain ACTV VeLa offices and ticket kiosks; pick one up at the ACTV office at Piazzale Roma upon arrival in the city (☎ 041-2747650; daily 7am–8pm).

For visitors planning an intensive look at Venice, there's a more expensive and comprehensive discount card simply called **VENICEcard** (☎ 041-5459611; www.alata.com), but it's mostly useful because it can be delivered directly to your home (at an additional fee, of course). The organizers of the discount card advertise that you can save up to €30 per day, with the card, but you'd have to use it for accommodations, all restaurants, theater performances, and every sight in town to achieve any great savings; it is definitely not worthwhile for people under 30, who pay less and benefit more from the Rolling Venice Card.

The city has two museum cards. The first is for all the attractions around St. Mark's Square (at €11 it's a good value). The second, a so-called **Museum Pass** (€16 adult), additionally gets you into Ca' Pesaro (the city's modern-art museum), Ca' Rezzonica (the museum of 17th-c. Venice), Palazzo Mocenigo (the costume museum), Murano's glass museum (Museo del Vetro), and Burano's lace museum (Museo del Merletto). The pass is only recommended if you're in town for more than 2 days—the chances of getting to the lesser museums if you have only 2 days are slim; and, as you know, there is more to Venice than museum-hopping.

The Architecture of Venice

Venice's buildings rest on flexible but immensely sturdy foundations made of pine and oak piles, driven into the layers of sand and clay at the bottom of the lagoon. These wooden piles are packed closely together in order to form a solid enough base on which the brick or stone buildings can rest. While the water of Venice served as a natural defense against invaders, making the construction of genuine fortresses unnecessary, it also meant that the structures were always damp inside. This is why there is seldom much happening on the ground floor of canal-side buildings; not only was this a place to load and offload boatfuls of people and supplies, but the open arcades served as "breathing room" for the entire building.

10am–4pm, Sun 2–4pm) has a history infused with pirate-style adventure. In 828, the remains of St. Mark the Evangelist were smuggled out of Egypt in a cask—some say it was filled with pickled pork, others wine, but whatever the substance, it was enough to deter Muslim guards from searching the casket, paving the way for one of the greatest heists in the history of Christianity. All this chicanery is actually recorded in one of the 17th-century mosaics above the entrance (see if you can spot it on the right). Fanciful as the story sounds, St. Mark—who had foreseen Venice as his final resting place in a vision—became the city's patron saint; if you cast your eyes to the very top of the central arch above the facade, you'll see a 15th-century statue of him, attended by angels. Also above the entrance are four horses, which are actually replicas of another stolen treasure, the Quadriga gilded bronze horses stowed today inside the Basilica.

The first church on this site burned down in the 9th century. The second version was torn down so that, during the 11th century, a far more flamboyant church could be built in direct imitation of Constantinople's Basilica of the Apostles. The main structure was built according to a Greek cross plan; the Oriental additions—perhaps most evident to the untrained eye in the five bulbous, onion-capped domes of the roof—remind us of Venice's connection with Byzantium. It grew and grew over the years, to be aptly nicknamed the "Golden Church," largely thanks to the endless plunder brought back from the Orient by Venice's thrifty marine fleet. Everything from columns to capitals to friezes were filched and used for the steady upgrade of the church. Of course, the building didn't exactly suffer from local neglect, and the ongoing attempts of various wealthy nobles to out-donate each other also contributed to the immense wealth of the Basilica.

For real gilt-edged sensory overload, join the queue and step inside. The visual decadence within the most riveting and spectacularly confusing church in the world, is a must-see. The queue for the Basilica may be long, but it usually moves at a steady pace; be prepared by keeping shoulders and knees covered—this is a house of worship, after all, and you'll be scanned, briefly, for modesty, as you enter. ***Note:*** If you have brought large bags (particularly backpacks) with you, follow the signs to the left-luggage facility.

Once you're allowed inside, study the **mosaics on the ceiling** of the atrium to the right of the entrance; you'll notice scenes from the Creation depicted in circles around the cupola. Beyond this is the Zen Chapel (Cappella Zen), where the life of St. Mark is depicted in a series of 13th-century mosaics.

Just beyond the main entrance, on your immediate right as you enter the atrium, look for the steep stairway marked **Loggia dei Cavalli;** note that you'll be charged €3 when you get to the top. This fee is for admission to the Galleria della Basilica, from which you can enjoy a quite enchanting bird's-eye view of the Basilica's interior, and get a closer look at some of the ceiling mosaics; in more prudish times these high-up, out-of-the-way vantage points would have served as the women's gallery.

Adjoining the gallery is the **Museo Marciano** (10am–4pm), where the real Quadriga **bronze horses** are kept. Although their origin is believed to pre-date Byzantium, the statues were stolen from Constantinople's Hippodrome in 1204 when Venice took part in the Fourth Crusade, and brought to Venice by Doge Enrico Dandolo. Also adjoining the gallery is the balcony above the entrance to the church; from here you can look back across the piazza and experience the crowds the way Venetian doges once did as they presided over important events that took place in the piazza below.

Returning downstairs via the same narrow stairway, turn right to head into the bosom of the Basilica, an enchanting, cavernous space lit by candles and decorated to every last inch with mosaics, frescoes, statuary, marble, and religious artifacts. Beneath you, the decorative mosaic floor is warped with age, spilling out as a dramatic tapestry of patterns and scenes; meanwhile, far above you, the domed ceiling glistens with gold leaf, particularly when the midday sun manages to penetrate

> *Venice is like eating an entire box of chocolate liqueurs in one go.*
>
> —Truman Capote

what few windows there are. Over the center of the church is the Ascension Dome, decorated by a 13th-century mosaic of Christ in Glory.

Deeper into the church, toward the right, is the **Tesoro (Treasury;** €2), with its small (though priceless) exhibition of the Basilica's most important treasures; a difficult-to-follow, over-the-top audioguide is included in the admission. This is also where the actual bones, teeth, and other relics of various doges and saints are kept, causing some visitors to make references to Dan Brown, author of *The Da Vinci Code.*

More worthwhile is a visit to the **Sanctuary** (€1.50), where the main altar is believed to be built over the remains of St. Mark. Alabaster columns, carved with **New Testament scenes,** support the green marble canopy *(baldacchino)* raised high above the altar. But the main reason to visit the Sanctuary is to have access to the fabulous 10th-century Pala D'Oro; perhaps the greatest treasure in the Basilica, it's a spectacular screen featuring 255 panels painted on gold foil and framed by silver gilt. The screen is further embellished with precious stones and pearls, but is incomplete thanks to some petty theft by Napoleon.

Before leaving the Basilica—which you should visit more than once—take time to meditate in the **Capella della Madonna di Nicopeia,** on the far left side of the church. Here, the pews face the Altar of the Virgin with its valuable

Madonna of Nicopeia icon. That image of the Madonna is believed to have protected Venice in times of war. The icon itself was pillaged from Constantinople, where it had long served as protection for the Byzantine army.

The other great sight off St. Mark's Square is the justly famous **Palazzo Ducale (Doge's Palace)** ✪✪✪ (St. Mark's Square; ☎ 041-5209070; www.museicivi civeneziani.it; a Museum Card €11 for adults, allows you entry into all the museums around St. Mark's Square; Apr–Oct daily 9am–7pm, Nov–Mar 9am–5pm). Passing through the vast array of rooms and halls here is like being transported through another age; unfortunately you may have to struggle against large groups of people to really get into the spirit of things. Your best bet is to try to get inside the moment the palace opens to visitors and avoid the crowds simply by staying ahead of them. Once you've passed through the ticket turnstiles (and I repeat: do this early), turn right and head directly for The Golden Staircase, which will take you into the heart of the place (you can return to study the courtyard later). Gilt-painted, this ceremonial staircase (completed in 1559) leads up to the government chambers as well as to the Doge's Apartments.

Bear in mind that the palace was constructed to serve several functions; not only was it the seat of government and the place where Venice's very extensive administrative duties were carried out, but it was also the home of the Doge and a ceremonial palace for receiving foreign dignitaries. The over-the-top decoration of the staircase and many of the official rooms was really a form of frivolous yet functional showing off, whereby the glory and might of the Venetian Republic was rubbed solidly in the eyes of anyone who cared to visit. It's up this staircase that ambassadors and emissaries would be led en route to their meetings with the Doge and his officials. The intention of the gilt decoration and marble statuary was to display the unquestionable wealth of the Republic.

There are other architectural details that serve as compensation for size (Venice, in anyone's terms, is tiny, and as a major power had to find ways of compensating); when you look at the upper levels of the palace from the courtyard, for example, note how clever design and large shuttered windows create the impression of regal, high-ceilinged floors, while in actual fact, they are a disguise for two floors of cramped offices.

The first landing off the Golden Staircase leads to the Doge's Apartments; keep moving right, and you'll first pass through the Scarlet Chamber, which was restored in 2005, with a recently rediscovered painting by Carpaccio. Beyond the Scarlet Chamber is the **Sala delle Mappe (Hall of Maps),** housing off-kilter cartographic murals of the 16th-century world, with Venice at its center, of course. Rooms in this section of the palace give some idea of the home life of the doges and their families; the Erizzo Room, for example—with its patterned silk-covered walls—is not unlike the styling of many of Venice's three-star hotel rooms. The adjacent **Grimani Room** features a number of **paintings of the city's symbol,** including Carpaccio's *The Lion of St. Mark* (1516); note how the lion's front legs rest on land while the hind legs are on the sea, symbolizing Venetian dominion over both. While you're on this floor, find the Philosopher's Room and ask for directions to Titian's *St. Christopher,* a fresco completed in just 3 days (it's hidden high above a doorway that opens onto a dead-end stairway).

If you've been impressed by the Doge's Apartments, prepare yourself for the glorious **works of art** decorating the official spaces **upstairs;** here the city's artistic masters—including **Veronese, Tintoretto,** and **Titian**—must have worked feverishly. Start in the official waiting room—or Anticollegio—where foreign emissaries would gaze on Paolo Veronese's *Rape of Europa* while waiting to meet with their hosts. Next, enter the **Chamber of the Full Council,** where Veronese glorified Venice in various allegorical paintings. In the adjoining Sala del Senato (Senate Chamber), where 300 members met to listen to reports and debate major issues, you'll notice many renditions of Christ by Tintoretto. Here, the role of the Lord appears to be to protect the Doge, and—by inference—Venice itself.

Venice's Great Lover

The most famous convict ever to cross the Bridge of Sighs into Venice's state prisons was Giacomo Girolamo Casanova, he of bodice-ripping world renown. Casanova, who earned universal recognition as an erotic hero who made love to incomparable numbers of women (122 of these adventures are recounted in his feisty, and undoubtedly exaggerated, autobiography), was actually busy with a great many activities other than satisfying his libidinal desires. Born in 1725 to theatrical parents, he was a sickly child who demonstrated considerable intellectual prowess. Between womanizing and boozing, he managed to earn a doctorate from the University of Padua and quickly rejected any plans he once had to join the priesthood.

Frequently afflicted with all manner of sexually transmitted diseases, he managed to build a prominent public image, traveling extensively through Europe and consorting with nobles, royals, and noteworthies, despite attempts by the Inquisition to challenge his moral virtue. After the love of his life, a Frenchwoman named Henriette, abandoned him, the heartbroken stud took up a career as a writer, which was cut short when he was convicted as a magician and placed in the prisons of the Palazzo Ducale. Apparently, Casanova managed to escape the supposedly impenetrable prisons, and later claimed to have slept with the chief of police's wife on the very same night that her husband was out searching for him!

After fleeing to Paris, Casanova's celebrity was much increased; he introduced the lottery to the French capital and made himself a millionaire through gambling and cheating. Always pursued by creditors, Casanova turned to spying in his later years, and eventually ended up as a librarian in Bohemia, where he set about putting his memoirs on paper. Venice practically ignored one of its most famous sons for years until finally, in the 1990s, the city hosted a Casanova exhibition, with only the smallest attention given to his most celebrated talent—as the world's original Casanova, the ultimate "Italian stallion."

The Secret Life of the Doges

If there's one Venetian encounter worthy of a splurge, it's the **Secret Itineraries tour** ✪✪✪ (bookings only by phone at ☎ 041-5209070; €15) of the Palazzo Ducale. Led by an expert on Venetian history and culture, the tour takes a small group of visitors to some of the many rooms in the palace that are kept locked to the general public; these are the secret chambers, passages, and stairways that allowed the machinery of the Venetian state to keep working independent of the luxury show that greeted official visitors to the palace. The tour reveals how the Doge was always carefully watched and supervised by an all-powerful Council of Ten, despite the fact that the immensely wealthy Doge was personally responsible for the upkeep of the palace. You'll also discover how Venice thrived on secrets, how spies and diplomats gathered valuable information from rival states, and how documents recording this information were kept—in triplicate—in the offices and halls of the palace.

For many, the highlight of the tour is learning more about Casanova, who escaped from the prisons here after blackmailing his guard and enlisting the aid of a priest who had been imprisoned for fathering a string of children. The tour also introduces you to clever psychological tortures: Prisoners were strategically jailed where they could see and hear terrible violence being done to another accused offender—this ensured that those next in line for the same punishment would confess more readily. You'll not only explore those secret rooms where the state machinery was operated by an army of bookkeepers and administrators, but—in the roof over the largest room in the palace—you'll get a sense of the complex architectural solutions keeping it all together.

On the ceiling is Tintoretto's *Triumph of Venice* (1587–97), a beautiful exercise in forced perspective, with earth in the distance, beyond the heavenly scene. For the best view of this ceiling fresco, stand near the doorway that leads into the Sala della Quatro Ponte. From here you can pass through quickly into the Chambers of the Council of Ten, where there is more work by Veronese in the room where judgments were uttered against an accused. In the adjoining **Sala della Bussola,** a wooden stairway entrance leads to every floor in the palace. The room itself is dedicated to justice. It was here that Venice's version of the CIA met to discuss matters of state security.

An extensive armory fills the next few rooms, where you should pause to enjoy the views over the city from the open windows. From the armory, head down to the L-shaped *liagò,* where you'll find a pair of marble sculptures of Adam and Eve by Antonio Rizzo. From the *liagò,* enter the Sala del Maggior Consiglio (Hall of the Great Council), a massive space filled with magnificent paintings combining mythical, religious, and Venetian imagery; it's also where you can't miss the largest oil painting on earth, *Paradiso* by Tintoretto. Measuring 23m (75 ft.) in length, it is above the seat that would have been occupied by the Doge during sessions of the Council. Above you, on the ceiling, is Veronese's *The Triumph of Venice.*

At the far end of the hall, you'll next see a long frieze of portraits of the Republic's first 76 doges. Look carefully, and you'll spot one faceless portrait—a black veil covers the face of Doge Marin Falier, who was executed for treason against the state and consequently dishonored by having his image removed. The portraits, which continue in the adjoining Sala dello Scrutinio, are also by Domenico Tintoretto.

Now head back through the Greta Council Hall and follow the signs pointing you in the direction of the prisons. When you come upon a series of air-conditioned rooms, pause to consider the works of Hieronymus Bosch in The Chamber of the Magistrato alle Leggi, where legal regulations were considered and decided by a special council. Bosch's depiction of Hell is particularly spooky, while his idea of Heaven includes a tunnel of white light often reported by those who claim to have died and returned to life. Equally exciting is Enrico van Bles detto il Civetta's *Hell,* which contains all manner of bizarre and torturous imagery.

Having thus had a sense of the spaces in which Venice's government authorities operated, you can now try to imagine yourself a condemned prisoner by crossing the **Ponte dei Sospiri (Bridge of Sighs).** This is where convicts on their way to the prisons said farewell to freedom and headed to lengthy internment or execution. At some point, you may feel lost in a tangle of prisons and passages (it's something of a mazelike complex), but simply follow the arrows and you'll eventually reach the **Sala dei Censori (Chamber of Censors),** where the city's small council of moral consultants met. On your way out, there's a small souvenir store, and an overpriced coffee shop.

Also worth visiting around St. Mark's Square: Rooms of the **Museo Civico Correr** ★ (in the Procuratie Nuove's Ala Napoleonica, Piazza San Marco; ☎ 041-2405211; €9 adults, €7 reduced, free with San Marco Museum ticket; Apr–Oct 10am–7pm, Nov–Mar 10am–5pm) display a broad array of art and memorabilia related to the culture of Venice. Starting with the androgynous angels of the neoclassical sculptor Antonia Canova, the tour goes into 20 rooms of historical items like coins, rare manuscripts, furniture, busts, paintings, and early maps of the city (just in case you thought getting around Venice is difficult today), always highlighting the line of doges as key figures in the city's proud history.

A highlight of the tour is the air-conditioned **Quadreria picture gallery** ★★ on the second floor. Though not in the same league as the Accademia (p. 321), it provides a useful understanding of how Venetian painting developed through Byzantine, Gothic, and Renaissance periods. Among the standout paintings is the so-called "Mannerist" work of Cosmé Tura, a *Pietà* (done around 1460), in which Christ is represented as an old man. Mannerism emerged as a counter-reaction to the careful balance and proportion of the High Renaissance; artists sought to deliberately distort physical proportions and use irrational space to generate an emotional effect. Although the movement is more directly associated with Rome, Florence, and Mantua, the artists of Venice also pursued their own Mannerist course, and this is evidenced in the distinctive styles of Titian, Jacopo, Tintoretto, and visiting Greek artist Domenikos Theotokopoulos, known as El Greco. The latter is the most famous of the Greek artists who trained in Venice (their works are in Room 41). Note the exaggerated Mannerism of his *Last Supper* (1641), which attempts to suggest religious tension.

It's Not Over Till the Fat Lady Sings

Venice was home to Italy's very first opera house, the Teatro di San Cassiano (1637), which gave way to the glorious **Teatro la Fenice (The Phoenix Theater)** ✪✪ (Campo San Fantin; ☎ 041-786575; €7; English tours at 12:20 and 3:20pm) in the 18th century. Celebrated as one of the world's great indoor opera spaces, the lavish arena had an unfortunate history of burning to the ground; in 1996—160 years after the last such disaster—the world mourned when the Teatro was once again gutted by fire because of the misdeeds of two lackadaisical electricians trying to cover up unfinished repair work. They are now sitting in prison, while—after years of painstaking redesigning, hard labor, and attention to decorative and fire-safety details—La Fenice is once again staging world-class performances. Reconstruction was based on plans by architect Aldo Rossi, who died before the project was complete, but who added a massive basement with water tanks designed to prevent future pyrotechnic disasters.

Much of the finer detailing of the theater's interior was re-created using close analysis of Visconti's first color film, *Senso* (1953); the first 10 minutes were shot inside La Fenice. Enter the 1,076-seat auditorium, and you are immediately struck by the glint of 24-karat gold leaf; around 1,672 sq. m (18,000 sq. ft.) of it was used throughout the building, most of it in the auditorium, where it sets off the frescoed floating cherubs and mermaidlike busts protruding from just beneath the ceiling. Above the velveteen Molteni seats, a massive chandelier hangs as if in homage to that famous scene in *Phantom of the Opera*. The reconstruction cost in excess of €50 million. If you're at all attracted to theater, dance, and opera, you should try to attend a performance here; see my discussion in "Nightlife" on p. 333.

Downstairs, the museum's rooms are dedicated to the more frivolous aspects of Venetian social life: Board games, gambling paraphernalia, and some ladies' footwear you really wouldn't want to get your feet into—one pair has 70cm (28-in.) platforms!

Two significant "towers" are also found on Piazza San Marco. As you face the Basilica, on your right is the rather humble **Campanile di San Marco (Bell Tower of St. Mark's)** ✪, which affords a 360-degree view of the city. Join the queue for the elevator which travels up almost 100m (328 ft.) to the bell stage, where you can squeeze past other tourists for this unique look at the city in splendid panorama. Originally built in the 12th century, the Bell Tower functioned as a beacon for passing ships; in 1609, Galileo used it to demonstrate his telescope to a group of local politicians. In 1902 it actually collapsed in its entirety and was rebuilt exactly as it had been a decade later. On May 9, 1997, eight armed men claiming to be "soldiers of the serenissima Venetian government" used a truck to break down the Campanile gates so they could climb the stairs to the top and hoist the flag of St. Mark, claiming that they wished to revive the Republic, some 200 years after its demise. Needless to say, their attempt failed and they were less than popular with local authorities. (*Tip:* An alternate high-altitude view of the city is from the bell tower of the Church of San Giorgio Maggiore; it costs somewhat less and is far less crowded.)

Although only open during special exhibitions, the **Palazzo Grassi** (☎ 041-5231680; www.palazzograssi.it) on Campo San Samuel is certainly worth a visit as a latter-day example of canal-side opulence. Owned by the Fiat motor company, the 18th-century neoclassical structure was designed by Giorgio Massari.

Querini Stampalia ★★ (Santa Maria Formosa, Castello 5252; ☎ 041-2711411; www.querinistampalia.it; €6; Tues–Sun 10am–6pm) is a 15th-century *palazzo* housing a foundation for the preservation and restoration of Venetian culture and art; there's a library and a museum which is crammed with period furniture and paintings by the likes of Bellini and Giambattista Tiepolo. Besides displaying impressive Renaissance paintings and Romanesque decoration, it presents regular

Catching Rays on the Lido

The Lido of Venice is one of the places where the modern seaside vacation first became popular. In the late 1800s, wealthy Europeans came here on the advice of their doctors to enjoy the sultry air and restorative effects of ocean salt water. The famous beaches of the Lido were lined with cabanas where aristocrats and well-to-do's could strip down to their cover-all bathing suits to maintain a sense of public dignity. It was along these salubrious shores that Thomas Mann set his study in morbidity, *Death in Venice,* which Visconti refashioned as a film set in the Hotel des Bains, the ultimate turn-of-the-20th-century resort.

Today Hotel des Bains continues to attract privileged summer vacationers intent on soaking up the sun while taking a dip in the warm and—some would say—polluted waters of the Adriatic. Unfortunately, catching rays on the Lido can be a pricey business; locals and seasonal visitors fork out hefty sums to occupy a beach cabana for a day or the entire season, the cost dependent chiefly on proximity to the water's edge. Those beaches directly in front of the posh hotels charge the earth, and there is little—besides the promise of swimming alongside some Italian celebrity—to make them particularly worth your own attention.

A far better idea is to catch a bus (or hire a bicycle from Bruno Lazzari, 21B Gran Viale Santa Maria Elisabetta; ☎ 041-5268019) and head for Alberoni, at the far end of the Lido, and acquire a tan where the locals come to play. The bathing establishments here, built under Mussolini, are a popular hangout for families and also attract a sizable gay beach culture. And you won't have to rent a cabana to enjoy the sand, sea, and sexy sunbathers.

exhibitions of provocative contemporary art. Look also for weekend recitals of music of the Renaissance and baroque periods held at the Foundation; your cheap concert ticket includes entry to the museum.

ATTRACTIONS IN SAN POLO & SANTA CROCE: THE RIALTO & BEYOND

Legend has it that the Rialto is where the very idea of Venice began; it was on this high bank *(rivo alto)* that some of the first settlers sought a new life. Today, the Ponte di Rialto (Rialto Bridge), which delivers tourists and locals to the famous markets of the Rialto, is geographically more or less in the very center of the city. Linking the *sestieri* (districts) of San Marco and San Polo, it's one of only three bridges spanning the Grand Canal. Lined with shops and practically always flooded with tourists, the existing bridge was constructed of stone after the original wooden bridge collapsed a number of times.

The Rialto Markets have stood at Venice's economic center for nearly 1,000 years, and they remain an interesting early-morning outing for those interested in watching fish being sold, or in buying fruit and vegetables for themselves. The fish market is open only in the morning; and when the crowds arrive and head for the souvenir stands, being here can become a hectic experience. While in the vicinity, you may want to pop into **San Giacomo di Rialto** (Campo San Giacomo; ☎ 041-5224745; Mon–Sat 9:30am–noon and 4–6pm), the city's oldest church, founded on March 25, A.D. 421—the same day as Venice itself.

As you head north out of the Rialto market area through San Polo toward Santa Croce, you'll see **San Cassiano church** (Campo San Cassiano; ☎ 041-721408; Mon–Sat 9:45–11:30am and 4:30–7pm), unimpressive from the outside, but (if it's open) really worth poking your head inside, specifically to take a look at Tintoretto's magnificent rendition of *The Crucifixion.* Campo San Cassiano was once the center of Venice's red-light district, and many of the buildings around this part of the Rialto area were once brothels; women-for-hire would lean from windows and beckon lasciviously to potential clients passing below. The nearby Ponte delle Tette is infamously named after that display.

There's no real way of telling where San Polo ends and Santa Croce begins, but there are two attractions in the latter area that will appeal to the museum-goer.

Galleria d'Arte Moderna ★★, which is housed in the Ca' Pésaro (Fondamenta Ca' Pesaro, Santa Croce 2070; ☎ 041-5241173; €5.50; Apr–Oct Tues–Sun 10am–6pm; Nov–Mar Tues–Sun 10am–5pm), includes a selection of modern and contemporary art principally by relatively unknown Italians. I have found the selection to be rather interesting, a handsome overview of the range of developments in Italian painting and sculpture in the modern age; you'll certainly get some insight into the often ambiguous playfulness of the Italian Modernists. As you enter the museum, for example, take a look at Giacomo Manzù's *Cardinal,* sculpted in 1955 and notice how his cloak obscures our ability to decide whether he's seated or toppling over.

What many visitors to Venice don't know is that the gallery also presents works by international masters, including unheralded works from the likes of Klimt, Kandinsky, Klee, Miró, Yves Tanguy, Henry Moore, Matisse, Jean Arp, Marc Chagall, and Max Ernst. But it's a better place to learn more about the lesser

Italian artists: the unfathomable sculptures of Medardo Rosso; the strange, ghost-like nudes of Cesare Laurenti; and Felice Casorati's humorous depiction of the banal.

Right around the corner from Cà Pesaro, and almost never visited (the ticket officer has assured me of this), is **Palazzo Mocenigo** ★ (Salizzada San Stae, Santa Croce 1992; ☎ 041-721798; €4), where you're forced to ask yourself where kitsch begins and ends in a city with so much rococo and baroque. Here's another opportunity to get a sense of the decadent Venetian home interiors of the 18th century. Formerly the residence of a family that bred seven doges, it was left to the city by Count Alvise Nicolò Moncenigo, who died a half-century ago, the last in his family line; today it's a costume and textile museum (which explains the general lack of public interest) that's worth a look if only for its opulent rooms.

One of the city's major repositories of art is preserved at the **Scuola Grande di San Rocco (Confraternity of St. Roch)** ★★★ (Campo San Rocco, San Polo; ☎ 041-5234864; www.scuolagrandesanrocco.it; €5.50 for adults over 18, €4 concession; Mar 28–Nov 2 daily 9am–5:30pm, Nov 3–Mar 27 daily 10am–4pm), the city's most important guild hall, and home to some extraordinary works by Jacopo Tintoretto. The **lower gallery** features paintings dedicated to the Virgin Mary; here, in the dramatic *Slaughter of the Innocents*, notice how the bravery of the women gives a feminist edge to Tintoretto's work. The painting also demonstrates the artist's ability to capture the chaos and drama of a spectacular action sequence, executed at a time when he was grieving the loss of one of his children. Upstairs, in the Sala Grande (Great Hall), you should be impressed by what is referred to as Tintoretto's Sistine Chapel, comprising a cycle of works submitted in fulfillment of a permanent contract with the Scuola. Vivid scenes from the Old Testament grace the ceiling, while New Testament images cover the walls; the hall is dominated by the central ceiling image of *The Miracle of the Bronze Serpent*, which suggests parallels between the afflicted, snake-bitten Israelites and the victims of Venice's plague (1575–76), when the city called upon St. Roch for aid. In contrast with other Venetians artists of the time, Tintoretto opted for darker tones, downplaying the use of color in order to evoke an atmosphere of somber spiritual contemplation. John Ruskin said *La Crocifissione (The Crucifixion)* was "above all praise"; seek it out in the **Sala dell'Albergo,** a side chamber off the Great Hall, which is also where you'll find *San Rocco in Glory* (it's on the ceiling). The latter is the painting which Tintoretto used to win the commission to supply the guild with all its canvases. Tintoretto outbid his peers by donating the completed canvas to the guild rather than simply providing sketches and ideas.

If you don't want to pay to visit the Scuola, at least step within the **San Rocco church** (free admission; 7:30am–12:30pm and 3–5pm), where you can see a few consolatory canvases by Tintoretto; the best are around the main altar, where St. Roch's ashes are kept. The church also features a glorious ceiling fresco with ominous perspective drawing the viewer's eyes up to the heavens.

Once you've absorbed as much Tintoretto as you can, set aside some time to do a comparative study of works by Titian, Bellini, and Donatello at the nearby **Basilica dei Frari** ★★, known locally as Santa Maria Gloriosa dei Frari (Campo dei Frari, San Polo 3072; ☎ 041-2728618; www.basilicadeifrari.it; Mon–Sat 9am–6pm, Sun 1–6pm), which is literally just around the corner. Built by the Franciscans, this vast Gothic pile is one of those "Where do I begin?" attractions, but it should give you some sense of the stylistic and creative developments between the late 1400s and early 1500s. Titian's *Assumption of the Virgin* over the main altar, completed in 1518, makes such revolutionary use of color and style that the church initially rejected it. Ironically, it was Titian's innovative use of brilliant, dramatic colors (in contrast to Tintoretto's more somber tones) that made him the city's darling, and the Frari now houses an immense neoclassical monument in his honor; you'll find it in the nave, across from the bizarre pyramidal monument honoring the sculptor Antonio Canova.

Completely upstaged by the Frari is the under-visited **San Polo Church** on the *campo* of the same name. It may be smaller and less famous, but it includes two paintings by Tintoretto, *The Virgin and the Saints* and *The Last Supper*. The church itself hearkens back to the 9th century, but was heavily reworked in the Gothic style during the 14th and 15th centuries. It has a somewhat unusual atmosphere with some odd decorative choices, like a *Madonna and Child* adorned with a set of metal thorns.

Somewhere along the border between San Polo and Dorsoduro is Campo S. Pantalon, the site of the terribly overlooked **San Pantaleone Church** (free admission; daily 4pm–6pm), which has, in my opinion, one of the most beautifully frescoed ceilings in Venice, depicting the martyrdom of San Pantaleone. Above your head, angels seem to disappear into the receding sky in an inspired manipulation of perspective that will leave you breathless.

ATTRACTIONS IN DORSODURO

Dorsoduro is filled with art galleries where you can buy originals and prints by contemporary artists, but for lovers of modern art, there's nothing to beat a visit to the world-class **Collezione Peggy Guggenheim** ★★★ (Calle San Cristoforo, Dorsoduro 701; ☎ 041-2405411; www.guggenheim-venice.it; €10; Wed–Mon 10am–6pm). This—one of the world's finest private art collections—is housed in the unfinished one-story Palazzo Venier dei Leoni, which Peggy Guggenheim purchased in 1948. You enter Peggy's home by way of the Nasher Sculpture Garden, which includes works by Ernst, Giacometti, Henry Moore, and Jean Arp. It's here that the patron's ashes are interred along with the many dogs she owned. Her museum surveys the major art movements of the 20th century; there are over 300 pieces in the permanent collection alone.

Introduced to modern art by Marcel Duchamp (whose work is on display here), Ms. Guggenheim at one stage set out to buy one artwork every day. Determined to protect and nurture the work of her contemporaries, she gathered a major collection. She poured energy (and money) into artists she believed in, collecting some of them as lovers, or even—in the case of Max Ernst—as a husband.

The collection includes groundbreaking works by international superstars: In the Surrealist Room, Dalí's contemplation of his own sexual awakening, evidently out of his anxiety resulting from fear of castration by his father *(Birth of Liquid Desires)* hangs next to Joan Miró's somber, hallucinatory *Seated Woman II*. René Magritte's famous simultaneous evocation of night and day in *Empire of Light* also shares the space. And so it goes . . . A house full of Ernst, Dalí, Miró, Picasso, Constantin Brancusi, Marc Chagall, Piet Mondrian, Jackson Pollock, and other innovators of modern art, laid out with a deep respect for the effect the different

The Cursed Palace

Next door to Palazzo Vernier dei Leoni is one of Venice's most gossiped-about buildings, the **Palazzo Dario.** Believed to be cursed, it is also considered the city's most haunted abode. Gabriele D'Annunzio, who lived across the Grand Canal, described it as "a decrepit courtesan, bowed beneath the pomp of her baubles." Ca' Dario was built in 1486 by Giovanni Dario; it supposedly brings outrageously bad luck to anyone who lives there, tragedy often spilling over into murder and suicide. As recently as 1992, the curse apparently moved the owner to shoot himself. Woody Allen, who loves the city, was apparently considering purchasing the empty-standing property until he heard of its mysterious reputation and abandoned his plan.

styles tend to have on the viewer. There are also several rooms dedicated to Italian innovators, like the Futurist Gino Severini and little-known Mario Sironi.

An excellent audioguide is available for €5; it's narrated by the gallery's director and forcefully presents details that bring the works and their relationship to Ms. Guggenheim to life. Better still, try to join one of the **free guided tours** (☎ 041-2405440401) presented from time to time.

There's an attractive art and gift shop attached to the Guggenheim, well worth a visit (see "Shopping in Venice," later in this chapter).

Gallerie dell' Accademia: A Venice Highlight

You can take a *vaporetto* directly to the **Gallerie dell'Accademia (Accademia Gallery)** ★★★ (Campo della Carità, Dorsoduro 1050; ☎ 041-5222247; www.gallerieaccademia.org; €6.50 entrance, or €11 for a 3-museum pass; Tues–Sun 8:15am–7:15pm, Mon 8:15am–2pm), getting off at the second-to-last stop before the Grand Canal spills out into the lagoon. Alternatively, experience the buzz of congested tourist crowds by walking the well-worn route "straight" from Piazza San Marco through Campo San Stefano (look out for Venice's very own leaning tower—the campanile of Santo Stefano church), and eventually crossing the Accademia bridge, arriving just a few steps short of the Gallery.

Ironically, the world has Napoleon to thank for this splendid collection of Venetian art; the impressive display was moved here in 1807, when Bonaparte closed down the church and took over the oldest of the city's six Scuole Grande (confraternity halls), packing the building with a formidable inventory of artistic plunder from churches around the city. A detailed study of the works—displayed more or less in chronological order—gives great insight into those qualities that define various stylistic epochs, from the 13th through 18th centuries.

Passing through the automated turnstile on the first floor, your visit starts in a vast gallery where the brothers of the Scuole met under the intricate ceiling painted by Marco Cozzi in the 15th century; look carefully at the proliferation of panels featuring eight-winged angels, and you'll see that each of their faces differs slightly from the next. **Room 1** is primarily concerned with artists influenced by the Byzantine and Gothic styles. The paintings of Paolo Veneziano, who is credited with initiating the Venetian school, suggest a confluence of Eastern and Western influences; the use of gold leaf to give a sheen to the backgrounds reflects Venice's close connection with Constantinople.

Behind Lorenzo Veneziano's *Annunciation with SS Gregory, the Baptist, James and Stephen* (1371) is the stairway leading to **Room 2,** where works by early-Renaissance masters (notably Jacopo Bellini and his sons, Giovanni and Gentile) begin to show the influence of principles of perspective and realism. Vittore Carpaccio's thrilling *Crucifixion and Apotheosis of the Ten Thousand Martyrs of Mount Ararat* (1515) is a standout favorite, one where you'll swear the artist tried to include all 10,000 willing victims.

As you move through the next few rooms you'll find Giorgione's stirring studies of humanity, *La Tempesta* and *La Vecchia,* which broke ground in their use of landscape to amplify atmosphere. For many, the highlights of the Accademia are the works by Titian, who is not much represented in other galleries or museums in Venice; you'll encounter his work in **Room 6,** alongside paintings by Tintoretto and Veronese (his *Venice Receives Homage from Hercules and Ceres* is particularly noteworthy).

When you reach **Room 8,** you'll see how the use of color has grown more vivid, taking on a quite extraordinary quality; notice, for example, Negretti's sumptuous use of color in *The Assumption.*

In **Room 10,** Titian's *Pietà,* impressive for its almost Impressionistic quality, shares space with huge canvases by Veronese and Tintoretto; look for Tintoretto's study of a group of Christians stealing St. Mark's body. And carefully scan Paolo Veronese's *Feast in the House of Levi* (1573), which was commissioned as *The Last Supper,* but was considered so defamatory that the artist was hauled before the Inquisition and ordered to remove details that were thought to corrupt the biblical event; clearly, he didn't comply. In this and subsequent rooms, pay attention to the distinguishing characteristics of High Renaissance masters Tintoretto and Veronese—the former played with light and the sensation of movement to bring drama to his canvases, while the latter is noted for his striking use of bold, vibrant colors. Baroque paintings (often by non-native Venetians) occupy **Room 11.** Here, Giambattista Tiepolo's *Castigo dei Serpenti* (*Miracle of the Bronze Serpent;* 1731–32) will remind you of a Hollywood disaster movie, its epic destruction rendered on a monumental scale; the damage to the canvas is a result of the work being rolled up for 60 years.

Go into **Room 13** for a look at Titian's *Madonna and Child,* and then pause in **Room 12** to consider Francesco Zuccarelli's *Baccanale* featuring maidens dancing sexily with a number of satyrs.

Head on to **Room 20,** where massive canvases by Carpaccio, Mansueti, and Gentile Bellini depict some of the major religious-historic events that have affected Venice. Notice Bellini's rendition of Piazza San Marco as it "was" in 1496, and Carpaccio's view of the Rialto Bridge (1494). Back then it was a wooden structure; the movable midsection is visible in the painting *Miracle of the True Cross at the Rialto Bridge.*

The work of Vittore Carpaccio (1460–1526) fills **Room 21;** the nine remarkable studies are from a series depicting the legend of St. Ursula transposed into

15th-century Venice. Your tour of the Accademia ends in the **Sala dell'Albergo.** Titian's *Presentation of the Virgin at the Temple* is the masterpiece beneath the gilded ceiling.

To get the most out of the gallery, join one of the **guided tours** (Tues–Sun 11am–noon; €3 per person, €4 for 2, €1 children 6–14).

For a time-capsule peek into the lavish home environments of 18th-century Venetian nobility, visit **Ca' Rezzonico** (Fondamenta Rezzonico, Dorsoduro 3136; ☎ 041-2410100; €6.50, €4.50 reduced; Apr–Oct Wed–Mon 10am–6pm; Nov–Mar 10am–5pm), a gorgeous *palazzo* that now serves as the Museo del Settecento Veneziano (Museum of 18th-Century Venice). Ca' Rezzonica was designed by Baldassare Longhena, who cut his architectural teeth on La Salute church (below). In later years it was home to the poet Robert Browning, who lived here until his death in 1889. The museum gives visitors some idea of the material and artistic beauty that Venetian aristocrats lavished upon themselves. The baroque ballroom certainly conjures up images of all-night debauchery under a magnificent frescoed ceiling by the artist Crosato; there are more ceiling frescoes by Tiepolo in the salons. While much of the furniture and decorative rococo detail may leave you cold (there's so much extraordinary beauty in Venice), there is an important selection of work in the upstairs portrait galleries. Amid the Tiepolos, Longhis, and Tintorettos are amusing renderings of daily life that provide insight into the very different worldviews of noble and working-class Venetians.

Toward the tip of Dorsoduro, where the Grand Canal flows into the lagoon, directly across the waters from Piazza San Marco, there seems almost always to be a group of tourists relaxing on the steps of the imposing **Santa Maria della Salute** ★ (Campo della Salute, Dorsoduro; ☎ 041-2743928; www.marcianum.it; daily 9am–noon and 3:30–6pm). La Salute, as it's known, has its own *vaporetto* launch. The *campo* that stretches between its steps and the waters of the Grand Canal provides a sense of open space that is lacking in most places this close to Piazza San Marco. The 17th-century church—built on an octagonal plan in the baroque style—commemorates the city's deliverance from the plague, and honors La Salute, the Virgin Mary of Good Health.

ACROSS THE GIUDECCA CANAL

From Dorsoduro's breezy Fondamenta Zattere, you look across the lagoon to the long island of Giudecca; few tourists ever venture here, which means that it has become a popular real-estate buy for non-affluent Venetians. But low rates probably won't last; when I was last in town, Madonna was looking to purchase there, and Elton John owned the "small" yellow house right next door to Palladio's La Zitelle Church.

Giudecca has often been associated with isolation and banishment; it's where problematic citizens have been sent to cool off, where the sick have been quarantined to prevent the spread of plague, and where Michelangelo spent time in exile from Florence. Despite a somewhat run-down appearance (many of its factories have long stood abandoned), its north-facing promenade offers superb views back toward Venice, and its ghostly quiet neighborhoods make for sublime exploration—largely because they're devoid of other tourists.

Church-Hopping

Avid church enthusiasts should purchase a **Chorus Pass** (☎ 041-2750462; www.chorusvenezia.org) admitting them to a large number of Venetian churches for €9 per adult (card-holding students under 30 pay €6). This brings about significant savings when you consider that each church usually charges €2.50 for entry. Note, however, that a few important churches do not participate, so consider carefully before buying a pass; the 15 churches covered by the pass are Santa Maria del Giglio, Sant Stefano, Santa Maria Formosa, Santa Maria dei Miracoli, San Giovanni Elemosinario, San Polo, Santa Maria Gloriosa dei Frari, San Giacomo dall'Orio, San Stae, Sant'Alvise, Madonna dell'Orto, San Pietro di Castello, Santissimo Redentore, Santa Maria del Rosario (Gesuati), and San Sebastiano. With the exception of the Frari, all of these are closed to the general public on Sundays during July and August.

It's easy to forget that beautiful churches are actually active sites of worship. If you'd like a more profound understanding of the relationship between Venetian churches and the city's cultural and artistic heritage, the Chorus Association provides that through thought-provoking guided visits to some of the major houses of worship; these take place on different days of the week, depending on the church. Choose between the Frari (Mon 11:30am), San Polo (Wed 11:30am), San Sebastiano (Thurs 2:30pm), and a combined tour of Santa Maria Miracoli and Santa Maria Formosa (Fri 11:30am). Tours cost €8, excluding the price of admission to the church (usually €2.50); they only operate March through June and September through December. To reserve, call ☎ 041-2424 before 5pm on the day before your intended visit; and be sure to stipulate an English-language tour.

One building definitely worth visiting is Palladio's other Giudecca church, **Il Redentore** (Campo del Redentore; ☎ 041-2750642; €2.50; Mon–Sat 10am–5pm, Sun 1–5pm), commissioned to celebrate the end of the plague that struck Venice in 1575. The church, with its massive dome and classical facade topped by statuary figures that seem always to be giving thanks, is the most prominent building on the island.

ATTRACTIONS IN CASTELLO

After pushing through the tourist throngs of St. Mark's Square, you may find a stroll along Castello's **Riva degli Schiavoni** ✸✸ to be restorative. Passing a number of remarkable *palazzi* (now mostly expensive hotels) on your left, and the lagoon with its boat traffic and nearby islands on the right, you can walk as far as the Giardini Pubblici, where Venetians go to relax on the grass or find shade under the trees; there are always children occupying the playground. It's here that one of Venice's major international art events, **the Biennale** ✸✸✸, erects the bulk of its exhibitions, in pavilions designed and built specifically for individual contributing nations.

Just before you reach the public gardens, you'll encounter Venice's renowned shipyard, the historically significant **Arsenale,** where the city's powerful mercantile and military fleets were assembled and repaired. The shipyard is very much a city-within-a-city. In its heyday, over 15,000 men would toil here on a seemingly endless supply of ships, often for military expeditions that demanded serious armadas. Legend recalls that in its busiest times the dockyard could complete an entire ship in 24 hours, or produce 100 warships in 2 months. But since the Arsenale is now administered by the Italian Navy, visitors generally don't get to tour this most interesting and unusual sight, which in many ways was the source of the Republic's maritime power and economic vitality for several hundred years. At the 15th-century gateway, four stone lions—the spoils of war—stand guard; one of them is believed to have been taken from ancient Athens, dating back over 2 millennia. For a bare glimpse inside the Arsenale, you need to be in Venice during the Biennale (see "Festival City," later in this chapter), when part of the dockyard opens up as an exhibition space. In May, a boating festival offers another opportunity to take a look at this fabled military institution.

As far as compact attractions go, **Scuola Dalmata di San Giorgio degli Schiavoni** ★★ (Fondamenta Furlani, 3259/A Castello; €3; Tues–Sat 9:30am–12:30pm and 3:30–6pm, Sun 9:30am–12:30pm) is among my favorites, mainly for its works by Vittore Carpaccio. The Scuole was established by Venice's Slavic population. The magnificent ground-floor interior is mainly covered with Carpaccio's early-16th-century paintings of the patron saints of Dalmatia, George, Jerome, and Tryphone. Note that during festivals the Scuola is only open in the morning.

Closely associated with an infamous nunnery whose cloistered ladies allegedly abandoned their vows, **San Zaccaria (St. Zacchary)** ★ (Campo San Zaccaria; ☎ 041-5221257; Mon–Sat 10am–noon, daily 4–6pm) is a Gothic church dating back to the 9th century but dominated by Coducci's 15th-century Renaissance facade. The body of San Zaccaria is proudly displayed in a glass enclosure, but it's the finely crafted work of Giovanni Bellini that really stands out here; his *Virgin and Child Enthroned with Four Saints* is done in classic Venetian style, particularly in the use of color and shade, and the magnificence of its fine detail.

It may be difficult to imagine today, but there was a time when horses were permitted on Venice's cobblestone walkways; you'll find evidence of this in an equestrian statue on **Campo Santi Giovanni e Paolo.** Depicting Bartolomeo Colleoni, this bronze Renaissance statue is by Andrea Verrocchio, a Florentine who taught da Vinci. The canal-side *campo,* which has several restaurants, is not only popular with early-evening romantics and wine tasters, but is worth visiting (even if it's not on most itineraries) for its enormous Gothic church, **Chiesa di Santissimi Giovanni e Paolo (Church of Sts. John and Paul)** ★★ (Campo SS. Giovanni e Paolo, Castello 6363; ☎ 041-2416014 or 041-5235913; €2.50; Mon–Sat 7am–12:30pm and 3:30–7pm, Sun 3–7pm), which stands next in line after St. Mark's Basilica in terms of importance to Venice. Built by the Dominicans between the 13th and 15th centuries, it is the final resting place of numerous venerable Venetians, among them 25 doges, and Titian, the city's favorite artist.

The church stands adjacent to the city's main hospital, which features a gorgeous 15th-century facade, harking back to its days as the Scuole di San Marco; by contrast, the church facade is beguilingly simple (as well as incomplete), but includes an outstanding stained-glass window on one side, allowing the sun's rays to cast brilliantly colored patterns into the church's vast interior. Inside are excellent artworks, including canvases by Veronese and Giovanni Bellini. It was Bellini who created the altarpiece near the mortal remains of the military hero Mercantonio Bragadin. Bragadin's fate was to be skinned alive by the Turks in the late 16th century, after a noble attempt to defend Cyprus—all this is pictured in the fresco below his urn. In fact, much of the commemorative effect of the church is linked with military heroism and victory; the lovely Capella del Rosario (Rosary Chapel) was built to celebrate and remember the defeat of the Turks at Lepanto in 1571, a major victory for the Republic. The chapel you see today is not the original 16th-century version, because that was gutted by fire in the 19th century, but the paintings on the ceiling are Veronese masterpieces, and well worth a considered look.

Heading back toward St. Mark's Square from Campo SS. Giovanni e Paolo, you should try to pass through Campo S. Maria Formosa, where there's a morning market and a number of relaxing cafes. It's also the site of Venice's first Renaissance-style church, built during the late 15th century; **Santa Maria Formosa** (☎ 041-5234645; €2 or free with Chorus Pass; Mon–Sat 10am–5pm, Sun 1–5pm) was founded (legend has it) after an instruction given to St. Magnus by a particularly alluring vision of the Virgin. You can witness an allegorical representation of the church's creation in the painting behind the main altar; it's by an 18th-century female, Giulia Lama. Also look for the beautifully restored 15th-century *Triptych of the Virgin of Mercy* by Bartolomeo Vivarini set in the marble altar, opposite the entrance, to your right. To your left are more exquisite paintings—*San Sebastian* and *Santa Barbara,* among others—by Jacopo Palma il Vecchio, whose execution of facial expressions is particularly remarkable.

ATTRACTIONS IN CANNAREGIO

If you've ever wondered where Shakespeare found the connection between Venice and a Jewish moneylender, pay a visit to Cannaregio's **Jewish Ghetto** ✚. This compact island has the distinction of being the world's first ghetto neighborhood, founded in 1516. Before that time, the Jews, who had settled in Venice in the early 10th century, were scattered across the city. Many worked as moneylenders or pawnbrokers after being forced out of their other professions during the early Middle Ages. Cannaregio was chosen because it was far from the city's centers of power. The term "ghetto" is derived from the fact that there were once two foundries—or *geto,* in Venetian dialect—in this district; the term became "ghetto" in the hard pronunciation of the Ashkenazi (German) Jews. Here, inhabitants had an enforced lock-in from midnight until dawn (and were forced to pay the Christian guards who barred the two access points on and off the island), while during the day they were required to wear a yellow hat. Because the community rapidly grew—from just 700 in the 16th century up to nearly 5,000 a century later—the area became known for its unique, multistoried buildings (to deal with the overcrowding). The Jewish community was a diverse one with Jews from all over the known world gathering here, each community founding its own synagogue. You'll see today the profound contrasts between the German synagogue (the oldest of the group) and the Turkish or Spanish synagogue.

During World War II, Jewish residents again suffered abhorrent treatment; having been declared enemies of the state, 104 people were rounded up and incarcerated on the night of December 6, 1943, and subsequently nearly 250 Jews were deported from Venice to concentration camps, where most of them perished. Sadly, only eight of the deportees have returned to their home city.

In contrast with its bleak history, the open square at the heart of this Jewish quarter, Campo del Ghetto Nuovo, is now a very pleasant place to watch all manner of daily life—including tour groups getting a very thorough look at some of the leaning nine-story apartment blocks; look especially for the two Holocaust monuments by Arbit Blatas.

There are five synagogues in the Ghetto. Two of these—the Scuola Grande Tedesca and the Scuola Canton—were built in the early 16th century on the top floors of adjacent buildings, which have now become the **Museo Ebraico di Venezia (Jewish Museum;** Campo del Ghetto Nuovo, Cannaregio 2902/b; ☎ 041-715359; www.museoebraico.it; €3; Oct–May Sun–Fri 10am–5:45pm; June–Sept Sun–Fri 10am–6:45pm). The exhibits within are of mostly 17th- and 18th-century Jewish artifacts. Of special interest are the tempera-painted marriage contracts, or *ketubah.* Look also for the lavishly decorated 17th-century Torah ark—next to it is a *ketubah* dating back to 1775. To learn more about the Ghetto and to actually see its synagogues, join the hourly tours departing from the museum from 10:30am until 5:30pm (June–Sept) or until 3:30pm (Oct–May); a combined €8 ticket will get you into the museum and onto one of the Ghetto tours.

Next to the museum is **Ikona Venezia,** a well-restored exhibition space and Venice's only permanent photographic gallery. It's owned and run by the charming Ziva Kraus, a resident in Venice for more than 30 years; she's usually on-site, and is a wealth of information on what's hot and happening in the world of art.

With its entrance hidden down a side-alley off Cannaregio's main drag, you need to look for signs pointing toward **Ca' d'Oro (House of Gold)** ★ (Calle Ca' d'Oro, Cannaregio 3933), so called because it was once largely covered in gilt, which played up the ornamentation of its fanciful facade. Ca' d'Oro is considered the single **best example of Venetian Gothic** architecture (which you need to witness from the Grand Canal). It was commissioned by Marino Contarini, of one

Visiting Venice's Ancient Jewish Cemetery

If your interest in Jewish culture extends beyond museums and synagogues, you may want to visit the ancient Jewish cemetery at San Nicolò, on the Lido. The grounds were granted to Venice's Jewish community in 1386, but the cemetery was closed down in the late 18th century, and remained shut for some 300 years. Recent restoration has meant that the cemetery has now reopened and can be visited with a guided tour; these are limited to a few days per week, and only on Sundays during the winter, although you can make special arrangements by reserving a guide in advance; call ☎ 041/71-5359 for information or to make arrangements.

of the city's wealthiest families, whose talents lay in creating matchless opulence, rather than in cohering to any single, recognizable architectural style. Accordingly, there was no end to the fussy detailing he brought about through the marriage of marble and expensive ultramarine, which kept master craftsmen busy for over a decade. Today, the early-15th-century palace serves as a government museum. **Galleria Giorgio Franchetti** (☎ 041-5222349; €5, €2.50 reduced; Tues–Sun 8:15am–7:15pm, Mon 8:15am–2pm) was named in honor of the baron who went to great efforts to restore the building to its original glory, and then filled it with fascinating works of art, including some remarkable ancient pieces.

Just a stone's throw (or a right and then a left turn) from the Fondamente Nuove *vaporetto* stop, is the imposing baroque facade of the beautiful **Chiesa dei Gesuiti** (Salizzada dei Specchieri; Mon–Sat 10am–2pm and 4–7pm, Sun 4–7pm), founded in the 12th century and reconstructed as recently as the 18th century. The church follows a typical Jesuit plan, with its white interior attractively inlaid with green marble and gilded stuccowork unique to Venice. Capped by sumptuous domes and a spectacular vaulted ceiling, it includes a number of lovely paintings; standouts are Jacopo Tintoretto's *Assumption of the Virgin,* and, to the left-hand side of the church entrance, Titian's somber *Martyrdom of Saint Lorenzo.* The main altar alone is worth the visit, particularly for the unusual representation of Christ holding a cross and sitting on a globe.

Of the Venetians whom I have pressed to name their favorite church, many are quick to cite **San Maria dei Miracoli** ★ (Rio dei Mirocoli; €2.50; Mon–Sat 10am–5pm, Sun 1–5pm). Despite an unprepossessing exterior, it has multihued marble throughout its rooms—lovely pinks, grays, and whites—and an impressive dome. Designed by Pietro Lombardo (and built 1481–89), it typifies Venetian Renaissance architecture, of which Lombardo became a master in his later life. You'll enter a beguilingly simple space, but look up at the vaulted ceiling and observe the 17th-century paintings of the prophets by Pier Maria Pennacchi and his students (it wouldn't hurt to have a pair of opera glasses or small binoculars with you). Very popular for weddings (it must be the pink and white marble!), the church takes its name from a precious icon of the Virgin (you'll see it above the altar) that was said to be responsible for a series of miracles in the 1470s.

One of the city's less frequented attractions is **Palazzo Labia** (Campo San Geremia, Cannaregio 275; ☎ 041-781277 to arrange a free visit; usually Wed–Fri between 3 and 4pm), once the home of Venice's flashiest family, known during the 18th century for their extravagant displays of opulence; allegedly, the Labias would throw furniture and jewels from their palace windows into the Grand Canal, to prove how little material wealth meant to them. You won't encounter gold tumbling from the windows of what is now home to a major Italian media corporation, but you can still visit the exquisite ballroom dominated by frescoes of Antony and Cleopatra by Giambattista Tiepolo. His portrayal of the Egyptian queen throwing pearls into vinegar is a wonderful echo of the Labia family's extravagant displays of wealth.

THE OTHER VENICE

In a city almost wholly devoted to the tourist trade, is it possible for the visitor to experience some of the life known to residents? It's not very easy.

Local activities include cycling on the Lido, or getting involved with one of the boating regattas staged during the rowing season; the non-competitive **Vogalonga Regatta** is held in May and has been one of the highlights of the Venetian calendar for over 3 decades. Just imagine being on one of the 1,500 man-powered boats that race out of St. Mark's Basin to remind Venetians of the continuing problem generated by the increasing number of engine-powered boats. Boats of every conceivable variety, shape, and size (as long as they can be rowed by humans, rather than powered by motors) gather in the waters opposite the entrance to the Doge's Palace; they then set off on a course that's roughly 30km (19 miles) in length, winding between a number of the lagoon islands and back to the Punta della Dogana via the Rio di Cannaregio. Most of the competitors belong to the local rowing clubs, but the number of foreign participants has been increasing steadily over the years; the regatta allows participants a unique opportunity to explore the lagoon and the city in a whole new way, all the while enjoying the spirited excitement of racing (but not really competing) against rowers and fun-lovers who include gondoliers, hard-training sportsmen, and locals in love with the city. To register for the event, visit **www.vogalonga.it**, where you'll also find links to rowing clubs that will help you find a vessel you can use for the event.

You can also let someone else do the rowing—a female gondolier, to be specific. Alex Hai came to Venice and fell in love. Not only with the city but also with the gondola. For years, Alex studied and practiced the art of the gondolier, and finally qualified for the stringent exams that protect the ancient craft. Unfortunately, gondoliers are nearly always Venetian-born, and certainly always male. Alex is neither, being a foreigner and a woman. While the rule book does not officially discriminate against women, the traditionalist men who control the examining body simply changed the rules each time Alex sat for the examination, and so she was repeatedly made to fail, a brutish political move that was to ensure that no woman ever again dare to covet the life of a gondolier.

But Alex persisted, and in July 2005, I attended a party to celebrate the imminent launch of her own gondola. She had earlier told me that she would take her gondola to the canals even if it took her the rest of her life. The good news is that Alex has achieved her dream, and is now available to travelers seeking **a very different gondola experience.** Alex is determined to bring romance back to what has become a hard-driving business. If you're keen to do it, Alex will also allow you to try your hand at steering the gondola, so you can grasp the difficulty of handling something that seems so marvelously simple, and her rides will take you to unexpected corners of the city. You can contact Alex directly, through her Association, Incantesimo Veneziano (☎ 348-3029067; alex@gondoliera.com).

The ancient art of gondola-building is dying, and the demand for the black-lacquered craft so intimately associated with Venice now far outstrips the ability of the few remaining master builders to supply them. Thom Price came from North Carolina a few years back, hoping to learn the boat-building technique as part of his college training; instead he opened his own building yard, and now actually runs courses in the basics of gondola building.

The opportunity to spend time in a real *squero* (boatyard) is unique. Workshops last 1-week and include demonstration **courses** for a thorough understanding **of how gondolas are made** and how they operate; there are even lessons in Venetian rowing, so this is not just for those of you who are handy with a power tool. The group spends mornings in the *squero,* while afternoons are devoted to visits around the city that further enhance visitors' appreciation of what makes Venice tick. You get to see the city's attractions in a whole new light, and meet artisans working on gondola-related crafts. This is a surefire way to feel less like an observer of Venetian culture, and more like someone who's actively involved. The bad news is that courses at the Squero Canaletto are infrequent and limited to 12 participants; this means doing some serious planning for your Venice trip. Contact Thom through his website (www.squero.com), or call when you're in town (☎ 041-2413963).

Finally, if you'd prefer something a little less physical, you might want to consider learning one of Venice's popular crafts. At **Ebrû,** on Campo Santo Stefano (San Marco 3471; ☎ 041-5238830; www.albertovalese-ebru.com), you can attend a variety of **classes in marble-paper production,** presented by the shop's owner, Alberto Valese. Paper-marbling is a technique that came to Venice from Persia via Turkey over 400 years ago; it involves creating elaborate, colorful motifs that imitate the veins in marble or stone in order to create a decorative effect on paper. Valese has been practicing this craft for decades and has exhibited around the world; classes take place at his home in Castello, accompanied by snacks and wine. A 3-hour introductory course costs €100. Weeklong intensive courses cost €350.

SHOPPING

Venice is wondrously overpriced. Everywhere you turn, some delightful item is available for purchase, and nine times out of ten, the price tag will be well over the normal market value. Retain your sanity by seeking out only those items that can't be found in any other city. When it comes to classic, quality goods like one-of-a-kind Murano glassware or a custom-made leather-bound book, then and only then should you open your wallet or purse. There's a great deal of craftsmanship worth investing in, but you'd best be on your toes.

The key to finding a good deal in Venice is to shop where tourists are not expected. If you can find an off-the-beaten-track shop in this city, the chances are you'll strike a bargain.

Venice's original markets are those of the Rialto, operating for over 1,000 years, and selling fresh produce and fish. While the fish market closes early, the numerous stalls vying for the tourist trade remain open all day; avoid these. You should also avoid spending your money anywhere in the vicinity of St. Mark's Square; browse if you must, but be warned that prices are high, and quality is largely dubious.

Fun Stores

Shopping really shouldn't be a chore, but in tourist-infested areas, it's easy to become jaded by the profusion of junk on offer as "unique" or "arty." To enjoy shopping here, tone down your expectations and indulge your more playful side, by taking time to appreciate the unusual, the unexpected, and the downright silly, bearing in mind that you need not buy anything at all.

ART, ANTIQUES & COLLECTIBLE ODDITIES

If there's one piece of kitsch that's worth considering, it has to be the striking Calendario dei Gondolieri (Calendar of the Gondoliers) available at just about every souvenir cart in town since 2002. The calendars are the brainchild of Piero Pazzi, and while they may not be Pirelli standard, the black-and-white images of 12 dashing young oarsmen will certainly remind you of your stay. Try the stands on the Dorsoduro side of the Accademia Bridge.

Dorsoduro is popping with art galleries and showrooms; at **BAC Art Studio** (S. Vio, Dorsoduro 862; ☎ 041-5228171; www.bacart.com) you can see posters being manufactured on the in-store press. Among the many lovely prints and original paintings, you'll find a large number of homoerotic angels by the artist Baruffaldi, and surreal images of the bespectacled bald man repeatedly painted by David Dalla, whose work is exhibited widely around the world.

I'm usually suspicious of gallery stores, but the **Museum Shop** (☎ 041-2405410; shop@guggenheim-venice.it) attached to the Peggy Guggenheim Collection (and directly managed by it) stocks some unique items. Besides the expected spate of arty reproductions, clever souvenirs, and elegant books (including an excellent children's guide to Venice), this is the place to pick up a pair of Peggy Guggenheim sunglasses, manufactured by Sàfilo, as well as a pair of leather open-toed sandals, manufactured by Rossimoda in gold and silver, and based on Ms. Guggenheim's very own design. For real Peggy G. fans, the shop also stocks copies of the millionaire's memoirs, *Out of this Century—Confessions of an Art Addict.*

For visitors who take their art far less seriously than Ms. Guggenheim did, there's **Art for Serious People** (Ramo dei Fuseri, San Marco 1862; ☎ 0415239884; www.dinodezorzi.com), where the emphasis is on getting a smile from passersby. The artist here is Dino de Zorzi, the London-born son of a gondolier. Dino works in Venice for most of the year, and attempts to paint with "the eyes of an adult and the hands of a child." His three-dimensional idiosyncratic artworks combine acrylic and silicone on wood, and though they make no pretense to be high art, they are delightful and fun, just like their creator.

If you are after more serious, collectible works, **Venezia, le stampe** (Calle Teatro Goldoni, San Marco 4606/B; ☎ 041-5234318) stocks a formidable range of antique prints, including original historic maps of Venice, etchings of *palazzi,* and architectural motifs.

One of the more unusual stores in Venice is **Forma** (Campo San Rocco, San Polo 3044; ☎ 041-5231794; 10am–6:30pm), promoting itself as the "Jurassic Shop." Forma stocks fossils, precious rocks, and geological finds, and also such bizarrely ornamental collectibles as crocodile skulls and butterflies. Perhaps it's strictly for collectors, but if you have a bent for archaeology, you'll find the store fascinating and well worth a look-see while you're near the Frari.

BOOKS

Libreria Mondadori (San Marco 1345; ☎ 041-5222193) is the largest bookstore in Venice, and can easily keep you browsing for hours; there's an excellent selection of tomes on the city, its history, and its art. Cultural events and book talks are occasionally held in the store's events area. Its management also often sets up a tent in summer directly in front of the train station, to display all manner of coffee-table books and academic works dealing with different aspects of Venetian life, culture, architecture, and art; come browsing here first for huge savings.

GLASSWARE & HANDICRAFTS

On the island of Giudecca, a restored 15th-century convent has become a center for Venetian artisans, who have banded together to establish a Venetian craft laboratory, **SS. Cosma e Damiano** (Giudecca 621/B-17). Here, you can see blacksmiths, glassblowers, and paper- and mask-makers in action, and possibly negotiate a good deal directly from the artist. The center also hosts fine artists, and there are plans to have an in-house theater association. For information, contact Ljupka Deleva, one of the resident artists (☎ 348-01055823).

For upmarket goods at a sensible price, **Marina e Susanna Sent** (Campo San Vio, Dorsoduro 669; ☎ 041-5200205; closed Tues and Sun in winter) is a fab boutique with classy, contemporary Murano glass sculptures and vases, colorful leather handbags, and unique glass jewelry.

Crossing the Rialto Bridge can drive you crazy if you encounter slow-moving hordes of tourists unable to decide in which direction to move; but there's one reason to make a point of stopping here—a visit to **Rivoaltus Legatoria** (Ponte di Rialto 11; ☎ 041-5236195; daily 10am–7:30pm). This is Venice's original handbound leather-journal and book emporium, which owes its success as much to superior craftsmanship as it does to Wanda and Giorgio Scarpa, the dutiful husband-and-wife team who've been here since the 1970s. Pick up a ready-made notebook or photo album for those special Venetian memories, or have that extra-special journal made-to-order.

Ebrû, on Campo Santo Stefano (San Marco 3471; ☎ 041-5238830; www.albertovalese-ebru.com), sells handcrafted marbled paper and original Venetian silks; it's well worth a visit for that more refined gift.

Ketty Parma is a young artist who, for nearly a decade, has been an innovator in traditional Venetian painting techniques. Her mosaics—made with handmade glass from Orsoni in the Ghetto—are stunning. Pay a visit to Ketty's small shop, simply for a taste of what it means to be an honest, hard-working artist in Venice; it's called **Alice Fine Arts Gallery 2** (Salizzada S. Antonin, Castello 3541/A; ☎ 041-5206790), and is an offshoot of her family's other gallery, **Alice in Wonderland** (Via Garibaldi, Castello 1639; ☎ 041-5287616; www.alicefinearts.com). Besides her own artwork, Ketty stocks authentic Murano glassware by Orlando Zonara, a 73-year-old glassmaker whose experience in the craft makes his work worth looking out for.

Just a few meters from the Guggenheim is **Dimitri Giannina and Ruth M. Scheibler's hic mosaico** (San Vio, Dorsoduro 717; www.hicmosaico.com; Thurs–Tues 9am–1pm and 2–7pm), a fascinating gallery of all things mosaic; there's even a selection of jewelry.

MASKS, COSTUMES & CLOTHING

Right near Campo dei Santi Giovanni e Paolo is **Laboratorio Artigiano Maschere** (Calle Barbaria delle Tole, Castello 6657; ☎ 041-5223110); working here is Giorgio Clanetti, one of several major figures responsible for reviving the Venetian art of mask-making.

Arguably the finest mask shop in Venice, **Ca' Macana Venezia** (Calle de le Boteghe, Dorsoduro 3172; ☎ 041-2776142; www.camacana.com), has such a good reputation that it was chosen to supply the masks worn in the orgy sequences in Stanley Kubrick's *Eyes Wide Shut*. You can attend mask-making courses here. The shop also sells gorgeous kaleidoscopes.

Family-owned and -operated **Schegge di Arlecchino** (Calle Longa, Castello 6185; ☎ 041-5225789; 10am–10pm), just off Campo Santa Maria Formosa, is another good place to study Venice's almost infinite variety of masks designed for Carnevale, and to buy one to take home with you. Delicately decorated masks are designed by Annalisa, who has been practicing her craft for the last 35 years; she's usually on-site hard at work, but is happy to talk with visitors about her masks.

You can also find some lovely leather and papier-mâché masks at **La Pietra Filosofale** (Frezzeria, San Marco 1735; ☎ 041528-5885), which carries many of the most unusual designs. For technophiles, there's a whole range of futuristic masks using wires and fuses. The small workshop also produces puppets, and makes for an entertaining visit; the last time I was here, one of the two owners played the guitar while his partner hummed along while working on his latest design.

If you're keen on one of those fun, funky shops found around Miami's South Beach, pop into **Penny Lane** (along Santa Croce's Salizzada S. Pantalon; ☎ 041-5244134), where you'll find new, vintage, and secondhand clothing stocked by the young owners, Luisa and Piero, who have a deep-seated aversion to what they call Italian fashion's obsession with Dolce & Gabbana. Although the space is small, you can browse for ages, while listening to old-flavored rock 'n' roll, searching for jewelry, bongs, cushions, and Dragonfly shirts with bright purple images of Jimi Hendrix—all very anti-Venetian!

Custom-made ("bespoke") shoes and original hats are what Venetian cobbler **Giovanna Zanella** (Campo San Lio, Castello 5641; ☎ 041-5235500) makes in her shop near the Rialto; take a look if you don't mind paying from around €150 for excellent quality apparel. Speak to Giovanna about those strange-looking slippers you'll see in shop windows; they're called *furlanes,* and are traditional gondoliers' shoes of velvet and brocade, available in various colors. Authentic *furlanes* have soles made from recycled bicycle tires.

NIGHTLIFE

The first source for all entertainment and nightlife needs is **HelloVenezia** (☎ 041-2424; www.hellovenezia.it; daily 7:30am–8pm), a hot line service that deals with ticketing and provides information about most cultural events, including the Biennale and shows at the various theaters.

FOR THE CULTURALLY INCLINED

No indoor experience can take your breath away quite like an evening at one of the world's great opera houses; my favorite night out in Venice invariably involves a presentation at **Teatro la Fenice** ★★★ (Campo San Fantin, San Marco 1965; ☎ 041-786575; www.teatrolafenice.it); there's a full program most of the year, and the main theater attracts some of the world's biggest names. Check out the program online in advance of your visit, and don't dally in making reservations.

Festival City

Revelries inspired by spiritual events are significant in the calendars of Venetians. Chief among these is the **Festa del Redentore,** held during the third week in July in celebration of the end of the tragic plague that crept through the city during the 16th century, killing upwards of 50,000 Venetians. Besides watching the fireworks (best seen from a boat on the lagoon), you can join in the celebrations by crossing the temporary bridge set up for the festival between Zattere and the island of Giudecca, where the Redentore church serves as a reminder of the city's salvation. During the original years of the celebration, the procession would have been led by the Doge himself, and the 311m (1,020-ft.) bridge would have been built on gondolas; today, there is no Doge, and heavier, more manageable barges are used for the construction of the bridge. The all-night event is usually accompanied by picnics and much drinking of wine. At sunrise, many of the younger revelers row out to the Lido.

The **Mostra Internazionale d'Arte Cinematographica (Venice Film Festival; ☎ 041-5218711; www.labiennale.org; from €5 a ticket)** is second only to Cannes as a center for European glamour, attended by movie stars and other celebrities from all over the world. Continuing for 12 days, the festival gets underway in late August and is centered on the Lido's Palazzo del Cinema. You can get in on some of the action by attending one of the public screenings.

Venice's **Esposizione Internazionale d'Arte della Biennale di Venezia (Art Biennale; ☎ 041-5218828; www.labiennale.org; tickets for main events €15, or €12 reduced)** is a highlight on the world's art calendar, offering visitors the chance to see some of the most unusual and experimental art on the international scene. Some of the exhibits are spread across the city, but the two main centers are at the Giardini della Biennale, where various nations have permanent exhibition spaces designed by native architects, and at the Arsenale.

Regata Storica is Venice's popular gondolier and rowing competition, held on the first Sunday of September. Most of the city comes out to watch the colorful processions and cheer their favorite team on to victory. In May, the Vogalonga is a major non-competitive regatta in which up to 1,500 watercraft "compete," starting in St. Mark's Basin.

Su e Zo per i Ponti, held on the second Sunday in March, is Venice's very own city marathon, made extra-grueling by the fact that runners have to cope with all those bridges.

Affordable tickets for the bigger events sell fast. While with sufficient planning you can purchase seats from €20, the same seats, cheapest in the house, ascend to €60 3 weeks in advance of the performance.

Dramas and musicals performed in Italian are presented at the **Teatro Goldoni** (Calle Goldoni, San Marco 4650/B; ☎ 041-2402011; www.teatrostabileveneto.it). Programs typically include works by Italian playwrights like Luigi Pirandello and, of course, Venice's own comic genius, Carlo Goldoni. There are also Italian versions of such international names as Goethe, Neil Simon, and Edward Albee, ensuring a varied and entertaining lineup; productions are often quite innovative and visual, so the language issue needn't be a problem. **Teatro Malibran** (Calle dei Milion, Cannaregio 5013; ☎ 041-786603) is another important venue, built where Marco Polo's family once lived and operating since 1678. The Malibran shares the theatrical program of La Fenice, so check out the main website for details.

Venice's popular Vivaldi performances keep a good number of musicians from going hungry; you'll frequently come across costume-clad students handing out brochures for these nightly events, most of which include some allusion to the Venetian maestro's *Four Seasons.* Arguably the city's best performing group is **Interpreti Veneziani,** a string ensemble that has performed across the globe, and that has been active in Venice since 1987. Concerts, which center on Vivaldi, but are not entirely limited to his oeuvre, take place in **Chiesa San Vidal** (San Marco 2862/B; ☎ 041-2770561; www.interpretiveneziani.com; €22, or €17 if you're under 25; 9pm). One of the many costume-wearing concert groups is **I Musici Veneziani** (www.imusicivenziani.com; ☎ 041-5210294; €22–€32, with a €5 reduction for students under 27), which usually puts on two different kinds of shows, performing every day during summer (mid-Apr through late Aug). Patrons can typically expect either Vivaldi's *Four Seasons* or an evening of "Baroque and Opera"; performances (9pm) usually take place in the Main Hall of the Scuola Grande di San Teodoro (Campo San Salvador) near the Ponte di Rialto.

If you prefer your classical music in a spiritual context, you can attend performances by Ensemble Antonio Vivaldi in the **San Giacometto** church (☎ 041-4266559; €20; Feb to mid-July at 8:45pm) at the Rialto Bridge.

Finally, the **Venice Jazz Quartet** gives outdoor concerts from late May until early July, and indoor concerts in November and December. Performances, which take place at the Palazzo delle Prigioni, are usually on Tuesday, Thursday, Friday, and Saturday, starting at 9pm; in winter there are earlier Saturday performances at 6pm. If you're a fan of Duke Ellington, Cole Porter, Miles Davis, Gershwin, and the like, these shows are highly recommended. Tickets cost €20 to €25; visit www.collegiumducale.com or call ☎ 041-984252 for details.

DRINKING & RELAXING

Venetians love to gather at their favorite watering holes for a drink. There are seldom any set times for this indulgence; whether it's mid-morning or early evening, the locals love to savor a glass of wine or a "spritz," a concoction of Proscecco and bitters that today is unique to Venice (it was brought here by the Austrians during the occupation). If you're fond of a relaxing drink, you'll find the city is alive with possibilities. The variety is much like what you'd expect in any major city: There are classy wine bars, publike student hangouts, and extremely posh hotel and restaurant bars where prices are so outlandish I won't bother to mention them.

I'll start by discussing a few of the smartish but affordable wine bars, where you can usually choose from a selection of *cicchetti* (hors d'ouevres) to quell any pangs of hunger that may accompany your thirst. After wandering through the

Rialto markets, I like to stop off at **Muro** ✸ (San Polo 222; ☎ 041-5237495; Mon–Sat), on the relaxed Campo Bella Vienna; this small, slightly trendy wine bar has a few tables outside and a chic upstairs restaurant serving tasty but pricey dishes like filleted turbot cooked with leek in white wine, butter, and thyme. Drawn by the relaxing lounge music, I soon find myself sipping spritz at the bar (topped by olives and other snacks) and ordering olive-oil-infused *cicchetti* (€1.30–€2) as an attractive alternative to a sit-down lunch. At night, a mixed, vibrant crowd often gathers outside with a glass of wine; if you're lucky you may be entertained by a small jazz group that sometimes keeps the party going till relatively late.

A similarly classy wine bar is **Enoteca Vinus Venezia** ✸✸ (Calle del Scaleter, Dorsoduro 3961; ☎ 041-715004; 10am–midnight), situated between Campo San Margherita and Campo dei Frari. You'll recognize it by the heap of corks displayed in the window. There's a small selection of glistening *cicchetti,* and bottles of wine are set in smart cherrywood racks behind the ebony stone-bar counter. There, Ricky, the smooth-talking barman, prefers nothing better than to fill up your goblet with a sought-after vintage from the Veneto (count on paying €2.50–€5 per glass); he'll gladly make a recommendation or let you taste a vintage if you're stumped for a choice. I get very comfortable at this bar, soothed by strains of gentle jazz music, and often notice that I'm the only non-Italian, amid a very well-behaved, sophisticated crowd.

For a slightly more formal atmosphere, you'll want to head over to nearby Campo della Guerra, and **Cavatappi** ✸✸ (San Marco 525/526; ☎ 041–2960252), an attractive wine bar with small kitchen; there are cheese-and-wine tastings and occasional jazz performances; also see "Dining for All Tastes," earlier in this chapter. Another contemporary-style drinking venue, best for a large glass of white wine, is the shimmering oval counter of the **Bacaro Lounge Bar** ✸ (Salizzada San Moisè, San Marco 1348; ☎ 041-2960687; daily 10am–2am), behind the Libreria Mondadori bookstore in "San Marco Space." Or try the **Impronta Café** ✸ (Calle dei Preti Dorsoduro 3815-3817; ☎ 041-2750386), where Paduan-born owner Massimo serves wine by the glass (€2–€4) or by the bottle; you can order from a selection of panini, salads, and affordable *primi* meals. The vibe here is funky; lounge tunes, stylish contemporary furniture, and large blackboards with chalked-up wine lists remind you that it's still brand new.

If you prefer a student crowd, head over to **Campo San Margherita** ✸✸; it's a veritable hotbed for youthful hormones, and the square seems constantly to be in motion. A number of the best resto-pubs here offer agreeable, fairly affordable menus, with portions that are usually generous. Billing itself as a "restaurant and champagne lounge," **Orange** ✸ (Campo Santa Margherita 3054/A; ☎ 041-5234740; www.orangebar.it; daily until 2am) is a friendly spot to sit and watch the action on the square unravel. Here, the bar staff, with their tongue-in-cheek Mafioso T-shirts, mix generous cocktails and head-spinning spritz concoctions; or you can choose from 60 different Italian wines, and another 20 imported varieties. In 2005, Orange opened its public rooftop terrace, which means that you can enjoy open-air dining while looking down on the square. Try the oysters and raw swordfish for something extravagant, or a good old-fashioned burger.

Across the way from Orange is **Margaret Duchamp** (Santa Margherita, Dorsoduro 3019; ☎ 041-5286255), which may not be quite as chic, but certainly attracts its share of students from Ca'Foscari university; drinks here are poured with a lighter hand than at Orange. Popular with artists and students, another friendly drinking spot with an affordable dining menu is **Imagina Caffè** (Ponte dei Pugni, Santa Margherita 3126; ☎ 041-2410625), around the corner from Orange. Park at a table outside and sip your drinks while watching the ebb and flow of crowds heading in and out of the square.

Over in Castello, but not far from Piazza San Marco, **Zanzibar** ★★ (Castello 5840; ☎ 339-2006831; daily 8am–2am) is a vibey canal-side bar and *paninoteca,* with a handful of outside tables. This place rocks at the evening hour, when a cool, funky crowd gathers for spritz and cocktails; you can munch on panini while listening to upbeat lounge tunes and enjoying the flow of human traffic. Zanzibar is situated just off Campo Santa Maria Formosa (which makes it a good place to stop after visiting the churches of Santa Maria Formosa and Santi Giovanni e Paolo, nearby); it's a relaxed and cheerful place for a sit-down glass of wine (served with a smile), but remember that drinks are cheaper if you stand at the bar.

Somewhere along Calle S. Pantalon, the sound of recorded international stars will draw you away from S. Pantaleone Church and into the **Capo Horn Pub** (Dorsoduro 3740–3741; ☎ 041-5242177). Inside, you'll almost always find a crowd of students snacking away on *cicchetti* and rapidly sipping their first drinks of the evening. Later, the group heads upstairs, which becomes a promising place to meet younger Italians.

As you wander west through Dorsoduro, you won't really know when you're in San Polo, but if you do end up there, try **Taverna da Baffo** (San Polo 2346; ☎ 041-5208862) for a late-afternoon drink; there are tables inside, where the atmosphere is that of a genuine tavern. Outside tables occupy a quiet canal-side square; at night students flock here in droves.

Finally, if you're in the mood for a mellow cocktail served at a cellar-style bar, there's very relaxed drinking to be enjoyed at Dorsoduro's **Cantina del Vino "già Schiavi"** ★ (Dorsoduro 992; ☎ 041-5230034), where locals gather for the evening's first spritz, or a glass of wine. Glass in hand, you can take a seat on San Trovaso bridge outside the entrance and watch as the evening strollers gather.

In the early evening, Dorsoduro's Zattere is where many Venetians head for a stroll or jog; it's also a good place for an ice cream from the well-known **Gelati Nico** (Zattere, Dorsoduro 922; ☎ 041-5225293), which has a few tables outside. You can also head over to a bar in the green hut in front of the Società p Azioni di Navigazione (Adriatica); here students gather at the lagoon-side tables to enjoy their first drink of the evening, listening to a local band. When I was last there, three guys produced relaxing tunes with a guitar, tambourine, and set of drums.

DANCE CLUBS

Here the opportunities are few. In the heart of the student district, between Campo Santa Margherita and Campo San Barnaba, **'Round Midnight** (Calle del Squero, Dorsoduro 3102; ☎ 041-5232056) advertises itself as a "DiscoClub," but such ambitions are undermined by flyers branded with chalky images of caftan-wearing saxophonists. It usually operates on Friday, Saturday, and some Thursday nights; doors open at midnight and "dancing" continues until 4am, making it a popular meeting point for late-night revelers when the other bars close. Nearby **Club Piccolo Mondo** (Dorsoduro 1056A; ☎ 041-5200371) is a smoky, boozy,

Romance in the Piazza

It's Tuesday night and there's life on the Piazza San Marco. The sextet at Caffè Florian has moved from Vivaldi's *Four Seasons* to Ravel's *Bolero* and the assembled crowd is delighted. The music pelting out of Florian, or Grand Caffè Quadri across the way, is available absolutely free of charge. Grab your partner and dance the night away right in the heart of St. Mark's, under the stars, in one of the world's most romantic cities.

popular nightspot with a good reputation; occasionally, the DJ (Michael the Mullet) puts on a good show. Meanwhile, in Cannaregio, **Paradiso Perduto** (Fondamenta della Misericordia, Cannaregio 2640; ☎ 041-720581) is a popular restaurant attached to a mildly bohemian nightspot known as Paradise Lost. Finally, **Casanova Discothèque** (Cannaregio 158A; ☎ 041-2750199) draws a young crowd.

ISLAND HOPPING TO MURANO, BURANO & TORCELLO

Getting to the islands of the lagoon is simple, especially if you have a *vaporetto* pass for 24 or 72 hours, which will allow you to go to each of the three most-visited islands in a single day without having to worry about paying for each leg of the journey. I strongly urge you to avoid the agency-operated tours that are touted in major tourist areas.

Murano ★ is celebrated almost exclusively for its glassware; this is where many innovations were developed to give the world better qualities and types of glass and mirrors. Today, there are two levels of glassmaking: ultradesigner chic for those with hard-wearing credit cards, and cheap trinkets that—while available for purchase on the island (and in shops around Venice)—usually come from China.

You can take time to admire the craftsmanship of some of the better glass factories (which are more like art studios), but you should know that you'll be the object of a sales pitch immediately following the demonstration. Some of the showrooms are enjoyable, but there is only so much colored and textured glass you can appreciate in a day.

One of the finest producers of high-end glassware is **Vivarini** (Fondamenta Vetrai, 138; ☎ 041-739285; www.formiaglass.it or www.vivariniglass.it), where the furnace of the Mian family has produced some of the most coveted glass pieces to come off the island. Only visit the **Museo Vetrario (Museum of Glass Art;** Fondamenta Giustinian, 8; ☎ 041-739586; €4 or free with San Marco ticket; Thurs–Tues 10am–4pm, Nov–Mar open till 5pm) if you have a serious interest in the history of glass production; while there are a few unusual and eccentric pieces here, it is otherwise a very dull exhibit of lifeless glassware.

A far better reason to hang around Murano is to try one of two worthwhile restaurants. **Ristorante Ai Pianta Leoni** (Riva Longa, 25; ☎ 041-736794) is opposite the museum, across the small canal, with a terrace on the water. The cuisine is Venetian, with delicious fish and meat dishes. **Trattoria "Busa alla Torre" da Lele** (Campo S. Stefano, 3, Murano; ☎ 041-739662) is tremendously popular, possibly because of the large personality of its charitable owner. Lele developed a close relationship with New York in the wake of the September 11, 2001, terrorist attacks by setting up a trust fund for the orphaned son of one of the victims. Now he brings New York City firefighters to Venice to take part in rowing regattas.

Vaporetti leave Murano every half-hour, headed for the fishing-village island of **Burano** ★★. Dominated by lace shops, Burano will strike you as one of the most colorful places on earth. Not much happens here, but just about every house is painted a different color, creating an immensely picturesque visual palette. And it really is a quiet, restful place with real village charm. There's an interesting church across the way from the Scuola dei Merletti, the lace museum where the art of lace-making is also taught.

To really escape humanity, catch *vaporetto* no. T from Burano to the island of **Torcello** ★★, where a once-substantial population has dwindled to a farcical number below 100. Nevertheless, traces of a prosperous past (this was also where Venice's first settlers came) still exist in its churches, particularly the 11th-century **Santa Maria Assunta cathedral** (☎ 041-730119; €3; Nov–Feb daily 10am–5pm, Mar–Oct daily 10:30am–6pm), celebrated for its excellent mosaics depicting vivid scenes of tortured sinners from the Last Judgment executed in the Byzantine style. Next door, Mass is still held at Santa Fosca church, while the campanile (€3) is great for panoramic views of the island and the lagoon.

The ABCs of Venice

American Express Located at **Salizzada San Moisè, in San Marco** (☎ 041-5200844; fax 041-5229937).

Banks ATMs (known here as Bancomat) are the most convenient way of accessing funds; there are ATMs at the airport and many all over the city. Most banks are **along San Marco's Calle Larga XXII Marzo,** and also **near Campo Manin;** try to get your banking done in the morning (8:30am–1:30pm) on a weekday.

Emergencies Dial ☎ **113** for any emergency. In case of fire, dial ☎ **115.** For an ambulance or other medical emergency, dial ☎ **118.**

Hospital Venice's hospital, **SS. Giovanni e Paolo** (Campo SS. Giovanni e Paolo;

☎ 041-5294111), is in Castello, and has an emergency room. A waterborne ambulance can be dispatched from here, and will transfer patients directly during an emergency.

Internet Inquire at your hotel about the Telecom communication center, where there's free Internet for 30 minutes. San Marco's Net House is on Campo San Stefano (☎ 041-2271190) and is open from 8am until 3am; you'll pay €7 per hour, discounted for students and Rolling Venice Card holders. A popular place to log on is Casanova (Lista di Spagna, Cannaregio 158/A; (☎ 041-2750199; 9am–1:30pm), charging €7 an hour, or €4 with student ID.

Police Call ☎ **113** in case of emergency; or alert the officers at the Pronto Intervento Stranieri (Fondamenta S. Lorenzo; ☎ **041-5284666**) in cases of theft and petty crime.

Post Office Venice's central post office (on **Fodaco dei Tedeschi;** ☎ 041-5289357; Mon–Sat 8:30am–6:30pm) is **near the Rialto Bridge.**

Restrooms In a city where you'll easily spend the entire day away from your hotel, it's good to know that there are public restrooms, particularly near the major tourist areas; these cost €.50 per entry.

Telephones The **dialing code** for Venice is **041.** To place an **overseas call,** dial ☎ **170** for assistance from an operator; for **general assistance,** dial ☎ **4176.** While there are many pay phones around the city, don't expect them to work; coin-operated machines are particularly temperamental.

Tourist Offices Venice Pavilion (☎ 041-5298711; www.turismovenezia.it) is the **main tourist office,** located in a lagoon-side building **near the Giardinetti Reale,** just moments from St. Mark's Square. Other offices are in strategic positions: **at the train station** (Cannaregio; ☎ 041-5298727); **across from the entrance to the Museo Correr; in St. Mark's Square's Procuratie Nuove** (☎ 041-5298740); **at the Garage Comunale, in Piazzale Roma** (☎ 041-2411499); and **on the Lido** (San Maria Elisabetta 6/a; ☎ 041-5265721).

8

Padua, Verona & the Dolomites

See why the Veneto's art treasures are strong competitors to the attractions of more heavily visited areas.

by Keith Bain

A WINGED LION, THE SYMBOL OF ST. MARK AND THE ONCE POWERFUL Venetian Republic, will be your constant companion as you tour the Veneto, the region that lies just inland of Venice, and was once its proud vassal. "Leo" is everywhere, a reminder of how and why the region became as rich as it now is in great works of art and architecture. Back in the days when the Venetians ruled trade and the seas, such Veneto cities as Padua and Verona were carefully nurtured as centers of art. Their Venetian overlords made a heavy investment to glorify their powers by employing only the top "interior decorators" and architects—Giotto, Veronese, Titian, Tintoretto, Tiepolo, and many more—to gild the *palazzi,* villas, churches, and government buildings of the region. Their work speaks to the legacy of abundance that for centuries defined the spirit of Venice, La Serenissima.

Of course, this region was important well before the Venetians took over. Verona, in particular, has the nickname "Little Rome" for its abundance of classical ruins and fortifications that hearken back to an age when gladiators were superstars and Christians were fed to the lions.

Enhancing the appeal of the great cities of the Veneto is the nearby mountainous area of the Dolomites. Along Italy's border with Mitteleuropa, these peaks inhabit a landscape so dramatically different from the flat Veneto that they might as well be a million miles apart instead of just a few hours away by bus or train. These mountains, separating the Veneto from the Germanic Tyrol, are a playground for outdoor thrill-seekers and nature-lovers. Here, in and around towns like Cortina d'Ampezzo, some of the best skiing and mountaineering is offered in one of the finest Alpine environments on the Continent.

It's the combination of these elements—classical, Venetian, and Alpine—that makes the region such a worthy destination for those who have already experienced Italy's major tourism triumvirate of Rome, Florence, and Venice. If you only have time for one or two of the sights in the region—perhaps in a day trip from Venice—Padua should be your pick, for its lively college-town atmosphere and exquisite frescoes by Giotto (it's also a quick 20-min. train ride from Venice). Those who have more time should include Verona, one of the prettiest medieval cities in Italy (and that's no small claim), which boasts the best collection of Roman ruins north of Rome itself.

Veneto

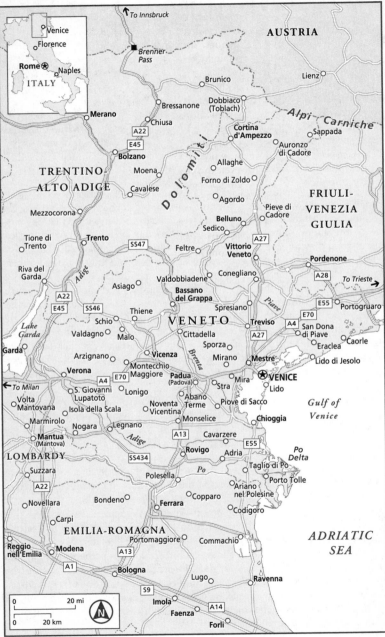

PADUA

When I first visited Padua, I arrived expecting some donkey-cart village populated by a fraternity of wizened academics, draped in ancient robes, paying eternal homage to Galileo Galilei, who taught here, at the country's second-oldest university, some 400 years ago.

My quixotic visions were quickly laid to rest when I discovered this to be very much a hip, happening city. Instead of doddering academics, I found the city's historical center to be a bustling student playground perfectly nestled among the ancient *piazze,* churches, and crumbling Roman fortifications. While thousands of young people come here to be educated, Padua receives millions of visitors paying their respects to St. Anthony, whose holy remains are enshrined in the city's fantastic, massive basilica. However, the city's most sublime crowd-puller has got to be the interior of the Scrovegni Chapel, covered with Giotto's fantastic legacy, a fresco cycle that—7 centuries ago—marked a shift in Western art.

DON'T LEAVE PADUA WITHOUT . . .

TAKING IN THE FABULOUS FRESCOES BY THE FATHER OF WESTERN ART Giotto's magical take on the drama and pathos of biblical narratives makes for Padua's finest 15 minutes. Unfortunately, that's as much time as you'll be allowed inside the Scrovegni Chapel, which is decorated with beautifully rendered episodes from the Gospels as well as a remarkable rendition of the nightmarish torments awaiting sinners condemned to eternal damnation.

RELIVING YOUR COLLEGE DAYS, THE PADUAN WAY When students at the University of Padua celebrate graduation, festivities take on a raucous, heady edge: The lively *goliardia* celebration is a blend of academic upheaval and pagan ritual that takes place in the vicinity of the **Palazzo del Bò** (p. 350). You can catch more than a passing glimpse of these public displays, usually held in July and September, after wandering through the historic courtyards of the Bò, Italy's second-oldest university, and where you'll find a statue of the world's first female university graduate. If you're not around for the graduation ceremonies, you can always join the pub-crawling students as they meander through the watering holes of the atmospheric Ghetto quarter.

PAYING YOUR RESPECTS TO BELOVED ST. ANTHONY Join the pilgrims who throng to the **Basilica di Sant'Antonio** (p. 350) to pay homage to the remains of the patron saint who is said to help bring back that which has gone missing or gotten lost. While visiting with spiritual devotees from around the world, you can take in the work of the great sculptor Donatello.

SEEING THE CITY'S MOST UNDERRATED ATTRACTION Visit the tiny, almost undetectable 12th-century **Baptistery** (p. 350), at the side of the Duomo. Here you'll discover an enchanting fresco cycle by Giusto de'Menabuoi. After your visit, you can join the beautiful people sipping drinks at the outdoor cafes at the edge of the Duomo's piazza.

A BRIEF HISTORY OF PADUA

Padua has had plenty of time to build a reputation as an important center. The Veneti tribe was settled here as early as the 6th century B.C., and in 45 B.C., the Romans set up camp here. In 602 A.D., when the Lombards marched across the Veneto, Padua was completely destroyed; only the ruins of the amphitheater, a few bridges, and parts of the city wall survive as reminders of Roman rule. Padua slowly rebuilt, taking 5 centuries to recover. By the time the university was established, in 1221, Padua had achieved political and economic stability.

Success made Padua desirable; in the early 14th century, the warring counts of the Carrara clan stepped in with new plans to put the city on the international map. A thriving city-state, Padua became a center of artistic and scientific excellence, able to lure preeminent artists like Giotto. Soon, the Carraras' expansionist passions inflamed the Venetian Republic, which was also seeking to make inland gains. So at the start of the 15th century, Venice moved on the city and absorbed it into the empire, of which it remained a part until the decline of La Serenissima, under Napoleon. After a short spell as an Austrian possession in the 19th century, Padua eventually became part of Italy in 1866.

LAY OF THE LAND

Of the **trains** leaving Venice each day, more than 80 stop in Padua, a mere 37km (23 miles) away; it's a quick journey of about 30 minutes, and you can expect to pay between €2.50 and €4.50. There are also trains connecting Verona (around 60 min.; from €2.50) and Milan (up to 3 hr.; from €11). You'll alight to find local buses waiting in the busy Piazzale Stazione; those numbered 3, 4, 8, 12, 18, A, M, and T (weekdays), or 8 and 32 (on the weekend) go downtown.

Less frequent, but equally affordable, are **buses** from Venice and Verona; these arrive at the **ACAP bus terminal** (Via Trieste, 40; ☎ 049-8241111; www.aps-online. it), which is particularly useful if you're only in town for the day because you'll get off close to the Scrovegni Chapel.

Padua's attractions are spread out, but are all generally within easy walking distance of one another; bus transport is free with the PadovaCard (p. 348).

ACCOMMODATIONS, BOTH STANDARD & NOT

If you're only in town for a short stay, I recommend staying in the center; you'll be close to most of the attractions, and will easily find a good deal. Padua also has a number of bed-and-breakfast options, and there's a hostel if you're on a very tight budget. The nearest camping site is far out of town.

Bed & Breakfasts

€€　Padua was the first city in Italy to discover bed-and-breakfasts as an alternative to traditional hotels; if you don't mind staying outside of the historical center, consider contacting the **Koko Nor Association** (Via Selva, 5; ☎ 049-8643394; www.bbkokonor.it; no credit cards), which has around 15 lodging options on its books. Most of these are homey, with an emphasis on affordability and hospitality. The great benefit is that you can use the kitchen to prepare meals, saving on hefty restaurant prices. Most of these lodgings are quite a distance from the center of Padua, however, and you'll need to consider the commute for sightseeing purposes. Through this agency, I recently stayed in Tibetan House, a large suburban apartment with Buddhist ornaments and wall-hangings, and a mellow 1970s atmosphere. There are three en suite bedrooms, a kitchen, lounge–cum–dining room, and a small terrace. While such accommodations are a good value, there were problems: My room was never serviced, my bathroom hadn't been properly cleaned, and I had to search around the apartment to find a towel. Breakfast was very much a help-yourself affair, and not very good. Koko Nor's rates vary according to facilities and proximity to the city; Tibetan House costs €70 for a double.

Hotels near the Center

€€   If you'd rather be in a hotel, you'll be glad to know that you can enjoy excellent value at **Hotel al Fagiano** ★ (Via Locatelli, 45; ☎ 049-8750073; www. alfagiano.it), which is also extremely cheerful. It's operated by the charming Amato Faggian, whose family has been in this 40-year-old hotel for 15 years, and has transformed it into something special. Guest rooms are lovely and spacious, neatly laid out, with very decent beds; upstairs rooms have timber beam ceilings and views of either the back garden or Sant'Antonio square (these rooms are particularly lovely in summer). What really makes this a standout choice, is the immense care that Amato's wife, Rosella, has taken in decorating the entire hotel (including the elevator) with her bright, contemporary collages and other artworks that may not look anything like Giotto's frescoes, but certainly echo the artistic heritage of the city. Expect to pay €77 for a double room, €55 for a single; breakfast is charged separately, and there's a €10 parking fee.

€€   Not nearly in the same league as Hotel al Fagiano, but a good €10 cheaper, is **Hotel Mignon** (Via Belludi, 22; ☎ 049-661722), which is on the road between Prato della Valle and Piazza del Santo. Guest rooms are smaller than those at Hotel al Fagiano, whose charm, flair, and professionalism Hotel Mignon can't match. Nevertheless, if you're simply looking for a decent hotel bed near the center, you could do worse.

€€€€   If you don't mind splurging, and want to be right in the heart of Padua's Ghetto, consider staying at the **Majestic Toscanelli** ★ (Via dell'Arco, 2; ☎ 049-663244; www.toscanelli.com). While there are ongoing renovations at the Majestic, it wears its dated, formal elegance with pride, clinging to its busy wallpaper and pink-green pastel trim. It's a small hotel, and many of the rooms also suffer from small bathrooms with even tinier showers. Nevertheless, the faux-antique furniture, loudly blowing air-conditioning, and views onto the streets of the Ghetto all add up to the closest thing you'll find to a hotel with historic ambience in this historic city. Double rooms go for €172 most times of the year, but last-minute specials via its website can drop the price to as little as €135 for a double (less for singles).

The Hostel Option

€   A great money-saver—if you're carrying a Hostelling International card (available on-site for €3)—is Padua's co-ed hostel, **Ostello Città di Padova** (Via Aleardi, 30; ☎ 049-8752219; www.ctgveneto.it/ostello). From Piazza Cavour it's a 1km (⅔-mile) hike, or twice that distance from the train station (to get there on foot from Piazzale Stazione, head due south along Corso Popolo, straight through the center until eventually you find yourself on Via Roma, turn right into Via Rogati, and then left into Via Aleardi, and continue to the end of the road); once there, you can rent a bike, however. There are cheap beds, costing about €15, in a large dorm (but note that you may find yourself sharing with non-travelers), or you can splurge on a four-person family room (about €60), or a prized double room (about €40). A shower and a very basic breakfast are included in the rate, but you'll have no access to your room between 9:30am and 4pm, and you'll have to observe a strict 11pm curfew, which may be a pity in this late-night student town. You can make use of in-house laundry facilities and the Internet (both charged). Reception is only open before 9:30am and after 4pm, so plan your arrival carefully. Rates are slightly higher for those who aren't Hostelling International members.

A Camping Site near Padua

€   Camping facilities are available from early March until mid-November at the **Montegrotto Terme** (Via Roma, 123/125; ☎ 049-793400; www.sportingcenter.it; no credit cards), some distance out of town. To get there, you'll need to either drive, or take a train and alight at Montegrotto, before setting off on a further 30-minute hike. Facilities are excellent (with showers and electricity connections). Rates average around €7 per person.

DINING FOR ALL TASTES

€-€€   For reliable pizza, served directly from a wood-fired oven amid a rowdy crowd of students, locals, and tourists, head for **Al Borgo** (Via Belludi, 56; ☎ 049/875-8857; Mon–Sat). Wonderfully unpretentious and conveniently located just off the Piazza del Santo, it charges decent prices for scrumptious food.

€-€€   Situated at the edge of the Prato square, **Zairo** ★ (Prato della Valle, 51; ☎ 049-663803; Tues–Sun 11:30am–3:30pm and 6:30pm–2am) is a large *osteria* with a formal indoor area and a more relaxed outdoor terrace, which can be lovely on a sunny afternoon or early evening. The clientele is a busy mix of hungry tourists and local families; when you get here, waistcoated, charmless waiters are quick to learn just how much you're willing to spend. "Ristorante? Pizzeria?" they'll inquire while looking you up and down, and then seat you according to what you intend to eat rather than where you'd like to be seated. In the evening, from around 8pm, smartly dressed locals start filling up the frescoed inside section dotted with classically inspired sculptures. Both menus are impressive, and the pizzas are quite excellent and reasonably priced; try the "Zairo" pizza for a perfect base heaped with shaved Parmesan. If you opt for the "Ristorante," there are plenty of interesting choices: marinated swordfish, goose, ham, bourguignon snails to start, a selection of homemade pastas, grilled turbot, and—if you're craving meat—a great filet topped with juicy boletus mushrooms.

€€   Also near Il Santo is the fairly elegant, if charmless, **Antica Trattoria dei Paccagnella** (Via del Santo, 113; ☎ 049-8750549), where I once asked the owner to recommend his most typically Padovani dishes. After a rigorous interrogation of the menu, he suggested the *baccalà mantecato* (dried codfish, boiled, skinned, and whipped up with olive oil, and then served with polenta), which makes a decent (though pricey) starter. Far better is Padua's traditional chicken dish, *bigoli con sugo di gallina imbriaga,* made with extra-thick spaghetti; it's wickedly good, although portions are small.

€€   In the center of town, **Ristorante Pizzeria PePen** (Piazza Cavour, 15; ☎ 049-8759483) offers a choice of indoor or outdoor seating, and a menu of pizzas and more substantial dishes that hasn't really changed in 23 years. If you're tired of pizza (which is quite average here), try the *gnocchi Verdi,* potato pasta stuffed with ricotta cheese radish and porcini mushrooms. You can also order that Paduan specialty, *fegato,* liver prepared with onions and served with polenta. Incidentally, right across from PePen is **L'Enoteca Santa Lucia** (Mon–Sat 6pm–1am) where you can choose to sample a selection of cheeses while enjoying a glass of wine.

€€€   If you're going to make an evening of it, and don't mind splurging on the best seafood in town, **Ristorante Isola di Caprera** ✹✹ (Via Marsilio di Padova, 11–15; ☎ 049-8760244; Mon–Sat) is the place worth dressing up for. Smart, classy, and certainly living up to its reputation, this place is so popular that you'll need to make reservations. Definitely.

WHY YOU'RE HERE: THE TOP SIGHTS & ATTRACTIONS

Padua's attractions are varied; it's not just Renaissance art and museums stuffed full of Roman rocks, although there's plenty of that, too. Venture through the narrow streets and alleyways of the atmospheric Ghetto, and you'll get a strong sense of history and an equally strong impression of student life. The university itself is something of an event, and its main building makes for a fascinating visit; if you hit town at the right time, the students' public graduation rituals can keep curious visitors entertained for hours. South of the center, the huge Il Santo basilica is visited by millions of pilgrims, who come to ask the city's patron saint for a blessing.

The central **tourist office** is in the Galleria Pedrocchi (☎ 049-8767927; www.apt.padova.it; Mon–Sat 9am–12:30pm and 3–7pm), where you can collect a wealth of information about the city and surrounding areas; there's also a booth on Piazza del Santo, and an office at the train station (☎ 049-8752077).

If you want an alternative look at the city, try contacting Antonio Altizio (☎ 347-7328053; aaltizio@hotmail.com); he works for Padua tourism, but occasionally indulges visitors with tours of some of the city's less familiar attractions and experiences.

Giotto's Sublime Frescoes & Nearby Museums

If you budget for only one attraction in Padua, make it the **Cappella degli Scrovegni (Scrovegni Chapel)** ✹✹✹ (Piazza Eremitani, 8, off Corso Garibaldi; ☎ 049-8204550/1 for information, or ☎ 049-2010020 to make a reservation; www.cappelladegliscrovegni.it; see below for admission fees and hours), which is decorated with Giotto's remarkable frescoes (he's widely considered the father of Renaissance art, and this chapel will show you why).

The chapel was built by Enrico Scrovegni in 1303 as a bid to try and atone for the sins of his father, a moneylender so despised that he was denied a Christian burial. (Dante features him by name in his *Inferno* in the seventh circle of hell, all rivers of boiling blood and Minotaurs, reserved for usurers, sodomites, and suicides). Enrico enlisted Giotto to cover the chapel walls in visual biblical narrative of the lives of Mary and Jesus, which he did between 1303 and 1306, bringing an experimental edge to the 38 panels here. His compositions are determinedly focused on storytelling; notice how the treatment of the space to create perspective, and the placement of the characters within that space, brings a laser-sharp focus to the central drama within each frame. Consistently, your eyes are drawn to the main action through the rhythms, lines, and character details within each picture.

From the visitor entrance, turn right and head toward the western entrance, which the Scrovegnis would have used. Interestingly, this is where Giotto chose to put his frightening fresco of *The Last Judgment*, no doubt intended as a warning to the living. In the fresco, as fiendishly imaginative and detailed as later Bosch scenes of hell, you'll witness horrendous tortures administered by hairy demonic figures, including one large monster that eats and excretes sinners. Throughout the church, notice Giotto's use of fine coloring—cobalt blues, rich reds—often in elaborate, exotic combinations. Notice also how, in nearly every fresco panel, Giotto stages an architectural device that pushes the illusion of perspective, and sets off the human figures, which have been endowed with realistic, detailed facial expressions (an innovation at the time). Pay careful attention to the panel depicting the Last Supper and you'll notice how Judas's halo is rendered black, a symbolic pointer to the betrayal (today, it is harder to perceive, as all the disciples' halos have darkened with time).

As a precautionary measure to prevent the atmospheric contamination of the frescoes, visits to the chapel are scientifically controlled, and last only 15 minutes per person. After pre-booking your visit, you'll wait in a video-viewing room for a quarter-hour air-purification process before being allowed into the chapel.

Saving with the PadovaCard

Save a bundle of euros by purchasing the **PadovaCard**, which will get you free admission into a wide range of attractions and also save you having to pay bus fare. Valid for 48 hours, or for the entire weekend if you buy it on a Friday, the ticket costs €14 and covers one adult and one child under 12. In addition to offering savings on entry at most museums, the card also attracts certain discounts at a number of shops and restaurants, on certain guided tours, bed-and-breakfast accommodations, and boat trips along the Brenta. It's a good idea to ask about discounts wherever you go in town; if you're driving, it also allows free parking in certain lots. The easiest place to purchase it is at the ticket office in the **Musei Civici Eremitani** (see below), when you should immediately book your visit to the Scrovegni Chapel. You can also contact the call center, **Telerete Nordest** (☎ 049-2010020; Mon–Fri 9am–7pm, Sat 9am–1pm).

In the same grounds as the Scrovegni Chapel, the ancient monastic cloisters of the Eremitani have become the **Musei Civici Eremitani,** which has a prestigious archaeological collection on the ground floor, and a gallery of works by the Venetian masters upstairs; Titian, Tiepolo, and Tintoretto are all featured, as are Bellini and Giorgione. Downstairs, there is a multimedia room, where you can watch a short documentary about Giotto and the Scrovegni Chapel, and learn about the career of the artist using various interactive exhibits.

The Eremitani friars were responsible for services at the nearby Eremitani Church, which you can visit to see lively frescoes by Guariento and Giusto de' Menabuoi (14th c.), as well as works by a young Andrea Mantegna (15th c.).

Entrance to the ticket office in the Musei Civici Eremitani complex is well signposted; this is where you can buy the money-saving PadovaCard (see box above). Alternatively, you'll pay €12 for joint admission to the chapel and the museums, including a mandatory €1 reservation fee. When purchasing your ticket, you must book a specific time for your chapel visit—be on time or you'll lose your chance to visit. The chapel is open 9am to 7pm year-round (excluding Jan 1, Dec 25–26, and May 1). In summer you can visit the chapel until 10pm; visits from 7 to 10pm cost €8. There's also a "Double Turn" promotional ticket for €11 plus €1 reservation fee; it's valid from 7 to 9:30pm and entitles the holder to spend 30 minutes in the chapel. When it gets busy, you may need to reserve a day in advance, but I've had no problem turning up in summer and getting an immediate chapel visit. The ticket office is open daily 9am to 7pm (Feb–Oct) and 9am–6pm (Nov–Jan).

Around the City Squares

A top activity in Padua is simply wandering from one lively square to the next; this will give you a strong sense of the very public lives led by the people who have populated Padua over the centuries. The *piazze* are where students gather between lectures, or to plot their evening on the town, which often starts out at one of the many bars or cafes.

By far the most famous cafe in town—and one of the most historically significant in Italy—is **Caffè Pedrocchi** ★ (Via VIII Febbraio, 15; ☎ 049-8781231), recognizable by its striking neoclassical entranceway guarded by two cheerless stone lions (it looks to me somewhat like an ancient temple). Designed in 1831 by Venetian architect, Giuseppe Jappelli, it was commissioned by Antonio Pedrocchi, a well-known cafe owner. It was here that students launched an uprising against Austrian rule in 1848. No visit to Padua is complete without grabbing a table on the open-air terrace of this beautiful cafe and raising an eyebrow at the passing pedestrian traffic. On Pedrocchi's upper floor, **Piano Nobile** (☎ 049-8205007) is a sort of museum to 19th-century refinement; the various rooms are decorated in different styles, kitschily drawing on Egyptian, Roman, and Greek influences. Today, parties and dinners are still hosted in the ballroom, which is dedicated to the notable musician Rossini. Also in the Piano Nobile is the recently established **Museum of the Risorgimento and of Contemporary Art** (☎ 049-8781231), which will only be of interest to history buffs with a particular bent for war stories. The exhibit covers the history of Padua from the fall of the Venetian Republic in 1797 until the Constitution of the Republic in 1948, with particular emphasis on the world wars and the impact of Mussolini.

The sheer historical weight of the centuries of learning that have gone on at the University of Padua makes a visit to its main building—the **Palazzo del Bò** ★ (Via VIII Febbraio; ☎ 049-8767927)—worthwhile. In the courtyard is a statue of the world's first female university graduate, Elena Lucrezia Corner Piscopia, who earned her philosophy degree in 1678; her feat represented a major leap in women's rights.

Bò is also home to the first permanent anatomy theater, set up in 1594; you can visit this claustrophobic-feeling circular auditorium (where medical students would witness cadavers being sliced up) by joining a tour of the Bò's most cherished rooms. These run Monday through Saturday, three times a day, and cost €3 per person; inquire at the university souvenir shop (in the Bò) about exact times, and be sure to ask what language the tour will be conducted in—on a recent visit, I found myself with a UN-affiliated guide who spoke everything but English. The tour includes the university's senate room, where velvet-upholstered seats are reserved for the institution's intellectual head-honchos; you also get to see the massive lectern built especially for Galileo, whose lectures were so popular they had to be staged in an extra-large room. The university opened in 1221, making it the second oldest in Italy.

Just steps from the Bò, pretty much slap-bang in the center of town, between Padua's markets on Piazza delle Erbe and Piazza della Frutta, is the **Palazzo della Ragione** ★ (☎ 049-8205006; €8; Feb–Oct Tues–Sun 9am–7pm, Nov–Jan 9am–6pm), originally constructed in 1218 and expanded in 1306 by one of the Eremitani monks. The vast single-room upper floor once constituted the largest upstairs hall in existence. Featuring an interesting 15th-century fresco cycle of more than 300 astrological and religious scenes by Nicola Miretto, the hall—or Il Salone—is capped by a massive wooden ceiling. It housed the law court until the late 1700s, but is now used for temporary exhibitions, often by important Italian artists. Also on permanent display is a massive wooden horse with overlarge testicles, and if that's not excitement enough, head for one of the balconies from where you can watch the scene on one of the *piazze* below; it's a wonderfully lively part of town.

On the ground floor of Il Salone is an 800-year-old covered market; between the butchers and fishmongers, you'll find coffee shops and wine merchants, where locals gather to gossip.

From Piazza delle Erbe it's a short walk along Via del Manin to Piazza del Duomo, the site of Padua's **Duomo (Cathedral;** ☎ 049-662814), supposedly built according to a plan by Michelangelo. What is worth a look here (besides the lovely students sipping drinks at the tables at the edge of the square), is the small 12th-century **Baptistery** ★★★ (☎ 049-656914; daily 10am–6pm), built in the Romanesque style; it features a mesmerizing fresco cycle by Giusto de'Menabuoi, a Florentine painter who worked here between 1375 and 1378. Entry to the Baptistery is free with the PadovaCard.

The Basilica & Surroundings

Padua's principal pilgrimage destination is the splendid **Basilica di Sant'Antonio** ★★, also known simply as **Il Santo** (Piazza del Santo; ☎ 049-8789722; Mon–Fri 6:20am–7pm in winter and 6:20–7:45pm in summer, Sat–Sun 6:20–7:45pm). This superb religious monument, completed in 1307, is topped by domes and heaven-reaching spires that cast a fantastic shadow over the square below, and suggest something of the region's Byzantine links. Inside this vast, cavernous brick church, I found myself mesmerized by the ongoing parade of serious pilgrims who had come to pay homage to their beloved St. Anthony; some had journeyed across the country, or from as far as South America to pay their respects to the saint who died just outside Padua in 1231. On the right, under a massive archway carved from marble, is the Tomba di Sant'Antonio, where pilgrims leave tokens of devotion and requests for aid from the patron saint responsible for the recovery of anything that's lost or gone missing (including fortunes, love, and health); as I watched devotees silently pray to Il Santo for aid, I quite definitely felt a surge in the energy around the tomb. Whether this is the spiritual being made manifest, or an aggregation of pure faith, the experience of being near the tomb is something quite extraordinary.

If you're lucky, one of the nuns or monks on duty will be able to chat with you in English to explain the significance of the various devotional acts happening around the church; alternatively, ask for the audio tour available at the front desk. You can also learn more about the saint's life by studying the bronze scenes around the tomb.

Some of the most important artworks in the church are the **relief carvings** and **bronze sculptures** of the high altar; these are **by Donatello,** and are said to have signaled Padua's first brush with the Renaissance in the mid-1400s. Behind the main altar is the Cappella del Tesoro, where more bits and pieces of the saint are preserved, including his tongue. St. Anthony's big day comes on June 13, when his feast is celebrated with a procession through the streets of Padua. An army of pilgrims follows his relics from the Cappella del Tesoro through town in a spectacular display of religious fervor and devotion.

Outside the church, the bronze equestrian statue is another early-Renaissance work by Donatello, his famous and important Monument to Gattamelata, which effectively altered the history of sculptural casting, not least of all because of its immense proportions.

If you head southwest from the Basilica, along Via Luca Belludi, you'll come upon the **Prato della Valle,** a large square famous more for its size than for anything else (until Russia joined Europe, it was the largest square on the Continent, an honor that now belongs to Moscow's Red Square). Now a recreational park, where families, students, and joggers spend time relaxing, sunbathing, playing ball, or attending small concerts, this elliptical expanse of paved tracks, pathways, a fountain, and grassy areas was originally a Roman theater. It's best on weekends, when the citizenry descends, and on Saturdays, when it hosts a lively market.

THE OTHER PADUA

My favorite Padua activity is watching the students celebrate upon receiving their hard-earned degrees. Despite the earnestness of the institution they attend, the graduation party is nothing short of medieval debauchery. The poor graduate's friends create massive posters depicting the "victim" of the ritual as a caricature surrounded by an uncensored history of his or her university adventures; judging from the lurid pictures, much of this revolves around sexual experimentation.

Dressed in a hideously unfetching outfit (perhaps a pair of underpants and rubber gloves), the candidate undergoes a variety of humiliating tortures, all the while being fed deadly alcoholic concoctions, much to the glee of the assembled crowd. It's a far cry from togas and mortar boards, and it says a great deal about the local sense of fun. You can catch sight of these ritualistically unceremonious ceremonies— called *goliardie*—around the Palazzo Bò, usually in July and September.

NIGHTLIFE

Many of the bars and cafes in and around the Ghetto are a great place to rub shoulders with the students of Padua University; cruise around the neighborhood until you find an atmosphere to your taste. Gearing itself to trendy adults, **Lounge Aperitif Miracle** (Via San Francesco, 15) lays claim to "probably the best barman in the world"; ask for Mauro Lotti by name, and then ask him to whip you up a superb martini. Alternatively, join the grownups at **Godenda** (Via Squarcione, 4/6; ☎ 049-8774192), a fabulous wine bar in the center of town. There's an excellent selection of vintages, and snacks and meals are available.

I'm a sucker for any venue that offers good people-watching, and one place I usually can't tear myself away from is the friendly **Paparazzi Fashion Café** (Via Marsilio da Padova, 17; ☎ 049-8759306; www.paparazzi.it; Tues–Sun 6pm–1am), where cool, funky types sip equally cool cocktails before heading for the clubs. Stand at the red marble bar, or grab a seat under the rows of paparazzi pics, while the DJ plays selections from his very own compilation album. Panini and fresh salads are also available, but you'd be forgiven for getting hung up on the cocktails and the human eye-candy. Note that while Paparazzi opens early, things only start heating up after 10pm.

The city's principal indoor theater is **Teatro Verdi** (Via dei Livello, 32; ☎ 049-8777011), which hosts classical music as well as professional comedies and dramas; the season runs from September through April or May. During summer, events at the Roman Amphitheater are particularly varied; expect Spanish salsa dancers, film screenings, and rock bands to fill a program that changes daily.

SIDE TRIPS FROM PADUA

Take one, or all three, of these worthwhile side trips from Padua.

The Riviera del Brenta

Palladian-inspired villas, built in the heyday of Venetian aristocracy, line the Brenta Canal, which stretches between Padua and Venice, providing a marketable venture for tour operators who've clung to Riviera del Brenta as the romantic term to lure visitors on expensive boats chugging up and down the waterways. A Brenta boat cruise isn't my favorite outing—they're expensive and crammed with boatfuls of package-deal groups. Nevertheless, the trip does allow you to observe around 3 dozen villas from the deck of the boat, stopping at three for a close-up inspection and tour. The inconsistent operating hours of these villas means that a boat cruise greatly eases the fuss you'll need to go through trying to plan your trip; there's not much emphasis on customer satisfaction, however, and some of the villa stops feel a bit truncated.

Popular cruises include **I Batelli del Brenta** (☎ 049-8760233; www.antoniana. it) and **Il Burchiello** (☎ 049-8206910; www.ilburchiello.it), both of which will rob you blind (you'll fork out around €70 for the cruise and three villas, before the optional lunch). You'll save a small fortune by arranging to see the Pisani and Fóscari villas by public transport; from Padua to Venice, there are **hourly ACTV buses** (€1.50; 90-min. trip) that go past both villas.

From Padua, the first mansion on the boat tour is **Villa Pisani** (Strà; ☎ 049-502074; €6, or €2.50 if you only visit the park and garden with its famous hedge maze; Oct–Mar 9am–4pm, rest of year 9am–7pm), built in the 18th century and chiefly known for the Tiepolo fresco on the ballroom ceiling. Commissioned for Doge Alvise Pisani in 1735, it was bought by Napoleon for his stepson in 1807; later, it became the site of the first meeting between Hitler and Mussolini in 1934.

The only Brenta villa designed by Palladio is **Villa Fóscari** (Mira; ☎ 041-5203966; www.lamalcontenta.com; €6; May–Oct only Tues–Sun 9:30am–noon and 2:30pm–6pm), which is also called Villa Malcontenta (The Unhappy Woman), and dates from the 16th century. If you arrive under your own steam, you'll need to have booked a guided tour, which costs €7. Near Fóscari is **Barchessa Valmarana** (Mira; ☎ 041-4266387 or ☎ 041-5609350; €6; usually open Apr–Oct Tues–Sun 9:30am–noon and 2:30–6pm), where visitors are led on a half-hourly guided tour.

Vicenza

The splendor of Vicenza is world renowned, and is principally associated with Andrea Palladio, the father of Renaissance architecture, who began his career here when he moved from Padua at age 16 to start his trade as an apprentice stone-mason. Today, thanks to Palladio (real name: Andrea di Pietro della Gondola), Vicenza is a UNESCO World Heritage Site, and a wealthy and prosperous one at that; besides the myriad architectural monuments, the city's business folk count textiles, gold, and silicon chips among the profitable enterprises that have upheld the entrepreneurial spirit of this lofty town.

In conjunction with UNESCO, the city's government has done a superb job of preserving its built treasures, making it feel much like a big-budget film set inviting close-up inspection to check that those buildings are really historical monuments. Walking through the cobblestone streets, you'll be struck by the sheer volume of imposing *palazzi* and gracious public buildings that loom, side by side, as testament to Palladio's stylistic coup; in the town alone, he was respon-sible for more than 10 different projects.

Vicenza is a mere 20-minute train ride from Padua (from €2.45), and there is no shortage of connections. You'll arrive at the station in **Piazza Stazione (Campo Marzio;** ☎ 0444-325046), from where you walk directly along the broad Viale Roma, lined with cheap stalls, until you reach the Piazza Castello. From here, the immense Corso Palladio sweeps northeast through the center of the town, practi-cally dividing it in two. As you head along Corso Palladio, wonderful monuments await your inspection.

Follow Corso Palladio to the very end, and you'll arrive at the helpful **tourist information office** (Piazza Matteotti, 12; ☎ 0444-320854; www.vicenzae.org; 9am–1pm and 2–6pm, mid-Oct to mid-Mar closes at 5:30pm), situated right next to two of the city-run attractions, both associated with Palladio. They'll tell where and how to purchase the cumulative admission ticket known as the **Card Musei** (€8), which gets you into the city's main museums. For €11 you can purchase the Card Musei e Palazzi which also gains you entrance to the Gallerie di Palazzo Leoni-Montanari, and to the Palazzo Barbaran if there is an exhibition.

IN SEARCH OF PALLADIO   Start by visiting the **Teatro Olimpico** ★★ (Piazza Matteotti; ☎ 0444-222101; admission only with cumulative ticket; Sept–June Tues–Sun 9am–5pm, July–Aug 9am–6pm), which is arguably Palladio's finest urban design, and one which he did not see completed (it was begun the same year that he died, and took 5 years to finish). Its historical significance is grounded in the fact that this was Europe's first indoor, covered theater, although the half-moon auditorium is strongly influenced by ancient arena-style design. The steep, raked auditorium seats as many as 1,000 patrons; the theater was inaugurated on March 3, 1585, with a performance of *Oedipus the Tyrant*. The execution of Palladio's design was so expensive that the city's academicians were forced to ask the Venetian Republic for financial aid.

Once you're inside the theater itself, go up to the top row (making certain not to walk on the seats), from where you'll get a proper idea of the grandeur of the space. The entire stage resembles a classical Italian street scene (supposedly Thebes), added by Palladio's student, Vincenzo Scamozzi, to force the illusion of perspective and depth; stone citizens stand in various poses, some gesturing, others playing out violent or heroic deeds from their own dramas.

On the other side of Corso Palladio, the **Museo Civici** ★ (Piazza Matteotti; ☎ 0444-321348; admission only with cumulative ticket; Sept–June Tues–Sun 9am–5pm, July–Aug 9am–6pm) occupies Palladio's Palazzo Chiericati. Its interior unfortunately has a government-run ambience, but includes an extensive collection of artwork by local masters (such as Bartolomeo Montagna, who founded the local Vicenzan school of painting), as well as more valuable paintings by the likes of Tintoretto (his St. Augustine healing the cripples is a favorite), Veronese, and Tiepolo.

Nearby, following signs from Corso Palladio, pay a visit to the **Church of Santa Corona** (Via Santa Corona, 2; 8:30am–noon and 2:30–6pm), built by the Dominicans in the 13th century, and notable primarily for two paintings: Giovanni Bellini's *The Baptism of Christ*, and *The Adoration of the Magi* by Paolo Veronese. Attached to the church is the city's museum of natural and archaeological history, well worth skipping.

Santa Corona is a good place to start a walking tour of *palazzi;* stroll north along Contrà Santa Corona until you reach the **Palazzo Leoni-Montanari** (€3.50, or included in the €11 Vicenza Card; Tues–Sun 10am–6pm, visitors can reserve admission for specific times at www.palazzomontanari.net) on your left. You can visit the art gallery here for the rather limited coverage of Veneto artwork, most of which is from the 18th century. Beyond the gallery, turn left and follow the road southwest until you reach Contrà Porti, lined with an exceptional number of Gothic palaces and several buildings by Palladio. Particularly noteworthy are Palladio's Palazzo Iseppo da Porto (which you'll pass on your right) and then the Palazzo Colleoni Porto, built in the 14th century.

On the corners of the intersection of Contrà Porti and Contrà Riale are the Palladian-designed **Palazzo Barbarano** (only open to the public during the temporary architectural exhibitions held here) at no. 11, and **Palazzo Thiene,** at no. 12, which now houses a bank. If you walk north along Contrà Riale, you'll come to the **Church of San Stefano** (only open early morning to 10am and early evening after 5:30pm), where there's a painting by Palma Vecchio. If you follow Contrà Riale in the opposite direction and turn left where it intersects with Corso Fogazzaro, you'll come to Palladio's most peculiar palace, the **Palazzo Valamarana** (at no. 16).

Continue along Corso Fogazzaro until you reach the Duomo, which was pummeled during World War II and then rebuilt. Turn into Contrà Garibaldi, and continue until you find the Piazzette Palladio. In front of you is Palladio's early masterpiece, popularly known as the **Basilica Palladiana** (Piazza dei Signori; ☎ 0444-323681), which is actually more an architectural solution than a building conceptualized from scratch. Local authorities approached Palladio to convert the existing (and collapsing) Palazzo della Ragione (which housed the Law Courts and the Assembly Hall) to something more fashionable (and stable). His revolutionary solution involved effectively creating a massive buttress out of two galleries enclosed by Doric pillars at the lower level, and Ionic pillars at the upper level. Destroyed during World War II, the copper-covered roof has been rebuilt; a menagerie of classical gods is featured along the balustrade.

The Basilica is surrounded on all sides by squares, the most important of which is the lively Piazza dei Signori, which separates the Basilica from Palladio's incomplete **Loggia del Capitaniato,** built to house the city's Venetian military might; the reliefs decorating it are a commemoration of Venice's 1571 vanquishing of the Turks at Lepanto. A lovely spot from which to take in the visual drama of the Basilica and the Piazza is the terrace of historic **Gran Caffè Garibaldi** (☎ 0444-544147; closed Wed), where a freshly made panino won't hurt your wallet too badly.

Vicenza's fresh-produce market occupies the Piazza delle Erbe, on the other side of the Basilica. Here, look for **Il Grottino** (closed Mon), a small watering hole that serves snacks; a cool crowd gathers here to listen to laid-back tunes in the evening.

If you are a fan of architectural marvels, it's important to include a trip to the **Villa Rotonda** ✦✦✦ (☎ 0444-321793; €3; Mar 15–Nov 4 Tues–Sun 10am–noon and 3–6pm), generally considered the finest of Palladio's buildings, and considered by those in the know to be the closest humanity has come to creating a "perfect" building. Built on a square plan, and capped by a dome, it was inspired by ancient Greek and Roman designs, and begun in 1567. Palladio's star student, Scamozzi, was responsible for seeing the project to its completion in 1592. The easiest way to get to the villa (also known as Villa Capra Valmarana) is on bus no. 8, but cycling or walking is also possible. There are two viewing alternatives: either observe from the gate, or pay to get into the grounds and see the exterior up close. On Wednesday and Saturday, you can also gain admission to see the interior of the villa, which costs €6.

From Villa Rotonda, you can walk to **Villa Valmarana "ai Nani"** (☎ 0444-543976; €6; hours vary), built by an admirer of Palladio in the 17th century; the real reason to visit is to see the splendid frescoes by Giambattista and Giandomenico Tiepolo. If you turn up when it's closed, it's always an option to pay a little extra to be admitted as scheduled times are terribly convoluted (inquire at the tourist office).

Overlooking the city of Vicenza, a 10-minute walk from Valmarana, is the 17th-century **Basilica di Monte Bérico** ★ (☎ 0444-320999; Mon–Sat 6am–12:30pm and 2:30–7:30pm, Sun 6am–8pm, with shorter hours in winter). The church is popular with pilgrims who believe that this was the very spot that the Virgin twice appeared to announce the city's delivery from bubonic plague, which struck Vicenza in 1426. In front of the Basilica, there's a relaxed cafe where you can have a drink and snack in the garden terrace, and enjoy the panoramic view over the city.

A BUDGET RESTAURANT   All that walking through the streets of Palladio's city will build up quite an appetite; to find a reliable, affordable *taverna*, turn off Corso Palladio into Contrà della Morette (which runs towards Piazza dei Signori) and look for **Antica Casa della Malvasia** (☎ 0444-543704), a spot that attracts a devoted local following. The cuisine is typical of the region, unpretentious and very good; and the menu of drinks, I must say, is spectacular.

Treviso

The low-key city of Treviso is easily overlooked by time-constrained tourists (many of whom merely think of this as a point of arrival for visits from the U.K. to Venice, typically with budget carrier Ryanair), but it makes for an attractive outing; its ancient system of canals quaintly set off the lively architecture (the houses often feature frescoed facades) of the historic center, extensively fortified by 16th-century walls. Much of the Treviso you see today resulted from extensive post-war restoration.

Treviso is small enough to get around without much hassle, but if you do require sightseeing assistance, head for the **tourist office** (Piazza Monte di Pietè; ☎ 0422-547632; www.provincia.treviso.it; closed Mon afternoon, 12:30–2pm weekdays, and 12:30–3pm weekends) slap-bang in the center of the town.

To reach the center from the train station (which is to the south of the center), head along Via Roma and farther as it becomes Corso dei Popolo, until you reach the Piazza dei Signori, at one end of the city's main street, Calmaggiore. Here stands the **Palazzo dei Trecento,** Treviso's 13th-century town hall (much rebuilt after destructive bombing raids on Good Friday 1944), and the more recent Palazzo del Podestà (from the 19th c.). Worth visiting here are the **San Vito** and **Santa Lucia churches** (free admission; daily 9am–noon), around the other side of the block. The chapel in the latter church showcases more work by Tomaso da Modena.

The city's 12th-century San Pietro Cathedral is farther along Calmaggiore, but has been maintained with limited success; you can visit in the mornings and after 3:30pm in the afternoon to see Titian's *Annunciation* (1570); however, you're likely to be far more impressed by the remains of the frescoed *Adoration of the Magi*, executed 50 years earlier by Pordenone.

Back toward the station, the **Church of San Nicolò** (Via San Nicolò; ☎ 0422-3247; free admission; Mon–Fri 8am–12:30pm and 3:30–7pm) stands near the city wall abutting the River Sile. The church was built by the Dominicans and features an extraordinary range of frescoes spanning several centuries. Of importance here are columns decorated with the work of the city's principal artistic contributor,

Tomaso da Modena (1325–79), who came to prominence in the north of Italy after the death of Giotto. Most of the works are of saints (Tomaso's Jerome and Agnes are standouts). There are bigger rewards in the next-door Sala del Capitolo, which you need to enter via the **Seminario Vescovile** (free admission; Mon–Fri 8am–12:30pm and 3–5:30pm, in summer until 6pm) to inspect the delightful portraits of 40 monks of the Dominican Order, preserved in Tomaso's somewhat droll style.

To the east of the center, not far from the town hall, the former church and convent of Santa Caterina has recently been transformed into the new **Museo Civico** (Via Santa Caterina; ☎ 0422-591337; €3; Tues–Sun 9am–12:30pm and 2:30–6pm), which holds Tomaso's impressive fresco cycle depicting *The Story of the Life of Saint Ursula.* Other important works that have been transferred here from the former museum include Titian's *Portrait of Sperone Speroni* and Bessano's *Crucifixion.* Outside the museum, in Piazza G. Matteoti, there's a pleasant market and a variety of stalls selling antiques.

A DINING SPLURGE   One of my favorite restaurants in the Veneto is Treviso's expensive **Don Fernando** (Via delle Absidi, 8/10; ☎ 0422-543354; closed Tues and Wed lunch) right near San Nicolò church. When the Buena Vista Social Club (from Cuba) was in town, they ate here 3 days in a row, and local vocalists and musicians regularly get up from their tables to serenade the other diners. It's a chic, classy place where you can expect Fernando himself to come and introduce the dishes to your table (the menu is very much a work in progress, but you can expect to pay €20–€30). You must order Carrello dei Bolliti, the fantastic meat stew, which has made a loyal following of Treviso's in-the-know foodies. Also wonderful is Mari e Monti, or "sea and land," a shellfish dish prepared with porcini mushrooms, rocket, and *granchio* sauce, and served with polenta. The selection of wines from the Veneto region is impressive, starting at €12 per bottle.

VERONA

Centuries ago, Shakespeare set a play about dizzying pubescent romance in a town he referred to as "Fair Verona." Today, mercurial Verona is far more romantic and charming than the Bard's brutal tragedy of star-crossed lovers suggests. Self-confident and stylish, Verona has the exuberant air of a city that knows it's beautiful enough to entertain visitors simply by being there.

Verona's visual drama and postcard-perfect feel have much to do with its medieval architecture pounded together from a generous supply of rose-colored limestone, quarried from the surrounding hills and known as *rosso di Verona.* Flower-filled balconies, like the one immortalized in *Romeo and Juliet,* protrude from noble houses, daintily overlooking the maze of cobblestone streets and lovely open squares; some of the buildings date back to the reconstruction that followed a catastrophic earthquake in 1117. Along with the historic houses are a number of elegant high-end boutiques, where visitors enjoy the pleasures of conspicuous consumption against the refined, historic backdrop of the city center. After Venice, this is the most visited city in the region, and once you spend a lazy day wandering its streets and seeing the sights, I think you'll understand its popularity.

DON'T LEAVE VERONA WITHOUT . . .

ACTING OUT YOUR OWN VERSION OF THE BARD'S ROMANTIC PLAY   Romantic strolls through the cobblestone streets and squares of Verona will evoke Shakespeare's star-crossed lovers, Romeo and Juliet. Wander around the oldest parts of the city, and you'll discover a city that beautifully combines historic heritage with contemporary prosperity; head for the **Piazza delle Erbe** (p. 364) and wend your way through, around, and under the remarkable buildings, statues, and archways left by the powerful Scaligeri clan who once ruled here.

SEEING AN OPERA   It's easily one of the grandest opera experiences on earth; massive outdoor extravaganzas played out in the 2,000-year-old **Arena** (p. 367), where gladiators once tore each other to pieces. Nowadays, the only uncivilized torture you'll witness happens to those spectators who've forgotten to bring a cushion. Most of the seating at the Arena is on the same cold, hard stone used centuries ago. Take something soft to sit on or be prepared to suffer: Operas are nothing short of 3 hours long.

TAKING IN 1,000 YEARS' WORTH OF ART   The **Museo Castelvecchio** (p. 368) is housed in a castle on the banks of the River Adige and is stuffed full of artwork from across the ages. How better to discover the who and how of Bellini, Carpaccio, Tintoretto, and Veronese—without the hassle of the crowds that heave through Venice's brilliant museums?

LEARNING ABOUT LOCAL WINES FROM A MASTER   Visit the tiny, cluttered **Enoteca dal Zovo** (p. 363) and you'll not only get to taste a selection of regional vintages, but you can also chat for hours with Oreste dal Zovo. He will introduce you to some romantic legends, most notably that of the Well of Love, which has inspired an impressive wine label that you can purchase here.

A BRIEF HISTORY OF VERONA

As suggested by the city's vast public Arena and superb collection of excavated ruins, Verona was a Roman stronghold, first occupied in 89 B.C. Its favorable position at the mouth of the Adige River made it a popular conquest, and it drew consistent attention from various Italian and Mitteleuropa invaders once the Roman empire fell. Verona's very own Della Scala (or Scaligeri) family put an end to the invasions when it came to power in the 13th century, holding considerable sway in Northern Italy. Much like the Medicis in Florence, this despotic family ruled Verona harshly, but at the same time beautified it immensely. They also forced the citizenry to pay taxes for expanding their miniature empire, and imported some of the region's best artists and architects. The Scaligeris were important patrons of the poet Dante.

The Della Scalas remained in power until 1387, when Milan's Viscontis took over briefly. In 1404, Verona fell into the welcome embrace of La Serenissima; Venice was developing its inland empire, and Verona happily remained under Venetian rule until 1797, when Napoleon got his claws into much of Europe. Later, in 1814, Verona—along with the whole of the Veneto—became part of Austria and only shook off foreign rulers when it joined the Kingdom of Italy in

1866. Today, she is a large, prosperous city, although the expanse of industrialization beyond the historical center is almost unnoticeable.

Verona's charms are complemented by her usefulness as a base from which to explore several other not-too-distant towns: Trent in the north, Mantua in the neighboring province of Lombardy, and Treviso, are all within easy reach of the city.

LAY OF THE LAND

Verona's **Stazione FS Porta Nuova** (☎ 8488-88088) is served by **direct rail connections** from most major destinations, including Rome, Milan, and Bologna. There are over 40 trains per day from Venice (the journey is around 90 min., and there are regular departures to and from the nearby towns of Padua, Vicenza, and Trent). **Buses** and **taxis** (for around-the-clock assistance, call **RadioTaxi:** ☎ 045-532666) constantly arrive in the adjacent Piazzale XXV Aprile concourse; from here, all buses head along Corso Porta Nuova in the direction of the city's historical center, about a kilometer northeast of the station; look for bus no. 11, 12, 13, 72, or 73 or—on the weekend—91, 92, or 93.

You can also **fly** directly to Verona's **Aeroporto Verona Villafranca** (☎ 045-8095666; www.aeroportoverona.it), 12km (7½ miles) from the center; there are regular shuttle buses to town. You can purchase a ticket (€3.60) from the driver.

Verona's historical center can be explored on foot, but if you require **public transportation,** there is a good, regular bus network; contact **AMT Public Transport** (☎ 045-8871111; www.amt.it).

ACCOMMODATIONS, BOTH STANDARD & NOT

Verona's accommodations aren't likely to blow you away. Yes, you can find comfort and stay well within your means, but the lack of historical authenticity in a city with such ancient roots may leave you longing for a broader selection of hotels. Prices are seasonal, and soar tremendously during the Arena's Opera Season, when it's sometimes impossible to find a vacant room anywhere in town. You'll pay around 50% more from mid-June through early October and over the Christmas to New Year's period.

€€–€€€   Let me kick off by introducing the **best value Verona has to offer: Hotel Aurora** (Piazzetta Novembre, 2; ☎ 045-594717; www.hotelaurora.biz) is everything a discerning traveler wants—a good location, right in the heart of the ancient city, just off the Piazza dell Erbe, and careful attention to details that, in this price range, are seldom even considered. Upon arrival, you'll find a flower and a chocolate on your pillow, and you'll be delighted by the neat, simple guest rooms, furnished with antique cupboards, and simply decorated with lithographs and paintings. Reserve room 5, which is best in terms of size. Bathrooms are a bit small, but the designers have made some effort to conserve space by making the bidet a foldaway. You can enjoy breakfast (included in the price) on a small terrace where you feel like you're part of the neighborhood. And music by busking musicians in adjacent Piazza dell Erbe often wafts up here, too. There are a few single rooms with shared bathroom facilities (€56–€68), while doubles cost €98 in the low season, and €130 during busiest times of the year.

€€   If you are in need of a touch more comfort, and would prefer to be in the vicinity of the Arena, **Hotel Torcolo** (Vicolo Listone, 3; ☎ 045-8007512; www.hoteltorcolo.it) is the ideal choice. Childhood friends and owners Silvia and Diana have fashioned a homey, comfortable, and exceptionally neat small hotel that's earned a fantastic reputation with frequent travelers (many of whom return year after year, particularly during opera season). The 19 guest rooms are well pro-portioned, cheerfully—if modestly—decorated, with wooden floors and shut-tered windows looking out over Verona's back streets. To my mind, the most important details here are the firm, comfortable mattresses. Each room is slightly different from the next, but they're all soberly tasteful, and there are a number of neat little single units for solo travelers; those on the third floor are warm in sum-mer, but have extra air-conditioning (you may struggle with the low ceilings, however). Prices fluctuate considerably, almost doubling during the popular opera season (when a double costs €112, which is still fairly reasonable). Breakfast is not always included in the rate; during the opera season expect to pay between €8 and €12, and if you bring your own vehicle, parking will set you back an addi-tional €10 to €15. Reserving a room here is not always easy, however. I once e-mailed for accommodations and the reply came that they were full; when I arrived in town and popped in for a visit, there were empty rooms. If you want a room here, be persistent.

€€–€€€€   Right next door to Giulietta e Romeo (see below) is the better-priced **Hotel Milano** (Vicolo Tre Marchetti, 11; ☎ 045-596011), a more down-home, less organized option than its more famous neighbor. Its rooms are pleasant, if a bit motel-like. Doubles start at €85, and go up to €160, making it €20 cheaper than the Giulietta. It's a somewhat dowdier, less spacious three-star option, so expect linoleum flooring and a tight squeeze in some of the rooms.

€€€–€€€€   Named for the romantic tale that has put Verona on the tourist map, **Hotel Giulietta e Romeo** ✹ (Vicolo Tre Marchetti, 3; ☎ 045-8003554; www.giuliettaeromeo.com) is a popular option in the center of town. The pinkish facade conceals neat, bright public spaces mostly painted an odd citrus yellow. Guest rooms tend to suggest a sense of space rather than being truly spacious; their appeal stems from being neat and clean, and the faint blue floral-patterned wallpaper and cherrywood refurbishment are quite pleasant. I haven't been overly impressed by the mattresses (they're not the firmest in town), but the cool white sheets at least hint at luxury. Bathrooms are quite small and pretty standard. Doubles start at €115. I must warn you, however, that if you arrive by car, you'll be paying €17 per night for parking. Bicycles are available for rent at €7 per day. If you're in town during the opera season, you'd better book your room a good 10 months in advance, and you'll need to stay for at least 4 days (one of which must be a Mon or Tues).

The Hostel Option

€   I wouldn't recommend Verona's co-ed hostel, **Ostello della Gioventù Villa Francescatti** (Salita Fontana del Ferro, 15; ☎ 045-590360) if you're on a tight schedule; it's situated some distance from the historical center, and involves a steep uphill climb along the road behind the Teatro Romano. Nevertheless, if you're here for several days and would prefer to keep a lid on that budget, make sure you've got your Hostelling International membership card and follow the yellow signs. Dorm rooms are spartan, and there are slightly more expensive family rooms, which you can book in advance. Despite the hike to the hostel, the hillside neighborhood is rather quaint, and the hostel has a lovely garden (something you won't find in most hotels in town). The major drawback is that you won't be able to access your room between 9am and 5pm, and you'll need to wait until reception opens at 5pm before you can check in. There's also an 11:30pm curfew, which is only relaxed for ticket holders during the opera season. The bed-and-breakfast rate is €16 per person, €19 per person in a family room.

A Camping Site Overlooking the City

€   On a hillside overlooking the city is the seasonal camping site, **Campeggio Castel San Pietro** (Via Castel San Pietro, 2; ☎ 045-592037; www.campingcastel sanpietro.com). Sheltered by trees, its site is charming, if a little cluttered in appearance (owing to its popularity); there are terraced areas for dining and for relaxing or soaking up the sun. Rates are very reasonable: €6 to €8 per tent and €6 per adult (€4 for children under 8). There's a further charge of €3.50 per motor car and €2 if you arrive on a motorbike. Tents are available for rental for those not carrying their own. To get there from the station, catch bus no. 41 or 95, and ask the driver where you should disembark; you'll have some walking (up a rather steep hill) to do before you arrive at the site, but once you do you can let your hair down. The campsite is operational from mid-May until mid-October.

DINING FOR ALL TASTES

There are many cafes throughout the center, and the area around the Arena is constantly abuzz with people-watching coffee-drinkers. It's really worth getting away from the most obvious spots to find charming *trattorie* hidden down quieter back streets; the selection below caters to most tastes, and allows you to get some idea of the peculiarities of local cuisine—especially the affection for horse and donkey meat.

€-€€   A particularly relaxed and pleasant cafe, **Al Ponte** (Via Ponte Pietra; ☎ 045-569608; Thurs–Tues till late), is named for the fact that it sits right on the edge of the River Aldige, and tables in the small terrace courtyard afford views of Ponte Pietra and Castel San Pietro. It's nothing sophisticated but has an extensive menu with light meals like panini, *tramazzini*, and a selection of salads.

€-€€   Another spot that's great for lunch—especially for vegetarians—is **Caffè Coloniale** (Piazza Viviani, 14C; ☎ 045-8012647), where you can grab a table on the pleasant roadside courtyard just around the corner from Casa di Giulietta. It's the type of place where subversive rebels wearing T-shirts bearing slogans like "Kill All Artists" hang out while ordering salads and super-strong espresso. I can recommend the Campestre salad—sliced apple, bacon, and huge chunks of Stracchino cheese, and drizzled with "healing" vinegar. Great warm vegetarian dishes (like aubergine baked with Parmesan cheese) and a selection of pizzas (try the red chicory) are also available.

€–€€   Disguised as a house of worship, **San Matteo Church** (Vicolo del Guasto, 4; ☎ 045-8004538; Mon–Sat noon–2:30pm and 6:30pm–12:30am) has been converted into a very affordable, atmospheric pizzeria (a basic marinara costs just €4). Situated down a quiet alleyway, off Corsà Porta Borsari, it's perfect for a quick meal, or one accompanied by plenty of wine.

€€   Just meters from the Arena, there are excellent pizzas to be had at **Le Cantine de L'Arena** ★ (Piazzetta Scalette Rubiani, 1; ☎ 045-8032849), which feels a bit like someone's eat-in kitchen, though it's dominated by a large, brick pizza oven stacked with bread boards and ham-shaving equipment. On one wall, a pair of frescoed cherubs seems to be cleaning the teeth of a crocodile. Pasta specials (for around €7.50) are chalked up on the board, but you should go for the pizzas which are among the best in town. On my last visit, I ordered a particularly scrumptious one called "Baito," piled full of Veronese cheese, fleshy boletus mushrooms, and mozzarella. The more adventurous can order pizza with horse meat (accompanied by arugula and Parmesan). Beneath the main dining room, an excavated space has been transformed into a beautiful underground cantina with archways and vaulted ceilings; in winter, it becomes the ideal setting for a hearty meal of grilled meat.

€€   Locals looking to introduce their foreign friends to the pleasures of authentic regional dining tend to head for **Osteria al Duca** ★★ (Via Arche Scaligeri, 2; ☎ 045-594474; closed Dec 24–Jan 7), a quaint family restaurant right across the way from the Scaligeri tombs. The restaurant is said to occupy part of what was once Romeo's family home, a 13th-century palace that was originally owned by the Della Scalas. Here, you're waited on by the family women; decked out in black, they squabble among themselves while clutching their notepads and trying hard to explain the menu in well-enunciated Italian. The homey vibe is maintained by the casual layout—diners share tables, and the family dog (a white Labrador) cruises about looking for a spot to nap. Try to arrive before 7:30pm, as it fills up quickly. Young Alessandro, whose family operates this lively eatery, explains that the food's authenticity is maintained by the firm grip his 70-year-old grandmother keeps in the kitchen. You'll recognize that local and regional specialties are the order of the day by the availability of horse-meat steak, horse tartar, horse prepared with Parmesan and rocket, and spaghetti served with donkey meat. But even simpler dishes, like the rich, creamy penne Romeo, which I had recently, are lovely; my pasta was rich with Gorgonzola cheese and sliced zucchini, and I finished off with a decadent portion of homemade tiramisu, which worked out to a very filling meal for just €10.

€€   Off a small courtyard square shared with a number of trendy shops, another of my favorite eateries in Verona is family-run **Ristorante Greppia** ★★ (Vicolo Samaritana, 3; ☎ 045-8004577; www.ristorantegreppia.com; Tues–Sun), which has specialized in Veronese cuisine for 30 years and maintains a sterling reputation throughout the city. Apparently, the secret lies in the traditional homemade pasta prepared by the family matriarchs. In winter, spring, and fall you can order "trolley meat" *(bollito misto con salse),* which is cut for you at your table and then prepared to suit your tastes. Among the selection of steaks, the *osso buco* is particularly wonderful, prepared in a local vegetable sauce and served with polenta. The only downside here? A €3 cover.

Vino Amore

A second "must visit" for wine lovers is Oreste dal Zovo's wonderfully over-stocked liquor store, **Enoteca dal Zovo** (Vicolo San Marco in Foro, 7; ☎ 045-8034369; www.enotecadalzovo.it), operating in the former arch-bishop's chapel since the 1950s. The walls are packed tight with booze, and the selection of wines is overwhelming, stacked between portraits of the city taken by Verona's very first photographer. If you're after a special bottle, ask for *Romeo and Juliet*-inspired "Well of Love" Valpolicella Amarone, one of the region's standouts; the well in question is just a few steps from the bottle store. Oreste and his American-born wife, Beverly, will also help you find rare vintages, or introduce you to some exotic-sounding liqueurs. The last time I was there, Beverly gave me an extensive tour of the neighborhood; if you want to get her chatting, ask to be shown the nearby Well of Love (Il pozzo dell'Amore). Enoteca dal Zovo is open daily 8am to 1pm and 2 to 8:30pm, and until 9pm over weekends; pop in around 5pm for a glass of wine.

€€-€€€   If you're interested in wine (drinking it, or even getting into heavy discussions about it), an evening at **Antica Bottega del Vino** ✹✹ (Via Scudo di Francia, 3; ☎ 045-8004535; www.bottegavini.it; Wed–Mon) should be a priority, even if it means going hungry for the next few days! You may be familiar with the branch that opened in New York in 2004—well, here's the original, which the Barzan family has been operating for almost 20 years. One thing you won't find on the NYC menu is horse meat *(pastissada di cavallo con polenta),* simply pre-pared with lemon and oil, and served with polenta, in the tradition of the region. Don't worry, though, there's plenty else to savor on the (moderately priced) menu, including bean soup *(pasta e fasoi),* tripe with Parmesan, sea bass with balsamic vinegar and rosemary, and green potato dumplings with pecorino cheese sauce; steaks here are also excellent and Florentine sirloin is served by weight. Ultimately, it's the ambience and selection of over 3,400 varieties of wine that draw the reg-ular clientele (and the regular awards from *Wine Spectator* magazine). The tables are dominated by large wine goblets, and everywhere you look are tempting bot-tles of wine, champagne, and vinegar urging you to blow your budget; recom-mended bottles are chalked up on the board behind the bar counter. If you're looking to buy wine to take home with you, you can also visit the bottle store right next door, La Bottega della Bottega.

WHY YOU'RE HERE: THE TOP SIGHTS & ATTRACTIONS

Verona's cobblestone streets, ancient Roman and Renaissance monuments, and romantic air, make it ideal for relaxed exploration. Specific sights are fairly spread out, but the strolls between them—most are located at the Piazza delle Erbe and over the Adige River, and close to the Arena amphitheater—are terrifically pleasant.

Saving with the Verona Card

The Verona Card is a money-saving tool for tourists, which nets users free bus trips, as well as access to all local museums, churches, and other monuments. It's valid for 1 day (€8) or 3 days (€12), and is available from all participating attractions, tobacco shops, and tourist offices (☎ 045-8068680; www.tourism. verona.it).

The **tourist information office** (Piazza Chiesa, 34; ☎ 045-7050088; www. verona-apt.net; usually open Mon–Sat 9am–8pm, Sun 10am–1pm and 4–7pm with shorter hr. in winter) works hard to supply maps and information about the city and surrounding area. There's an office near the Arena (Via degli Alpini, 9; ☎ 045-8068680; www.tourism.verona.it; Mon–Sat 9am–6pm) and one at the train station (☎ 045-8000861; Tues–Sat 8am–7:30pm and Sun–Mon 10am–4pm).

If you'd like to be guided around the city, you can join one of the walking tours starting at the equestrian statue of Vittorio Emanuele II, in the Arena Square, every evening at 5:30pm (Apr–Sept). Contact **Juliet & Co.** (☎ 045-8103173; www.julietandco.com) for information; tickets cost €10, children are free.

Piazza delle Erbe & Northwestern Verona

The original, fortified Verona was centered on its ancient Roman forum, which became the site of the city's medieval market, popular for its sale of exotic herbs, spices, and other lifestyle goods imported through Venice's bustling trade port. Today it is still known as the **Piazza delle Erbe,** and vendors still man the stalls at what is an irresistibly lively and eclectic market. Besides fresh goods from nearby farms, many of the umbrella-canopied stalls hawk VERONA-emblazoned souvenirs, while some crafty artists sell handmade reproductions of famous paintings. At the northwestern end of the square is the baroque-style **Palazzo Maffei,** built in the 17th century, and worth a close-up look for the classical statuary atop the balustrade—gods and goddesses from the ancient pantheon. In the square, the column nearest the palace is topped by the winged lion of St. Mark, symbolizing Venetian rule. Nearby, the beautiful 14th-century fountain is capped by a Roman statue inappropriately known as the Madonna of Verona.

To the east of the fountain, you'll find the Arco della Costa or "arch of the rib"; pass under the hanging whale rib in order to reach **Piazza dei Signori** (also called Piazza Dante), a quiet square where you'll instantly feel as though you've escaped the crowds. The square is centered on a statue of the great poet, Dante, who found refuge in Verona under the Scaligeris after fleeing Florence for political reasons.

The architecture around the square is worth some attention. Directly across from the Arco della Costa is the 13th-century home of the Scaligeri family. Dante stands facing the **Palazzo della Ragione (Palace of Reason),** built in the 12th century in the Romanesque style; visit the courtyard behind the imposing facade, and pay particular attention to the Gothic-style stairway, built in the mid–15th century. Back in the square, look at the **Loggia del Consiglio,** a Renaissance-style council chamber, behind Dante; statues of several important Romans who were born in Verona are featured here.

Continue through the Piazza dei Signori, under the archway directly opposite the arch of the rib. On your right you'll see some unusual Gothic funerary sculpture—the elaborately decorated 14th-century Scaligeri Tombs, with spiking turrets issuing toward the heavens. The level of detail hints at the perceived importance of these rulers, now guarded by stone warrior saints. The raised outdoor tombs all but completely conceal the 7th-century **Santa Maria Antica church,** which served as the private chapel of the Scaligeris; above the side entrance to the church is the tomb of Cangrande I, and above that is a copy of his equestrian statue (the original is at the Castelvecchio Museum).

Two blocks north of the tombs is the **Basilica di Sant'Anastasia** ★ (Piazza Anastasia, Corso Anastasia; ☎ 045-592813; www.chieseverona.it; see "Church Savings," below, for admission info; Mar–Oct Mon–Sat 9am–6pm, Sun 1–6pm; Nov–Feb Tues–Sat 10am–4pm, Sun 1–5pm) with its incomplete facade, currently undergoing restoration. Begun in 1290 for the hard-line Dominicans, the church took over 200 years to build, and serves as an excellent example of Italian Gothic architecture. Erected on a near-perfect cross plan, it features a vast Romanesque interior of soaring arches supported by massive pillars; there are 16 chapels scattered along the sides of the church.

Casa di Giulietta

Call me a cynic, but the only thing I find romantic about the famous **Casa di Giulietta** (Via Cappello, 23; ☎ 045-8034303; €4, but for an extra €1 you can also visit Juliet's tomb; Tues–Sun 8:30am–7:30pm, Mon 1:30–7:30pm, last admission at 6:45pm)—Verona's most popular attraction—are the thousands of couples who crowd in here each day and give themselves over to the suspended disbelief that this was ever the home of anyone even remotely connected to the love-struck Juliet, or the Capulet clan. (In fact, rumor has it that this building was a brothel in a former incarnation.) You enter Juliet's courtyard via a small arcade, covered with graffitied messages of love. To keep the hopefuls amused, there's a bronze statue of Juliet in the small courtyard below; visitors queue up to have their picture taken, usually while grabbing her left breast—an odd tradition that has left it buffed to a high gloss. Meanwhile, the interior of the *palazzo* has a rather cheap pseudo-museum atmosphere, packed full of assorted portraits of the young lovers who made the city so famous. You'll also have to get into the *palazzo* if you feel the need to be photographed on Juliet's balcony.

Those who decide to visit Juliet's tomb can simply walk to the Capuchin Monastery of San Francesco al Corso, where her sarcophagus is found in the lovely medieval cloister.

Among the standout Gothic elements of the interior are the *gobbi*, carved hunchback beggars who are permanently buckled under the weight of the holy water fonts at the entrance. Do look for Claudio Ridolfi's Christ being scourged at the pillar in the Rosary Chapel, which reminds me of a scene from Mel Gibson's *Passion of the Christ;* and then look up to inspect the damaged but incredible 15th-century fresco over the dome. In the Giusti Chapel, which is intended only for legitimate worshiping visitors, see if you can spot the tourists on their knees pretending to pray so that they can check out the paintings, and then join them. In the Pellegrini Chapel, the 24 terra-cotta tableaux tell the story of the life of Christ; while above the chapel is Pisanello's famous fresco of *St. George Freeing the Princess of Trebisonda,* considered the most important work in the church.

From Sant'Anastasia, head along Via Duomo to get to **Il Duomo** ★ (☎ 045-592813; €2; Mar–Oct Mon–Sat 9:30am–6pm, Sun 1–6pm, Nov–Feb Mon–Sat 10am–4pm, Sun 1:30–5pm), the city's imposing 12th-century church complex, recognizable by its red and white stripes. The Romanesque facade features a double-level porch around the main doorway, which is guarded by two bellicose stone griffins; you can't get in through there, however, as the tourist entrance is around the side of the building.

Inside, magnificent detailing abounds, accompanied by the droning of recorded, chanting monks creating an atmosphere of religious melancholy. You really need to spend time looking at each of the chapels around the church; as you enter, the first one on your left features Titian's *Assumption* (1530); take the time to find Liberale da Verona's surprising, sublime *Adoration of the Magi.* In the Chapel of the Madonna, note how—in the spirit of baroque overkill—devotees with their offerings have transformed the Virgin into something more reminiscent of a Versace or D&G advertisement than a religious icon. In the half-dome of the main chapel, pay some attention to those delightfully cheerful frescoed figures by Francesco Torbido, rendered in 1534.

Attached to the main church is **Sant Elena Cathedral** (Verona's first cathedral) and the baptistery; en route to these, you'll pass through an area of excavation, where the archaeological remnants of an ancient church have attracted the attention of coin-tossing believers. The baptistery—known as San Giovanni in Fonte (St. John of the Spring)—is an especially solemn space enclosed by walls of exposed pale brickwork, creating a ghostly atmosphere, which I love for the large baroque crucifix that hangs like a giant mobile from the wooden beams of the ceiling.

Church Savings

Admission to Sant'Anastasia costs €2.50 (€1 concession), but if you're planning to visit other churches, you might just as well purchase the €5 (€4 concession) combined church ticket, which will also get you into the San Zeno, San Fermo, and San Lorenzo churches, as well as into the Duomo complex during the afternoon. Better still, purchase the Verona Card for major savings (see box, above).

It's a Dog's Life

The name Scaligeri comes from the Latin word for ladder *(scala)*, a feature on the family crest of Verona's most famous rulers. But it was from the domestic animal on the coat of arms that the Scaligeri patriarchs took their names: Mastino I (Mastiff the First) was the first in the line, while others in the dynasty included Cangrande I (Big Dog the First) and Cansignorio (Head Dog). Look for the dogs supporting a ladder on Big Dog's tomb.

Across the River Adige: The Teatro Romano

Over the River Adige, across the Ponte Pietra, you'll come to a lovely hillside neighborhood around the Castel San Pietro complex. At its base, excavated from beneath a labyrinth of medieval structures, is the ancient **Teatro Romano (Roman Theater)** ✯ (Rigaste Redentore, 2; ☎ 045-8000360; €3; Tues–Sun 8:30am–7:30pm, Mon 1:30–7:30pm), probably dating back to the 1st century B.C. Around the theater, with its original stone semicircular seating plan, a cluster of ancient buildings vividly recalls the city's original Roman occupation. Archaeologists think that the hillside location of the outdoor theater was the site of the very first human settlements in Verona. Today the theater offers lovely views of the city, and while the program content has certainly been modernized, attending a show here is a wonderful way of transporting yourself back to the days when theatrical performances and spectacles were the primary entertainment. A visit to Teatro Romano can be combined with a tour of the town's small, on-site **archaeological museum** (Museo Archeologico). Note that the open-air theater offers an experience entirely different from that of the spectacular Roman Arena down in the city center.

The Roman Arena

The 2,000-year-old **Arena di Verona** ✯✯✯ (☎ 045-8003204; €4; Tues–Sun 8:30am–7:15pm), on the edge of Piazza Brà, is arguably the most important Roman structure in Northern Italy, and certainly the best-preserved Roman amphitheater anywhere. Once located outside the walls of the city, the Arena was a massive entertainment stadium seating nearly 30,000 citizens who would flock here regularly to watch gladiatorial combat, mock battles, and thrilling naval displays for which the Arena was flooded. It also hosted public executions and bullfights, but such bloodfests have now given way to opera and music concerts that draw equally spirited—if more civilized—crowds. Facing the central performance space are 44 tiers of stone seats, reached via a thorough system of well-preserved stairways and passages.

Frankly, the best way to see and experience the Arena is to pick up a ticket for one of the performances during the world-renowned opera season; if you're in town for Verdi's *Aida,* do not pass on the opportunity to see it. The spectacle of witnessing the world's third-largest amphitheater fill up with excited spectators (many of whom would never consider going to the opera) is quite thrilling. On Mondays and during the Opera Season, admissions run 1:30 to 7:15pm.

The Castle & Other Churches

Verona's main art museum, **Museo Castelvecchio** ✗ (Corso Castelvecchio, 2; ☎ 0495-8062611; €4; Tues–Sun 8:30am–7:30pm, Mon 1:30–7:30pm), is less than 10 minutes by foot south from the Arena, at the end of Via Roma. Built on a bank of the River Adige between 1355 and 1375, Castelvecchio is very much a castle, and served as both a military fortress (to ward against foreign invasion and popular uprisings) and a residence for the various rulers of Verona before being transformed into a museum in the 1920s. Attacked by the Nazis during World War II, the structure you see today is a meticulous restoration by acclaimed Venetian architect Carlos Scarpa, who not only repaired the damage done by bombs but also by the 1920s restoration—when ugly Gothic and Romanesque features were added.

I'd proceed briskly through the first few rooms of the museum, which feature fairly prosaic Roman and early-Christian art, glasswork, and jewelry. It's the fierce attempts at realism of the early-Renaissance painters that are the glories of this museum, notably in the works of Tintoretto, Tiepolo, Veronese, and Bellini, which you'll see throughout. As well, give some time to the Venetian painters featured in the **Pisanello Room (Room 10),** many of them combining a sense of Gothic refinement with Byzantine embellishments. Note in particular how the background of Gothic rocks in Jacopo Bellini's *Saint Jerome in the Desert* heavily suggests the appearance of the Dolomite mountain ranges. Upstairs, the picture galleries continue, and although I feel that there's way too much to take in, there are several wonderful works worth seeking. Among them are Francesco Bonsignori's *Madonna and Child,* executed when he was just 20 years old; and Girolamo dai Libri's colorful *Madonna of the Umbrella* (which suggests that doggie parlors were already in vogue during the 16th c.). **Room 22** is where you'll find works by Venice's great masters, Tintoretto and Veronese.

From Castelvecchio, it's a short walk—mostly along the River Adige—to get to the remarkable **Basilica San Zeno Maggiore** ✗✗ (Piazza San Zeno, 2; ☎ 045-592813; Mar–Oct Mon–Sat 8:30am–6pm, Sun 1–6pm; Nov–Feb Tues–Sat 10am–4pm, Sun 1:30–5pm), a mammoth 12th-century church featuring quintessential Romanesque striped brickwork, and dedicated to Verona's patron saint, San Zeno, whose remains are preserved inside in a downstairs crypt. San Zeno hailed from Africa and was the city's bishop in the 4th century. Before entering, spend some time giving your attention to the lovely facade, with its fantastic "Wheel of Fortune" rose window above the entrance. The doors themselves are particularly noteworthy. Made of wood, they're plated with 48 bronze panels featuring biblical scenes and important moments from San Zeno's life. Thrown into the mix are more bizarre images of dubious origin and meaning; see if you can figure out what that woman is doing with those two crocodiles attached to her breasts! Above the doorway is a relief sculpture in which the saint can be seen overcoming Satan. On either side of the doorway are splendidly ornate relief carvings, helping to make this one of the most celebrated Romanesque churches in Italy.

Sunday Savings

With the exception of Casa di Giulietta and the Arena, all of Verona's most important museums are free on the first Sunday of every month. Arena admission is reduced to €1 on this day (but, alas and alack, there's no break given at Juliet's touristy home).

The splendid detail continues inside, where you'll notice that the nave resembles the keel of a ship, and the walls are covered with early frescoes and later prayers to the patron saint, graffitied on the walls by earnest citizens during desperate times. Andrea Mantegna's 15th-century *Madonna and Child* triptych can be viewed at the altar, but it's also worth seeking out the polychromatic statue of the spectacularly jolly San Zeno, carved out of marble in the 12th century, and fondly referred to as "San Zeno Laughing." Attached to the church is a cloister enclosing a lawn courtyard, and there's a 72m (236-ft.) campanile (bell tower), the construction of which began in 1045. An antiques market held in Piazza San Zeno on the third Saturday of every month is definitely worth a visit.

If you are fascinated by Italian religious architecture, and if you have the time, you may consider visiting two other early churches, both in proximity to the Arena. **San Lorenzo** is a Romanesque church built in 1117 on the site of an earlier Christian building, according to a Latin cross plan. Extraordinarily, the facade features Norman towers from the 15th century.

Finally, the 11th-century **San Fermo Maggiore** (Stradore San Fermo; ☎ 045-592813) is a colossal structure featuring four naves, and composed of two halves: the lower original part is Romanesque, and the 14th-century upper part is Gothic. A visit inside reveals two entirely competing moods and styles, all under a vaulted wooden ceiling that suggests the shape of an upside-down boat. A fresco by Antonia Pisanello is the star artwork among a number of lovely paintings from the 14th and 15th centuries.

THE OTHER VERONA

Today, Verona's most spectacular battles take place not in the Arena but at the Marc'Antonio Bentegodi Stadium, where the city's population turns out en masse to witness magnificent **soccer matches.** Verona boasts two important European clubs: **Chievo Verona,** once a B-league team, is now considered one of the country's finest teams, while **Hellas Verona** remains a favorite despite dropping to the B-league. The stadium, which has hosted the World Cup, has a capacity of 39,000 and is home to both the city's teams, which enjoy a hard-core fan base.

The stadium is about a kilometer west of the city center, and is a great place to rub shoulders with real locals. It's easy enough to walk to, but even easier to get there by bus: Nos. 11, 12, and 13 all run from the historic center to the stadium. The ticket offices are outside the stadium, or purchase online from the team website at www.chievoverona.it.

NIGHTLIFE

If you're lucky, you may just be able to catch a performance of *Romeo and Juliet* at the intimate outdoor **Teatro Romano,** where a **Shakespeare Festival** ✖✖ is held annually from June through early September. I saw a thoroughly entertaining Italian version of the tragic romance in 2005, with such visually dynamic

---

Rock Opera

When **opera season** ✖✖✖ rolls around, the unassuming town of Verona raises its head and prepares for an influx of cultured nobility; suitably attired and ready to be escorted to their €150 seats, this refined set—who turn up to give standing ovations to some of the finest voices on earth—make one forget that the Arena was initially intended for Roman spectacles of violence and bloodshed that wowed up to 30,000 people per sitting.

The season runs from mid-June until the end of August, the highlight usually being performances of Verdi's *Aida*. The version of this staged during the 83rd season, in 2005, featured mind-boggling scenery and staging by Franco Zeffirelli (who is known for directing a big-screen, men-in-tights version of *Romeo and Juliet* back in 1968), with colossal gold pyramids and sphinxes filling the stage; even those of us sitting far away could appreciate the spectacle. *Aida* is probably the one show you must consider booking for in advance; tour leaders practically insist that their groups attend this show, and the midrange reserved seats are often sold out (particularly on weekends). Bear in mind that while the rock-bottom tickets being sold for €10 to €17 may sound like a bargain, there will be some obstruction of your view because you'll be watching the show from the side of the stage.

You can purchase tickets for the opera at the box office beneath the Arena itself (Via Dietro Anfiteatro, 6/B); credit cards are accepted, although the phone line is frequently down, so it's a good idea to take cash just in case. You can also phone in your booking (☎ 045-8005151) or use the Web, www.arena.it, where you can also get program details.

Note: If you're attending a performance of the opera season, bring a cushion, or rent one on your way into the Arena. If you fail to heed this warning, you'll be using your backside to polish some of the same hard rock as Roman spectators did nearly 2,000 years ago, and you'll regret it deeply. Binoculars are handy too!

The **Associazione Culturale Orpheus** (Chiostro S. Luca, Corso Porta Nuova, 12; www.operainconcerto.it; €15) isn't exactly competing with the opera at the Arena, but it offers alternative concert performances on a much smaller scale between late June and early September. Orpheus presents a very mixed bag of concerts, usually boasting one or two of the minor "stars" from the main Arena program as guest soloists.

staging that I didn't need to understand a word that was being said. The Teatro Romano also hosts summer musical performances, as well as contemporary dance shows and ballet. The Verona Jazz program is particularly impressive, drawing an outstanding international lineup. **Theater tickets** are available at the **box office** on Piazza Brà (☎ 045-8077500 or 045-8066485; www.estateteatraleveronese.it); in purchasing them, note that it's more expensive to sit on reserved plastic chairs nearer the stage, but that you have a more authentic experience by paying less and taking a cushion for a place with the plebes on the original stone seats a little further back.

Drinking & Relaxing

Although it's expensive, my favorite venue for pre-opera drinks is **Via Roma 33 Café** ✪✪ (Via Roma, 33; ☎ 045-591917), where contemporary stylishness draws Verona's definitive "in" crowd, who are, in turn, served by beautiful waiters and waitresses. You can sit under umbrellas outside, or enjoy the chilled, cosmopolitan ambience of the all-white interior. Although a cocktail here will set you back a whopping €3.50, it's likely to be the best mixed drink you'll enjoy anywhere in the Veneto—and served with a dazzling smile.

The best place to enjoy a drink while taking in the splendid view over the city is **Mako** ✪ (☎ 045-8340648; summer only 10am–2am), which is situated on the hill above the Teatro Romano, in the same complex as Castel San Pietro. This cool open-air cocktail lounge/bar is where modern-day Romeos and Juliets sink deep into Bali-style sofas, surrounded by barrels of bamboo stained in pastel pink, purple, and lilac; there's live music at night, and you can order snacks (€2.50–€5), try out various wines, or have an excellent cocktail (mojitos and margaritas are €6), or even log on to the Internet.

SIDE TRIPS FROM VERONA

You can take two worthwhile side trips from Verona.

Mantua

Mantua's historical center is all cobblestone streets, Roman ruins, and classical monuments, and its interlocking squares in the heart of the city easily evoke a sense of Middle Ages bonhomie. Fashioned out of muddy marshland, this small Lombardy city, called Mantova in Italian, was the home of Virgil and is believed to be where the blood of Christ is kept in a crypt, having been brought here by the soldier who pierced his side while he hung upon the cross. Mantua was also a creative center for a number of good Renaissance artists, many of whom were sponsored and subsidized by the city's powerful Gonzaga clan.

Although they started out as peasants (originally named Corradi), the Gonzagas emerged as one of Europe's most prosperous and powerful dynasties, ruling here with an iron fist for almost 4 centuries and improving their political interests through a series of tactical marriages that expanded their power and improved their bloodlines. The spirit of acquisition that drove the Gonzagas has all the elements of a good melodrama, which you can get a feel for by visiting their vast palace complex, still rich with artistic treasures. Thankfully, the wealthy Gonzagas also fostered a period of intense cultural development, centered on their patronage of architects and artists. Whatever your feelings are regarding factual and mythical history, Mantua is hugely romantic, and well worth a visit; unencumbered by tourist hordes, it's a most convenient side trip from Verona.

Get up early to catch the 9:33am **train** from Verona (€2.30), which will allow you to spend a full day enjoying the many sights. *Warning:* Don't visit Mantua on a Monday, when nearly every attraction in town is closed.

From the train station, you can take **bus no. 1** directly into the historical center, which you can also reach on foot (count on about 10 min.). Here, with its entrance on Piazza delle Erbe, you'll find an extremely thorough **Ufficio Informazioni Turistiche (Tourist Information Office;** Piazza Montegna, 6; ☎ 0376-328253; www.turismo.mantova.it; Mon–Sat 8:30am–12:30pm and 3–6pm, Sun 9:30am–12:30pm), with reams of ideas for how you can spend your day, and maps that will help you find your way.

The tourist office has its entrance directly opposite the small round **Rotonda di San Lorenzo** (free admission; daily 10am–1pm and 2–6pm), the city's oldest church, originally built in the 11th century. Although it has been partially demolished and rebuilt, there are still some 800-year-old frescoes on display.

Around the corner, the imposing facade of the Renaissance-era **Basilica of St. Andrea** ✭ (Piazza Montegna; ☎ 0376-328504; free admission; daily 8am–noon and 3–7pm) looms gracefully over Piazza Montegna. Commissioned by Lodovico II Gonzaga and designed in monumental style by Leon Battista Alberti, this church centers on a holy crypt in which soil soaked with the blood of Christ is kept. The sacred relic was supposedly brought to Mantua by Longinus, the Roman soldier who pierced Christ's side while he was on the cross, and its authenticity was demonstrated when a visiting pope claimed that it cured his gout. You can visit the crypt with permission for €1; those in town on Good Friday can witness a procession in which the relic is paraded through the city streets. Above the altar of the crypt is the Octagon, and above this is the church's main dome, decorated with a fresco featuring a frenzy of activity. The first chapel on the left is also the final resting place of Andrea Mantegna, the much sought-after court painter employed by the Gonzagas during the 15th century.

Mantegna is celebrated as the most important investment the Gonzagas made in a long and sensitive relationship with the arts. Sure, they mostly enjoyed having themselves painted, but they also supported artists like Titian and Pisanello, thus inadvertently making a valuable contribution to museums around the world. To see Mantegna's famous rendition of the Gonzagas, visit the fascinating **Palazzo Ducale** ✭ (Porto Sordello; ☎ 0367-224832; www.mantovaducale.it; €6.50; Tues–Sun 8:45am–7:15pm), a city-within-a-city that was the Gonzaga family home, a palace that expanded along with their wealth and means. Pressed for time, I'd single out the Camera degli Sposi, one of the apartments of Isabelle d'Este, who married Francesco Gonzaga at the end of the 15th century; here, Mantegna spent 9 years capturing life at court in his famous fresco cycle, which is a marvel of Renaissance painting.

Amid the palace's maze of architectural styles, you'll encounter hundreds of treasures of the Renaissance and Roman eras, although it remains a sore point that many of Mantegna's canvases have been removed to other museums across the globe. Pisanello's frescoes decorate the **Sala del Pisanello;** his 15th-century celebration of the Arthurian legends remained under plaster until rediscovery in 1969. Also worth a look is the **Apartment of the Dwarves (Appartemento dei**

Nani) with its miniature version of the Vatican's holy staircase, built to amuse the "little people" who were members of Isabella's court.

Hedonism and frivolity are the principal qualities that defined the design and decoration of the **Palazzo Te** ✪✪ (Viale Te; ☎ 0376-323266; €8, €2.50 concession; Tues–Sun 9am–6pm, Mon 1–6pm), my favorite attraction in Mantua, about 20 minutes south by foot from the center. It was here that Isabella's fun-loving son Frederico Gonzago sought refuge from the rigors of court life. He commissioned Giulio Romano to build this beautiful Mannerist suburban villa as an unabashed tribute to worldly pleasures; throughout the palace, frescoes depict horses, cherubs, and classical myths with an overtly erotic edge. In the splendid **Sala dei Giganti (Room of the Giants),** the dramatic perspective of the ceiling fresco forces the spectator to share the experience of imminent collapse as the crumbling slopes of Mount Olympus bring about the defeat of the Giants at the hands of Jupiter and the gods.

SAMPLING THE TASTE OF MANTUA   Even more so than Verona, Mantua is horse-meat country. To sample this classic Roman delicacy, visit the 250-year-old **Antica Hosteria Leoncino Rosso** (Via Giustiziati, 33; ☎ 0376-323277; Mon–Sat noon–3:30pm and 7–10:30pm, Sun noon–3:30pm), right in the historical city center. There's plenty to choose from the menu of Mantuan, Italian, and Roman dishes. I like to order a variety of dishes, starting with Mantuan garlic salami *(salame mantovano),* which is particularly good with the house tap wine. Some of the more exotic dishes include risotto with Mantua sausage, macaroni with stewed horse meat *(maccheroni con stracotto),* or you can go for plain horse stew. If, like me, you're not into equine meat, try the superbly roasted guinea fowl, or rabbit stuffed with olives. Most dishes are under €10. Note that the restaurant is closed for half of August.

Trent

The Adige River links Verona with the gorgeous Alpine town of Trent, 101km (63 miles) to the north. Here, betwixt soaring mountains a sense of meditative calm prevails, making this a tranquil respite from the busier cities. Of course, the laid-back atmosphere you'll experience in this sun-drenched valley town is in stark contrast to the town's history as the seat of powerful Church overlords: Trent was ruled by dynastic bishops from the 10th century until the 1700s. It was here that furiously militant Christianity exercised a fierce grip during the 16th century, when the Catholic Church staged its Council of Trent in response to Martin Luther's Reformation on the other side of the Alps. Stern meetings, held over 18 years, were designed to halt the spread of the Protestant gospel before it oozed into Italy; it was during these sessions that a blueprint for the coming Inquisition was established. Many of the town's attractions remain suffused with the legacy of the Council's proceedings.

There are frequent **trains** from Verona to Trent, and the trip lasts around 1 hour; you save €3 by taking the regional, slightly slower train (70 min. rather than 58 min.), which costs €4.65; visit www.trenitalia.com for full schedules. From the train station, walk along Via Pozzo until you get to Piazza del Duomo (just keep on going as Pozzo changes its name along the way), which centers on a fountain statue of Neptune. Here, cafes fill the square in front of the rather ordinary-looking Duomo; it's also where you can pop into the **tourist office** (Via Manci, 2; ☎ 0461-983880; www.apt.trento.it; daily 9am–7pm). Pick up the euro-saving **Trento Card** for €9 here, which allows free entrance to all museums, and saves on public transport for a 24-hour period (there's also a 48-hr. version with added benefits for €14). The card also allows free bicycle rentals and discounted meals at some restaurants.

Construction of the **Duomo** (☎ 0461-234419; free admission, although there's a €1 admission to the crypt; Mon–Sat 9:30am–12:30pm and 2:30–6pm) was initiated in the 13th century, and it was here that the Council announced many of its decisions, particularly after its most important meetings were held here in the Chapel of the Crucifix, recognizable by its massive cross. Beneath the altar of the main church are the foundations of the 6th-century Basilica Paleocristiana, an early church where the remains of some of the first prince-bishops of Trent are buried.

There's a museum in the Palazzo Pretorio attached to the Duomo; the **Museo Diocesano Tridentino** (☎ 0461-234419; www.museodiocesanotridentino.it; €3 adults, €.50 teens; Wed–Mon 9:30am–12:30pm and 2–5:30pm) is in a 13th-century palace where the city's prince-bishops lived like nobility. Besides a collection of artistic treasures from the Duomo, the museum provides a pictorial account of the proceedings of the Council of Trent; the paintings here documenting its activities are akin to our modern "artist's renditions" of courtroom proceedings.

From Piazza del Duomo, follow the *palazzo*-lined Via R. Belenzani until it meets Via Roma, where you turn right to head east until you reach the Piazza della Mostra, across from which is the **Castello del Buonconsiglio** (☎ 0461-233770; www.buonconsiglio.it; €5; Apr–Sept Tues–Sun 9am–noon and 2–5:30pm, Oct–Mar 9am–noon and 2–5pm), on the eastern outskirts of the center. A repository for the city's art treasures, collected by Bernardo Clesio (a powerful ruler of Trent), this was another venue for the Council of Trent. Comprising two castles in a single complex, the original medieval Castelvecchio was extended in the early 16th century when the Magno Palazzo was added. Within the Castello complex is the **Museo Provinciale d'Arte,** and within its Torre dell'Aquila (Eagle Tower) is the *Ciclo dei Mesi (Cycle of the Months),* a marvelous fresco cycle presenting 15th-century court and country life. To ascend the Eagle Tower, you need to reserve in advance and cough up €1 extra.

Between the Duomo and the Castello, you can also visit the **Roman ruins of the Tridentum** (Piazza Cesare Battisti; www.provincia.tn.it; €2; June–Aug Tues–Sun 10am–noon and 2:30–7pm, Sept–May 9am–noon and 2:30–6pm). Discovered by archaeologists during the 1990s, the ruins date back to 1000 B.C., and include extensive Roman roadways and sewage systems. This important site is on view from a new visitor center.

For a superb bird's-eye view of Trent, you can catch a ride in the **Funivia Trento** (☎ 0461-822075; €.80), a cable car departing every 15 to 30 minutes from Ponte di San Lorenzo (southwest of the train station) to ascend to the lofty heights of the mountain village of Sardagna on the slopes of Monte Bondone.

A further attraction that can be added to your visit to Trent is the **MART** (Corso Bettini, 43, Rovereto, 25km/16 miles south of Trent; www.mart.trento.it; Tues–Sun, 10am–6pm, Fri until 9pm), Italy's largest modern-art museum, which opened in December 2002. Over and above the permanent collection of almost 10,000 paintings, sculptures, and other works, there's a lineup of temporary exhibitions.

It's a good place to learn more about 20th-century avant-garde art and the Futurist movement, dominated here by Italian works. If you purchase the 48-hour version of the Trento Ticket, admission is free; otherwise it costs €8. If you're feeling active, you can cycle there using the cycle track along the Adige River, or catch bus no. 301 from the station.

For a quick bite: Drop into **Scrigno del Duomo** ✦ (Piazza del Duomo, 29; ☎ 0461-20030; www.scrignodelduomo.com; daily 11am–3pm and 6pm–12:30am), a chic little wine bar that features imaginatively prepared Italian fare with *primi* in the €6 to €8 range.

CORTINA D'AMPEZZO

The craggy, soaring peaks of Italy's Alpine Dolomite range are unmistakable; like a massive coral reef ripped from the sea, strung with conifers and laced with snow, these mountains have a look distinct from any other major range in the world (they also have some of the most exotic-sounding names: Cristallo, Tofane, and Sorapiss). Picturesque Cortina d'Ampezzo, at the center of it all, has been drawing skiers for over a century, its reputation cemented when the Olympics were held here in 1956. Today it's prime schussing ground for the designer set, *the* place to ski side by side with European jet-setters and celebrities who, during the season, multiply by five-fold the 7,000-strong population of this village. When it's not a bustling ski-resort, it becomes a center for hard-core hikers and climbers, who are challenged by the endless selection of routes on offer.

DON'T LEAVE CORTINA D'AMPEZZO WITHOUT . . .

RIDING THE ARROW IN THE SKY   The **Freccia nel Cielo** (p. 379) is one of Italy's great funicular experiences, taking you from Cortina's Olympic Ice Skating Stadium to the lofty heights of the incredible Dolomites. Views from the top—3,163m (10,377 ft.) above sea level—are unforgettable.

SKIING THE PISTE WITH YOUR SUPERSKI PASS   Cortina is considered the top ski resort in the country, and it would be unthinkable to miss the opportunity of tackling at least a few of the 18 ski areas accessible with the very reasonably priced **Dolomiti Superski pass** (p. 380).

LAY OF THE LAND

There is no direct rail service to Cortina; the **nearest railway** is in Calalzo di Cadore, 35km (22 miles) south. From Calalzo, there are **regular bus services** to Cortina; try either **Dolomitibus** (☎ 0437-217111; www.dolomitibus.it) or **ATVO** (☎ 041-5415180). Calalzo is serviced by fairly regular trains from Venice and Padua, but you should consult the schedules on www.trenitalia.it to determine which of these are direct, as some routes may be fairly convoluted. The entire journey from Venice to Cortina takes around 3½ hours. If you're traveling from Rome, Eurostar Italia has daytime services to Mestre (mainland Venice), from where there are **shuttle buses** to transfer you directly to Cortina; these shuttles are scheduled to coincide with your train times (for details, contact **Servizi Ampezzo:** ☎ 0436-867921). You can also catch a **direct bus** from Venice to Cortina; it takes the entire morning (departing 7:50am), but the affordable (€11) and scenic journey makes it worthwhile.

During peak season—the so-called "white weeks" of winter—buses deliver hotel guests directly from Venice and Treviso airports to their hotels; this happens on Saturday and Sunday. An excellent source of information regarding shuttle services into Cortina is www.dolomiti.org, a superb regional resource.

Cortina has its own **urban bus service** (Dolomiti Bus information: ☎ 0436-867921; Mon–Fri 8:15am–12:30pm and 2:30–6pm, Sat 8:15am–12:30pm), which operates various routes and is useful for getting to out-of-town cable cars and hotels that aren't in the center. Bus tickets (€.80) are available from *tabacchi* and bars near the bus stops; if you're planning to make frequent use of the bus, buy books of tickets (€8 for 12) or get a weeklong Guest Card pass (€10). There's also a round-the-clock **taxi service;** call **RadioTaxi** (☎ 0436-860808).

ACCOMMODATIONS, BOTH STANDARD & NOT

Cortina's accommodations aren't cheap, and the popularity of the resort with up-market travelers means those winter prices are not going to drop in a hurry. Out-of-season, Cortina is quiet and low-key, and hotel prices ease up; some even close down during the slowest periods. But when the snow falls and demand skyrockets, so does the cost of a bed in even the simplest of hotels; also, high-season demand makes it virtually impossible to secure a bed without several months' advance reservation. *Note:* Some hotels will ask you to stay for a full week during high season; at best they might offer discounted rates for extended stays.

The best way to save on lodging is to stay in a private home; visit the **tourist office** (Piazzetta San Francesco, 8; ☎ 0436-3231) to see what's on offer. Its website (www.infodolomiti.it) also carries extensive listings of other alternative lodging options, including farm stays and bed-and-breakfasts. If you're the genuinely outdoorsy type, you can forgo hotel accommodations altogether, and head out (on a mapped hike) with your camping equipment and a plan to make use of one of the many **refuges** dotted around the d'Ampezzo area; these operate in the summer period from late June until late September. The tourist office and its website (see above) have information about the refuges.

Standard Hotels in Cortina

Cortina's great boom happened in the 1950s when the town prepared for the crowds attending the Olympic Games; ideas about hotel style have not exactly moved on since then and accommodations remain simple and a trifle "cottagey," with plenty of wood paneling and floral bedspreads.

€€–€€€   If you're arriving by bus and want to be near the center, there are more than enough options right near the bus terminal. Unpretentious and unassuming, **Hotel Cornelio** (Via Cantore, 1; ☎ 0463-2232 or 0436/2535; www.hotel cornelio.com) offers value and a welcoming attitude. When I last stayed here during low season, its rather tiny single rooms were among the cheapest I could find (€45, including breakfast), although prices do drop even lower as you head out of town. Rooms are almost entirely done in wood, so there is some creaking and groaning, and you have a good idea of when your neighbor is flushing the loo or moving around the room, but that's pretty much standard for Cortina. Even my tiny room had a small terrace with a Dolomite panorama, and given the dearth of good dining options in the town, you could do worse than to use the in-house *ristorante,* where regional dishes are served.

€€–€€€   The town center is where you'll find **Hotel Montana** (Corso Italia, 94; ☎ 0436-862126; www.cortina-hotel.com), which is comfortable and affordable—more so if you stay for periods of 7 days or longer (in popular Feb, you'll generally pay €880 for a double for a 1-week stay, while the Jan rate is €550). There are also some excellent online specials from time to time; I recently found a weekly rate of €175 per person for October. Guest rooms are mostly spacious, with wooden floors and typical, quaint styling; ask for one with a balcony affording views of the Dolomites. Only breakfast is served, but there are a number of cafes nearby where you can eat cheaply, or picnic in your room with supplies from the nearby supermarket.

€€–€€€€   If you are traveling with your own vehicle, you might want to consider the charming, homey **Hotel Menardi** ★ (Via Majon, 110, ☎ 0436-2400; www.hotelmenardi.it), which somehow feels just the way an Alpine retreat should. The hotel has been a family concern since the early 20th century, when the Menardis moved from farming to hosting guests and travelers. Guest rooms start at about €45 per person. Rooms vary considerably, too, but they're all fairly spacious, with pine floors, pine walls, pine cupboards, and a pine desk; fabrics are eclectic with fussy patterns. Rooms in the 15-year-old annex are larger and carpeted (they're also a touch more stylish and modern); I would advise asking for a first-floor corner unit, where you can enjoy breakfast on your wooden balcony while enjoying views of the surrounding mountains. In the annex, the Menardis have added a wellness center where you can defrost in the Jacuzzi or sauna or steam bath, or enjoy a deep tissue massage. The warm atmosphere pervades the public spaces, from the lobby area, filled with statues of the Virgin, to the cozy bar, where a fire is lit in winter, and the downstairs wine nook (a typical feature of Dolomite homes), where tastings are sometimes held.

€€€   Another well-priced option is **Hotel Villa Gaia** (Via Guide Alpine, 96; ☎ 0436-2974; www.hotelvillagaia.it), which has benefited from a refreshing makeover. It may not be the most fabulous hotel in town, but there's a quaintness about the place that seems to underscore the keenly low prices. Open year-round, the peak season rate (other than the Christmas to New Year's period) is €120 double, including breakfast; there are additional discounts for weeklong stays during the popular "white weeks." Guest rooms are simple, with wood-paneled walls and the usual, basic styling; some of the rooms have spectacular views from tiny terraces.

€€€–€€€€   While Menardi's charms are mostly concerned with its large garden that's dotted with wooden barrows of colorful flowers, I must tell you that **Hotel Ambra** ★ (Via XXIX Maggia, 28; ☎ 0436-867344; www.hotelambracortina. it), situated in the center near the town's church bell tower, is smarter and offers cheaper rates during most of the winter season (although it's pricier in summer, when it seems to attract a steady, loyal following). Ambra is the hands-down winner for value with a sleek design. There may not be as much space at Ambra (it's a much smaller hotel, with just 25 rooms), but a sense of calm and order prevails. What you need to consider is that Menardi generally offers its best rates based on half-board lodging. While Menardi charges €130 per person sharing in February, Ambra's rate for 2006 is €90. In my opinion, you save more by reserving at Ambra and spending some of the extra cash on a good meal.

The Camping Option

€   In Località Fiames, 5km (3 miles) north of Cortina, but still on the urban bus route (take bus no. 1 to the access road), is **International Camping Olympia** (☎/fax 0436-5057; www.campingolympiacortina.it), which has good facilities (including a restaurant, bar, swimming pool, and sauna) and is open year-round. Adults are charged between €4.50 and €7.50, depending on the season. The campsite also offers bunk beds in dorms (€20).

Closer to town, in Campo (2km/1¼ miles south), are a number of other camping sites, including **Rochetta** (☎ 0436-5063) and **Cortina** (☎ 0436-867575).

DINING FOR ALL TASTES

If you're looking to make up a **picnic basket,** the best pastries and breads in town are available from **Panificio Alvera Pasticceria** at Corso Italia, 191. The busy store also sells treats that you can take home as gifts, including regional specialties such as bottled fruit fermented in grappa, and various jams and preserves. Farther along Corso Italia, toward the town center and near the church, I have found plenty of goodies at the supermarket, **La Cooperativa di Cortina** (☎ 0436-861245; www.coopcortina.com).

Cortina's restaurants offer the opportunity to try both authentic Tyrolean cuisine and Italian food with a Germanic edge. Expect to find plenty of meat, including sausage, veal, and venison on the menu. Asparagus, wild mushrooms, and radicchio are widely used, often in hot, creamy sauces, while ravioli stuffed with beetroot is well worth seeking out.

Simple dishes and snacks are available at several of the terraced cafes along the popular pedestrian drag, Corso Italia.

€€   You'll find plenty of choice at **Pizzeria Ristorante Ghedina al Passetto** (Via Marconi, 8; ☎ 0436-2254; www.alpassettoghedina.it), smack in the center of town. Usually packed with skiers, this well-priced, wood-paneled restaurant is filled with the aroma of good, wholesome food. While there are plenty of pizzas and pastas, it's the regional specialties that deserve attention: Tyrolean balls with melted butter and Parmesan, and Tyrolean dumpling soup, especially. Simple main courses include plenty of meat and sausage dishes to stave off the cold; beef filet in a vodka sauce, or sausage prepared in a cabernet sauce and served with polenta, are some of the more elaborate offerings. Wine is served by the glass, the bottle, or the carafe, and the tiramisu here is famous with good reason.

€€   Just east of town is the popular **Al Camin** (Via Alvera, 99; ☎ 0436-862010; Tues–Sun noon–3pm and 7–11:30pm), where you'll find the kind of authentic fare that's usually only served in local homes. I especially enjoy the *knederli,* the region's liver-flavored dumplings. First courses here range from €7 to €10 and are served up in a rustic dining hall, centered on an old stone fireplace.

WHY YOU'RE HERE: THE TOP SIGHTS & ATTRACTIONS

The best sights in and around town are natural ones; come here any time of year and you'll view spectacular mountain scenery. Stony peaks rise from valleys that are carpeted by lush forest and meadows, and that are dotted with quirky Alpine houses.

For all sorts of skiing and hiking information, you can start by dropping in at the **tourist office** (Piazzetta San Francesco, 8; ☎ 0436-3231; www.infodolomiti. it; daily 9am–12:30pm and 4–7pm). Another excellent source of information is **Cortina Turismo** (Via Marconi, 15/B; ☎ 0436-866252; www.dolomiti.org), which supplies an outstanding map of footpaths in the mountains around town.

Of course, you don't have to be a skier or rock-climber to appreciate the high-altitude Alpine peaks; simply hop on a funicular to enjoy a steady, no-hassle climb through achingly beautiful mountain scenery. Funiculars generally run from mid-July to late September and from mid-December until May 1; departures start at 9am and run every 20 or 30 minutes until 4 or 5pm. The aptly named **Freccia nel Cielo (Arrow in the Sky)** ✪✪ (☎ 0436-5052 for information), provides the most breathtaking ascent in the region; departures are from the ground station not far from Stadio Olimpico del Ghiaccio (Olympic Ice-Skating Stadium). You can travel as far as the second stop—Ra Valles (altitude 2,550m/8,364 ft.)—for €20 round-trip; once there, you can sit back and take in the ragged Dolomitic peaks while enjoying a drink on the terrace of the bar. For €24 you can head all the way to the top and back—the final station, Tafano di Mezzo, is a magnificent 3,163m (10,375 ft.) above sea level.

If you want to enjoy at least one cable-car ascent, but can't afford the Arrow in the Sky, consider the popular **Funivia Faloria,** which operates from a station southeast of town; the excursion costs only €8 round-trip, and you can spend the money you've saved at the bar of the Faloria Refuge (2,123m/6,963 ft.), where you can relax on the terrace enjoying panoramic views of the Dolomites and Cortina town.

More adventurous visitors should start by contacting **Gruppo Guide Alpine** (Corso Italia, 69/4; ☎ 0436-868505; www.guidecortina.com), which offers a range of activities for beginners and experts. Many of the adventures are snow-related, and the guides here will lead you on all manner of ski adventures, including danger-free snowshoeing and more daring ice-climbing. In the snow-free seasons, they provide experts in hiking, rock-climbing, and mountain biking. There are a number of specialized programs for children and also for older adventurers. With more than 55 years in the business, and nearly 30 guides aged 27 to 65, the company has a sterling reputation; its outings may well be the highlight of your visit to Italy.

There's all manner of adventurous fun to be had at the **Cortina Adrenaline Center** (☎ 0436-860808; www.adrenalincenter.it), based at the Pista Olimpica di Bob (Olympic bobsled arena). You can take on canyoning, rafting, hydrospeeding, kayaking, mountain biking, and—if you're truly brave—try "Taxi Bob Wheel," a thrilling, 110kmph (68 mph) simulation of the bobsledding experience, only with tires and a brake system! A further activity for those wishing to test their mettle is the army training course type Adventure Park, where, armed with climbing gear and pulley attachments, you swing on vines, pull yourself along ropes, and traverse mountain bridges.

Skiing the Dolomites

Cortina's reputation as Italy's leading ski resort is not to be scoffed at; slopes and facilities are top-notch, and fine ski routes are easily accessible thanks to the system of funiculars. Cortina has 8 ski areas and there are another 10 within easy reach, all of which fall under the scheme covered by the **Dolomiti Superski pass,** which allows unlimited skiing and ski-related travel (on shuttle buses, funiculars, and chairlifts) for a predetermined period; you'll have access to 1,220km (756 miles) of ski runs and 450 chairlifts. Prices vary according to the number of days you choose, starting with a 1-day pass at €38 during high season (children and seniors pay a discounted rate); by comparison, a 7-day pass costs €206 for the same period. High season generally runs from around December 24 to January 7 and February 5 through March 11; there are slight savings during the lower season (mid-Jan and mid-Mar). To get your pass, or for more information, go to **Dolomiti Superski** (Via di Castello, 33; ☎ 0436-862171; www.dolomitisuperski.com), where you can also explore a number of savings schemes.

For those who prefer independent adventures, the terrain around Cortina draws hard-core cyclists keen to develop their mountain-biking stamina. There are some easier routes out of town, or you can stick to the roads (although you should be wary of heavy traffic during certain periods); you can **rent bikes** from **2ue & 2ue** (Via Roma, 70; ☎ 0436-4121; www.dueduecortina.com), which offers special deals on family rentals, and which can give you advice on where to peddle.

Activities

On those days when the weather doesn't cooperate, you can cruise through the center of town, exploring picturesque Corso Italia or browsing boutiques aimed at high-end spenders. There are a couple of churches, expensive art galleries, and even a **Museum of Modern Art** (Via del Parco, 1; ☎ 0436-2206; www.musei. regole.it; adults €5, seniors and students and children 6–14 €3, free for children under 6; Jan–Easter daily 4pm–7:30pm, June and Sept Tues–Sun 10am–12:30pm and 4–7:30pm, July–Aug and Christmas holidays daily 10am–12:30pm and 4–8pm, call for appointment when museum is closed). Architecture is a blend of stone structures (such as the Santi Filippo e Giacomo church in the center) and Alpine buildings constructed over the years since the town became a popular stopover venue in the mid-1800s.

Besides the many outdoor pursuits offered in the area, you can also visit the Olympic ice-skating arena, **Stadio Olimpico del Ghiaccio** (Via del Stadio; ☎ 0436-4380; skate rental and admission €8.50), which has two ice-skating rinks open to the public.

Milan & the Lake District

The wealthy region of Lombardy combines commerce with high living.

by Reid Bramblett

MILAN IS THE GLITZY CAPITAL OF LOMBARDY (LOMBARDIA), ITALY'S MOST prosperous region. Its factories largely fuel the Italian economy, and its attractions—high fashion, fine dining, hopping dance clubs, and da Vinci's *Last Supper*—have much to offer the visitor. But there's much more than a sophisticated city to Lombardy. To the north, the region bumps up against craggy mountains in a romantic lake district, and to the south it spreads out in fertile farmlands fed by the mighty Po and other rivers.

Lombardy has a different feel from the rest of Italy. The *Lombardi,* who descended from one of the Germanic tribes that overran the Roman empire, and who have over the centuries been ruled by feudal dynasties from Spain, Austria, and France, are a little more Continental than their neighbors to the south; indeed, the *Lombardi* are faster talking, faster paced, and more business-oriented. They even dine differently, tending to eschew olive oil for butter and often forgoing pasta for polenta and risotto.

The Italian lakes have entranced writers from Catullus to Ernest Hemingway. Backed by the Alps and ringed by lush gardens and verdant forests, each lake has its own charms and, accordingly, its own enthusiasts. Not least among these charms is their easy accessibility to many Italian cities, making them ideal for short retreats: Lake Maggiore and Lake Como are both less than an hour from Milan, and Lake Garda is tantalizingly close to Venice and Verona. Each of these world-renowned resorts—Como (the choicest), Maggiore (speckled with elegant islands), and Garda (a windsurfing hot spot, and microcosm of Italy, with the Mediterranean lemon groves and vineyards of the south gradually shading to Teutonic schnitzel and beer on the north end)—can make for a great 1- or 2-day break from Italy's sightseeing carnival.

DON'T LEAVE MILAN & THE LAKE DISTRICT WITHOUT . . .

PAYING HOMAGE TO DA VINCI AND MICHELANGELO You'll find *The Last Supper* in Santa Maria delle Grazie and the *Pietà,* Michelangelo's last work, inside the medieval Castello Sforzesco.

CLIMBING TO THE ROOF OF THE DUOMO Wander amid the Gothic buttresses and statue-topped spires for a citywide panorama.

SEEING THE BRERA AND AMBROSIANA PICTURE GALLERIES   They feature plenty of stunning work by the Old Masters.

TAKING A WINDOW-SHOPPING SPIN   Walk past the high-end boutiques in Milan's Golden Rectangle, and then go on a budget shopping spree through the stock shops and outlets of Corso Buenos Aires.

INDULGING IN THE NIGHTLIFE   The converted warehouses along the Navigli canals are always hopping after dark.

FERRYING BETWEEN LAKE MAGGIORE'S BORROMEAN ISLANDS   You can tour the palaces of one of Lombardy's last remaining Renaissance-era noble families and watch the peacocks wander their exotic gardens.

MILAN

Milan (Milano) is Italy's financial center, business hub, and fashion capital, as well as one of its most industrialized major cities. That also means it's crowded, noisy, hot in summer; damp and foggy in winter; and distinctly less easygoing (and more expensive) than most Italian cities.

Milan reveals its long history in monuments, museums, and churches—its cathedral is one of Europe's great Gothic structures, and another church contains Leonardo da Vinci's *Last Supper.* This sophisticated city also supports a thriving cultural scene embracing La Scala (one of the world's top opera houses), high-fashion boutiques and shows, and a throbbing nightlife.

LAY OF THE LAND

Think of Milan as a series of concentric circles radiating from the central **Piazza del Duomo,** the Cathedral Square. Within the inner circle, once enclosed by the city walls, are many of the churches, museums, and shops that'll consume your visiting hours. For a general overview, obtain one of the serviceable maps with a street index that the tourist offices provide for free.

The city's major neighborhoods encircle the hub, Piazza del Duomo. Looking east from the Duomo, you can see the imposing **Castello Sforzesco,** at one end of the well-heeled **Magenta neighborhood.** You can walk to the Castello in about 15 minutes by following Via Orefici to **Piazza Cordusio** and from there Via Dante. The other major draw in Magenta is **Santa Maria delle Grazie** *(home of The Last Supper);* to reach it, leave Via Dante at Via Meravigli, which becomes Via Magenta and leads to the church (total walking time from Piazza del Duomo to the church is about 20 min.).

Heading north from Piazza del Duomo, walk through the city's glass-enclosed shopping center (the world's first), the **Galleria Vittorio Emanuele II.** Emerging from the northern end of the Galleria, you'll be in **Piazza della Scala,** steps away from Milan's famous opera house, **La Scala.** A walk northeast of about 5 minutes along Via Manzoni takes you to Via Montenapoleone and the **Quadrilatero d'Oro,** the city's high-fashion shopping district, the epicenter of Italian design. A walk of about 10 minutes northwest of Piazza della Scala along **Via Brera** brings you into the atmospheric **Brera neighborhood,** where cobblestone streets and old *palazzi* surround the city's major art collection, the **Pinacoteca di Brera.**

Another neighborhood to set your sights on is **Ticinese/Navigli,** often referred to just as the Navigli, which translates as "canals." A 15-minute tram ride due south of Piazza del Duomo, the Navigli's old quays follow what remains of an elaborate canal system, designed in part by Leonardo da Vinci, that once laced the city. The moody charm of this area isn't lost on prosperous young Milanese, who are converting old lofts and moving into former quarters of the working classes. The attendant bars, shops, and restaurants on the ground floors have sprung up to serve their needs. It's also the only part of Milan open in August. You can walk to the Navigli in about 30 minutes from Piazza del Duomo by following Via Torino south to Corso Porta Ticinese, but a tram ride (or the Metro to Porta Genova) will get you there more quickly, in about 15 minutes.

GETTING THERE

Both of Milan's **airports** are operated by **SEA** (☎ 02-74852200; www.sea-aeroporti milano.it). **Milan Malpensa,** 45km (27 miles) northwest of the center, handles most international flights. For general information, call ☎ 02-74852200 or 02-76800613. A 40-minute **Malpensa Express train** (☎ 02-20222; www.ferro vienord.it/webmxp) costs €11 and heads half-hourly to the Cadorna train station in western Milan—*not* to the larger and more central Stazione Centrale (you'll have to take the Metro to get there). More convenient are the Malpensa shuttle buses, which run every 20 to 30 minutes and will take you directly to a bus stop on the east side of Stazione Centrale in 50 minutes. Your choices are **Malpensa Bus Express** (☎ 02-33910794), which costs €5.50, or the cheaper **Malpensa Shuttle** (☎ 0331-258411)—same exact service at a lower price: €5. The trip into town by taxi costs a whopping €60 to €75.

The airport called **Milan Linate,** only 7 km (4 miles) east of the center, handles some European flights (which are increasingly being moved to Malpensa) and domestic flights. For information, dial ☎ 02-74852200. **Starfly buses** (☎ 02-58587237) run from Linate to Stazione Centrale every 20 to 30 minutes; allow 20 minutes for the trip, which costs €3. For €1 you can also take city bus no. 73 to and from Linate from the southeast corner of Piazza San Babila, a few blocks east of the Duomo. The trip into town by taxi costs about €12 to €18.

By train, Milan is 552km (343 miles) northwest of Rome (hourly trains; 4½–6 hr.), 288km (179 miles) northwest of Florence (hourly trains; 2¾–4 hr.), and 257km (160 miles) west of Venice (half-hourly trains; 2½–3½ hr.).

The **Stazione Centrale,** a vast fascist-era structure, is about a half-hour walk northeast of the center, with easy connections to Piazza del Duomo in the center of downtown by Metro, tram, and bus. The stop on the Metro for the train station

Tip for Departing Passengers

If you're going to the airport to leave on a flight, make sure you call the airline beforehand to find out which terminal you need, as Malpensa's Terminal 1 and Terminal 2 are actually several kilometers apart.

Milan

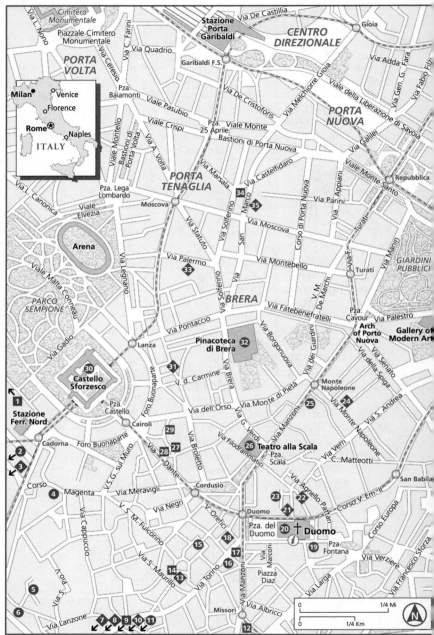

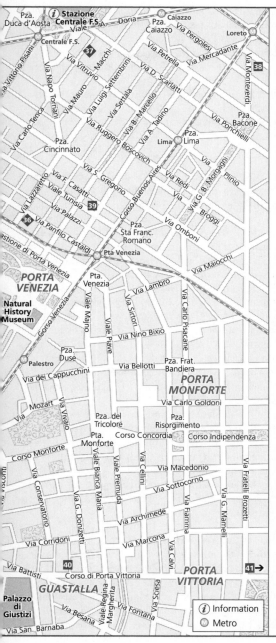

is "Centrale F. S." To get downtown, the Metro is fastest (10 min.), but if you want to see something of the city en route, take bus no. 60 from the station to Piazza del Duomo. If you decide to walk, follow Via Pisani through the district of high-rise office buildings around the station to the equally cheerless Piazza della Repubblica, and from there continue south on Via Turati and Via Manzoni to Piazza del Duomo.

Chances are you'll arrive at Stazione Centrale, but some trains serve Milan's other train stations: Stazione Nord (with service to/from Como, among other cities), Porta Genova (with service to/from Alessandria and Asti), and Porta Garibaldi (with service to/from Lecco).

GETTING AROUND

An extensive and efficient **Metro** (subway system), **trams,** and **buses** make it very easy to move around Milan. The Metro closes at midnight, though buses and trams run all night. Tickets good for one Metro ride (or 75 min. worth of surface transportation) cost €1. You can also get a *carnet* of 10 tickets for €9.20, or purchase unlimited-ride tickets good for 1 day (€3) or 2 days (€5.50). Tickets are available at Metro stations and at newsstands. You must stamp your ticket when you board a bus or tram—you can be slapped with a hefty fine if you don't. For information about Milan public transportation, visit the information office in the Duomo metro stop (☎ 02-72524301 or 800-808181; www.atm-mi.it).

The main Azienda di Promozione Turistica del Milanese (APT) **tourist office** is in the Palazzo del Turismo (Via Marconi, 1, on the south side of Piazza del Duomo; ☎ 02-72524301; www.milanoinfotourist.com). There is also an extremely well-hidden office in Stazione Centrale (☎ 02-72524360). To find it, as you exit the train platform into the main commercial hall—before taking the escalators downstairs to the ticketing areas—head to your left and look for the side corridor on the right whose entrance is lined in flashing neon lights. The tourist office is down that corridor, just past the rock shops flanking either side.

These offices issue maps, museum guides, hotel and restaurant listings, and other useful information, but because they're now privately run, they charge nominal fees for the majority of the more useful materials. The tourism section of the city's website (**www.turismo.comune.milano.it**) is also helpful, as is **www.museidel centro.mi.it,** which covers several of the minor, special-interest museums in the historical center. The private **www.hellomilano.it** is particularly good for events. They publish a monthly events newspaper, free at the tourist offices; online, click on "What's On" for the events calendar.

ACCOMMODATIONS, BOTH STANDARD & NOT

Most Milan hotels are oriented toward business types, with precious few left over for the relatively few tourists who don't high-tail it for more popular cities such as Venice or Florence. It's difficult to find rooms in *any* price category when fashion shows and trade fairs are in full swing (often Oct and Mar). Many hotels raise their prices at these times, too. August is low season, and hotels are often willing to bring prices down considerably (though you really don't want to be here), as they will sometimes do on slow weekends. Always ask for the lowest possible rate when booking and be prepared to bargain.

Though they won't book a room for you, the tourist office (see "Getting Around," earlier in this chapter) will help you track down hotels within your budget (and, if you go to the main office in person, will even call around for you).

Bed & Breakfasts in Milan

Milan doesn't go in much for alternative accommodations. There are only 18 registered B&Bs in the entire city, and few of them are anywhere near the historical center, nor do they offer particularly good savings over hotels.

€€–€€€   There is, however, a clutch of them in the residential district just north of the Navigli, packed with locals' restaurants and low-key bars, and within about a 10-minute walk from a Metro stop. Closest to the Navigli are the three €120 rooms at **Cocoon** (Via Voghera, 7; ☎ 02-8322769 or 349-8606014; Metro: Porta Genova). A few blocks farther north you'll find the three €110-to-€120 attic rooms at **Alle Dolce Vite** (Via Cola di Rienzo, 39; ☎ 02-4895-2808; www.la dolcevite.net; Metro: S. Agostino), with a lovely garden. Between Piazza Vesuvio and Piazza Po, **Bed and Bread** (Via Vetta d'Italia, 14; ☎ 02-468267 or 333-8396441; www.bedandbread.it) offers three small but nice rooms for €100 to €110 and a denlike shared living room with a DVD player and low vaulted brick ceiling. You can always find a handful of other B&Bs, as well as apartments for short-term let, at the official tourist office site www.milanoinfotourist.com and at the private broker www.friendly-home.org.

Hotels near the Duomo

€€   The **Hotel Speronari** ★★ (Via Speronari, 4; ☎ 02-86461125; hotel speronari@inwind.it; Metro: Duomo) is where I usually stay when I come to town: It's a budget hotel—€76 for a double without private bathroom, €96 with bathroom—in a deluxe location, tucked into a tiny pedestrian side street between Via Torino and Via Mazzini near the church of Santa Maria presso S. Satiro. The staff is earnest, and the rooms are basic but done well: cool tile floors, functional furnishings, ceiling fans, and brand-new cot springs. Even those without full bathroom have a sink and bidet, and all, save a few of those without bathrooms, have TVs. Rooms on the third and fourth floors are brighter, and those on the courtyard are a tad quieter than rooms facing the street (there are convenient trolleys a half-block in either direction, but they come with a distant but noisy rumble for rooms on the street side). Credit cards are accepted, but they'll round the room price down if you pay cash.

€€   A 15-minute walk south of the Duomo, the **Hotel Aliseo** (Corso Italia, 6; ☎ 02-86450156 or 02-804535; Metro: Missori) offers a lot of comfort in addition to its good location and great rates: €60 to €75 for a double room without bathroom, €80 to €100 for one with. The management is friendly, and rooms are furnished with pleasant modern pieces and decent beds (no phones, though). Rooms without bathroom come with a tiny washroom with sink and a bidet, just no toilet or shower (large, spanking-clean bathrooms are in the hallway). Rooms on the street side open to small balconies, but are noisier than those overlooking the *cortile*. The Aliseo—which used to be called the Ullrich—books up quickly, so be sure to call ahead.

€€–€€€ The narrow Via Santa Marta is a slice of old Milan, cobblestoned and lined with charming old buildings, one of which houses the **Hotel Santa Marta** ★ (Via Santa Marta, 4; ☎ 02-804567; www.hotel-santamarta.it; Metro: Cordusio or Duomo). Recent modernizations have preserved the old-fashioned ambience while adding such modern comforts as air-conditioning, but rates for a double have stayed around €120 to €130 (dropping to €80 on weekends; spiking to €190 during trade fairs). It's also across the street from one of the city's most atmospheric restaurants (La Milanese; see below), and a short walk from the Duomo and other sights. The tile-floored guest rooms are comfortable and decorated with a matter-of-fact fashion sense; some are cramped and others are quite large, and there's a renovation scheduled for August 2006. If they're full, they'll send you to their sister hotel, the Rovello (see below).

The Magnificent Midrange Hotels of Via Rovello

Halfway between the Duomo and the Castello, just above Piazza Cordusio, a quiet side-street angles off the wide, cafe-and-shop-lined artery of Via Dante. It's called Via Rovello, and it's home to a trio of wonderful midpriced hotels that put you in the heart of the action—no more than a 10-minute stroll from the castle, Duomo, Brera museum, and La Scala opera house—yet tucked away from the busy streets.

€€–€€€€ The 10-room **Hotel Rovello** ★ (Via Rovello, 18; ☎ 02-86464654; www.hotel-rovello.it; Metro: Cordusio) was also completely renovated in 1999 with striking results. The unusually large guest rooms occupy the first and second floors of a centuries-old building and incorporate many of the original architectural details, including exposed timbers and wood-beamed ceilings. Handsome contemporary Italian furnishings are set off by gleaming hardwood floors, the tall casement windows are covered with attractive fabrics, and walls are painted in soothing green and gold tones. The orthopedic mattresses are covered with thick quilts for a homey feel. Many of the rooms have dressing areas in addition to the large new bathrooms. A breakfast of rolls and coffee is served in a sunny room off the lobby.

€€–€€€€ Unlike its neighbors, the **London Hotel** ★ (Via Rovello, 3; ☎ 02-72020166; www.hotellondonmilano.com; Metro: Cordusio) sticks to its old-fashioned ways—and lower prices: Doubles without bathroom go for €100 to €130, with bathroom for €120 to €150. The big fireplace and cozy green velvet furniture in the lobby say a lot about the comfort level and friendly atmosphere that bring many guests back time after time. Just beyond the lobby, there's a bar where beverages are available almost around the clock; guests can purchase cappuccino or a continental breakfast in the morning. Upstairs, the rooms look as if they haven't been redecorated in a number of decades, but they're roomy and bright, and the heavy old furnishings lend a charm very much in keeping with the ambience of the hotel. Rooms on the first floor tend to be the largest, and they get smaller as you go up.

€€€ A recent renovation has brought **Hotel Giulio Cesare** ★ (Via Rovello, 10; ☎ 02-72003915; www.giuliocesarehotel.it; Metro: Cordusio) thoroughly up-to-date, with a grandiose marble lobby and a handsome lounge and bar area with deep couches—though management can be a bit brusque. The rooms are contemporary chic, with starkly modern minimalist furnishings, but do reflect the building's centuries-old heritage with their tall windows and high ceilings. Some are quirkily shaped, and a few singles are cramped. Doubles go for €150.

Cheap Hotels Far East of the Duomo

€€   Though tiny **Hotel America** (Corso XXII Marzo, 32, in the block east of Piazza Emilia; ☎ 02-7381865; www.milanohotelamerica.com; Metro: Porta Vittoria, though it's more convenient by tram/bus: 12, 27, 45, 60, 66, 73, or 92) is a bit off the beaten track, in a middle-class neighborhood a 10-minute tram ride east of Piazza del Duomo, the young owner and his family work overtime to make this *pensione* one of the best lower-priced lodgings in Milan. The €52-to-€62 rooms (€68 if you want a private bathroom) occupy the fourth floor of an apartment house, with streamlined, wood-veneer modern furnishings and, in many, a thematic stars-and-stripes decor—which is taking the theme a bit too literally. Guests are welcome to join the resident innkeepers in the living room and watch TV. The Rolling Stone music club, a venerable fixture on the Milan nightlife scene, is on the ground floor of the building, a good reason to ask for a room facing the quieter *giardino* courtyard (room 10 even has a balcony).

€€–€€€€   The family-run **Hotel Pavone** ✦ (Via Dandolo, 2, off Corso di Porta Vittoria; ☎ 02-55192133; www.hotelpavone.com; tram: 12, 23, 27, 60, or 73) is around the corner from the Palace of Justice, about a 15-minute walk east of the Duomo in a neighborhood more geared to business than to the tourist trade. Rooms run €90 to €19 and tend to be a bit sparse, with gray tile floors and no-nonsense Scandinavian-style furniture, but they were spruced up in 2003 with new linens and decor. Most are unusually large and cloaked in a silence unusual for big-city Milan (rooms 12, 14, 16, or 18, all of which overlook a garden, are the quietest of the bunch). Many rooms are outfitted as triples and are large enough to accommodate an extra bed, making this a fine choice for families.

Cheap Hotels near Stazione Centrale & Corso Buenos Aires

€€   The Bianchi family is genuinely welcoming to the many English speakers who find their way to their **Hotel Kennedy** (Viale Tunisia, 6; ☎ 02-29400934; www.kennedyhotel.it; Metro: Porta Venezia), a block from the southern end of Corso Buenos Aires. Their homey establishment on the sixth floor of an office-and-apartment building (there's an elevator) is sparkling clean and offers basic accommodations in large, tile-floored rooms that cost €52 to €80 for a double without private bathroom, €65 to €120 for one with bathroom. Room 13 has a terrace, while room 15 has a small balcony that even glimpses the spires of the Duomo in the distance. Amenities include a bar in the reception area, where coffee and soft drinks are available, as is a light breakfast of brioche and coffee that doesn't cost much more than it would in a cafe.

€€   Occupying an old house on a quiet residential street off the north end of Corso Buenos Aires, the **Hotel Paganini** ✦ (Via Paganini, 6; ☎ 02-2047443;

Metro: Loreto) has minimal public areas (except for a reception area with a self-serve espresso machine), but the guest rooms are large, bright, and embellished with tile floors, high ceilings with elaborate moldings, solid beds, and banal modular furnishings—all for just €63 for a double. The one room with a bathroom is just inside the entrance, with wood floors, a ceiling decorated with molded stuccoes, and plenty of elbowroom for €83. The shared bathroom facilities are modern enough and kept spanking clean by the owners, who are happy to point their guests to restaurants and sights. The best rooms are in the rear, overlooking a huge private garden. There is much to be said for this location: The Stazione Centrale is only a 10-minute walk way down Via Pergolsi, and if shopping is on your agenda, the nearby Corso Buenos Aires is one of the city's bargain fashion meccas.

Hotels Worth a Splurge

€€€–€€€€   Tucked away in a residential neighborhood of apartment houses and old villas near *The Last Supper*, the **Ariosto** ✹✹ (Via Ariosto, 22; ☎ 02-4817844; www.hotelariosto.com; Metro: Conciliazione) is a refreshingly quiet retreat—all the more so because many of the newly refurbished rooms face a private garden, and some open onto balconies overlooking it. All the rooms are decorated with wood-and-wicker furnishings, shiny parquet floors, and hand-painted wallpaper, and while most are decently sized, singles tend to be skinny. Many of the doubles have separate dressing areas off the tile or stone bathrooms, which are equipped with hair dryers (and a few with Jacuzzis). The rack rate for doubles is €220, but that's only applied during trade fairs, and may be discounted by as much as 45% during slower periods.

€€€€   If the charmingly funky **Antica Locanda Solferino** ✹✹✹ (Via Castelfidardo, 2; ☎ 02-6570129 or 02-6592706; www.anticalocandasolferino.it; Metro: Moscova or Repubblica) in the artsy Brera neighborhood hadn't been discovered long ago by members of the fashion world and film stars—this was Marcello Mastroianni's preferred Milan hostelry—you would consider it a find. The €200-to-€220 rooms have more, shall we say, character than they do modern comforts, but the eclectic smattering of country antiques and Art Nouveau pieces more than compensates for the absence of minibars. Nor do the repeat customers seem to mind that some of the bathrooms are miniscule (though modern), or that there is no lobby or breakfast room (coffee and rolls are delivered to your room). So be it—this is a delightful place to stay in one of Milan's most enticing neighborhoods, and reception manager Gerardo Vitolo is very friendly. The rooms on the tiny courtyard are quieter, but those on the street have plant-filled balconies (the best is room 10 on the corner, if you don't mind a tub rather than a shower).

DINING FOR ALL TASTES

The Milanese are more willing than Italians elsewhere to break the sit-down-meal tradition and grab a sandwich or other light fare on the run. And with so many students and young professionals, Milan has no shortage of *pizzerie* and other low-cost eateries.

Restaurants near the Duomo

€   **Luini** ★★ (Via S. Radegonda, 16, 2 blocks east of the Galleria Vittorio Emanuele II; ☎ 02-86461917; www.luini.it; no credit cards; Tues–Sat and Mon until 3pm, closed Aug; Metro: Duomo) has been a Milan institution since 1948, and it's so good they've even opened a branch in London. You'll have to elbow your way through a throng of well-dressed patrons at this stand-up counter in order to plunk down €2 to €3 for the house specialty: *panzerotto,* a pocket of pizza crust stuffed with all sorts of ingredients, including the basic cheese and tomato.

€   Busy **La Crêperie** (Via C. Correnti, 21, an extension of Via Torino, about a 10-min. walk southeast of Piazza del Duomo; ☎ 02-8395913; www.la-creperie.it; Mon–Sat, closed July 15–Aug 25; Metro: Sant'Ambrogio) is an ideal stop for a light lunch or a snack while visiting the nearby church of Sant'Ambrogio or Museo Nazionale di Scienza. Crepes come in both the meal (prosciutto, cheese, and so on) and the dessert variety (I recommend the Nutella, with its creamy hazelnut-chocolate spread). They've recently expanded beyond crepes to serve other foreign and exotic hand-held foods, such as *hot dogs americani* and waffles.

€–€€   **Peck** ★★ (Via Spadari, 9; ☎ 02-8023161; Mon–Sat, closed Jan 1–10 and July 1–20; Metro: Duomo) is Milan's most famous food emporium, its glittering cases filled with a wonderful selection of roast veal, risottos, *porchetta,* salads, aspics, cheeses, pastries, and other fare from its exquisite larder for €3 to €12. You can eat at the stand-up bar where, especially around lunchtime, it can be hard to find elbowroom, or you can put together a gourmet picnic to go.

€€–€€€   For a sit-down meal, head to Milan's most classic restaurant since 1933, **La Milanese** ★★★ (Via Santa Marta, 11; ☎ 02-86451991; closed Tues, Dec 25–Jan 8, Apr 24–May 2, and July 20–Aug 31; Metro: Cordusio), tucked into a narrow lane in one of the oldest sections of Milan just west of the Duomo. In the three-beamed dining room, Milanese families and other patrons share the long, crowded tables. Giuseppe prepares traditional Milanese fare, and you can even try their twin specialties—without pigging out—*risotto e osso buco,* a half-portion each of *risotto alla milanese* (rice cooked with saffron and beef marrow) and perfect *osso buco* (tender veal shanks on the bone) for just €21.

Restaurants in Magenta & Brera

€   Any time one of my Milanese friends says "Hey, let's go get pizza!" they invariably take me to **Pizzeria Grand'Italia** ★★ (Via Palermo, 5; ☎ 02-877759; no credit cards; Metro: Moscova). It serves up a huge assortment of salads, pizzas, homemade pastas, and *focacce farcite* (focaccia bread stuffed with cheese, mushrooms, and other fillings) along with wine and oil from the Furfaro family's farm in Tuscany. Rather than get a whole pie, you get one thick-crusted mega-slice topped however you like it. The late hours make this a prime nightspot, and part of the fun is watching the chic, young Milanese stopping buy for a snack as they make the rounds of the nearby Brera district bars and clubs.

€€   The main business at **Latteria** ✹✹ (Via San Marco, 24; ☎ 02-6597653; no credit cards; Mon–Fri, closed Aug; Metro: Moscova) was once dispensing milk and eggs to a press of neighborhood shoppers, but now the emphasis is on serving the La Brera neighborhood delicious, homemade fare in a room decorated with paintings and photographs of roses. The minestrone and other vegetable soups are delicious, as are the many variations of risotto, including the typical *riso al salto*, a delicious dish of leftover *risotto alla milanese* that is fried with butter. The menu changes daily, and the friendly staff, including owners Arturo and Maria, won't mind explaining the different dishes. The place is tiny, doesn't take reservations, and is immensely popular, so arrive right when it opens at 7:30pm—or wait until 9pm or later, when a few tables will free up as the early-dining tourist clientele clears out and the locals take over.

Restaurants near Stazione Centrale & Corso Buenos Aires

€   If you're looking for an excellent, cheap, and quick meal near the train station, head to the nearby branch of **Brek** (Via Lepetit, 20; ☎ 02-6705149; www.brek.com; closed Sun lunch; Metro: Stazione Centrale), one of the world's best quick-casual food chains. Even when the Italians do something as low-concept as a cafeteria, they can't help but make it fashionable and pour their hearts into the quality of the food. At the various food-prep stations, the friendly and helpful staff make pasta and risotto dishes on the spot, and roast pork, veal, and chicken to order. The large selection of cheeses would put many a formal restaurant to shame, and you can even get excellent wines in tiny bottles. Best of all: Almost every dish goes for just €3 to €8. There's another branch at Via dell'Annunciata, 2 (☎ 02-653619), just off Piazza Cavour, a 5-minute walk from the Brera museum, the shops of the Quadrilatero d'Oro, and the Giardini Pubblici park.

€€€€   Decidedly more upscale, and a few blocks from the southern end of Corso Buenos Aires, is the worthy splurge of **Joia** ✹✹ (Via P. Castaldi, 18; ☎ 02-2049244; www.joia.it; Mon–Fri, closed Aug; Metro: Repubblica), once called by Michelin the best vegetarian restaurant in Europe. (Translation: Book ahead, and bring your credit cards.) The innovative vegetarian creations of Swiss chef Pietro Leemann—a welcome respite from Northern Italy's orientation to red meat—incorporate the freshest vegetables and herbs in a seasonally changing menu. You can even fiddle around with the traditional Italian menu, ordering first courses as main courses, and many of the main courses can be served as appetizers. The one drawback is the price: €17 or €18 for first courses—whew! They've recently opened a **branch** at Corso di Porta Ticinese, 106 (☎ 02-89404134; closed Mon lunch and Sun), in the hopping Navigli district.

Restaurants in the Navigli

You can't swing a salami without smacking some place in which to eat or drink along the quays of Milan's defunct canal system. The former warehouses are now packed with bars, pubs, *pizzerie, trattorie,* and restaurants. Here are a few of my faves.

€   The most popular pizzeria in the Navigli, **Premiata Pizzeria** ✹ (Via Alzaia Naviglio Grande, 2; ☎ 02-89400648; closed Tues lunch; tram: 3, 15, 29, 30, or

Cafes & Gelaterie

€ **Bar Zucca/Caffè Miani** (at the Duomo end of the Galleria Vittorio Emanuele II; ☎ 02-86464435; www.caffemiani.it; Metro: Duomo) is best known by its original name, Il Camparino. It's the most attractive and popular of the Galleria's many bars and introduced Italy to Campari, the country's ubiquitous red cordial. You can linger at the tables set up in the Galleria for views of the Duomo's facade, or in one of the Art Nouveau rooms inside.

€ You can find organic gelato at the **Gelateria Ecologica** (Corso di Porta Ticinese, 40; ☎ 02-58101872; Metro: Sant'Ambrogio or Missori), in the Ticinese/Navigli neighborhood. It's so popular, there's no need for a sign out front. Strollers in the atmospheric Brera neighborhood sooner or later stumble upon the **Gelateria Toldo** (Via Ponte Vetero, 9; ☎ 02-8646-0863; Metro: Cordusio or Lanza), where the gelato is wonderfully creamy and many of the *sorbetto* selections are so fruity and fresh they seem healthy.

€ The **Pasticceria Confetteria Cova** (Via Montenapoleone, 8; ☎ 02-76000578; Metro: Montenapoleone) is approaching its 200th year in refined surroundings near the similarly atmospheric Museo Poldi-Pezzoli. It's usually filled with shoppers making the rounds in this high-fashion district. You can enjoy a quick coffee and a brioche at the long bar, or take a seat in one of the elegant adjoining rooms.

€ The **Pasticceria Marchesi** (Via Santa Maria alla Porta, 13; ☎ 02-862770; Metro: Cordusio) is a distinguished pastry shop, with an adjoining wood-panel tearoom. Because it's only steps from Santa Maria delle Grazie, you can enjoy the old-world ambience and a cup of excellent coffee (or one of the many teas and herbal infusions) as you dash off postcards of *The Last Supper*. Of course, you'll want to accompany your beverage with one of the elegant pastries, perhaps a slice of the *panettone* (cake laden with raisins and candied citron) that's a hallmark of Milan. No one prepares it better than they do at Marchesi.

---

59) stays packed from early dinnertime until the barhopping crowd stops by for late-night munchies. The restaurant rambles back forever, exposed copper pipes tracing across the ceilings of rooms wrapped around shaded outdoor terraces set with long, raucous tables. Seating is communal and service hurried, but the wood-oven pizzas are excellent (€6–€12). If you're hungrier, there's a long menu of pastas and meat courses, while those with lighter appetites can enjoy a selection of salads (€5–€9), or cheese or salami platters made for two (€14).

€€ **Al Pont de Ferr** ★★ (Ripa di Porta Ticinese, 55, on the Naviglio Grande; ☎ 02-89406277; tram: 3, 15, 29, 30, or 59) has long been one of the more respectable of the Navigli joints, with tables set out on the flagstones overlooking the canal (regulars know to bring tiny cans of bug spray to battle the mosquitoes in summer). The €9 risotto is livened up with a guinea fowl *ragù*, Camembert, and milk; and the €9 oven-baked rosette of fresh pasta is inventively stuffed with Prague ham, cheese, and walnut. There's a surprisingly good selection of half-bottles of wine, but most full bottles start at €15 and go senselessly higher. On the whole, portions could be a lot larger, but you gotta love a place whose menu opens with the quip, "Good cooking is the friend of living well and the enemy of a hurried life."

€€–€€€€   **Ponte Rosso** ✦ (Ripa di Porta Ticinese, 23, on the Naviglio Grande; ☎ 02-8373132; Tues–Sat, Mon lunch only; tram: 3, 15, 29, 30, or 59) is an old-fashioned trattoria on the canal, a long railroad room crowded with tiny tables and a short, simple menu of simple, hearty home cooking. The owner hails from Trieste (which explains the old Triestino photos on the walls), so kick a meal off with a €10 *antipasto di salami misti,* a mixed platter of cured meats from the Friuli region, famous for producing San Daniele, the most delicate prosciutto in Italy. In fact, dishes on the always-changing menu hail from all corners of Italy, from Milanese risotto with saffron (€10), to homemade Ligurian *stracetti maccheroni* with pesto (€10), to Sardinian spaghetti *con la bottarga* (dried fish roe) with crumbled sheep's cheese (€12).

WHY YOU'RE HERE: THE TOP SIGHTS & ATTRACTIONS

Despite hosting some major sights—Leonardo da Vinci's *Last Supper;* the gargantuan Gothic Duomo bristling with statues, spires, and pinnacles; the Old Masters in the Brera and Ambrosiana picture galleries; the fashion boutiques; and La Scala opera house—Milan is not a place that rewards folks who linger too long.

Sure, it's a nice enough town, with great restaurants and a hopping nightlife. But when you compare this dingy, gray, work-oriented city with beauty queens like Venice, Florence, and Rome, or with the charms of Tuscan hill towns, Sicilian villages, or the resorts of the coast or the nearby lake district, Milan just doesn't hold a candle. For that reason, give Milan a day or two to hit the highlights, and move on.

Luckily, Milan's airport is second only to Rome in international arrivals, so it's easy to route yourself through here, spending the first or final night of your holiday in the city in order to knock off that *Last Supper* and maybe catch an opera at world-renowned La Scala.

Il Duomo (The Cathedral)

When Milanesi think something is taking too long, they refer to it as *la fabbrica del Duomo* (the making of the cathedral). It took 5 centuries to complete Milan's magnificent Gothic **Duomo** ✦✦✦ (Piazza del Duomo; ☎ 02-72022656; www. duomomilano.com; daily 7am–7pm; Metro: Duomo), which was begun by the ruling Visconti family in 1386. The last of Italy's great Gothic structures is the fourth-largest church in the world (after St. Peter's in Rome, Seville's cathedral, and a new one in Ivory Coast), with 135 marble spires, a stunning triangular facade (currently under restoration wraps), and 3,400-some statues flanking the massive but airy, almost fanciful exterior.

The cavernous interior, lit by brilliant stained-glass windows, seats 40,000 but is unusually spartan and serene, divided into five aisles by a forest of 52 columns. The poet Shelley used to sit and read Dante amid monuments that include a gruesomely graphic **statue** of *St. Bartholomew Flayed* ✦ and the tombs of Giacomo de Medici, two Visconti, and many cardinals and archbishops. Another British visitor, Alfred, Lord Tennyson, rhapsodized about the view of the Alps from the **roof** ✦✦✦ [kids] (elevators on the church's exterior northeast corner for €6; stairs on the exterior north side for €4; Nov 14–Feb 13 daily 9am–5pm, Feb 14–Apr 30 and Oct 10–Nov 13 daily 9am–6pm, May 1–Oct 9 daily 9am–6:30pm), where you get to wander amid the Gothic pinnacles, saintly statues, and flying buttresses. You are joined high above Milan by the spire-top gold statue of *Madonnina* (the little Madonna), the city's beloved protectress.

> "How glorious that Cathedral is! Worthy almost of standing face to face with the snow Alps; and itself a sort of snow dream by an artist architect, taken asleep on a glacier. "
>
> —Elizabeth Barrett Browning, in a letter from 1851

Back on terra firma, the cathedral's **crypt** (€1.55; daily 9am–noon and 2:30–6pm) contains the remains of San Carlo Borromeo, one of the early cardinals of Milan and a member of the noble family that still owns much of the prime real estate around Lake Maggiore (later in this chapter). A far more interesting descent is the one down the staircase to the right of the main entrance, to the **Battistero Paleocristiano S. Giovanni alle Fonti** (€1.50; Tues–Sun 9:45am–12:45pm and 2–5:45pm), the ruins of a 4th-century baptistery believed to be where St. Ambrose baptized St. Augustine.

The Duomo houses many of its treasures across the piazza from the right transept in a wing of the Palazzo Reale devoted to **Museo del Duomo** (Piazza del Duomo, 14; ☎ 02-860358; €6; daily 10am–1:15pm and 3–6pm). Among the legions of statuary saints are a significant painting, **Tintoretto's** *Christ at the Temple,* and some intriguing displays chronicling the construction of the cathedral.

The best place from which to admire the Duomo facade is an outdoor table at Caffè della Zucca, the bar that invented Italy's consummate aperitif, Camparisoda. This genteel cafe lies at the entrance to the elegant **Galleria Vittorio Emanuele II** ✦✦, Milan's late-19th-century version of a mall. This wonderful steel-and-glass-covered, cross-shaped arcade is the prototype of the enclosed shopping malls that were to become the hallmark of 20th-century consumerism—though it's safe to say that none of the imitators have come close to matching the Galleria for style and flair. The designer of this urban marvel, Giuseppe Mengoni, didn't live to see the Milanese embrace his creation: He tripped and fell from a

A Duomo Combo

Catch the elevator to the Duomo's roof and see the cathedral museum together with a €8 Combination Ticket.

Milan Itineraries

If you have only 1 day in Milan

Book ahead—at least 2 weeks in advance if possible—for the very first entry time of the day (8:15am) to see **Leonardo da Vinci's** *Last Supper.* Head east to Milan's gargantuan **Castello Sforzesco** for Michelangelo's final *Pietà* and a clutch of fine Renaissance paintings. Stroll down the largely pedestrianized Via Dante, pausing for a cappuccino break in one of its many cafes, to Piazza del Duomo and Milan's enormous Gothic **Duomo.** Be sure you make it up onto the roof—my favorite Milan experience—to duck under buttresses and wend your way between the statue-topped spires for thrilling citywide panoramas that, on the few winter days when industrial smog doesn't interfere, stretch all the way to the Alps. Join the throngs of locals and businessmen on break and grab a *panzerotto* from **Luini** for a typical Milan lunch on the go, and then wash it down with a view of the Duomo facade and Italy's prototypical aperitif, a Campari-soda, in the very bar that invented it, **Caffè della Zucca.**

Amble through the glass atrium of the historic **Galleria Vittorio Emanuele II,** ending up in front of **La Scala** opera house, where you can visit the operatic collections in its **Museo Teatrale** and check into last-minute tickets for that night's performance. While you window-shop the world-famous boutiques of **Quadrilatero d'Oro,** pop into the private collections of the **Museo Poldi Pezzoli** for 30 minutes, whetting your appetite for the artistic giants in the **Pinacoteca di Brera,** where you can peruse the paintings until they kick you out at 7:30pm. Hop on a tram down to the **Navigli,** Milan's trendiest restaurant district and nightlife scene, strung out along the remnants of the city's old canals.

girder a few days before the Galleria opened in 1878. His shopping mall par excellence provides a lovely route between the Duomo and Piazza della Scala and is a fine locale for watching the flocks of well-dressed Milanese.

The Last Supper

What draws so many visitors to Milan is the *Cenacolo Vinciano,* better known to English-speakers as **Leonardo da Vinci's** *Last Supper* ★★ (Piazza Santa Maria delle Grazie, 2, a wide spot along Corso Magenta; ☎ 02-89421146; www. cenacolovinciano.it; €6.50 plus a required booking fee of €1.50; Tues–Sun 8:15am–7pm; Metro: Cardona or Conciliazione). From 1495 to 1497, Leonardo da Vinci painted this poignant portrayal of confusion and betrayal for the wall of the refectory in the Dominican convent attached to the church of Santa Maria delle Grazie. Aldous Huxley called this fresco the "saddest work of art in the world," a comment in part on the deterioration that set in even before the paint had dried on the moisture-ridden walls. The fresco got a lot of well-intentioned but poorly executed "touching up" in the 18th and 19th centuries, though a recent lengthy

If you have only 2 days in Milan

On Day 1, start off at the **Pinacoteca Ambrosiana** when it opens (10am) for 90 minutes of Old Masters (Raphael, Caravaggio, da Vinci) before moving on to see Bramante's illusory architectural masterpiece inside the tiny church of **Santa Maria Presso S. Satiro,** and then plunge right into the sights around Piazza del Duomo: the **Cathedral** itself (don't forget the roof!), a light lunch at **Caffè della Zucca,** and a stroll through **Galleria Vittorio Emanuele II** to La Scala opera house (give its **Museo Teatrale** 30 min. of your time, and check into buying tickets for tonight's—or tomorrow's—performance). End the day as above, window-shopping the **Quadrilatero d'Oro,** visiting the **Museo Poldi Pezzoli,** and touring the **Pinacoteca di Brera** until it closes—but instead of heading to the Navigli tonight, stick around the Brera neighborhood, which is also chock-a-block with bars and pubs and great restaurants.

Start Day 2 at the medieval **Castello Sforzesco.** On your way to see **da Vinci's** *Last Supper* (book tickets for noon), stop into the **Museo Archeologico** to see how the Roman town of *Mediolanum* grew to become the metropolis of Milan. Take lunch at the bistrolike Art Nouveau **Bar Magenta,** and head south to the gorgeous 4th-century church of S. Ambrogio and the nearby **Museo Nazionale della Scienza,** filled with scale models of Leonardo's inventions. Make your way east to the ancient church of **San Lorenzo Maggiore,** and then stroll south a few blocks to jump into the pub, jazz club, and restaurant scene of the Navigli.

restoration has done away with all that over-painting, as well as tried to undo the damage wrought by the clumsy patching and damage inflicted when Napoleon's troops used the wall for target practice, and from when Allied bombing during World War II tore off the room's roof, leaving the fresco exposed to the elements for 3 years.

In short, *The Last Supper* is a mere shadow of the work the artist intended it to be, but the scene, which captures the moment when Christ told his apostles that one of them would betray him, remains amazingly powerful and emotional nonetheless. Only 25 people are allowed to view the fresco at a time, with a 15-minute limit, and you must pass through a series of devices that remove pollutants from clothing. Accordingly, lines are long and tickets are usually sold out days in advance. I'm serious: If you don't book ahead—preferably a week or two in advance—you'll most likely be turned away at the door, even in the dead of winter when you'd expect the place to be empty (tour bus groups swallow up inordinately large batches of tickets, leaving precious few for do-it-yourself travelers).

Milan by Tram

For an excellent overview of the city, hop aboard vintage 1920s tram no. 20, distinguished by CIAOMILANO emblazoned on its sides, for a tour with commentary in English and five other languages. The 1¾-hour tours are hop-on/hop-off for a full day and run daily at 11am and 1pm (also 3pm in summer) from Piazza Castello (Metro: Cairoli). The only drawback: It costs a whopping €20. For more details, call ☎ 02-33910794.

Often overlooked are the other great treasures of the late-15th-century **Church of Santa Maria delle Grazie** itself (☎ 02-48014248; Mon–Sat 7:30am–noon and 3–7pm, Sun 7:20am–12:15pm and 3:30–9pm, may close earlier in winter; Metro: Cardona or Conciliazione), foremost among them the fine dome and other architectural innovations by one of the great architects of the High Renaissance, Bramante (one of the architects of St. Peter's in Rome). To one side of the apse, decorated in marble and terra cotta, is a lovely cloister.

Other Outstanding Sights

The **Brera** ✸✸✸ (Via Brera, 28; ☎ 02-722631; www.brera.beniculturali.it; €5; Tues–Sun 8:30am–7:30pm; Metro: Lanza or Montenapoleone) is one of Italy's top museums of medieval, Renaissance, and 20th-century paintings, including the world's finest collection of Northern Italian works. The concentration of so many masterpieces in this 17th-century palace is the work of Napoleon, who used the *palazzo* as a repository for the art he confiscated from public and private holdings throughout Northern Italy; fittingly, a bronze likeness of the emperor greets you as you enter the courtyard.

Just to give you a sampling of what you'll encounter in these **40 or so rooms,** three of Italy's greatest masterpieces hang here: Andrea Mantegna's amazingly foreshortened *Dead Christ* ✸✸✸, Raphael's *Betrothal of the Virgin* ✸✸, and Piero della Francesca's *Madonna with Saints* ✸✸ (the Montefeltro Altarpiece). It is an indication of this museum's ability to overwhelm visitors that the last two absolute masterpieces hang near each other in a single room dedicated to late-15th-century works by Tuscan and Umbrian masters.

Among the other important works are Jacopo Tintoretto's *Finding of the Body of St. Mark* ✸, in which the dead saint eerily confronts appropriately startled grave robbers who come upon his corpse, and several by Caravaggio, including the masterful *Supper at Emmaus* ✸✸. Just beyond is a room devoted to works by foreigners, among them Rembrandt's *Portrait of a Young Woman.* Given Napoleon's fondness for the Venetian schools, it is only just that the final rooms are again filled with works from that city, including Canaletto's *View of the Grand Canal.*

Sights between the Duomo & the Brera

The stunning treasure trove of antiques and Bellinis, Botticellis, and Tiepolos in the private **Museo Poldi Pezzoli** ✸✸ (Via Manzoni, 12; ☎ 02-794889; www.museopoldipezzoli.it; €7; Tues–Sun 10am–6pm; Metro: Duomo or Montenapoleone) leans a bit toward Venetian painters (such as Francesco Guardi's elegantly moody

Grey Lagoon), but also ventures widely throughout Italian painting—Antonio Pollaiuolo's *Portrait of a Young Woman* is often likened to the *Mona Lisa*—and into the Flemish school. It was amassed by 19th-century collector Giacomo Poldi-Pezzoli, who donated his town house and its treasures to the city in 1881. CD-ROM terminals let you explore bits of the collections not currently on display, especially arms and armor, the best of which is housed in an elaborate *pietra serena* room designed by Pomodoro. Pick up a free audioguide in English at the ticket desk.

Milan's renowned opera house, **Teatro alla Scala** ★★ (Piazza della Scala; ☎ 02-72003744 or 02-860775 for the box office; www.teatroallascala.org; Metro: Duomo or Montenapoleone), was built in the late 18th century on the site of a church of the same name. La Scala is hallowed ground to lovers of Giuseppe Verdi (who was the house composer for decades), Maria Callas, Arturo Toscanini (conductor for much of the 20th c.), and legions of other composers and singers who have hit the high notes of fame in the world's most revered opera house. La Scala emerged from a multiyear restoration on December 7, 2005—the traditional gala opening night—and between opera, ballet, and orchestral performances, the theater now maintains a year-round schedule. Treat yourself to an evening performance; the cheap seats start at just €10.

With restoration now complete, the **Museo Teatrale alla Scala** (☎ 02-88792473; €5; daily 9am–12:30pm and 1:30–5:30pm; Metro: Duomo or Montenapoleone) has also moved back into its permanent home just to the left of the main entrance. The operatic nostalgia includes such mementos as Toscanini's batons, a strand of Mozart's hair, a fine array of Callas postcards, original Verdi scores, a whole mess of historic gramophones and record players, and costumes designed by some of Milan's top fashion gurus and worn by the likes of Callas and Rudolf Nureyev on La Scala's stage.

Sights between the Duomo & *The Last Supper*

The collection of the **Pinacoteca Ambrosiana** ★★ (Piazza Pio XI, 2; ☎ 02-806921; www.ambrosiana.it; €7.50; Tues–Sun 10am–5:30pm; Metro: Cordusio or Duomo) focuses on **treasures from the 15th through the 17th centuries:** An *Adoration* by Titian, Raphael's cartoon for his *School of Athens* in the Vatican, Botticelli's *Madonna and Angels,* Caravaggio's *Basket of Fruit* (his only still life), and other stunning works hang in a series of intimate rooms. Notable (or infamous) among the paintings is *Portrait of a Musician,* attributed to Leonardo da Vinci but, according to many scholars, of dubious provenance; if it is indeed a da Vinci, the haunting painting is the only portrait of his to hang in an Italian museum. The adjoining Biblioteca Ambrosiana, open to scholars only except for special exhibitions, houses a wealth of Renaissance *literaria,* including the letters of Lucrezia Borgia and a strand of her hair. The most notable holdings, though, are da Vinci's *Codice Atlantico,* 1,750 drawings and jottings the master did between 1478 and 1519. These and the library's other volumes, including a rich collection of medieval manuscripts, are frequently put on view to the public; at these times, an admission fee of €10 allows entrance to both the library and the art gallery.

Though it's been clumsily restored many times, most recently at the end of the 19th century, the fortresslike **Castello Sforzesco** ★★ (Piazza Castello; ☎ 02-88463700; www.milanocastello.it; €3; Tues–Sun 9am–5:30pm; Metro: Cairoli, Cadorna, or Lanza) continues to evoke Milan's two most powerful medieval and

Renaissance families, the Visconti and the Sforza. The Visconti built the castle in the 14th century and the Sforza, who married into the Visconti clan and eclipsed them in power, reconstructed it in 1450. The most influential residents were Ludovico il Moro and Beatrice d'Este (he of the Sforza and she of the famous Este family of Ferrara), who commissioned the works by Bramante and Leonardo da Vinci in the kilometers of rooms that surround the Castello's enormous courtyard.

The castle's salons house a series of small city-administered museums known collectively as the **Civici Musei Castello Sforzesco**—which were, up until the city got greedy in 2005, always free. Ah, well. They're still worth the relatively small admission charge for the *pinacoteca*, with its minor works by Bellini, Correggio, and Magenta, and the extensive holdings of the Museo d'Arte Antica, filled with Egyptian funerary objects, prehistoric finds from Lombardy, and several giant tapestries in a room containing historical musical instruments. The biggest draw is the final work of an 89-year-old Michelangelo, his unfinished ***Rondanini Pietà*** ★★, a work so intense and abstract it almost seems to prefigure 20th-century art. Apparently, the master was dissatisfied partway through—or there was a flaw in the material—and he started reworking the piece, but died before he could finish; look for an extraneous arm from the earlier version.

The most fascinating finds in the **Civico Museo Archeologico** ★ (Corso Magenta, 15; ☎ 02-86450011; €2; Tues–Sun 9:30am–5:30pm; Metro: Cadorna) are the everyday items from Milan's Roman era—tools, eating utensils, jewelry, and some exquisite and remarkably well-preserved glassware. The exhibits fill a 16th-century monastery with Greek, Etruscan, and Roman pieces from throughout Italy; there's also a section devoted to ancient remains from Ghandara, India. You can get a glimpse of Roman architecture in the garden: two Roman towers and a section of a road, part of the walls enclosing the settlement of *Mediolanum*, once capital of the Western Roman empire.

If you didn't get enough of Leonardo da Vinci with the *Last Supper*—or just want to see another side of his genius—check out the scale wooden models of many of his most amazing inventions at the **Museo Nazionale della Scienza e della Tecnologia Leonardo da Vinci** ★ 🄺🄸🄳🅂 (Via San Vittore, 21; ☎ 02-48555331; www.museoscienza.org; €8, though families pay €6 per adult plus €3 per child under 18; Tues–Fri 9:30am–5pm, Sat–Sun 9:30am–6:30pm; Metro: Sant'Ambrogio), including submarines, helicopters, and other engineering feats that, for the most part, the master only ever invented on paper. This former Benedictine monastery and its beautiful cloisters are also filled with planes, trains, carriages, sewing machines, typewriters, optical devices, and other exhibits, including enchanting re-creations of workshops, that make up one of the world's leading collections of mechanical and scientific wizardry.

From here, you're just 2 blocks from one of the most underrated sights in Milan, the Basilica di Sant'Ambrogio (see below), which lies in the neighborhood south of the Duomo.

A Trio of Top Churches South of the Duomo

In the 4th century A.D., Milan was (briefly) the capital of the Western Roman empire—and the capital of Western Christendom. Long before the bishop of Rome turned the papacy into the most powerful center for the church, it was the bishop of Milan who called the shots, and the greatest bishop of 4th-century Milan was St. Ambrose.

Little remains of the first **Basilica di Sant'Ambrogio** ✦ (Piazza Sant'Ambrogio, 15; ☎ 02-86450895; www.santambrogio-basilica.it; Mon–Sat 7am–noon and 2:30–7pm, Sun 7am–1pm and 2–8pm; Metro: Sant'Ambrogio), constructed by the saint on this site, but the 11th-century structure built in its place (and renovated many times since) is remarkable. It has a striking atrium, lined with columned porticos, and a brick facade with two ranks of *loggie* flanked by bell towers. Look carefully at the door on the left, where you'll see a relief of St. Ambrose. Note the overall effect of this architectural assemblage because the church of Sant'Ambrogio set a standard for Lombard Romanesque architecture that you'll see imitated many times throughout Lombardy. On your wanderings through the three-aisled nave you'll come upon a gold altar from Charlemagne's days in Milan, and, in the right aisle, the all-too-scant remains of a Tiepolo fresco cycle, most of it blown into oblivion by World War II bombs. The little that remains of the original church is the Sacello di San Vittore in Ciel d'Oro, a little chapel in which the cupola glows with 5th-century mosaics of saints (€2; enter from the right aisle). The skeletal remains of Ambrose himself are on view in the crypt. As you leave the main church from the left aisle you'll see one of the "later" additions, by the great architect Bramante—his Portico dell Canonica, lined with elegant columns, some of which are sculpted to resemble tree trunks.

What makes the beautiful church of **Santa Maria Presso S. Satiro** (entered down a short alley on the east side of Via Torino, just south of Via Speronari and Piazza del Duomo; ☎ 02-874683; Mon–Fri 7:30–11:30am and 3–7pm, Sat 9:30am–noon and 3–7pm, Sun 8:30am–12:30pm and 3–7pm; Metro: Duomo or Missori) so exquisite is what it doesn't have—space. Stymied by not being able to expand the T-shaped apse to classical Renaissance, cross-shaped proportions, the architect Bramante designed a marvelous relief behind the high altar that creates the illusion of a fourth arm. The effect of the *trompe l'oeil* columns and arches is not entirely convincing but is nonetheless magical. Another gem lies to the rear of the left transept: the Cappella della Pietà, so called for the 15th-century terracotta *Pietà* it now houses, but built in the 9th century to honor St. Satiro, the brother of St. Ambrose, and covered in lovely Byzantine frescoes and Romanesque columns.

Set back from the road beyond a free-standing row of 16 ancient Roman columns (probably from the 2nd c. A.D.), the **Chiesa di San Lorenzo Maggiore** ✦ (Corso di Porta Ticinese, 39; ☎ 02-89404129; www.sanlorenzomaggiore.com; daily 7:30am–12:30pm and 2:30–6:45pm; Metro: Missori) is further testament to the days when the city was the capital of the Western Roman empire. The 4th-century early-Christian structure has been rebuilt and altered many times over the centuries (its dome, the highest in Milan, is a 16th-c. embellishment), but retains the flavor of its roots in its octagonal floor plan and a few surviving remnants. These include 5th-century mosaics—one depicting a beardless Christ—in the Cappella di Sant'Aquilino, which you enter from the atrium (€2). A sarcophagus in the chapel is said to enshrine the remains of Galla Placidia, sister of Honorius, last emperor of Rome, and wife of Ataulf, king of the Visigoths. Just where Ms. Placidia ended up is a point of contention. Her official mausoleum is one of the mosaic masterworks of Ravenna, but she is most likely buried in Rome, where she died. You'll be rewarded with a glimpse of even earlier history if you follow the stairs from behind the altar to a cryptlike room that contains what remains of a Roman amphitheater.

THE OTHER MILAN

Unlike other Italian cities, Milan doesn't give much thought to tourism beyond its major sights. Sure, it has a vibrant cultural scene; a busy schedule of events, exhibitions, and trade fairs; and a fashion industry that, outside of the boutiques, keeps itself behind closed doors and invitation-only parties. But because most of Milan's cultural events are conducted in Italian only, they're a bit inaccessible to the visitor who doesn't speak the language. Which brings me to the first way to break out of the tourist mold in Milan.

Parla Italiano?

Lots of foreigners come to Milan for business reasons, many on frequent visits or for stints of a few months or longer, so the city is better equipped than most with language schools—especially the kinds devoted to getting you up to speed quickly, teaching you how to get by in everyday conversation rather than mucking about for weeks with obscure verb conjugations. All of these institutions offer lengthy courses spread over many weeks or months; I'll just mention the courses they offer that last a week or two and are thus better suited to tourists.

The **Scuola Leonardo da Vinci** (Via Darwin, 20; ☎ 02-83241002; www.scuola leonardo.com) has been teaching Italian to foreigners since 1977; 2 weeks of 40 lessons in small classes (12 people maximum) cost €280. The **International House Milano** (Piazza Erculea, 9; ☎ 02-86457408; www.ihmilano.it) offers two levels of 2-week courses: 15 hours per week for €290, or 20 hours per week for €385. You can also get one-on-one intensive lessons for €44 per hour plus a €60 enrollment fee, though you have to sign up for a minimum of 20 hours—that means an investment of at least €940. **Accademia di Italiano** (Via P. Paleocapa, 1; ☎ 02-87388760; www.aimilano.it) teaches small classes (no more than six), with an intensive 2-week course totaling 40 hours of lessons (8 hr. a day) for €305.

The **Società Dante Alighieri** (Via Napo Torrani, 10; ☎ 02-6692816; www.societadantealighieri.org) has the benefit of pedigree—it's been around since 1889—and offers one-on-one lessons from €35 per hour. Don't confuse that one with the **Instituto Dante Alighieri** (Piazzale Cadorna, 9; ☎ 02-72011294; www.dantealighieri.org), which has also been around a while (established 1923); it offers two levels of short-term courses consisting of 45-minute lessons. It's pricier than the others, but has the benefit of some 1-week options: Semi-intensive courses for 1 week (25 lessons; €635) or 2 weeks (50 lessons; €1,160), and intensive courses for 1 week (35 lessons; €790) or 2 weeks (70 lessons; €1,445). You can also get individual tailored courses, starting at €560 for 15 lessons.

Attend Mass in a Historic Church

The Milanese may worship the almighty euro Monday to Friday, and pray for bargains on haute couture during Saturday-morning shopping sprees, but come Sunday they remember that they're Italian—and Catholic—and show up for

Mass. As so much of Milan's urban fabric is made up of gray, utilitarian architecture lining broad boulevards strung with tram lines and teeming with traffic, it comes as a bit of a shock to realize that the city is also home to some stupendous churches—a heritage from its 4th-century role as a capital of Western Christianity.

On Sundays, dress to the nines (this *is* Milan, after all) and take your pick of churches for Mass, from the huge, echoing nave of the Gothic **Duomo** (Sun at 7, 8, 9:30, 10, and 11am and 12:30 and 5:30pm—plus lauds at 10:30am and vespers at 4pm), to that hidden jewel box of Renaissance architecture, **Santa Maria Presso S. Spirito** (Sun at 10am or 6pm). Perhaps the most evocative spaces, though, are those 4th-century churches just south of the center: the elegant Romanesque interior of **Sant'Ambrogio** (a popular place, with Sun Masses scheduled at 8, 10, and 11am—that one's in Latin—and at 12:15, 6, and 7pm) or the ancient octagon of **San Lorenzo Maggiore** (Sun at 9:30, 11:30am, and 6pm—or, for an odd experience, pop into the 4pm Mass in Tagalog; this church serves as a cultural center for Milan's sizeable Filipino community).

Shop with the Locals

So many people come to Milan for the shopping, but so very few can afford the prices in the Quadrilatero d'Oro boutiques. That's why the real Milanesi don't bother buying there; they just window-shop and pause for see-and-be-seen drinks at Cova. When it actually comes time to break out the credit cards, most Milanesi head instead for two neighborhoods where prices are cheap, stock shops abound, and midpriced middle-class goods take precedence over Prada and Armani designs.

To the northwest of the historical center lies *the* **neighborhood for true bargain hunters,** the grid of streets southeast of the train station surrounding the broad **Corso Buenos Aires** (follow Via Vitruvio from Piazza Duca d'Aosta in front of the station; Metro stops Lima and Loreto are the gateways to this bargain stretch). This wide boulevard is home to a little bit of everything, from shops that hand-sew men's dress shirts to CD megastores. As it crosses Piazza Oberdan/Piazza Venezia heading south, it becomes Corso Venezia and the stores start moving up the scale.

Men will want to stop at **Darsena** (Corso Buenos Aires, 16; ☎ 02-29521535), where you just might find an Armani suit or jacket at a rock-bottom price. **Calzaturificio di Parabiago** (Corso Buenos Aires, 52; ☎ 02-29406851) shods men and women fashionably at reasonable prices, with an enormous selection and a helpful staff. For designer shoes at a discount, look no further than **Rufus** (Via Vitruvio, 35; ☎ 02-2049648; Metro: Centrale F.S. or Lima), which carries men's and women's styles from lots of labels for under €100.

Spacci Bassetti (Via Procaccini, 32; ☎ 02-3450125; Metro: Garibaldi F.S., but closer on tram 33 or 94) is a discount outlet of the august Bassetti line of high-quality linen, and the huge space offers the luxurious towels and sheets at excellent prices. They also have regular (non-discount) stores at Corso Buenos Aires, 52 (☎ 02-29400048; Metro: Lima), and Via Botta, 7A (☎ 02-55183191; Metro: Porta Romana), near the Navigli.

The other hunting ground for discount fashions is south of the historical center in the **Navigli district** (starting at the south end of Corso di Porta Ticinese; Metro to Porta Genova, or trams to Piazza XXIV Maggio). Women can shop at **Eliogabaldo** (Piazza Sant'Eustorgio, 2; ☎ 02-8378293; Metro: S. Agostino), where some of the offerings may be secondhand, but only in the sense that a model donned them briefly for a show or shoot.

Biffi (Corso Genova, 6; ☎ 02-8375170; Metro: S. Agostino) attracts fashion-conscious hordes of both sexes in search of designer labels and the store's own designs. One more Navigli stop, and again well stocked with designer wear for men and women—but especially dresses (no changing rooms, so come prepared)—is nearby **Floretta Coen Musil** (Via San Calocero, 3; ☎ 02-58111708; Metro: S. Agostino), open Monday through Saturday, afternoons only from 3:30 to 7:30pm; credit cards are not accepted.

CHIC SHOPPING

For the best discounts, you want to "Shop with the Locals," as detailed above. But bargains be damned, the best spot for fashion gazing and supermodel-spotting is along four adjoining streets north of the Duomo known collectively as the **Quadrilatero d'Oro (Golden Quadrilateral):** Via Montenapoleone, Via Spiga, Via Borgospesso, and Via Sant'Andrea, lined with Milan's most expensive high-fashion emporia. (To enter this hallowed precinct, follow Via Manzoni a few blocks north from Piazza della Scala; San Babila is the closest Metro stop.)

The main artery of this shopping heartland is Via Montenapoleone, lined with chi-chi boutiques and the most elegant fashion outlets, with parallel Via della Spiga running a close second.

If your fashion sense is greater than your credit line, don't despair: Even the most expensive clothing of the Armani ilk is usually less expensive in Italy than it is abroad, and citywide *saldi* (sales) run from early January into early February, and again in late June and July.

Even if your wallet can't afford it, stop by to browse the new flagship **Armani megastore** (Via Manzoni, 31; ☎ 02-72318630; www.armani-viamanzoni31.com; Metro: Montenapoleone). To celebrate 25 years in business in the summer of 2000, Giorgio opened this new flagship store/offices covering 743 sq. m (8,000 sq. ft.) with outlets for his high-fashion creations, the Emporio Armani and Armani Jeans lines, plus the new Armani Casa selection of home furnishings; flower, book, and art shops; a high-tech Sony electronics boutique/play center in the basement; and an Emporio Café and branch of New York's Nobu sushi bar.

Books

Milan has two English-language bookshops. **The American Bookstore** (Via Camperio, 16, at the corner with Via Dante; ☎ 02-878920; Metro: Cordusio) and **The English Bookshop** (Via Ariosto, at Via Mascheroni, 12; ☎ 02-4694468; www.englishbookshop.it; Metro: Conciliazione).

The glamorous outlet of one of Italy's leading publishers, **Rizzoli** (in the Galleria Vittorio Emanuele II; ☎ 02-8052277; www.libreriarizzoli.it; Metro: Duomo), also has some English-language titles (in the basement), as well as a sumptuous collection of art and photo books.

If it's a bargain on bookish souvenirs you're after, **Remainders** (in the Galleria Vittorio Emanuele II; ☎ 02-86464008; Metro: Duomo) hawks glossy coffee-table tomes and art books at half price and, on the second floor, offers cut rates on English-language books—just a few novels, plus lots of art and academic books.

High Fashion at Low Prices

Inspired by the window displays in the Quadrilatero, you can scour the racks of shops elsewhere for designer seconds, last year's fashions, imitations, and other bargains. The best place to begin is **Il Salvagente** (Via Fratelli Bronzetti, 16, off Corso XXII Marzo; ☎ 02-76110328; Metro: San Babila), where you can browse through an enormous collection of designer clothing for men, women, and children (mostly smaller sizes) at wholesale prices. **Dmagazine** (Via Montenapoleone, 26; ☎ 02-76006027; Metro: Montenapoleone) may sit on the boutique-lined main shopping drag, but its merchandise is pure discount overstock from big labels such as Armani (I saw slacks for €99), Prada (how about a sweater for €72?), and Fendi (designer scarves for €44 anyone?).

Italian Design

The top name in Italian homeware design since 1921 has been **Alessi** (main showroom: Corso Matteotti, 9; ☎ 02-795726; www.alessi.com; Metro: San Babila; sales outlet: Via Montenapoleone, 19; ☎ 02-7602-1199; Metro: Montenapoleone), which just since the late 1980s has hired the likes of Michael Graves, Philippe Starck, Frank Gehry, and Ettore Sottsass to design the latest in teakettles, bottle openers, and other housewares.

The 1980s was really part of a renaissance of Italian industrial design. This is the era when design team **Memphis** (Via della Moscova, 27; ☎ 02-6554731; www.memphis-milano.it; Metro: Turati), led by Ettore Sottsass, virtually reinvented the art form, recruiting the best and brightest architects and designers to turn their talents to lighting fixtures, kitchen appliances, office supplies, and even furnishings. Italian style has stayed at the very top of the designer homewares market (well, sharing popularity space with Scandinavian furniture) ever since. Part of the Memphis credo was to create the new modern, and then bow out before they became establishment, so they self-destructed in 1988, though you can still find their influential designs in many homeware shops, and in the main showroom.

Linens

For Milanese design with which to dress the bed, visit **Frette** (Via Visconti di Modrone; ☎ 02-777091; www.frette.it; Metro: San Babila). This outlet branch of the high-fashion linen house offers the line of tablecloths, towels, robes, and bedding that it supplies to the world's top hotels at substantial discounts. They have other stores at Via Montenapoleone, 21 (☎ 02-783950; Metro: Montenapoleone), Via Manzoni, 11 (☎ 02-864433; Metro: Montenapoleone), Corso Buenos Aires, 82 (☎ 02-29401072; Metro: Lima), Corso Vercelli 23/25 (☎ 02-4989756; Metro: Conciliazione), and Via Torino, 42 (☎ 02-86452281; Metro: Duomo).

The elegant swirling paisleys of **Etro** (Via Montenapoleone, 5; ☎ 02-76005049; www.etro.it; Metro: Montenapoleone) have been decorating the walls, furniture covers, and accessories in some of Italy's richest and aristocratic homes since 1969. They've since expanded into full lines of clothing and leather goods, as well as perfumes and accessories (available at the branch on the corner of Via P. Verri and Via Bigli, ☎ 02-7600-5450; Metro: Montenapoleone).

NIGHTLIFE

On Wednesdays and Thursdays, Milan's newspapers tend to devote a lot of ink to club schedules and cultural events. If you don't trust your command of Italian to plan your nightlife, check out the tourist office on Piazza del Duomo—there are usually piles of flyers announcing upcoming events. The tourist office also keeps visitors up-to-date with the *Hello Milano* (www.hellomilano.it) free newspaper and *Milano Mese,* the official events, exhibitions, markets, and trade fairs monthly.

The Performing Arts

For the lowdown on Milan's premier opera house, **Teatro alla Scala** ✹✹✹, see p. 399.

Milan's **"Giuseppe Verdi" Symphony Orchestra** plays at the **Auditorium di Milano,** a renovated 1930s movie house at Via S. Gottardo, 42/Largo Gustav Mahler (☎ 02-83389222; www.auditoriumdimilano.org; Metro: Duomo, then tram no. 3 or 15). Concerts run from late September to May, usually on Thursdays at 8:30pm, Fridays at 7:30pm, and Sundays at 4pm.

Pubs

A publike atmosphere, induced in part by Guinness on tap, prevails at Liberty-style **Bar Magenta** (Via Carducci, 13, at Corso Magenta; ☎ 02-8053808; closed Mon; Metro: Cadorna), in the neighborhood for which it takes its name. One of the more popular La Brera hangouts, with a young following, is **El Tombon de San Marc** (Via San Marco, 20, at Via Montebello; ☎ 02-6599507; closed Sun; Metro: Moscova), which despite its name is an English pub–style bar and restaurant.

Among the Navigli nightspots (growing in number all the time) is **El Brellin** (Vicolo della Lavandaia, off Alzaia Naviglio Grande, 14; ☎ 02-58101351; closed Sun; Metro: Genova F.S.), an intimate, canal-side piano bar with its own mini-canal. **Birreria La Fontanella** (Alzaia Naviglio Pavese, 6; ☎ 02-8372391; closed Mon; Metro: Genova F.S.) has canal-side tables outside in summer and the oddest-shaped beer glasses around—that half-a-barbell kind everyone seems to order is called the "Cavalliere."

A Jazz Club

Since Capolinea got ousted (warning: the club's name is still there at Via Ludovico il Moro, 119, but it is *not* the old jazz club where the greats came to play; rather, it's some pathetic mimic of it slapped together by the next-door neighbors who forced the original owners out of this space), the best venue on the jazz-club scene is the Navigli's **Le Scimmie** (Via Ascanio Sforza, 49; ☎ 02-89402874; www.scimmie.it; closed Tues; Metro: Porta Genova), where shows start at 10:30pm and the cover ranges from free to €8—plus it has its own bar-boat moored in the canal.

Nightlife Tip

The Navigli/Ticinese neighborhood is currently on the rise as Milan's prime night turf, though the Brera retains its pull with night owls as well.

Discothèques

The dance scene changes all the time in Milan, but at whatever club is popular (or in business) at the moment, expect to pay a cover of €5 to €20, depending on how good-looking and/or female you are. Models, actors, sports stars, and the attendant fashion set favor **Hollywood** (Corso Como, 15; ☎ 02-6598996; www.discotecahollywood.com; closed July 23–Sept 7; Metro: Moscova), which is small, chic, and centrally located in La Brera.

Grand Café Fashion (Corso di Porta Ticinese, 60, at Via Vetere; ☎ 02-89400709 or 0336-347333; Metro: Porta Genova) is a multipurpose nightspot halfway to the Navigli with a restaurant open from 9pm and a disco nightly from 11:30pm. It brings a beautiful crowd to the Ticinese neighborhood, where they dance the night away, sometimes to thematic evenings like Latino Mondays and, er, lap-dance Sundays.

Milan's most venerable disco/live music club is **Rolling Stone** (Corso XXII Marzo, 32, just east of Piazza Emilia; ☎ 02-733172; www.rollingstone.it; closed Sun–Mon; tram: 12, 27, 45, 60, 66, 73, or 92), in business since 1982. Most of the performers these days are of a rock bent, and the club is as popular as ever.

The ABCs of Milan

Consulates The **U.S. Consulate** at Via Principe Amadeo, 2/10 (☎ 02-290351; Metro: Turati), is open Monday to Friday 9 to 11am and 2 to 4pm. The **Canadian Consulate** at Via Vittor Pisani, 19 (☎ 02-67581; Metro: F.S. Centrale or Repubblica), is open Monday to Friday 9am to noon. The **British Consulate** at Via San Paolo, 7 (☎ 02-723001; Metro: Duomo), is open Monday to Friday 9:15am to 12:15pm and 2:30 to 4:30pm. The **Australian Consulate** at Via Borgogna, 2 (☎ 02-77704217; Metro: San Babila), is open Monday to Thursday 9am to 5pm, Friday 9am to 4:15pm. The **New Zealand Consulate** at Via Guido d'Arezzo, 6 (☎ 02-48012544; Metro: Pagano), is open Monday to Friday 8:30am to 5pm.

Crime For police emergencies dial ☎ **113.** There is a **police station** in Stazione Centrale. The main Questura (police station) is just west of the Giardini Pubblici (**Via Fatebenefratelli, 11;** ☎ 02-62261; Metro: Turati), though the entrance for the office for foreigners and passport problems is at Via Montebello, 26 (☎ 02-62265777; Metro: Turati). Milan is generally safe, with some notable exceptions, especially at night, including the public gardens, Parco Sempione, and the area to the west of Stazione Centrale. The train station is notorious for pickpockets, whose favorite victims are distracted passengers lining up for the airport buses at the east side of the building. You should likewise be vigilant for pickpockets on all public transportation and in street markets.

Drugstores Pharmacies rotate 24-hour shifts; look for signs posted in most pharmacies announcing which shops are open all night on any given day. The **Farmacia Stazione Centrale** (☎ 02-6690935), **in the main train station,** is open 24 hours daily and some of the staff members speak English. There are also **night pharmacies** at **Piazza del Duomo, 21** (☎ 02-86464832), **Corso Buenos Aires, 4** (☎ 02-29513320), **Via Boccaccio, 26** (☎ 02-4695281), **Viale Lucania, 10** (☎ 02-57404805), **Piazza V Giornate, 6** (☎ 02-55194867), and **Via Stradivari, 1** (☎ 02-29526966).

Emergencies The general number for emergencies is ☎ **113.** For the Carabinieri police, call ☎ **112.** For first aid or an ambulance, dial ☎ **118.** For a fire, call ☎ **115.**

Hospitals For an ambulance, call ☎ **118.** The Ospedale Maggiore Policlinico **(Via Francesco Sforza, 35;** ☎ 02-55031; www. policlinico.mi.it; Metro: Duomo or Missori) is centrally located, a 5-minute walk southeast of the Duomo.

Lost Property The city-run *ufficio oggetti rinvenuti* **(lost-and-found office)**—where you check for items lost on the street or public transportation—is just south of Piazza del Duomo **(Via Friuli, 30;** ☎ 02-88453907; Metro: Duomo or Missori) and is open Monday to Friday 8:30am to 4pm. The *oggetti smarriti* (lost objects) at Stazione Centrale (☎ 6371-2667) is located in the same office as the luggage storage and is open daily from 6am to 1am.

Post Office The main post office, Poste e Telecommunicazioni, is just west of Piazza del Duomo, at **Via Cordusio, 4;** (☎ 02-72482126; www.poste.it; Metro: Cordusio). Windows are open Monday to Friday 8am to 7pm and Saturday 8:30am to noon. Most branch offices are open Monday to Friday 8am to 2pm, Saturday 9:30am to 1pm.

Taxis To find a taxi in Milan, walk to the nearest taxi stand, usually located near major *piazze* and major Metro stops. In the center, there are taxi stands at Piazza del Duomo and Piazza della Scala. Or call a radio taxi at ☎ **02-4040,** 02-8383, 02-8585, 02-4000, or 02-6969 (the desk staff at many hotels will be happy to do this for you, even if you are not a guest). Cab meters start at €3.10, and add a surcharge of €3.10 at night, €1.55 on Sundays.

THE LAKE DISTRICT

Poets, composers, and mere mortals have been rhapsodizing about the Italian lakes for centuries—most vocally since the 18th century, when it became de rigueur for travelers on the Grand Tour to descend through the Alps and enjoy their first days on Italian soil on the shores of the lakes.

LAKE COMO ★★★

If you have time for only one lake, make it Como. The first sight of the dramatic expanse of azure Lake Como, ringed by gardens and forests and backed by the snowcapped Alps, has a history of evoking strong emotions. Over the centuries, the lake has inspired poets (Lord Byron), novelists (Stendhal), composers (Verdi and Rossini), and plenty of less famous visitors.

The lake has drawn everyone from deposed queens (George IV of England exiled Caroline of Brunswick here for her adulterous ways) to well-heeled travelers, and is still sought after by the rich and über-famous. George Clooney recently moved into the neighborhood, buying a villa from Teresa Heinz and her hubby, Senator John Kerry—it featured as the bad guy's home in *Ocean's Twelve*.

Aside from its emotional pull, Como is also just an enjoyable place to spend time. Less than an hour from Milan by train or car, its deep waters and verdant shores provide a wonderful respite from modern life. Tellingly, Lake Como served as a backdrop for the romantic scenes in *Star Wars II: Attack of the Clones*—one of the very few settings in the film *not* created entirely by CGI computer programs. I guess even George Lucas realized that Como was a place of such unearthly beauty as to need little digital touching-up.

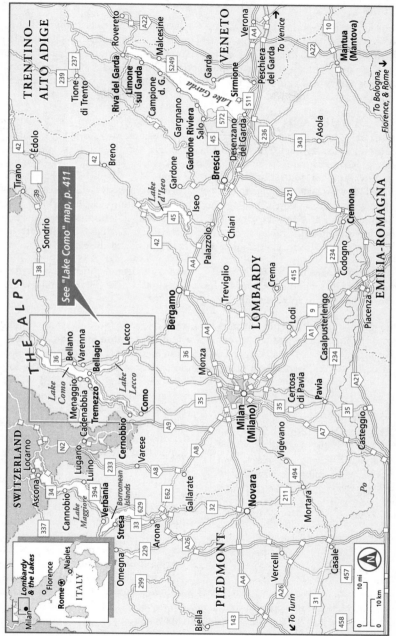

See "Lake Como" map, p. 411

Como

The largest and southernmost town on the lake isn't likely to charm you. Long a center of silk-making, this city—which traces its roots to the Gauls, and after them, the Romans—bustles with commerce and industry. You'll probably want to stay in one of the more peaceful settings farther up the lake, but Como amply rewards a day's visit with some fine Renaissance churches and palaces and a lovely lakefront promenade.

LAY OF THE LAND   Como is 78km (47 miles) northeast of Milan. One to three trains hourly connect Milan and Como's Stazione San Giovanni on Piazzale San Gottardo (regional trains from Milan's Piazza Garibaldi station take 55–65 min.; high-speed trains from Milan's Stazione Centrale station take 35–40 min.).

The **regional tourist office** (Piazza Cavour, 17; ☎ 031-269712 or 031-3300111; www.lakecomo.org; sometimes closed Sun in winter) dispenses a wealth of information on hotels, restaurants, and campgrounds all around the lake. There is also a **city tourist office** (☎ 031-3371063) in a little trailer that keeps moving around but is always somewhere near Piazza del Duomo; currently it's parked on Via Maestri Comacini, around the right side of the cathedral.

ACCOMMODATIONS & DINING   Como's moderately priced hotel scene is pretty slim pickings, but I do have a few suggestions for travelers on a budget and those who wish to splurge a bit.

€   If you're really pinching pennies, you could do worse (not much worse, mind you) than the seven bare-bones rooms above the **Ristorante Sociale** (Via Maestri Comacini, 8; ☎ 031-264042), tucked under an arcade next to the Duomo's right flank. Its big selling points: a prime location next door to the Duomo and double rooms that go for just €40 without private bathroom, €50 with. The **restaurant** ★—which features simple dishes at low prices; closed Mondays—far outshines the rooms. This is where Comaschi go to dine after a play at the Teatro Sociale (the restaurant's walls are plastered with playbills and signed actor photos), where the local soccer team celebrates its victories, and where the local equivalent of the ladies' auxiliary meets to have long, voluble conversations while enjoying one of the best fixed-price menus on the lake. For €16 you get a choice of four *primi,* four *secondi,* a side dish, and water or wine—though they usually give you both at no extra charge. Just steer clear of the fish—it's frozen . . . rather scandalous for a place located just 2 blocks from the fishing boats bobbing in the harbor.

> ❝This lake exceeds any thing I ever beheld in beauty, with the exception of the arbutus islands of Killarney. It is long and narrow, and has the appearance of a mighty river, winding among the mountains and the forests. ❞
>
> —Percy Bysshe Shelley, writing about Lake Como in a letter from 1818

€€€-€€€€   You can get far nicer rooms—but at a much higher rate of €128 to €198 for a double—at the **Hotel Metropole Suisse** ★ (Piazza Cavour, 19; ☎ 031-269444; www.hotelmetropolesuisse.com). This massive 1892 hotel closes

Lake Como

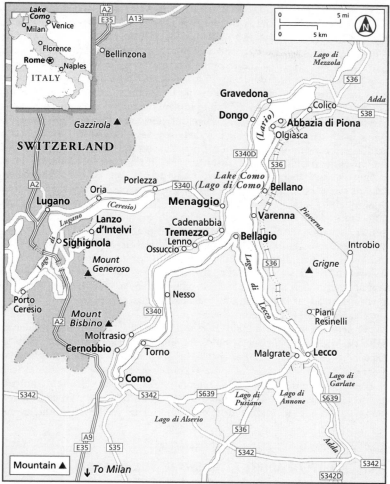

one side of Como's main square, and while accommodations vary—some carpeted with nice contemporary furnishings; others older with wood floors, brass beds, and embroidered upholstery—almost all overlook the lake, at least partially (the best with full-on views from small balconies). The corner bar/lounge has picture windows for lake views, and the restaurant (under separate management) has tables out on the piazza.

€ I'd take dinner at the Sociale, above. But the best lunch spot is **Pasticceria Monti** (Piazza Cavour, 21; ☎ 031-301165; Wed–Mon), a busy cafe on the main lakefront piazza and one of Como's favorite places to gather and watch passersby. They make excellent sandwiches and other light fare from €2.50, including daily pasta dishes, not to mention sublime coffee, pastries (from €1.50), and gelato (from €1).

WHY YOU'RE HERE: THE TOP SIGHTS & ATTRACTIONS   Part Gothic and part Renaissance, Como's **Duomo** ★★ (Piazza del Duomo, in the center of town just off the lake; ☎ 031-265244; daily 7:30am–noon and 3–7pm) is festooned with exuberant masonry and sculpture. Statues of two of the town's famous native sons, Pliny the Elder and Pliny the Younger, flank the main entrance. Inside, beneath an 18th-century dome by Juvarra—the architect who designed much of Turin—is a lavish interior hung with mostly 16th-century paintings and tapestries, with lots of helpful leaflets in English to explain the major works of art.

The black-and-white-striped 13th-century **Broletto (Town Hall)** abuts the Duomo's left flank, and adjoining it is the **Torre del Comune.** As a study in contrasts, the starkly modernist and aptly named **Casa del Fascio,** built in 1936 as the seat of the region's fascist government, rises just behind the Duomo.

Como's main drag, **Corso Vittorio Emanuele II,** cuts through the medieval quarter, where wood-beamed houses line narrow streets. Two blocks south of the Duomo, the five-sided **San Fedele** (Piazza S. Fedele; daily 8am–noon and 3:30–7pm) sits on a charming square. Though largely 12th-century, parts of the church, including the altar, date from the 6th century.

To see **Como's most alluring church,** though, you've got to venture into the dull outlying neighborhood southwest of the center where, just off Viale Roosevelt, you'll come to the five-aisle, heavily frescoed **Basilica of Sant'Abbondio** ★★ (☎ 631-3388111; daily 8am–6pm, except during weddings, which are hugely popular here), a Romanesque masterpiece from the 11th-century lined with great 14th-century frescoes.

Lakeside life revolves around **Piazza Cavour** and the adjoining **Giardini Pubblici,** where the circular **Tempio Voltano** (☎ 031-574705; €3; Tues–Sun 10am–noon and 3–6pm, Oct–Mar 2–4pm) houses memorabilia that'll enlighten you about the life and experiments of native son and electricity pioneer Alessandro Volta.

For a quick retreat and some stunning views, take the **Brunate funicular** (Lungo Lario Trieste; ☎ 031-303608; €4.10 round-trip; every 15 min. in summer, every 30 min. in winter) for a 7-minute ride up to the top of the forested

---

A Word about Alternative Accommodations on the Lakes

With the exception of the B&Bs noted below, the lake region is a bust when it comes to finding alternative accommodations. Como itself has only four B&Bs (all too far out of town to be feasible); Bellagio has only one in town (the recommended restaurant, Barchetta—see below—rents five rooms for €80 each); Varenna has none. On Lake Garda, it's a similar story: Sirmione has precisely zero B&Bs or rental rooms (it would be hard to find a place to stick them because almost every building is already a hotel). Riva del Garda has one B&B (out on the very edge of town), and of the dozen *affittacamere* (rooms for rent), only one is in the center; the others are either up near the suburb of Arco or in places no visitor would want to lodge.

hill above the town. The tourist office has maps that detail several trail hikes from the top.

Bellagio

Bellagio is often called one of the most beautiful towns in Italy. Nestled amid cypress groves and verdant gardens, its earth-toned old buildings climb from the lakefront promenade along stepped cobblestone lanes. It has become a popular retreat for everyone from Milanese out for a day of relaxation to Brits and Americans who come to relax for a week or two.

It also occupies by far the loveliest spot on the lake, the section known as the Centro Lago where the three legs of Lake Como meet. Bellagio is at the tip of the peninsula at this fork with frequent ferry service, making this a great base for exploring Varenna (see below) and other spots on the nearby shores of the Centro Lago.

LAY OF THE LAND   There are one to three SPT **buses** (☎ 031-247111; www.sptcomo.it) per hour from Como (70-min. trip), where you can get train connections. **Ferries** (☎ 800-551801 or 031-579211; www.navigazionelaghi.it) from Como take 2 hours; hydrofoils 35 to 45 minutes. Schedules vary with season, but from Easter to September a ferry or hydrofoil makes the trip from Como to Bellagio and other towns along the lake at least hourly. The picturesque lakeshore **road** from Como, the SS583, can be very crowded in summer, so allow at least an hour of traveling time by car.

Bellagio's **tourist office** is at Piazza della Chiesa, 14; (☎ 031-950204; www.bellagiolakecomo.com), a steep 1½ blocks up from the port.

ACCOMMODATIONS & DINING IN BELLAGIO   Note that a wider selection of moderately priced hotels can be found across the lake from Bellagio, in Varenna (see below). If you're traveling on a budget, your best bet is to lodge there and then simply make Bellagio a day trip.

€€   The best deal is the little **Giardinetto** (Via Roncati, 12, just off Piazza del Chiesa; ☎ 031-950168; closed Nov–Mar; no credit cards), at the top of town. The rooms are basic, but quite large and bright, with solid old armoires, big windows, and—in the better rooms—box-spring-and-mattress beds rather than the standard cots. The best part: Doubles cost a mere €52 to €55 (breakfast tacks on another €6 per person). Most rooms overlook a gravelly grapevine-covered terrace, where you're welcome to bring your own food for an alfresco meal, and those on the upper floors even catch a glimpse of the lake from their balconies (especially rooms 18–20). Some, though, are on the airshaft or even come with no window whatsoever.

€€-€€€   The 10 simple rooms at the **Suisse** ★ (Piazza Mazzini, 23; ☎ 031-950335; Oct–Nov and Dec–Feb closed Wed), a 15th-century lakeside villa right on the main harbor square, have a pleasant but budget decor: parquet floors, stylish solid-wood furnishings with lovely inlaid or carved details, and plain bathrooms. Not only do you get water views, but the €100 to €154 for a double room includes half-pension at the restaurant, so it's like getting two meals a day for free. What's more, the restaurant is pretty good—Italian fare year-round, with an inventive fusion flair in summer—served either alfresco under the arcades, in a plain ground floor room, or in the understatedly elegant upstairs dining room, with a decorated ceiling and a lake-view terrace.

€€-€€€€   Spend a bit more to splurge on Suisse's neighbor, the 150-year-old **Hotel Du Lac** ★★ (Piazza Mazzini, 32; ☎ 031-950320; www.bellagiohoteldulac. com; closed early Nov to Easter), run with an air of graciousness and old-fashioned comfort by the Leoni family. Downstairs, a bar opens onto the arcaded sidewalk, there is a series of pleasant sitting rooms, and meals are served in a nicely appointed dining room with panoramic views of the lake (half-board is an extra €15 per person). Each of the smallish guest rooms is unique, though they tend toward cushy armchairs and a nice smattering of antiques and reproductions, many with balconies or terraces, and cost €110 to €180 for a double. There's a rooftop sun terrace with sweeping lake views, and free access to the Leoni's nearby sports center with a pool, tennis courts, and a children's center.

€   **Bar Café Rossi** ★ (Piazza Mazzini, 22/24; ☎ 031-950196; Oct–Mar closed Thurs) is one of the nicest of Bellagio's pleasant lakefront cafes, tucked under the arcades of the town's main square. You can dine at one of the few outside tables or in the delightful Art Nouveau dining room with its intricate tilework, carved wood cabinets, and stuccoed ceilings. Wine and the excellent house coffee are available all day, but a nice selection of pastries and sandwiches (€2.50–€4) makes this a good stop for breakfast or lunch.

€-€€   **La Grotta** (Salita Cernaia, 14; ☎ 031-951152; credit cards accepted only for bills totaling more than €21; closed Nov 15–Dec 25 and Mon Oct–June) is tucked away on a stepped street just off lakefront Piazza Mazzini, and has a cozy, informal series of vaulted-ceiling dining rooms with extremely friendly service, not to mention a wide-ranging menu. Most of the regulars come for the fish specials, including lake trout (€12), or the delectable pizzas (€5–€10) that are the best for miles around (I've made sure of this by sampling them six or seven times).

€€€   **Barchetta** ★★ (Salita Mella, 13; ☎ 031-951389; www.acena.it/la barchettadibellagio; closed Nov–Mar and June 15–Sept 15 Tues–Wed at lunch) is one of Bellagio's best restaurants, specializing in fresh lake fish (try the perch or angler fish). In all but the coldest weather, food is served on a bamboo-enclosed heated terrace. Most of the pastas are innovative variations on traditional recipes, such as *ravioli caprino* (with goat's cheese, topped with pear sauce) and savory risotto with hazelnuts and pistachios. Book ahead.

BELLAGIO'S GARDENS   One of Bellagio's famed gardens surrounds the **Villa Melzi d'Eril** (☎ 031-950204; €5; late Mar to early Nov daily 9am–6pm), built in 1808 by Francesco Melzi, a friend of Napoleon and an official of his Italian Republic. The villa was later the retreat of Franz Liszt and is now the home of Count Gallarati Scotti, who allows the public to stroll through his acres of manicured lawns and fountains and visit a pavilion displaying a collection of Egyptian sculpture.

Bellagio's other famous gardens are those of the **Villa Serbelloni** ★ (☎ 031-951555; €6.50; Apr–Oct, tours Tues–Sun at 11am and 4pm), occupying land once owned by Pliny the Younger and now in the hands of the Rockefeller Foundation.

You can visit the gardens and villa on twice-daily guided tours (reserve ahead), about 1½ hours long, in Italian and English (tours require at least six people to depart). You meet at the little tower on the backside of Piazza della Chiesa.

Varenna

You can happily spend some time clambering up and down the steep steps that substitute for streets in this charming fishing village on the eastern shore of the lake, just 10 minutes by ferry (5 min. by hydrofoil) from Bellagio. There's a tiny **tourist office** at Piazza S. Giorgio/Via IV Novembre (☎ 0341-830367; www.aptlecco.com).

The hilltop ruins of the **Castello di Vezio** (☎ 335-465186; www.castellodi vezio.it; €4; 10am to sunset, Apr–Oct daily, Feb, Mar, and Nov Sat–Sun only, Dec Sun only, closed Jan) lie a 20-minute hike above the town. The main reason for a visit is to enjoy the stunning views of the lake, its shoreline villages, and the backdrop of mountains at the northern end.

The gardens of the **Villa Monastero** ★ (☎ 0341-830129; www.villamonastero. org; €2; Mar–Oct daily 9am–7pm) are more easily accessible at the southern edge of town along Via IV Novembre, and you can reach them by following the series of lakeside promenades through the old town from the ferry landing. This villa and the terraced gardens that rise from the lakeshore were once a not-so-spartan monastery—until it was dissolved in the late 17th century, when the nuns in residence began bearing living proof that they were on too friendly terms with the priests across the way. If you find it hard to tear yourself from the bowers of citrus trees and rhododendrons clinging to terraces, you'll find equally enchanting surroundings in the adjoining gardens of the **Villa Cipressi** (☎ 0341-830113; www.hotelvillacipressi.it; €2; Mar–Oct daily 9am–7pm).

ACCOMMODATIONS & DINING   As I said before, a stay in Varenna is one of the best options for value-conscious travelers (and the village is also quite lovely in its own right).

€€–€€€   You'd have to look hard to find a more pleasant retreat by the lake than the **Milano** ★★ (Via XX Settembre, 29; ☎ 0341-830298; www.varenna.net; closed Dec–Feb), an old lakefront house renovated into a boutique hotel by Bettina and Egidio Mallone, a friendly young Italian-Swiss couple. The modern common area now has a TV with satellite channels and computer with free Internet. The rooms were overhauled in 2003 with new beds and antique-style furnishings, and spanking new bathrooms as of 2004. All rooms have balconies. Rooms 1 and 2 (which open onto a wide terrace) and rooms 5 and 6 have full-on lake vistas (doubles €130–€145); the others overlook the neighbor's pretty garden with askance lake views (doubles €120–€130). In summer, breakfast is served on the outdoor terrace, as are the €25, three-course dinners, available upon request Monday and Wednesday through Saturday. They also have an apartment nearby (no views, though) that they'll rent out—preferably to families or groups of four—for €55 per person, including breakfast back at the hotel.

€€–€€€€   If you enjoyed your tour of Varenna's lush gardens (see above), there's no need to leave. The 16th-century **Villa Cipressi** ★★ (Via IV Novembre, 18; ☎ 0341-830113; www.hotelvillacipressi.it; usually closed late Oct to Mar, but some years open year-round) was converted to a hotel nearly 2 centuries ago, and though it's geared toward hosting conferences, other guests can book, space permitting. Though the rooms have been renovated without any attempt to retain historic character, they're extremely large and attractive. Not every room gets a lake view (doubles €120–€150), but all save a few small ones on the road side enjoy marvelous views over those famous gardens (and they cost less: €100–€120). Suites (€120–€150) take advantage of the high ceilings and contain loft bedrooms, with sitting areas below that can easily fit a couple of single beds (€45 extra) for families.

€€€   One of your most memorable experiences in this region could be a meal at the romantic **Vecchia Varenna** ★★ (Via Scoscesa, 10; ☎ 031-830793; www.vecchiavarenna.it; closed Mon and Jan), on a terrace over the water or in a beautiful stone-floored room with white stone walls. The kitchen makes the most of local herbs and vegetables and, of course, the bounty of the lake—*quadrucci* (pasta pockets) are stuffed with trout (€11), and one of the best of the many risottos combines wild mushrooms and *lavarello* (a white fish from the lake; €11). The grilled lake trout stuffed with mountain herbs is sublime (€15). Reservations are required.

LAKE MAGGIORE

Anyone who reads Hemingway's *A Farewell to Arms* will recognize this lake and its forested shores. That's just the sort of place Lake Maggiore (Lago Maggiore) is: a pleasure ground steeped in associations with famous figures—Flaubert, Wagner, Goethe, and Europe's other great minds seem to have been inspired by the deep, moody waters backed by the Alps—and not-so-famous wealthy visitors. Fortunately, you need be neither famous nor wealthy to enjoy Maggiore, which is on the Swiss border just a short dash east and north of Milan.

Stresa & the Borromean Islands

Strolling and relaxing seem to be the main activities in Stresa, a pretty little place with a long lakefront promenade, a lively center, and a bevy of restaurants and hotels that range from the expensive and splendid to the affordable but comfortable. Sooner or later, though, most visitors climb into a ferry for the short ride to the trio of famed islands just off Stresa's shore, the Isole Borromee.

LAY OF THE LAND   Stresa is 80km (48 miles) northwest of Milan, linked by 20 **trains** daily (58–84 min.). The **tourist office** is at the ferry dock (☎ 0323-31308; www.lagomaggiore.it, www.illagomaggiore.com, or www.stresa.it), closed Sundays November to April.

Cumulative Ticket

You can get a cumulative ticket covering both Isola Bella and Isola Madre for €15. Audio tours help make sense of it all for €3.50 each or €5 to rent two sets of headphones.

Making the Most of Your Time Here

To squeeze as much of Stresa's sights in as you can in a day, note that the ferry back from the Isole Borromee stops first at the Mottarone Funivia area before chugging down the coast to the center of Stresa and the main docks. You can hop off here either to (1) ride the cable car up the mountain (€13 round-trip, or €7 one-way and walk or bike—€21 rentals—back down), or (2) simply walk back into Stresa itself along a pretty lakeside promenade, past crumbling villas and impromptu sculpture gardens, in about 20 minutes.

ACCOMMODATIONS IN STRESA & THE ISLANDS   This is one of the few places in the region where the options include both standard hotels and more interesting B&B accommodations.

€€   For much of the spring and summer, the street in front of **Hotel Primavera** ★★ (Via Cavour, 30; ☎ 0323-31286; www.stresa.it; closed Dec 20, and some years Jan–Feb) is closed to traffic and filled with flowering plants and cafe tables. The relaxed air prevails throughout this bright little hotel a block off the lake in the town center. The tile-floored rooms are furnished in functional walnut veneer and go for €75 to €105. Many rooms have balconies just wide enough to accommodate a pair of chairs; a few on the fourth floor even get a sliver of lake view around the apse and stone bell tower of the Duomo.

€€   The same family runs the more modern, though equally priced **Hotel Meeting** ★ (Via Bonghi, 9; ☎ 0323-32741; www.stresa.it; closed Dec some years, Jan–Feb others), named for its proximity to a conference center. It's a 5-mintue walk from the lakefront in a quiet and leafy setting—though light sleepers on the back may notice the trains passing in the distance. The Scandinavian rooms are big and bright, and all come with balconies.

€€   Just uphill from the train station—and an unfortunate 10-minute walk from the center of town and the lakeside—the family-run **Mon Toc** ★ (Via Duchessa di Genova, 69; ☎ 0323-30282; www.hotelmontoc.com; closed Jan or Nov) is surrounded by a private garden for an almost countrylike atmosphere. The functional €78 doubles are unusually pleasant for a hotel this cheap (though a few of the tidy bathrooms are of the miniscule, molded, airplane variety). The friendly owner refuses, out of honesty, to call the sliver of lake visible over the rooftops from the second-floor rooms a "lake view."

If you don't luck out with those, there are always the bland rooms at the **Fiorentino** (see "Dining in Stresa," below).

DINING IN STRESA   As befits the select nature of the area, the restaurants of Stresa are also quite special.

€–€€   It's hard to find friendlier service or homier trattoria-type food in Stresa than at the **Hotel Ristorante Fiorentino** (Via A. M. Bolongaro, 9–11;

A Few B&B Options

€€ There's only one B&B in the heart of Stresa—but it's a doozy, right across the street from the lake. At her **Il Viaggiatore** (Corso Italia, 38; ☎ 0323-934674; www.bb-ilviaggiatore.it), Rosanna rents two large, homey rooms with killer lake views for €70 to €80. They share a kitchen, and Rosanna is an avid outdoorswoman and rock climber who helps run a guide service for hiking and climbing in nearby Piemonte parkland.

€€€ For a truly unique lake experience, stay on the Isola Superiore itself. From March to October, the **Verbano** ★ (see "Dining in Stresa," above) rents some beautiful lake-view rooms in the villa upstairs for €148 per double.

€€ Cheaper—but only open in summer (Apr–Sept)—are the €60-to-€70 doubles at **Chez Manuel** (Via Di Mezzo, 41; ☎ 0323-31165; www.bedandbreakfast stresa.com; closed Oct–Mar), with wood floors, blond furnishings, a shared kitchen, and rooftop views.

☎ 0323-30254; www.hotelfiorentino.com; closed Nov–Feb), especially at these prices—the €14 *menu turistico* is a steal. Everything that comes out of the family-run kitchen is made fresh daily, including cannelloni (€6) and other pastas. You can dine in a big cozy room or on a patio out back in good weather. As you might have guessed from the name, they also rent rooms—quite nice, if boring, ones at just €74 to €80 per double.

€-€€ Most of Stresa seems to congregate in the **Taverna del Pappagallo** (Via Principessa Margherita, 46; ☎ 0323-30411; www.tavernapappagallo.com; no credit cards; closed Tues–Wed except in summer) for the most popular pizza in town (€4.20–€10). But just about all the fare that comes out of the family-run kitchen is delicious, including delectable homemade gnocchi (€6.20) and such dishes as grilled sausage with beans (€8). Weather permitting, try to dine at one of the tables in the pleasant garden.

€€-€€€ **Verbano** ★★ (Isola Superiore; ☎ 0323-32534; www.hotelverbano. it; closed Jan and sometimes Wed in winter) has a fairy-tale location on the point of the "Fisherman's Isle," taking up the jasmine-fringed gravelly terrace next to the hotel. The waters lap right up to the wall and the views are over the back of Isola Bella and the lake around you on three sides. The cooking needn't be anything special given its location in a prime tourist spot, but surprisingly it's almost as lovely as the setting. First courses cost just €5 to €10, and include such delectables as a *zuppa di verdure* (vegetable soup), hearty with barley and grains; and a *paglia e fieno* ("hay and straw") mix of regular (yellow) and spinach (green) tagliatelle noodles in a *ragù* made of scorpion fish, carrots, and zucchini. Definitely leave room for a grilled lake trout accompanied by rice stained black with squid ink. March to October, they also rent some beautiful rooms in the villa upstairs for €148 per double.

EXPLORING THE ISLANDS   Since the 12th century, the Borromeo family has owned these three islets, which float in the misty waters off Stresa and entice visitors with their stunning beauty. Isola Bella and especially Isola Superiore have villages you can hang out in for free, but Isola Madre consists solely of the admission-charging gardens.

Isola Bella ✹✹ (☎ 0323-30556; www.borromeoturismo.it; €10; Mar 25–Oct 22 daily 9:30am–5:30pm) remains true to its name, with splendid 17th-century gardens that ascend from the shore in 10 luxuriantly planted terraces. The Borromeo *palazzo* includes a room in which Napoleon and Josephine once slept.

The largest and most peaceful of the islands is **Isola Madre** ✹✹ (☎ 0323-30556; www.borromeoturismo.it; €9; Mar 25–Oct 22 daily 9am–5:30pm), all 8 acres of which are covered by the Orto Botanico, teeming with exquisite flora and exotic, colorful birds. The villa in the center of it all was built in 1518 to 1585 and is still filled with Borromeo family memorabilia and some interesting old puppet-show stages.

Most of Isola Superiore, also known as Isola dei Pescatori (Fishermen's Island), is occupied by a not-so-quaint old fishing village—every one of the tall houses on this tiny strip of land seems to harbor a souvenir shop or pizza stand, and there are hordes of visitors to keep them busy.

Public **ferries** (☎ 800-551801 or 0322-233200; www.navigazionelaghi.it) leave for the islands every half-hour from the big building with triple arches on Stresa's Piazza Marconi. Round-trip tickets to any one island cost €5.20 (Isola Bella or Isola Superiore) to €7 (Isola Madre), so it's far more economical to get a €10 day pass allowing you to ride as much as you'd like. You'll see other ticket booths and touts dressed as sailors who will try to lure you aboard; avoid these overpriced private hucksters and stick with the public ferry service.

LAKE GARDA

Lake Garda (Lago di Garda), the largest and easternmost of the lakes, laps against the flat plains of Lombardy and the Veneto at its southern extremes, and in the north, where it juts into the Trentino-Alto Adige region, becomes fiordlike and moody, its deep waters backed by Alpine peaks. All around the lake, Garda's shores are green and fragrant with flowery gardens, groves of olives and lemons, and forests of pines and cypress.

This pleasing, vaguely exotic landscape has attracted everyone from the poet Gabriele D'Annunzio to the dictator Benito Mussolini who, retreating with his Nazi minders, founded the short-lived Republic of Salò on the lake's western shores (where he ultimately was captured and killed by Partisans).

Long before them, the Romans discovered the hot springs that still gush forth at Sirmione, the famed resort on a spit of land at the lake's southern reaches. Today's visitors come to swim (Garda is the cleanest of the major lakes), windsurf (Riva del Garda, at the northern end of the lake, is Europe's windsurfing capital), and enjoy the easygoing ambience of Garda's many pleasant lakeside resorts.

Sirmione

Garda's most popular resort sits on the tip of a narrow peninsula of cypress and olive groves that juts due north from the center of the lake's southern shore.

Despite an onslaught of visitors, Sirmione manages to retain its charm (though just barely in the heaviest months of July–Aug). Vehicular traffic on the narrow, marble-slab streets is kept to a minimum; only by booking a hotel within the old city can you get your name on the list of cars allowed past the guard at the lone city gate. The emphasis here is on strolling, swimming in waters that are warmed in places by underwater hot springs, and relaxing on the sunny terraces of pleasant lakeside hotels.

LAY OF THE LAND   Sirmione lies just off the A4 **autostrada** between Milan, 127km (76 miles) to the west, and Venice, 149km (90 miles) to the east. **Train** connections are via nearby Desenzano (20 min. from Sirmione by half-hourly bus), which is on the Milan–Venice trunk line. There are trains almost every half-hour in either direction, stopping in Verona (25 min.), Venice (1½–2½ hr.), and Milan (1–1½ hr.).

Hydrofoils and ferries operated by **Navigazione Lago di Garda** (☎ 800-551801 or 030-9149511; www.navigazionelaghi.it) ply the waters of the lake. One or two hourly ferries and four daily hydrofoils connect Sirmione with Desenzano (20 min. by ferry; 10 min. by hydrofoil). Two daily ferries and three daily hydrofoils connect Sirmione with Riva (almost 4 hr. by ferry; 2 hr. 10 min. by hydrofoil). Service is curtailed from October to April.

The **tourist office** is just outside the old town near the castle (Viale Marconi, 2; ☎ 030-916245 or 030-916114; www.bresciaholiday.com; Nov–Mar closed Sat afternoon and Sun).

ACCOMMODATIONS & DINING   Sirmione's gaggle of moderately priced hotels book up quickly in July and August, which is when they charge the higher rates quoted below. The tourist office will help you find a room in your price range on the day you arrive, but they won't book ahead of time.

€€   One of Sirmione's best-value lodgings is also one of its most romantic. The **Grifone** ★★ (Via Bocchio, 4; ☎ 030-916014; www.sirmionehotel.com; no credit cards; closed late Oct to Easter) is a vine-clad stone building with fantastic views of the neighboring castle and lake from its simple, plain, pleasant, and remarkably cheap (€55 double) rooms. Top-floor rooms (36–42) even have small balconies. There's also a shady patio off the lobby and a small pebble beach. Brother and sister Nicola and Cristina Marcolini oversee the hotel and adjoining restaurant with a great deal of graciousness, carrying on several generations of a family business.

€€   The family-run **Corte Regina** ★ (Via Antiche Mura, 11; ☎ 030-916147; www.corteregina.it; closed Nov–Mar) doesn't enjoy the lake views of the Grifone, but this attractive hotel—housed in a stone building fronted by a vine-shaded terrace on a narrow side street—has nicer rooms and just as friendly a welcome for €70 to €95 for a double. The large tile-floored rooms have been recently renovated, with contemporary furnishings under modern wood-beamed ceilings and new bathrooms.

€€–€€€   Ezra Pound once lived in the pink-stucco **Hotel Eden** ★ (Piazza Carducci, 17/18; ☎ 030-916481; www.hoteledenonline.it; closed Nov–Easter) on a quiet side street leading to the lake in the center of town. The Eden has been modernized with taste and an eye to comfort, and the management is both friendly and helpful. You can see the lake from most of the attractive, contemporary rooms (€120–€170 doubles; breakfast €10), whose mirrored walls enhance the light and lake views. The marble lobby opens to a delightful shaded terrace and a swimming pier that juts into the lake.

€€€–€€€€   If you're looking for more of a resort hotel (or just something open through much of the off season), the modern **Olivi** ★★ (Via San Pietro, 5; ☎ 030-9905365; www.gardalake.it/hotel-olivi; closed Jan) offers a taste of the high life at fairly reasonable rates: €132 to €200 for two. It's not directly on the lake—which you can see from most rooms and the sunny terrace—but instead commands a hilltop position near the Roman ruins amid pines and olive groves. The rooms are decorated in varying schemes of bold pastels and earth tones, with dressing areas off the bathrooms, and balconies. There's a large pool in the garden and, to bring a lakeside feeling to the grounds, an artificial river that streams past the terrace and glass windows of the lobby and breakfast room.

€€   You can get a quick pizza (€7–€11) with a view of the lake from the terrace at **L'Archimboldo** (Via Vittorio Emanuele, 71; ☎ 030-916409; Wed–Mon).

€–€€   For better pizza—but no view—head to **La Roccia** (Via Piana, 2; ☎ 030-916392; closed Thurs and Nov–Mar), serving excellent food in unusually pleasant surroundings, especially if you sit in the large garden. The menu features more than 20 wood-oven pizzas (€4.50–€9), plus plenty of traditional pastas, including lasagna and excellent cheese tortellini in a cream-and-prosciutto sauce (€8).

€€   You'd think that a location smack in the heart of the main drag's boutiques and *gelaterie* would turn any restaurant into a pricey and awful tourist trap. That, normally, is too true—but not in the case of Sirmione's **Ristorante Al Progresso** ★ (Via Vittorio Emanuele, 18–20; ☎ 030-916108; closed Thurs off season and either Nov–Dec or Dec–Jan, depending on flow of tourism), an appealingly plain spot with a touch of style, low prices, and quite excellent home cooking. Fresh lake trout (€9.50) is often on the menu—simply grilled or served *al sirmionese* (boiled with a house sauce of garlic, oil, capers, and anchovies)—as is a tangy €9 *scaloppine al limone,* veal in a sauce made from fresh lemons grown on the lakeshore.

EXPLORING SIRMIONE   In addition to its attractive though tourist-shop-ridden old town, Sirmione has many lakeside promenades, pleasant beaches, and even some open countryside where olive trees sway in the breeze. Anything you'll want to see can be reached easily on foot, though an open-air tram makes the short run out to the Roman ruins from the northern edge of the old town (except 12:30–2:30pm).

The moated and turreted **Castello Scaligero** ★ (☎ 030-916468; €4; Tues–Sun 8:30am–7pm) still guards the only land-side entrance to the old town. Built in the 13th century by the Della Scala family, who ruled Verona and many of the lands surrounding the lake, the castle warrants a visit mainly for the views from its towers.

From the castle, Via Vittorio Emanuele leads through the center of the town and emerges after a few blocks into the greener, garden-lined lanes that wind through the tip of the peninsula to the **Grotte di Catullo** ★ (☎ 030-916157; €4; Mar–Oct 14 Tues–Sun 8:30am–7pm, Oct 15–Feb Tues–Sun 8:30am–4:30pm). Whether these extensive ruins at the northern tip of the peninsula were actually once the villa and baths of the pleasure-loving Roman poet (and Sirmione native) Catullus is open to debate. But their presence here, on a hilltop fragrant with wild rosemary and pines, demonstrates that Sirmione has been a deservedly popular retreat for millennia, and you can wander through the evocative remains while taking in wonderful lake views.

If you want to enjoy the lake's clean waters, head to the small **Lido delle Bionde beach,** near the castle off Via Dante. In summer, the beach concession rents lounge chairs with umbrellas for €5 per day, as well as kayaks and pedal boats (€8 per hr.).

Riva del Garda

Riva del Garda is not just a resort but also a real town (the northernmost on the lake), with medieval towers, a nice smattering of Renaissance churches and *palazzi,* and narrow cobblestone streets where the everyday business of a prosperous Italian town proceeds on its alluring way.

LAY OF THE LAND   Riva del Garda is roughly 2 hours by **bus** from a number of nearby cities and lake towns, including Trent (24 buses daily), Verona (16 buses daily), Brescia (5 buses daily), the busy **train** station at Desenzano (6 trains daily; see "Sirmione" for details), and Sirmione (although from there only the 4:30pm run is direct; for all others, you must transfer at Peschiera).

It's far more genteel—if slower—to arrive by **boat** (☎ 800-551801; www.navigazionelaghi.it). Schedules vary with the season, with very limited service in the winter, but in summer you can opt for one of three daily hydrofoils (80 min. from Gardone, 2hr. 10 min. from Sirmione), or the two daily ferries (2¾ hr. from Gardone, almost 4 hr. from Sirmione).

The fastest way to Riva **by car** is the A22, which shoots up the east side of the lake (exit at Mori, 13km/9 miles east of Riva). It's far more scenic to drive along the western shore, past Gardone, and along the beautiful corniche between Riva and Salò that hugs cliffs and passes through kilometer after kilometer of tunnels.

The Riva del Garda **tourist office,** which supplies information on hotels, restaurants, and activities in the area, is near the lakefront (Giardini di Porta Orientale, 8; (☎ 0464-554444; www.gardatrentino.com or www.garda.com). It's closed Sundays April to June 15 and September 16 to October; closed weekends November to March.

ACCOMMODATIONS & DINING   Perhaps the least pretentious of the lake towns, Riva del Garda has a handful of affordable options for travelers.

€   **La Montanara** (Via Montanara, 18–20; ☎ 0464-554857; closed Nov–Easter), for example, ain't fancy, but it's cheap. The exceedingly basic, midsize rooms (€36 doubles) are squirreled away above an equally inexpensive trattoria in an old *palazzo* in a quiet part of the *centro storico.* It's all a bit down at the heels, but immaculately kept, with a picture or two framed on the whitewashed walls to relieve some of the spartan-ness. The four rooms without private bathrooms have at least a sink, and cost just €32. The two units on the top floor are the best for their general brightness and high ceilings.

€€   The management at **Hotel Portici** (Piazza III Novembre, 19; ☎ 0464-555400; www.hotelportici.it; closed Nov–Mar) pays much more attention to their ground-floor restaurant/bar under a portico of the main square than they do to the hotel, but perhaps that's because their rooms are mainly booked by tour groups—keeping this central and surprisingly reasonable choice off the radar of more independent travelers. Sadly, its location in the upper leg of the piazza's L-shape deprives almost all rooms of a lake view—and the functional units are boringly modern to boot, done up in a monotonous blue tone. Still, for these low prices—doubles from €64 to €100, depending on the season—you can easily cross the piazza to a cafe to get a view.

€€–€€€€   For a bit more scratch you can move across the piazza to **Hotel Sole** ★★ (Piazza III Novembre, 35; ☎ 0464-552686; www.hotelsole.net; closed Nov to mid-Mar except at Christmastime and during frequent trade fairs), one of the finest hotels in town with a wonderful location right on the lake. The management charges a fair price yet still lavishes attention on the hotel's rooms and guests, with amenities from a casual cafe with lakeside terrace, to a rooftop solarium with sauna, to free bikes for guest use. This place screams class: a lobby filled with rare Persian carpets and abstract art, a sweeping circular staircase, and warm and luxurious rooms fitted with tasteful furnishings and marble-trimmed bathrooms. The best rooms are outfitted in antique style with balconies and lake views costing €112 to €180 for a double. Penny pinchers can get a modern-functional room overlooking the square and town for €96 to €160. Half-board in the formal restaurant is a steal at only €8 extra per person; full-board costs €15, but then you couldn't dine out.

€€–€€€   If the restaurants attached to the hotels above don't satisfy, indulge in the Teutonic side of this Trentino town at the noisy indoor beer garden of **Birreria Spaten** ★ (Via Maffei, 7; ☎ 0464-553670, closed Wed and Nov–Feb), occupying the ground floor of an old *palazzo*. Many of the German and Austrian visitors who favor Riva opt for the schnitzel-and-sauerbraten side of the menu, but you can also enjoy a pasta like *strangolapreti* (spinach-and-ricotta dumplings in a butter sauce; €8), one of 30 pizzas (€5–€9), or a simply grilled lake trout (€15). If you can't decide, the €14 Piatto Spaten is an ample sampler of Tirolean specialties: *cotechino* (spicy sausage), *wurstel, canederli* (a giant bread dumpling), a ham steak, and sauerkraut.

EXPLORING RIVA DEL GARDA   Riva's old town is pleasant enough, though the only historical attractions of note are the 13th-century **Torre d'Apponale** and, nearby, the moated lakeside castle, **La Rocca.** Part of the castle interior now houses an unassuming **museum of local art and crafts** (Piazza C. Battisti, 3; ☎ 0464-573869; www.comune.rivadelgarda.tn.it/museo; €3; 10am–6pm, Mar 19–June 12 and Oct closed Mon).

Get Physical in Riva

At the beach next to the castle you can rent rowboats or pedal boats for about €6 to €7 per hour (buy 2 hr., get a third free) from March to October daily 8am to 8pm.

For a more adventurous outing, check out the **windsurfing** at the **Nautic Club Riva** (Via Rovereto, 44; ☎ 0464-552453; www.nauticclubriva. com). Boards rent for €17 for an hour, €24 for 2 hours, or €39 all day. Multiday and weekly packages, as well as lessons, are also available.

You can rent **mountain bikes** from **Superbike Girelli** (Viale Damiano Chiesa, 15; ☎ 0464-556602) for €4 per hour or €10 per day, or from **Fori e Bike** (Viale dei Tigli, 24; ☎ 0464-551830) for €8 to €13 per day (the higher price for the better mountain bikes).

Most years, the tourist office runs a few **free guided tours** in English—weekends around the town itself, Tuesdays and Fridays to sights in the surrounding area. You must book in advance, by 5pm the previous day, at ☎ **0464-554444.**

The main attraction is the lake itself, which Riva takes advantage of with a waterside promenade stretching for several kilometers past parks and pebbly **beaches.** The water is warm enough for swimming from May to October, and air currents fanned by the mountains make Garda popular for **windsurfing** year-round (see "Get Physical in Riva," above).

10 Turin & the Alps

Olympic glory is only part of the story.

by Reid Bramblett

IT'S OFTEN SAID THAT TURIN IS EITHER THE MOST FRENCH CITY IN ITALY or the most Italian city in France. And it makes sense: From the 13th century until Italy's 1861 unification (when the city served briefly as the new country's capital), Turin was home to the House of Savoy, whose last three monarchs—Vittorio Emanuele II, Umberto, and Vittorio Emanuele III—became the first kings of Italy. The Savoys were as French as they were Italian, with holdings that extended well into the present-day French regions of Savoy and the Côte d'Azur. The city's Francophile 17th- and 18th-century architects laid out broad avenues and airy *piazze* and lined them with low-slung neoclassical buildings.

Turin is also called the Italian Detroit, but that's largely because Fiat and tire manufacturer Pirelli are based here. In every other respect, the comparison is unfair. Turin is, in fact, the most genteel and elegant city in all of Northern Italy.

Wedged into Italy's northwest corner, Turin is capital of the Piemonte (Piedmont) region, "at the foot of the mountains," which are, in this case, the Alps. Dramatic peaks are visible throughout the Piemonte, most of which rises and rolls over the fertile foothills that produce a rich bounty of cheeses, truffles, and, of course, wines—among them some of Italy's most delicious reds: Barbaresco, Barbera, and Barolo (the last considered one of Italy's top beefy, yet structured, wines).

TURIN

Most visitors come to Turin with business in mind, but those who take the time to look around the historical center will find fine museums, excellent restaurants, and a sophisticated city with scads of old-fashioned class.

As I write this, Turin is in the final stages of gearing up to host the 2006 Winter Olympics. *Palazzi* are wrapped in scaffolding, streets and squares torn up to put in new parking lots and a subway system, and Piazza Castello is being transformed into a medals stage for the ceremonies. The promises are that the city will be brighter and better than ever, with long-closed sights such as the Palazzo Madama finally reopened to the public. (At press time, the *palazzo* was scheduled to reopen in the fall of 2006.)

This also means that you should take assertions of fact in this chapter with a grain of salt, as everything from open hours and admission prices to how the city infrastructure will operate after the Games is still up in the air as we go to press.

Piedmont & the Valle d'Aosta

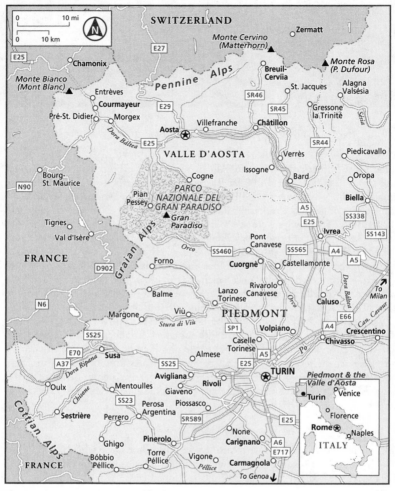

LAY OF THE LAND

Turin lies 669km (415 miles) northwest of Rome, and 140km (87 miles) east of Milan. For now, the city's main train station is Stazione Porta Nuova, just south of the center on Piazza Carlo Felice, at the intersection of Turin's two major thoroughfares, Corso Vittorio Emanuele and Via Roma. There are, on average, one to two trains per hour to and from Milan (2 hr.), Venice (5–6 hr.), and Genoa (2 hr.), and nine trains daily to and from Rome (7–9 hr.).

There are long-term plans to move the bulk of train services from Porta Nuova to the Porta Susa station, west of the center on Piazza XVIII Dicembre, which currently merely connects Turin with outlying Piemonte towns—though, given the chaos surrounding the Olympics, just when that will happen is anybody's guess.

Domestic and international flights land at the **Caselle International Airport** (☎ 011-5676361; www.turin-airport.com), 16km (10 miles) north of Turin. **SADEM Buses** (☎ 011-3000611; www.sadem.it) run between the airport and the Porto Nuova train station every half-hour to 45 minutes; the trip takes 40 minutes and costs €5 (€5.50 if bought on the bus).

Turin's refined air becomes apparent as soon as you step off the train into the mannerly 19th-century Stazione Porta Nuova. The stately arcaded Via Roma, lined with shops and cafes, proceeds from the front of the station through a series of *piazze* toward the Piazza Castello and the center of the city, about a 15-minute walk.

> ❝ This is a remarkably agreeable place. A beautiful town, prosperous, thriving, growing prodigiously, as Genoa is; crowded with busy inhabitants; full of noble streets and squares. The Alps, now covered deep with snow, are close upon it, and here and there seem almost ready to tumble into the houses. The contrast this part of Italy presents to the rest of Italy is amazing. ❞
>
> —Charles Dickens, in a letter from 1853

The circular Piazza Carlo Felice, directly in front of the station, is built around a garden and surrounded by outdoor cafes that invite even business-minded Torinese to linger. A few steps farther, Via Roma opens into the Piazza San Carlo, which is flanked by the twin churches of San Carlo and Santa Christina. The Palazzo Madama, at the end of Via Roma, dominates the main Piazza Castello. Flanking the north side of the piazza is the Palazzo Reale, residence of the Savoys from 1646 to 1865, whose gardens provide a pleasant respite from traffic.

From here, a walk east toward the Po River along Via Po takes you through Turin's university district to one of Italy's largest squares, the much-elongated Piazza Vittorio Veneto. At the end of this elegant expanse sits the Po.

The **main tourist office** is a pavilion called "Atrium" in the middle of Piazza Solferino (☎ 011-535181; www.turismotorino.org or www.comune.torino.it; daily 9:30am–7pm). There's also an office in the airport, and another at the Porta Nuova train station. You'll find more information on the surrounding region at **www.regione.piemonte.it.**

ACCOMMODATIONS, BOTH STANDARD & NOT

The **tourist office** (☎ 011-535181; www.turismotorino.org) will book hotel rooms for free, but only 48 hours in advance of your arrival (for B&Bs, a week in

---

City Bus & Tram Tickets

It's easy to get around central Turin on foot, but there's also a vast network of **GTT (Gruppi Torinese Trasporti;** ☎ 800-019152; www.comune.torino.it/gtt) trams and buses. Tickets are sold at newsstands: €.90 for a single, 70-minute ride; €3 for 24 hours. The Torino Card (later in this chapter) gets you free travel for 48 hours.

Musical September

September is the month to enjoy classical music in Turin. More than 60 classical concerts are held on stages around the city during the monthlong **Settembre Musica festival** (☎ 011-4424777; www.settembremusica.it).

advance). Frustratingly, the city's tourist office doesn't list *affittacamere* (rental rooms), which range in price from €20 to €80 for a double, though most are in the €30-to-€40 bracket. While you can get a list of the 36 rental rooms in Turin from the **Piemonte Region's official site** (www.regione.piemonte.it), you have to use the Italian-language version of the site; the stripped-down English version doesn't include lodging info. As a shortcut—though, given how websites are sometimes reorganized, a deep link such as this might eventually go out of date—try typing in www.regione.piemonte.it/turismo/ricettivita.htm to go directly to the lodgings search-engine page. Just click "Affittacamere" on the left. On the next page, select "Torino" in the Provincia column, and a list of towns will pop up in the Comune column to the right. Scroll down to select "Torino" again, then click "Cerca." Follow the same steps from that main lodging page to search for *campeggi* (campgrounds), *agriturismi* (farm stays), *ostelli* (hostels), *case vacanze* (residence hotels and vacation rentals), and other options. There are a number of good, affordable options, which are fairly represented on the site, for those willing to surf a bit.

You also could simply contact **NorthWestWay/The Salt Way** (☎ 0183-930244; www.northwestway.it), which rents 10 apartments scattered about town, sleeping anywhere from two to six people, for a minimum of 3 nights. They range from basic to quite cushy, so ask a lot of questions before you book if particular amenities are important to you. Prices start at €42 to €50 for two people, €55 to €70 for three, or €70 to €95 for four.

Bargains in the Historical Center

€€   I just love it when a hotel with one of the best locations in town also happens to be one of the cheapest. Tiny **Albergo San Carlo** ✦ (Piazza San Carlo, 197; ☎ 011-5627846; www.albergosancarlo.it) isn't fancy, with knocked-about-but-nice antiques mixed with the functional furnishings, little Persian rugs by the beds, and quirky touches like the crystal chandelier in room 12, or the marble-topped dresser and carved headboard in room 7. But the price—€70 for a room without private bathroom, €90 for one with—can't be beat, and the location is phenomenal: It occupies the fourth floor of the 17th-century Palazzo Isnardi di Caraglio, flanking the east side of elegant Piazza San Carlo. Ask to see several rooms, as they differ dramatically in space and atmosphere. The five rooms on the piazza side have sloping mansard ceilings with dormer windows, and tend to be larger (if a tad noisier) than rooms 1 to 7 in the back.

€€-€€€   A few blocks west, just south of Piazza Solferino, are the twin hotels **Artuà & Solferino** ✦ 🧒 (Via Brofferio, 3, off Corso Re Umberto; ☎ 011-5175301; www.artua.it)—20 rooms evenly split between the fourth floors of neighboring buildings (you check in at the reception for the "Solferino" half). This is a real

Turin

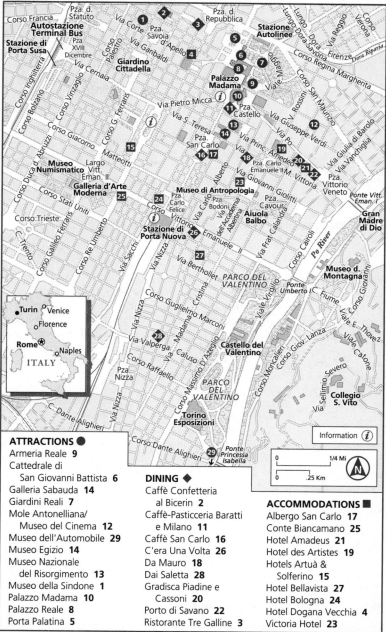

ATTRACTIONS ●

Armeria Reale **9**
Cattedrale di
San Giovanni Battista **6**
Galleria Sabauda **14**
Giardini Reali **7**
Mole Antonelliana/
Museo del Cinema **12**
Museo dell'Automobile **29**
Museo Egizio **14**
Museo Nazionale
del Risorgimento **13**
Museo della Sindone **1**
Palazzo Madama **10**
Palazzo Reale **8**
Porta Palatina **5**

DINING ◆

Caffè Confetteria
al Bicerin **2**
Caffè-Pasticceria Baratti
e Milano **11**
Caffè San Carlo **16**
C'era Una Volta **26**
Da Mauro **18**
Dai Saletta **28**
Gradisca Piadine e
Cassoni **24**
Porto di Savano **22**
Ristorante Tre Galline **3**

ACCOMMODATIONS ■

Albergo San Carlo **17**
Conte Biancamano **25**
Hotel Amadeus **21**
Hotel des Artistes **19**
Hotels Artuà &
Solferino **15**
Hotel Bellavista **27**
Hotel Bologna **24**
Hotel Dogana Vecchia **4**
Victoria Hotel **23**

Information (i)

Weekend Hotel Bargains

Turin is such a business-oriented city that rooms are actually cheaper on the weekends, when hotels have to scramble to fill beds. Some 32 Turin hotels (all in the three- to five-star category) offer a "Week-end à Torino" promotion; 24 of these hotels charge between €82 and €100 per person for a room for 2 nights (Fri–Sat), breakfast, a 48-hour Torino Card (a €15 value), and a little extra that varies from hotel to hotel—could be free parking, a box of chocolates, or a CD of classical music.

Of the hotels recommended in this book, those participating include the **Hotel Amadeus** (€90 per person; a free guided tour of the city and "typical Torinese gift"), the **Artuà** (€99 per person; free tour and parking), and the **Hotel des Artistes** (€99; breakfast in bed and a bottle of local wine). The city tourism office (www.turismotorino.org) has a full list of participating hotels.

---

family-run joint; the owner's kids leave toys scattered and hang around the breakfast room/lounge to watch cartoons or videos on the communal large-screen TV. The rooms are simple—creamy wood floors, beat-up white lacquer modular furnishings, and small, but nice, new bathrooms—but the place is full of thoughtful extras, like high-speed Internet access for €3 a day, and a sauna/hydromassage unit in Solferino. You can even save a few bucks by opting for a €75-to-€90 "standard" room (smaller or noisier, with sloping roofs and older furnishings, and no breakfast) instead of a €100-to-€130 "comfort" double.

€€–€€€   The best value for your money in the center—€105 for a double, falling to €85 Friday to Sunday nights—is the **Hotel Dogana Vecchia** ✪ (Via Corte d'Appello, 4, at Via Milano; ☎ 011-4366752; www.hoteldoganavecchia. com) installed in the old 18th-century Customs house, just a few blocks west of Piazza Castello (and a few blocks east of the wine bars and *trattorie* around Piazza Em. Filiberto). The hotel's an odd marriage of fading old-fashioned style and bland modernity, the bright and friendly reception giving way to dimly lit corridors with frilly moldings decorating the vaulted high ceilings. Try to snag one of the "Antiche" rooms, which have been left with a splash of style (stucco decorations, crystal chandeliers, herringbone wood floors, Art Nouveau bed frames and wardrobes), instead of a "standard" room with lower ceilings, modern terrazzo flooring, and insipid functional units. Want to save even more? They don't advertise this fact, but the hotel retains a few older rooms without private bathroom, which sell for around €40, breakfast not included.

Hotels near Piazza Vittorio Veneto

€€–€€€   A pair of good-value hotels sits on one of Torino's arcaded boulevards leading from the city center east toward Piazza Vittorio Veneto and the river. **Hotel Amadeus** ✪ (Via Principe Amadeo, 41 bis; ☎ 011-8174951; www.turin hotelcompany.com) has the slight edge of affordability—€85 per double on the weekends, €120 during the week—and a bit more of a swank feel, with coffered edges to the ceilings, textured wallpaper, colorful fabrics and carpets, and well-lit marble bathrooms. Rooms ending in -03 are the largest—though none are really that spacious—but for optimum quiet pick a room ending in -04 or -05, facing the back courtyard.

€€€   Solo travelers take note: Both the Amadeus and its neighbor, **Hotel des Artistes** (Via Principe Amadeo, 21, at Via Accademia; ☎ 011-8124416; www.des artisteshotel.it), feature extra-wide *francesina* beds in their single rooms. Otherwise, the €125 doubles at the Hotel des Artistes are bland but comfy. The hotel received a functional overhaul 3 years ago, with bathrooms jammed into room corners as an afterthought and heavy drapes over the double-paned windows.

Hotels near the Train Station

Unlike the areas around train stations in most large cities, the Porta Nuova neighborhood is semi-stylish and perfectly safe, and many of the city's hotels are here, just a 10-minute stroll south of the central sights.

€€   In fact, for €95 per double you can have a room in a gracious 18th-century apartment house directly across the street from the station at the family-run **Hotel Bologna** ✦ (Corso Vittorio Emanuele II, 60; ☎ 011-5620290 or 011-5620193). Some rooms are quite grand, incorporating frescoes and fireplaces. Others have been renovated in sleek modern style with laminated, built-in cabinetry and glossy wood floors. Still others fall in between, with well-maintained 1970s style furnishings and linoleum flooring. Whatever the vintage, all of the rooms are spotlessly clean, nicely maintained, and were overhauled in the fall of 2005.

€€   Step off the elevator at the simple, sixth-floor **Hotel Bellavista** (Via Galliari, 15, between Via S. Anselmo and Via Principe Tomasso; ☎ 011-6698139), on a

---

A Worthy Splurge

€€€€   Pass through the doors of a plain-looking building between the Via Roma and the river, and you'll think you're in an English country house. That's the idea at the **Victoria Hotel** ✦✦ (Via Nino Costa, 4, a tiny street, unlabeled on most maps, off Via Giuseppe Pomba between Via Giolitti and Via Cavour; ☎ 011-5611909; www.hotelvictoria-torino.com), and the Anglophile decor works splendidly. The lobby resembles a drawing room, with floral sofas, deep armchairs, and a view onto a garden. The glass-enclosed breakfast room feels like a conservatory. "Standard" guest rooms—€163 per double—are handsomely furnished in a chic style that soothingly combines contemporary and traditional styles, with mahogany bedsteads and writing desks, and rich fabric wallcoverings and draperies. "Deluxe" accommodations (€183 double), each with a distinctive look, are oversize rooms furnished with carefully chosen antiques and such flourishes as canopied beds and richly upholstered divans.

quiet street in the residential neighborhood between the station and Parco del Valentino, and you'll find a sun-filled corridor brimming with houseplants and opening onto a wide terrace. The 18 rooms are airy and comfortable but uninspired, with functional modern furnishings. Most, though, afford pleasant views over the surrounding rooftops—the best stretching across the river toward the hills. What most rooms don't have is a private bathroom, though the several communal facilities are well placed, only steps away from most rooms. The seven doubles with bathroom go for €65 to €70; those without go for €55 to €60. Breakfast is not included, but rolls and coffee at the bar area go for a reasonable €3 to €5.

€€€   Costing a bit more than its neighbors (€120 for a double)—but with oodles more class—is the fading glory of the **Conte Biancamano** (Corso Vittorio Emanuele II, 73, at Corso Umberto 5 blocks west of the station; ☎ 011-5623281; www.hotelcontebiancamano.it). Admittedly, most of that class is limited to the grand public rooms—all frescoed ceilings and fancy stuccowork. The guest rooms are rather plain, suffering from a kind of mod furniture that must have looked oh-so-stylish in 1984. Rooms on the back courtyard are considerably quieter than those on the front, which overlook one of the busiest roads in Turin.

DINING FOR ALL TASTES

The Piemonte region stretches from the Po plains through the Langhe and Roero wine hills, to the mountain villages of the Alps. This vast geographic diversity—not to mention a heavy influence from neighboring France—informs the local cuisines you'll find in city restaurants. Piemontese cooking is big on meats stewed in red wine, the most favored being *brasato al barolo* (beef or veal braised in Barolo). The best dish with which to kick off a meal is usually only available in winter: *bagna cauda,* literally translated as "hot bath," a plate of raw vegetables that are dipped into a steaming sauce of olive oil, garlic, and anchovies.

Two local pastas dishes you will encounter are *agnolotti* (a thick pasta tube often stuffed with an infusion of cheese and meat) and *tajarin* (a flat egg noodle that may be topped with porcini mushrooms, sauce made with walnuts, or the local delicacy that is perhaps the region's greatest contribution to Italian cuisine: the white truffles of Alba). Italian Alpine cuisine leans toward polenta (a cornmeal mush varying from soupy and sticky to almost cakelike), and stews thick with beef and red wine (the best of which is a typical dish from neighboring Valle d'Aosta: *carbonada*).

€   For picnic pickings—or merely a look at the bounty of the surrounding farmlands—wander through the extensive outdoor food market at Porta Palazzo, Monday through Saturday from 6:30am to 1:30pm (also Sat 3:30–7:30pm). If all you want is a quick sandwich, head to **Gradisca Piadine e Cassoni** (Via Principe Amadeo, 41A; ☎ 011-8159331; Mon–Fri, Sat until 3pm), where Carmela or Alessandro will knead and cook a flatbread while you wait, and then stuff it with your choice of fillings for €2.50 to €5.

€€   One of the few kitchens in Turin that remains open until 10pm, **Dai Saletta** ✪ (Via Belfiore, 37, just south of Via Oddino Morgari; ☎ 011-6687867; Mon–Sat) turns out a nice selection of homey trattoria fare in a cramped dining room several long blocks south of the train station. Homemade pasta dishes are delicious and cost just €8. Try the hearty *tortelloni alla salsiccia* (a large pasta shell stuffed with sausage) or *peposelle* (a thick pasta tossed with Gorgonzola and walnuts).

€€ **Da Mauro** (Via Maria Vittoria, 21, between Via Bogino and Via San Francesco da Paola; ☎ 011-8170604; no credit cards; Tues–Sun) is more relaxed than many Torinese restaurants, and if the informal ambience and the menu remind you of regions farther south, your instincts are right. The family who owns the restaurant emphasizes Tuscan dishes, though the menu seems to run the gamut of Italian cooking. There are several spicy pasta dishes, including deftly prepared cannelloni for €6, and the meat courses are similar to those you would find in Tuscany—simply grilled or roasted steak, pork chops, and game birds for just €6.20 to €7.50.

€€ **Porto di Savano** ✪✪ (Piazza Vittorio Veneto, 2; ☎ 011-8173500; Wed–Sun, Tues dinner only) is probably the most popular trattoria in Turin. Seating is family

---

Turin's Renowned Cafes

Cafe-sitting is a centuries-old tradition in sophisticated Turin. Via Roma, and the *piazze* that open off of it, is lined with gracious salons that have been serving coffee, and the world's first aperitif—that Turin invention called vermouth—for decades. Espresso and pastries are the mainstays of every cafe's menu, but most also serve chocolates—including the mix of chocolate and hazelnuts known as *gianduiotti*—that are among the city's major contributions to culinary culture.

€ **Caffè Confetteria al Bicerin** ✪ (Piazza della Consolata, 5; ☎ 011-4369325; www.bicerin.it; Thurs–Tues) claims to be Turin's oldest continuously operating cafe (since 1763). It is famous for the illustrious clientele, which has included Nietzsche, Dumas, and Puccini, as well as for its signature drink, the *bicerin* (local dialect for "something delicious"), a heady combination of coffee, hot chocolate, and cream. The house pastries are exquisite.

€ Part of the pleasure at stylish **Caffè-Pasticceria Baratti e Milano** (Piazza Castello, 27; ☎ 011-4407138; Tues–Sun), opened in 1875, is watching a diverse clientele sipping espressos and munching on the delicious house pastries—the crowd ranges from auto executives to students from the nearby university, and from elegantly clad shoppers to visitors to the nearby museums.

€ The classic **Caffè San Carlo** ✪ (Piazza San Carlo, 156; ☎ 011-5617748; www.caffesancarlo.it) opened its doors in 1837, and ever since has been an essential stop on any tour of Turin, accommodating patrons beneath a huge chandelier of Murano glass in a salon that houses a remarkable assemblage of gilt, mirrors, and marble. An adjoining frescoed tearoom is quieter and only a little less grand.

style, at long tables that crowd a series of rooms beneath old photos and mementos, and the typically Piemontese fare never fails to please (all the more so on Sun, when many other restaurants in central Turin are closed). Several variations of gnocchi are usually made fresh daily, as is the Piemontese flat noodle *tajarin* (€7.50), and *agnolotti al sugo d'arrosto* (cheese-stuffed pasta in a roast pork *ragù;* €8). They also honor an old working man's tradition: At lunchtime, Monday through Saturday only, you can order a *monopiatto,* which consists of a plate of hearty pasta (€8.30) or a meat dish (€10) with a dessert, coffee, and either water or wine included in the price—one of Turin's great bargains.

Worth a Splurge

€€€€   Arriving at **C'era Una Volta** ✪✪✪ (Corso Vittorio Emanuele II, 41, next to Libreria Zanaboni at Via Goito; ☎ 011-6504589; Mon–Sat)—which translates as "Once Upon a Time,"—you'll feel as if you've entered a bit of a time warp: a large, old-fashioned second-floor dining room filled with heavy old tables and credenzas, and a highly professional waitstaff that seems to have been in place, unchanged, since the 1950s. Until recently, the restaurant only offered a set-price tasting menu (€24–€26) of authentically Torinese dishes that never stopped coming; if you choose this option, don't bother making plans to eat for the next 24 hours. But due to popular demand the restaurant has introduced a la carte choices as well. The menu changes daily, but might include crepes with ham and cheese, risotto with artichokes, a carrot flan, rabbit stew, or a slice of beef with polenta. A meal like this deserves a fine Barolo—and almost always requires that you book ahead.

€€€€   Another Torino classic, **Ristorante Tre Galline** ✪✪ (Via Bellezia, 37; ☎ 011-4366553; Tues–Sat, Mon dinner only) has been one of the city's most popular eateries for more than 3 centuries, a bright wood-paneled room with friendly, professional service and a five-course gourmand's tasting menu that's a steal at €35. The salami are hand-carved at your table for an appetizer, and the daily changing menu mixes Torinese and Piemontese specialties with slightly creative dishes using local ingredients. Some of their better creations include *agnolotti* (meat-filled pasta ringlets) in a pink *ragù* (€9), risotto with basil and truffles (€13), *carré d'agnello in crosta di erbette* (lamb cooked with herbs; €15), and rabbit cooked in apple vinegar (€16). If you don't book ahead, don't expect to get in.

WHY YOU'RE HERE: THE TOP SIGHTS & ATTRACTIONS

Though best known for its famed shroud, Turin has a number of worthy sights and attractions, from world-class museums to art-filled churches. Allow a full 2 days to explore the town fully.

Around Piazza Castello

Don't be misled by the baroque facade on the **Palazzo Madama** ✪ (Piazza Castello; ☎ 011-4429912; www.palazzomadamatorino.it; €9; Mon–Wed and Fri–Sat 10am–7pm, Thurs 10am–11pm, Sun 10am–8pm), which was added by architect Filippo Juvarra in the 18th century. If you walk around the exterior of the *palazzo*—named for its most popular resident, Madama Reale, aka Marie Christine of France—you'll discover that the massive structure incorporates a medieval castle, a Roman gate, and several Renaissance additions. Juvarra also added a monumental marble staircase to the interior, most of which has been

The Torino Card

A €15 Torino Card (sold at the tourist office) will, for 48 hours, grant you plus one child under 12 discounts on concerts and the like, free admission to 82 museums (including all those mentioned here), discounts on cultural events, and free public transport within Turin. For €17, your card is valid for 72 hours.

given over to the far-reaching collections of the Museo Civico di Arte Antica. The holdings focus on the medieval and Renaissance periods, shown off against the castle's unaltered, stony medieval interior. One of Italy's largest collections of ceramics is here, as well as some stunning canvases, including Antonello da Messina's *Portrait of a Man*. I can't say much more about the museum or *palazzo* because it was closed for years to undergo extensive restorations and is scheduled to reopen after this book goes to press, in the fall of 2006.

The **Palazzo Reale (Royal Palace)** ✪ (Piazzetta Reale/Piazza Castello; ☎ 011-4361455; www.ambienteto.arti.beniculturali.it; €6.50; Tues–Sun 8:30am–7:30pm) is the former royal residence of the House of Savoy. Begun in 1645 and designed by the Francophile count of Castellamonte, it reflects the ornately baroque tastes of European ruling families of the time—a fact that will not be lost on you as you pass from one opulently decorated, heavily gilded room to the next. (The Savoys had a keener eye for painting than for decor, and most of the canvases they collected are in the nearby Galleria Sabauda.)

What's most notable here are some of the tapestries, including those depicting the life of Don Quixote, in the Sala delle Virtu (Hall of Virtues) by the finest workshop in baroque-era Europe, the royal French manufacturer Gobelins; and the collection of Chinese and Japanese vases in the Sala dell'Alcova. One of the quirkier architectural innovations, an antidote to several monumental staircases, is a manually driven elevator from the 18th century.

One wing houses the **Armeria Reale** ✪ (Piazza Castello, 191; ☎ 011-543889; www.artito.arti.beniculturali.it; €4; Tues–Sat 1–7pm, Sun 10am–7pm), one of the most important arms and armor collections in Europe, especially of weapons from the 16th and 17th centuries. This sight was closed when I researched this guide, but was set to reopen by the time you arrive.

Behind the palace, and offering a refreshing change from its frippery, are the **Giardini Reali (Royal Gardens),** laid out by Le Nôtre, more famous for the Tuileries and the gardens at Versailles.

Just north of the Piazza Castello and the Royal Palace sits the bland facade of the **Cattedrale di San Giovanni Battista** ✪ (Piazza San Giovanni; ☎ 011-5661540 or 011-4361540; daily 8am–12:30pm and 3–7pm). Far more interesting is the single chapel inside the cathedral's pompous, 15th-century interior—the baroque **Cappella della Santa Sindone,** occasional home to the controversial **Santissima Sindone (Shroud of Turin;** see below). Even without the presence of one of Christendom's most precious relics—only rarely on view in a silver casket elevated on the altar in the center of the room—the chapel is still well worth a visit. Restored after a 1997 fire (one of many the shroud has miraculously survived, with occasional singeing, over the centuries), the chapel is somberly clad in

The Shroud of Turin

The shroud of Turin is said to be the piece of fabric in which the body of Christ was wrapped when he was taken down from the cross—and to which his image was miraculously affixed. The image on the fabric is of a man 5 feet 7 inches tall, with bloodstains consistent with a crown of thorns, a cut in the rib cage, cuts in the wrists and ankles, and scourge marks on the back from flagellation.

Recent carbon dating suggests that the shroud was manufactured sometime around the 13th or 14th centuries. But the mystery remains, at least in part because no one can explain how the haunting image appeared on the cloth. Debunkers constantly attempt to create replicas using lemon juice and the sun, mineral pigments, even aloe and myrrh (the last because, according to funerary traditions at the time, Jesus' body would likely have been treated with these oils before being wrapped in the shroud). Every few years, a new crop of naysayers publishes the results of their adventures in fakery, and a competing crop of faithful apologists points out how the success of newly made facsimiles doesn't necessarily negate the authenticity of the Turin shroud itself. Additional radio carbon dating has suggested that, because the shroud has been exposed to fire (thus affecting the carbon readings), it could indeed date from around the time of Christ's death. In the end, faith and science are unlikely to reach agreement (unless, of course, science suddenly decides the shroud is genuine). Despite scientific skepticism, the shroud continues to entice hordes of the faithful.

The shroud was last on display during Italy's Jubilee celebrations in 2000. Technically, it shouldn't be on display again until the next Jubilee, in 2025, but it pops up every 5 to 15 years for special occasions. (Rumor has it that the shroud may go on permanent exhibit, either in the cathedral or in its own space.)

Until such a display exists, to see the shroud you'll have to content yourself with three alternatives: a series of dramatically backlit photos near the entrance to the Cappella della Santa Sindone, a replica on display in the church, and a museum devoted to the relic, the **Museo della Sindone** (Via San Domenico, 28; ☎ 011-4365832; www.sindone.org; €5.50; daily 9am–noon and 3–7pm).

black marble. But, as if to suggest that better things await us in the heavens, it ascends to an airy, light-flooded, six-tiered dome, one of the masterpieces of Italian baroque architecture.

In front of the cathedral stand two landmarks of ancient Turin—the remains of a Roman theater and the Roman-era city gate **Porta Palatina,** flanked by twin 16-sided towers.

The Top Museums

Turin's magnificent **Museo Egizio** ★★★ 🧒 (Via Accademia delle Scienze, 6; ☎ 011-5617776; www.museoegizio.org; €6.50; Tues–Sun 8:30am–7:30pm) is the world's largest Egyptian collection outside of Cairo. This was, in fact, the world's first Egyptian museum, thanks to the Savoys' habit of ardently amassing artifacts throughout their reign, and the museum continued to mount collecting expeditions throughout the early 20th century. Of the 30,000 pieces on display, some of the more captivating exhibits are in the first rooms you enter on the ground floor. These include the 15th-century B.C. Rock Temple of Ellessiya, which the Egyptian government donated in gratitude for Italian efforts to save monuments threatened by the Aswan Dam. The two nearby statuary rooms are staggering both in the size and drama of the objects they house; notable among the objects are two sphinxes and a massive, richly painted statue of Ramses II. Smaller objects—mummies, funerary objects, and a papyrus Book of the Dead—fill the galleries on the next floor. The most enchanting exhibit here is the collection of everyday paraphernalia, including eating utensils and shriveled foodstuffs, from the tomb of the 14th-century B.C. architect Khaie and his wife.

The Savoys' other treasure trove, a magnificent collection of European paintings, fills the salons of the **Galleria Sabauda** ★★ (Via Accademia delle Scienze, 6; ☎ 011-547440; www.artito.arti.beniculturali.it; €4; Tues and Fri–Sun 8:30am–2pm, Wed–Thurs 2–7:30pm), upstairs in the same building as the Egyptian collection. The Savoy's royal taste ran heavily to painters of the Flemish and Dutch schools, and the works by van Dyck, van Eyck, Rembrandt, and van der Weyden, among others, comprise one of Italy's largest collections of northern European paintings. In fact, two of Europe's most prized Flemish masterpieces are here: Jan van Eyck's *Stigmata of St. Francis* and Hans Memling's *Passion of Christ.* Italian artists, including those from the Piemonte, are also well represented; one of the first canvases you see upon entering the galleries is the work of a Tuscan, Fra Angelico's sublime *Virgin and Child.*

The **Mole Antonelliana** ★★ (Via Montebello, 20; ☎ 011-8125658; www.museonazionaledelcinema.org; Tues–Fri and Sun 9am–8pm, Sat 9am–11pm) is by a long shot Turin's most peculiar building; in fact, it's one of the strangest structures anywhere. It consists of a squat brick base, a steep conelike roof supporting several layers of Greek temples piled one atop the other, and a needlelike spire, all of it rising 166m (552 ft.) above the rooftops of the city center—a height that, at one time, made the Mole the world's tallest building. Begun in 1863 and designed as a synagogue, the Mole is now a monument to Italian unification and architectural hubris and, as of 2000, home to the thoroughly fascinating **Museo Nazionale del Cinema (National Film Museum)** 🧒 (€5.20 for just the museum, €6.80 for the museum plus an elevator ride).

Cumulative Ticket

A cumulative ticket to both the Egyptian Museum and the Sabauda Gallery costs €8.

The museum's first section tracks the development of moving pictures from shadow puppets to kinescopes. The rest is more a tribute to film than a true museum, offering clips and stills to illustrate some of the major aspects of movie production, from *The Empire Strikes Back* storyboards to the creepy steady-cam work in *The Shining*. Of memorabilia, masks from *Planet of the Apes, Satyricon,* and *Star Wars* hang together near *Lawrence of Arabia*'s robe, Chaplin's bowler, and *What Ever Happened to Baby Jane?*'s dress. Curiously, most of the clips (all in Italian dubbed versions), as well as posters and other memorabilia, are heavily weighted toward American movies, with exceptions mainly for the major players of European/international cinema like Fellini, Bertolucci, Truffaut, and Wim Wenders.

Even if you skip the museum, you can ride the dramatic glass elevator (€3.60 for the ride) to an observation platform at the top of the spire, an experience that affords two advantages: The view of Turin and the surrounding countryside, backed by the Alps, is stunning; and, as Guy de Maupassant once said of the Eiffel Tower, it's the only place in Turin where you won't have to look at the damned thing.

THE OTHER TURIN

To understand Italy—or at the very least to learn the stories behind Cavour, Garibaldi, Mazzini, Vittorio Emanuele II, Massimo d'Azeglio, and the people after whom most of the major streets and *piazze* in Italy are named—you need to brush up on the Risorgimento, the late-19th-century movement that launched Italian unification. While any self-respecting town in Italy has a museum dedicated to it, Turin's **Museo Nazionale del Risorgimento** (Via Accademia delle Scienze, 5; ☎ 011-5621147; www.regione.piemonte.it/cultura/risorgimento; €5; Tues–Sun 9am–7pm) is the best of the bunch. After all, much of the history of Italy's unification played out in this Turin *palazzo,* which was home to unified Italy's first king, Vittorio Emanuele II, and later became, in 1861, the seat of its first parliament. Documents, paintings, and other paraphernalia recount the heady days when Vittorio Emanuele II banded with General Garibaldi and his Red Shirts to oust the Bourbons from Sicily and the Austrians from the north to create a unified Italy. The plaques describing the contents of each room are in English, and the last rooms house a fascinating collection that chronicles Italian fascism and the resistance against it, which evolved into the Partisan movement during World War II.

As befits a city responsible for 80% of Italian car manufacturing, the **Museo dell Automobile (Automobile Museum;** Corso Unita d'Italia, 40; ☎ 011-677666; www.museoauto.it; €5.50; Tues–Sun 10am–6:30pm) is a shiny collection of most of the cars that have done Italy proud over the years, including Lancias, Isotta Frashinis, and the Itala that came in first in the 1907 Peking-to-Paris rally. Among the oddities is a roadster emblazoned with the initials ND, which Gloria Swanson drove in her role as faded movie queen Norma Desmond in *Sunset Boulevard.* The museum lies well south of the center; take bus no. 34 or 35, or tram no. 1 or 18.

But that's just a museum displaying a century's worth of Fiats. To really get behind the scenes, get a glimpse of industrial Turin at its best on the 3-hour **Turismo Industriale tour** (run by the tourist office; €5; Mar–Dec 2, 4 times a month). On a rotating schedule, this bus tour visits one of Turin's top industrial or design firms—most frequently *il grande* Fiat itself (usually once a month), but also one of a quartet of pen makers (from Aurora's classy engraved fountain pens to Lecce Pen's famous biodegradable ballpoint) as well as a trio of top-notch design firms. These include Bertoni (designing Fiats and Lancias since the 1920s—not to mention cars for MG, Maserati, Aston Martin, BMW, Volvo, Ferrari, and the incomparable Lamborghini Countach), Giugiaro (a firm that helped assemble the winning Olympic bid), and Pinin Farina (their 1947 Cisalpino high-bullet train was the first vehicle ever honored by New York's MoMA as one of the "eight wonders of our time").

The tourist office runs intriguing **themed walking tours on Saturday evenings** (book ahead; ☎ 011-535181; www.turismotorino.org; €6 each). Among the themes are a "Tasty Turin" tour of historic cafes. "Literary Turin" visits places where Nietzsche, De Amicis, and Alfieri lived. "Turin is Cinema" highlights film locations around town; "Aperitif under the Mole" is a stroll to cafes and funky bars to sample Turin's famous pre-meal alcoholic innovation, the aperitif; and "Walks Under Artist's Lights" visits locations where you can admire Turin's contemporary art. All tours are in Italian, English, and French, and depart at 6pm from the Atrium info pavilion on Piazza Solferino. Oddly, and unfortunately, the "Your First Time in Turin" Saturday morning tours are done only in Italian (the tour is in two halves: a 10am city tour and an 11:30am Egyptian Museum tour; do either for €6 or both for €7). Holders of the Torino Card get 20% to 25% off all tours.

Somewhere (☎ 011-6680580; www.somewhere.it), a private tour agency, runs another series of guided tours. Get the dirt on the city's secret side with either the "Magic Turin" tour, which traces the city's traditions of black and white magic (meet at Piazza Statuto; €20; Thurs and Sat at 9pm), or on the "Underground Turin" tour, which takes you under the baroque *palazzi* to cellars, air-raid shelters, and other spaces laced with stories of mystery, intrigue, and murder (meet at Piazza Vittorio Veneto; €25; Wed and Fri 8:30pm). Gourmands in a hurry might prefer the "Dinner Tram," a gourmet meal, with a guide and a sax player, aboard a trolley car converted into a roving restaurant (meet at Piazza Carlina; €45; Sat 9pm), or the "AperiTram," which is the same deal, only instead of food you sip cocktails while getting a city tour by trolley (meet at Chiesa Gran Madre di Dio; €15; Fri 7:30 and 8:30pm). Torino Card holders get a 20% discount on "Magic Turin" and "AperiTram."

A SIDE TRIP FROM TURIN

The little town of Cogne (29km/18 miles south of Aosta; seven buses daily, 50 min.) is the most convenient gateway to the **Parco Nazionale del Gran Paradiso**, one of Europe's finest parcels of unspoiled nature—a third of it lies on the Piemonte side of the regional boundaries, accessible from Turin.

The former hunting grounds of King Vittorio Emanuele II comprise this vast (3,626 sq. km/1,400 sq. miles) and lovely national park. In five valleys of forests and pastureland, many Alpine beasts roam wild—including the ibex (a long-horned goat) and the chamois (a small antelope), both of which have hovered near extinction in recent years. Cogne also offers some downhill skiing, but it is better regarded for cross-country.

Humans can roam these wilds via a vast network of well-marked trails. Among the few places where the hand of man intrudes ever so gently on nature is in a few scattered hamlets within the park borders and in the **Giardino Alpino Paradisia** (☎ 0165-74147; €2.50; daily July–Aug 10am–6:30pm, June and Sept 10am–5:30pm), a stunning collection of rare Alpine fauna near the village of Valnontey, 1.6km (1 mile) south of Cogne.

The park actually has five entrances (three on the Valle d'Aosta side, two on the Piemonte), and seven info centers, but the **main information center** is in the Piemonte village of **Noasca** (Via Umberto I; ☎ 0123-901070). There are also offices in **Turin** (Via Della Rocca, 47; ☎ 011-8606211) and **Aosta** (Via Losanna, 5; ☎ 0165-44126), but perhaps the best stop is the tourist office at the park entrance in **Cogne** (Via Bourgeois, 34; ☎ 0165-74040; www.cogne.org), providing a wealth of information on hiking and skiing trails and other outdoor activities in the park and elsewhere in the region. You can also get info at **www.pngp.it** and **www.parks.it**.

COURMAYEUR & MONT BLANC

The one-time mountain hamlet of Courmayeur is now the Valle d'Aosta's resort extraordinaire, a collection of traditional stone buildings, pseudo-Alpine chalets, and large hotels catering to a well-heeled international crowd of skiers. Even if you don't ski, you can happily while away your time sipping mulled wine while regarding the craggy bulk of Mont Blanc (called Monte Bianco on this side of the border), which looms over this end of the Valle d'Aosta and forms the snowy barrier between Italy and France. The Mont Blanc tunnel, which can zip you into France in just 20 minutes, reopened in 2002, 3 years after a devastating fire.

The cable-car system up Monte Bianco actually begins not in Courmayeur, but in La Palud, outside the village of Entrèves, 3km (2 miles) to the north, a pleasant collection of stone houses and farm buildings surrounded by pastureland. Quaint as the village is in appearance, at its soul Entrèves is a worldly enclave with hotels and restaurants that cater to skiers and outdoor enthusiasts who prefer to spend time in surroundings quieter than Courmayeur.

LAY OF THE LAND

The Valle d'Aosta is a region best explored by car, but if you're coming by public transportation, first you have to get to the regional capital of Aosta, 113km (68 miles) northwest of Turin and about 35km (21 miles) east of Courmayeur-Entrèves. Aosta is served by 12 **trains** a day to and from Turin (2–3hr.), and 10 trains daily to and from Milan (3–4 hr., with a change in Chivasso).

Thirteen daily **buses** (☎ 0165-262027) connect Aosta with Courmayeur (1 hr.). Buses also run between Courmayeur's Piazzale Monte Bianco and Entrèves and La Palud (10 min.), at least every hour, more often in summer (☎ 0165-841305).

By car, the A5 autostrada is the fastest way from Aosta to Courmayeur (less than 30 min.)—but you spend much of that time in tunnels. For more scenery, hop on the parallel SS26, which winds through villages and suburbs but takes a good hour.

The villages themselves are tiny and walkable.

The **tourist office** in Courmayeur (Piazzale Monte Bianco, 8; ☎ 0165-842060 or 0165-842072; www.courmayeur.net or www.regione.vda.it/turismo)

provides information on hiking, skiing, and other outdoor activities in the region, as well as hotel and restaurant listings (though note that in the off seasons of Dec 1–24 and January 7 to late April, it's open only Sat–Sun).

ACCOMMODATIONS AROUND MONTE BIANCO

€€–€€€ **La Grange** ★★ (c.p. 75, 11013 Courmayeur-Entrèves; ☎ 0165-869733, off season ☎ 335-6463533; www.lagrange-it.com; closed May–June and Oct–Nov) may well be the most charming hotel in the Valle d'Aosta. This converted barn in the bucolic village of Entrèves is ably managed by Bruna Berthold. None of the rooms are the same, though all are decorated with pleasing antique and rustic furnishings; some have balconies overlooking Mont Blanc, which quite literally hovers over the property. The stucco-walled, stone-floored lobby is a fine place to relax, with couches around a corner hearth, a small bar area, and a prettily paneled room where the lavish buffet breakfast is laid out. There is an exercise room and a much-used sauna. The highest rates of €130 for a double are only charged December 26 to January 6 and February 5 to March 5; otherwise doubles go for a wonderfully low €80 to €100.

€€–€€€ In winter, the pine-paneled salons and cozy rooms of the chalet-style **Edelweiss** ★ (Via Marconi, 42; ☎ 0165-841590; www.albergoedelweiss.it; closed May–June and Oct–Nov) attract a friendly international set of skiers. In summer, many Italian families spend a month or two at a time at this hotel, near the center of Courmayeur. The Roveyaz family extends a hearty welcome to all and provides modern mountain-style accommodations and free bikes (just a few; first-come, first-served). Many rooms—which range from €70 to €125, depending on the season—open onto terraces overlooking the mountains, and the nicest rooms are those on the top floor, tucked under the eaves.

DINING FOR ALL TASTES

€€ I never expected to find fresh fish at the foot of Mont Blanc, but that's just what you can enjoy at a table in front of the hearth of cozy **Ristorante La Palud** (Strada la Palud, 17; ☎ 0165-89169; Thurs–Tues) in the little cable-car settlement just outside Entrèves. Seafood isn't the only option here at 1,290m (4,300 ft.), however. Plenty of Valdaostana specialties are on hand, and *primi* rarely cost more than €10: mountain hams, creamy *polenta concia* (cooked with Fontina cheese and butter), and, in season, *cervo* (venison). The best dessert is a selection of mountain cheeses. The wine list borrows heavily from neighboring Piemonte, but includes some local vintages.

Drinking with the Best of Them

€ **Caffè della Posta** (Via Roma, 51; ☎ 0165-842272) is Courmayeur's most popular spot for an après-ski grog. Since it opened 90 years ago, it has been welcoming the famous and not so famous into its series of cozy rooms with a fire roaring in the open hearth.

A Marvelous Splurge

€€€€   The atmosphere at the popular and cheerful **Maison de Filippo** ✪✪ (Loc. Entrèves; ☎ 0165-869797; www.lamaison.com; June and Oct–Nov closed Tues), in Entrèves, is delightfully country Alpine. Dinner, an endless parade of Valdaostana dishes, is so generous you may not be able to eat again for a week—which more than makes up for the steep €40 price tag. Daily menus vary but often include an antipasto of mountain hams and salamis, a selection of pastas filled with wild mushrooms and topped with Fontina and other local cheeses, and a sampling of fresh trout and game in season. Service is casual and friendly. In summer you can choose between a table in the delightfully converted barnlike structure or on the flowery terrace. Reserve in advance.

ACROSS MONT BLANC BY CABLE CAR

One of the Valle d'Aosta's best experiences is to ride the series of **cable cars** (☎ 0165-89925; www.montebianco.com; for hours and prices, see "Schussing the Slopes," below) from La Palud, just above Entrèves (10 min. from Courmayeur

Schussing the Slopes

Recreation draws many people to the Valle d'Aosta—hiking in summer, sure, but especially the skiing. You'll find some of the best downhill skiing and facilities at Courmayeur, Breuil-Cervínia (the Italian side of the Matterhorn, here called Monte Cervino), and in the Valle di Cogne/Gran Paradiso. Ski season starts in late November/early December and runs through April, if the snow holds out, reaching its height mid-January through mid-March.

At Courmayeur and Breuil-Cervínia, expect to pay €32 to €38 for daily lift passes, depending on the season. Cogne is less expensive, with daily passes running around €15 to €20. Multiday passes, providing access to lifts and slopes of the entire valley, run €99 for 3 days, €129 for 4 days, and so on, with per-day rates on a sliding scale that end up at 14 days for €351.

One money-saving option is to take one of the Settimane Bianche (White Week) packages—room and board and unlimited skiing—available at resorts throughout the Valle d'Aosta; such packages cost around €300 to €500 at a midrange hotel.

Cross-country skiing is superb around Cogne in the Parco Nazionale del Gran Paradiso, where there are more than 48km (30 miles) of trails.

For more **skiing info,** call ☎ 0165-238871 or go to www.skivallee.it. For more on all sorts of outdoor activities in the region, contact the tourist boards of **Aosta** (☎ 0165-236627; www.regione.vda.it/turismo), **Breuil-Cervínia** (☎ 0166-949136; www.montecervino.it or www.cervinia. it), and **Cogne** (☎ 0165-74040; www.cogne.org).

Mont Blanc Hours & Prices

Hours for the Monte Bianco/Mont Blanc cable cars vary wildly, and service can be affected by weather conditions (winds often close the gondola between Helbronner and Aiguille du Midi). For a report of **weather** at the top and on the other side, dial ☎ **0165-89-961** or go to www.fondazionemontagnasicura.org or www.ohm-chamonix.com.

In theory, the cable cars run roughly every 20 minutes from 7:20am (8:20am in fall and spring) to 12:30pm and again 2 to 5:30pm (July 22–Aug 27; closed Nov 2–Dec 10). The last downward run is 5:30pm in summer and 4:30pm in winter. The Hellbronner–Aiguille du Midi gondola is only open May through September.

The ride to Punta Helbronner costs €32 round-trip, or €88 for the family pass (two adults and two kids). From Helbronner to Aiguille du Midi, you must buy tickets at Helbronner for an additional €17. To continue all the way from Helbronner to Chamonix in France costs €41 *each way*—which is why it makes more sense to buy the €82 "Trans Mont Blanc" tickets at La Palud, which includes all five cable-car rides, from La Palud up over the top and back down to Chamonix, and then a bus ride through the Mont Blanc tunnel back to Italy.

From approximately June 25 to September 4, a few pricing rules change. The family ticket rises to €98, and the system of discounts gets confusing. In summer, children 5 to 11 get 50% off, children 12 to 15 get 25% off, and adults over 60 get a 10% discount. In winter, kids 5 to 11 still get 50% off, but older kids pay full price, and the age for seniors rises to 65 (but the discount also rises, to 20% off).

---

on hourly buses), across Mont Blanc to several ski stations in Italy and France, and finally down into Chamonix, France.

You make the trip in stages—first past two intermediate stops to the last aerie on Italian soil, Punta Helbronner (20 min. each way). At 3,300m (11,000 ft.), this ice-clad lookout provides stunning views of the Mont Blanc glaciers, the Matterhorn, and other peaks looming in the distance. (In summer, you may want to hop off at Pavillion Frety, before you get to Punta Helbronner, and tour a pleasant botanic garden, **Giardino Alpino Saussurea;** daily June 24–Sept 30.)

For sheer drama, continue from Punta Helbronner to Aiguille du Midi in France dangling in a tiny gondola more than 2,300m (7,544 ft.) above the Géant Glacier and the Vallée Blanche (30 min.). From Aiguille du Midi you can descend over more glaciers and dramatic valleys on the French flank of Mont Blanc to the resort town of Chamonix (50 min.).

11 The Cinque Terre, the Portofino Promontory & Genoa

Northwest Italy is a hot new travel destination.

by Pippa de Bruyne

MY FRIENDS ACCUSE ME OF EXAGGERATING THE BEAUTY OF THE LIGURIAN Coast. They chuckle when I tell them how, at night, I'd watch the moon cast a silver crease across the bay while church bells tolled the hour in a village that time forgot. "Isn't the area overrun with tourists?" they ask. "Don't you need to go elsewhere to see the best art and architecture?"

I answer "yes" and "yes," but add that it doesn't really matter. The Cinque Terre and other parts of Liguria do swarm with tourists in the summer and fall; and you won't see the type of really important art and architecture that abounds in the hill towns of Tuscany, Rome, and Venice. But these are small quibbles when you're there hiking the hills, walking the cobblestone streets, or drinking the local wine. There's a reason why this ancient land has become one of the top honeymoon destinations in all of Italy: So much of what you experience here is impossibly romantic, with exquisite vistas around nearly every corner.

Mother Nature was kind to Italy, but in Liguria her generosity knew no bounds. The coastline forms a graceful arc, rising sharply into the foothills of the Appenines, affording dizzying views of the sea that laps its shores.

West, toward the French Riviera, is the Riviera di Ponente, its crescent-shaped bays and sandy beaches spawning a seemingly endless string of resort towns, including the grand old dowager San Remo. East, toward the Tuscan coast, lies the Riviera di Levante, home to the glamorous Portofino promontory and the medieval villages that cling to the jagged cliffs and terraced vineyards of the Cinque Terre.

> There is nothing in Italy more beautiful to me than the coast between Genoa and La Spezia.
>
> —Charles Dickens, 1845

This eastern stretch of shore, a mere 2- to 3-hour drive from Florence and Milan, is the coastline at its finest, its precipitous slopes punctuated by hidden inlets and rocky coves, where boats bob and ancient abbeys cluster. Watch weather-beaten old-timers bent double under sacks of grapes, or wander the medieval lanes of villages seemingly untouched by time, and you'll be hooked forever.

DON'T LEAVE THE LIGURIAN
COAST WITHOUT . . .

TOASTING THE SETTING SUN WITH GOLD   The Riviera di Levante is famous for its sunsets, and justifiably so. Not only do its sheer cliffs afford huge, humbling views of this blazing show but they also produce one of Italy's most delicious wines—the much-vaunted golden Sciacchetrà—a perfect match to toast the sinking sun.

GETTING LOST IN GENOA   It's been 160 years since Charles Dickens enthused on the wonders of losing yourself in the labyrinth of Europe's largest preserved medieval city, but it is still enthralling. Set aside a day to explore this fascinating honeycomb of narrow lanes, and simply wander at will.

PICNICKING IN THE PARKS   Among my most memorable meals are Ligurian picnics, with fresh (and cheap!) ingredients culled from the delis and *focaccerie* that line the main street of every village. In Portofino, you can picnic on stone benches in the shadow of a church; in Santa Margherita Ligure, in the gardens of a 17th-century villa overlooking the sea; and in the Cinque Terre, on the private terrace of your rented apartment or hotel.

HAVING YOUR SEAFOOD ON THE ROCKS   There's something deeply satisfying about eating seafood while gazing into the azure depths of the sea—especially when you're so close you can hear the breakers. Many Riviera restaurants offer this pleasure, but three personal favorites are **Trattoria dö Spadin** (Punta Chiappa; p. 465), **La Camogliese** (Camogli; p. 463) and **Santa Chiara** (Genoa; p. 474).

THE CINQUE TERRE NATIONAL PARK

The Cinque Terre has a long history—an amphora bearing its ancient name was discovered in the ruins of Pompeii—but this sleepy land of gravity-defying vineyards and intact medieval villages catapulted into the global spotlight only after it was declared a UNESCO World Heritage Site in 1997. The past decade has brought an unprecedented growth in tourism, and the Cinque Terre (pronounced "*chink*-weh *teh*-reh," literally meaning "five lands") is today one of Northern Italy's top draws, with September bringing hordes of hikers flourishing walking poles, while June and August find the villages jam-packed with Italian families.

Even if this is your first visit here, it's not hard to discover the reasons for its popularity. Walk along a cliff pathway and the stupendous view of clear blue waters will stop you in your tracks. Above and below are the terraced vineyards that cascade like hooped petticoats down the mountains, supported by mile upon mile of dry stone walling—a backbreaking feat that took over a millennia to create.

Across the bay, tiny villages cling to jagged cliffs like medieval building blocks. And when evening falls, there is still one more impressive show—the sinking sun turns the sea into a caldron of gold.

The Ligurian Coast

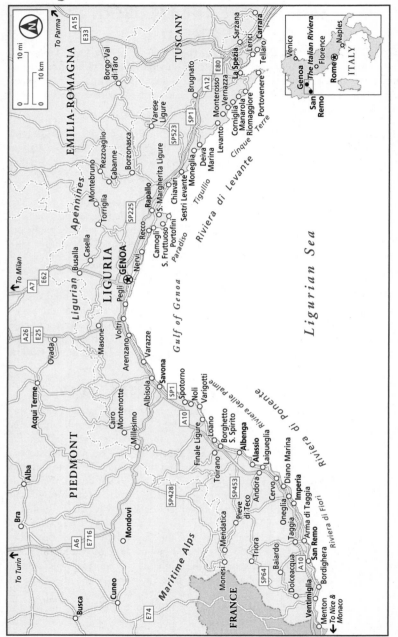

The principal activity in the Cinque Terre is hiking, but the evening is my favorite part of the day: settling down to a hearty meal in town and, later, having the tangle of romantically lit medieval *caruggi* (alleyways) at my disposal.

LAY OF THE LAND

The Cinque Terre was founded in the early Middle Ages, after the ever-present threat of Saracen pirates had finally dwindled, and each village still retains a distinctive character, even though now it's only a few minutes by train from one village to another. You'll want to settle on one before leaving home (not least because, having dragged your luggage up steep hills and then lugged it up six flights of stairs, you're unlikely to want to move again). Ask any group of travelers which of the five villages makes the best base and you're likely to get five different answers. To me, the village you choose is less important than whether you can bag a room with a terrace or balcony, preferably with a table and chairs overlooking the sea. Of course, in peak season you may have to take whatever you can get. Below—from east to west—is the lowdown on the five villages.

RIOMAGGIORE   This is arguably the most authentic of the villages, with a strong resident Italian community that gets on with life regardless of the annual incursion of tourists. It also seems to appeal to a younger crowd, probably because it also has the best-value accommodations in the Cinque Terre, with a handful of very good agents managing privately owned holiday apartments. This is the best village in which to find a small self-catering apartment, with a *terrazzo* from which to watch the passing parade, or a sea view to toast the sunset.

MANAROLA   Clinging to the stark gray crags above crashing breakers, Manarola is the village most exposed to the elements. It's also more isolated than neighboring Riomaggiore, a mere 20-minute stroll away but more than double that by car. With no natural harbor, fishing boats clutter the narrow streets, hoisted safely away from the frothy fingers of the sea by a crane. Behind the boats are convivial *trattorie* and *ristoranti* (friendlier than in smug Vernazza), packed to the brim with as many domestic as foreign tourists. Stroll to Punto Bonfiglio, the headland across the harbor, for lovely views of the village, or take the bus up to Volastra, the tiny rural hamlet set high above its seaside counterparts, and arguably the most tranquil place to base yourself in the entire Cinque Terre (see "Accommodations & Dining," below, for more details).

CORNIGLIA   Perched some 100m (328 ft.) above the sea, with no harbor, Corniglia is the oldest of the five villages, and has spectacular views. For most visitors the main drawback is its location. But while it's a schlep to get up here if you've missed the (more or less) half-hourly shuttle from the station, once you arrive you'll enjoy the most splendid views in the region. Besides Volastra, Corniglia is the most peaceful of the villages, with the sound of passing trains muffled by tunnels way below. Corniglia also lays claim to the region's best beach, the nudist Guvano (reached by following the signs from the north side of the railway station; €3.50).

VERNAZZA   With a long harbor affording picture-perfect views of its bobbing boats, ruined 12th-century castle, Gothic church, and dinky town square, Vernazza is the most popular of the five villages. It's almost as pretty as Portofino, and has seen little change in over a century. The only village with a natural harbor, it enjoyed a dominant position in regional trade and a natural sense of superiority. Its prominence is evident in the gorgeous detailing you'll see throughout the village, and in the high degree of civic pride. Its houses are immaculately kept, and carefully spaced trees line the main drag and pretty harbor piazza. However, it's totally insufferable in peak season—at least after 10:30am, when the ferry disgorges its first full load of visitors, topped off every hour by the train. Thankfully things do settle down at night: The village's day-trippers leave, and you can wander its romantically lit alleyways and find a table at its harbor piazza. Some of the best dining is to be had here, and it's worth eating here one evening, even if you're staying elsewhere (trains run well into the night). Accommodations here comprise a large selection of mostly tiny rooms.

MONTEROSSO AL MARE   Monterosso is more resort than village, with two sandy beaches and a plethora of accommodations options (it has the only real hotels in the Cinque Terre). In short, Monterosso has been entirely given over to tourism. It has facilities typical of the Riviera's resorts—beachfront bars and rows of umbrellas and beach chairs for hire. (Incidentally, there's free access to the beach only where you see no umbrellas.) Not surprisingly, there are fewer stairs and hills to negotiate here than in the rest of the Cinque Terre. In a region lacking "to do" sites, it also has one of the few listed attractions: the 17th-century Chiesa del Convento del Cappuccini, perched on a hillock in the center of town. It's also worth taking a look in the adjacent Church of San Francesco to view the 17th-century van Dyck painting of the *Crucifixion*, as well as work by the prolific Ligurian artist Luca Cambiaso. The biggest drawback here is that, even when night falls, the voices you hear all around you are unlikely to be Italian, and the "new" residential part of town, west of the railway station, is ugly; make sure you book in the more charming historical center, accessed through a large tunnel (though to be sure, walking through here on a weekend feels like you're being processed through a sausage factory). Perhaps it's obvious, but I'd be remiss if I didn't say that Monterosso al Mare is my least favorite village in the Cinque Terre.

GETTING THERE

Given the torturous roads and lack of adequate parking facilities (a privilege for which you also have to pay around €12 per day), the Cinque Terre is best accessed **by train.** Trains run the length of the coast from dawn to around midnight once or twice an hour. Genoa, home to the closest international airport, lies 70 to 90 minutes west by train; La Spezia, the eastern gateway, can be reached in a mere 10 to 20 minutes. (Incidentally, Florence lies about 2 hr. away via La Spezia—and a mid-morning intercity connection costs as little as €7.50.) A fun way to get here is **by boat**—ferries ply the waters from as far afield as the Tuscan Archipelago in peak season (July–Aug), but there are regular trips running from Portovenere and the Portofino promontory from Easter to the end of October (for contact details, see "Getting Around," below).

GETTING AROUND

Travel between the villages is also easiest and quickest **by train** (it usually takes about 5 min. to go from one village to another); a ticket costs between €1.10 (weekdays) and €1.20 (weekends), and is valid for 6 hours, so you can use it more than once to get between the villages during this time (don't forget to validate it before travel at the yellow machines posted at stations).

But because most of the journey is through the mountains, this is not the most scenic way to travel, so plan to incorporate at least one **boat** trip into your hiking itinerary (it takes 25 min.–2 hr. to walk between villages; see below). Boats working the water on this stretch of coast include those of the **Consorzio Marittimo Turistico "5 Terre Golfo dei Poeti"** (☎ **0187-732987;** www.navigazionegolfo deipoeti.it); they run from Riomaggiore from about 9:20am (from Monterosso at about 10:30am) till 5pm (later in peak season); there is no service from November to March. You can purchase a ticket from Monterosso to Riomaggiore for €8; return is €12. The cheapest run is between Monterosso and Vernazza, at €5.

Travel within the villages is only possible **on foot**—easy enough, given their tiny size. Almost all tourist services—ATMs, grocers, wine shops, delis, and various eateries—are strung along the main street that runs up from each harbor. The park also has methane **buses** running relatively regular services (hourly or twice

The Cinque Terre Cards: A Stacked Deck?

The 1-, 3-, or 7-day **Cinque Terre Cards** (€5.40, €13, and €21 respectively) entitle you to unlimited train trips between La Spezia and Levanto, unlimited bus trips within the park, and free access to the park's coastal path (usually a €3 entry). The 1-day Cinque Terre Ferry/Boat Card (€14) also includes unlimited 24-hour access to the ferries working the coast. While this is a convenient way to get around (no standing in lines to purchase additional tickets), it does not represent a real savings unless you're packing in a very full day with more than two train trips and additional activities, such as mountain biking or horseback riding (discounts for card holders). Cards can be purchased from any of the park offices (located at all the five village train stations as well as at La Spezia and Levanto), though I'd calculate carefully before actually purchasing one.

hourly) from the villages via the parking lots (no cars are allowed in the villages) up to the hillside hamlets dotting the coastline. Tickets range from €1.50 to €2.50.

ACCOMMODATIONS & DINING

As the majority of accommodations listed are in medieval buildings, there are (with the exception of Monterosso) no large hotels, and each operator offers only a handful of rooms—often booked months in advance. That's why I've included a fairly numerous selection.

The following discussion includes the very best available accommodations village by village, and the top dining choices in each. Given the tiny size of the villages, there are an amazing number of restaurants to choose from, but with few exceptions, all share almost identical menus (as do almost all restaurants on the Ligurian coast). Pesto is featured without fail, as is every conceivable combination of seafood. It is virtually impossible to have a truly bad meal here, so stroll around the village and survey all the options before making a choice. While dining in the Cinque Terre is by no means prohibitively expensive, it's not cheap, either; be prepared for €6 to €9 per person for a *primo* course, plus a €2 to €3 *coperto,* or cover charge. If you're willing to shell out a little more on a top meal, dine at the costlier of my recommendations and make up the difference with plenty of picnics (see "Delicious. Cheap. Local. Making Meals from the Village Deli," on p. 459).

Hotels & Restaurants in Riomaggiore

The pickings for the budget-conscious traveler in Riomaggiore are rich indeed, with a broad selection of apartments and private rooms, well managed for their absentee landlords by the holiday-letting agents whose offices line Via Colombo. You can take a virtual tour of these rental agents by visiting www.emmeti.it; click on "Hotels-Accommodation," then "Liguria," then "Residences-Flats," and all nine agents will pop up, some with photographs of the flats being offered.

€–€€€   The most efficient and helpful outfit by far is **Mar Mar** ✦ (Via Malborghetto, 4; ☎ 0187-920932; www.5terre-marmar.com), not least because there is a friendly, intelligent, and very helpful English voice on the other end of the line (ex-Californian Amy joined in 2003 as an office assistant, and is now a partner). E-mail your requirements (sea view and/or balcony, one or two bedrooms, equipped kitchen or kitchenette, dining room, and so on) and the response—often accompanied by photographs—comes with clear, truthful descriptions of what's available. Dorm rooms cost between €15 and €20 per person (there's 24-hr. access); rooms with private bathrooms €60 to €80; and privately owned apartments €65 to €90. Apartments sleeping four to six people can cost up to €120. Mar Mar also acts as an informal tourist bureau, arranging twice-weekly wine tastings and kayak rentals, and even assists with laundry.

€€–€€€   If you'd prefer to have more hotel-like facilities, with breakfast thrown in, I have two recommendations. Both properties are situated a little way above the village center (out of earshot from the train but a bit of a schlep if you're burdened with heavy luggage). **Locanda Cinque Terre** ✦✦ (Via de Batté, 67F; ☎ 0187-760538; www.cinqueterreresidence.it) is the more modern complex (a rather good re-interpretation of the slim historic buildings in the heart of Riomaggiore). It is well maintained and outfitted with modern conveniences, and some units open onto small terraces. It doesn't have the views of Villa Argentina (below), but Locanda Cinque Terre offers excellent value and a more personal feel, with hands-on owners at your beck and call.

€€–€€€   A stone's throw from Locanda Cinque Terre is the stalwart **Villa Argentina** ✦ (Via A De Gasperi, 170; ☎ 0187-920213), a small hotel with a slight

---

Accommodations Tip

Levanto and **Bonnasola** are neighboring towns on the western outskirts of the park and a smart option if you want to get away from it all in high season; both are well connected by train and boat to the five villages. Levanto is larger, with a hard-working tourist bureau and a wide selection of hotels and restaurants, most of which offer better value than nearby Monterosso. But in the beauty stakes the hands-down winner is the tranquil seaside village of Bonnasola, where **Villa Belvedere** (Via Ammiraglio Serra, 3; ☎ 0187-813622; www.bonassolahotelvillabelvedere.com) is a real find. A double suite with balcony and sea view will run you €95; €130 for half-board during August. Arrange for a free shuttle to pick you up from the train station. The Villa owners also have the best-located restaurant in the Cinque Terre, **L'Antica Guetta** (Via Marconi, 1; ☎ 0187-813797), which is right on the beach. Wear a swimsuit under your clothes, and plan a lazy afternoon soaking up the sun. L'Antica Guetta is worth the 10- to 20-minute train trip from any of the villages.

Before You Book

In the past, most visitors would plan only an overnight stay in the Cinque Terre and then very much regret that decision. Since 2000, though, the average stay has increased to 3 nights. You'll likely want that much time, too—it's only after sundown that the villages empty of day-trippers and you can wander the fascinating *caruggi* alone, or sit in the shadows beside the old-timers as they gossip about the day. Three nights also gives you the opportunity to tackle two different hikes, and time to relax along the way. Some questions to ask before booking:

What type of lodging should I seek?   You'll come across three types of accommodations in this region: hotels, B&Bs, and *affittacamere* (rooms for rent). The truth is that there's no difference between the three in price (in fact, these towns are so small that when one lodging raises or lowers a rate, all of its neighbors tend to follow suit). And there's very little difference in terms of visitor experience. Outside of Monterosso, many of the places that bill themselves as hotels are actually more like well-run B&Bs—sometimes without the breakfast. Family-operated, they are perfectly comfortable (despite their tiny rooms) and scrupulously clean, but with absolutely no facilities. You'll rarely have air-conditioning, a television, or a bathtub, not to mention much space or soundproofing. Most B&Bs are as efficiently run as these so-called hotels, but have perhaps one or two fewer rooms. *Affittacamere* have much the same look, but may give you a smidgen more privacy—they tend to be self-contained units, with no other guest rooms in the building. Another advantage of *affittacamere* is that some come with kitchenettes for no additional cost.

Standards are high at all three, but for peace of mind, always look for the park's "Mark of Quality," a gray stone plaque placed prominently outside the building. All rooms that have earned this designation are also listed in the "Ospitalità nel Parco" booklet, found at any park outlet. Or stick to the recommendations listed here. (Note that if breakfast is not

nautical theme and artworks by one of the Cinque Terre's most respected artists (you'll see his murals all over Riomaggiore, in fact). Like most hotels in the Cinque Terre, the rooms (€90–€130), though nothing to write home about, are functional—book one with a sea-facing terrace and the view more than makes up for the dull decor.

€   Eating comes next. If seafood's your bent, there's only one place to be: right on Riomaggiore's harbor, at **La Lanterna** ★★ (☎ 0187-920589), where even the pickiest seafood lover will not find fault. *Primi* range between €6.50 and €8 (no *coperto;* tips welcome) but splurge on the seafood antipasto (small €9.50; large included, every village has plenty of bar/cafes serving good cappuccino and fresh pastries every morning, and this can entail quite a savings.)

How do I go about making reservations?   If a hotel won't respond to your e-mails or faxes, you should phone. Sometimes proprietors have a minimal understanding of English or—especially in the case of *affitta- camere*—are unwilling to hold a room too far in advance (too many bad experiences with people who don't turn up). If you don't mind traipsing around a bit, you might want to wait till you get here: You'll ultimately find a bed, but not the best room.

Must my room have a view?   Given the popularity of the region in high season, it's worth booking well in advance if you want to bag a room with a terrace and/or a sea view—and given the beauty of the sunsets and the tiny size of most rooms, believe me, you do. Rooms with views usually cost the same as those without, so, when reserving, always ask for a room with a balcony and sea view, and then double-check whether this is what you'll be getting before you hand over the cash (note also that many hoteliers won't guarantee a sea view for, say, 1 night, in case they get a longer booking for that particular room).

How far is it from the rail track?   Because trains run all night, light sleepers should pick lodgings as far away from the rail tracks as possible. Many travelers don't realize how thin the walls can be, so pack earplugs if you're a light sleeper.

Are there discounts for paying in cash?   If you are prepared to wait till you get here before finding a room, it's worth knowing that most people are happy to give a cash discount of 5% to 10% (for rentals longer than 1 night, of course).

€13). With eight or nine varieties of fish, each prepared differently, this is a great introduction to the coast's bounty. This place is tiny, so make reservations.

€€   Both of our hotel choices (above) are within easy walking distance of Riomaggiore's best restaurant (and one of the top five in the Cinque Terre): **Ripa del Sole** ★★★ (Via de Gasperi, 282; ☎ 0187-920143; www.ripadelsole.it). It has lovely views from its terrace, service is unpretentious, and the food is superb. Almost all the *primi* cost a flat €9.50 (*coperto* €2.50), making the choice that much more difficult: fresh tagliatelle with lobster? gnocchi with scampi and white truffles? *pansotti* with butter and sage? *Secondi* here are an especially good value—sea bass filet oven-cooked with potatoes and the region's famous Taggiasche olives (unpitted, though, which is irritating) is a mere €8.

Hotels & Hostels in Manarola & Volastra

€   The Cinque Terre's only official **youth hostel** is in Manarola: **Albergo della Gioventù Ostello** (Via Riccobaldi, 21; ☎ 0187-920215; www.cinqueterre.net/ostello). Clean and functional, it's in a good location (a short stroll from the train station and harbor), and offers same-sex, six-bed dorms with shared bathrooms, as well as family rooms (all with bunk beds) with private bathrooms. Prices range from €18 to €22. There are a number of auxiliary services, from Internet facilities to hiking and snorkeling gear for rent, and it's not as impersonal as a large city hostel. But lockout (10am–5pm) and the late-night curfew have me longing for Mar Mar's more relaxed and informal dorms in Riomaggiore (see above).

€€   Manarola has only three designated hotels, of which the charming **Ca' D'Andrean** (Via Discovolo, 10; ☎ 0187-920040; www.cadandrean.it), located in the heart of the old village in an old winery, offers the best service. Comfortable double rooms, some with terraces, go for €75 to €88; breakfast is an additional €6 per person.

€€   Closer to the harbor, **Marina Piccola** ★ (Via Birolli, 120; ☎ 0187-920103; www.hotelmarinapiccola.com) enjoys a better location, with some rooms overlooking the sea—request a sea view and/or terrace or balcony; room 10 is a particularly good choice. Doubles go for €85 to €105. Marina Piccola is also the best restaurant in the village, with tables right on the harbor; average *primo* is €8; *coperto* is €2.50. (Budget hunters may want to investigate the en suite room with private entrance just a little farther up from the Piccola's restaurant—you'll get the same sea view for only €60; contact Nella Capellini—who speaks limited English—at ☎ 0187-920135 or 3201-964550.)

€€–€€€   Located higher up, with great village and sea views, is Manarola's most popular B&B, **La Toretta** ★★ (Via Rollandi, 58; ☎ 0187-920327; www.torrettas.com). Run by the affable Gabriele Baldini as efficiently as a hotel (a great breakfast on the terrace in the morning; wine tastings in the evening), all rooms (€50–€120 double) open onto the requisite small terrace with sea views. He also has a student room that has two single beds and a private bathroom for €30 per person, as well as apartments.

€€   But for the best views in the entire Cinque Terre, head up to **Volastra** (buses connect the two towns almost every hour, from 7am to 9:30pm), where the **Luna Di Marzo** ★★ (Via Montello, 387; ☎ 0187-920530; www.albergolunadi marzo.com), from its top-floor corner room with large terrace, has the best view in the park. A new custom-built hotel, Luna Di Marzo enjoys an extraordinary position on the edge of the village, with distant views of tiny Manarola and Corneglia, and a horizon so big it curves at the edges. The rooms, which are outfitted with the usual bland, mass-produced furniture and fittings, are the most spacious in the region, and cost €90 (if it's available don't think twice before spending the extra €10 required for room 8 and plan to have at least one romantic candle-lit picnic on your terrace; rooms 5, 6, and 9 share the same stupendous views but with windows at waist height).

€€   Running to the east along the ridge are also a few B&Bs worth looking into: **Ca'del Michelè** (☎ 0187-760552; www.cadelmichele.com; four rooms, two with sea view) and **Il Vigneto** (☎ 0187-762173, ask for Patrizia; www.ilvigneto5 terre.com; 6 rooms, 2 with sea views; lovely roof terrace). Rooms at both properties run about €60 to €70.

Hotels & Rooms in Corniglia

€€   Corniglia has only one hotel, and it's among the most authentic and inexpensive options in the region: The **Cecio** ★★ (Via Serra, 58; ☎ 0187-812043; simopank@libero.it) is small (only eight rooms), family-owned, and very laid-back—when you book, ask to speak to manager (and self-proclaimed tiramisu maestro) Giacinto, the only one with a reasonable command of English (you can also call him on his cellphone: ☎ 3343-506637). For the best views, book room 3 (a great corner room), 2, 4, or 5; these will run you a mere €60 for two people. There is a restaurant downstairs and you can picnic on the rooftop.

€€   **La Terrazze** ★ (Via Fieschi, 110; ☎ 3498-459684; www.eterasse.it) is the classiest of the *affittacamere* (rooms for rent), not least because the two en suite rooms (double €90) open onto the most charming terraced garden (shared with an upstairs two-bedroom apartment), shaded with lemon and olive trees bedecked in candles and colored baubles.

€€–€€€   The best restaurant in the village is **Mananan** (Via Fieschi, 117; ☎ 0187-821166). Owned by Agostino Galletti (who makes a most sublime ricotta and herb ravioli, topped with a walnut sauce), this authentic trattoria is housed in a charming 18th-century wine cellar. It's best to call ahead because Agostino only opens when he's feeling up to it (if you're stuck, the Cecio, just outside the historical heart, serves a rather good pesto). Prices vary greatly, but you can get a *primo* here for about €15.

Be Aware of the Seasons

Peak season runs from mid-June to August, when the villages are packed with Italian families taking their annual holiday, and continues full steam into September, when hikers arrive in droves, and the harvesting of grapes begins. Crowds are particularly evident on weekends, when day-trippers arrive from the landlocked hinterland. Easter and May are also busy times, but you're more likely to negotiate a discount then—at the very least, hoteliers are refreshed and ready to face the season with a friendlier face than at the tail end of an exhausting September. Many businesses close from November to March; others offer up to 50% discount on lodgings and the like.

Hotels & Restaurants in Vernazza

Vernazza has only three hotels, but these are not really different from the *affitta-camere* (rooms for rent) lodgings everywhere, and a trained service culture is almost entirely lacking.

€–€€   An exception is **Albergo Barbara** ★★ (Albergo Barbara, Piazza Marconi, 30; ☎ 0187-812398; www.albergobarbara.it), which boasts friendly, professional service from husband-and-wife team Giuseppe and Patricia (whose excellent English and helpful advice are a bonus). It offers nine simple rooms, located on the top floors (there's no elevator) of a building right on Piazza Marconi, the main harbor square. The two en suite rooms with sea view (€80 double) are the best, but the two double rooms in the attic, which share a bathroom (each with in-room basin), are the best value at €48.

€€   The longest-running hotelier is **Gianni Franzi** (☎ 0187-821003; www.giannifranzi.it), with a range of rooms in two separate buildings a short but steep haul from his trattoria. Choose between the slightly larger rooms—with private bathrooms but no views—or the prettier rooms with sea views from the small Juliet-style balconies but dank, shared bathrooms. Decor is a rather charming blend of hand-me-downs and antiques—a welcome break from the mass-produced chip and pine found elsewhere. Gianni also manages a few independently owned rooms scattered across town (if you can book "Stalin," you'll be perched on a seaside cliff and have the most stupendous view in Vernazza). Gianni's is a very efficient family-run organization, but be prepared to deal with the tight-lipped Marisa, Gianni's wife. Still, with rooms charged at €65 (shared bathroom) and €77 (en suite), it offers well-pitched value (note that in peak season you may need a minimum 2-night stay).

€€   Of the myriad *affittacamere* available, look into the four studio-type apartments overlooking the harbor square offered by **FrancaMaria** (☎ 3287-1219728 or 0187-812002). One even has a small dining room and a kitchenette (€90–€110); son Giovanni also has three rooms but these are poky. Make sure you're booking a room overlooking the Piazza Marconi. Alternatively, there are the four rooms (most overlooking Piazza Marconi) offered by **Martina Callo** (☎ 0187-812365; roomartina@supereva.it) for €50 to €80 (room 3, which has a terrace, is the one to go for here). There are also five rooms available from **Affita Camera da Annamaria** (☎ 0187-821082) for €60 to €85; it's located on Via Carattino—again, ask for a room with a terrace. **Mamma Rina** (☎ 0187-812025) is another that offers rooms with terraces, which have hill views; these come with private bathrooms but they are not en suite and go for €60. **Maria Taddei** (3474-977748; mflorisa@hotmail.com) has a small apartment overlooking Piazza Marconi for €65 to €70, or contact **Tilde** (☎ 3392-989323); they have a studio with lovely sea view for €70.

€€   Vernazza is generally thought to have the region's best restaurants and **Gambero Rosso** ★★★ (☎ 0187-812265), located in an old wine cellar that has tables on Piazza Marconi (the main harbor square), invariably tops the Cinque Terre list. I think it's a case of the most attractive girl getting the glances, but hey,

Vernazza sure is pretty—and even more so when you're eyeing the spread on Gambero's classy white-starched tablecloths lit with candles. The staff is a tad irritating—a request for olive oil and balsamic (to accompany the bread) is often met with an upturned nose, which is cheeky, given that the *coperto* (service charge) is €3, the highest in the village. But Gambero's food more than makes up for this. Light and fragrant *primi* (average €9.50; average *secondo* €11) are clearly made fresh to order. It's hardly surprising that Gambero Rosso earned two stars in the highly respected *Ristorante di Veronelli 2005.*

€€   Almost next to Gambero is Vernazza's oldest trattoria, owned by main man **Gianni Fanzi** ★ (☎ 0187-821003). With service tipped in its favor and meals coming in slightly cheaper (average *primo* €8.50; *coperto* €2.50), it's the best dining option in the village. And if you're tiring of the usual variations of seafood pasta, Gianni does a mean veal roast for a mere €7.50.

€€   You might want to climb the stairs to **Al Castello** ★★ (☎ 0187-812296). Named after the castle (whose entrance is a few steps higher) where guards kept a look out for marauding pirates, this is a great luncheon refuge from the crowded streets below, and at dinnertime, when the lights start to twinkle below, you'll feel as if you're floating. It's the same menu you'll see everywhere—with *primi* ranging between €8 and €10, and *coperto* coming in at €2—but the seafood is good and fresh, and the view is certainly worth the climb.

Hotels & Restaurants in Monterosso

With Monterosso awash in three-star lodgings falling in the €100-to-€150 category, and most of the one- and two-star hotel options offering very poor value, this is not a good base for budget hunters. But it will suit those wanting more hotel-like facilities, or a beach holiday.

€€   Well-situated on the beachfront, but with no frills whatsoever, is the one-star **Agavi** (Via Fegina, 30; ☎ 0187-817171; hotel.agavi@libero.it), a stone's throw east of the station on Via Fegina; a sea-facing room here costs between €70 and €100.

€€   **Villa Pietrafiore** (Località Pietrafiore; ☎ 0187-817311) is a long walk from the train station (don't do this with heavy luggage), but has a wonderful location above the town, with sea-view rooms going for €60 to €90.

€€–€€€   With its room prices ranging from €90 to €117, **La Colonnina** (Via Zucca, 6; ☎ 0187-817439; www.lacolonninacinqueterre.it), hidden behind a lovely, leafy entrance, is reasonable but also bland and sterile—only book here if all else fails (and do try for one of their four double rooms that open onto a garden terrace). Like other places around here, it fills up months in advance.

€€€   The best beachfront options are **Hotel Baia** (Lungo Mare Fegina, 88; ☎ 0187-817512; www.baiahotel.it) or neighboring **La Spiaggia** (Via Lungo Mare, 98; ☎ 0187-817567; www.laspiaggiahotel.com), both on Lungomare Fegina, the beachfront road that leads to ugly Fegina. If you get a sea-facing room at either of these (try Baia first, where the decor is marginally better), you'll more than likely tout Monterosso as the best of the Cinque Terre's villages. But don't stay if there are no sea-view rooms left.

€€€€   A little farther along (through the tunnel) is the only beachfront option in the historical section, located on what is often referred to as "fishermen's beach." All the rooms at **Hotel Pasquale** ★★ (Via Fegina, 4; ☎ 0187-817550; www. pasini.com) have sea views; the hotel is also relatively tasteful and at €135 a good value option, given that it's both beachfront and old town.

€€€€   If there are no sea-facing rooms available in the beach hotels, your best bet in Monterosso is **Villa Steno** ★ (Via Roma, 109; ☎ 0187-817354; www.pasini. com). It's a modern building in a tranquil location above the old town; most rooms come with a private sea-view balcony or little garden furnished with table and chairs, ready for the evening sundowner and picnic. A double goes for €140.

€€€€   Alternatively, if Villa Steno is full, try **Locanda Il Maestrale** ★ (Via Roma, 37; ☎ 0187-817013; www.monterossonet.com). With only six rooms (€100–€130 for doubles; €170 for suites), some with lovely frescoed ceilings, and stylish public rooms, this is as close as the Cinque Terre gets to a boutique hotel. But it's a little stuffy.

€€€   Stuffy is not a word you'd use for the down-to-earth **Albergo Marina** (Via Buranco, 40; ☎ 0187-817613; www.hotelmarinacinqueterre.it) or its neighbor **Albergo Amici** (Via Buranco, 36; ☎ 0187-817544; www.hotelamici.it). Neither offers much in terms of facilities, looks, or price (€100–€130 and €105–€135, respectively), but I'd give Marina the first go: It has a more personal feel, with the entire family (three generations) very hands on, and the dinner—sometimes served in the roof garden—is a very worthwhile €10 per person if you go for the half-board option. Then again, the larger Amici has the better roof garden (replete with lemon trees and a sea view), and is a little better maintained.

€   Possibly my favorite place in Monterosso is the village's oldest wine cellar, **L'Enoteca Internazionale Di Barbieri Susanna** ★ (Via Roma, 62; ☎ 0187-817278). The selection on its shelves is almost overwhelming (over 1,000 labels), so take a seat at one of the rustic timber tables outside and sample a few (€2.50–€4 per glass). But first line your stomach with fresh bruschetta (€3–€5); toppings range from the simple (slices of fresh tomato with whole basil leaves and olive oil) to the sublime (fresh anchovies marinated in lemon juice and topped with tomato, mozzarella, capers, and oregano). This is also the ideal place to sample a good Sciacchetrà—order it with a side of bruschetta topped with Gorgonzola and candied fruit.

€€   Given its small size, Monterosso has a remarkable selection of traditional restaurants, but the hands-down winner is **Ciak La Lanterna** ★★★ (Piazza Don Minzoni, 6; ☎ 0187-817014). Ciak excels not only with food (a bit of a splurge, with *coperto* at €3 and *primi* around €11) but also atmosphere. Pick a table inside and you'll be sandwiched among loud Italian families, around which waiters scurry like soldier ants to serve the hungry masses.

Delicious. Cheap. Local. Making Meals from the Village Deli

Invariably, one of the best meals that I have in the Cinque Terre is a picnic lunch composed of a few slices of *coppa di parma*, a small bunch of arugula, a plum tomato, a wedge of olive-studded focaccia, and a bottle of chilled Vermentino—all enjoyed on my private terrace overlooking the main street in Riomaggiore. Every village has at least two superb delis and/or *enotece*, as well as tiny *focaccerie*, where wood-burning ovens churn out large squares of fresh focaccia. For best value in providing picnic fixings, head straight for one of the **Coop 5 Terre** shops located on the main streets of Riomaggiore, Manarola, and Vernazza.

For a picnic in Corniglia, you'll find the delightful **A Bütiega** on Via Fieschi, 142 (the main lane). And Monterosso has plenty of *prodotti tipici* shops, a few good bakeries, and a supermarket.

WHY YOU'RE HERE: EXPLORING THE NATIONAL PARK

The Cinque Terre is crisscrossed with a network of well-marked trails (58 at last count). Some pass within leaping distance of the crystal-clear waters of the sea, some through cultivated terraces and the fragrant vegetation of the Mediterranean flora. All hikes are listed, together with the estimated times to complete each segment, in "The Park By Foot," which is available at the park offices. (Though not always in English, paths are clearly marked/numbered and can be used in conjunction with the advice set forth below.) **Park office headquarters** are in Riomaggiore (Via Telemaco Signorini, 118; ☎ 0187-760000; www.parconazionale5terre.it).

By far the most popular trail is the **coastal "blue" path** (referred to as *sentiero azzuro*, or simply "no. 2") that **links the five villages.** To walk any stretch of the coastal blue path you have to pay a daily entry fee of €3 (all others hikes are free); you purchase your ticket between 8am and 8pm from any of the park offices, located at all five village train stations or at trail heads. If you wish to complete the full coastal walk (Riomaggiore to Monterosso), set aside an entire day (if you're reasonably fit it should take about 5 hr. without stops), and bear in mind that it's easier to walk from east to west—that is, to set off from Riomaggiore and to end in Monterosso.

A less arduous plan is to **walk from Riomaggiore to Vernazza.** It's a 3-hour hike, which includes a 20-minute amble between Riomaggiore and Manarola, called the **dell'Amore** (a name that is more evocative than the actual walk); the satisfying 45-minute stride between Manarola and Corniglia; and the final tiring but very rewarding 2-hour stretch from Corniglia to Vernazza. (The latter is the most attractive part, so if you have time for only one good walk, make it this leg.) From Vernazza, I suggest you catch the ferry to Monterosso (€5; one almost every hour), and then take the train back to your home base. But if you're fit and up for it, do tackle the final stretch between Vernazza and Monterosso, generally considered to be the most challenging, with the undulating path taking another 2 hours. It's almost as rewarding as the Corniglia/Vernazza leg.

Walks That Include a Visit to the Sanctuaries

Like most of Liguria's coastal towns, the five villages all have sanctuaries built high up in the hillsides; it was to these that villagers would beat a hasty retreat when sighting the masts of pirates on the horizon. Time allowing, incorporate at least one of the Cinque Terre sanctuaries (also known as shrines) into your hiking program, of which the following two are especially recommended:

The **Sanctuary of Soviore,** located above Monterosso, is possibly the oldest place of worship in Liguria, with ruins and early records dating pilgrimages to this point way back in A.D. 740. Today the principal reason to make the 90-minute pilgrimage to the "new" 18th-century sanctuary is the view: On a clear day, you can see as far as Corsica and the Tuscan archipelago. To get here, either catch the bus that runs from Monterosso or head up path no. 9, and then east along path no. 1. Descend back to the coast to visit the **Sanctuary of Reggio,** surrounded by century-old ilexes, before passing through vineyards and olive groves into Vernazza.

For even more awesome views, plan a trip up to the **Montenero Sanctuary.** A number of attractive paths lead there, but if your knees have seen better days, simply catch one of the buses that run from Riomaggiore to Biassa and ask to be dropped off at the closest point to the sanctuary; from here it is about 20 minutes up a footpath. As a place of refuge, the Montenero Sanctuary dates back to 1335, but today it is particularly popular with wedding parties, not least because the park authorities have opened a rather good *ristorante* in the vaulted 14th-century refectory; it also offers 15 (very spartan) cottages on the grounds, but with the mandatory 20-minute walk uphill with luggage, this is only for diehard hikers and solitude seekers. For restaurant or cottage bookings, call ☎ **0187-760528** (www. manario.it).

Tips to Avoid the Crush

Whatever hiking trail you choose, be prepared for columns of fellow walkers winding their way along the coast if you're here during September (or May, to a lesser extent), when the weather is optimal.

The only way to avoid the frustrating crush is to **start early**—sunrise if possible—and have breakfast in a village along the way. If you're not an early riser, **opt for one of the less popular paths;** generally, the higher up you go, the less traffic you'll come across, with the highest path (no. 1) virtually free of any hikers. Paths that lead east of Riomaggiore are also practically empty. Note that you needn't climb all the way to these higher routes; conserve your energy by catching a bus to one of the hillside hamlets—for example, from Manarola to Volastra, and then walk through vineyards along path no. 6d to the small settlement of Porciana before descending into Corniglia via path no. 7.

Eating on the Hoof: The National Park Restaurants

The Cinque Terre Park authorities run a number of restaurants and refreshment points situated on the hiking routes—you can reach these on foot, or simply catch one of the park buses in hillside hamlets. Most feature great views and offer simple fare typical of the region; for good value, try the €15 "hiker's meal" (comprising a *primo, secondo* (usually fish), dessert, glass of red or white wine, water, and coffee). It's an excellent value given that this includes the iniquitous *coperto* (note that if you order any items from the a la carte menu, the €2 *coperto* will be charged).

The following four refreshment points can be utilized as great pit stops while hiking: The **Dell'Amore** (☎ 0187-921026), located on Lovers Lane between Riomaggiore and Manarola. Second, located in the hills almost halfway between Corniglia and Vernazza, **San Bernardino** (☎ 0187-812548) makes a perfect halfway break, with lovely views back to Corniglia. Third, **Montenero** (☎ 0187-760528), the starting point to most mountain-bike trails and a number of walks, serves traditional meals in a vaulted, whitewashed 14th-century refectory. Finally, **Monesteroli** (☎ 0187-758214; reached by Biassa bus from Riomaggiore), is one of the most charming venues, with warm golden hues off set by avocado-green lampshades, and where you can enjoy a splendid *vista con mare* from the terrace in the evening.

Alternatives for Exploring the Park

Another good way to get off the overburdened coastal track is to explore the higher routes on **horseback** or **mountain bike.** Guided horseback excursions (summer to Sept 15; 9am–12:30pm and 5–8pm) aimed at beginners (90 min.; €25 or €20 with Cinque Terre Card), minimum-experience riders (2 hr.; €25 or €20 with Cinque Terre Card), and experts (4 hr.; €50 or €35 with Cinque Terre Card) can be arranged through any of the **park information points** (☎ 0187-920633). There are also four well-marked mountain-bike trails, most of which start from the **Montenero Sanctuary** (☎ 0187-760528), where you can also rent the cycles and any other gear you may need (€4 for a half-day; €2.50 with Cinque Terre Card).

Better still, get out your swimsuit and explore the translucent waters of this beautiful coastline. A dinghy should cost in the region of €40 to €60 for 4 hours (plus fuel), or you can rent a kayak for around €7 an hour (look for the rental signs at Riomaggiore harbor or at the sandy cove at Vernazza's harbor). Alternatively, contact Kate (☎ 3288-426885; www.fishnet.it) for **guided coastal tours** by boat (€80 per hr.; maximum seven persons; discounts for half- or full days). Incidentally, Kate, who has been living in Monterosso for the past 15 years, also offers wine tastings (€60) and full-day tours covering the five villages (€250).

THE OTHER CINQUE TERRE

For a less-touristy approach to the region, try one of the following activities.

Worshipping with the Locals

One of the greatest challenges facing the Cinque Terre is the decline in full-time residents, and with an aging population, the Cinque Terre is in danger of losing its cultural traditions. Attending 11am Sunday Mass with the villagers in one of their Gothic-style churches (each sporting a beautifully carved marble rose window, proof that the villagers were turning a reasonable profit in the Middle Ages) is one of the best ways to experience an authentic slice of village life. Other times for Mass are as follows: 4pm on Saturday and Sunday (Riomaggiore and Vernazza); 5pm on Saturday (Manarola); 5:30pm on Saturday and Sunday, and 9am on Sunday (Monterosso).

Making Wine & Perfect Pesto

In 2005, park authorities launched a new series of guided tours showcasing traditional activities, including *Wild Nature and Cultivated Terraces* and *Cookery Lesson in Montenero* (both tours, departing Manarola and Riomaggiore, respectively, at 9am; €30 including lunch, after which you are brought back to the starting point). On the former tour, you are taken for a walk through the vineyards behind Manarola, given a short lesson on local grape cultivation, introduced to the vintners, and, finally, provided a glass of wine during lunch at Gli Ulivi, in Volastra. In *Cookery Lesson in Montenero,* you walk up to the Montenero Sanctuary, where you are given a demonstration on the traditional way to make pesto (Liguria's most famous culinary export), and then enjoy the results in Montenero's 14th-century refectory, where its *ristorante* is located. All park tours (including those of guided hiking trails) run once a week on specified days only; to learn more, contact ☎ 0187-760000 or agenziaviaggi@parconazionale5terre.it.

THE PORTOFINO PROMONTORY

This pristine piece of coast, a jutting triangle that divides the Golfo Paradiso from the Golfo Tigullio, was a favored haunt of Hollywood stars and jet-set moguls in the 1950s, and its villages and towns still ooze the kind of sophisticated charm their cousins south of Genoa have long since sacrificed to mass-market tourism.

Portofino is glamorous with chichi boutiques hawking everything—from Pucci to Picasso—to socialites who teeter along its cobblestone lanes in high heels. Neighboring **Santa Margherita Ligure,** on the other hand, is larger and less pedestrian-friendly but has the slightly faded elegance of an aging Hollywood star—great bone structure and still beautiful. East of Santa Margherita, where the promontory joins the mainland, is the bustling harbor town of **Rapallo,** which has its fair share of Liberty-style (Art Nouveau) buildings and palm-lined promenades. But the encroachment of bland, modern structures now detracts from what must once have been the equal of Santa Margherita Ligure.

Of all the harborside settlements, my favorite is **Camogli,** a tiny fishing village that lies west of Santa Margherita, on the western flank of the promontory. Once mother to the legendary Mille Bianchi Velier (1,000 white ships) that set sail from here, it's an unpretentious beauty with a pedestrian promenade that follows a pebble beach. Tall, narrow houses—decorated with restrained *trompe l'oeil* detailing and green shuttering—stand near the shore. It's a relatively undiscovered gem, with an excellent selection of good-value restaurants and hotels. Even the **ferry trips** (☎ 0185-772091; www.golfoparadiso.it) are significantly cheaper if taken from here. Come as a day-tripper, but if you regret not basing yourself here, you'll find suggested lodgings below.

LAY OF THE LAND

Like everywhere else on this stretch of coast, getting to **Camogli** and **Santa Margherita Ligure by train** is easy (and cheap): It takes about an hour to get here from Monterosso (€9.70–€11; 20–26 trains daily), and half that from Genoa (€2.20). Traveling by car can be tedious, with parking anywhere carrying a price tag that pushes up your daily hotel budget by as much as 30%. And that's if parking is available at all (don't make the mistake of parking illegally, a misdemeanor for which you'll pay €100 in Portofino). If you want independence from public transport, it's better by far to hire a **scooter;** call **GM Motor Center Rent** (☎ 3294-066274; €40 per day).

From **Santa Margherita,** there is only one (narrow) road **into Portofino** (the southern tip of the triangle); the **bus** journey between the two takes about 15 minutes and costs €1.30. You can also get there **by boat** (€4.50). Buses run with equal regularity for the same price between Santa Margherita and Rapallo.

Portofino can only be reached **by foot** (around 5 hr.) or **by boat** from Camogli (a very pleasurable journey with two possible stops along the way—the first at Punta Ciappa where there is a truly great trattoria, the second at the San Fruttuoso Abbey; see top sights below). To get between Camogli and Santa Margherita, you can either take the 10-minute train journey (runs hourly or twice hourly; €1.10) or the more scenic 25-minute bus journey.

PICK OF THE PROMONTORY: ACCOMMODATIONS & DINING

In addition to the following hotels, you can also stay at the Abbey of San Fruttuoso (see "Waiter, Could You Order My Boat?" below).

Hotels & Restaurants in Camogli

€€   For the most peaceful stay on the Ligurian coast, and for an array of good-value dining options, the pretty fishing village of Camogli can't be beat. Bargain hunters should look no further than **La Camogliese** (Via Garibaldi, 55; ☎ 0185-771402; www.lacamogliese.it), where rooms are light, bright, and relatively spacious (there's even a small writing desk!), and someone is always on hand at reception to assist with queries. Doubles range from €70 to €87. Book the corner room on the second floor if possible; it costs no more and has the best views. The hotel also has five rooms with small balconies overlooking the stream that runs into the ocean.

€€   Another good bet, on the other side of the harbor, is **Locanda Il Faro** (Via P. Schiaffino, 116–118; ☎ 0185-771400), a small hotel efficiently run by the

Amendola family, with en suite rooms (ask for a sea view) that cost between €70 and €95; private bathrooms (but not en suite) go for €60 to €85. The Amendolas' restaurant, on the ground floor, has an excellent reputation.

€€   But if you don't mind a 5-minute walk to the beach, **Affittacamere da Roberto** (Via S. Bartolomeo, 27; ☎ 0185-774094; www.camogliroberto.it) offers two independent studio apartments located in the olive groves behind town. Surrounded by trees, they offer a rural ambience (good for families), yet are minutes from the promenade action (€60–€80 double).

€€-€€€€   If you have a little more money to burn, **Hotel Casmona** (Salita Pineto, 13; ☎ 0185-7700156; www.casmona.com), in a 19th-century seafront villa, enjoys the best location, right on Via Garibaldi, the seafront promenade. Almost all rooms boast idyllic sea views and cost between €85 and €145, depending on the season.

€€€€   **Cenobio dei Dogi** ★★ (Via Cuneo, 34; ☎ 0185-7241; www.cenobio.it) is by far the best hotel in town, and, given what you get for your money elsewhere on the promontory, it's a very good value. Once the country retreat of Genoa's doges, it is perched above the sea at the edge of the village, with expansive views looking back on Camogli and the entire coastline—a truly wonderful location, with a range of rooms to suit your budget. Doubles cost from €150 to €217.

€€   At lunchtime, head for Via Garibaldi (the seafront promenade), where you'll find the most wonderful seafood restaurant in a tiny timber Swiss-style chalet cantilevered over Camogli's pebble beach. With great sea views, old-fashioned decor, and personal service (I drank the proprietor's Vermentino wine recommendation, Il Monticello, for the duration of my most recent trip), **La Camogliese** (☎ 0185-771086) is a lunch experience that evokes a Riviera holiday: a dreamy afternoon spent slurping up the most memorable seafood pasta. *Primi* are around €8.50, *coperto* €2.10.

€€   Other top Camogli picks are **Ristorante Rosa** ★★★ (☎ 0185-773411) for superb sea bass and great sea views, tiny **Da Paolo** ★★★ (☎ 0185-773595) for seafood so fresh it's almost still moving (the owners have their own boat), and **La Cucina di Nonna Nina** ★★ (☎ 0185-773835) for traditional Ligurian cuisine. The latter is *the* place for pesto and very popular with the locals—make sure you book early or you'll end up in the plastic tent behind the actual restaurant. You'll pay between €8 and €12 for *primi* at all three.

Hotels & Restaurants in Santa Margherita Ligure

€€   With a bustling, jet-set atmosphere, its bars and cafes buzzing with people (and the streets with cars and scooters), Santa Margherita Ligure is more glam-town than laid-back village. And it attracts the lion's share of tourists. Run by one of Santa's many eccentric and gruff hoteliers, the Liberty-style **Hotel Villa Anita** (Viale Minerva, 25; ☎ 0185-286543; www.hotelvillaanita.com) is my first choice in this price category, and with a small playground and outdoor table tennis, it's ideal for families. Conveniently located in a tranquil neighborhood a few minutes' stroll from the seaside action (and town center), nothing much has changed since the Tarellas opened their doors 40 years ago—but that is precisely its charm. Ask for a room with a terrace or a balcony (room 4 is a good choice). Doubles range from €60 to €100.

€€   Also recommended is the popular **Hotel Conte Verde** (Via Zara, 1; ☎ 0185-287139; www.hotelconteverde.it), located 100m (328 ft.) from the seafront, and an easy stroll from the station. Alessandro is unwilling to be pinned down on price but on one recent day in September he was charging €90 for a double (reduced to €80 for a 3-day stay). Every room is different in size and individually decorated—if you are staying for more than 1 night, request a room with a terrace.

€€€   The best non-budget option is the centrally located **Hotel Jolanda** ★ (Luisito Costa, 6; ☎ 0185-287512; www.hoteljolanda.it), a wonderful over-the-top creation of glamorous Miriam Pastine. Given the atmosphere of decadence and old-fashioned luxury (there's plenty of wood paneling and gilt mirrors), it's a very good value; opt for the superior category (standard is tiny) or splurge for a huge suite. Doubles start at €100.

€€€€   Santa Margherita's sweeping promenade is lined with large Liberty-style hotels—sadly, staff at most of these gorgeous old piles don't understand the first thing about service, with the stellar exception of the (very) **Grand Hotel Miramare** ★★★ (Via Milite Ignoto; ☎ 0185-287013; www.grandhotelmiramare.it). Dressed in antiques and pretty touches, with floor-to-ceiling windows and large bathrooms overlooking the sea, its interiors are equaled by the magnificent exterior. Hardly surprising, then, that it is still the most popular and romantic option in Santa Margherita almost 60 years after Laurence Olivier and Vivienne Leigh chose to honeymoon here. Doubles cost from €239 to €356, including breakfast.

Waiter, Could You Order My Boat?

€-€€   There is something wonderfully romantic about having to catch a boat to get to your restaurant table, something which **Trattoria La Cantina** (☎ 0185-772626) and **Da Giovanni** (☎ 0185-770047) have certainly capitalized on over the years. Both are fortunate enough to be located in the tiny village of San Fruttuoso, the latter enjoying the greater fame, but both play to packed houses. Lesser known, and even more stunningly situated, is **Trattoria dö Spadin** ★★ at Punta Chiappa (you can't miss the sign as you approach; ☎ 0185-770624). Though food is a tad pricey (*primi* €13; *coperto* €3), it is classic *cucina povera*—simple, fresh, light, and delicious—but the cost may have as much to do with the glorious location as it does with the fare. The restaurant faces Camogli and the entire Golfo Paradiso, and it's sandwiched between the startling blue sea, which crashes below your seat, and a tiny kitchen that looks like it's been styled for a cookbook on Riviera cuisine. Pack your swim gear, and, after coffee, wander down to the harbor and wade in the ocean. My idea of heaven.

A Splurge in the World's Most Romantic Hotel

€€€€   Relaxing on the terrace at the **Splendido** ★★★ (Viale Baratta; ☎ 0185-267801; www.hotelsplendido.com), you know you're in heaven: The moon rises above the billionaires' boats bobbing in the harbor below, and twinkling lights outline the distinctive shape of Mount Portofino, its cypruses like dark exclamation marks against the lush hillside. Then the tinkling of the piano starts up, and you're humming along: "a kiss is just a kiss . . ." Whether you're here just to sample Corrado Corti's superb fare at La Terrazza (bank on around €215 for two with wine), or booked in for the evening, you'll have the time of your life.

The Splendido is unlike any other hotel I've ever visited. With tight building restrictions in the park, nothing much has changed in this sprawling villa since Bogart and Bacall frequented the bar, or since Garbo came "to be alone." Staff members are unusual, with quirky personality and charm counting for more than coiffed looks and A+ diplomas in hotel management, and many have been here for years: 3 decades for barman Antonio Beccalli, who has mixed cocktails for the likes of Madonna and De Niro. By the time dinner is over, and you find yourself twirling around the bar to some cheesy love song crooned by an incorrigible flirt ("chosen just for you, madam"), you feel truly at home. And the thing is, for that night, you are.

€€–€€€   There are no surprises at **Il Faro** (Via Maragliano, 24a; ☎ 0185-286867), with all the usual suspects typical of Ligurian fare, and plenty of seafood. But the three-course menu at €25 is a bargain; there's also no *coperto* charged here. **Trattoria Cesarina** (Via Mameli, 2c; ☎ 0185-86059) is another regularly lauded restaurant—Fabrizio changes his small menu almost daily, depending on his mood and what's available at the market; *primi* here range between €12 and €15.

€€€   Santa Margherita is also where the most creative cooking is happening: Head for Slow Food member **Piccolo Ristorante Ardiciocca** ★★★ (☎ 0185-281312; www.ardiciocca.it), and you'll be stumped with a choice of intriguing combinations (nettle ravioli with walnuts and thyme? risotto with Taleggio cheese and pears?) as well as the more predictably delicious selections—sea bass cooked with lemon leaves and served with fresh mayo. Count on spending at least €14 before you've ordered a drink.

Hotels & Restaurants in Portofino

For an additional dining option, see **à crêuza du Gio,** below, under "Why You're Here: The Top Sights & Attractions."

€€€€   This postcard-perfect village is *the* place for people-watching, and while you could settle for just doing dinner here (a far more convivial affair than lunch), it's rather marvelous to wander from the cobblestone streets to your own bed without having to worry about bus or ferry schedules. Portofino isn't cheap, but this is your chance to overnight in one of the prettiest places on earth, along with the privileged few bobbing in the bay. Either book yourself into **Hotel Eden** (☎ 0185-269091; www.hoteledenportofino.com), which has doubles for €140 to €160, and which is a few strides from the harbor. Or—if the occasion warrants it (and surely you can find a reason?!)—extend the mortgage and book into the Splendido (see "A Splurge in the World's Most Romantic Hotel," above).

€   Bizarrely enough, I recently had one of my cheapest meals (a most delicious Stracchino cheese pizza for €7) in Portofino. **El Portico** is a few steps down Via Roma (the lane that runs up from the harbor to the bus stop; ☎ 0185-269239), and right opposite the Pucci shop, so you can watch (as I did) middle-aged socialites parade in Pucci cat-suits for their bored husbands while the butler waits outside.

WHY YOU'RE HERE: THE TOP SIGHTS & ATTRACTIONS

The **Abbey of San Fruttuoso** (☎ 0185-772703; €4, children €2.50; May–Sept daily 10am–6pm, Mar–Apr and Oct Tues–Sun 10am–4pm, Dec–Feb only for holidays, closed Nov) is the oldest remnant of the Benedictine empire that flourished along this coast between the 13th and 18th centuries. Tucked away in a beautiful cove between Portofino and Camogli, this modest complex—built with money from the once-powerful Doria clan—was the heart of the Order, with jurisdiction over some 10 churches, a few as far afield as Sardinia. Today San Fruttuoso is still only accessible by boat or on foot; sadly that does not mean it isn't crowded with day-trippers who come in by the boatload. For the most atmospheric visit, try to get here early; alternatively, settle into one of the seven rooms on offer at **Da Giovanni** (☎ 0185-770047; €180 double, steep given that rooms share bathrooms) and you can have it all to yourself in the evenings when the day-trippers finally leave.

But the real treasure lies in San Fruttuoso's bay. Seventeen meters (56 ft.) below the surface of the translucent water is **Il Cristo degli Abissi (Christ of the Abyss)** ★★★, his arms outstretched and eyes ever-imploring since being submerged here in 1954. On the last Saturday in July, garlands of flowers float down in memory of all those who have lost their lives at sea. You'd have to be made of stone not to be moved. You can either swim or dive out to the statue (**B&B Diving Centre;** ☎ 0185-772751; www.bbdiving.it), or hire the services of a water taxi.

Less visited but equally worthwhile is the **Abbey of La Cervara** (Via Cervara, 10; ☎ 0185-293139; www.cervara.it), situated high up on a headland east of Portofino village. It has beautiful sea views from the Belvedere Terrace, but the gardens are the real delight here, particularly the immaculately maintained Renaissance-style **Monumental Garden,** with box hedges pruned in rigid geometrical shapes. It's open only on the first and third Sunday of the month (☎ 800-652110; visite@cervara.it), but if gardens are your thing, head for Santa's **Villa Durazzo** (☎ 0185-293135; free admission; summer Tues–Sun 9:30am–6:30pm, winter closes 4:30pm), clearly visible on the hill around which the town spreads. While it's not essential that you enter the 17th-century villa (worthwhile only if you're not planning to see the *palazzi* in Genoa), the elevated and shady gardens, with their classical statues and pruned hedges, are a great place to enjoy a little peace and quiet, and an ideal spot for a picnic. (On the staircase alley that leads up to the garden from Piazza Martiri della Libertà, you'll find à crêuza du Gio (☎ 0185-280438), where the bearded Gio takes his ingredients very seriously and serves up great pizza and focaccia slices; he also stocks ice-cold beers. The views of the bay are lovely, and there are plenty of strategically placed park benches.

Next to the gardens (9am–7pm in summer) is the lovely **Chiesa San Giacomo;** it's worth checking out the baroque interior and the frescoed ceiling dripping with chandeliers, proof that Santa Margherita has long enjoyed the patronage of the wealthy.

A Few Good Walks

If you want to picnic in Portofino, head up to **Chiesa di San Giorgio** and settle on the stone benches that line the church wall facing the Golfo Paradiso—there's a little fresh-produce shop on the staircase that leads up to the church (or you can take your pick from the deli in Via Roma). Most people feel compelled to walk up to the 16th-century Fortezza di San Giorgio, or **Castello Brown** (named after Montague Yeats Brown, the 19th-c. British consul in Genoa who briefly owned it), and beyond to the Faro that marks the promontory tip. If it's a busy day, ditch this and head up one of the Portofino Park's trails.

Perhaps it's because most people in Portofino walk only when there's a luxury shop beckoning at the end, but the park trails are usually a great deal less congested than the Cinque Terre's, even in peak hiking season. All are well marked, and big intersections have maps showing the trail network.

For a highly recommended, brisk 90-minute walk, follow the trail from Portofino to Pietre Strette (which has picnic tables), and then head down to San Fruttuoso, taking the less direct path (for more expansive views) via Base Zero. Another recommended route from Pietre Strette is to follow the level trail (marked with red triangles) to Semaforo Nuovo—the coastal views here are splendid. Double back to the intersection where a map shows you the descent to San Rocco and Punta Chiappa, where you can catch a well-deserved ferry home.

GENOA

"Ever been to Marseilles? Well, Genoa is worse." This was a pretty standard response from the few people I knew who had actually been to Genoa before I made my first visit to the city, in 2005. Which is why I was shocked back then to find myself wandering the narrow winding alleyways of its ancient heart—the largest preserved medieval center in Europe—totally enraptured. I marveled at the myriad tiny bustling shops, their shopkeepers seemingly unaware of the magnificence of their vaulted ceilings, frescoed alcoves, and marble pillars. How misinformed its detractors were! This was like stepping into a massive film set, an urban labyrinth designed for a scene from the Middle Ages, yet bizarrely with all the actors in 21st-century fashions.

The contrasts everywhere are extreme: Right next to the cafe, which looks just as it did when Verdi took his coffee here 150 years ago, a small furniture boutique showcases the best in modern Italian design; glamorous middle-age women, wearing chunky jewelry and dark shades, stride past veiled Muslim shopkeepers; and a few steps past gloomy lanes where prostitutes eye potential customers, a white-aproned fishmonger digs his fingers into a silver mountain of perfect *acciughe,* the contents of his stall so fresh it smells of the sea. It's exotic, and best of all, this "secret, inward-looking casbah city" (as Renzo Piano, Genoa's celebrated architect, fondly describes it) is relatively undiscovered. All around you are the lilting sounds of Italian, with barely another tourist in sight. Given that its urban regeneration dates back a mere decade, it's simply a matter of time before this "Venice without water" joins the list of must-see destinations in Italy.

Beyond the labyrinthine *centro storico,* which abuts the Porto Antico (home to the largest aquarium in Europe), Genoa is not a conventionally attractive city. It has a large industrial sector leading to massive urban degeneration, and many of its hillsides are blighted by ugly apartment blocks dating from the 1960s. To get the most out of your stay (and, yes, Genoa definitely warrants a few nights), base yourself in the *centro storico* and confine yourself to exploring the many attractions that lie within this charming medieval village—a virtual island within a city that sprawls 34km (21 miles) along the coast.

A BRIEF HISTORY OF GENOA

Genoa has always been a mercantile city. By A.D. 1000, Genoa was already minting its own money. Its power lay in its ability to dominate the Mediterranean, with superior boat-building skills and a ready army of mariners. The end of the medieval period saw a gradual waning in Genoa's maritime dominance, but the ruling oligarchy, made up of a few powerful families—headed in the mid–16th century by Admiral Andrea Doria, a naval genius—had by now diversified into banking and financing, and thrived on exploiting the political intrigues of the times. By loaning money to the various monarchs embroiled in imperialist wars, and charging a whopping 10% to 40% interest for the favor, Genoa, already impossibly wealthy, became the most glamorous city in Europe, so much so that the period between 1550 and 1650 became known as the "century of the Genoese," and the city as La Superb (The Proud).

But fortunes declined as emerging nations aggressively moved into the shrinking Mediterranean trade arena (sapped, ironically enough, by the discovery of Atlantic trade routes by Columbus, now one of Genoa's most famous sons, but forced at the time to turn to Spain to fund his ambitious journey). By the beginning of the 19th century, Genoa found itself stagnating economically, but politically it remained a hotbed of plot and intrigue. Stirred by the speeches of Giuseppe Mazzini (born here in 1805), the fiercely determined Giuseppe Garibaldi sailed from Genoa

> " *Gold is born in the Americas, dies in Seville, and is buried in Genoa.* "
>
> —A popular 16th-century saying, referring to the power of the Genoese bankers of the time

to Sicily with his "thousand Red Shirts" in 1860, and so set in motion the force that would flatten all resistance to the unification of Italy.

The 1900s saw the maritime city turn into a major industrial center, much of it state-controlled, and huge urban construction projects that led to the visual decay of the city. Many middle-class Genoese fled to the outlying green hills. It was only in 1992, when the 5th centenary of the voyage of Christopher Columbus appeared on the events calendar, that the city fathers awoke from their long slumber and kick-started various urban renewal projects. The process was further stimulated by the city's hosting the G8 summit in 2001, and being designated Cultural Capital of Europe in 2004. With a record 3.2 million visitors last year, it would seem that Genoa the Proud is on the rise once again.

LAY OF THE LAND

Aeroporto Cristoforo Colombo (www.airport.genova.it) is 20 to 30 minutes from the old city center. A **taxi** ride costs €25; the VolaBus 100 only €3 (it runs every half-hour). You can also get to Genoa **by boat** from Sardinia and Sicily, or from various points along the Ligurian coast. Based in Camogli, Golfo Paradiso ferries (www.golfoparadiso.it) serve the east coast, including Cinque Terre and Portofino. Homegrown **Consorzia Liguria ViaMare** (☎ **010-265712;** www.liguria viamare.it) covers the same area as well, offering harbor tours, whale-watching trips, special night trips, and a few stops along the west coast; both depart from the Porto Antico.

Your energies should be focused on Genoa's medieval heart, the *centro storico,* and the best (and usually only) way to get around this pedestrian area is on foot. If you're arriving **by train,** alight at **Stazione Principe** (home to a small but excellent tourist bureau; pick up a copy of the detailed city map, which has every street in the medieval city marked). Walk down Via Balbi to Via Garibaldi (the northern borders of the historical area), stopping off to view a few museums, and then lose yourself in the *centro storico,* which bleeds out into the Porto Antico, home to the aquarium (a 10-min. direct walk from the station).

If you're overnighting in the "modern" side of town, get off one stop earlier, at **Stazione Brignole.** From here catch a bus (€1) to Piazza Ferrarri (the eastern boundary of the old town) and head west.

If you'd like to get a better sense of the city, including its hillside neighborhoods, the 3-hour **Girocittà bus tour** (☎ 010-5959779; €13) gives an insight into the extraordinary variety of Genoa, and includes a short walking tour of the historical center. More satisfying and focused **walking tours** (historical center or the interiors of the *palazzi* that line Via Garibaldi) are offered once weekly from June to mid-September; both are fascinating and an unbelievably good value at €5. To find out when these are running this year, call ☎ **010-2359331** or e-mail anna.daneri@virgilio.it.

Note: The one time you don't want to be in Genoa is during the Salone Nautico Internazionale (International Boat Show) held every year in October (see www.fiera.ge.it for exact dates). Prices skyrocket and you'll be lucky to find a bed.

ACCOMMODATIONS, BOTH STANDARD & NOT

€   Genoa's upscale **youth hostel** (Passo Costanzi, 120n; ☎ 010-2442457; www. ostellionline.org), rated as one of the best in Europe, is large, clean, and functional, with great views of the port, and at €15 a night offers the cheapest bed in town. Its biggest drawback (besides the institutional atmosphere) is that it's a 20-minute bus trip from town, and another 5 to 10 minutes into the medieval center (bus no. 40 from Brignole station; from Principe station you need to change from no. 35 to 40). Stay there only if you're on the strictest of budgets.

An Unwelcome Visitor to Genoa

In July 2005, more than 100 people were admitted to hospitals with fevers, headaches, and watery eyes after spending the day at the beach. The culprit? An increasingly warm Mediterranean sea has led to toxic warm-water algae blooming this far north for the first time. Before taking to the waves, check the status of the water with your host or nearest tourism bureau.

The following suggestions (with the exception of Villa Pagoda) are all conveniently located in the medieval heart of the city:

€€–€€€€   **Hotel Colombo** (Via Porta Soprana, 27/59R; ☎ 010-2513643; www.hotelcolombo.it), a two-star hotel in the historical center (within spitting distance of the 12th-c. Porta Soprana), is my hands-down favorite budget lodging in the city, with small rooms (average-size for historical Genoa, though) but really quirky decor (upturned turn-of-the-20th-c. trunk as TV table, ostrich-feather cushions on wrought-iron chairs, secondhand Corbusier classics—you get the picture). Doubles go for €85 to €100. Patrizia, a delightful bohemian, keeps upgrading as the money comes in—next year sees her seventh-floor roof terrace, with lovely city views (and already dressed with lemon trees and blooming geraniums pots), turned into the breakfast room.

€€   On the other side of the historical center (off Via Balbi, and very close to Stazione Principe), **Agnello D'Oro** (Via Monachette, 6; ☎ 010-2462084; www.hotelagnellodoro.it) is a charming and rather more old-fashioned *albergo*, where hands-on owner Concetta acts as an informal tourism bureau (despite limited English). Rooms average around €80 for two, breakfast included—ask for one of the top-floor garret rooms for best views (room 56 is the best one in the house).

€€–€€€€   For a more traditional hotel-like experience, the recently renovated three-star **Hotel Helvetia** (Piazza Nunziata, 1; ☎ 010-2465468; www.hotelhelvetia genova.it) offers the best value for the money in its price bracket; ask the charming manager Nedo (source of great restaurant recommendations) for a room on the second floor with a terrace facing the piazza (overlooking one of the city's open-air hubs). Doubles range from €75 to €105. You'll feel like you're still in the old city, but without the claustrophobia of its narrow lanes.

€€–€€€€   Moving up the scale (and comfort zone) Best Western has two excellently located hotels in the old city, of which **Hotel Metropoli** (Piazza Fontane Marose; ☎ 010-2468888; www.bestwestern.it/metropoli_ge) offers better value. Rooms (€89–€165) are somewhat bland but come with the expected modern conveniences, and reception staff is very helpful. Before you book either of these however, do check whether the **Jolly Hotel Marina** (Molo Ponte Calvi, 5; ☎ 010-2511320; www.jollyhotels.com) has any specials. It's a super four-star hotel floating on the harbor waters (spitting distance from the aquarium; €150 a night for a double was an excellent value in 2005).

€€€€   But should the occasion require (or budget constraints allow), the 11-room **Locanda di Palazzo Cicala** (Piazza San Lorenzo, 16; ☎ 010-2518824; www. palazzocicala.it) is worth every cent. It's Genoa's only boutique hotel, and by far its best, located in a beautifully restored 17th-century palace overlooking the San Lorenzo Cathedral and a small piazza. Furnishings are a veritable catalog of modern design classics mixed with a smattering of antiques, all beautifully offset against the stucco decorations and high vaulted ceilings; bathrooms are tiny but state-of-the-art. Rooms go for €170 to €200, but check the Internet for special deals.

€€€€   If you'd prefer not to be in the city itself, Genoa's other top choice lies in the garden suburb of Nervi (a short train journey away) at the gorgeous **Villa Pagoda** (Via Capolungo, 15; ☎ 010-3726161; www.villapagoda.it). This romantic villa (apparently built by a rich merchant in the hopes that he could import his mistress here) is a tiny four-star hotel with five-star service (unmatched in Genoa), and a superb chef (no reason to dine anywhere but on their terrace, cooled by sea breezes). Nervi has a wonderful seaside walkway, and plenty of parks and villas to explore, the most famous of which houses Liguria's finest modern-art collection. Bag the top-floor room—all billowing white curtains and sea views—and you have the makings of a very romantic evening. Rooms cost from €195 to €390.

DINING FOR ALL TASTES

€   For **drinks and canapés only,** start your evening at **Café Garibaldi** (off Via Garibaldi; ☎ 010-2470847). The huge gilt mirror behind the bar reflects a group of elegant gray-haired women reclining on antique couches while they pick at plates of appetizers; behind them, seated between marble pillars, young trendies get down to some serious drinking. It's early evening and the locals are celebrating. Hardly surprising: Get here between 6 and 8pm and you are welcome to help yourself to the wonderful aperitif buffet—free as long as you order a drink (€4 for their famous Shakerati).

€€   Because Café Garibaldi is overpriced for dining, you'll want to wander down to **Squarciafico** (Piazza Invrea, 3r; ☎ 010-2470823), another atmospheric vaulted cellar in a 15th-century *palazzo* near San Lorenzo Cathedral. *Primi* run around €9.50 (*coperto* €2) and are well worth it—the "cantina" is renowned for its simple but innovative approach to traditional recipes (like adding fresh mint to traditional *acciughe* pasta).

€€   **Sopranis** (Piazza Valoria, 1R; ☎ 010-2473030) is another of Genoa's best-value restaurants. Service is a real joy and the food (predominantly pizzas at around €7.50) is good. Set in a small and cozy cross-vaulted room dating back to 1594, Sopranis has an atmosphere more exclusive than similarly priced venues.

€€   Located in the harbor (about a 10-min. walk from Via Garibaldi) is another extremely popular restaurant with locals: **Antica Osteria di Vico Palla** (Vico Palla, 15/R; ☎ 010-2466575), the perfect place to discover authentic Ligurian cuisine. The atmosphere is fantastic: The tiny space buzzes with large Italian families and their friends, as well as with loud waiters laden with plates of traditional fare (try the mandilu silk-handkerchief lasagna; the ravioli stuffed with fish, prawns, and mushrooms; or the *trofie al pesto*, served here with potatoes and green beans). *Primi* average around €9.

Ligurian Cuisine

Ligurians are proud of their traditional dishes, which is no doubt why most menus are virtually identical, with the presence of the coast exerting an indomitable influence. Seafood aside, Liguria's most famous export is **pesto**—that fragrant blend of fresh basil, garlic, pine nuts, pecorino and Parmesan cheeses, and olive oil (because of its low acidity, Ligurian olive oil is said to be among the finest in Europe). It's often served with green beans and potatoes, and is best sampled with the local pasta, *trenette* or *trofie*. Both are slightly more robust than your average pasta, being thickened with potato; *trofie*—short, slim, twirled dumplings—are truly unique, and considered the ideal partner for pesto.

Liguria is also the birthplace of **focaccia,** a thick bread made with olive oil, usually salted or topped with softened onions or olives, but also made with a variety of other toppings. Be warned that some can be incredibly oily—always ask for a tiny sliver (you're charged by weight) before committing to a large slice. *Focaccia con formaggio* is another must try—two layers of pastry oozing with Stracchino cheese. Ligurians also have a way with *acciughe*—fresh anchovies—which you should definitely try (select *acciughe* marinated in lemon and olive oil, and buy a small tub at a deli, where it costs a quarter of the price charged by restaurants). Then eat it with a slice of plain focaccia.

Other dishes to look for include ***pansotti,*** pasta parcels sometimes stuffed with *preboggion* (a paste of wild herbs that grow on the coast, including the fragrant borage) and cheese, and served with a walnut sauce or with olive oil and sage; ***cima ripiena*** (stuffed cold veal); ***pesce al sale*** (fish coated in rock salt and oven-baked); ***polpo in umido con potate*** (octopus stew with potatoes and olives); ***torta verde*** or ***pasqualina*** (layers of thin pastry filled with vegetables, often spinach); ***capponata*** (bread soaked in vinegar with a mix of anchovies, tuna, eggs, basil, tomatoes, and beans); and the ubiquitous ***fritto misto alla ligure*** (mixed selection of fried shellfish and calamari).

The region is not generally known for fine wines, but there are a few exceptions, notably Rossesse, a delicious red from a small region of which Dolceaqua (near San Remo) is the center. The Cinque Terre is better known for its whites, of which Vermentino is serviceable (Pope John Paul II was apparently a fan and regularly requested cases to be sent to the Vatican), but don't leave without sampling a really good Sciacchetrà, the dessert wine from the Cinque Terre, where 10 kilograms (22 lb.) of "raisins" produce only 1.5 liters (50 oz.).

€€–€€€   If you're looking for a taste of the Italian Riviera in an untouched medieval fishing village, catch the bus to Boccadasse, and take a table at **Santa Chiara** (Via Capo Santa Chiara, 69r; ☎ 010-3770081), where Luisa and her husband Luigi serve wonderful seafood on rocks beaten by the sea. And the restaurant has stunning views that stretch all the way east to Mount Portofino, which is why you won't even wince at the €4 *coperto* (average *primo* €10; *secondo* €13). You can sit in the cool whitewashed rooms, with excellent art on the walls and perfectly framed views through the windows; however, I would opt for a table on the edge of the terrace, where you can take in the variegated blues and greens of the coastline.

€€€€   If you enjoy people-watching, head for **Le Colonne di San Bernardo** (☎ 010-2461252), a similarly gorgeous venue akin to Café Garibaldi, and located on one of Genoa's oldest streets (a few steps down from Piazza San Bernardo). Owned by the colorful Michele Serrano, an ex-actor/journalist/antiquarian, he attracts a like-minded clientele (like Lordana, owner of Art B&B, and Lorenzo, owner of Via Garibaldi 12), for whom he creates rather interesting recipes (Lorenzo loves his signature lobster and *martini bianco pasta,* priced at €18).

WHY YOU'RE HERE: THE TOP SIGHTS & ATTRACTIONS

With some 30 museums clamoring for your attention, Genoa offers that typical Italian dilemma—so much to see, so little time. That said, my top picks are all within walking distance of each other on pleasant streets from which vehicular traffic is banned. Your stroll will include the following:

1. The *centro storico.* This is the city's ancient heart, dating between the 12th and 16th century, where space constraints forced its inhabitants to build ever upwards, resulting in a sort of medieval Manhattan. The converging buildings create narrow, twisting lanes, which every now and then open onto "breathing spaces": tiny squares, often lined with cafes or bars. You might want to ignore the stops I advise below and just lose yourself here.
2. The **Strada Nuova,** the city's famous Renaissance streets. These include Via Garibaldi, created in the mid–16th century and known as Rue des Rois (Street of Kings) and Via Balbi, created in the early 17th century. Both are living proof of the city's historical high point, when its wealthiest flexed gilded financial muscles by creating semi-private streets wide enough for new carriages, from which they would enter mansions that were the envy of Europe.
3. **Porto Antico,** home to Europe's largest aquarium. Besides offering that structure, the harbor affords a pleasant albeit touristy stroll (particularly at night, when the views of the terraced city are splendid), and is a must-see for anyone traveling with kids.

Centro Storico ★★★

From Via Garibaldi, you can plunge directly into the labyrinthine *centro storico* and get thoroughly lost—even armed with a map, you'll be tempted to take a short cut only to find yourself a few steps from where you started. If you'd like to see a house museum, with a smaller but more focused art collection, stop at **Palazzo Spinola** (Piazza Pellicceria, 1; ☎ 010-2705300; free admission with museum card; Tues–Sat 8:30am–7:30pm, Sun 1–8pm). It displays a smaller but better selection of artworks than those in the Musei di Strada Nuova (including a particularly haunting *Ecce homo* by Antonello da Messina, and fine portraits of Genoese patrons by Rubens and van Dyck). Artworks have detailed descriptions in English, and the attic (take a look at the rooftop to see where the Genoese servants would come up for air) has textiles and ceramics that provide insight into the life and times of one of Genoa's wealthiest families, who donated the house to the city after extensive bomb damage in World War II.

From here you should head in the general direction of Palazzo Ducale and San Lorenzo Cathedral, cut through **Campetto**—one of the old city's most charming "breathers"—and pass **Piazza Matteo,** the Dorias' old stamping grounds (before Admiral Andrea, Genoa's uncrowned king, moved up and out, building his **Palazzo del Principe Doria Pamphilj,** located just beyond the Stazione Principe).

A hodgepodge of Romanesque, Gothic, and baroque styles, **San Lorenzo Cathedral,** the city's religious heart, is nevertheless an interesting stop, particularly if you set aside the time to visit the Cathedral's **Museo del Tesoro** (☎ 010-2471831; €5.50; Mon–Sat 9am–noon and 3–6pm). Worth visiting for Franco Albini's 1950s interior design alone, the Treasury claims to house the ashes of St. John the Baptist—a claim dating back to 1099, when the Genoese soldiers who played a crucial role in liberating the Holy Land during the First Crusade returned triumphant, bearing the saint's remains. Besides the purported ashes, the treasury houses a number of fascinating relics (including a green glass bowl said to be the Holy Grail, and the platter upon which the martyr's head was presented to Salome).

Behind the cathedral, alongside the 16th-century **Palazzo Ducale** (now an important exhibition space featuring the city's best temporary exhibitions; to find out what's showing, visit www.palazzoducale.genova.it), is **Del Gesù,** built by the Jesuits between the 16th and 19th centuries. This is Genoa's finest baroque church, with a wealth of marble and gilded plaster covering every crevice (so much so that some of the city's more puritanical citizens have suggested that God is offended by such vulgarity).

From Del Gesù you can wander up to the twin-towered A.D. 1155 **Porta Soprana** (avoid the nearby house museum purporting to be where Columbus grew up; it's a total rip-off, with nothing of interest inside), or slip through to **Piazza Ferrari.** Personally I'd plunge back into the mysterious honeycomb, heading farther south to the oldest part of the city to view the Genoese church that tops my list: the restrained, serenely beautiful Romanesque **San Donato,** a million miles from the baroque style of Del Gesù, yet only a short stroll away, down Via Pollaiuoli. Surrounded by 11th-century city walls, it was untarnished by the baroque fever that gripped the city some 600 years later; its simple interior is a touching ode to a millennium of faithful worship. Holy Mass begins at 6pm Monday to Saturday; 10:45am on Sunday.

From here you can either take a look at the impressive **Faculty of Architecture,** located in the nearby Convent of San Silvestro (there are great views of the city from here), or head downhill along Via dei Giustiniani or Via Canneto il Lungo, passing Muslim butchers, bars, and the **Bottega di Barbiere** (Vicolo Caprettari, 14), a gorgeous barbershop and one of Genoa's many Art Nouveau treasures—to the Porto Antico.

Via Garibaldi (Strada Nuova) ★★

"I'm overwhelmed, struck, in rapture; my eyes are full of gold, marble, crystal," wrote Charles Dupathy, declaring: "If you want to see the world's most beautiful street, go to Strada Nuova in Genoa." Strada Nuova, now known as Via Garibaldi, must have been a real eye-opener when it was built 500 years ago as an elite new street to house Genoa's five wealthiest families. From the filthy, tangled web of the city's medieval center, you would have suddenly stepped into a wide street lined with Renaissance mansions, each covered in *trompe l'oeil* paintings, with chandeliers dominating the frescoed and gilded entry halls.

Today most of the palaces on this pedestrians-only street are home (aptly enough) to large banks and financial institutions. If you have to change money, do so at the **Bancho di Chiavari,** where you can admire the still magnificent remnants of its frescoes and marble columns. Then walk across to Palazzo Podesta to admire the grotto and fountain in its small courtyard.

But if you have only limited time, make **Via Garibaldi 12 ★★★** (☎ 010-2530365; Tues–Sat 10am–2pm and 3:30–7pm), your chief port of call; it's the most glamorous shop in Genoa, and residents joke that people get married just so they can post their wedding list here. You'll be bowled over by the contrast of seeing a large selection of the world's modern-design classics set within rooms that boast 16th-century pillars and ceiling frescoes. In the dining hall, with its 18th-century gilded ceiling and mirrored walls, you'll find a Zahar Hadid sofa that's curved like a snake.

At the opposite end from the Bancho is the **Musei di Strada Nuova complex** (☎ 010-2758098; €4, or purchase a €9 museum card here for free entry to all the top museums; Tues–Fri 9am–7pm and Sat–Sun 10am–7pm). The complex comprises Palazzo Rosso and Palazzo Bianco—housing what is billed as **Genoa's finest art collection**—and the grand Palazzo Tursi, which has an eclectic group of exhibits, including a Guarneri-designed violin belonging to Paganini (the great virtuoso who played the violin so seductively that his straight-laced listeners likened him to the devil), letters written by Columbus, and a fascinating coin collection that charts Genoa's mercantile history. Viewing the art collections is not essential (though there are a few Caravaggios as well as some works by the Flemish masters Rubens and van Dyck, who were very popular with the Genoese fat-cats of the time), but it's worth entering the *palazzi* just to marvel at the lavish decoration and fine proportions that inspired Rubens to publish a book of his drawings of the Strada Nuova.

A Savings Tip

Genoa's best bargain is the **museum card,** which costs €9 and provides 24-hour free entry to 20 museums (including all those listed here), as well as reduced fare at top attractions like the aquarium; €10 includes free 24-hour bus travel; and €15 buys you 3 days—just make sure one of your free days doesn't fall on a Monday, when most of the museums are closed. Purchase the card from the bookshop adjacent to the Strada Nuova museum complex in Via Garibaldi.

Built in the style of Via Garibaldi by the Balbi and Durazzi families in the early 1600s, **Via Balbi** is Genoa's equally famous street. However, its traffic makes it less pleasant than the pedestrians-only Via Garibaldi, and there is one stop really worth making: the **Palazzo Reale** (Via Balbi, 10; ☎ 010-2710211; €4; Tues–Wed 9am–1:30pm, Thurs–Sun 9am–7pm). This is by far the most beautiful and luxurious of Genoa's palaces, not least because it was home to the Savoyard royals, who spared no expense in outdoing every other home in the city. They covered every inch with gold and created a hall of mirrors that challenged the supremacy of the Palace at Versailles as *the* royal residence in Europe. Unless you wait for the half-hourly guided tour (which is recommended, though the rooms do have brief historical descriptions), you can nip through in about 20 minutes, by which time your neck will be aching (not for nothing did Gustave Flaubert wax lyrical about "the beautiful ceilings of the palaces of Genoa, under which it would be such a delight to love").

Porto Antico ★

The **Porto Antico (old port)** 🧒 is indeed very touristy, but it's also a balm for beleaguered parents, who come here in droves to visit Europe's largest **Aquarium ★** (☎ 010-2345; www.acquario.ge.it; €13 adults, children 4–12 €8; daily 9:30am–7:30pm). Designed by Genoa's most famous architect, Renzo Piano, it looks appropriately enough like a container ship filled with watery exhibits, and has certainly put the wind back into Genoa's tourism industry, attracting an annual average of 1.2 million visitors. All in all, 4 million liters of fish-filled waters are on view, with tanks containing full Caribbean coral reefs, dozens of sharks, dolphins, and more. Most children who visit—even those who have seen it before—are awestruck. Exploring is very straightforward: A walkway takes you past 71 tanks hosting some 600 species. Set aside around 2 hours to cover it all.

From here, families with kids should walk over to the nearby **Città dei Bambini** (☎ 010-2475702; €5 adults, €6 children; 10am–5:50pm, visits organized into hour-long sessions, reserved in advance), Italy's first center of science, designed for children 3 to 14. Activities are divided by age, and though much is in Italian, even children who only speak English find it fascinating.

Renzo Piano also designed the Porto Antico's **Bolla** biosphere, a large sci-fi ball housing tree ferns and birds, and the **Bigo.** Supposedly evoking the harbor-side cranes, but more like tentacles of a giant submerged arthropod, the Bigo hoists a **glass elevator** ascending 60m (197 ft.), where you can enjoy a panoramic view of Genoa (€4; daily 10am–6pm); equally impressive is to simply take a stroll here at night and look back at Genoa, its undulating hills glittering with pin-prick jewels of light. It's beautiful and part and parcel of the great surprise that is Genoa.

THE OTHER GENOA & THE ITALIAN RIVIERA: LIFE, DEATH & ART

She steps out of the Mercedes in a swirl of lace and satin, resplendent with joy as only a bride can be. The waiting groom holds her in delight; when he kisses her, the glamorous guests (no one out-glams the Italians) raise a small cheer. This is a typical scene outside the **Municipio offices** in Palazzo Tursi on Via Garibaldi, a public ritual repeated throughout the day until the flagstones are pale with confetti and rice. September is usually the best month for **weddings,** but who knows when the spirit of romance will blossom for Genoese lovers? Get here on a Saturday morning in summer and you'll more than likely be part of the genial crowd that wishes the bride and groom well.

Tipping the other end of the emotional scale is a visit to **Cimitero Monumentale di Staglieno** ★★★ (bus no. 31 from Stazione Brignole). The Genoese have been burying their dead in this lush, parklike cemetery since 1844, and it is both graveyard and museum, featuring the work of some of Italy's most talented stonemasons (incomparably better than the city's truly dead masonry museum, Museo di Sant'Agostino). Filled with mossy tombs and imploring angels, grieving maidens and Gothic spires, it is a deeply moving and atmospheric place, and it's still used daily by the Genoese who honor their dead.

If you're traveling on your own, or want the inside track on what's happening in Genoa, you simply must stay as Loredana Galante's guest at her small **B&B** (☎ 338-8834826; www.loredanagalante.it; €50 single, €90 double). With an infectious laugh and delightful sense of humor, 35-year-old Loredana is one of Genoa's foremost artists (specializing in conceptual and performance art) and meeting her is like finding your long-lost cousin in Italy. Loredana's stylishly renovated apartment is full of her quirky artwork, and she hosts regular themed parties (a recent one had everyone arriving with a book, and reading passages aloud). Time your visit to coincide with one of these *feste* and you'll get to know some of Genoa's most interesting citizens. But don't expect to get to bed early.

If you're frustrated by how few Ligurians speak English (and you will be), it's time to learn Italian. The focus of Genoa University's annual **summer school** (aimed predominantly at descendants of Ligurian emigrants) is designed to improve spoken Italian, with grammar courses pitched at four different proficiency levels. It is also a crash course on Italian culture and history, with guest speakers from various faculties speaking on anything from Italian cinema and art to contemporary politics (in Italian, of course). While there is an entry exam, it is not necessary to be fluent in Italian (one woman I met could not speak a word when she first arrived, and was receiving one-on-one tutorials as a result). The course, which is usually scheduled for 2 weeks in September, is held at Villa Durazzo in Santa Margherita Ligure and costs €500 (tuition and lunch included). For an application form, write to **Segreteria del Centro Internazionale di Studi Italiani dell'Università,** Via Balbi, 5, 16126 Genova; for more information on the course, you can also contact Mrs. Burley, one of the language teachers, at pburley@libero.it.

The city is not really a shopping destination, but it's still a great place to check out **atmospheric *caruggi*—**hardware shops, picture framers, and the like—which cater primarily to residents rather than to tourists.

Of course, **Via Garibaldi 12** (see above), is a destination in its own right, and just the place to pick up a Renzo Piano cutlery set. And do pop into **Upim,** a department store, and the antiques shop **Galleria Imperiale,** both on the **Campetto,** a small square in the heart of the historical center; these two stores are worth browsing just to look at the interiors.

Campetto leads into Via degli Orefici (Street of Goldsmiths) and Piazza Soziglia, where you will find the sweet shop **Pietro Romanengo** (no. 71r). Nothing has changed here since it first opened its doors in 1814, including the recipe for its "rosolio drops." Those are the rose oils in which Catherine de Medici is said to have bathed. Mixed with lemon, peach, anise, lime, and orange, they make a sublime combination.

A SIDE TRIP FROM GENOA

The coastline that stretches west of Genoa, known as the Riviera di Ponente, must once have been a paradise. Large bays backed by lush vegetation and shimmering mountains create ideal conditions. But as is so often the case, its beauty has been marred by the crush to exploit its charms, from a lengthy sprawl of seaside resorts and ugly apartment blocks swamping the medieval centers to the acres of plastic tunneling that produce the cut flowers of the Riviera dei Fiori. It has little to recommend it to the time-pressed traveler, with the exception perhaps of **San Remo,** a 4- to 5-hour train trip from Genoa.

This grand old resort town took shape in the 1860s, when a Piemontese, Pietro Bogge, built the first Grand Hotel des Londres (still operational). A decade later, the ailing Russian Empress Maria Alexandrovna arrived, fleeing the humiliation of her husband's infidelity. She proceeded to find solace in her brief sojourn here and brought along the origins of a sizable Russian community. The spires of its Russian Orthodox church are now as much a part of San Remo's character as its Art Nouveau casino, built in 1905. After Maria Alexandrovna's departure, San Remo's exotic glamour was sustained by an interesting array of entrepreneurs, artists, and aristocrats (including the composer Tchaikovsky and Swedish scientist Nobel), and 190 villas and 25 hotels were built between 1874 and 1906 to accommodate them.

Nowadays the town has no real identity beyond tourism, so the experience is a little hollow, not least because a few town-planning catastrophes have all but ruined her once beautiful visage. Besides trying your luck at the pretty **casino** (☎ **0184-534001;** men must wear jacket and tie), there isn't that much to see or do in town itself, so your hotel choice is rather crucial here.

€€   Among a number of hotels along the Corso dell'Imperatrice, **Lolli Palace** (☎ 0184-531496; www.tourism.it) currently offers the best value. Doubles range from €78 to €140.

€€€€   Among the upscale choices, the grand **Royal Hotel** (Corso dell'Imperatrice, 80; ☎ 0184-5391; www.royalhotelsanremo.com) is pricey at €220 to €400 (check the Internet for deals), but still a relatively good value given its high standards, grand rooms, and old-fashioned luxury.

I'd opt to base myself in nearby **Dolceaqua,** an inland medieval village that is one of Italy's most beautiful towns (Monet was inspired to paint it) and where the Rossesse, Liguria's best red wine, is produced. Dolceaqua is gorgeous and feels relatively undiscovered, yet has a sophisticated **tourism office** (www.dolceaqua.it), excellent wine-tasting venues, and a number of charming, inexpensive B&Bs.

€€   The pick of the B&Bs are **Dei Doria** (Via Barberis Colombo, 40/44; ☎ 0184-206343; www.deidoria.it; €80–€85 double), with great views; the classy **Talking Stones** (Via San Bernardo, 5; ☎ 0184-206393), with three en suite rooms for €60; and quaint **Raimondo** (Via San Bernardo, 17; ☎ 0184-206110; raimondo yvonne@libero.it; €60 double).

12 Naples, Pompeii & the Amalfi Coast

Meet the unusual Neapolitans, and then tour ·
one of the most awesome coastlines on earth.

by Barbie Latza Nadeau

IT'S A PLACE WHERE PEOPLE WEAR THEIR EMOTIONS ON THEIR SLEEVES. IT'S a boisterous, pulsating city, with a flavor and cuisine all its own. It's fun and unforgettable. And yet legions of people are terrified at the thought of making a visit to Naples because this metropolis of just over a million people has the dubious honor of being Italy's crime capital and home base to the Camorra, the country's largest organized-crime outfit. Even though the Camorra hasn't killed a tourist in years, not even accidentally, the perception that mobsters and thugs roam the Neapolitan streets is enough to sway many would-be visitors from including Naples in their travel plans.

But to skip Naples out of fear of its reputation is the real crime. Naples is a city so vibrant it seems to be *writhing* with energy and passion, which can be downright contagious. And don't wait. Legendary Naples is disappearing fast, being replaced by everything from modern conveniences to traffic rules.

It's impossible to miss the urban renewal in progress. At the time of this writing, almost every major square in the city center is a construction site for an elaborate, new underground metro line that should go into operation sometime before 2008. The skyline is spiked with large construction cranes and many of Naples's churches are hidden under scaffolding. Museums are being revitalized. Meanwhile, there's a genuine attempt to limit some sections of the old center to pedestrian traffic.

The Neapolitans will try to convince you that they're the only real Italians left—or, for that matter, who have ever existed. They are ardent ambassadors for themselves, and will give you dozens of reasons why their city is the best in the country. And they may have a case. Naples could be considered one of Italy's most rewarding destinations. Whether you're quietly pondering an ancient relic at a world-class museum or dodging mopeds on the narrow cobblestone streets of the historical center, spending time here is like getting a shot of adrenaline; it's impossible not to come away at once overwhelmed and invigorated. Yes, the traffic *is* deadly, and the winding streets *are* crowded with helmet-less prepubescent kids careering around pedestrians and trinket peddlers. Pollution is a genuine problem, too, from pungent litter to toxic emissions from vehicles that have likely never been street-legal. And there's a good chance that someone will take advantage of you somehow, whether by merely pilfering a couple of extra euros for a taxi ride or double-charging you for bread at a trattoria. But, I promise, if you can turn a blind eye to its faults, Naples will win you over.

DON'T LEAVE NAPLES WITHOUT . . .

WALKING DOWN THE SPACCANAPOLI   Quaint and quiet it is not, but walking down the long strip known as the Spaccanapoli (so called for the way it "splits" the city in two) is exhilarating. Shop owners, selling everything from handmade nativity ornaments to Pulcinella, a classic Neapolitan mask with the nose in the shape of a beak, haggle with both locals and *stranieri* (foreigners). Nearby antiques sellers hawking silver sets and antique print figurines vie for available space on the cobblestone streets and church steps. It's here that Neapolitan culture is most revealed, and most accessible.

LISTENING TO MUSIC   No matter what your musical interests, you shouldn't leave Naples without savoring *la canzone napoletana*—the traditional Neapolitan song. It's easy to find, too. Whether you've booked a seat for a famous opera at the San Carlo Theater or you happen to catch the fishmongers at the Porta Nolana market as they belt out "O Sole Mio," it's hard not to appreciate the way Neapolitans love to share their music.

GOING UNDERGROUND   Naples has been able to capitalize on its incredibly well-preserved underground network of tunnels and caves, which have housed everything from graves and clandestine worshipers to cisterns of drinking water. Take one of the guided tours offered by **Napoli Sotterranea** (p. 495), but only if you aren't thick at the waist or claustrophobic—some of the unlit tunnels are just a foot wide.

CATCHING A VIEW   The best place to gaze out over the Bay of Naples is from the terrace of the glorious **Certosa di San Martino monastery museum** (p. 502) or nearby **Castel Sant'Elmo** (p. 503). Or, if you are down at the waterfront, the expanse of the bay from atop the **Castel Nuovo** (p. 498), across from the ferry port, is a good option. Better still—if you don't mind a short hike—is the perspective from the top of **Monte Echia** (p. 500).

HAVING A PIZZA   Neapolitans truly believe that they invented pizza and that Neapolitan pie is second to none. One of the best places to decide for yourself is at **Pizzeria Gino Sorbillo** (p. 490). Claiming that 21 family members have all been *pizzaioli* (professional pizza makers), this restaurant has been a staple in the historical center since 1935, and the pizza is nothing short of amazing.

DINING ROMANTICALLY ALONG THE WATERFRONT   In the shadow of the Castel dell'Ovo is a small restaurant mecca known as the **Borgo Marinaro** (p. 501), which is basically a tiny fishing village stuck onto the edge of the city. Many of the restaurants are carbon copies, romantic all the same, offering only slight variations of classic Neapolitan seafood dishes, but one stands out among the rest. **Zi Teresa** (p. 491) was a famous eatery after World War II and still meets the test of time.

SPLURGING AT THE GRAN CAFFÈ GAMBRINUS   Okay, so the iced tea costs you upwards of €6—but the glass is big, and it buys you a seat to the sidewalk show. This is the best place to people-watch in Naples, and maybe even in all of Italy. The waitstaff must have trained hard to be this *un*friendly, but that somehow adds to the appeal. Deals (no doubt some on the shady side) have been brokered at this famous bar on the **Piazza del Plebiscito.** Neapolitans doll up to saunter by the outdoor tables in what is a cross between a fashion show and a vaudeville act. The Gambrinus has been graced by everyone from Oscar Wilde to Bill Clinton.

GOING TO MARKET   Fighting your way through either the Pignasecca market, in the heart of the Spanish Quarter, or the fish-and-vegetable market, at the Portanola gate, will bring you perhaps the truest taste of local flavor in the city. So what if you don't actually need to buy anything?

SHARING A GOOD GLASS OF LOCAL WINE WITH A LOCAL   Southern Italian wines are fast growing in popularity and quality, as evidenced by the new crop of wine bars and wine-tasting venues in the city. Join the locals in their relatively new pastime of wine tasting. Many of them, sponsored by Slow Food (p. 592), offer a great chance to meet the locals.

A BRIEF HISTORY OF NAPLES

Naples is one of the most precariously situated cities on the planet. The historical center sits at the base of one of the world's most dangerous volcanoes, Mt. Vesuvius. From atop the volcano, it looks as if the city slid down the mountainside, stopping just short of the Tyrrhenian Sea and leaving a scattering of villages along its flanks. But, in fact, the region around Naples was settled from the sea inward and upward, with the Greeks likely the first to have arrived, in the 8th century B.C.

Naples was first called Neapolis, meaning "new city." Together with nearby Cuma, the ancient region was a powerful trade center and a force to be reckoned with, not to mention an attractive acquisition for invading tribes like the Etruscans and Romans who were lured by its climate and the beauty of the coastline. It was the Romans who finally captured Neapolis from the Greeks around 326 B.C., and quickly connected the new city to the eternal city by the Appian Way, literally paving the way for its destiny as a cultural center.

Even from the beginning, life has never been particularly easy for the Neapolitans. Over the centuries, Mt. Vesuvius has erupted, pushing the villages back down toward the sea; and wars and conflicts have diminished much of its former glory. The scars of World War II, for example, are evident in the pocked churches and quiet plaques that mark the sites of destroyed treasures. More recently, decades of crime, high unemployment, and corruption have taken a toll on everything but the city's unique spirit.

As you visit Naples, you'll easily spot the evidence of its rich and varied past. The **historical center,** a UNESCO World Heritage Site, still follows the same street pattern the Greeks used. In the area of **Santa Lucia,** along the waterfront to the north, you'll see where the Normans left their statues and castles. Palaces along the entire **waterfront,** like the Palazzo Reale, were shaped by numerous occupations. The palace, built by the Spanish viceroys in the 17th century, was expanded by the Bourbon monarchs in the 18th century and decorated in its present neoclassical design by the French in the 19th century. Back from the water in the grid-work section known as the **Spanish Quarter,** the influence of Spain's rule still rings in the local dialect and most of the surnames of the locals.

Directly above these areas are the **Vomero** and **Capodimonte** hills, where the monastery of San Martino and the remains of catacombs testify to later Christian influences. Contemporary Naples has been built snugly around the monuments of its past. Ancient churches and convents sit among the modern buildings in more recently developed areas of the city, like the main **industrial port** to the south. And all along the northern shoreline, especially near the **Mergellina** port and the **Posillipo,** modern apartment blocks are perched above ancient caves and ruins.

LAY OF THE LAND

Naples is serviced by the relatively small **Capodichino International Airport** (Via Umberto Maddalena, 192; ☎ 081-7896259), with regular direct flights from major European cities. There are no direct flights to Naples from North America or Asia. The airport is only 6km (3¾ miles) north of the city, so getting in is fast and relatively easy. There's a regular ANM **bus** (no. 14) directly to Piazza Garibaldi, the primary train and bus terminus in the city center, for under €2, but you'll still have to get to your hotel from there. A **taxi** direct from the airport should cost between €12 and €25, depending on the disposition of the driver.

One of the easiest ways to visit Naples from other cities in Europe is **by train.** Tickets within Italy can be booked online at www.trenitalia.com, but tickets still have to be collected at self-service kiosks in the train station. A one-way ticket from Florence to Naples is around €42, from Milan to Naples around €56. For local trains running to Pompeii or the Amalfi Coast, check schedules with www.vesuviana.it. Trains cost around €2.50 from Naples to Pompeii. Those who might consider a day trip from Rome to Naples (or vice versa) should know that while the trip costs a reasonable €18, and the ride is a little under 2 hours, delays and cancellations (especially for the last train of the day) are common on this route and might throw a wrench in your plans. To help **plan your train travel** in this region, consult **Campania Transport** (www.campaniatrasporti.it), which covers all networks in the region.

The city's **main Centrale train station,** on Piazza Garibaldi, is not the most pleasant point of arrival, as most of the parking area in front is (at press time) a giant construction site for the new underground metro system. The station, however, is well connected to the city center and the port. But while many of the center's hotels are within walking distance, it's not easy to maneuver your way out of the area and through the multitude of scams that await you. A taxi into the center should cost around €8. So long as you check that the meter is running, you'll get to your hotel without blowing your budget.

From Naples, it's easy to go **by boat** (**Tirrenia ferries;** ☎ 081-8449297; www.tirrenia.it; or **SNAV ferries;** www.snav.it) to Sicily, to the main villages and towns along the Amalfi Coast, and even to coastal towns in Northern Italy. The average ferry trip to Amalfi is just under 2 hours, with stops at Positano and Sorrento. It takes just over half an hour to get to Capri, and only 15 minutes longer for Ischia. The ferries to Sicily take 8 to 10 hours. Most trips are overnight journeys with sleeping cabins available for an additional €40 (another €10–€15 on top of that for a private berth).

In Naples, there is no shortage of boat companies that will ferry you from the coast to the islands. Simply go to the ferry dock at Molo Beverello (the port of Naples, across from the gloomy fortress), where you'll find ticket stands for all the major companies at a fixed kiosk. You can browse the signs posted above each company's name, listing the next departure and destinations. There's no need to book ahead but you should be wary of anyone selling a service without tickets, unless you actually see the boat, or better yet, are on it. Some so-called private tour companies are just scams.

You can generally buy your tickets the same day you're traveling, but be sure to check whether the boats are delayed by choppy seas or other unforeseen problems. The most efficient of the line is **Metro del Mare** (☎ 199-600700; www.metrodelmare.com), which operates huge no-nonsense hydrofoils. What they offer is more like a bus service on the water than a Mediterranean cruise, but they're generally on time and will almost always get you where you're going.

GETTING AROUND

The best way to get around Naples is as a very alert, quick-footed pedestrian. **City buses** (www.sita-on-line.it) are almost always packed and do get stuck in traffic—it's faster to walk. The city is adding to its already impressive underground system, **Metronapoli** (www.metro.na.it), with new subway stops now under construction (you won't miss them) at many of the city's major *piazze*. Until the new lines are completed in 2008, the subway is not to be considered for travel in the city center, although it is very efficient to get to outer areas like Capodimonte. The **funicular system** (☎ 800-568866; www.metro.na.it), also run by Metronapoli, is useful to get to the top of the Vomero.

INTRODUCTORY TOURS

If you aren't able to trek around the cobblestone streets or climb the hills, consider using the hop-on **City Sightseeing Napoli** (Piazza del Municipio; ☎ 081-5517279, www.napoli.city-sightseeing.it; €18 adults, €9 child, €54 family). These top-down bus tours have become standard in Italian cities since 2000. They are a great way to see the city quickly, though they are limited to three routes, so offbeat exploration is not an option. Drivers speak English, and you buy your ticket, which is valid for 24 hours, from the attendant on the bus. You can get off at any stop and get back on when the bus passes by again. The whole tour takes about an hour and 15 minutes. All three routes have audio narrations in eight languages, and all leave from the busy Piazza Municipo behind the Castel Nuovo. Those who have time for only one tour will probably want to hop aboard Route A buses as they cover most of the city's highlights.

> ❝ *If Napoli, Italy's southern capital, was a man, it would be the 'bad boy' of every woman's dreams.* ❞
>
> —Francesca Di Meglio, Italian-American journalist, 2004

Napolijamm (Via Sannio, 9; ☎ 081-5621313 or 393-9164547; €18) is one of Naples's more interesting guided walking-tour companies, offering a range of itineraries. I'd recommend the blue tour, which takes you around sites of miracles and mysteries. You need to book at least 24 hours in advance, and tours start promptly at 9:30am. The tour lasts 4 hours but is worth it if you have time.

ACCOMMODATIONS, BOTH STANDARD & NOT

Anyone who has fallen for the chaotic charms of Naples knows that an overnight stay in the city core is a must. Whether you choose a funky hotel around the Scappanapoli or a waterfront room with a view, sleeping in the city is a far better choice than in the suburbs. The all-inclusive tourist hotels on the outskirts should be saved for those simply transiting to Pompeii (p. 508) and the Amalfi Coast (p. 510), and even then they are probably best avoided. Also best avoided is sleeping in the Spanish Quarter. There are a few reputable hotels there, but safety is not guaranteed—and if you can't leave your room for dinner, why bother?

HOME STAYS

Three really excellent Web-based services are available for finding out-of-the-ordinary accommodations in Naples and along the entire Amalfi Coast. **My Home Your Home** ★★★ 🏠 (Via Duomo, 196; ☎ 081-19565835; www.myhomeyour home.it) offers some choice apartments, many of them converted attics and walled-off sections of larger apartments. Most run around €90 a night for a bedroom, bathroom, kitchen, and living area. This is a particularly suitable option if you have children because you'll have kitchen access, and most of the owners will provide extra beds or fold-out sofas to accommodate everyone. Here, too, you'll find extraordinary (read: expensive) opportunities, such as renting the top floor of the 10th-century Badia di Santa Maria Olearia monastery (complete with Guido, the caretaker, at your disposal) for a week, for six adults, for around €2,500—if you're looking to justify such an expense, it only comes to about €60 a day per person).

Another service that tends to provide more economical options is **Rent A Bed** ★ (Vico Sergente Maggiore, 16; ☎ 081-417721; www.rentabed.com). It's the best source for finding rooms in occupied private apartments, farmhouses, and even docked boats in Naples and along the Amalfi Coast. Prices start at around €21 a night per person, and rarely top €100. Of the many I recently inspected, not one was a disappointment, whether it was a sun-drenched, chic Scandinavian-modern place in the historical center (€90) or a very simple but white-glove-clean apartment in the residential hill zone (€40). The website gives full details and photos, and has expanded its service to the Amalfi Coast and islands. Don't try to find hotels here, though; they don't have enough listed. Instead use the Rome-based **www.venere.it** ★★★, which is a growing **hotel-booking service** that is both reliable for online booking and easy to use.

HOTELS IN THE HISTORICAL CENTER

You have several good choices for safe, affordable, and comfortable accommodations in the historical center, depending on your own priorities and budget. They start on the high end with a string of old-style luxury hotels, like the Grand Hotel

Naples Accommodations & Dining

Information
Lighthouse
Metro

OTTOCALLI

PARCO DI CAPODIMONTE

Via di Milano

Via del Capodimonte

Via Capodimonte

ARENACCIA

Albergo dei Poveri

ORTO BOTANICO

CAPODIMONTE

Corso A. di Savoia

Via Santa Teresa

Via Vincenzo Irolli

Salita Capodimonte

Via Miracoli

Via Michele Tenore

Via S. Antonio Abate

Via Foria

Corso Garibaldi

Via Arenaccia

Via Casanova

Airport ↗

VASTO

Piazza Cavour

Via Materdei

Via Stella

Via Carbonara

Via Salvator Rosa

National Archaeological Museum

Piazza Cavour

SANTA CHIARA

Duomo

2

Via Anticaglia

Via Tribunali

3

Corso Novara

Stazione Centrale

Piazza Garibaldi

Centrale

7

6 **5**

4

V. del Sole

V. Paladino

Via Vicaria Vecchia

Corso Umberto I

8

9

Via E. Pessina

Montesanto

Piazza Dante

Via B. Croce

Via Biagio dei Librai

Via Duomo

Corso Garibaldi

Stazione Circumvesuviana

FUNICULAR

Stazione Cumana

10

Università

Piazza del Mercato

Via Monteoliveto

Via Toledo

Via Nuova Marina

Via Marinella

National Museum of San Martino

11

Via A. Diaz

Corso Vittorio Emanuele

QUARTIERI SPAGNOLI

Via Medina

Via A. Depretis

Via Cristoforo Colombo

Bacino del Piliero

Stazione Marittima

FUNICULAR

12

Via S. Carlo

Maschio Angioino (Castel Nuovo)

13

Palazzo Reale

Molo Beverello

Bacino Angioino

14

Via Chiaia

Piazza del Plebiscito

Piazza d. Martiri

17

SANTA LUCIA

15

16

Via S. Lucia

Via N. Sauro

18

To Chiaia & Mergellina

Morelli

Via Partenope

Golfo di Napoli

Castel dell'Ovo

19

Venice

Milan

Florence

Rome

Naples

ITALY

Sicily

ACCOMMODATIONS ■
Albergo Sansevero
  Degas **10**
Caravaggio Hotel **3**
Chiaia Hotel
  de Charme **14**
Hotel Ausonia **16**
Hotel Canada **15**
Hotel Neapolis **6**
Napolit'amo **11**
Sansevero d' Angri **2**
Soggiorno SanSevero **9**

DINING ◆
Amici Miei **17**
Antica Trattoria
  da Carmine **4**
Brandi **13**
Campagnoli **5**
Da Ettore **18**
Donna Teresa **1**
Sorbillo **8**
SorRiso Integrale **7**
Trattoria
  San Ferdinando **12**
Zi Teresa **19**

Vesuviano and Santa Lucia along the waterfront Via Partenope, charging upwards of €300 a night. But the farther from the waterfront you go, the better deal you'll find. **High season** in Naples and the Amalfi Coast begins at Easter and runs through September. Many smaller hotels are actually closed (especially on the islands) for the rest of the year, with a handful opening at Christmas time.

€€   The best deal in the historical center of Naples is one of a trio of hotels all using the name **Sansevero** (www.albergosansevero.it). These distinct properties all start at €95 a night for a double including breakfast, and are tucked inside some of the city center's most exquisite old *palazzi*. The best of the bunch is the **Albergo Sansevero Degas** ★★ (Calata Trinità Maggiore, 53; ☎ 081-5511276), whose rooms are enormous and luxuriously appointed. The appeal here is to history: The rooms once belonged to the French Impressionist painter Edgar Degas.

The second choice is the **Soggiorno Sansevero** ★★ (Piazza San Domenico Maggiore, 9; ☎ 081-5515742). This one belonged to the Prince of Sansevero (an eccentric noble who lived in the 1700s), and the rooms are stunning for the price, with characteristic arches and period furniture.

The third, and perhaps most interesting, is the imposing former palace that now houses the **Sansevero D'Angri** ★ (Piazza VII Settembre, 28; ☎ 081-210907). The Italian patriot Garibaldi once stayed here. The side reception rooms have original frescoes and 17th-century parquet floors. The problem with this place is that it's a bit creepy—namely, it borders the Spanish Quarter, which is not the safest part of downtown Naples, and the views from most of the rooms are of an old, decrepit building that looks as though it's about to collapse. Its interior, with dusty velvet curtains and a sense of faded glory, makes it more like a haunted mansion than a glorious old palace. The bathrooms are gigantic by Italian hotel standards, and the beds are great, but you may sleep with one eye open.

€€   If you must check your e-mail daily or can't live without a PC, stay at the **Hotel Neapolis** ★★★ (Via Francesco del Giudice, 13, along the Via Tribunali; ☎ 081-4420815; www.hotelneapolis.com), where each room has its own computer with free Wi-Fi. Rooms themselves are medium-size and nicely appointed with cable television (you can watch BBC World in English). Doubles usually range between €70 and €80 a night. Bathrooms are typically tiny (the type of room where the toilet gets wet when you take a shower) and it's a tossup whether the mattresses or the walls are thinner. Nevertheless, it's a great option from which to explore the area. Ask for one of the rooms with a tiny balcony facing the Via Tribunali so that you can enjoy a bird's-eye view of the lively Neapolitan lifestyle spilling out onto the alleyways below. The street entrance to the hotel is somewhere between quaint and off-putting, as is the case with almost all hotels in the city center. Here you have to walk through a courtyard shared by the entire *palazzo*, so you may trip over a tricycle or get dripped on by the wet laundry hanging overhead.

€€€€   Not far from here is the more expensive and relatively new **Caravaggio Hotel** ✦✦ (Piazza Riario Sforza, 157, behind the Duomo; ☎ 081-2110066; www.caravaggiohotel.it). This property is definitely designed for a more upscale market, with wonderful in-room amenities and gorgeous exposed stone walls and colorful mod furnishings. Rooms have original wooden ceilings and some have nice-size balconies with chairs; all have views of the back of the Duomo and the charming little Piazza Riario Sforza, where a group of local elders gathers on the benches each morning. Rooms are almost double the price of the Hotel Neapolis, above, starting at €190 for a double, breakfast included. Still, it's an appealing hotel, and because it's so new, its beds are ultrafirm (not having had the time to sag). Caravaggio has the definite feel of a luxury hotel in the making. For not much more, you can stay at one of the luxury hotels on the waterfront overlooking the Bay of Naples, but you certainly won't find anything this nice in the heart of the historical center.

A HOTEL IN THE SPANISH QUARTER
€€   Up the busy Via Toledo, as close to the Spanish Quarter as you'd want to stay, is the nicely priced **Napolit'amo** ✦✦ (Via Toledo, 148; ☎ 081-5523626; www.napolitamo.it). Its rooms start at €80 for a double and are exceptionally large—a perfect option if you're traveling with kids. The beds are solid and all the rooms facing the Via Toledo have balconies.

A HOTEL IN SANTA LUCIA
€€   Farther down toward the very expensive hotels on the waterfront is the best find in downtown Naples: **Chiaja Hotel de Charme** ✦✦✦ (Via Chiaia, 216; ☎ 081-415555; www.hotelchiaia.it). It wasn't so long ago that a lively brothel next door serviced many of the city's politicians and bankers, but the hotel recently bought it to add to its eclectic collection of individually designed rooms. This place simply oozes with character. The furnishings are all original antiques, most of which belonged to the former owner, the Marquis Nicola Lecaldano Sasso III. Nobody seems to remember who the Marquis was or what he did, but his taste in furniture was wonderful. The double rooms have enormous beds (not just two singles pushed together), and come with Jacuzzi tubs and tiny balconies overlooking the Via Chiaia.

HOTELS NEAR MERGELLINA
€€   The farthest from the city center that you might want to stay is near the Mergellina port. Here two hotels stand out above the rest. The legendary **Hotel Canada** ✦ (Via Mergellina, 43; ☎ 081-680952; www.canada.hotel-napoli.it) leads the list. Never mind the strange collection of art, this hotel is reliable and comfortable and the price is fair. Rooms start at €65 double and most have views of the sea.

€€   Not far away is the slightly bizarre **Hotel Ausonia** (Via Francesco Caracciolo, 11; ☎ 081-682278). Rooms start at €90 and have a slightly offbeat nautical atmosphere (think portholes and lots of knots), but this hotel has long been a favorite with returning clientele. The owners are personable and accessible.

DINING FOR ALL TASTES

It is often said that you can eat better in Southern Italy than anywhere else in Europe. Indeed, the food in Naples is virtually always fresh, recipes are original, and presentation is generally spectacular. Sun-ripened tomatoes and buffalo mozzarella (made from water-buffalo milk), capers, and unique pastas like cavatelli (made with only durum wheat and water) are popular on most menus. In Naples, a classic dish is *spaghettini alla puttanesca,* made with fresh tomatoes, garlic, anchovies, capers, and olives. Grilled swordfish and shellfish are also standard fare, and grilled cheeses and a wide variety of vegetables, from eggplant to wild chicory, round out most menus. Desserts in the south tend to focus on candied fruits and nuts, or on the old standby: gelato.

In general, reservations are rarely required in Naples mostly because no one ever seems to answer the phone to take them. I've marked below the restaurants you should attempt to call first to secure a place. For a **map of Naples's restaurants,** see p. 486.

RESTAURANTS IN THE HISTORICAL CENTER

€ If your idea of a typical Neapolitan trattoria is a tiny restaurant with small tables piled high with good food, **Antica Trattoria da Carmine** ★★ (Via dei Tribunali, 330; ☎ 081-294383) should be your first stop, especially if your time in Naples is short. It's only open for lunch, but after eating here you won't need more than a sliver of pizza for dinner. The restaurant will serve only what's in season, and then only if it's fresh—which means that the menu is usually pretty slim. That being said, portions are hefty, and the tabs are low, with most *primi* going for just €5. The chef has been known to come out of the kitchen after you've ordered to explain that he's run short of an ingredient or is unhappy with a piece of fish, and to tell you what you should order instead. Take his advice: This is exactly the type of experience you came to Naples for.

€ One of the strangest and most wonderful dining experiences you may have in the heart of the old center of Naples will be at **Campagnoli** ★★★ (Via dei Tribunali, 47; ☎ 081-459034). When you walk in the door, you'll be sure you've made a mistake (or, more likely, that I've made a mistake in recommending this place), but wander past the rows of dusty wine bottles to the back dining room and rouse the owners from their television program or poker game to get you a table. The food is incredibly simple, but so fresh, so flavorful, and so authentic it's impossible to be disappointed (especially considering that not one of the *primi* is over €5). You can't reserve here, so Saturday nights, when the locals show up in full force, are best avoided. Don't be surprised if they ask you to write your own bill from the chalkboard listings on the side wall.

€€ Do not even dream of coming to either **Amici Miei** ★★ (Via Monte di Dio, 78; ☎ 081-7644981; reservations recommended) or the similar **Trattoria San Ferdinando** ★★ (Via Nardones, 117; ☎ 081-421964) without an appetite. These are classic Neapolitan restaurants—copious helpings, service with a twinkle in the eye—and you'll talk about them long after your trip. The house pasta at Amici Miei is the *paccheri Amici Miei* for €8, made with eggplant and ultracreamy Gorgonzola sauce. Grilled meats are the other specialty.

The San Ferdinando specializes in fish plucked right from the waves, and their menu changes more often, but standards like *pasta e fagioli* for €7 and pasta with calamari, €8, are always good. Grilled squid is also a perennial on the menu (and highly recommended).

Pizza in the Historical Center

€   The three generations of *pizzaiole* at **Pizzeria Gino Sorbillo** ★ (Via dei Tribunali, 32; ☎ 081-446643) may convince you that Neapolitan pizza is the best on the planet. The menu is extensive and they spare nothing when it comes to fresh ingredients and overall appeal. In fact, you can make it through an entire pie without encountering any soggy crust, and each pie has that delicious smoky undertone that only the best pizzas have (most simple pies start at just €2.50). The place has the feel of a diner; your silverware arrives in a wicker boat wrapped in a napkin. It has more rave reviews than Taillevant in Paris (or at least that's the way it looks from the wall of self-acclaim at the front, where Sorbillo displays every article ever written about the restaurant—and there are many). If you have only 1 day in Naples, and are dying to see if the pizza really is better than it is at home, this is the place to put that proposition to the test.

A Vegetarian Restaurant in the Historical Center

€   Vegan-friendly, but not at all foodie-unfriendly, **SorRiso Integrale** ★★ (Vico San Pietro a Majella, 6, Piazza Bellini; ☎ 081-445026) is that rarest of heath-food restaurants in that it coaxes sinfully delicious flavors out of all those good-for-you foods. The cuisine can best be described as fusion, with Asian and Arab specialties alongside classic Italian cuisine, all of it made with only organic veggies. The mixed plate, brimming with vegetarian couscous and potatoes, is the best deal for €7, and you can easily split it between two. My only quibble is with the ambience. If you can get a table outside, you'll dine under monstrous rubber trees, but, inside, the atmosphere is reminiscent of a college dorm. Never mind, the food is wonderful, and you can stock up on healthy goodies for the next day at the store in the main lobby.

RESTAURANTS IN SANTA LUCIA

€€   If you can ignore the multitude of national flags outside the building, or the curiously well-spoken English of the waiters, you can still have a genuine Italian experience at **Brandi** (Salita Sant'Anna di Palazzo; ☎ 081-416928; reservations recommended), possibly the most famous Naples pizzeria (though I prefer Sorbillo for its lack of pretense). This is where dignitaries dine "with the locals" when they come to town, and the pizza is darn good. You'll be biting down on history here, too: The owner of Brandi created the classic Pizza Margherita (€5) for Princess Margherita di Savoy, Queen of Italy, back in 1889 (and she liked it so much she gave permission for her name to be affixed to the dish).

€   The pastas and *secondi* on the restaurant menu at Brandi are nearly three times the price of the pizza, so stick to the pies and have your pasta in a more local place like **Da Ettore** (Via Santa Lucia, 56; ☎ 081-7640498), about 10 minutes down toward the Castel dell'Uovo. Da Ettore is a down-home cafe in a swank part of Naples, utterly out of place thanks to its no-frills decor, but swarming with locals most nights nonetheless. You'll find all the classic Neapolitan dishes here, with most pastas selling for just €6. They're good, as are the calzones, but I particularly like the vegetable dishes (the perfect eggplant Parmesan, for starters). Try to to get a table outside if the weather is nice.

RESTAURANTS ON THE WATERFRONT

€€€   Hands held across the table, couples gazing dreamily iris into iris, romantic conversations, surprise proposals: These are common sights at the restaurants of the Borgo Marino, where romance isn't just in the air, it's on the menu and playing footsie under the table. All of this loving is inspired by the lovely waterside views from each terraced restaurant (when the weather is chilly, they bring out heaters rather than close these money-making terraces). The best of these restaurants is the legendary **Zi Teresa** ✹✹ (Borgo Marinaro, 1; ☎ 081-7642565; reservations recommended), which Norman Lewis wrote about in *Naples '44*—a must read if you really want an eye on the Neapolitan mentality during World War II. The former dive, named for a favorite aunt, is now a swank restaurant on an expansive terrace. But even though it's pricier than the *trattorie* in the center core, it's still a very good value—for fresh seafood and fresh pasta, in particular—especially compared to what you get in cities like Rome for these prices. If you watch what you order, you can easily get a filling and delicious plate of pasta, a salad, and a carafe of the house white for around €20, including service.

RESTAURANTS IN VOMERO

€€€   Up on the Vomero, the best choice you can make is the cozy **Donna Teresa** ✹✹ (Via Michele Kerbaker, 58; ☎ 081-5567070; reservations recommended), a terrifically popular restaurant with locals, especially at lunchtime, so you really must book ahead. Once you've eaten here, you will understand the appeal—the food is marvelous, hearty, and unique. A favorite on the menu is the *pasta patata e provala* for €12, a casserole of pasta, potatoes, and smoked cheese.

WHY YOU'RE HERE: THE TOP SIGHTS & ATTRACTIONS

SIGHTSEEING IN THE HISTORICAL CENTER

It is in Naples's center that the raw Neapolitan energy is most evident. Here you can get a genuine sense of what this city is really all about. This part of town also has some of the city's best museums and most venerable churches. Window-shop along the Spaccanapoli (made up of the Via Benedetto Croce, Via San Biagio dei Librai, and Via Vicaria Vecchia) and the Decumano Maggiore (now called the Via dei Tribunali).

Museums & Sights in the Historical Center

The crown jewel of the Neapolitan museum scene is the **National Archaeological Museum** ✹✹✹ (Piazza Museo Nazionale, 19; ☎ 081-440166; www.marketplace.it/museo.nazionale; €6.50; daily 9am–7:30pm). This is Europe's oldest and, experts agree, most comprehensive archaeological museum.

Naples Attractions

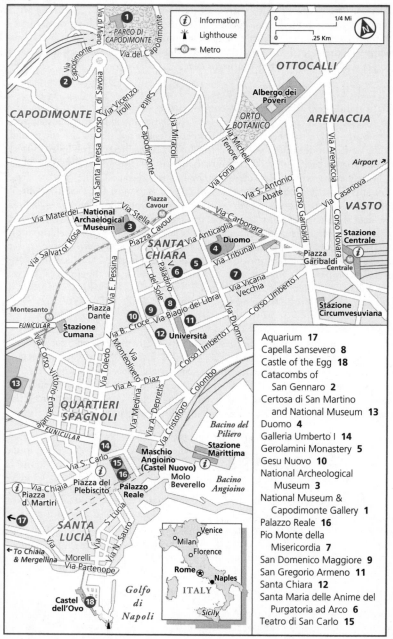

Information ⓘ
Lighthouse ⚓
Metro Ⓜ

0   1/4 Mi
0   .25 Km

PARCO DI CAPODIMONTE ❶

Via di Miano

Via Capodimonte

CAPODIMONTE ❷

Via del Capodimonte

OTTOCALLI

Albergo dei Poveri

ORTO BOTANICO

ARENACCIA

Via Arenaccia

Airport ↗

Salita Capodimonte

Via Vicenzo Irolli

Corso A. ip Savoie

Via Santa Teresa

Via Miracoli

Via Michele Tenore

Via Foria

Via S. Antonio Abate

Corso Garibaldi

Via Casanova

VASTO

Via Materdei

Piazza Cavour

Via Stella

Via Salvator Rosa

National Archaelogical Museum ❸

Piazza Cavour

Via Carbonara

Via Anticaglia

SANTA CHIARA

Duomo ❹

Stazione Centrale

Piazza Garibaldi

Centrale ⓘ

Via E. Pessina

V. del Sole

V. paladino

❻ ❺

Via Tribunali

Pio ❼

Via Vicaria Vecchia

Corso Umberto I

Via Biagio dei Librai

❽

Montesanto

Piazza Dante

❿ ❾

Corso Umberto I

FUNICULAR

Stazione Cumana

Via B. Croce

⓫

⓬ Università

Stazione Circumvesuviana

Via Toledo

Via Monteoliveto

Via A. Depretis

Via A.

Via Medina

Via A. Diaz

Colombo

Corso Umberto I

Via Cristoforo

❸ QUARTIERI SPAGNOLI

Corso Vittorio Emanuele

FUNICULAR

Bacino del Piliero

Stazione Marittima

⓮

Via S. Carlo

⓯ ⓰

Maschio Angioino (Castel Nuovo)

Molo Beverello

Bacino Angioino

Via Chiaia ⓘ

Piazza del Plebiscito

Palazzo Reale

Piazza d. Martiri ⓘ

⓱

SANTA LUCIA

← To Chiaia & Mergellina

Morelli

Via Partenope

S. Lucia

Via N. Sauro

Golfo di Napoli

Castel dell'Ovo ⓲

Venice

Milan

Florence

Rome ✪ ● Naples

ITALY

Sicily

Aquarium **17**
Capella Sansevero **8**
Castle of the Egg **18**
Catacombs of San Gennaro **2**
Certosa di San Martino and National Museum **13**
Duomo **4**
Galleria Umberto I **14**
Gerolamini Monastery **5**
Gesu Nuovo **10**
National Archeological Museum **3**
National Museum & Capodimonte Gallery **1**
Palazzo Reale **16**
Pio Monte della Misericordia **7**
San Domenico Maggiore **9**
San Gregorio Armeno **11**
Santa Chiara **12**
Santa Maria delle Anime del Purgatoria ad Arco **6**
Teatro di San Carlo **15**

Campania Artecard

The region of Campania offers a useful **integrated ticket** system (☎ 800-600601; www.campaniartecard.it) that is a great investment if you plan to go to at least two museums or archaeological sites, including many regional sites like those in Pompeii and Caserta. Even if you are only in the city for a day or two, the savings are substantial. Youth cards are reduced in price and offer free admission to all sites.

- **€13 adults:** Free entrance to two sights and half-price for the others in Naples and the Phlegrean Fields, plus free unlimited use of public transportation. Must be used within 3 days.
- **€25:** Free entrance for two sights and half-price for the others in Naples, the Phlegrean Fields, Caserta, and the archaeological areas of Capua and Paestrum, plus free unlimited use of public transportation. Must be used within 3 days.
- **€28:** Free entrance to all sights in Naples and region, but no public transportation. Must be used within 7 days.

You can buy the card at any of the sights, train stations, hotels, and some tobacco shops. In theory the card is also supposed to allow you to cut long lines at ticket stands, but in most cases, you still have to go to the ticket agent to validate the card.

On the **lower floor** surrounding an open courtyard, you'll wander through a massive collection of statues and bronze works. Most of these pieces were excavated from digs in the Roman Forum and along the coast of Campania, between Naples and Sorrento. If you're pressed for time, head straight up the original open stairway to the mezzanine floor, and feast your eyes on some extraordinary mosaics. The best of these is the large *Alexander the Great defeating Darius,* found in the House of Faun, one of the finest examples of private architecture found in Pompeii. There are 1.5 million tiny tiles in this 3-by-6m (10-by-20-ft.) mosaic masterpiece, which was dug out from under the crusted lava and reconstructed here at the museum.

The **mezzanine** is where you'll see the best of the artifacts and relics carefully removed from the lava-encrusted ruins of nearby Pompeii, Herculaneum, and Stabiae. Check out the ancient coins and the unbroken pottery—the latter seems impossible when you consider that all of these pieces were covered by 2.7m (9 ft.) of smoldering ash and pumice almost immediately after Mt. Vesuvius's A.D. 79 eruption.

To get an idea of just what kind of people the ancient Pompeiians were, don't miss the seriously erotic art that is kept in the **Gabinetto Segreto (Secret Room)** on the mezzanine. It's open to the curious public but closely monitored. The guard at the door blocks anyone under 11 from entering, and takes special care

Naples Itineraries

If you have only 1 day in Naples

Start with an early breakfast (*sfogliatella* and cappuccino) along the **Spaccanapoli**. Take in the **Gesù Nuovo** church on Piazza del Gesù and make sure you see the cloister adjacent to the church of **Santa Chiara** just next door. Then head up to the **National Archaeological Museum** in the city core. Round out the morning with the **Castel Nuovo** and **Palazzo Reale** on the waterfront. If this is your only meal in Naples, make it a pizza lunch at **Pizzeria Gino Sorbillo**. Spend the afternoon at the **Certosa di San Martino** high above the city. If there is still time, take the engrossing underground tour 40m (131 ft.) below the city center offered by the cultural association **Napoli Sotterranea**.

If you have only 2 days in Naples

Buy an Artecard (p. 493), which gives you free public transportation (land and sea) and free entrance to three museums (plus half-price on the rest). Again, start the first day with an early-morning breakfast on the **Spaccanapoli**.

On the first day, add the **Cappella Sansevero** and the **Duomo** to your morning walk, and then take in the **National Archaeological Museum** (closed Tues). Spend the rest of the day in the center, visiting the **Castel Nuovo** and the **Palazzo Reale**, and add to them the **Teatro di San Carlo** and the gorgeous **San Francesco di Paola church** on the Piazza del Plebiscito. If you've done all that by late afternoon, take a boat tour around the Bay of Naples to the **Posillipo**. Finish up the evening by either splurging for a romantic dinner down on the waterfront at **Borgo Marino** under the shadow of the **Castel dell'Ovo** or enjoy a cheap and authentic Neapolitan pizza at **Sorbillo** on Via Tribunali.

On your second day, head up to the **Certosa di San Martino** (closed Wed) as early as you can and catch the views from the terrace or from the old monastery windows. Then walk down the slope to the **Castel Sant' Elmo,** and head straight for the terrace which is shared with the local Carabinieri. Also up on the hills above the city center, don't miss the **National Museum of Capodimonte** and the **Catacombs of San Gennaro,** Naples's patron saint. After you've done the upper reaches, head back down and catch the underground tours by **Napoli Sotterranea.** Follow that up with some shopping on the Via Toledo and treat yourself to a cold drink at the **Garinbus** on Piazza del Plebiscito before heading out of town.

If you have 3 days in Naples

Follow the same 2-day itinerary above. On your final day—adjust your schedule to account for museum closings on Tuesdays and Wednesdays— take a side trip to **Pompeii** or the **Phlegrean Fields** to see **Cuma** and **Pozzuoli.**

that no one shoots pictures in here. The museum also has masterpieces from the Farnese collections, including sculptures of the Farnese Bull and Hercules. It's hard to do justice to this museum in under 2 hours unless you go directly to the mosaics and Pompeii artifacts. A useful museum map, sold in the bookshop across from the ticket booth, will help you weed through the exhibits that don't interest you.

A note on directions: Don't be confused by the subway entrance right below the National Archaeological Museum, which is unfortunately also marked MUSEO. The only entrance to the museum is upstairs on the raised terrace.

The nearby **State Archives** (Piazzetta Grande Archivo, 5; ☎ 081-204491; www.archivi.beniculturali.it/sitoenglish.html; free admission; Mon–Fri 9am–6pm, Sat 9am–1pm) has more to offer than rooms of documents. The setting is what you're really here for because the archives are kept in a former 9th-century monastery comprising four unique cloisters, each with entrancing artwork.

A definite must-do is a tour given by **Napoli Sotterranea** ✪✪✪ (entrance at Piazza San Gaetano, 68; ☎ 081-296 944; €9; tours Mon–Fri at noon, 2, and 4pm with a special 9pm tour on Thurs and a 6pm tour on weekends). These private, guided tours in English, Italian, or German take you some 40m (131 ft.) under the city center to explore the labyrinth of tunnels that have served as aqueducts, catacombs, clandestine worship space, and, most recently, a garbage dump. Pro-Mussolini graffiti line the walls of the ancient cisterns. One especially poignant exhibit is a cordoned-off area with a rusty child's tricycle and several tiny beds, from the days when these caves were used as bomb shelters.

The second part of the tour will take you down just below street level, above the aqueducts, where you can see the initial excavation of a massive ancient theater. The entrance is worth the visit alone, as the tour guide takes you into a tiny apartment and literally pushes a bed out of the way to reveal a hidden stairway. It's simply fascinating to note that the modern-looking "box" almost directly in the middle of the underground excavation is the floor and sewer piping of someone's modern kitchen in the apartment block above. This is one of the most fascinating tours in Naples today, but don't take it if you're claustrophobic or stocky; some of the tunnels are shoulder-width.

Schedules Mean Nothing

Italian museums are notorious for changing hours and closing dates for no apparent reason and with no notice. In theory the hoteliers in the city should know of any changes, but it's possible you will arrive at the door of a major venue only to find it closed for some obscure reason. Impromptu strikes by both museum workers and transport drivers are common, too, and there is general lack of regard for printed timetables. At the time of this writing, the National Archaeological Museum is closed on Tuesdays and the Castel Nuovo, Certosa di San Martino, and Castel Sant'Elmo are closed on Wednesdays. There is no "free entrance day" in Naples such as you have in Rome and other Italian cities, so use your Artecard (p. 493) to get the best deals.

Churches in the Historical Center

The archaeological museum is at the edge of the historical core of the city, an easy launching point for visiting Naples's most venerable churches, including its main basilica, **Il Duomo** ✪✪✪ (Via Duomo, 147; ☎ 081-449097). If you're coming from other Italian cities like Rome or Milan, you may be disappointed by its drab neo-Gothic facade. But venture in and you'll be justly rewarded by the stunning interior built between the 1200s and 1300s. It holds many remnants of the two previous churches that occupied this site, including much of Naples's oldest church, the 4th-century Basilica di Santa Restituta, which now serves as the chapel on the right-hand side. The left-hand nave leads to the **archaeological area** (€3; Mon–Fri 9am–12:30pm and 4:30–7pm, Sun 9am–1pm) and to more remains of the Basilica di Santa Restituta. These excavations are worth exploring to see the ancient Greek and Roman columns that remain. Remnants of an old Greek road will give you an idea of the level of ancient Neapolis.

Back inside the church, most of the relics have to do with San Gennaro, Naples's patron saint. There are frescoes of the saint's life, statues of his contemporaries, and a bust with his skull bones inside. Beside the main altar are two vials said to contain his congealed blood. In May, September, and December, the Neapolitan faithful (and curious tourists lucky enough to be in town for the spectacle) crowd into the tiny Chapel of the Treasury to witness a miracle, as a vial of St. Gennaro's blood liquefies. Legend tells us that this miracle will save Naples from disaster. It's hard not to get caught up in the moment and even to believe the legend because the last time the blood failed to liquefy was in 1944, when Mt. Vesuvius last erupted.

The area between the Spaccanapoli and Via dei Tribunali is rich with churches, cloisters, and monasteries. Each has its own story to tell, though unfortunately, not many offer any sort of explanation. If you see a nun or priest lingering around the naves, don't be shy about asking questions. More often than not, they will speak some English and many are happy to help if they know the answers. You might even be lucky enough to get a quick private tour, or be let into a locked room. On the other hand, there is just as good a chance that you'll be greeted with an annoyed shrug.

You can wander in and out of the tiny churches and chapels in this area if you've got the time, but definitely save time for the area's two most famous churches that border the Piazza del Gesù (see below). And don't be put off by the heavy police presence and the seemingly random searches they conduct on local thugs and suspicious-looking tourists. It's not uncommon to watch as an attempted arrest leads to a foot chase down the narrow streets by the police, so stay alert and stay out of their way.

On the piazza, just past the permanent police barricade, is the **Gesù Nuovo** ✪✪ (Piazza del Gesù; ☎ 081-5518613). This former 15th-century *palazzo* is now a church with a baroque interior **full of fabulous art,** from the Cosimo Fanzago sculptures of David and Jeremiah to the enormous 1725 fresco *Expulsion of Heliodorus from the Temple* by Francesco Solimena. Off to the left is a room of relics dedicated to the popular local saint Giuseppe Moscati, who tended medically to the poor. The walls are lined with a bizarre collection of golden syringes and notes of thanks offered up by the faithful who came here to ask the saint for health. There's even a handwritten note on the left-hand side announcing when the local vicar will let the devoted into a private sanctuary to kiss the saint's relics.

Never on a Sunday

Unless you're prepared to attend Mass, don't even think about visiting Naples's churches on Sunday mornings. You'll be hushed and rushed out of the nave before you can make the sign of the cross. Churches open as early as 6:30am; almost all are open by 8am. They close again around noon, some as late as 1pm. (The churches tend to open again at 4pm and close by 9pm). Stay away from churches during unannounced services like funerals and weddings, no matter how tempting it may be to steal a peak at a gorgeous bride. In time, she'll be out on the church steps for all to see.

Adjacent to the piazza, through a decaying 14th-century arch, is the austere church of **Santa Chiara** ✫ (Via Benedetto Croce; ☎ 081-5526280). Most of the church was destroyed by a World War II bombing in 1943, so the interior is largely unembellished. The fire that followed the bombing took 6 days to put out, and destroyed all the original Gothic and baroque features and frescoes by masters like Giotto. Local children play soccer in front of the main entrance in the summer, and a slew of gypsy women line the steps asking for a little *spicci,* or small change. The main draw here is its 14th-century **cloister** ✫✫✫ (€4 for cloister and museum) around the back on the left side. It's hard to believe you're still in the center of Naples when you step into this peaceful haven. And it's no surprise that these serene gardens are a frequent meeting point for Neapolitan elders, who sit on the always-cool stone benches along the perimeter. If you follow these old-timers in, watch how the ticket seller casually walks away to let them pass by without paying. But stay away from the maze of colorful benches in the center; these are strictly off-limits, and if you try to sit here, a SWAT team of church officials will stop you. Nevertheless, look closely at the details of the tiles, which range from floral landscapes to happy village scenes from the 18th century. The adjacent **museum** (9:30am–1pm and 2:30–5:30pm) is largely unimpressive except for the remnants of the church from before the war.

There are two fascinating **smaller churches** in this quarter. First is the Gothic **San Domenico Maggiore** ✫ on the piazza of the same name, which was built right on top of the church of Sant'Angelo a Morfisa. Small chapels on each side are named for those who took solace here, like Giordano Bruno, who was burned at the stake in Rome's Campo de' Fiori; and St. Thomas Aquinas, who stayed here in the 13th century and whose chapel features an icon that is said to have spoken to him. The second of these smaller churches is the **Capella Sansevero** ✫✫ (Via Francesco de Sanctis), with an astonishing sculpture of the *Veiled Christ* by Giuseppe Sanmartino, which will make you rethink any preconceptions you had about the limitations of marble.

Also worth a look is the **Pio Monte della Misericordia** ✫✫ (Via Tribunali, 253), with its own **Caravaggio masterpiece,** *Le Sette Opere di Misericordia (The Seven Acts of Mercy).* If you've got the time, you should also check out **San Gregorio Armeno** (Via San Gregorio Armeno, 44). Visit this church on a Tuesday to witness a miracle similar to that at the Duomo, this time when the congealed blood of St. Patrizia liquefies to ensure the fertility of the Neapolitans, and the birth of babies. This church, incidentally, was built on the site of an ancient temple to the fertility goddess Ceres. Nearby you'll find the city's best *presipe* (nativity scene) artisans. The figurines are marvelously detailed, and make fine souvenirs.

Closer to the Via dei Tribunali, don't miss the Renaissance **Gerolamini Monastery** (Via Duomo, 142), with its 60,000-volume library of ancient books and documents. It's not just the books you come to see but also the inner garden of the cloisters, filled with lemon trees. You pass through the garden on your way to the library and its adjacent gallery, with fascinating works by Luca Giordano, like his *Mourning the Death of Christ* (studied for its grotesque style). Also worth a look here is the baroque church of **Santa Maria delle Anime del Purgatoria ad Arco** ⭐ (Via Tribunali, 39). You'll easily spot this church by the funerary decorations on its facade, including skulls and bones on the columns. Inside, take a quick peek at the sculpted skull with wings and crossbones of the church's designer Cosimo Fanzago, the region's king of baroque architecture. Next, head straight down to the cemetery, open only from 11:30am to 12:30pm, Monday through Saturday. Here the eerie custom of praying for souls in purgatory is a testament to the religious fervor of many Neapolitans, who fill up the pews each day. From here you can peek through the side grates at piles of bones and skulls that were said to have been "adopted" by women married to soldiers during the war. These women would care for the skulls and even sleep next to them in the absence of their husbands.

Sights in Santa Lucia

The grime and edginess of the old historical center and Spanish Quarter seem to melt away when you enter the Santa Lucia and waterfront area. Whether you're having a glass of wine and people-watching on Piazza Trieste e Trento or at the nearby Piazza del Plebiscito, or knocking around the Palazzo Reale or Castel Nuovo, there's little in what is referred to as Royal Naples that doesn't impress.

Castel Nuovo ⭐⭐ (Largo Castello, entrance from Piazza Municipio; ☎ 081-7952003; €5; Mon–Sat 9am–7:30pm) is probably the first thing you see, after Mt. Vesuvius, if you're arriving in Naples by boat. Its stoic exterior is a mainstay in the waterfront skyline, with its five towers and stark Renaissance doorway. Enter from the back off the Piazza Municipio and head straight to the top for the view of the harbor. Don't miss the bronze doors by Guglielmo Monaco, complete with an embedded cannonball. The museum specializes in 19th-century Neapolitan artists, but only a few works are outstanding, including Vincenzo Caprile's *Vecchia Napoli*, which shows the famous Zizze fountain in its original glory. More captivating than the museum is the **Cappella delle Anime del Purgatorio,** which has very vivid, if unnerving, frescoes of life in purgatory and the various forms of torture. The Sala dei Baroni is where the modern-day Neapolitan City Council meets, and can easily be skipped.

Next door is the **Palazzo Reale** ⭐ (entrance near Piazza Trieste e Trento, at present the main entrance at Piazza del Plebiscito is closed; €4; 9am–8pm, closed Wed), which is not to be confused with the Palazzo Reale, high on the Capodimonte hill. This one is a natural accompaniment to the nearby Castel Nuovo. Its main courtyard and charming gardens are free, and Neapolitan nannies bring the city's wealthy children here to play. Once inside, you'll find the Grand Staircase and the royal apartments are the most fascinating aspects of the palace. These glorious living quarters were built for the Spanish royalty in 1600; later the Bourbon kings and queens ordered their expansion. It's easy to imagine the extravagant goings-on under the ornate frescoes. The best rooms are the Court Theatre, with its ornate ceiling, the Ambassadors' Hall, the Palatine Chapel, and the library with its million-plus volumes.

Adjacent to the Palazzo Reale is the extraordinary **Teatro di San Carlo** ★★ (Via San Carlo, 101–103; ☎ 081-7972111; www.teatrosancarlo.it; guided tour €2.50; tours at 2, 2:30, 3, and 3:30pm). This is Europe's oldest working theater, built in 1737 over a period of just 8 months. Tickets start around €75 during the opera season, and are available online or at the box office beside the main entrance. In Italy, the San Carlo season is second in fame only to La Scala in Milan, and its curators are working to bring back the famous 18th-century comic operas (Opera Buffa). If you can't make it for a performance, don't miss the guided tours.

Sights from Piazza Trieste e Trento to the Waterfront

Just across the street from Teatro di San Carlo are the adjoining squares of **Piazza Trieste e Trento,** with its hectic traffic circle and buzzing cafes, and the **Piazza del Plebiscito.** From the **Bar del Professore** on the Piazza Trieste e Trento, you can access a slightly hidden underpass leading to the strange **Napoli nella Raccolta de Mura** (free admission; 9am–7pm), a funky underground museum celebrating the golden age of Neapolitan music. It's worth a peek, if just for a few minutes. The adjacent Piazza del Plebiscito is one of Naples's most recognizable squares; its Roman Pantheon knock-off church of **San Francesco di Paola** is embraced by two colonnades of Doric columns. Built in 1817 by King Ferdinand to celebrate Naples's escape from French rule, the church lacks the warmth of other city-center churches. This one is purely neoclassical, but the Neapolitans don't seem to like it—which is not surprising. The church is much more impressive from the outside, so if you're pressed for time, skip the inside.

The piazza, a major hub for Neapolitan celebrations, outdoor concerts, and political rallies, is another matter. It's hard to imagine now, but this square used to be nothing more than a giant parking lot until the city closed it to traffic in 1994 to welcome the G8 conference. From this square, you can head down to the main ferry port or cross over to the museums of Castel Nuovo and Palazzo Reale.

The other streets around this area comprise Naples's main shopping district (p. 504). The Via Toledo (officially called, but rarely signposted as, Via Roma), heading north from the port, is full of upper- and midrange stores. But better than that is the afternoon "street theater" here, when, starting around 5pm, it seems that every Neapolitan is out for an early-evening *passeggiata*—a parade of color and emotion. The area is tops for people-watching. Head toward the Piazza del Plebiscito and you can reach the lovely Via Chiaia, a pedestrian zone that attracts as many street performers as window-shoppers. Via Chiaia feeds into the designer shops around Piazza dei Martiri (see "Shopping," below).

Borgo Marinaro & the Waterfront

You are perfectly poised in this waterfront district to stroll past the grand hotels along busy Via Partenope and down to the **Castel dell'Ovo** (Via Partenope; ☎ 081-2464111 or 081-7640590; free admission; Mon–Fri 9am–6pm, weekends 9am–1pm). Inside the castle itself there isn't much to see except the view—if you can get to it. This castle, the oldest in Naples, almost always seems to be in some sort of transition, whether it's a new excavation or a general shoring up of the ancient walls. Most of the building is closed to the public and used as office space, so unless there's an exhibit of interest, there's little reason to schedule a visit. More interesting in this area is the **Borgo Marinaro** ✸✸, a tiny fishing village that's attached like a barnacle onto the side of the city center. There are some apartments, but the dock area is mostly sidewalk cafes and seafood restaurants overlooking the expensive yachts and fishing boats moored here. It's a vibrant spot in the summer, but a little off-putting in winter.

If you're more interested in actually seeing Naples than in being seen down in the fashionable part of town, head up to the summit of the **Monte Echia** ✸✸, which was originally settled in the 7th century B.C. as the city of Parthenope. Getting here is a short but grueling hike up the hill from the Piazza Carolina, just behind the north end of the Piazza del Plebiscito. When you reach the Via Egiziaca a Pizzofalcone, just keep climbing until you reach the top and are presented with spectacular views. There's a garden here where you can ponder for a spell before heading down the other side, taking the hairpin stairs past houses until you reach the **Chiatamone,** just in front of Castel dell'Ovo.

Corso Umberto I

You're likely to see the grungiest part of Naples first if you arrive by train near Piazza Garibaldi and down the busy Corso Umberto I. At this writing, the streets here are made even more chaotic by the massive cranes and loud, choking construction sites for the city's new metro stations. But this part of town also has its charm. It's here that the city's many immigrants set up stalls and shops, giving the city an almost Middle Eastern feel. Here, too, is Chinatown.

There are many **churches** in this area, but the two most noteworthy are the **Chiesa di Santa Maria del Carmine** (Piazza del Carmine; ☎ 081-201196), which has a massive fireworks display from the bell tower each July 16 that you can see from all along the flanks of Mt. Vesuvius; and the **Chiesa di San Pietro ad Aram** (Corso Umberto I, 292; ☎ 081-286411). Both are uniquely Neapolitan and steeped in religious tradition. At San Pietro ad Aram, for example, you can visit the crypt of the unknown martyrs supposedly buried behind the white walls. You can buy red votive candles on the way down, and join the prayers of the ultrafaithful, who hum Gregorian chants as they reach out toward the wall—it's a magical experience and a very good introduction to the religious fervor of the Neapolitans.

Celebrations in May

The best cultural event this side of Rome is Naples's **Maggio dei Monumenti** (**Monument of May;** ☎ 081-2471123), when the city is alive with cultural activity. Owners of impressive *palazzi,* which are generally closed to the public, open their doors for a peek inside. The city sponsors open-air concerts, exhibits, and street fairs in non-conventional places and out of the way *piazze.* You could wander around Naples every day of the month without repeating your steps. It's a cultural bonanza well worth planning your trip around.

La Sanità & Capodimonte

The hill and valley of Capodimonte and La Sanità are as contradictory as Naples gets. The residential streets below are congested and dirty, and there don't seem to be any businesses other than motorcycle repair shops. Up above, on the Capodimonte, are some of Naples's best attractions, starting with the exquisite **Palazzo Reale di Capodimonte** ✪✪✪ (Parco di Capodimonte; ☎ 081-7499111; €7.50, reduced price after 2pm; Tues–Sat 10am–7pm, Sun 9am–2pm). This massive structure was intended as a hunting lodge for Charles VII of Bourbon in 1738, but during its construction it evolved and became what it is today: a palace housing the art collections of Charles and his mother, Elisabetta Farnese. In 1860, the museum expanded to house Naples's Gallery of Modern Art. In 1957 it evolved again to become the Museo Nazionale di Capodimonte and Farnese Collection. It is widely considered one of the world's best Renaissance and post-Renaissance art collections, with some 160 rooms spread out over three floors.

Don't try to do the whole museum in one visit—there is simply no way you can survive that much art in one dose. Instead, dedicate a couple of hours to the highlights, including the *Crucifixion* (1426) by Masaccio, in **Room 3;** *Madonna with Baby and Angels* by Botticelli, in **Room 6;** *Danae* by Titian, in **Room 11;** and Raphael's portraits of Pope Paul III. Once you've seen those, snoop around the **Gallery of Rare Objects** to view such treasures as the gold-embossed dining table of Cardinal Alessandro Farnese. There are also porcelain collections in the Royal Apartments that are spread through **rooms 31 to 60,** and intricately woven Belgian tapestries on the second floor. **Room 78** is dedicated entirely to Caravaggio's *Flagellation* (1607–10).

The museum is set inside the former 130-hectare (321-acre) hunting reserve called the Parco di Capodimonte. There are five lakes, several villas, and an old porcelain factory inside, but unless you're in Naples for an extended stay and have already explored the rest of this fascinating city and environs, this park is probably not worth your time.

Instead, head down to the catacombs of **San Gennaro** ✪✪ (Via Capodimonte, 16; ☎ 081-7411071; €5; 45-minute guided tours only at 9, 10, 11am, and noon). The entrance is hidden back behind the **Chiesa di Madre di Buon Consiglio,** on the left side. These are Naples's oldest and most intriguing catacombs, dating back to the 2nd century. There are two levels of catacombs, complete with frescoed ceilings, pillars, and arches holding up the passageways among the tombs. Naples's patron saint and the catacombs' namesake, San Gennaro, was moved here in the 5th century when the site became a must-see for religious pilgrims.

When you're exploring this part of Naples, it's impossible not to notice the beautifully tiled dome of the **Chiesa Santa Maria della Sanità** (Via della Sanità, 124). Below this church, known to locals as the Chiesa di San Vincenzo, are some other interesting **catacombs** (€5; guided tours Mon–Fri at 9:30, 10:15, 11, and 11:45am and 12:30pm) with remnants of mosaics and some weathered frescoes. The guide explains how corpses of the middle class and poor were left in the fetal position to signify that human beings should leave the world as they entered it. Wealthy families apparently stuck the skulls and assorted bones of their dead into walls, and had frescoes of skeletons painted around them. You'll see the stone chairs where corpses were placed to decompose for this macabre wall art. The tour takes about half an hour and is as grisly as it is engrossing.

Mergellina & Posillipo

The port of Mergellina has a real waterfront feel. The trendy cafes, wine bars, and restaurants here are a lively place to spend a summer or fall evening, but on a cold winter day, you'll be positively miserable here. Along the promenade from Castel dell'Ovo (p. 499) to the Mergellina is a charming park called **Villa Comunale** (May–Oct 7am–midnight, the rest of the year until 10pm). Tucked inside this park is the **Acquario** (☎ 081-5833111; €1.50; Tues–Sat 9am–6pm, Sun 9:30am–7pm). The first aquarium in Europe open to the public, it is likely to be closed for renovations when you visit.

The highlight of this part of town is the **Posillipo,** one of the most romantic spots in Naples, judging by the many couples who visit. The modest will turn their eyes from the activity in the cars that line the streets on the main Via Petrarca. For others, it will be voyeur's paradise. In summer, this is the best place in Naples to sunbathe, if you don't mind paying for beach space. These beaches are not suitable for children, though, because the water is deep and the shoreline is unpredictable and hard to navigate. It's an enchanting area to explore if you have time (and good shoes), with highlights like the **Grotta di Seiano** ✫ (Discesa la Gaiola, 36, or Discesa Coroglio; ☎ 081-7952003; for private guided tours; bus: 140), a 720m (2,400-ft.) tunnel with many galleries and stunning views of the sea right off the Pisillipo cape. Tours cost about €15 a head.

Vomero

Until the 1800s, this area was nothing more than a grassy field, accessible only by the winding steps of the Pedamentina a San Martino. These steps are still intact, and I highly recommend them as a way to get back down to center city in about 15 minutes. But going up these steps should best be avoided unless you're a glutton for punishment, or in great shape. Most people prefer to take the funicular or bus instead.

The present-day Vomero is a swank residential area that is not very enticing compared to the vibrant city core below. But Vomero is worth visiting, if only for the glorious **Certosa di San Martino** ✫✫✫ (Largo San Martino, 5; ☎ 081-5781769; €6; Thurs–Tues 8:30am–7:30pm; metro to Vanvitelli, funicular Montesanto to Morghen, or bus no. 4), the large monastery that dominates the hill above the city. This is inarguably **one of the highlights of Naples.** Built as a Carthusian monastery in the 14th century, it now houses an art museum, a mind-boggling display of nativity scenes, a cloister, and a glorious church, not to mention the best view of the Bay of Naples. When you enter the courtyard, pass the ticket stand and bookstore, and head left through the first set of arches, directly past the ornate carriages and out onto the tiled overlook. Here you can't help but be transfixed by the view of both the terraced gardens that seem to cascade down the hill, and the whole of historical Naples. You can pick out the Spaccanapoli from here and count the domes and spires of the city's numerous churches below. Ships and ferryboats dot the turquoise waters. Whether it's the tranquil atmosphere of the monastery or the improved quality of the air, there's something completely mesmerizing about the view from here, which should definitely be savored.

Bloody Naples

Naples is often called the "city of blood," but not because of Mafia activity. This is a city where religious rites border on spectacle, and nothing is so fascinating as watching congealed blood liquefy in front of thousands of parishioners. If you want to catch that phenomenon, try one of the churches listed below. (But go early if you want to get a glimpse of the vials before the miracles happen.)

- ◆ **San Gennaro at the Duomo:** First Saturday in May, September 19, and December 16.
- ◆ **St. Patrizia at the church of San Gregorio Armeno:** Every Tuesday, August 25, and on request if parishioners insist.
- ◆ **San Giovanni Battista at the church of San Gregorio Armeno:** August 29.

The rest of the museum is also captivating. One highlight is the **Sezione Presepiale,** which houses a stunning collection of nativity scenes, all hand-carved over the past 4 centuries. The **Cuciniello presepe** spans the width of the room, with a landscaped scene of Christ's birth, made from wood, cork, papier-mâché, and terra cotta. Carry on through this part of the museum and out into the **Great Cloister,** a serene oasis except for the odd display of skulls along the railings. On the far side of the cloister is a tiny waiting room where one of several friendly experts are only too happy to take you through the locked portion of the museum. Though none of the escorts speaks English, each is very animated and proud to be assigned to this collection of art. There is a fascinating collection of old maps and scenes of Naples, along with ebony boxes and intricate clocks. Most people come here to see the famous Pietro Bernini work, *Madonna and Child with the Infant John the Baptist.*

I recommend that you pass through a door, covered by a velvet curtain, just off the Great Cloister, for a peek at some frescoes by important Neapolitan artists. You can also wander the terraced gardens and visit some of the smaller rooms of the old monastery, but make sure you head back out to the tiled overlook for another view of Naples before leaving.

Down the road from the Certosa di San Martino is the odd **Castel Sant'Elmo** (Via Tito Angelini, 22; ☎ 081-5784030; €2; Mon–Tues and Thurs–Sat 8:30am–7:30pm, Sun 9am–6:30pm). It was originally built over the site of a 13th-century church, and it affords stunning panoramas over the bay and Mt. Vesuvius. It's basically the same view that you get from the Certosa, but it has the added bonus of an unobstructed view of Mt. Vesuvius.

THE OTHER NAPLES

Churches and museums are central to any visit to Naples, but it would be a shame not to stop and take in the local color. Sit at an outdoor table at the **Café Diaz** (Piazza Santa Maria Maggiore della Pietrasanta) or down farther at the **Lontano**

da Dove (Via Bellini, 3). There are very few tourists here, and you won't pay an exorbitant table charge (as you would on the Piazza Trieste e Tridente).

The performance begins in the morning with the buzz and roar of mopeds and tiny delivery trucks zipping through the crowds, laden with fresh bread and other products. In the late afternoons in the winter, these streets are filled with smocked school children playing soccer. In the summer, you'll see the Neapolitan elders— in windows and on street corners—catching up on neighborhood gossip. It's common to witness heated marital spats, passionate romantic trysts, near-fatal car accidents, and Neapolitan road rage, often in the same moment, and sometimes in the same family. This unbridled passion is what makes Naples so off-putting, and so captivating.

Saunter farther down the Spaccanapoli and browse through the doll hospital **Ospedale delle Bambole** (Via S. Biagio dei Librai; see below), and the nearby stores selling doll parts, from tiny feet to heads. Up the **Via San Sebastiano,** which connects the Spaccanapoli to the **Via dei Tribunali,** you'll find stores selling music and musical instruments, some so unique you'll just have to stop to ask for a demonstration. At the top of the street, cross under the **Porta Alba** arch and look through the used bookseller's offerings. Or cross the **Via dei Tribunali** into the lovely **Piazza Bellini,** which is home to great restaurants and a worthy magnet for Naples's bohemian crowds. There are even cordoned-off ruins here, as if to remind you that Naples's history began long before the trendy cafes occupied this spot.

Keep wandering until you get to the **Via Toledo,** also known as the Via Roma. This is the city's main shopping street and one of the most congested footpaths in the city. Cross over to the **Spanish Quarter,** but only during the day and only when you see the streets crowded. This is the seediest part of downtown Naples,

Surviving the Neapolitan Market

No description can do justice to the sensory overload this market experience produces. There's so much going on, it's almost impossible to capture it with a camera. Naples's most famous **Mercato di Porta Nolana** ✪✪✪ (mornings along the Via Cesare Carmignano and Via Sporamuro) can be overwhelming and downright frightening. No matter what street you approach from, you'll end up walking through the vegetable market to the fishmongers, whose yelps and howls are unnerving. Most visitors don't need fresh fish, but these people are so colorful, it's a shame not to start up a conversation with them. Many know some English and will show off their seafood, especially when it's still alive. If you have the kids along, don't be surprised if they're soon holding squid and starfish. Soon you'll get a lesson in how to cook the fish, and if there is an open jar of home-canned sardines nearby, you'll be obliged to take a taste. These burly men are possibly the most gentle Neapolitans around, and it would be a shame not to get to know them before leaving the country.

and home to the Camorra and other thriving crime gangs. It's worth a quick exploration, though, to see firsthand the *casa bassa,* the classic Neapolitan apartment dwelling on the ground floor. Residents' doors and windows are invariably open. Here, too, you'll see religious demonstrations in the form of neon shrines to the Madonna and ornate crucifixes against a sea of billowing laundry. But be careful here—it's easy to get lost in the maze of streets, and you may feel uneasy as conversations almost always halt when strangers pass by. The area is best avoided late at night.

SHOPPING

Even though there are designer stores down the Via Calabritto toward the Piazza dei Martiri, shopping here is just not the same as it is in Rome, Milan, or Florence. In Naples, you should hunt and peck for bargains and one-of-a-kind objects like handmade jewelry and nativity, or crèche, ornaments. And don't plan to spend a single euro in the middle of the day: Most shops close from around 1 to 4pm for the still-observed "siesta."

BOOKS & MAPS

There is a great selection of stores selling rare and used books along the **Via Port'Alba.** Many of the books are English translations of European titles. Many more are Italian translations of English titles. Some of the most intriguing titles are shelved in the stands in front of the stores. Owners don't mind if you browse through them.

Feltrinelli is the usual choice for maps, books, music, and stationery. In Naples, **Libreria Feltrinelli** (Piazza dei Martiri/Via Santa Caterina a Chiaia, 23; ☎ 081-2405411) is a three-story structure with lots of books in English.

You'll also find some wonderful old books and maps at the **Colonnese** (Via San a Maiella, 33; ☎ 081-459858; www.colonnese.it) down in the historical center. They also carry famous Neapolitan tarot cards, some books on witchcraft, and a stunning collection of medical texts. It's the best place in town for reprint lithographs and maps.

ECCENTRISM AT ITS BEST

Perhaps the strangest collection of shops are the ones selling doll parts along the **Spaccanapoli,** toward the Via Duomo. Also here is the **Ospedale delle Bambole** (Via San Biagio dei Librai, 81; ☎ 081-203067), a doll hospital where you can get your doll fixed up for under €60. Check out the window displays in the nearby stores. Most have rows of doll heads, piles of legs, and boxes of doll arms and hands. Walking down this street (away from the Via Duomo) in the late afternoon, you'll find antiques sellers who display their wares on old bedsheets on the sidewalks and church steps. One of the most enchanting shops on this street is the **Secretiello** (Via San Biagio dei Librai, 18; ☎ 081-5523009), which is full of treasures disguised as junk. Very little has a price tag, and the owner will bargain in English. Here you'll find silverware and teapots with family crests and a curious collection of silver chains. These items make wonderful souvenirs because most are uniquely Neapolitan. There are picture frames, tiny coffee spoons, and napkin rings that are long out of production.

FASHION

High-fashion shops like **Ferragamo, Armani, Gucci, Versace,** and **Valentino** all have boutiques around **Piazza dei Martiri.** For more moderate fashion prices, you can't go wrong at **Carla G** (Via Vittoria Colonna, 15, Chiaia; ☎ 081-400005; bus C25), which offers very up-to-date fashion options at much more reasonable prices (but certainly not with the impressive labels).

Italy's three mainstay department stores are all easily accessible. **La Rinascente** (Via Toledo, 340; ☎ 081-411511; bus: R1, R2, or R4) is a moderately priced store with clothing, undergarments, and perfume. **Coin** (Via Scarlatti, 88/100, Vomero; ☎ 081-5780111; funicular Montesanto to Morghen, funicular Centrale to Fuga, funicular Chiaia to Cimarosa, or bus no. C36) sells clothing, undergarments, perfume, and shoes. **Upim** (Via Nisco, 11, Chiaia; ☎ 081-417520; bus: C25) is a bargain shop with good quality merchandise, clothing, undergarments, and toys.

KITSCHY SOUVENIRS

Most of the main *piazze* have mobile stands selling the standard issue T-shirts and soccer jerseys for €5. There is one store, though, that is a cut above: **Napoli Mania** (Via Toledo, 312–313; ☎ 081-414120; www.napolimania.com) has everything Neapolitan, including original T-shirts designed by the clever owners.

MUSIC

Neapolitan music is world renowned, and there are more musical-instrument sellers per capita here than in any other Italian city. Most dealers are on the **Via San Sebastiano,** where it's not uncommon to witness recitals and practice sessions. There are also two music schools on the nearby Via Tribunali. In the morning, you can often hear students of classical piano through the open windows.

NATIVITY SCENE

The best place to buy nativity paraphernalia is the **Via San Gregorio Armeno.** Since 1025, Neapolitans have taken great pride in the creation of figurines, stables, and other accessories for the Christmas crib. Just look up at the Certosa di San Martino to see what craftsmanship goes into these works of art. But it's not all serious. You can even pick up some Bill Clinton and Monica Lewinsky nativity figurines. Each year local and international newsmakers are reincarnated into Mary and Joseph, and you never know whose face will grace the tiny baby Jesus figurines. Among the best of the more traditional shops are **Maria Costabile** (Via Benedetto Croce, 38; ☎ 081-5591186), which does a great job with tiny food and animals, and the slightly more upscale **Giuseppe Ferrigno** (Via San Gregorio Armeno, 8; ☎ 081-5523148), a long-established haven for collectors.

SWEETS

One of the few chains in Naples is the line of sweets shops called **Gay-Odin** (Via Toledo, 214; ☎ 081-400063), named after founder Isidore Odin, who fell in love with his beguiling assistant Onorina Gay. Five locations sell scrumptious handmade chocolates and ice cream. It's a great place to pick up gifts as well.

Another great spot for handmade treats is award-winning **Dolce Idea** (Via Solitaria, 7/8; ☎ 081-7642832), which has three branches in the city. Famous for the chocolate sculptures, they also do a great job with packaging for the trip home.

Limoncello!

To some folks, Italy's *limoncello* is a nectar from the gods. It's a sweeter *digestivo* than Grappa, but no less potent. You should only drink it ice cold. It's an exceptional treat when mixed with Prosecco (Italy's version of champagne), and delicious on ice cream. But it's dangerously strong, with around 35% alcohol content, which is hidden by its sweet taste. *Limoncello* is made from lemon peels, and when done right, it has no artificial preservatives or coloring. Italians, especially in the south, believe that it's a digestive aid after a big meal. It's hard to argue the merits of sipping a cold shot of the stuff, especially when your waiter offers you a free glass at the end of a meal. In many of the small *trattorie* off the tourist tracks, it's not uncommon for waiters to lug a frosty bottle to your table *"a casa"* (on the house). You cannot miss the numerous stores selling the sweet stuff, but the best place in Naples to buy it and learn about the process is **Limone'** (Piazza San Gaetano, 72; ☎ 081-299429; 10am–2pm and 4–8pm). They peel the lemons by hand and make their own *limoncello* right here using time-tested recipes. You're free to watch the process.

The basic recipe:

> 10 thick-skinned lemons
>
> 1 liter pure alcohol (or vodka)
>
> 2 pounds white sugar
>
> 2 liters water

Peel the lemons (remove wax first if necessary), put lemon peels and alcohol in an airtight container, and leave in the dark for 1 week, after which time the alcohol should be yellow. Bring sugar and water to boil for 10 minutes, and then let cool to room temperature. Strain the alcohol into the cooled syrup, pour in funky bottles, and seal. The experts say *limoncello* should be stored at room temperature when unopened, but in the freezer when preparing to serve it.

NIGHTLIFE

The funny thing about Naples is that despite its incredibly vibrant energy during the day, there is very little that goes on late at night. You'll find a handful of nightclubs and discos, but the Neapolitans seem to prefer lingering over a long meal to going out and dancing. Expect very few live music **concerts** and virtually no bigname performers brave enough to come to Naples. Check the schedules at **Palapartenope** (☎ 081-5700008; www.palapartenope.it) on the off chance something is going on in town during your stay.

Generally, if you're looking for a **club** or **bar,** your best bet is the historical center. Piazza Bellini is a popular hangout, where you can sip cocktails and beer at quaint outdoor tables at any of the bars. A favorite is the **Intra Moenia** (Piazza

Bellini, 70; ☎ 081-290720; www.intramoenia.it), which also serves light snacks and late-night munchies. Or head to the seaside along the Chiaia and Mergellina, where the same places that gave you a morning cappuccino will serve you a glass of wine by the water's edge.

LIVE MUSIC

For live jazz, which is oddly popular here in the land of the Neapolitan love song, try **Bourbon Street** (Via Bellini, 2; ☎ 328-0687221; www.bourbonstreet club.it). Someone plays every night, but listen closely before you pay your cover charge. The best disco is **Ex-ess** (Via Martucci, 28/30; ☎ 081-2461729), but don't underdress—a bouncer at the door won't let you in unless you fit in.

For classical events, check out the **San Carlo** (Via San Carlo, 101–103; ☎ 081-7972111; www.teatrosancarlo.it; guided tour €2.50) and the **Festival Musicale di Villa Rufolo** (www.rcs.amalficoast.it) down the coast in Ravello.

DAY TRIPS FROM NAPLES

There are some indispensable stops outside of Naples, and you won't forgive yourself if you miss them.

MT. VESUVIUS

Mt. Vesuvius is a natural disaster waiting to happen. Over 3 million people live on its flanks and down the crusty lava path to the Bay of Naples. It smolders constantly, drawing warnings from volcanologists, who consider it one of the most dangerous volcanoes in the world.

That really should not deter you from seeing it, however; the experts at the **Osservatorio Vesuviano** ★★ (☎ 081-7777149; www.ov.ingv.it; free admission; 10am–1pm weekends) monitor this giant so closely that even the slightest earth tremor sets off a buzz of activity. The observatory has survived seven eruptions and has an interesting museum with lots of models and movies.

Much like the Leaning Tower of Pisa before they shored it up, Vesuvius is definitely a "see it while you can" venue. It's a national park, a fertile agricultural zone, and a UNESCO Biosphere Reserve. The best way to visit is to take **Trasporti Vesuviani** (☎ 081-5592582; €3 round-trip) from Pompeii to the so-called **1,000 Car Park.** From here, you can make a 30-minute hike (walking sticks are around €2) to peer into the 200m (656 ft.) cone and its fumaroles, which emit a thick steam. This is the only place from which you can truly get a sense of the havoc Vesuvius caused to the towns below during its A.D. 79 eruption. From this vantage point on top, you can easily make out the lava fields, overgrown with lush vegetation. From here it's also easy to see how much of Pompeii, Herculaneum, and other villages are still unexcavated.

POMPEII & HERCULANEUM

Down below, **Scavi di Pompeii** ★★★ kids (Via Villa dei Misteri, 2; ☎ 081-5365154; www.pompeiisites.org; integrated ticket for nearby sites €8.50, €14 with Herculaneum, see below; daily Apr–Oct 8:30am–7:30pm, last entrance 6pm, rest of year until 5pm, last entrance 3:30pm) is where most tourists go to see the damage caused by Vesuvius when it erupted on August 24, A.D. 79. For 18 hours, according to archaeologists and historians, hot ash and pumice rained on the city of Pompeii, collapsing roofs and filling in every conceivable gap with a soft powder that solidified to a thickness of 9m (30 ft.) in some places. Lava eventually ran over the top of the ash-covered wasteland. Seventeen hundred years later excavations began to reveal what was underneath.

This is a massive archaeological site with many similar, well-preserved ruins. The first mistake is to try to see it all, unless you have ample time and lots of energy. The second mistake is to wander aimlessly. It's an easy place to get lost; without a map, the sites are hard to identify, and in all honesty, everything may start looking the same after an hour or so.

Pick up a map at the newly revamped entrance just across from the train stop for Scavi di Pompeii, and head straight for the **Forum,** the mosaics in the **House of the Tragic Poet,** and the bronze statue in the **House of Faun.** You may also enjoy a peek at the erotic art in the **House of the Vetti,** and a quick walk through the giant **Amphitheater.** Farther afield, though still inside the site, is the **Villa dei Misteri.** On the walk back out you'll pass the ancient tombs of Pompeii, which stood outside the city walls, as was the custom of the time. The casts of victims from the **Garden of Fugitives** have been placed inside movable display cases; the curators relocate them based on the season and weather. Ask where they are when you buy your tickets.

Old Pompeii is worth seeing, but staying in new Pompeii is not worth it. The new town is dismal and expensive, with only a handful of hotels. Make this a day trip either from Rome or Naples. (It's also doable by train from Sorrento or by bus from any of the towns along the coast.)

In some ways, nearby **Herculaneum Scavi** ★★★ 🅺🅸🅳🆂 (Corso Resina, 6; ☎ 081-7390963; €8.50 or €14 with Scavi di Pompeii; daily Apr–Oct 8:30am–7:30pm, last entrance 6pm, the rest of the year until 5pm daily, last entrance 3:30pm), in the village of Ercolano, is preferable to Pompeii, because, though smaller, it's better preserved and less crowded with tourists. The excavations here are not marked as well as Pompeii's, so this is an ideal place to hire an authorized guide. Legally, they can't charge for tours inside the excavations, but they do expect a tip. Herculaneum has many more intact structures than Pompeii, with rooftops and multistory houses, because this town was buried quickly in volcanic mud while Pompeii was covered slowly with the ashen rain. If you go down to the old shoreline, you can see many of the 250 skeletons that were unearthed in the 1980s, and the layers of volcanic deposits that stopped at the sea. These excavations are a fraction of the size of Pompeii's and both sites can be explored on the same day. Give yourself a couple of hours here with a good map (always get the most updated version from the ticket booth because many excavations are ongoing, especially at the time of this writing).

GREEK RUINS & THE PHLEGREAN FIELDS

The coastline west of Naples is dotted with spectacular ruins tucked amid the badly planned suburbs of the city. The best are **Cuma** (Via Montecuma; ☎ 081-8543060) with its **Cave of the Sibyl,** and the **Parco Archeologico** (Via Fusaro, 75, Baia; ☎ 081-5233797), with its **ruined baths** and **mosaics.** You can visit both of these sites with a combined ticket for €4. To reach them, take the local train line from Naples, toward Pozzuoli (20-min. trip).

Herculaneum

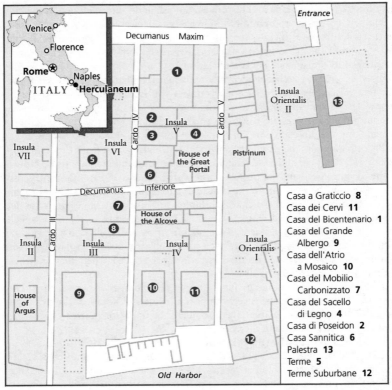

Casa a Graticcio **8**
Casa dei Cervi **11**
Casa del Bicentenario **1**
Casa del Grande
 Albergo **9**
Casa dell'Atrio
 a Mosaico **10**
Casa del Mobilio
 Carbonizzato **7**
Casa del Sacello
 di Legno **4**
Casa di Poseidon **2**
Casa Sannitica **6**
Palestra **13**
Terme **5**
Terme Suburbane **12**

SIDE TRIPS TO THE AMALFI COAST
& NEARBY ISLANDS

If you make it as far south as Naples, you've simply got to check out at least one of the nearby islands and the Amalfi Coast, which is one of the most dramatic stretches of coastline in Europe. But weaving down the treacherous stretch of highway that hugs the coast in a local blue bus or sweating it out by train from Naples are no longer the favored ways to get to the coastal towns. Now there are myriad ferries and hydrofoils (see below) to choose from, all offering exquisite views of the coast—and of those big blue buses often stuck on hairpin curves.

To go **by water** from Naples to the towns along the Amalfi Coast, or to the islands of Caprior Ischia, you have two choices. You can go from the main ferry and hydrofoil port at **Molo Beverello** (you'll have many more options here) or from the smaller marina of **Mergellina.** But before you just get in line at the ticket counter for the next boat out of Naples, it's well worth walking down to the dock to see exactly what kind of boat you're booking a seat on. Some are open-topped

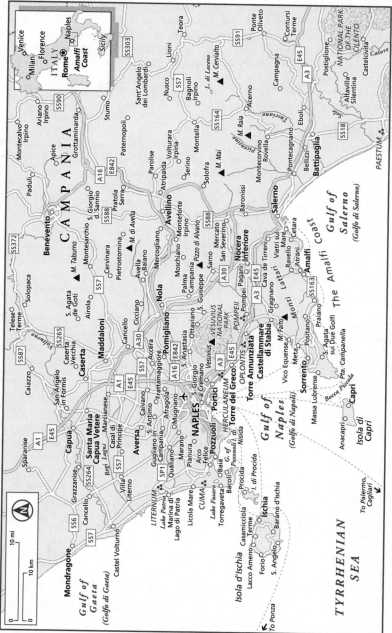

cruisers that are driven with the same reckless abandon as a Neapolitan taxi. Others are large, no-nonsense hydrofoils that are basically aqua buses. These things matter if you have luggage or children, as many of the boats are jammed with little or no room for luggage. See below for ferry information.

For info on local **SITA (blue) buses,** call ☎ 081-6106711, or check out schedules at www.sita-on-line.it. Buy your tickets at tobacco shops before boarding. For train information from Naples to Sorrento or Salerno, use the **Circumvesuviana line** (☎ 081-8780862; www.vesuviana.it).

THE ISLANDS

In what should be considered nothing short of miraculous, the tiny islands of Capri (*cap*-ree), Ischia (*isk*-ee-ah), and Procida (*pro*-she-da) manage to remain enticing in spite of the hordes of summer invaders who storm the shores every day from about April through October. Overcrowded boats stream from the mainland to these islands like ants to cupcakes, but the masses are absorbed and the islands rarely seem crowded, except in town centers.

From Naples to the Amalfi coast

Deciding between boat or bus to reach the Amalfi Coast from Naples is a matter of taste and budget. Trains go to Salerno for €10 by way of Sorrento, but you'll have to take a bus or boat from there to the smaller villages. I do not recommend **renting a car** because traffic has gotten out of hand in recent years and the roads can be harrowing. Anyway, rental cars are so expensive in Italy that boats are a much more economical option.

By Bus The most economical option is the bus, but it's also the most time-consuming. The SITA bus leaves hourly (€3.20) but takes a solid 2½ hours, longer when traffic is bad at the height of the summer. Weekday tickets for travel between Naples and Amalfi are €6.40, €5.40 on the weekends. With these tickets you can get off at any of the stops along the way. You can purchase tickets at the kiosks in the bus terminus at the Central Station in Piazza Garibaldi or at any *tabacchi* along the perimeter of the square. Bus tickets for return trips from Sorrento, Positano, and Amalfi are also available at self-service kiosks or at the *tabacchi* at each terminus.

By Boat The average cost of a straight 85-minute run between Naples and Amalfi by boat is €10 one-way. This is the best option for scenery and ease—the boats are generally covered and you usually have concessions on board. The seas in the summer are rarely choppy, but in winter the timetables can be iffy owing to rough seas.

A Suggested Itinerary

Base yourself in **Amalfi** and explore the coast from there. It's my favorite of the villages at night, so you can easily spend your days out exploring and your evenings in this enticing village. **If you have 3 days,** take an early ferry from Amalfi to **Sorrento** and climb up into the town. Spend an hour or so exploring the churches and shops before heading to the island of **Capri** for lunch. There is plenty to do on Capri until sunset, so take the last boat back to Amalfi and watch the sun set along the coast. Have a late dinner here and take a stroll along the shoreline.

On your **second morning,** head straight to **Positano** on an early ferry and take your breakfast at one of the many cafes along the ferry dock. Then hike up to the town, climbing the stairs (which are the streets) to the busy road on top. Don't forget to look back at the seascapes below. Once on top, stroll down the main road, stopping in shops along the way until you get back down to the church below. Depending on your penchant for pottery and linen clothing, this can take anywhere from an hour to a whole morning. Head back to Amalfi for lunch and then take the short walk to the nearby beaches of **Atrani** for some serious sunbathing. (The beaches here are cheaper and much less crowded.)

On your **third morning,** take the €1 bus up to **Ravello,** one of the loveliest towns along the drive, hanging some 330m (1,100 ft.) above the sea. It's a steep road, almost 6.4km (4 miles) long, with many hairpin turns, so tour buses tend to skip it; coming here, you'll be able to escape the worst of the crowds. From the main square, walk to the aristocratic, 15th-century Villa Cimbrone. Tour the vaulted cloisters and ruined chapels and enjoy the evocative views over the bay. Stay for **lunch in Ravello** before heading back down to Amalfi. A good choice is **Cumpa' Cosimo** (☎ 089-857156; main courses €11–€29). The menu focuses on a range of homemade pastas. If you're heading back to Naples to catch a flight or train, take a ferry instead of the blue buses (unless the seas are rough). In high season, the boat trip is likely to be shorter, as buses can get caught in hour-long traffic jams.

Capri ★★★

Capri is the romantics' favorite. This island practically demands public displays of affection, so why not join the fun? When you get to the main port of **Porta Grande,** head straight for the town of **Capri,** taking the funicular (€1.70) from the main port. There are plenty of convertible taxis, too, if you've got luggage, but if you're on a day trip, walk up the zigzagged streets to the top. Stop often and gaze over the stone walls at the coastline below and the turquoise sea beyond.

The most crowded spot you'll encounter on the entire island is the Piazzetta, the main square, where visitors sit at restaurants under a ring of colorful umbrellas. These places charge a hefty price for even a glass of water, but they're the ultimate place to people-watch. The square is where those who have come here to shop cross paths with nature-lovers and honeymooners. There is so much going on here, it's difficult to catch it all. Unfortunately, there's nowhere to sit but at one of the four restaurants, and loitering in front of any of them isn't tolerated. Customers are paying for the view, after all.

The city of Capri publishes a seasonal magazine called *Capri Press Guide Magazine* in English and Italian, available at most coffee bars, hotels, and stores, with maps of nature walks and events. Following these very detailed itineraries will allow you to check off all the highlights of the island, though roaming aimlessly will do you no harm. For the best **views of the cliffs,** follow along to the **Arco Naturale** ★★. The expensive boutiques and hotels are all along the Quisisana. Be sure to visit the old monastery of **Certosa di San Giacomo** on the far end of Via Matteotti, which has been recently restored thanks to a European Union grant. It was here in 1656 that the Carthusian brotherhood of San Giacomo, facing a plague, literally sealed themselves inside instead of tending to the sick, as they were expected to do. The Capresi people, angry at being abandoned, threw the corpses of the plague victims over the monastery walls.

You can't go wrong stopping by the **Giardini di Augusto** (open dawn to dusk) to relax in the **cultivated gardens,** or visiting the lookout point indicated on the signs as the **Belvedere di Tragara** ★★★. From here you can see the famous **Faraglioni rocks** protruding from the sea.

Anacapri ★★, on the other side of the island, is like the country cousin of the posh town of Capri. More rural than its swank counterpart, it has a slight bohemian vibe. It is often said that until the mid–18th century, most of the people in Anacapri had never been to the town of Capri—and vice versa. And the accommodations here are much more economical, though the atmosphere is definitely more provincial.

The highlights of Anacapri are the detailed majolica tiles on the floor of the church **Chiesa Monumentale San Michele** (Piazza San Nicola; €1; 9:30am–6pm), in the main piazza, and the **Villa San Michele** (Viale A. Munthe; ☎ 081-8371401; €5; daily Nov–Jan 10:30am–3:30pm, Mar 9:30am–4:30pm, Apr–Oct 9:30am–5pm), which was the home of the Swedish author Axel Munthe. The appeal here is the tranquil gardens and songbirds.

One of the most enchanting adventures you can have on Capri is a visit to the **Grotta Azzurra (Blue Grotto)** ★★★ (9am to 1 hr. before sunset). Entrance is €4, but it will cost you at least four times as much to get there from the Marina Grande. The average fare is €12 (€8 for the motorboat trip to and from the cave and another €4.30 for the rowboat into the cavern). It's worth the cost because the blue light inside the cave is mesmerizing. Geologists believe that this is a cave that actually sank into the water, which accounts for its almost unnatural light effects. It is dreadfully crowded in the summer months, but a great spot the rest of the year.

€€ **If you're staying on Capri** (and you shouldn't feel that this is a requirement unless you're on your honeymoon or have just won a cache of cash), the best deal is **Il Girasole** (Via Linciano, 47; ☎ 081-8372351; www.ilgirasole.com) just out-side Anacapri; its owners will kindly fetch you at Marina Grande if you let them know what ferry you are on. The rooms are tidy and all have terraces drenched in bougainvillea vines, plus there is a modest swimming pool and four iMac com-puters for guests needing to check e-mail. Rooms start at €95, though those are the first to go.

€€–€€€   Even though it's almost impossible to get in, it's worth calling **La Tosca** (Via Birago, 6; ☎ 081-8370989; www.caprionline.com/latosca) to see if they might have a room available. This is absolutely the best deal on the island, with rooms ranging from €63 to €125, but at the time of this writing the next available room (there are only 12) was 6 months down the road. If your trip is planned that far ahead, book here. It's well located, its rooms are sunny and warm, and its owners make you feel like a real Capresi. Repeat customers almost always get a room when they call again.

€€€€   Most other hotels are pricey, but what you get is a night or two on a paradise island—no secret to the hoteliers. The best of the overpriced is the **Luna** (Viale Matteotti, 3; ☎ 081-8370433; www.lunahotel.com), which has outstand-ing sea views and an Olympic-size swimming pool. Rooms (€175–€240) are slightly dated, but—with such amazing views—who cares?

Dining on the island of Capri is also expensive, but it's almost always worth it. Capri is home of the famous mozzarella and tomato *caprese* salad, and other regional dishes like *ravioli caprese,* and the Capresi are rightfully proud of their cuisine.

€€   A restaurant that doesn't feel touristy, which is unusual because this island is 100% dedicated to tourism, is **La Pergola** (Via Traversa Lo Palazzo, 2; ☎ 081-8377412). Its owner/chef grows his own lemons for his house specialty of green ravioli with lemon and cream.

€€   Behind the Piazzetta is the always simple and reliably filling food at **La Cisterna** (Via Serafina, 5; ☎ 081-8375620). The owner is gloriously jolly and makes sure you are happy with your meal. It's the type of classic Caprese trattoria that makes you wonder why you'd ever dream of spending more money than this on food. Try the classic *caprese* salad for €7.

€€€   Down near the Arco Naturale there's a wonderful dining experience to be had in **Le Grottelle** (Via Arco Naturale, 13; ☎ 081-8375719), which specializes in grilled fish, rabbit, and chicken. But the real draw here is the atmosphere—the restaurant is tucked inside two natural caves, and the ambience, especially at night, could not be more romantic.

€€€   A sure bet in Anacapri is **Le Arcate** (Via de Tommasso, 24; ☎ 081-8373325). Open year-round, this is one of the few local restaurants that tourists and locals agree on. Pasta dishes and shrimp with lemon sauce are favorites among locals. The pizzas are more than adequate, though no one on Capri seems able to produce a pie as good as the best on the mainland.

Other Islands of the Amalfi Coast

Capri isn't the only island here but it's the most picturesque and certainly the most romantic. If you aren't bothered by lack of amenities, you should consider a day trip to **Ischia,** which is a quick boat trip from Naples, Capri, or the coast. You can tour the island on the local bus for under €5. You'll also want to leave time for a dip in its therapeutic thermal waters, which are popular with many German tourists. Go to www.ischiaonline.it for general information; www.venere.it has the best hotel deals.

Procida, used as a movie set for *The Talented Mr. Ripley,* is a small, peaceful island that you may want to consider visiting. With so many alternatives, I wouldn't stay here unless you had time to spare. For more information, check out www.procida.net.

SORRENTO ✪

It is no coincidence that many visitors to the Amalfi coast choose Sorrento as a base. This is both its appeal and its biggest problem. The town, which sits high above the sea, is known for its gorgeous cliff-top views. But Sorrento is also beholden to tourists, and it's hard to find anyone here who isn't sustained by the tourism industry. This explains why the town has numerous comfortable and often expensive hotels and restaurants, and also why it's the least traditional and "authentic" of the Amalfi Coast towns. Still, it's well connected by trains and is easy to navigate in English. The old town sprawls out from the main square, Piazza Tasso, and most of the best hotels are around the Via Capo, the busy coastal road. In the summer months, it's mandatory to book ahead.

For private apartments in Sorrento and all along the coast, check out **www.sorrentotourism.it**, which is updated frequently.

€€ **Bed & Breakfast Casa Astarita** ✪✪✪ (Corso Italia, 167; ☎ 081-8774906; www.casastarita.com) is the best deal in town. What started as a summer business out of their home for the Astarita sisters has turned into one of Sorrento's loveliest bed-and-breakfasts. While the rooms are gorgeous—colorful majolica-tile floors, family antiques—it's the warm atmosphere of the common parlor, where the friendly hostesses often socialize with guests over glasses of house-made *limoncello,* that makes this such a great choice. Rooms start at €80 a night for a double. Breakfast is homemade by Signora Annamaria.

€€ **Hotel De'sire'** (Via Capo, 31b; fax 081-8781563) overlooks the sea and offers some of the brightest rooms in Sorrento at an incredible price, starting as low as €60 in the off season. The highlights of this hotel are a private elevator down to the beach and the panoramic terrace above.

€€–€€€ **Hotel Il Faro** (Via Marina Piccola, 5; ☎ 081-8781390; www.hotelilfaro.com) is another good value, with rooms starting at €100 a night (add €10 a day for a room with a sea view), which is definitely on the economical end along this coast. Room decor is stuck in the 1970s, and the breakfast is mediocre (with no fruit included), but with the money you save, you can go out for a morning meal in the old town.

You don't come to Sorrento to eat. On the whole the food here is forgettable, with the same seafood menus and decor at each restaurant. These carbon-copy eateries offer an overall bland dining experience with the following exceptions:

€   For an outstanding lunch that is slightly different—think octopus in tomato sauce, or a terrific spaghetti with clams—go to **Angelina Lauro** ★★ (Piazza Angelina Lauro, 39–40; ☎ 081-8074097). It's a self-service buffet with extraordinary homemade food and a large local following. Pasta dishes start at just €3 and are almost always excellent.

€   A charming restaurant frequented by locals is **O'Parrucchiano** (Corso Italia, 67; ☎ 081-8781321;www.parrucchiano.com), which has been in the same family since it opened in 1868. Its first owner left the seminary to found the original trattoria, and when his friends came to visit, they taunted him that he hadn't become a parish priest, or *parrucchiano* (hence the name of the restaurant). It's a jungle in here, but a romantic one, with plants and foliage everywhere. The specialty of the house is cannelloni—the waiters claim that the dish was actually created here.

€€   If you're looking more for character than for cuisine, try **Ristorante il Buco** ★★ (Rampa Marina Piccola, 6; ☎ 081-8782354; www.ilbucoristorante.it), just outside Sorrento's old town. Built inside an abandoned wine cellar, all curved ceilings and ancient stone, its dishes are varied and generally satisfying, accompanied by a superb wine list. It's a favorite among locals, so you'll actually hear Italian spoken here, not the usual tourist potpourri of English, German, and French.

POSITANO ★★

Positano is still widely considered the jewel of this stretch of coastline, but in catering to an ever more affluent and prestigious set of guests, this little village of 3,800 has all but out-priced itself to the average tourist. It's almost impossible to find a double room for under €150, with most hovering around €225 a night. And a growing trend toward "child-free" establishments further defines this area as a romantic honeymoon or anniversary spot, or a place for wealthy pensioners.

There's no real reason to stay in Positano unless you're lucky enough to find an apartment or private room, but even those cater to the fatter wallets. Fortunately, the town is easy to visit. It's well worth a walk up the steps and down the busy shopping streets. **The only real sight,** other than the obvious views of the sea and coastline, is the often photographed church **Chiesa di Santa Maria Assunta** (Piazza Flavio Gioia; 8am–noon and 3:30–7pm). The reason you come here is to explore the stepped streets, window-shop, and take in the views from along the cliffs. Try to stick to the northern side of town if you want to avoid the crowds. The best way to explore is just to wander and climb, turn the corners, and follow your instincts. You cannot get lost here—the only ways to go are up or down.

If you are determined **to stay in Positano,** first check **My Home Your Home** ★★★ kids (Via Duomo, 196; ☎ 081-19565835; www.myhomeyourhome. it), which has a few affordable-for-Positano apartments and rooms within homes for just over €100 a night. Bear in mind that the cheapest rooms in Positano are often booked a season ahead, and a good deal is hard to find.

€€   Another viable option for Positano is the tiny **Pensione Maria Luisa** ★★ (Via Fornillo, 42; ☎ 089-875023; www.pensionemarialuisa.com). Rooms in the summer are €80 with a terrace, but hard to book because they often fill up many months in advance. Rooms are tiny and not air-conditioned, but the price is the best in Positano.

€€€   If you don't mind spending a little extra, you won't completely break the bank at the **Hotel Pupetto** (Via Fornillo, 37; ☎ 089-875087; www.hotelpupetto.it), where rooms start at €147 and are modest but comfortable.

Meals in Positano are also over-priced though it has to be said that the food is generally exceptional.

€€   The locals eat at **'O Guarracino** (Via Positanesi d'America, 12; ☎ 089-875794), one of the few restaurants that is open year-round. The view from the long terrace is outstanding, and the food is reliably satisfying. Plates are seasonal and generous, most starting at €10. The clientele, many of whom are expats with summer homes here, don't take kindly to tourists, though, so it's best to try to fit in.

€€   Another reasonable dining option is the restaurant and cooking school in the nearby village of Montepertuso. At **Il Ritrovo** ★★ (Via Montepertuso, 77; ☎ 089-812005; www.ilritrovo.com), everything is either made by hand (the pasta), home grown (the vegetables), or home raised (the rabbit and chicken), and most plates are around €10. This is a great choice in the summer, but its cozy fireplace gives it even more appeal in the winter. And management will even chauffeur you to and from Positano in a little minibus. It's one of those places you'll long to return to. They also offer a daylong cooking class for €150.

AMALFI ★★★

Amalfi is a suitable alternative to both Positano and Sorrento. It has a far more interesting history than any other village on the coast, and was once a thriving fishing port with a population of 70,000 along either side of the river that divides it. The major trade route between Tunis, Constantinople, and Beirut went through the town, and much of the local architecture reflects these influences. But what makes Amalfi a better choice than the others is that there's still a sense of community that doesn't revolve around tourism. Sometimes, especially in the off season, you actually get the feeling that the locals could live without you—and that, oddly enough, is a welcome change from the neighboring towns of Positano and Sorrento.

Amalfi has a very impressive cathedral **Cattedrale di Sant'Andrea (Church of St. Andrew)** ★★★ (Piazza Duomo; ☎ 089-871059), on the main square. Up the stairs and around the back is the **Chiostro del Paradiso** (€2.50). Don't miss the crypt with the tomb of St. Andrew, the church's patron saint. There are few better places to sit at sunset than the stairs leading up to this magnificent church. From down below in the piazza, if you're lucky, you'll get to watch a bride perform the accomplished art of stair-climbing in stiletto heels and a long dress.

Amalfi also has a couple of fascinating museums, including the **Museo della Carta** ★ (Palazzo Pagliara, Via delle Cartiere, 23; ☎ 089-8304561; www.museodellacarta.it; €3.40; daily summer 10am–6pm, winter until 3pm), which received

European Union funding to refurbish its original paper presses dating back to the 14th century. Amalfi is believed to be the first European city to produce paper rather than import it. The museum is a great place to buy lovely handmade paper as a gift or souvenir. The guided tours are worthwhile.

Closer to the waterfront is the **Museo Civico** (Piazza del Municipio, 6; ☎ 089-8710107; free admission; daily 8am–2pm and 3–8pm), which has revolving exhibits that include many fine local artists.

For private apartments and rooms, which is a great way to spend an extended stay here, the ultimate choice is **www.amalfiaccommodation.com**. They seem to have the cream of the crop, and if what you're looking for is not listed on their website, the proprietors of this agency will find it for you. You may have to pay cash, as you often do when you rent an apartment along the coast, but this also gives you a little room to haggle. Sometimes owners will knock off half a day's board if you do pay in cash, and if they don't suggest this, don't be shy about asking. Private apartments are rarely licensed and fees are therefore up to the owner's discretion. The above website also handles *agriturismo* (farm stay) options on the coast, but these aren't recommended here because almost all are far from the sea view. Stick to the towns when you're visiting the Amalfi coast—that's where the appeal is and that's why you're here. Save the *agriturismo* stays for Tuscany and Umbria—no one in Italy does it better than they do.

€€   **Hotel Amalfi** (Vico dei Pastai, 3; ☎ 089-872440), run by the Lucibello family, is clean and reliable. Rooms, which start at €55, are modest, but they come in a variety of configurations and the owners will move beds in and out as needed. If you've got a big group, they also rent out guest apartments nearby starting at €140 a night, with eat-in kitchens, two bedrooms apiece, a pull-out bed in the living room, and balconies overlooking a quiet street. Either the hotel or the apartments are a perfect option for those traveling in groups, and there's even a parking lot (around €10 a day). Owners will usually refer you to similar hotels if they're booked, and almost invariably do whatever they can to make sure you come back.

€€   Down on the waterfront inside an old pasta factory is **La Bussola** 🧒 (Lungomare dei Cavalieri, 16; ☎ 089-871533; www.labussolahotel.it). Rooms here, starting at €95, are comfortably large with balconies right on the waterfront. This is perfect for the elderly, and for those traveling with young kids, because you won't have to navigate steps and alleyways to find your way home at night when the streetlights are dim. From here you're a few minutes from the ferry port and bus terminal, making it an excellent hotel from which to explore the entire coastline.

€€€   A worthy splurge in Amalfi is the **Cappuccini Convento** ★ (Via Annunziatella, 46; ☎ 089-871877; www.hotelcappuccini.it), set in a 12th-century Franciscan monastery high on the hill. This is a memorable place to stay, wonderfully isolated, with sweeping views, especially if you stroll along the cliff-side monk's walk. Some aspects of the service could be improved (the towels, for example, could all use replacing) and there's the feel of dampness in the walls, mainly because of the age and location (it's literally blasted into the cliff). But rooms start at €125, and the drawbacks are worth overlooking for the ambience. A nice double room will cost considerably more if you want a view, but that's not necessary because the view is almost always accessible from the terraces. It's certainly not worth the extra money if all you'll be doing in your room is sleeping.

€   If you're planning to spend the day at the beach or touring the coast by boat, pick up your lunch before you head out at **Pizzatteria Mediterranea** (Via Lorenzo d'Amalfi, 9), which has excellent spinach-filled pastries and fresh pizzas.

€€   Relatively new, but headed for great acclaim, is **Maccus** ★★★ (Largo S. Maria Maggiore, 1–3; ☎ 089-8736385; www.maccusamalfi.it), which may well offer the tastiest food in the region. It's also a festive place as its young owners host wine and food tastings in conjunction with Slow Food (p. 592). They also have jazz nights, literary dinners, and other events that cater to trendy residents more than to tourists. Most plates hover around €9, but you'll want to have more than one, to enjoy the atmosphere. It's a great place to meet locals and people-watch. Dinner is late on Saturday nights because the outdoor seating is in the piazza at the entrances of the church of Santa Maria Maggiore and the Chiesa dell'Addolorata: The tables can't go up until Mass has ended and the churchgoers have dispersed.

€€   Not far across the main street is the **Cantina San Nicola** ★★ (Salita Marino Sebaste, 8; ☎ 089-8304549), a little gem tucked inside an old monastery. The atmosphere is deliciously medieval, and the food is delightful. There are wine tastings on Tuesday and Thursday nights in the dining room, and the menu changes according to the season (with the exception of Grandma Margherita's meatloaf, which is a great choice year-round at just €12).

€€€   The favorite restaurant for locals and visitors alike for the last 100 years or so has been **Da Gemma** (Via Fra' Gerardo Sasso, 10; ☎ 089-871345). But as it gains in popularity, it has become increasingly expensive. The rooftop terrace overlooking the main square is the payoff, but still it's pricey. Gemma was the current owner's mother, and her recipe for *zuppa di pesce* is memorable, but costs €14. There are Middle Eastern desserts like eggplant dipped in chocolate, and wonderful local wines. The drawback here, other than the unnecessarily high prices, is that everyone knows about this restaurant, so advance booking is mandatory.

RAVELLO

Ravello is a sophisticated, cultured, and exquisite village of just 2,500 permanent residents, perched high above the cluttered coast. You'll sense the aristocratic air the minute you step off the local bus or pull into the main parking lot, and it's almost never crowded, and always serene. There's also no noise from traffic, and somehow the air just seems better up here. But all this comes with a price. Ravello is a very expensive place to stay. Still, for just €1, and without staying over, you can take the 15-minute bus from the bus terminal on the waterfront in Amalfi to the heart of this paradise.

Start with the **Villa Cimbrone,** which is about a 20-minute walk from the last bus stop through some of the quaint neighborhoods that cling to the cliffs. As you wind through the narrow, stepped streets, look below to terraced hills overgrown with lemon trees and vineyards, which cascade down to the turquoise sea below. Designed by Lord Grimthorpe (who also designed Big Ben in London), this 20th-century villa is nothing short of heavenly. The gardens are perfectly cultivated, with the smell of lavender and chamomile wafting through the air.

Make your way next to the **Belvedere Cimbrone,** a lookout point, for an unmatchable vista down the coastline. There is a standard-issue and modestly priced snack bar nearby where you can have an iced tea or glass of wine on the lawn before heading back down to the main square. You don't need much more than an hour, excluding the walk up, to tour the gardens of Villa Cimbrone.

Once you have finished here, head back down toward the main square and the Duomo, which was founded in 1086 and has undergone countless renovations and reincarnations. The small **Museo del Duomo** inside is badly designed and has a hard-to-find collection of imperial and medieval artifacts, but keep searching, following the corridors until you get there.

Calendar Highlights for Touring the Amalfi Coast

January   January 6 is the Feast of the Epiphany. On January 17, Neapolitans celebrate O Cippo 'e Sant'Antonio by throwing their unwanted belongings, from old clothes to tattered furniture, in piles throughout the city and then setting them afire.

February   Late in the month, Carnevale, a countrywide festival, is celebrated mostly by children in wildly expensive costumes parading through the streets and throwing colored confetti.

March/April   Easter and Holy Week.

May   The first Sunday of the month is the day the blood of San Gennaro should liquefy; to find out for yourself, head to the Duomo for morning Mass. Maggio dei Monumenti (p. 500) also takes place this month.

July   A fireworks display in Piazza del Carmine on July 6 celebrates the feast of Madonna del Carmine. The Neapolis Rock Festival (www.neapolis. it) is also this month.

August   Ferragosto, or the Feast of the Assumption, is on August 5.

September   On September 19, San Gennaro's blood is put to the test again.

December   December 8 is the Feast of the Immaculate Conception. Christmas is, of course, on December 25. The Feast of San Stefano is celebrated on December 26. And finally, join in the Capodanno, New Year's Eve celebrations, on December 31.

Next head to **Villa Rufolo,** beside the Duomo tower; the famous **Ravello Music Festival** (www.ravelloarts.org) is held here each summer, and it's worth whatever effort you can make to attend at least one concert. The stage juts out from the edge of the garden cliff, suspending the performers over the sea. The Villa Rufolo was founded in the 11th century. Richard Wagner composed an act of *Parsifal* here, and Boccaccio was so moved by the spot that he included it in one of his tales.

OTHER TOWNS TO CONSIDER

Several other villages along the Amalfi coast are worth exploring, at least for an afternoon. **Scala** and **Minori,** toward Salerno, are both enchanting and largely undiscovered. **Atrani,** just beside Amalfi, is an up-and-coming town with a wonderfully quaint beach and lots of "real" fishermen who sell their catch on the rocks. Inland from the coast are great options as well. **Paestum,** which was originally known as Poseidonia, has a wonderful excavation of Greek ruins and what archaeologists have termed the best Doric temples in existence, and I prefer it to the Parthenon. Don't discount **Caserta** either, if you have time to dawdle. This is an important stop 19km (12 miles) north of Naples, with one of Italy's largest palaces (120 rooms built around four inner courtyards) called **Reggia di Caserta** (Via Douet, 2; ☎ 082-3321400; €8 or €4 for just the gardens; call for open hours).

The ABCs of Naples & the Amalfi Coast

American Express Call ☎ 800-872000

Area Code 081 for Naples and the Amalfi Coast.

Business Hours Banks and public offices are officially open 8:30am to 1:20pm and 2:45 to 3:45pm, though nothing really gets going until around 9am. Churches are open 8 or 9am to 1 pm, and then again from 4 to 6 or 7pm. Coffee bars open around sunrise and many close late in the evening. Restaurants generally do not open until 12:30pm for lunch and 7:30pm for dinner.

Currency Exchange A great many *cambio* centers are found around Naples and the Amalfi Coast, but make sure their rates are up-to-date. You cannot go wrong with **Banco di Napoli** (Via Toledo, 177/178; ☎ 081-7924567) for money transfers.

Doctors For **medical advice** by telephone, call ☎ 081-2542424 in central Naples; ☎ 081-7613466 area from Posilipo to

Chiaia; ☎ 081-983292 in Ischia; ☎ 081-5266954 in Pozzouli; or ☎ 081-5780760 in Vomero.

Emergencies Carabinieri (police): ☎ **112;** fire department: ☎ **115;** ambulance: ☎ **118** or rush to a *pronto soccorso* (below).

Hospital An emergency room in Italy is called *pronto soccorso.* Those in Naples with 24-hour service are **Cardarelli (Via Cardarelli, 9,** Vomero; ☎ 081/7471111) and for children **Santobono (Via M Fiore, 6,** Vomero; ☎ 081-2205797). On Capri: **Ospedale Capilupi (Via Provinciale Anacapri,** Due Golfi; ☎ 081-8381205). In Sorrento: **Ospedale Civico (Corso Italia;** ☎ 081/5331111).

Internet Access In Naples, there's **Clic Net** (Via Toledo, 393; ☎ 081-5529370; www.clicnet.it; €3 per hour or €5 for 2 hr.; 9:30am–9:30pm) or **Internet Bar** (Piazza Bellini; ☎ 081-295237; www.internetbarnapoli.it).

Newspapers & Magazines Major national Italian news dailies *Corriere della Sera* and *La Repubblica* have special *cronaca* sections for individual cities with local listings of events. *Qui Napoli,* a free magazine issued by the Naples Tourist board, has the most comprehensive listings in both English and Italian. *Le Pagine dell'Ozio* is a monthly guide to events and a comprehensive listing of bars, restaurants, and nightlife options.

Pharmacies Pharmacies stagger their nighttime and Saturday hours. A list of pharmacies (with addresses) that are open at given times is posted beside all pharmacy doors.

Post Office Naples's main post office is at **Palazzo Centrale della Posta,** Piazza Matteotti (Toledo; ☎ 081-5511456), open weekdays until 7pm, Saturday in the morning only.

Restrooms The best bet for a safe, clean toilet in Naples is at a coffee bar or a department store on the Via Toledo. Restrooms at major sights (not churches) generally have an attendant who will charge about €.50 for the service, and sometimes for the toilet paper.

Safety Even though it has a bad reputation, Naples is a relatively safe city.

Pickpockets around the tourist sights are standard, as in most Italian cities, only here they seem a little less obvious. There aren't blatant groups of gypsies, but there are skilled moped drivers who can grab a purse strap before you know what happened. Don't wander through the Spanish Quarter at night. Don't flash your diamond necklace around Piazza Garibaldi. Don't pull out a wad of money in a clip anywhere. Don't go out with anything you can't afford to lose; most hotels have wall safes where your passport and valuables are safer than on your person.

Transit Info You can get **24-hour traffic reports** (☎ 166664477) at a cost of €.60 per minute.

The main website for transportation in and around Campania is **www.campania trasporti.it**. Each entity of the public transportation network has its own contact information. For **bus service** in Naples, contact **ANM** (☎ 800-639525 toll free; www.anm.it). **Boat timetables** are published daily in the Neapolitan newspaper *Il Mattino*. **Water-taxi service** (☎ 800-547500 or 081-8773600; www.taxidelmare. it) is very expensive: One-way between Capri and Ischia costs €494; round-trip between Capri and Positano costs €832.

13 The Bucolic Charms of Puglia

Moderately priced villages, a fascinating history, and an enchanting countryside—why discerning travelers try to keep Puglia to themselves.

by Barbie Latza Nadeau

WHAT'S THE "NEXT TUSCANY"? MANY SAY PUGLIA, THE REGION THAT stretches from Tremiti to the very bottom of Italy's boot heel. So much of what makes Tuscany captivating—expansive views of vineyards and olive groves, as well as a very distinct cuisine and wine—is mirrored here in Puglia (minus the heavy influx of tourists, at least for now).

Puglia, which in English is sometimes called Apulia, boasts monumental castles built by Frederick II, and remnants of ancient fortresses. Magnificent natural wonders, like rare limestone caverns and underground rivers, are rewarding to explore. Tiny working-class fishing villages overflow with hidden treasures, from exquisite baroque churches to well-preserved mosaics. The area is largely rural, its country roads flanked with stone fences, its hills dotted with conical *trulli* houses.

Puglia is also one of the few places in Italy where centuries-old customs endure. You can still find matriarchs rolling pasta by hand in the back alleys of coastal towns like Gallipoli, and it's common to hear a Greek dialect spoken on the eastern tip of the peninsula. English words almost never appear on menus in Puglia, and prices rarely exceed €12 a head for a delectable three-course meal including some of Italy's best local wine.

But it's wise to remember that Puglia is not Tuscany—not yet, anyway. And its museums, though ample, are not on par with those in Rome, Naples, Venice, and Florence. Much of what's on display is mainly for those who already have a keen knowledge of Italian history and the country's national heritage. While tourists are welcome, you will never feel particularly catered to here.

Touring Puglia is sometimes a challenge. Public transportation is marred by sporadic schedules and confusing routes, which often name townships rather than particular cities. Restaurants open very late for dinner, and service staff, even in hotels, rarely speak even basic English. It's still primarily a region where Italians unwind, explore their history, and enjoy some of the country's most unusual cuisine. Of course, that makes Puglia a great place to meet locals.

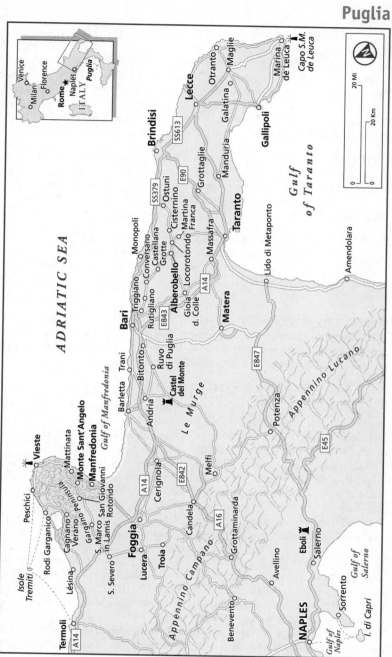

Puglia

ITALY

Venice
Milan
Florence
Rome ★
Naples
Puglia

ADRIATIC SEA

Isole Tremiti

Termoli
A14

Peschici
Rodi Garganico
Lésina
S. Severo
S. Marco in Lamis
S. Giovanni Rotondo
Cagnano
Verano
Gargano peninsula
Mattinata
Vieste
Monte Sant'Angelo
Manfredonia
Gulf of Manfredonia

Foggia
Lucera
Troia
Cerignola
Candela
Grottaminarda
A14
E842
Melfi
A16

Barletta
Trani
Andria
Bitonto
Ruvo di Puglia
Castel del Monte
Le Murge

Bari
Triggiano
Rutigliano
Conversano
Monopoli
Castellana
Grotte
Alberobello
Locorotondo
Gioia d. Colle
Matera
E843
A14

Ostuni
Cisternino
Martina Franca
Grottaglie
Massafra
Taranto
E90
SS379

Brindisi
SS613

Lecce
Otranto
Galatina
Maglie
Marina de Leuca
Capo S.M. de Leuca

Manduria
Gallipoli

Gulf of Taranto

Lido di Metaponto
Amendolara

Potenza
Appennino Lucano
E847
E45

Appennino Campano
Avellino
Benevento
Eboli
Salerno
Gulf of Salerno
Sorrento
I. di Capri
Gulf of Naples
NAPLES

20 Mi
20 Km

525

DON'T LEAVE PUGLIA WITHOUT . . .

POKING AROUND CAVES, CAVERNS & RAVINES   One of Puglia's great treasures is its many caves and caverns. Some are the conventional stalagmite-stalactite variety, like the spectacular **Grotte di Castellana** (p. 534), near Bari. More unusual is the deep cave in which the altar of the Santuario di San Michele in Monte Sant'Angelo is found. It is also well worth the journey along winding roads to take a day trip to Matera, just across the border into the province of Basilicata, to amble around the ruins of this eerie city carved into the ravines.

SPOTTING *TRULLI*   Almost everyone associates Puglia with the strange ice-cream-cone-shaped structures called *trulli*, but nothing really prepares you for the sight of these elfin houses. A drive along the back roads of the Itria Valley is a great way to see the ancient *trulli* between **Ostuni** (p. 536) and the *trulli* capital of **Alberobello** (p. 534).

NOTING THE LECCESE BAROQUE   Ornate baroque can be overwhelming under the best conditions, but there is something almost subtle about the specialized designs found in **Lecce** (p. 538), which is why they are known as Leccese baroque. This captivating city is the jewel of southern Puglia and should not be missed.

SEEING THE GARGANO PROMONTORY   The lush green Foresta Umbra of the **Gargano Promontory in northern Puglia** (p. 530) literally sprouts from the surrounding farmlands that make up the spur of Italy's boot. This environmentally friendly spot is a camper's paradise and a nature lover's dream.

A BRIEF HISTORY OF PUGLIA

Puglia is basically the heel of Italy's boot, surrounded by the Adriatic and Ionian seas. Because it's the first piece of land jutting out to the east, it served as the point of entry for most invasions into Italy. In fact, Puglia has been conquered, claimed, or rebuilt by the Greeks, Byzantines, Romans, Normans, and Spanish.

The most obvious influence in Puglia's history was that of Frederick II of Hohenstaufen, who reigned as Holy Roman Emperor until he died in 1250. His interests were nature and geometry, and the architecture he inspired is stunning. You won't see much in Puglia that he didn't build or otherwise influence.

Today, Puglia is a vital agricultural and fishing center, with its low, rolling hills producing more grain, tomatoes, lemons, and olives than any other Italian province. Eighty percent of the durum wheat for Europe's pasta industry is produced here, and almost all of Italy's olives for oil are grown here, as well as some of the country's most legendary grape vintages like Primitivo red and Salento whites. Puglia alone produces more wine than Germany does. The fishermen along the Adriatic coast are the county's most prolific. Across the peninsula along the Ionian coast, the mussels and clams are highly sought after.

The northern plains are oddly similar to the United States heartland, where agriculture reigns. It's perfectly normal to see a giant John Deere tractor on the medieval streets of villages like Lucera. Here, farming is the most lucrative business around.

Avoiding the Scams

Puglia is a great contradiction. It's extremely friendly and inviting by day, but can be disturbingly unwelcoming at night outside the tiny villages and medieval *piazze*. And just pause some evening on the southern beaches and you'll see helicopters patrolling the seas for traffickers of everything from clandestine humans to illegal arms and contraband cigarettes.

Puglia is also known for a couple of scams:

- **Mopeds:** In Brindisi, young thugs may bump your car with their mopeds and plead injury, but the minute you get out, you become vulnerable. Drive, instead, to a busy street or gas station and ask for help. Chances are, once you drive away, they will move on to the next victim.
- **10-euro bills:** An otherwise innocent-looking person will ask change for a 10; you kindly hand them legitimate coins and bills and you end up with a famously counterfeit tenner.

LAY OF THE LAND

You'll need your own transportation in Puglia. Trains and buses connect the major towns, but the local services to some of the smaller villages, which really hold the most appeal, are so sporadic you can waste an entire day getting to a sight that is really worth only an hour. This is especially true in summer when schedules are particularly sporadic.

Anyway, it's easy to drive here. The highways are not as traffic-laden as those in the north, and getting around cities like Foggia, Lucera, and Lecce is much simpler than, say, Rome or Milan.

Navigating the region isn't difficult, either (but be sure to buy a detailed map like Touring Club Italia's "Puglia"). Highway numbers are not always well marked but the towns are all amply signposted (though some road signs are stacked so high you will have to stop at the various forks in the road to read them). Keep in mind that **blue signs** point you to towns and villages, while **brown signs** indicate heritage sites. But be warned that many inventive entrepreneurs use the same style of brown signs to try to lure unknowing travelers.

Puglia bus and train schedules change frequently. Check **www.trenitalia.it** for the most updated **train schedules.** To navigate around the smaller towns, check schedules on the **www.ferroviedellostato.it.** For the **Gargano area,** check schedules with **www.ferroviedelgargano.com.** Perhaps most important of all is the **calendar of scheduled strikes** (transport and other), found on one of the most consulted websites in the country: **www.commissionegaranziasciopero.it.**

For updated information on **bus lines** and timetables, consult **www.sitabus.it** or call ☎ 0881-773117.

Puglia is quite large (400km/248 miles long), so you'll need to plan your time wisely to see the best it has to offer. If you've got 4 or 5 days, split the province into north and south of Bari, and explore both areas separately. If you have only

Maps

Touring Club Italia (www.touringclub.it) has the best maps for navigating this region. You can pick up a map at most newspaper stands and bookstores. You can also study the complete highway system and check traffic reports on **www.auto strade.it**, which is also a good tool for planning your itinerary.

a couple of days and have to choose between north and south, head south to see the *trulli* and to saunter around the Leccese baroque villages here. The beachfront isn't nearly as nice as that along the northern coast, but this area really offers a lot more in terms of the diversity and range of true Pugliese culture and history.

In **the north,** the two best hubs are the medieval village of **Lucera** (p. 529) and the coast of the **Gargano Promontory** (p. 530), which fills the spur of Italy's boot. Lucera is really an optimal base with its wonderful local color, and it's an easy drive from there to the Gargano Promontory. If you prefer the beach, however, go directly to the Gargano coast, where there is really no major difference between **Vieste** (p. 531) and **Peschici** (p. 531), the area's two most picturesque seaside locales. But if you turn your Puglian visit into a beach vacation, you will miss most of what the area has to offer.

In **the south,** the city of **Lecce** (p. 538) is the unquestionable top choice in which to stay. This lovely town is coming of age; it's culture-rich and just a short drive from anywhere you'd want to go in the Salento peninsula. But a second option, especially if you're keen to experience local culture, is the charismatic hilltop village of **Ostuni** (p. 536), the so-called "white city," just off the main highway between Bari and Brindisi. This town is bursting with local flavor (but lacks the number of accommodations choices you find in Lecce). A recent effort by the city to upgrade restaurants, wine bars, and shops is paying off, making Ostuni a great spot for experiencing some of the best local food and wine. Here, too, you are in *trulli* country, and just a short drive out of the village will put you on some of the most fascinating back roads of the entire region.

If, instead, you prefer a slightly offbeat adventure, head down to the Ionian side of Puglia and settle in at the ancient seaport village of **Gallipoli.** Here you are still less than 1½ hours from Brindisi and around an hour on good highways from the main attractions like Lecce and the *trulli* area. But take heed: This little fishing village is not nearly as developed as Ostuni. But it *is* romantic and quiet, and a great spot for mixing with locals, sunbathing on free beaches, and eating fresh seafood for next to nothing. The best mussels *(cozze)* and clams *(vongole)* in all of Southern Italy are found near here.

THE NORTH

Although, as I've said, your two best hubs for touring the north are Lucera and the Gargano Promontory, two sights—the offshore Isole Trimeti and the historic Castel del Monte—are of such importance in this northern area that I've broken out a discussion of them in the pages that follow.

LUCERA ★★★

If you base yourself in Lucera, you'll experience one of Puglia's premier examples of a **reincarnated Arab village.** In the early 13th century, the entire Saracen population was removed from Sicily and relocated here within the city walls. But far from being persecuted as they were in so many other parts of the province, the Arab community was allowed by Frederick II to worship freely and live according to their customs, in exchange for providing security for the kingdom.

Much of what the Sicilian Saracens built was destroyed by the French after Frederick II, but hints of the past are evident in the form of Arabic carvings that are still found on some cornerstones in Lucera, and in the local museum filled with exhibits of Arabic-scripted pottery and depictions of the original village. This small village is now the cultural capital of the area, and has more wine bars and restaurants per capita than any other town in the area. On August weekends, the local wine club turns a section of the historical center into a giant candlelit wine-tasting venue, where for €10 you buy a glass with a little canvas pouch and wander from piazza to piazza to taste the best of the local vintages.

Lucera's touted tourist sights are not what make the town worth visiting. Instead, come here to mix with locals and to get a real sense of how southern Italians on this side of the country live. Rather than being turned off by a constant barrage of *stranieri* (foreigners), the Pugliese of Lucera are very open and genuinely interested in sharing their town with visitors, which is a relatively new phenomenon here. It's not uncommon to strike up a conversation with someone at the coffee bar or local trattoria, or to be given a local gift like a jar of preserves or bottle of local wine from those you befriend. There is a sense of pride about Puglia and considerable community spirit in Lucera, and the people here are aware that they can benefit from tourism dollars.

The heart of Lucera is its central square, the **Piazza del Duomo.** Especially in the summer, locals from this small city and surrounding towns gather here for an evening stroll or to take part in one of the community's many events (see an events listing at **www.luceraweb.net**). The square is flanked by the 14th-century **Duomo** ★ (7:30am–12:30pm and 4:30–8pm), one of the few remaining examples of Angevin architecture in the country. It was built after the death of Frederick II on the site of a mosque, after the Angevins defeated the Arabs here. It's majestic and nothing short of the town's community hall, where the local choir practices, town meetings are held, and locals gather to pray.

Nearby, a much more dramatic 4th-century church, the Gothic **Chiesa di San Francesco** ★★, has original frescoes and a display of vestments worn by the local saint, Francesco Antonio Pasani, known as Padre Maestro. Lucera's other attraction is the **Castello** (follow signs from Via Bovio and Via Federico II to Piazza Matteotti; Tues–Sun 8am–2pm and 4–8pm, closed winter afternoons), built by Frederick II in 1233 on the highest hill at the edge of town. The pentagon fortress walls around the castle were once topped with 24 towers, and extensive renovations in recent years uncovered the last of these towers after an earthquake in 1980 had all but destroyed the structure. From this vantage point, you'll get a rare glimpse of the expanse of the Tavoliere Plain with its low, rolling farmland that spreads out around Lucera.

Accommodations & Dining in Lucera

€€   A few new bed-and-breakfasts are currently popping up in Lucera, but hands down, the best place to stay is at the more traditional **Albergo Al Passetto** ★★★ (Piazza del Popolo; ☎ 0881-520821), which offers very comfortable rooms and unique ambience—the hotel itself is built right into the fortification wall that surrounds the city—for around €70 a night. Book early, though, as this is the only hotel inside the city walls.

€   **Al Federiciano** ★★ (Via Caropresa, 9; ☎ 0881-549490) is a top pick for dining. It's definitely on the spartan side decor-wise, but they do an *orichette* (ear pasta) with seafood that you will remember years later. If the weather is nice, ask to sit out on the upper terrace.

€   A handful of new restaurants in Lucera are capitalizing on its growing popularity and serving authentic local cuisine. If you've only got a few days, try the **Tavernetta** ★★ (Via Schiavone, 7–9; ☎ 0881-520055), tucked away on a tiny dead-end street behind the Duomo. Its pasta dishes are generous for the price and the pizzas, which start at €3.50, are overflowing with fresh ingredients that vary by season.

THE GARGANO PROMONTORY ★★★

The unrivaled other draw of the north is the Gargano Promontory (www.parks. it/parco.nazionale.gargano/Eindex.html), home to Italy's last original forest, the **Foresta Umbra.** This lush national park is made up of ancient beech trees and giant oaks. As you'd expect, it tends to be a haven for Italians in RVs in the summer months, making travel through winding park highways slow and cumbersome (unless you can manage the drive mid-week, or mid-morning, when the campers are mainly all in place). There are outstanding walking trails here, but you need to stop at the main visitor center to get the most updated maps. The open trails vary depending on seasons, which are spectacular as leaves change and flowers blossom, and are also affected by wildlife migrations. So don't use an old map. And don't just drive through here; lovely as the drive is, it's worth getting out to explore and picnic.

The Gargano Promontory is also the site of the ancient **Pilgrim Trail,** which follows the narrow road connecting the towns of **Monte Sant' Angelo** ★★★ with its **Santuario di San Michele Arcangelo (Sanctuary of Archangel Michael)** ★★★ (free admission; July–Sept 7:30am–7:30pm, Oct–June 7:30am–12:30pm and 2:30–5pm) to **San Giovanni Rotondo** ★. Both are natural magnets for religious visitors, but also offer sweeping views and fascinating architecture. The main altar of the sanctuary, for instance, is built inside a cavern far below the church of the same name. Legend has it that the archangel Michael first appeared here in A.D. 490 and his footprint is enclosed behind glass for all to see just behind the altar. Even on the hottest summer days, the religious "fashion police" will stop you at the entrance to the grotto and give you a blue or yellow cape to cover up any offensive skin you may be showing, namely exposed bellies, legs, and shoulders.

Outside the church, climb the hill to the **Castle** (€1.80; same hours as Santuario di San Michele Arcangelo), where you should go directly to the top to catch the view of the terra-cotta rooftops of the cascading town of Monte

Sant'Angelo and the carpet of treetops that make up the national park farther afield. On clear days you'll see the Gulf of Manfredonia and the Adriatic Sea, which is largely populated with trolling fishing boats and naval ships scouting for terrorists and traffickers.

About 25km (16 miles) down the winding roads is the more religiously significant village of **San Giovanni Rotondo** ✸ which is the burial site of Italy's beloved Padre Pio, a Capuchin friar who's a national hero in Southern Italy for his ability to heal by touch. His picture (the one of the kindly, bearded monk with a frayed frock and fingerless glove) dominates restaurants, coffee bars, and newspaper stands from Bari to Naples to Rome. This is an especially significant stop for Catholics, but because the tiny village receives over 200,000 religious pilgrims a year, it may be worth skipping during the summer months (unless you are a pilgrim). In addition to the tomb of Padre Pio in the sanctuary below the church, you'll find a 14th-century church of **Sant'Onofrio,** with a baptistery, and a 16th-century church of **Santa Maria delle Grazie.** Monte Sant'Angelo is much more rewarding, and both areas should be avoided on September 8 and June 29, which are religious feast days marked by huge crowds.

If you're in search of a beach holiday, consider either **Vieste** ✸✸ or **Peschici** ✸ the two main seaside villages perched on and above the coast. The best beaches are between these two villages, and the main road is lined with hotels and camping spots. The towns are similar, with Vieste edging ahead slightly for its tourist amenities. It has a better **Duomo** and another Frederick II **castle,** which is closed to the public and used as an Italian military base.

Because most people travel this coastline from Manfredonia on up, Peschici, which is farther down the coast, is far less developed than Vieste. But Peschici is starting to see a number of new restaurants and hotels. It also has fun street names like Via Malconsiglio (bad advice) and Via Buonconsiglio (good advice), not to mention the Vico Purgatorio (purgatory). This town is high above the coastline and you'll want to think about that vertical positioning if you're here for a beach holiday—getting to the sea means traversing many steps.

Accommodations & Dining on the Gargano Promontory

€€ **Hotel del Seggio** (Via Veste, 7; ☎ 0884-708123) is one of the incomparable deals on this coast. For €65 you get a large double room with a balcony and view of the Adriatic Sea. The owner is a bit standoffish, but the rooms are nicely appointed, comfortable, and quiet.

€€ **Hotel Degli Aranci** (Piazza Santa Maria delle Grazie, 10; ☎ 0884-708557; www.hotelaranci.it) is another top option, with rooms just €100 for a double during high season. But be sure to ask for one of the "new rooms," which have been refurbished with hardwood floors and marble bathrooms. The older rooms are not that great, which is why the refurbishment is in progress.

€€–€€€ At **Agriturismo Madonna Incoronata** 🧒(Mattinata; ☎ 0884-582317; www.agriturismogargano.it) you can choose between a variety of outbuildings on an old farm, which are now comfortable bungalows with full kitchens. The smallest one-room apartments start at €66 in low season and €86 in high season, and the largest three-bedrooms are €148 at the most. This is a very viable option if you've got children, and a great choice if you don't mind giving up such amenities as daily linen and restaurant service. Minimum stay is 2 nights.

ISOLE TREMETI

In the summer months, most everyone who spends time on the Gargano coast makes the short 40km (25-mile) ferry trip to the Isole Tremiti, which consists of the distinctively different islands of San Domino, known for its lush green natural habitat; San Nicola, distinguished by its crags and cliffs; and the untamed Capraia, which is mostly wilderness. These islands have been used almost exclusively for confinement and contemplation, from their beginnings as a Benedictine monastery (which still stands) to their role as a jailhouse for political prisoners in the 1920s and 1930s. Now visitors can choose from nature hikes, bird-watching, swimming, or church-gazing. But staying on the islands is not recommended because accommodations are limited and expensive, and there simply isn't enough to do here to warrant more than a morning or afternoon excursion. The most **efficient and affordable ferries** are those operated by **Adriatica Navigazione** (www.tirrenia.it), which has frequent service during the summer and should get you there for around €10 one-way.

CASTEL DEL MONTE ✯✯✯

The last must-see stop in northern Puglia is the impressive, if a little out of the way, 13th-century UNESCO World Heritage Site, Castel del Monte (west of Andria on highway S170; www.castellipuglia.org/en/monte.html; €3; Apr–Sept 8:30am–7pm, rest of the year 9am–2pm, closed Sun). This is another Frederick II fortress, which nobody, not even the local tourist authority, can exactly explain. The massive octagonal castle, built between 1229 and 1249, is a perfect mix of mathematical and astronomical precision, and affords some peculiar optical illusions as you wander through the eight 25m-high (82-ft.) octagonal towers. From every point you see octagonal glimpses of the sky and the shadows within the castle's courtyard form more octagons. The number eight is symbolic in astronomy and religion, and many believe this castle is the perfect symbol of the union of the infinite and finite. Each room has floors originally laid with hexagon-patterned marble and adorned with Muslim influences like double-painted arches, some of which remain in the eighth room from the stairway. From the fifth room you explore what used to be an aviary for falcons. From the terrace, note the double-slanted roof, which diverted rainwater to both a holding tank and into the castle's bathrooms.

The castle sits high above the plains and some say it was a hunting fortress, though history books claim it has never been inhabited. Regardless, you'll marvel at the ancient architecture. You can see it perched on its high hill for miles as you approach, and it's probably the most organized tourist spot in Puglia. You must park 2km (1¼ miles) below the castle, in the public lot, which has a handful of sandwich bars, picnic areas, and public toilets; €3 covers all-day parking and the ride on the shuttle bus, which leaves every 15 minutes. Two restaurants are found at the top near the castle, along with a souvenir shop selling bits of armor and medieval fridge magnets. Just don't leave until you've walked around the entire perimeter of the castle to survey the countryside.

THE SOUTH

Here the big decision is Bari versus Ostuni. My preference is the latter.

BARI

There is often a sense of obligation to visit any area's largest city and provincial capital. Bari (on the A14 or S16) is that town and it is *maybe* worth an hour or two, or a lunchtime stroll through the old town, especially if you're going there anyway for a ferry connection. But there is absolutely nothing here that you can't see a better, quainter, quieter version of elsewhere in the province.

If you do find yourself here before a ferry connection and need to kill time, keep in mind that Bari's legendary reputation for petty crime is exaggerated, though not completely unwarranted. There are suspicious characters lurking around the ferry port and a concentration of gypsy kids in the center, but if you're aware of their presence and vigilant, they likely won't bother you.

When touring Bari, go directly to the **old town,** a maze of tiny streets carefully designed to block the strong winds off the Adriatic Sea and to confuse the enemies that tried to take the town. It works—and it makes it very hard not to get lost. You won't go too far astray, though, as the old city is surrounded by water on three sides and butts up against the modern city on the other. A good starting point is **Piazza San Nicola** and the **Basilica di San Nicola,** with its classic Romanesque architecture. This is the most clearly marked square in the city. Just wander through the maze to the **Piazza Odegitria,** which is the closest piazza to the waterfront and where the city's medieval **Cathedral di San Sabino** and bell tower stand tall.

From here you can easily visit the Swabian **Castello Normanno-Svevo** (Piazza Federico II di Svevia, 4; ☎ 080-5286263; €2; Thurs–Tues 9am–7pm), which is another of Frederick II's great architectural feats. There is a moderately interesting museum with rotating exhibits and a permanent collection of plaster casts from the statues in various churches and town squares around the province, but nothing worth more than a half-hour of browsing. Indeed, Bari isn't worth too

---

Cheap Sleeps for the Under-30 Crowd

If you are under 30, you are eligible for a fine initiative called **Stop Over in Bari** (Via Nicola, 47; ☎ 0881-5214538). Call ahead and organizers will set you up with low-priced rooms in quaint hotels, or with private rooms in houses, and give you a pass for free public transport and free admission to the museums, plus free bike rental and meal coupons. Book as far in advance as you can, though, because the best rooms go fast.

If you're over 30, don't sleep here unless you absolutely have to in order to catch an early ferry—Puglia has more interesting places in which to spend the night.

much of your time; the restaurants on the waterfront just off the old town tend to prey on the captive tourists waiting for ferries to Greece. If you are there at mealtime, go instead toward the Piazza Mercantile for better food at slightly better prices—the **Mercantile** (Piazza Mercantile, 15; ☎ 080-5210124) does a nice *orchiette* with tomato and pecorino cheese for €5.

LE MURGE

Just north of Bari, a 150-by-50km (93-by-31-mile) limestone plateau called Le Murge reaches inland from the sea. The terrain here is marked by caves and ravines and dotted with little villages. An intriguing spot is the caves at **Castellana Grotte** ★★ (☎ 081-4998211; €8 short tour, €15 for longer tour; Oct–Mar 8:30am–12:30pm, year-round 2:30–6:30pm), which are a visually stunning labyrinth of stalactites and stalagmites twisting from the cavern floors and ceilings. There are two options for seeing the caves, both through guided tours (of which only one is an abbreviated English tour at varying times, but there isn't enough narration to warrant planning your day around it, so just take the Italian tour). The shorter, 1km (⅔-mile) tour lasts about an hour and is best if you've got kids because you won't want to subject them to a longer distance than that. Far more interesting, however, is the 3km (2-mile) tour that lasts around 2 hours and includes the Caverna Bianca, which is a large opening in the deepest part of the cave network that is lined with glassy, shimmering stalactites. These caves were used primarily as a landfill for the area's trash until 1938, when they were explored fully and now are one of the most educational stops in the province. Bring a long-sleeve shirt—it's always 60°F (16°C) inside the caves.

THE ROAD TO *TRULLI* COUNTRY

The rural highways through the Itria Valley to Ostuni are lined with vineyards, ancient olive trees, almond groves, and peach and cherry orchards, which makes a leisurely drive through the back roads one of the great pleasures of exploring this part of southern Puglia. This is also where you begin to see the conical houses called *trulli,* which are whitewashed stone huts with stacked gray slate-tile roofs. Many *trulli* rooftops are painted with astrological signs and almost all of them in this area are inhabited.

Few people really seem to know why these structures exist, but the most credible local legend states that they were originally built as a way to avoid housing taxes (because they had only stacked rocks and no mortar, they theoretically weren't houses). There is, after all, an old Italian proverb, *"Fatta la legge, trovato l'inganno"* ("As the law is made, the deception is found"), which still holds true today. Another believable piece of *trulli* trivia is that when a baby was about to be born, the man of the *trulli* would build another room with its own cone, so anyone passing by could easily see how many children each family had, and thus how fortunate they were.

The **capital of the *trulli* area** is the Disney-esque town of **Alberobello** ★★, which has 1,500 of these dwellings, now mostly housing trinket peddlers, wine bars, and clothing shops. You should definitely stop here, but the best part of Alberobello is across the Largo Martellotta, away from the tourist mecca into the residential zone around the Piazza M. Pagano. These *trulli* are still primarily private houses, and a quiet walk-through will give you a better idea of how the population lives. The

Go If You Must, but Don't Tell Anyone

If you are traveling with children, you know that the caves and *trulli* will only hold their attention for so long, and endless winding roads in the back seat are no picnic. There is a diversion, but only in an emergency. The bizarre **Zoosafari e Fasanolandia** 🧒 (Fasano exit off Hwy. 16, south of Bari; ☎ 080-4413055; www.zoosafari.it; hours vary, see website; €13, free for children under 4) is just what the kids ordered, but may leave adults aghast. Here on the Puglian plains is Italy's only driving-safari complete with lions, tigers, and bears, not to mention elephants, ostriches, penguins, camels, and zebras. There's also a dolphin and otter show in the main lake and a reptile house and butterfly exhibit in the zoo. If that's not enough, there's a children's theater, a water slide, a full playground, a sprawling amusement park, and a fully stocked junk-food paradise for the kids. The highlight (close your eyes here, Mom and Dad) is the monkey train on which spectators crowd into caged cars and ride through the monkey pen in a strange, reverse zoo effect while monkeys clamor all over the cages to look inside.

In theory, this is somewhere between a Mediterranean version of Sea World and a real African safari—but it's basically a zoo run by carnies. The pens are somewhat rusty and the animals are crowded, but the kids will love it and you can probably get a lot of very good behavior in exchange. There is easily enough to do to spend the entire day here, but, please, only in an emergency.

---

houses are so tiny that it is common to see residents either dining at a table outside the kitchen doors or visiting with friends on chairs in the alleyways.

€€€€   There are very few restaurants to choose from in Alberobello. **Il Poeta Contadino** (Via Indipendenza, 21; ☎ 080-4321917) is on the expensive side, starting at €25 for a large plate of pasta, water, and cover charge. The ambience is warm and the food is very good.

€   Its exact opposite is the greasy spoon down the street, **3M** (Via Indipendenza, 9; ☎ 080-4325432), where the pasta starts at €5, with no table charge at all. You can even ask for your water all *rubinetto*, straight from the tap, for free.

If you are looking for **gifts to take home,** duck into **Tholos Wine Bar di Luigi Minerva** (Via Monte S. Michele, 20; ☎ 080-4321699; www.trullodelgusto.it), where you can sample some wonderful local wines, salami and cheese, and local confections. They will package and ship gifts for you.

   Don't overnight in Alberobello unless you are dying to sleep in a *trulli*. (And even then, there are many self-catering *trulli* farther from town, in the countryside.) You should be able to find a *trulli* for about €75 a night, or €450 a week, but you almost always have to use an agency for booking. The best agencies are the **Immobiliare Fittatrulli** (☎ 0881-722717) and **Trullidea Case Vacanze** (www. trullidea.it), but these can be expensive (over €200 a night).

OSTUNI ★★

A better place to lodge than Alberobello is the hilltop town of Ostuni, which is known locally as *la città Bianca,* or "the white city," for the way its whitewashed historical center is visible from miles around. This little hilltop village, founded in the 9th century, oozes character and, in recent years, has made itself into a truly (not to be confused with *trulli*) worthy destination. Some streets are reminiscent of the stepped towns along the Amalfi coast, though you've got a distinctively North African feel here with arched stairways connecting houses and restaurants.

This is a fun city in which to walk, and there always seem to be free concerts, art exhibits, and the like. Just keep climbing up the maze of winding streets from the main square at Piazza della Libertà, until you reach the pinnacle of Ostuni, on which stands a completely out-of-place 15th-century **Gothic church** with a red-brown exterior and a green-and-yellow-tiled cupola. It's like a peacock among doves in this whitewashed town. Stand back as far as you can to take in the detailed Gothic facade, which is divided into three sections with pilaster strips. Above each door is a carved rose window with 24 external arcades representing the 24 hours of the day. The inside of the church is standard-issue for Puglia, with its requisite marble floors and ornate ceiling, but it does offer more than most churches. Keeping with the calendar theme, the 12 arched internal arcades represent the months of the year, and the seven angel heads represent the days of the

---

A Back-Roads Drive from Ostuni to Alberobello

The towns between Alberobello and Ostuni lie along one of the most picturesque highways in all of Puglia. Try the following route (see the map on p. 525):

1. Leave Ostuni for **Cisternino,** one of Italy's most beautiful villages (14km/8¾ miles on Hwy. 604).
2. Head 9km (5½ miles) down the highway to **Martina Franca** to take in some of the area's best baroque architecture outside of Lecce, on the **Chiesa di San Martino.**
3. Go another 9km (5½ miles) on Highway 172 to **Locorotondo,** often referred to as the "balcony" for the way the highway overlooks the valley below. This is one of the best areas in which to pick up some local wines like Primitivo.
4. Now you have an 8km (5-mile) jaunt, on Highway 604, to **Alberobello.**

Note: If you are inclined, stay on Highway 604 and visit Noci, or head up Highway 172 to see the Grotto di Putignano.

week. Outside the church, you can catch a panoramic view across the olive groves to the sea.

Accommodations & Dining in Ostuni

€–€€   The hotel scene in Ostuni is quite pricey, which makes little sense except for the fact that it's such a dynamic city to visit. But the B&B market is competitive and very viable. **Bed & Breakfast Sole Blu** and the adjacent apartment **Casa Colombo** (Via Vittorio Emanuele, 16; ☎ 0831-303856) are like staying at grandma's house when it comes to decor, but the prices are very reasonable at just €30 a person for the B&B and €80 a night for the two-bedroom apartment.

€€–€€€   Also try **Bed & Breakfast in Ostuni** (Via Leonardo Clemente, 20; ☎ 0831-304684; www.bb-ostuni.it), which is a little bit pricier at €90 to €120 a night, but with a far more refined ambience. Here the mini-apartments are round-roofed huts in the heart of the city. They're nicely appointed but, like all Ostuni homes, are noticeably lacking windows. Nonetheless, this is a super spot.

€   As Ostuni makes its mark as a tourist town, lots of little restaurants are opening all the time, but two older establishments remain superior. **Spessite** (Via Clemente Brancasi, 43; ☎ 0831-302866) is down a series of stepped streets from the main cathedral, and is a local favorite for the seafood pastas. Sunday mornings here are packed with locals, so don't even try unless you speak the local dialect. Other times of the week, you can usually get in without a reservation. Fresh seafood dishes like the pasta *scoglio* are €8.

€€   Or try **Porta Nova** (Via Petrarolo, 38; ☎ 0831-331472; closed Wed). It's a little bit more expensive, but the panoramic view from the terrace is worth it. Its dishes are also somewhat more creative than the Spessite's, and the locals who eat here tend to drive nicer cars (and park them at the entrance). The specialty of the house is seafood and the chef is a local hero.

FROM BARI TO BRINDISI BY THE COAST

The coastal towns between Bari and Brindisi are mostly busy fishing ports and strange beach-club enclaves. There isn't much appeal on this stretch of coast beyond the towns of **Torre a Mare,** which is perched above a set of coastal caves, **Polignano a Mare,** with its medieval old center, and **Monopoli,** which is a bustling seaport almost halfway between Bari and Brindisi. In Monopoli, you should see the **Museo della Cattedrale** (**Largo Cattedrale;** ☎ 080-748002; €1; daily 9am–1pm and 5–8pm) for its religious art. Along this route is the excavated villa that Emperor Trajan built in the 1st century A.D., called **Egna'zia** (Via Appia Traiana free admission; 8:30am–sunset); it's just south of Monopoli.

At a gloriously lush nature reserve, **Torre Guaceto** ^{kids} (Via Piazzetta, A/32, Serranova di Carovigno; ☎ 0831-989885; www.riservaditorreguaceto.it), you can take a **bicycle trek** for €15, kids 4 to 14 €7 (Wed and Sat at 4:30pm, bicycle and child seat included) or a **guided hiking trek** for €10, kids 4 to 14 €4 (Tues and Fri; departure times given when you make a reservation). Walks last about 3 hours and will take you all around the "humid zone," a natural habitat for cranes, egrets, and red herons, primarily comprising small lakes, reed thickets, and wild grasses.

The beaches here are free and lightly populated, even at the height of summer. The Torre Guaceto nature group also offers **snorkeling adventures** (Apr–Oct by appointment at ☎ 0831-989885; equipment provided) for exploring the Adriatic's sea plants and sea life. These are well-done, professional expeditions and a great way to explore the Adriatic Sea.

BRINDISI

Farther down the coast from here is Brindisi, which you should avoid unless you must make a ferry connection there; the town's poor reputation has been confirmed by serious attacks against tourists—women especially—even in broad daylight. This is the place where traveling in a group is recommended, even when you're just waiting for a ferry. (Most ferry connections to Greece and Croatia leave in the evening, so you should easily be able to avoid sleeping in Brindisi.)

There are, however, some worthwhile sights in this ancient port town. Among the best to see are the 1st-century B.C. **Colonna Romana,** on top of Virgil's Steps, which marks the end of the Via Appia that once ran all the way from Rome's Porta Capena. There is also an 11th-century **Duomo** (Mon–Fri 7:30am–12:30pm and 4:30–7:30pm) on the center square and the **Museo Archeologico Provinciale** (☎ 0831-221401; free admission; Mon–Fri 9am–1:30pm, Tues and Thurs also 3:30–6pm, and Sat–Sun 9am–1pm) nearby, which is overflowing with various artifacts found along the Via Appia.

LECCE ★★★

One of the cities that makes Puglia and the Salento Peninsula captivating is undoubtedly Lecce. It's a true crossroads, connecting easily with anywhere else you'd want to go in the area, and as cosmopolitan as it gets in Southern Italy, thanks in part to the bustling university at its heart. Lecce is often referred to as the "Florence of the South," and is special not only for the cultural energy that abounds here but also for its architecture, the exquisite style of Leccese baroque. For reasons that remain unknown, the architecture of Lecce evolved directly from the Romanesque to the high baroque, skipping the Gothic stage. That is emphasized here by the extensive use of the quirky, fanciful symbols that were popular in the Middle Ages, but rarely used elsewhere on baroque churches: snarling dragons, griffins, placid mermaids, pelicans, and a menagerie of other pagan symbols. These fantastic beasts are carved in exquisite detail, thanks to the use of a local sandstone that's particularly soft and malleable when first quarried, hardening after long exposure to the air. The plasticity of this stone allowed the carvers here to give free rein to their imaginations, and the abundance of swoops, curlicues, and various doodads on the buildings can have an almost psychedelic effect.

Many of Lecce's churches were designed by Antonio Zimbalo, whom locals still refer to as *"Zingarello,"* or gypsy. His eye for detail and pure flamboyance are evident in the city's major churches like the 17th-century **Basilica della Santa Croce** ★★ (on the Piazza della Santa Croce), which took 150 years to decorate. The facade is marked by two balconies on which a heavy concentration of ornate faces, flowers, and fauna ooze out from the stone. Zimbalo's other Leccese masterpiece is the **Church of San Giovanni Battista** ("del Rosario" on some maps), near Porta Rudiae on the southwest edge of the old center. Here, too, the mix of pagan and Christian symbols is particularly noteworthy and the details are so fascinating and complex that it's hard to pull yourself away. Look for the cherubs' faces, the fantastic monsters, and the fruits and flowers in his designs.

There's no better activity than simply strolling the city, and you should start your walking tour of Lecce from the Piazza Sant'Oronzo (but first get a coffee at one of the many cafes that line the open-air excavations of a 1st-c. B.C. Roman amphitheater). From here, you can easily explore the mishmash of churches that clutter the streets leading to the other main square, Piazza Duomo, and Lecce's main cathedral (with two facades, a bell tower, and a cloister worth visiting). At the far end of the Piazza Duomo is the Bishop's Palace, with a pretty little fountain in the center courtyard that you can visit for €1.50. The other Leccese baroque churches you should see are **Santa Chiara, San Matteo, Sant'Irene,** and **Santa Teresa,** but rather than looking for them, wander the town and stumble upon them. This is not the type of place where you'll want your nose in a map, and the city center is small and easy to navigate. Directions to all the churches are well marked with brown signs.

Accommodations & Dining in Lecce

€€   Try to stay overnight in Lecce. There are tidy little B&Bs like the **Centro Storico B&B** (Via A. Vignes, 2b; ☎ 0832-242727), which offers a comfortable triple room with kitchenette for just €65. If you don't mind stairs (46 in all and no elevator), an even more inviting B&B is the **Bed and Breakfast Prestige** ★★ (Via Santa Maria del Paradiso, 4; ☎ 0832-243353). Double rooms are under €80 a night, and most rooms face the church and bell tower, which tolls hourly.

€   If you can only stay for one meal in Lecce, take it at the **Trattoria Cucina Casareccia** ★★ (Via Colonnello Costadura; ☎ 0832-245178), which is actually the living room of a private home that has been converted over time into a family restaurant. What's on the menu is basically whatever Grandma decides to cook, but you'll eat well for around €10 including wine.

€   A more adventurous culinary choice, though hardly as appealing in terms of atmosphere, is **Alle due Corti** (Via Corte dei Giugni, 1; ☎ 0832-242223), which serves a local dish called *tajeddha*—a lasagna-style layered dish made with mussels, rice, and potatoes. It may sound a little bit questionable, but it's actually quite delicious. Alle due Corti also serves another local delicacy, *cavallo,* which is horse meat.

Shopping in Lecce

Shopping in Lecce is probably best limited to food and wine. Shops cater to locals first, and one of their favorites is **Panetteria Valentina** ★★ (Via Petronelli, 3; ☎ 0832-300549), which specializes in regional delicacies like pasta, cookies, and fig paste. It also has a great selection of fresh stuffed-pizza breads to nibble on while you make your way around town. The owner is a delightful elderly man who all but hand-feeds you his goods, so don't be shy—it's great fun to sample. Another fine purchase for sweet gifts is the local handmade chocolate from **Maglio Arte Dolciaria** (Via Templari, 16; ☎ 0832-243816; www.cioccolatomaglio.it), which also has shops in Bari and Maglie nearby. The chocolate-covered figs here are indescribable and the staff members will package your sweets.

A Day Trip to Matera

One of the most intriguing places you can visit on a trip to Puglia is **Matera** ★★★, which is actually in the neighboring region of Basilicata. It's only a few kilometers over the border and definitely should be included in a Puglian vacation. The haunting **ruins,** called the *sassi* (www.sassiweb.it; follow the numerous road signs to find them), are one of Italy's saddest post–World War II stories. Around 20,000 peasants lived in this village, which was literally carved out of two sides of a ravine. The houses were cavelike, windowless structures that often held an entire family and its animals. Malaria was rampant and poverty killed many of the children. Most famously, Carlo Levi wrote about his sister's visit here in his book *Christ Stopped at Eboli,* in which he related her description of children with "wizened faces of old men" reduced to skeletal frames from starvation, heads crawling with lice. It was this description that prompted the Italian government to finally pour money into the poorest areas of Italy's south to eradicate malaria. In 1960, the city built a new town above and moved the remaining 15,000 residents out of their squalor.

Today when you visit the site, the cityscape is eerie and completely, utterly shocking, even though some of the old *sassi* have now been reclaimed by artists and wine bars are being rebuilt into funky houses. Mel Gibson filmed the crucifixion scene of *The Passion of the Christ* here, with very little change to the backdrop. To tour the area, start with a couple of the **six rock churches** built into the caves. The local tourist authority offers an integrated ticket for €6 for entrance to all six churches (or €5 for three churches, €2.50 for one church). There is also a guided tour available, priced according to the number in the group, but it will never cost more than €15, including entrance to all six churches.

You should plan to spend a half-day or more in Matera if you really want to grasp what this city is all about. There is a lot to explore—don't cut your time too short, but it's not an easy, or great, place to spend the night, so make it an early-morning day trip and get back to your base by nightfall.

SALENTO PENINSULA

From Lecce, you can easily explore the entire Salento region, including the island town of **Taranto,** which has superb Greek excavations from the villages that made up the colonies of greater Greece *(magna graecia)*. These are well displayed at the **Museo Archeologico di Taranto (Archaeological Museum of Taranto;** two entrances: Via Corso Umberto I, 41, Palazzo Pantaleo, and Via Corso V. Emanuele; ☎ 099-4532112; €8, free for students under 18 and for seniors over 60; Mon–Sat 9am–2pm, Sun 9am–1:30pm). Taranto is an industrial town whose many factories and port are marked by unpleasant odors. It's nice enough to walk around here, but there are better places to stay. The old town is an island attached by a bridge to the more modern city. Don't miss the lively morning fish market, and the cathedral, which used to be a mosque, in the center square.

THE OTHER PUGLIA: GALLIPOLI ★★★

Just down the road from Taranto, Gallipoli attracts local Italian tourists who come to relax in the village square or along the sandy beaches. The old town is also an island like Taranto, but this city has much more appeal, perhaps because the main industry is small-time fishing, and it's mesmerizing to stand on the promenade above the port and watch the fishermen untangle their nets by hand at the end of the day.

This is another whitewashed city and a place made famous in ancient times as a seaport from where olive oil was exported. It now thrives more on domestic tourism, with about 10% of its ancient houses offered up as self-catering rentals in the summer. Along these streets are everything from tomatoes sun-drying on the walls to town elders playing cards outside their kitchen doors. There aren't many true attractions, but do stop inside the **Duomo,** on the piazza of the same name. Gallipoli is also a wonderful **beach haven,** with a string of free beaches sprawling out on either side of the city.

14 Sicily

It's fiery, friendly, and utterly unlike any other region of Italy.

by Barbie Latza Nadeau

NO MATTER HOW YOU ARRIVE ON THE ISLAND OF SICILY—WHETHER straight into the bustling confusion of Palermo, by sea through the historically perilous Straits of Messina, or by air under the shadow of Mt. Etna's volcanic plume, you cannot escape the other-worldly feeling that defines this island. In many ways, Sicily is the "other" Italy, a region so steeped in uniquely Sicilian tradition that it hardly seems related to the mainland. Instead, Sicily is more like a fiery, distant cousin, and almost everything, from the unique twang of the local dialect to the spicy food, is intensely indulgent and surprisingly unlike what you may expect.

Most of what is considered Sicilian—from city names to social habits to desserts—is derived from ancient Arabic culture. Add to that a breathtaking terrain that often feels exotic, with prickly-pear cactuses growing along the roadsides and palm trees lining the village streets. Mix in a healthy dose of mob history and legendary passion—both romantic and religious—and you've begun to scratch the surface of what it is to be Sicilian and what you should look for when you visit.

> ❝To have seen Italy without having seen Sicily is to not have seen Italy at all, for Sicily is the clue to everything. ❞
>
> —J. W. Goethe, *Journey To Italy*

This unique heritage is one that these island people are intensely proud of. Most here feel that they are Sicilians first, Italians second. There are even old-time Sicilians who brag that they have never been off the island. Once you've visited, it's not hard to see why they would never need to go anywhere else.

DON'T LEAVE SICILY WITHOUT . . .

TEMPTING FATE ON A LIVE VOLCANO   Sicily is home to some of the world's most active volcanoes, which are welcoming spots for nature lovers and armchair volcanologists alike. The massive Mt. Etna, on the eastern coast, and the extremely active volcanic island of Stromboli, off the northern coast, are part of a volcanic arc that also includes the active volcanic islands of Vulcano and Lipari. These are milder in temperament, but still rewarding natural wonders to explore. A relatively new range of **volcano tours** (p. 569) makes it easy (and safe) to get close.

VISITING NORMAN PALERMO   All over the city of Palermo you'll stumble upon buildings with Norman, Arab, Byzantine, French, Roman, and Greek influences. The **Palazzo dei Normanni** (p. 548) and the **Cathedral** (p. 550) highlight any walking tour of Sicily's capital city.

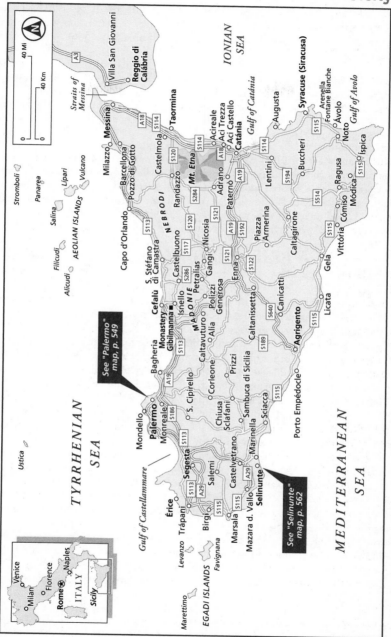

See "Palermo" map, p. 549

See "Selinunte" map, p. 562

APPRECIATING WORLD-CLASS BYZANTINE-ARAB MOSAICS No one combined Arab artistry with Byzantine decadence better than the ancient Sicilians. Enjoy these on a morning visit to **Monreale** (p. 556), just outside Palermo.

GOING GREEK Some of the best preserved Greek ruins in the world are in Sicily. Don't miss the Doric temples in the archaeological park near Agrigento, on the island's southern flank, or the ruins of the **Greek Theater of Taormina** (p. 570), high above the island's eastern shore. You can also visit stunning cities like Siracusa and Gela to see Greek ruins.

ATTENDING A PUPPET SHOW First performed in the 18th century to give commoners a chance to enjoy theater without paying for live performers, Sicilian puppet theater has enjoyed a long tradition. Today the best theaters are in Palermo, Siracusa, and Cefalù. Performing *Pupi* are still hand carved, following traditional methods, and each of the theaters has an adjacent museum where you can see the puppets up close. Handmade puppets also make a perfect Sicilian souvenir.

A BRIEF HISTORY OF SICILY

Sicily's tenuous position—strung between North Africa and the European mainland, just 160km (100 miles) from Cap Bon in Tunisia on one side and 3km (2 miles) from Calabria in Italy on the other—has made it a natural stepping stone for settlers and invaders throughout its long history. Rock carvings on the island date the first humans on Sicily to 12,000 B.C.

Sicily's Hellenistic cities—Siracusa and Catánia and what is now Messina—were founded in the 6th through 8th centuries B.C. by the Greeks, who later built vast temples, which still stand near Agrigento. Throughout the 4th and 5th centuries B.C., the Carthaginians of North Africa fought the Greeks—and later the Romans—for control and turned the island into a bloody battlefield. After the fall of Rome, Sicily labored under many occupations before returning to the Arabs in the 9th century, when Islam became the official religion. The Arab rulers tolerated Christianity and Judaism on Sicily.

When the Normans regained control of the island in the 11th century, Sicily began its Golden Age, still clinging to its ancient rituals but relying more and more on Greek, Arab, and Byzantine influences. Sicily fell to the French in the 13th century and was repeatedly sacked and oppressed for the next several hundred years. The Sicilians eventually reacted to this oppression by forming their own secret society, which they called "Mafia," a term derived from the Arabic word for "refuge." In the 1700s, this secret society, by then also known as the Cosa Nostra, began distributing a picture of a black hand, which was a formal request for protection money. Those who didn't pay faced misfortune—or worse. The Cosa Nostra is still a force in Sicily today, though it's unlikely that you'll be aware of its presence. They do not target tourists.

One delight in visiting Sicily is viewing its many pasts, one layer upon the other. Phoenician ruins on the western coast (now anchored by modern-day Palermo) lie below Norman-Arab castles and churches. Fine examples of Byzantine architecture are within walking distance of early Gothic churches.

Sicily in Threes

The Greeks called Sicily "Trinacria," which means three angles. The symbol of Sicily, and the perfect gift by which to remember your trip, is a three-legged bowl, pin, or pendant of the same name.

Medieval fortresses and baroque palaces are only a short drive apart. By the 19th century, Sicily and Naples formed a sovereign kingdom called the "Two Sicilies," which unified with Italy in 1861. After unification, Sicily became part of Italy's "poor south," and its problems were largely ignored by the Italian government.

Today Sicily exists primarily as an agricultural region, its economy heavily subsidized by tourism and profits manipulated by an ever-efficient Mafia. Efforts to turn the region into a mini–Silicon Valley are beginning to see results, but organized crime and local corruption are still factors in everyday life.

LAY OF THE LAND

Sicily, the largest island in the Mediterranean, is surrounded by the Ionian, Tyrrhenian, and Mediterranean seas, each of which gives the island a different character. Traveling around the coast is for most visitors far more rewarding than attempting the mountainous and largely rural interior. The towns I encourage you not to miss are **Palermo** (p. 548) and **Cefalù** (p. 557), to the north; **Messina,** to the northeast; **Taormina** (p. 570), **Catánia** (p. 568), and **Siracusa** (p. 566), to the east; and **Agrigento** (p. 563), to the south.

GETTING ON & OFF THE ISLAND

Palermo is accessible **by ship** from Naples and other European ports. You can also **fly** from Rome into **Palermo's Falcone-Borsellino Airport** or **Catánia's Fontanarossa Airport.** If you're set on seeing the Aeolian islands, you can sail there from Naples, tour the tiny islands, and then take another ferry to the "mainland" of Sicily. If you take the popular overnight **ferry** from Naples to Palermo, you should wake up just in time to see the sun rising over the rocky terrain. Flying into Catánia's airport at the foot of Mt. Etna is also an unforgettable experience, especially if the volcano is acting up.

Another option is to take the **train** from Rome (11–13 hr.) or Naples (9–11 hr.) to Palermo. You can also disembark sooner, in Taormina. Trains from all over Europe arrive at the port of Villa San Giovanni, where they roll onto enormous barges for the 1-hour trip across the Straits of Messina to Sicily. It's expensive, but you can rent a couchette for the trip. On you're way home, nothing is more fun than sleeping on the overnight train from Taormina, and waking up refreshed in downtown Rome.

Those choosing to fly get the best deals from **Meridiana** (www.meridiana.it), Italy's low-cost **budget airline,** which often has fares of €29 and up (one-way) from Rome, Florence, or Milan to Catánia. As with discount carrier Ryanair, there are lots of restrictions and hidden fees, so be sure to read all the fine print before booking.

Ferries to & from the Island

You can reach Sicily by ferry from Naples, Genoa, Livorno, and Reggio di Calabria through these major ferry lines:

* **Traghettionline** (☎ 010-582080; www.traghettionline.net)
* **Grandi Navi Veloci** (☎ 058-6409894 in Livorno, ☎ 010-589331 in Genoa, ☎ 091-587404 in Palermo; www1.gnv.it)
* **Tirrenia Navigazione** (☎ 199-123199; www.tirrenia.it)
* **Trenitalia** (☎ 090-661674; www.trenitalia.it; runs 20 boats a day from Reggio di Calabria to Messina)
* **TTT Lines** (☎ 095-7462187; www.tttlines.it)

Most visitors take the overnight ferry from Naples. The cost to Palermo is €40 per person for a deck seat (add €75 per person for a private cabin with bathroom) and €80 for a compact car. Those going overnight from Naples to Catánia pay more for a deck seat or a berth in a private cabin; cars on this ferry are €100.

The car ferry across the Straits of Messina (from Calabria to Sicily) is a shorter, 25-minute ride, with departures every 20 minutes or so throughout the day. Tickets can be purchased at Villa San Giovanni in Calabria (you'll have to jump out of your car and run to the little house with your car-rental form and license-plate number) and cost from €17 per car, or just €1 for foot passengers. Ferry information can be had from **Tourist Ferry Boat s.p.a.** (☎ 090-3718510 in Messina, or 090-361292 in Villa San Giovanni).

Alitalia (www.alitalia.com) and **Airone** (www.airone.com) are the other major players on these routes, with the following average round-trip rates:

* €85–€105 Rome to Palermo (price varies by day of week and time of day),
* €150 Florence to Palermo,
* €220 Milan to Palermo.

From Falcone-Borsellino Airport, it's simple enough to hop a Trinacria express train (running every half-hour 5:30am–10pm for the 1-hr. ride to Palermo; cost €4.50). A local bus also leaves the main terminal every half-hour from 8:45am to 11pm, and, if traffic is light, takes the same amount of time as the train (cost €4.80). Taxis to Palermo are pricey at €50, though, depending on traffic, you may get where you're going a bit faster this way.

GETTING AROUND THE ISLAND

It's a snap to hop from one town to another, thanks to efficient **rail** and **bus lines.** Local trains are run by **Trenitalia** (☎ 892021; www.trenitalia.it), which has a very helpful and easy-to-use website in English. Bus service on the island is not quite as reliable as train service, except within towns. For **public transportation,** try **www.sicilia.indettaglio.it**, which has a searchable database for bus routes, or ask for tickets and information at *tabacchi* in individual towns.

Sicily Itineraries

If you have only a few days in Sicily

Spend your time in **Palermo.** This is a smart port of entry by air or sea from mainland Europe, especially if you're coming from Rome or Naples. As the island's capital, Palermo serves as its cultural and financial hub, and enjoys a broad range of well-priced hotels and restaurants, as well as ample public transportation. Palermo also offers an intimate glimpse of Sicily's distinct brand of chaotic charm—from its eclectic multicultural architecture to its many museums with their comprehensive collections of Greek, Etruscan, and Roman artifacts. Based in Palermo, you can easily explore the northern coast from Trapani to Cefalù with or without your own transportation, and even zip down to the Greek ruins near Agrigento or Selinunte in just over an hour by car, bus, or rail.

If you have only 5 days in Sicily

Consider arriving in Palermo and spending half your time there, and then heading down to the Greek city of **Siracusa** for a stay in or near the old center, which is on the island of Ortygia. From here you can explore **Mt. Etna,** the popular (and expensive) resort town of **Taormina,** and the southern coast. If you're traveling by air, leave the island from **Catánia** (many airlines will allow open-flight tickets to and from Sicily at no extra charge).

If you have more than 1 week in Sicily

Divide your time between Palermo and Siracusa, as above, and add a day or two on the **Aeolian islands,** the string of volcanic islands just off the coast of Sicily, which offer everything from watersports to beachcombing to volcano tours.

Driving is also a pleasure, as you'll be cruising some of the country's best highways, thanks to the organized-crime syndicates that reportedly dominate public works contracts. Say what you will, they keep the roads in top-notch shape.

You'll save 30% to 60% on **car rentals** by bypassing the international chains and renting from such Italian companies as **Maggiore** (www.maggiore.it) or **Sicily by Car** (www.sbc.it). While their daily rates are comparable—be sure to shop around—Sicily by Car consistently has the best weekly rates for a compact rental at €80 for 5 to 7 days (Maggiore's weekly rate comes to €180; other car companies charge even more).

PALERMO

In many ways Palermo is the essence of Sicily. It's a city that combines tarnished gems like the Kalsa district, its buildings still pocked from World War II and years of neglect, with dazzling jewels like the Norman Palazzo and city cathedral.

The city reached its heyday in the 800s to 900s, when it flourished under Arab rule. In 973 it was famously described as the "city of 300 mosques." During this period and for the next century, when it was reclaimed by the Normans, Palermo was considered one of the grandest cities in Europe. Much of the architecture you see today, from smooth pink domes to Gothic spires to Byzantine basilicas, are remnants of this era.

Even during the Norman occupation, Palermo remained a bridge between East and West—look closely at the great Catholic buildings here, like the city's massive cathedral, and you'll notice that the columns are inscribed with verses from the Koran. The city was and is multicultural not only in its eclectic architecture but in its sultry charm. Over the centuries, various rulers tried to impose logic on the city plan, building arrow-straight streets (like the Via Toledo and Via Maqueda, which intersect at the heart of the city—the Quattro Canti—dividing it into four distinct districts), but Palermo couldn't be tamed, as you'll see when you wander along the narrow, meandering back streets. Here you'll come upon tiny shops selling exotic textiles and ebony statues alongside conventional Italian pottery, and stumble on small ethnic restaurants abutting traditional Italian *trattorie*. Over the years, Palermo has been inhabited by Jewish merchants, Turkish and Syrian craftsmen, Persian artists, Spanish royalty, and Mafia dons—and each faction has left its mark.

LAY OF THE LAND

You're most likely to arrive **by air** at the Falcone Borsellino–Punta Raisi Airport, 31km (19 miles) west of the city center; **by sea** at the main Port of Palermo, just minutes outside the city center; or **by rail** at the main train station, Palermo Centrale, on Piazza Giulio Cesare, just east of the center core. New Palermo is not worth visiting; you'll want to spend your time in the historical center with its web of narrow, winding streets, bisected by two pencil-straight thoroughfares, the Via Vittorio Emanuele and the Via Maqueda. These streets intersect at Palermo's core, the **Quattro Canti (Four Corners)**, at the Piazza Vigilena. The Palermo Tourist Board runs a number of green tourist kiosks, marked INFO POINT, in central Palermo, offering free maps and event listings.

The Quattro Canti is the best point of reference for exploring the city. Four diverse neighborhoods sprawl back from the square, recognizable by four distinct, sculpture-laden baroque facades that hug the tiny intersection. Each of the facades is divided into three parts representing a different theme. The fountains depict the four seasons. The niches on the middle level are adorned with statues of Spanish kings. The top levels carry the statues of Palermo's many patron saints, complete with crowns and crests. Locally, this tiny square is known as the Theater of the Sun for the way in which its features are lit by the sun, or lost in shadows, at different times of day. Back from each corner are the four distinct districts of historical Palermo that are to be explored separately: the Alberghia, Il Capo, Vucciria, and La Kalsa.

ALBERGHIA   The heart of Norman-influenced Palermo and the most multicultural section of the city is Alberghia. The streets here are lined with ethnic restaurants that offer some of the best alternatives to Italian cuisine in the country. Start sightseeing here at the **Palazzo dei Normanni** (Piazza Indipendenza, 1;

Palermo

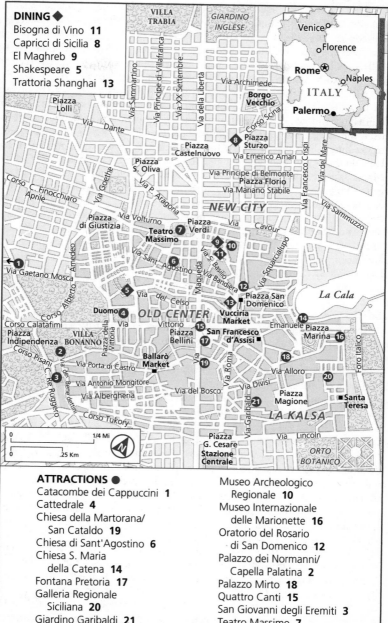

VILLA TRABIA

GIARDINO INGLESE

Venice

Florence

Rome

Naples

ITALY

Palermo

Piazza Lolli

Via Sammartino

Via Principe di Villafranca

Via XX Settembre

Via della Libertà

Via Dante

Via Archimede

Borgo Vecchio

Corso Scina

Piazza Castelnuovo

Piazza Sturzo

Via Emerico Amari

Piazza S. Oliva

Via Principe di Belmonte

Piazza Florio

Via Mariano Stabile

Via Francesco Crispi

Via del Mare

Via Sammuzzo

Corso C. Finocchiaro Aprile

Via Goethe

Via P. Aragona

NEW CITY

Piazza di Giustizia

Via Volturno

Via Cavour

Teatro Massimo

Piazza Verdi

Via Squarcialupo

Amedeo

Via Gaetano Mosca

Via Sant' Agostino

Via Maqueda

Via S. Basilio

Via Bandiera

La Cala

Via del Celso

Piazza San Domenico

Duomo

OLD CENTER

Vucciria Market

Emanuele

Piazza Marina

Corso Alberto

Corso Calatafimi

Vittorio

Piazza Bellini

San Francesco d'Assisi

Piazza Indipendenza

VILLA BONANNO

Piazza della Vittoria

Ballarò Market

Via Roma

Corso Pisani

Via Porta di Castro

Via Antonio Mongitore

Via Alberghería

Via del Bosco

Via Divisi

Via Alloro

Foro Italico

Santa Teresa

Piazza Magione

LA KALSA

Corso Tukory

Via Garibaldi

Via Lincoln

Piazza G. Cesare

Stazione Centrale

ORTO BOTANICO

0   1/4 Mi
0   .25 Km

☎ 091-7054317; €5 adults, €2.50 students, includes the Cappella Palatina; Mon–Sat 8:30am–noon and 2:30–5pm, closed Sun afternoon and holidays), a complex of palaces built by Arabs in the 9th century (its current Arab-Norman facade was last reworked in the 17th c.). The main palace is now the seat of the Sicilian parliament. Its halls are closed to the public during parliamentary sessions, primarily Tuesday through Thursday. When it's open, you can wander through the smaller reception rooms to the massive main hall with its ornate, gilded ceiling. Through the windows you can see Palermo's skyline and distant mountains. The Royal Apartments are not always open to the public except for the Byzantine Sala dei Venti. If it's open, be sure to follow the signs to the **Sala di Ruggero II,** which was King Ruggero's rapturously lovely bedroom, encrusted with mosaics of colorful peacocks and amorous leopards, and nearly as beautiful as the Cappella Palatina (see below). Outside, walled ornate gardens, called the Parco d'Orleans, have been planted over the centuries with African kapok trees, exotic rare orchids, and imported banyan trees.

From here you come to **the one "must-see" sight of Palermo,** the **Cappella Palatina** ✖✖✖ (in the Palazzo dei Normanni; ☎ 091-7054879; Mon–Fri 9–11:45am and 3–5pm, closed weekend afternoons). This is Palermo's most popular tourist attraction—with long lines to prove it. The interior of the small chapel, built by Roger II when he ruled Sicily in 1130, is an explosion of precious gems and shiny mosaics covering every square inch of space. Tiny marble tiles are inlaid with gold leaf or painted to look like lapis and designed to depict stories from the Old Testament and Sicilian history. The gold and silver backing of the tiles makes them glitter. The facial expressions are more realistic and emotionally compelling than one would expect from mosaics. Art historians agree that they're among the finest in the world, equal to anything you'll see in Ravenna, the Italian city best known for mosaics. Other notable works of art in the chapel include the exquisite mosaic-encrusted throne in the nave and the traditionally Islamic *muqarna* design on the ceiling, created by North African artisans in the 12th century (a surprising element in a Christian chapel).

To the south of the Palazzo dei Normanni is the **Chiesa di San Giovanni degli Eremiti** ✖ (Via dei Benedettini; ☎ 091-6515019; €4.50; Mon–Sat 9am–1pm and 3–7pm, Sun and holidays 9am–12:30pm), where the frescoes are seriously worn. Spend your time instead wandering through the lush green cloister; it belonged to the Benedictine convent that once occupied this church. From here you can study the intricate weave of Norman and Arab architecture. The five red domes are of Arab construction. For many, this church represents the harmonious blending of cultures, which is the basis of Sicilian history.

IL CAPO The labyrinth of streets that makes up the Il Capo district—across the Corso Vittorio Emanuele and back from the Quattro Canti—is home to many of Palermo's most imposing attractions. The main **Cathedral** ✖✖✖ (Corso Vittorio Emanuele; ☎ 091-334376; www.cattedrale.palermo.it; free admission; Mon–Sat 7am–7pm, Sun 8:30am–1:30pm and 4–7pm) sprawls over a flat, palm-tree-lined square that seems out of place among the tightly clenched apartment blocks that surround it. The Cathedral has undergone many major metamorphoses over the centuries. It was built by Archbishop Gualtiero Offamilio in 1184 on the site of a crumbling basilica, and transformed into a mosque during a period of Arab control. It was restored again to a Christian church by the Normans. Each transformation left architectural additions: The twin towers were added in the 14th century, the three-arched portico made its appearance in the 15th century, and the towering, somewhat ugly baroque cupola was the fault of architect Ferdinando Fuga in the 18th century. As with many of Palermo's great churches, the inside is relatively barren. But the tombs of famous Norman rulers, including Roger II and Frederick II, are worth a peek.

Also worth a visit in this district is the **Chiesa di Sant'Agostino** (Via Sant'Agostino; daily 8am–noon and 4–5:30pm), a classic Gothic church complete with a rare-for-Palermo 14th-century rose window. In the 15th century, the side portal, which is now a defining feature, was hastily added. Many of Palermo's churches are austere shells tucked inside lavish exteriors, but the artwork inside Sant'Agostino is downright decadent. It's a popular wedding spot, though, especially on Saturday around lunchtime, when multiple wedding parties chat and men scurry about, changing flowers between ceremonies.

VUCCIRIA The liveliest of Palermo's districts is the downtrodden Vucciria, which has transformed itself in recent years from the center of Palermo's poverty and crime to a quaint, offbeat village with a colorful daily street market, a new crop of boutiques, and some of Palermo's best museums.

Top on the list is the **Museo Archeologico Regionale** ★★ (Via Bara all'Olivella, 24; ☎ 091-6116805; €4.50; Mon–Fri 8:30am–6pm, Sat–Sun and holidays 8:30am–1:30pm), a world-class showcase of Sicilian antiquities—Etruscan, Roman, and everything in between. The museum contains over 10,000 Etruscan artifacts, making it one of the largest such collections anywhere, as well as 5th-century Phoenician sarcophagi, Greek carvings, bronze statues, and the world's largest collection of ancient ship anchors. The museum is straightforward to navigate, with exhibits on either side of a lush, tranquil cloister. The ground-floor exhibits include Phoenician, Greek, and Egyptian sculptures and artifacts. The highlights of the collection, also housed on the ground floor, are the sculptures, or *Metopes*—all of them unearthed at the seven Greek temples of Selinunte (p. 561)—including Hercules entangled with an Amazon, Actaeon fighting off angry dogs, and Perseus beheading the Gorgon. They're beautiful and a must-see, especially if you plan on visiting the temples themselves later in your visit. Off the main exhibit room is a tiny room lined with 19 lions' heads that were spouts for a massive fountain (59 lion heads in all) from the Templo della Vittoria in Selinunte. The halls upstairs are lined with Etruscan vases and mirrors, and other treasures.

Palermo's churches are largely used by the island's devout, who frown upon visitors entering during Mass. Endure their wrath and be sure to peek inside the **Chiesa di San Domenico** (Piazza San Domenico; ☎ 091-5844872; Mon–Fri 9–11:30am, Sat–Sun 5–7pm), with its monumental baroque facade and high bell towers. It was built in 1640, and its facade was added more than a century later. Inside are the tombs of Sicilian nobility and high-ranking politicians like former Prime Minister Francesco Crispi, making it comparable to the Pantheon in Rome in terms of cultural and historic significance. The inner church is inlaid with marble designed by famous marble craftsman Antonello Gagini and members of the

Gagini school. Also don't miss the **Oratorio del Rosario di San Domenico** (Via dei Bambinai, 2; Mon–Fri 9am–1pm, Sat 2–5:30pm) and the **Oratorio del Rosario di Santa Zita** (Via Valverde, 3; Mon–Fri 9am–1pm and 3–6pm, Sat 9am–1pm), which sit just behind the church. Inside these marble chapels are some of Palermo's finest stuccowork, done by Giacomo Serpotta, who labored from 1686 to 1718 to carve the dozens of cherubim who frolic on the altars, their faces eerily lifelike. The Oratorio del Rosario di Santa Zita was damaged by heavy bombing during World War II, and major works of art have not yet been restored. Miraculously, these little angels survived, and are worth seeing. The oratories are sometimes not open at the posted times, but ask inside the church and the custodian will open the door for you. In the Oratorio del Rosario di San Domenico, check out the columns to the right of the altar. The lizard is meant to depict strength and courage. Above the altar is a cupola painted with gawking knights, noble ladies, and young boys who seem to be peering down as you stare up.

LA KALSA   Once plagued by poverty and its natural consequences, crime and corruption, the district of La Kalsa was on the black list of most visitors for decades. Mother Theresa even set up a mission here to help the city's poorest victims. But now, after several decades of revitalization, La Kalsa is one of the bright spots of Palermo and home to some of its most compelling museums and churches. Give yourself a few hours and start a thorough exploration of this district at the Quattro Canti, with its web of streets winding around **La Martorana and Chiesa di San Cataldo** ★★ (Piazza Bellini, 3; entrance to San Cataldo €1; Mon–Sat 8:30am–1pm and 3:30–5:30pm, closed Sun afternoon). These two churches have teetered between Christian and Muslim worship for centuries and today represent Palermo's unique, multilayered religious past. La Martorana, also known as the **Chiesa dell'Ammiraglio,** was built by the Syrian Emir George of Antioch in the 12th century as a mosque, though it was never used as one. Keen eyesight—or better yet, good binoculars—will help you see the Arabic lettering repeating "Allah" around the base of the cupola. The Greeks took over the church shortly after it was built between 1140 and 1158, and covered the interior with glittering mosaics depicting scenes of George of Antioch hiding from the Virgin Mary, and local honcho Roger II with a crown reportedly given to him by Christ. In 1433, the church became a Benedictine convent, and the good, if shortsighted, sisters reworked it by destroying the Norman apse, adding some flowery baroque design to the facade and replacing many of the mosaics with now-faded frescoes. In the 1930s, the church was returned to the Greek Orthodox community of Palermo, which still celebrates the Greek Mass here. A bonus to visiting this church is the sense of cultural understanding and acceptance this church seems to invite, as visitors of varying religions come to pray.

Adjacent to La Martorana is the rustic church of **San Cataldo,** housed in an intimate structure topped with three classic red Arab-Norman domes. The interior of the church is completely devoid of decoration except for its wrought-iron cross. It's also completely lit by candles (the church was never wired for electricity) and the flickering lights against the worn wooden benches and brick arches give it a deeply serene, spiritual aspect that's quite moving. If you're lucky, you'll visit San Cataldo when one of the local clergy is humming prayers.

Farther into the winding web of streets in La Kalsa is Sicily's most impressive art museum, and one of the finest collections in Italy, the **Galleria Regionale Siciliana** ★★★ (Via Alloro, 4; ☎ 091-6230011; €4.50; Tues–Fri 9am–2pm, Tues–Thurs also 3–8pm). The setting couldn't be more ideal: The 15th-century **Palazzo Abatellisis** is a superb example of Catalonian-Gothic architecture—all Spanish-style mullioned windows and narrowing towers. Though it was nearly destroyed by bombs in World War II, it was tastefully restored in 1954 and has housed this collection of sculpture and paintings, dating from the Middle Ages through the 18th century, ever since. The inner courtyard is lined with rows of marble sculptures from the Romanesque era through the 16th century. A closed hall surrounding the courtyard houses wooden sculptures from the 12th to the 16th centuries and delicate stone statues from the 14th and 15th centuries. The museum's prize work of art is the intricately detailed bust of Eleonora of Aragon, created by Francesco Laurana in 1471 and widely considered to be his master-piece. Farther along, the mural-size *Triumph of Death* fresco—painted in the 15th century by an unknown artist, or, some believe, a collection of artists—depicts Death as a fiendish fellow on horseback, shooting arrows at the local youth, who dodge them and dart away. On the mezzanine you can sit and ponder this depiction of death on a lone bench that hangs perilously close to the railing-free edge.

If you've got kids in tow, don't miss the **Museo Internazionale delle Marionette** 🧒 (Via Butera, 1; ☎ 091-328060; www.museomarionettepalermo.it; adults €3, children €1.50; Mon–Fri 9am–1pm and 4–7pm; Sat 9am–1pm), which celebrates the art of puppetry, as much a part of the Sicilian life as sunshine. Here you'll find over 3,000 puppets ranging from traditional Italian puppets from the theaters of Naples and Catánia, to a small collection of international puppets from China, India, Turkey, and Africa. Every Friday afternoon the curators hold a show (check the website for schedules).

Not far from the puppet museum is Palermo's oldest tree, a 150-year-old tan-gled *ficus benjamin* that reaches 25m (82 ft.) and covers the midsection of the **Giardino Garibaldi** (Piazza Marina; free admission). This garden is a calm oasis in the middle of an often overwhelmingly hectic city and a great spot to bring a pic-nic lunch. The benches stay cool under the shade of the tree, even in the most grueling heat.

Beyond the historical center, Palermo quickly becomes suburban, and tiny boutiques are replaced with supermarket-style chain stores and old *palazzi* give way to modern, post-war apartment blocks. There's not much to see or do in these neighborhoods, and they should be avoided.

ACCOMMODATIONS BOTH STANDARD & NOT

The historical center is the most enjoyable place to stay in Palermo. Many of the city's best-priced hotels are right around the Via Roma, between the train station and the Quattro Canti. But there are two spots in particular that will give you a better taste of local flavor than a standard hotel.

€   Staying at **Giorgio's House** (Via A. Mongitore; ☎ 091-525057; www.giorgios house.com) is a bit like finding that long-lost Sicilian cousin we all wish we had. Giorgio will take care of everything, from picking you up at the airport to plan-ning your itinerary. He'll take you around the city or highlight your map so you can do it yourself. There are only three rooms for rent here, each of which is impeccably clean with large comfortable beds and luxurious bedding, so book as soon as you know your dates. Prices are €29 per person for a double room for up to 2 nights, and €26 a person for 3 nights or more. Giorgio will also organize windsurfing courses, sailing courses, and wine tastings. Nothing you suggest is beyond this Sicilian's reach. This is truly living like a local.

€€   The **Casa Giuditta** (Via Savona, 10; ☎ 328-2250788; www.casagiuditta. com) is another dream spot in Palermo, where you'll feel as if you're staying with relatives (ones you like!), or at least with good friends. The Casa Giuditta is, by definition, a bed-and-breakfast, but it has the distinct feel of a private holiday home. It has double rooms for €78 and gives discounts for families and longer stays. They also have six-person apartments in the center of Palermo for just over €100 a night. Rooms are comfortable and private. You'll feel as though everyone at the front desk knows your business, but there's a wonderful intimacy about this hotel that you'll remember long after you've left.

€€   You don't need to pay more than €100 for a hotel room in Palermo, so staying at the **Hotel Tonic** (Via Mariano Stabile, 126; ☎ 091-581754; www.hotel tonic.com) can be considered a splurge. I list it because it has a sense of style that gives it a much more pricey feel. The rooms (€100 for a double) are elegantly appointed with antique furniture, rich bed linens, velvet curtains, and ample pillows. Unusual for Italy, the rooms are spacious, with enormous beds and lots of floor space. All rooms come with phone, safe, and wet bar. You won't get the personal service offered at Giuditta or Giorgio's, but this is the best choice for those who prefer a more anonymous hotel setting.

DINING FOR ALL TASTES

It's difficult to dine poorly in Palermo—even the street food is top quality. But instead of eating on the main thoroughfares where restaurants tend to cater to group tourists, try delving deep into the individual districts, where you'll find tiny restaurants with uniquely Sicilian fare.

€   One of the most unique dining experiences you can have in Palermo is on the balcony of the **Trattoria Shanghai** ★ (Vicolo dei Mezzani, 34; ☎ 091-5897025). Getting to the restaurant is half the adventure. You'll enter through the door of a typical historical Palermo apartment building and follow the signs upstairs. There you'll go into the tiny apartment-cum-restaurant. The owner and his children will probably be sitting watching TV in the kitchen and will barely look up to greet you before nodding or pointing to a table (it's a bit odd—and you may feel as though you're crashing someone's mealtime rather than going to a restaurant—but the cooking more than makes up for it). Choose a seat on the balcony overlooking the Vucciria market; depending on the crowds and availability, what you order is often lifted before your eyes in a tattered wicker basket from the vegetable stand below. A simple and filling plate of sardine and tomato pasta costs just €4; other pastas and vegetable dishes, just as fresh and delicious, range from €4 to €6. You'll want to order multiple courses just to stay and enjoy the Palermo life below.

€   African cuisines are popular in Palermo. For good, authentic Tunisian dishes, head to one of the city's oldest dining establishments, **El-Maghreb** (Via Bara all'Olivella, 75; no phone). Here you can enjoy *shwarma* and kabobs for €3 to the sound of Arabic music. The ambience is rustic, with whitewashed walls and wrought-iron tables, and the atmosphere is casual and friendly.

€   If you're looking for something less substantial, the **Bisogno di Vino** (Via Giacalone, 2; ☎ 348-3824787) combines light dishes with quality wines in a junglelike atmosphere, with rubber plants outside. This is Palermo's answer to bar food in the sense that the offerings are more for nibbling, but you can easily fill up on the cheese and sausage plate for just €4 coupled with a €2 glass of Sicilian white wine.

€€   For reasonably priced seafood and a warm atmosphere, try **Capricci di Sicilia** ✹✹✹ (Via Instituto Pignatelli, 6; ☎ 091-327777), which fills up first with locals, especially on weekends. Sardine, broccoli, and sea urchin pasta is the specialty for €8, but you can also rely on the antipasto bar for €6, especially for lunch. This is a tiny spot that feels very local and intimate.

€€   It's difficult to spend too much on a meal in Palermo. A splurge here means spending €10 to €12 on a plate of pasta. If you're in the mood for "going all out," head straight to **Shakespeare** (Salita Artale, 5; ☎ 091-7495205), in the shadow of the cathedral. The food here tastes as though it's worth much more than you're paying, with healthy portions of seafood (try the seafood packet in phyllo pastry) for just €11. This is where trendy professional Palermitans come for a night out, so you'll get a good glimpse of local life. Don't be in a hurry, though; this is a restaurant for lingering over your meal and savoring the local energy.

THE OTHER PALERMO

Straight back toward the harbor from the San Domenico church and oratories is the cacophonous, crowded, exhilarating morning market, **Mercato Vucciria,** which is best known for its swaying carcasses of meat hanging from the awnings over a fog of dry ice; and its live seafood "demonstrations," in which the fishmonger ends up swallowing some sort of squirmy, live sea creature as the gathering crowd gasps in disgust. How entertaining is this? Look up and you'll see the elderly Palermo residents hanging perilously out their windows to watch the morning spectacle as if it were a television sitcom.

Here, among the stalls and decaying buildings, you'll get an idea of the local Palermo palate and how it differs from others across the country. Almost every stand sells hot peppers, exotic spices, and other condiments that you won't find in mainland Italian cuisine. You'll also see couscous instead of pasta, Asian rice, and oddly shaped imported vegetables. Don't be shy about asking questions. The vendors will welcome you and explain the produce and how to prepare it. You'll likely be offered wedges of ripe fruit or chunks of raw vegetables dipped in open jars of hot peppery confections if you feign even the slightest interest. The seafood dealers will dish out cooked mussels and clams on request, and the butchers always seem to have some cured meat to nibble on. Never mind if you don't understand them, their gestures will generally get the point across, and you'll come away feeling like a local—and satisfied enough to skip lunch.

NIGHTLIFE

Palermo's 19th-century opera house, **Teatro Massimo** (Piazza Teatro Massimo; ☎ 091-6053111; www.teatromassimo.it; adults €3, seniors and students €2; guided tours every half-hour Tues–Sun 10am–3:30pm), dominates the cityscape. It's been a controversial site, ravaged by corruption and nearly razed during World War II, but today it's a well-respected institution, adequately (if not spectacularly) serving those with cultural tastes. Performances are second tier, as few big name performers make it to Sicily, and the sets and performances are several rungs down from what you'd find in Naples, Venice, or Milan. Tickets start around €19 and go up to €100. Outside in the courtyard, a lively mix of buskers give entertaining outdoor street performances, vying with one another for the crowd's loose change.

A SIDE TRIP FROM PALERMO

Just 8km (5 miles) from the city center is the day-trip destination to end all day-trip destinations, the magnificent **Cattedrale di Monreale** (Piazza Duomo, Monreale; ☎ 091-6404413; free admission, recommended audioguide €4; daily 8am–6pm), one of the most spectacularly mosaiced churches in Christendom. You thought St. Mark's in Venice was over the top? Wait until you enter this giant complex, the last of the Norman Sicilian cathedrals—an amalgam of different styles, with elements from Muslim, Byzantine, and Romanesque architecture added over the years. Inside, a whopping 6,340 sq. m (68,243 sq. ft.) of gold mosaics are plastered over every conceivable space, from the arched apse ceiling to the sanctuary aisles. Of special note are the luminous scenes from the Old

---

Mafia Tours of Corleone

Just 60km (38 miles) out of Palermo, toward the center of the island, is the famous Mafia haven of Corleone. Seeing the sheer number of construction cranes that dot the city sky, it's not hard to believe that organized crime is still an integral part of everyday life here. Many of the city center's buildings are under scaffolding, which in Sicily usually means that money is being laundered through bogus construction contracts. But you aren't here to linger; you're here to visit the Mafia museum, officially called the **Centro Internazionale Documentazione sulle Mafie e sul Movimento Antimafia** (Palazzo Provenzano, Via Orfanotrofio; ☎ 091-8463655; free admission; Mon–Sat 9am–1pm and 3–7pm, Sun 9am–1pm), which is a serious look at Italy's fight against organized crime. There are reams of court documents, displays of bullets from famous hits, and an uncomfortable number of bloody pictures of arrests, murders, and maimings. It's worth coming here to understand Italy's struggle to stamp out the Mafia. The fact that this museum even exists in what is widely known as the heart of Mafia country is a testament to the fact that the struggle is getting results. At the time of this writing, the Mafia museum was under a veil of scaffolding, too.

Testament over the nave, and the **Christ Pantocrator,** in the main apse, whose eyes seem to follow you as you roam the church (it's an optical illusion but fun to see). The artists were Venetians and Sicilians who were perfecting mosaic techniques during the 12th and 13th century; in certain areas, the work gets a more experimental edge to it. The complex also houses a lovely and contemplative Benedictine cloister set with 228 twisted columns inlaid with mosaics.

CEFALÙ

The second city of the northern coast is the tiny town of **Cefalù,** famous for its giant head-shaped rock, **La Rocca,** which is accessible by a winding staircase called the **Salita Saraceno.** You may want to base yourself in Cefalù, especially if you plan to explore the Aeolian islands, which are accessible from the harbor here, but accommodations are often expensive. The charm of Cefalù is the way its medieval old town is so carelessly scattered along the coast, providing frequent glimpses of the sea. It's enough to spend your time here just wandering around the historical city center, dipping into the main monasteries built by Frederick II and Roger II, or gazing at the enormous and clumsy **Duomo di Cefalù** (Piazza del Duomo; ☎ 0921-922021; free admission; daily 8am–noon and 3:30–7pm), with its two towers that seem to converge at the top (an optical illusion, of course). The church was built by Roger II, supposedly to fulfill an impulsive promise he made to God when his ship was caught in a storm off the coast. The interior of the church has an 1150 mosaic of an emotional Christ holding a Bible.

ACCOMMODATIONS

Staying in Cefalù can be pricey because of growing interest in this coastal town, but there are still a few options if you book early.

€€ **Villa Gaia** (Via V. Pintorno; ☎ 0921-420992; www.villagaiahotel.it) offers good-size double rooms for €140 during the summer months and €98 in the off season. The rooms are very clean with large beds, and many have sea views. Even though the hotel is close to the city center, most rooms are in the back, so street noise is minimal. This is a hotel that fills up seasons ahead by returning customers, so book as far in advance as you can.

€€€ Another good value hotel, though not as charming as the Villa Gaia, is the reliable old **Astro Hotel** 🧒 (Via Roma, 105; ☎ 0921-754639; www.astro hotel.it), which is straight out of the 1960s, decor-wise. It's clean, though, the rooms are ample, and the bathrooms are large by Italian hotel standards. A single room starts at €60, doubles at €110. A bonus is the different types of beds, especially if you're traveling with kids. Ask for cots, baby beds, or whatever you need, and the staff members are likely to come through.

DINING FOR ALL TASTES

Dining well in Cefalù takes a bit of work. Restaurants catering to tourists have raised prices and lowered quality, but there are a few holdouts from a time when quality was all that mattered.

€ Of all the restaurants on the main square, Piazza del Duomo, the only one offering good value is the **Ostaria del Duomo** (Piazza del Duomo; ☎ 0921-421838). Expect very filling plates of traditional Sicilian cuisine, mainly seafood-based, for under €10. They have an extensive wine list, even by the glass, and the view of both the imposing cathedral and the evening *passeggiata* complete the dining experience.

€€ Another good bet is **Al Gabbiano** (Lungomare G. Giardia; ☎ 0921-421495), on the waterfront, which offers a decisively romantic dining experience. The specialties are seafood—I like the swordfish rolls for €11, but pastas are also available and are a decent deal at €7.

AEOLIAN ISLANDS

Wildly diverse and seductively appealing for anyone in search of an island getaway, Sicily's Aeolian islands are among the best offbeat escapes in the Mediterranean. The tiny islands are the peaks of a 3,000m (9,840-ft.) volcanic mountain range that was formed more than a million years ago. Today two of the islands, Vulcano and Stromboli, still smolder and sizzle, but the rest are largely dormant. In the warmer months, hydrofoils and ferries leave from Cefalù, Milazzo, and Messina, and hop from island to island. The main island is Lipari and almost all mainland ferries stop here first. A standard fare from Milazzo to Lipari (about a 2-hr. journey), with one or more side trips to other islands, is €11. The hydrofoils, of course, are faster and more expensive.

Hydrofoil & Ferry Travel Times from Lipari

Destination	Hydrofoil Travel Time	Ferry Travel Time
Alicudi	2 hours	N/A
Filicudi	1 hour 30 minutes	N/A
Panarea	50 minutes	N/A
Salina	35 minutes	45 minutes
Stromboli	1 hour	3 hours 45 minutes
Vulcano	10 minutes	25 minutes

LAY OF THE LAND

I recommend that you base yourself in **Lipari,** as it offers the widest range of rooms and apartments. As the capital of the Aeolian islands, it also has the most to see. The **Citadel** is the focal point in the only real town in the Aeolians. Start at the Via del Concordato, with its 17th-century **Cattedrale di San Bartolomeo** and its 12th-century Benedictine cloister. Then head straight for the **archaeological dig,** which is a quarry for the nearby **Museo Archeologico Eoliano** (Via del Castello; ☎ 090-9880174; €4.50; daily 9am–1:30pm and 3–7pm). You can easily spend a few hours poking around the vases, sculpture, and other ancient artifacts in the two buildings that make up this museum. German and Italian tourists come here for the clear waters, the snorkeling, the scuba diving, and its beaches.

The most popular beaches are at Canneto, a 20-minute walk north of the town, and Spiaggia Bianca, a bit farther north. This second beach was named for its white sands, an anomaly on the islands, whose sands are mostly black.

Panarea is a ritzy resort island, complete with Greek-style whitewashed villas and very expensive restaurants. Sleek yachts cater to movie stars and wannabes. Paparazzi speedboats circle the islands like pesky mosquitoes. There's a fascinating 23-hut **Bronze Age Village** on the southern shore, but most of the best artifacts are on display at the Archaeological Museum in Lipari. The island is busy in August, and then sinks into a heavy lethargy for the rest of the year.

Unlike Vulcano and Lipari, **Salina** is wooded and speaks to visitors who love the outdoors; hikes take you to the volcanic peaks of **Fossa delle Felci** and **Madonna Del Terzito.** Religious pilgrims trek through the valley between the two during the mid-August Feast of the Assumption (which can be a reason to stay away at this time). The island produces vegetables, citrus, and Malvasia wine.

Stromboli is best at night, when the fireworks from the very active volcano light up the night sky and make the water look like a blazing pool. Almost everything on this island revolves around the volcanic activity. There are a handful of tour operators who specialize in guided visits to the volcano. My favorite is **Magmatrek** (Via Vittorio Emanuele; ☎ 090/986-5768; www.magmatrek.it), which offers a marvelous 5-hour evening trek for €22 (departs daily 4pm, Mar–June).

Vulcano, the archipelago's second largest island after Lipari, is fascinating if you're into live volcanoes and inexpensive spa treatments. The Fossa di Vulcano crater is a steamy reminder that this island is very much alive. The mud at the **Laghetto di Fanghi** is therapeutic. Sulfur bath treatments are synonymous with Vulcano for Italians who summer on Sicily. Access to the public mud baths is €1.50, which includes entrance to the steaming pools and beach. Hotels along the coast offer treatments, including massage and shower starting at around €35. You may not want to stay overnight because the smell of sulfur can be overpowering after a few hours.

Filicudi and **Alicudi,** two small, isolated islands, are perfect for nature lovers. They're also great for tent campers and those who don't need amenities. If camping is not for you, this is a fine island to visit for an afternoon hike; just take a ferry from one of the other islands.

ACCOMMODATIONS ON THE AEOLIAN ISLANDS

€ You can spend a lot of money to sleep on the Aeolian islands, and because it can take a couple of hours to get here from the mainland, a day trip really isn't advisable. The best deals are on Lipari, where you should get in touch with legendary **Diana Brown** (Vico Himera, 3; ☎ 090-9812584; www.dianabrown.it). She has double rooms starting at €40 and self-catering mini-apartments with kitchenettes starting at €40 per person. When her B&B is full, she'll go out of her way to help you find something else.

€€–€€€ If Diana can't help, try the **Hotel Oriente** (Via G Marconi, 35; ☎ 090-9811493; www.hotelorientelipari.com). Beds are on the small side, and the atmosphere borders on cluttered, with antique farm tools lining the white walls, but the Oriente is cozy and inviting. The best part of the hotel is the garden and a staff of locals who are intensely protective of their island, but generous with its secrets.

€€€   On Stromboli, my favorite place to stay is **La Locanda del Barbablu** (Via Vittorio Emanuele, 17–19; ☎ 090-986118; www.barbablu.it), with small but comfortable rooms starting at €120.

WESTERN SICILY: TRAPANI PROVINCE

This is Muslim Sicily and, surprisingly, the home of the famously sweet Sicilian Marsala wine. Unfortunately, it's become touristy and expensive in recent years, but the byproduct is a full agenda of community activities, mostly centered in the provincial capital of Trapani. During the summer there are outdoor plays, concerts, and fairs almost every weekend. This area makes a fun-filled day trip from Palermo, but staying here isn't recommended unless you're willing to spend a lot for very little. The region around Trapani is one of Sicily's richest, producing coral, tuna, and salt. Don't even bother looking at Trapani until you get past the concrete jungle on the outskirts and dive into the old historical center, which is a fine mess of tangled streets that intersect with Via Garibaldi and the Corso Vittorio Emanuele. Once here, don't miss the **Cattedrale di San Lorenzo** (Corso Vittorio Emanuele; ☎ 0923-432111), styled in classic 18th-century baroque.

Erice: Honeymooner Heaven

The city of Trapani is not the province's favorite city. That honor goes to medieval **Erice,** which is known for its Carthaginian walls still covered with Punic etchings and symbols, and for the lovely 14th-century Duomo, Chiese Matrice, at its heart. The city was founded by early-Mediterranean settlers known as the Elymians, who worshiped the goddess of fertility (known as Astarte to the Elymni, Aphrodite to the Greeks, and Venus to the Romans). Early Elymni art depicts her annual winter departure with a random escort to her shrine in what is now El Kef in Tunisia. When she returned, springtime began in Sicily. Tiny Erice, dramatically perched high in the mountains (at 743m/2,437 ft.), is one of my favorite medieval towns in Europe. It's overcrowded with tour buses during the day, so it's important to stay overnight and have it to yourself. Superstitious Sicilians who wish to honor the goddess of fertility honeymoon here even today. Many couples who are hoping to begin a family book a room in one of the small *pensioni* that line the narrow cobblestone streets. Romans practiced a form of holy prostitution by keeping women of the night (and day) in the city temple to service the local men. Erice is also deliciously famous for its sweet cakes. They are replicated all across the island, but none as wonderfully decadent as the originals here. If you'd like your own romantic tryst, try the reasonably priced **Edelweiss** (Cortile Padre Vincenzo; ☎ 0923-869158), where rooms start at €82 per double, per night.

EGADI ISLANDS

A quick trip to one of the three islands that make up the Egadi archipelago is a good way to round out your tour of this section of Sicily. Ferries run from Trapani and Marsala, take about 10 to 20 minutes, and cost between €2.50 and €6, depending on the season.

Levanzo is best known for its **Grotta del Genovese** with its cave etchings of bison and deer—animals one doesn't automatically associate with Sicily. Visiting the caves is an adventure unto itself because you must first locate the custodian, **Signor Natale Castiglione,** who will either be at his souvenir shop just behind the port or at ☎ 339-7418800 (ncasti@tin.it). For €5.50 (by foot) or €12 (by boat), he'll take you deep into the caves. You can try to find the caves yourself, but they're not well marked and the trek with Mr. Castiglione is far more colorful.

For a taste of island wildlife, head to the car-free **Marettimo** and pick up a local hiking map. This is also a good island for swimming, sunbathing, or fishing (contact the **San Giuseppe Association** at ☎ 0923-923290).

Farther out to sea is the largest of the islands, **Pantelleria,** which is just 80km (50 miles), from the Tunisian coast. This island, a short flight from Palermo or a 4-hour ferry ride from Trapani, is hugely popular with wealthy Italians and foreign movie stars, but the real allure is its volcanic landscape. Near Montagna Grande, the island's primary, 823m (2,743-ft.) volcano, are 24 red craters made from red volcanic rock, which contrast dramatically with the black lava terrain. Add to that lush vineyards and exotic plant life, like caper bushes, and you'll understand Pantelleria's allure.

SELINUNTE

Like so many of the ancient ruins you see across Italy, Selinunte reminds me of how fleeting empires can be, and how even the most magnificent buildings and cities decay and disappear. One of the mightiest and most powerful of the Greek outposts, Selinunte was founded in the 7th century B.C. by immigrants from Syracuse who thrived in this coastal locale, building temple after temple as a thank you to the gods for their generosity. The statues and friezes they created for these temples now fill the museums in Palermo; once you've seen them, you'll want to journey to their source. At the height of its glory, the ancient city had some 100,000 residents. The death blow came in 250 B.C., when Carthage pillaged Selinunte not once but twice. It was forgotten until the 16th century, when Sicilians started to settle this area once again.

Getting There

Selinunte is 122km (76 miles) southwest of Palermo and 113km (70 miles) west of Agrigento. If you're driving from Palermo or Agrigento, allow at least 2 hours. The easiest way to get there without your own wheels is by train to Castelvetrano. Shuttle buses for €2.50 (get your ticket first in the *tabacchi* inside the train station) run half-hourly from the train station to the site.

Touring the Ruins

When you approach the archaeological grave-land, you'll be overwhelmed by its haunting desolation. The ruins of the once-mighty temples, most of them built

Selinunte

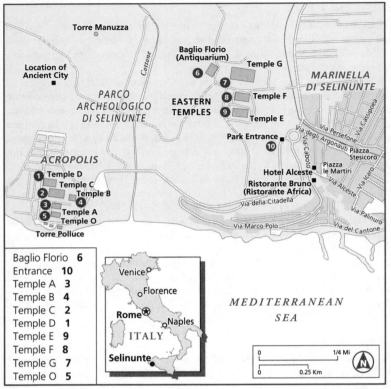

Baglio Florio	**6**
Entrance	**10**
Temple A	**3**
Temple B	**4**
Temple C	**2**
Temple D	**1**
Temple E	**9**
Temple F	**8**
Temple G	**7**
Temple O	**5**

in the 5th century B.C., lie in vulnerable heaps along the cliff tops above the sea. They fell in stages, as mighty earthquakes shook this region.

There are two main areas: the **Acropolis** and the **Eastern Temple** ★★ kids (☎ 0924-46251; €4.50; Mon–Sat 9am to 1 hr. before sunset, Sun 9am–noon and 3–7pm). In the Acropolis the temples are brilliantly named A, B, C, D, E, F, G, and O. Ask for the free site map at the ticket stand (they won't offer it unless you ask). The oldest is **Temple C,** dedicated to Apollo, which was built in the mid–6th century B.C. Many of the exhibits in Palermo's archaeological museum (p. 551) were unearthed at Temple C, including the Gorgon mask. The next oldest is believed to be **Temple D,** which was built in the late 6th century B.C. and dedicated to Neptune. The Eastern Temple, dominated by **Temple G,** is a short walk up a gravel road. The most endearing of all these temples is **Temple E,** partly because it was so completely reconstructed in the 1950s, and partly because of the way the columns reflect the sun and cast shadows on the plateau. These are magical ruins, which you can wander around for hours. They're also especially child-friendly, with bathrooms, refreshment stands, and lots of wide-open spaces.

AGRIGENTO

You must fit a trip to the Greek ruins of Agrigento into your Sicilian agenda. But you should not stay there overnight. Much of the area is marred with unfinished shells of buildings that are built quickly at night before local authorities can stop them. Known as *abusivismi,* they are built without permits, often, it is said, for the financial benefit of some organized-crime syndicate, and many end up being abandoned. Many of them are plainly visible from the **Valley of the Temples** ✿✿✿ (Archaeological Park, Via dei Templi entrance indicated by signposts; €6; western zone daily 8:30am–7:30pm, eastern zone daily 8:30am–10pm). Founded a century after Selinunte, Agrigento followed much the same arc—slowly growing to prosperity, expanding its population, investing in its temples—until its run-ins with the ferocious Carthaginians. The city became a colony of Carthage until 210 B.C., when it fell into Roman hands.

GETTING THERE

Agrigento is an easy day trip from Palermo on the northern coast or from Siracusa on the southern coast. Interurban **buses** run hourly from both cities to Agrigento for around €6 and take about 2 hours. Check the seasonal schedule at any *tabacchi.* Try to avoid buses on Sundays, when schedules rarely apply. **Trains** are more reliable, departing for the 2-hour trip from Palermo's central station every 2 hours to Agrigento. The cost is €6.70. From Siracusa, consider taking a **chartered excursion** booked through Sicily's tourism bureau (**www.compagniasicilianaturismo.it**). These are van tours that shuttle small groups to a site for around €35. The train from Siracusa is trickier; you must first travel to Catánia and then switch to Agrigento; the trip can take 4 to 6 hours each way. In **your own car,** the drive from Palermo takes about 2½ hours.

TOURING THE RUINS

The archaeological park and museum, which lie in the plain below the town, are all you really need to visit on this part of the southern coast. It can be uncomfortably hot here in summer, so to beat the heat start in the western zone in the early morning, break up the day with a leisurely lunch, and a visit to the museum, and then head to the eastern zone, which is open until 10pm. Better yet, come in the off season. In the late winter, from February to early April, the whole valley is covered with almond blossoms.

The western zone is dominated by the **Temple of Zeus,** which was never completed, thanks to a Carthaginian battle and a subsequent earthquake. Had it been finished, it would have been the largest temple ever built, with 20m-high (66-ft.) Doric columns. Here you'll find the famous 8m-tall (26-ft.) *telamon* (atlas), meant to support the structure. The nearby **Temple of Dioscuri (Temple of Castor and Pollux)** is composed of fragments from different buildings. At various times it honored Castor and Pollux (twin sons of Leda); Demeter (Ceres), the goddess of marriage; and Persephone, the personification of spring. Across the Via dei Templi is the eastern zone of the archaeological park. This is a far more complex area, home to the oldest and most impressive of the temples. The first to your right after the entrance is the **Temple of Hercules,** which was built in the 6th century B.C. to honor, yes, Hercules. At one time it ranked in size with the Temple of Zeus. Today only eight pillars are standing. As you wander through the site, peek out at the distant sea, a reminder that these temples stood as a beacon to sailors and shone brightly through the day under the brutal Sicilian sun, the gold decorations no doubt adding to the sparkle. The next large temple is the nearly intact **Temple of Concord,** with its 34 columns. In the 4th century A.D. it was consecrated as a basilica, which saved it from abandonment. The original intent of this temple is a mystery; it was only named the Temple of Concord in 1748, when it was restored to the state that you see today.

The last of the major temples in the eastern zone is the **Temple of Hera,** which was used for sacrificial offerings (the red is not remnant blood, though, but the scars of fires during various wars).

The **Museo Archeologico** (Via dei Templi; ☎ 0922-40111; adults €4.50, students and seniors €2; Mon 9am–1:30pm, Tues–Sat 9am–6pm) is a comprehensive museum with very detailed explanations in both Italian and English of the many artifacts unearthed in this area. Of note are the prehistoric findings from the area and a plan of the ancient city of Akragas (the old Greek name for Agrigento). The prize piece is the red ceramic krater from 490 B.C. that was used to mix wine and water. Many similar kraters were illegally excavated from ruins in this area and sold illegally to American museums. This museum also has a full *telamon* and several *telamon* heads similar to the one found above in the Temple of Zeus.

RAGUSA

The province of Ragusa is rich in history and largely untouched by the outside world. Most Sicilians believe it is the most authentic of Italy's provinces, thanks to the absence of foreign invasions in modern times. Sicilian poet Gesualdo Bufalino appropriately calls it *un isola nell'isola* (an island within the island). Virtually no tourists come here and for me to urge you to start the trend seems almost sacrilegious. But it's such a wonderfully intriguing place, where unmarked roads wind through Sicily's own private backyard. Villas stand perched on hills overlooking cascading vineyards and orchards, and small towns like Modica magically appear in the valleys. There is very much a *cultura contadina,* or peasant culture, here, which I hope will not soon succumb to the pressures of modernity. This is primarily a wine-and-beef-producing area with pockets of oil production. Its asphalt is so durable that it's exported to weather-challenged countries like England.

Start in the provincial capital of **Ragusa** ✖✖. Originally a Norman fortress, it grew to become one of the most important Hellenistic cities of the 5th through the 1st centuries B.C. Then an earthquake in 1693 destroyed much of this island and reduced the thriving city of Ragusa to rubble. Surviving businessmen built a new city, Ragusa Alta, on the top of the hill rather than along its flanks, but diehard Ragusans refused to accept this new location and rebuilt a baroque version of ancient Ragusa exactly where it had been: clinging to the hillside. Today the ornately baroque town at the base of the hill is known as Ragusa Bassa, or simply as Ibla, and is unique on the island for its dazzling display of hillside architecture. It's hard to imagine churches built in a more precarious setting.

The two Ragusas coexisted separately until 1926, when they were officially joined as one municipality. Ragusa Alta has some baroque churches that are worth a peek, but your real gratification will come from spending a few hours wandering through the medieval streets of Ibla, below. The largest church, **Basilica di San Giorgio,** on Piazza Duomo, is so ominously top-heavy that it's a bit unnerving to stand near it. Midway up the massive steps, look directly up at the statues, which give the impression of movement—a trick that the famous architect Rosario Gagliardi repeated across this province in the many churches he designed, including the modest church of **San Giuseppe.**

Ragusa's whimsy continues all along its quaint streets. The **Palazzo Arezzo,** just off the Piazza Duomo, is covered with hedgehog sculptures. Nearby, at the **Circolo di Conversazione,** is the old haunt of Ragusa nobility, who came here to gain inspiration from the statues—of Michelangelo, Galileo, Dante, and Bellini—that still grace the somewhat faded interior.

As rich as the physical attributes of Ragusa seem, it's the people who make this place so special. There is still a sense of nobility among those who live in Ibla. If you take a leisurely lunch or morning coffee in the main Piazza Duomo square, you're likely to see working-class men kissing their superiors' hands when they greet them. The people here are welcoming to strangers and will go to great lengths to explain what's worth seeing in their town. There's a gracious friendliness here that could soon be spoiled by mass tourism, but for now few tour buses intrude on the quiet, and you should come and enjoy the tranquillity while it lasts.

From Ragusa (or Siracusa, below) try to make a side trip to **Modica,** which is a stunningly situated town that seems to spill into the valley from the top of two high hills. A monstrous auto bridge cuts the valley view in half from below, but does save hours in driving time by going over the valley rather than around it. Like Ragusa, Modica is divided into upper and lower sections and has been a victim of natural disasters for centuries. You may not want to base yourself here, but do stop by to see the glorious baroque **Chiesa di San Giorgio** in Modica Alta that sits atop a 250-step stairway. Modica was known as the Venice of the south until a devastating flood in 1902 wiped out the canals. The rivers have now been diverted and the gaps filled with cobblestone streets, perfect for walking.

ACCOMMODATIONS & DINING

€€ Staying here is not easy because hotels are scarce and amenities are few and far between. There's a perfect solution in the one-stop hotel and restaurant that has evolved from a four-room bed-and-breakfast, and that has handled basically all the city's visitors for decades. **Il Barocco** (Via Oranotrofio, 29; ☎ 0932-663105; www.ilbarocco.it) now offers lovely double rooms with original antiques, large bathrooms, and sweeping views of the town or valley below from €80. A suite costs €100. The restaurant is a true find on the island, offering authentic southern Sicilian cuisine like vermicelli with *seppie* and creative seafood dishes based on the season for well under €10 a plate. There is even an ice-cream parlor with freshly made flavors based only on seasonal fruits.

€ A much more spartan place to sleep—though it's great if you have kids—is the tiny **Le Fiorere** (kids) (Via Maria Paterno Arezzo, 104, corner of Piazza Duomo; ☎ 0932-621530; www.bblefioriere.it), which has two mini-apartments with stoves and fridges for just €30 low season, €40 high season, including breakfast and parking. The rooms are not swank, but they're the next best thing to living in a Ragusa apartment. The owners even bring up morning breakfast from the coffee bar below.

€€–€€€   The finest restaurant in Ibla is **Il Duomo** (Via Bocchieri, 31; ☎ 0932-651265), just a block from the cathedral in the old town. Try the bread homemade from local wheat, and dip it in some of the 20-odd types of olive oil. Menus change with the seasons, and main courses range from €9 to €16. Also near the cathedral is **La Bettola** (Largo Camerina, 7; ☎ 0932-653377), with its kitschy, 1940s pre-war decor. My favorite dishes are the homemade penne and the herb-infused chicken breast.

SIRACUSA

Siracusa was the most important of all the Greek cities on the coast of Sicily. In its prime, it took on both Carthage and Rome. The modern town of Siracusa has little to recommend; what visitors flock here for is the **historic island of Ortygia,** one of my favorite places on earth. Ortygia, the Old City, has been inhabited for thousands of years. The Duomo is here, as well as many ancient ruins, small crafts shops, boutiques, and charming, family-run restaurants. And, of course, there's the sea slapping relentlessly against the shore.

If you have your own transportation, approach Siracusa by the coast. Mt. Etna looms overhead, with its plume of smoke billowing in the wind. Over the centuries, Siracusa produced some of Sicily's most creative thinkers, from the Greek poet Epicharmus to the physicist and mathematician Archimedes, to the winner of the 1959 Nobel Prize for Literature, Salvatore Quasimodo. It also offers travelers a good number of choices, and good value, for both dining and sleeping.

ACCOMMODATIONS & DINING

Siracusa has a wide range of places in which to sleep, partly because in summer a number of families convert their homes into makeshift B&Bs. I'd start with **www.sleepinsicily.it**, which offers rooms in places like the **Hotel Residence Siracusa,** in the heart of Ortygia, for as little as €50 a night. These can only be booked through this website. Listings change often from season to season, but all the rooms I saw were spotlessly clean and comfortable, with friendly hosts.

€€€   By far the favorite hotel for return visitors is **Domus Mariae** (Via V. Veneto, 76; ☎ 0931-24854; www.sistemia.it/domusmariae), a converted convent attached to a working convent (which rents out rooms as well, when the hotel is full). Domus Mariae is known for its impeccable, friendly service, perhaps because it's run by nuns who seem to live vicariously through their visitors, always curious about the day's excursions and genuinely pleased to meet new people. The rooms are large, especially considering the locale in the center of Ortygia, with colorful, modern furnishings. You can almost always get a sea view if you book ahead, and you can just as easily get a discount on your room if you forfeit the view. Double rooms start at €105 without a view, €135 with a view. The one oddity here: Rooms are cleaned only every other day.

€€ A close second to the Domus Mariae is the slightly cheaper **Hotel Gutkowski** (Lungomare Vittorini, 26; ☎ 0931-465861; www.guthotel.it), in a light blue building that often blends perfectly with the sky outside, and a modern, minimalist decor that sometimes feels a little out of sync with this ancient town. Water pressure is a big problem here, and the bathrooms are tiny, even by Italian standards. Never mind—doubles are a reasonable €90, and the rooms, though somewhat bare, are large.

€ **La Siciliana** (Via Savoia, 17; ☎ 0931-68944) is known for its good food and reasonable prices. Sit as a sidewalk table, if you're lucky enough to get one, or inside, near a wood-burning pizza oven. More ambitious meals might include grilled swordfish with herbs, or spaghetti *alla Norma* with eggplant. Main courses are €6 to €14.

€€–€€€ Another option is **Minosse di Visetti** (Via Mirabella, 6; ☎ 0931-66366), on an obscure alleyway in the center of town. Go for the plate of fresh mussels with cherry tomatoes, or the *zuppe di pesce,* one of the best-tasting fish soups in town. Main courses are about €9.80 to €19.

ATTRACTIONS IN ORTYGIA

I suggest that you cross the bridge onto the island, and start walking. Go where your heart and mind lead you; it's too small an area, bordered by the sea, for you to get lost. Along the way you'll pass the major points of interest, including the **Piazza del Duomo,** one of the loveliest squares in Italy, bordered by baroque-faced palaces. Looming high above the square is the **Cathedral** ✮✮ (daily 8am–noon and 4–7pm), the former Greek Temple of Athena, with its 5th-century Doric columns providing the main support and needed balance against the gaudy baroque shell. The main altar is another surviving remnant from the Greeks, who first settled this island. The original temple was topped with a shiny golden statue of Athena that was visible from the sea and beckoned sailors to the island. Across from the cathedral is the **Palazzo Municipale,** which was built in 1629 by Juan Vermexio. His signature carving of a lizard can still be seen on the left-hand side. Below this palace are the remains of an Ionic temple that can be visited by asking the doorman inside. On the cathedral's southern flank is the **Palazzo Arcivescovile,** which holds a library of 13th-century documents. On the northwest side of the piazza is the striking **Palazzo Beneventano del Bosco,** with its lovely courtyard. On the southwest side is the **Chiesa di Santa Lucia alla Badia.**

As you continue through the twisting streets of Ortygia, you'll stumble upon the **Fontana Aretusa,** a rare freshwater fountain that once served as the city's main water supply. During the summer, migratory ducks paddle around the fountain. Smart cafes line the surrounding sidewalks, where teens gather until late in the evening. Deeper into the heart of the town, you'll come to the **Piazza Archimede,** with a fountain that seems to draw the crowds for the evening *passeggiata.* Walking to the boardwalk that skirts the island, you'll pass the former Jewish Ghetto and the recently unearthed **Jewish Miqwe** (Via GB Alagona, 52; ☎ 0931-22255; €5; daily 10am–7pm), consisting of three freshwater pools, used for ritual bathing, and a private pool for the rabbi.

ATTRACTIONS ELSEWHERE IN SIRACUSA

There is plenty to do in Siracusa outside the old town of Ortygia, starting with what is unquestionably one of the finest archaeological museums in Italy, the **Museo Archeologico Regionale "Paolo Orsi"** ★★★ (Via Cadorna; ☎ 0931-464022; €4.50, or €6 when combined with Parco Archeologico della Neapolis, below; Tues–Sat 9am–2pm). Sector A of the museum offers insight into the island's Stone Age and Bronze Age cultures, with rare prehistoric tools on display. Sector B focuses on the Greek and Roman settlements in the Siracusa area. It's here you'll find the museum's most important possession, the headless *Venus Landolina,* from the Hellenistic period in the 2nd century B.C. The last sector is primarily home to artifacts found in eastern Sicily, including sculptures found near Agrigento. The Greek vases have great style and elegance.

The nearby **Parco Archeologico della Neapolis** (Via del Teatro; ☎ 0931-66206; €4.50, or €6 when combined with Museo Archeologico; daily 9am–2pm) is an excellent accompaniment to the museum. Pick up a map with your ticket because this is a working excavation in a constant state of evolution. Don't miss the **Latomia del Paradiso (Garden of Paradise)** on the north side of the park. The Greeks used this as a prison work camp, forcing penitents to mine limestone blocks. At the center is a man-made grotto called the **Orecchio di Dionisio.** Twenty-three meters (75 ft.) high and 65m (213 ft.) deep, it was used for theatrical performances after the prison closed down. Nearby is the **Grotta dei Cordari,** a pillar-supported cave where rope was manufactured. In the park you'll find the gigantic **Teatro Greco (Greek Theater),** one of the greatest ancient theaters, which could seat 16,000 people. The Italian Institute for Drama presents plays here in the summer in even-numbered years. Across the park is the **Anfiteatro Romano (Roman Amphitheater),** which is Italy's third largest. During the 2nd century A.D., gladiators fought to the death here, and mock sea battles were staged for the people of Siracusa and surrounding villages.

CATÁNIA & MT. ETNA

Catánia is a working-class town that relies far too heavily on Mt. Etna tourism. It's not worth feeding into the overpriced frenzy and kitschy volcanic souvenirs that seem to dominate Sicily's second city. It just doesn't have the same sort of wonderful chaos as Palermo, nor does it possess the warm charm of Siracusa. You should only swing through Catánia for a coffee break on your way up or down Mt. Etna, or if you're going to or coming from Fontanarossa Airport.

You must go through at least the outskirts of Catánia to see Sicily's best natural disaster in waiting, **Mt. Etna** (get latest information from Parco Naturale dell'Etna, Via Etna, 107, Nicolosi; ☎ 095-821111; daily 9am–2pm and 4–7pm; www.parcoetna.ct.it; or from the Linguaglossa tourist office, Piazza Annunziata, 5; ☎ 095-647-352; daily 9am–3pm; www.prolocolinguaglossa.it). No matter what, you should always check with the authorities before starting up the peak. This is Europe's largest active volcano and, as recently as 2001, the monster showered the city of Catánia with ash, and lava seeped within kilometers of the tiny village of Nicolosi—where residents brought out their trusty relics of Sant'Agata to ward off the volcano's wrath (Sant'Agata, by the way, has been called on to protect this tiny village for centuries). Again in 2002, the mountain stirred, this time

Volcano Tours

- **Centro Ippico Amico del Cavallo** (Via A. Gramsci, 27, Misterbianco; ☎ 095-461-882) offers horse rides through the farmland surrounding the volcano (7-hr. return) plus additional treks for 2 or 5 days.
- **Ferrovia Circumetna** (Via Caronda, 352a, Catánia; ☎ 095-541250; www.circumetnea.it) has day treks that include transport from Catánia for around €25.
- **Natura e Turismo** (Via R Quartararo, 11, Catánia; ☎ 095-911505) offers expert treks around the craters with a volcanologist. Prices vary greatly depending on who is available and the size of your group.

from the northern flanks, and hot lava wiped out a stylish ski resort and much of a lush pine forest. Mt. Etna has four summit craters and 200 cones (major and secondary). No one is allowed all the way up to the summit craters, but many of the nearby cones are approachable by guided tour. It's strongly recommended that you not try to explore the cones on your own. The expert source for up-to-date information on volcanic activity is **Etna Online** (**www.etnaonline.it** in Italian, or **boris.vulcanoetna.com** in English). The lava near the cones is hot and slippery, and while the park officials will gladly sell you a ticket to the highest point for €4.50, they don't check your footwear or give much in the way of eruption advice. There is, however, a tiny disclaimer on your ticket that releases them from responsibility should an eruption occur.

DINING FOR ALL TASTES

A good meal in Catánia is inexpensive and easy to find. Fresh seafood is standard in most restaurants and street snacks range from *crispelle* (fritters made with either anchovies or ricotta cheese) to *arancini di riso* (round rice balls in a light batter). Desserts in Catánia are worth skipping lunch for. The famous *Olivette di Sant'Agata,* named for the patron saint who has protected this city against Mt. Etna's wrath for centuries, is a layered cake with almond paste, identifiable by its green coloring.

€ If you're planning to dine in Catánia, try the tiny **Pesce Cotto** (Via S. Sofia, 103b; ☎ 095-515959), but go early or book ahead because this perfect little trattoria has only three tables. The eatery survives on a substantial takeout business, which is also a viable option for food on the road or a picnic in the park. You can't choose your meal, though, because you'll be served exactly what the chef is making that day. You can eat in the restaurant, with wine, for less than €10.

€ A reliable choice for lunch or dinner is one of Catánia's oldest restaurants, **Turi Finocchiaro** (Via E. Reina, 13; ☎ 095-7153573). The antipasti selection, displayed on a massive table near the entrance, is really enough for lunch. For bigger appetites, the seafood dishes are fresh daily and cost around €9 for ample portions.

€   For late-night snacks and bar food, try **Guliven's** (Via Crociferi, 69; ☎ 095-311192), which offers the type of memorable experience you hope for. The outdoor tables butt up against the steps to the nearby church, on which live music, poetry reading, and other events are held throughout the year. The specialties here are dinner salads, cheese and salami plates, and stuffed sandwiches served with cold white wine.

TAORMINA

Taormina is the Positano of Sicily. It offers similarly spectacular sweeping views from its terraced perch above the sea, and is laced with wonderfully decadent romantic hotels and restaurants, giving it a general feel of luxury. But, just like Positano, it's a gorgeous resort town that has priced itself out of the average tourist's pocketbook. If Ragusa is the most authentic of Sicily's villages, Taormina is the least. English is spoken everywhere here, and tour buses have their own parking lot below the city. But it's still a worthwhile stop on a drive along the coast, or as a day trip from either Siracusa or Palermo to see the Teatro Greco (Greek Theater), and to walk and shop along its narrow main street. The city's **Teatro Greco** kids (Via Teatro Greco; ☎ 0942-232220; adults €4.50, seniors and students €2; summer daily 9am–7pm, Nov–Mar until 4:30pm) shouldn't be missed. It was so perfectly built in 3 B.C. that you can still sit in the spectator seats and watch the natural dialogue of sea and sky. Colonnades added by the Romans in A.D. 2 frame the changing set, and even now the local community theater performs here with no man-made props.

The rest of Taormina can be enjoyed by simply walking along the main streets, which are lined with gift shops, some reasonably priced. You can see Mt. Etna from many vistas, and there are churches like the baroque **Chiesa San Giuseppe** and the 13th-century **cathedral** that are worth a look. In summer you can also go down to the sea and waste a glorious day or two hanging out on the beaches. A 12th-century clock tower at the entrance of the **Borgo Medievale** marks the entrance to the city's old town. For even better views of the seaside below, climb the **Monte Tauro** and gaze out over the Saracen castle ruins.

ACCOMMODATIONS

Staying in Taormina is not cheap, especially when you consider the inflated restaurant prices that are practically unavoidable. A few nicely priced hotels are available, but it's essential to book early because these are the fastest to go.

€€   **Hotel La Campanella** (Via Circonvallazione, 3; ☎ 0942-23381; no credit cards) is a great choice if you're fit—there are over 100 steps from the street to the entrance of this tiny 12-room hotel, and at this price, just €80 for a double, you'll have to lug your bags up yourself. The rooms are simple but clean, and you can enjoy breakfast and a drink on the hotel's lush rooftop garden with views of the sea. The center of town is about 10 minutes away on foot, but the walk is picturesque, passing through a residential district.

€€   The **Hotel Condor** (Via Dietro Cappuccini, 25; ☎ 0942-23124; no credit cards) is another gem among the sparkling jewels of Taormina. It's above the town but the 10-minute walk to the main street is an easy jaunt on steps and sidewalks with hand rails. The 12 rooms are airy with large beds, spacious bathrooms, and gorgeous sea views. Doubles start at €76. The hotel also has a delicious restaurant with its own *nonna* behind the stove. The Condor is harder to get into than La Campanella because returning guests tend to book months in advance, but it's worth the effort.

CENTRAL SICILY

If you're traveling from Palermo to Agrigento, or from Palermo to Siracusa, don't miss the **Villa Romana del Casale** (near Piazza Armerina; ☎ 0935-680036; www. villaromanadelcasale.it; adults €4.50, seniors and students €2; daily 8am–6:30pm). This is widely considered the most significant Roman site on the island for its magnificent mosaics. The villa was built in the early 4th century, probably by Maximianus Herculeus, who ruled with Diocletian from A.D. 286 to 305. It was abandoned over time, ravaged by wars, and then buried under many feet of mud in a torrential storm in the 12th century. It remained covered for more than 700 years. Only in the 1950s did true excavation begin, and it still continues in various parts of the villa. The whole compound consists of some 40 rooms, most of which are still set with original mosaics. Don't attempt this site without one of the official maps—the routes change and new rooms are continually opened to the public (and others continually closed for further restoration). The most important mosaics, in the *palestra,* portray scenes from the Circus Maximus in Rome. These are the only ones of their kind in Italy. Farther along the **eastern part of the villa** is a great corridor with a mosaic hunting scene, *Ambulacro della Scena della Grande Caccia,* depicting African animals that were brought to Rome for battles with gladiators. In the **Sala delle Dieci Ragazze** are the oft-photographed bikini-clad women (note the physiques of these ladies and the jam-jar barbells they're lifting). If it's open, also try to get a glimpse of the elliptical courtyard.

Shopping on Sicily

Sicily is not a shopper's paradise. Focus your purchases on artisan items like leather goods and shoes, some of which are still handmade in villages like Taormina. Among the souvenirs representing the soul of the island are colorful pottery, handmade puppets, and jewelry. The three-legged Trinacria is said to represent the three points of Sicily.

15 The Essentials of Planning

by Bill Fink

PLANNING CAN MAKE OR BREAK A TRIP, ESPECIALLY WHEN IT COMES TO pricey Italy. In the pages that follow, we'll cover all the essential information, from when to go, to where to book, to what travelers with special needs—families, people with disabilities, and others—need to know before they hop on the plane.

WHEN TO VISIT

Spring and fall (Apr to early June and Sept–Oct), are the best times to visit Italy. Temperatures are lower, crowds are fewer, and the country is open for business. Late June through August, tourists overrun the country, the sun is blazing, and 90% of the country is on vacation in August (mostly at the same beach), with many hotels, restaurants, and some sights closed. November through March is the cheapest time to visit, with most hotels charging off-season rates and airfares being significantly less expensive. But, like in August, many locals take vacation during this time, which means a shortage of good restaurant and hotel options, and limited hours at sights.

Italy's Major Festivals

You may want to gear your visit to one of the following special celebrations. Yes, prices for hotels will be at their peak during these times, but the excitement of seeing these events may well make the splurge a worthy one.

Spring

Easter Holiday Celebrations: Virtually every city in Italy has a series of traditional celebrations during Holy Week. The Vatican is obviously at the center of things, with the Pope leading a procession across Rome. On Easter Sunday he blesses the huge crowds from his balcony at St. Peter's. Florence and Orvieto have similar celebrations, known as **Scoppio del Carro (The Explosion of the Cart),** on Easter Sunday. A mechanical dove drops from a wire to ignite a cart full of fireworks, while oxen pull the cart in a procession around town to the Duomo.

Maggio Musicale Fiorentino (Apr–June): Opera, ballet, and modern music are presented in major Florence theaters and there are some free piazza concerts.

Corso dei Ceri (Race of the Saints' Candles; May 15): Gubbio becomes a mob scene for this race of three 9m-tall (30-ft.) shrines up the streets and the mountain above the town.

Summer

Festival di Ravenna (mid-June to July): Ravenna hosts a world-renowned classical-music festival, with ballet and opera performances also on the roster.

Calcio in Costume (late June): Florence stages a series of medieval rugby matches with players in traditional costume, with the finals around June 24.

Spoleto Festival (June–July): Spoleto hosts an annual music-and-arts festival that features some of the top performers in the world.

Festa di San Pietro (late June): In honor of St. Peter's feast day, Rome holds a series of ceremonies around St. Peter's Basilica.

Giostra del Saracino (mid-June): Jousting matches are staged in Arezzo's main square, with processions of costumed characters across town.

Shakespeare Festival (July): Verona hosts a series of plays, ballets, and music related to Shakespeare.

Il Palio (July–Aug): Siena's major event is a crazy bareback horse race around the central piazza. Neighborhoods hold parties in support of their team during this 2-month time period. The races take place July 2 and August 16.

Verona Opera Season (early July to late Aug): Verona's famed outdoor opera season takes place in its large Roman amphitheater.

Umbria Jazz (mid-July): Perugia's annual world-class jazz festival attracts top names to every venue in the city.

Festa del Redentore (late July): Venice's "Feast of the Redeemer" celebrates the town's freedom from the plague in 1578.

The third weekend in July is marked with fireworks, boating events, and other festivities.

Festa International di Musica Antica (mid-July): Italy's largest Renaissance and baroque music festival is held in Urbino.

Venice International Film Festival (late Aug to early Sept): This is akin to France's Cannes Film Festival.

Fall

Regata Storica (early Sept): Venice's annual gondola and boat festival, with processions through the canals and races on the first Sunday in September.

Festa dell Uva (Sept): Chianti's annual grape harvest and wine-swilling festival happens in Impruneta, the last Sunday in September, with historical processions and plenty of tastings. Also check out the Chianti Classico festival the second Sunday of the month, in Greve.

Winter

La Scala Opera Season (early Dec to early Nov): Milan's renowned opera house features the world's finest singers.

Christmas festivities: Major celebrations in cities across Italy are highlighted by the Pope's blessing Christmas Day in St. Peter's Square, and by the display of the Virgin's girdle in Prato.

ENTRY REQUIREMENTS

International visitors to Italy must have a valid passport that expires at least 6 months later than the scheduled end of their visit.

For Residents of the U.S.: Whether you're applying in person or by mail, you can download passport applications from the **U.S. State Department** website at http://travel.state.gov. For general information, call the **National Passport Information Center** (☎ 877/487-2778).

For Residents of Australia: You can pick up an application from your local post office or any branch of Passports Australia, but you must schedule an interview at the passport office to present your application materials. Call the **Australian Passport**

The Climate at a Glance

Italy has hot, dry summers, with temperatures reaching the 90s (30s Celsius) and higher from Florence southward, and unless you get up into the Alps, the northern towns don't get a whole lot cooler. In winter, northern regions of Italy have rain and some snow, but from central Italy on south it usually doesn't get much cooler than the 50s (10s Celsius), though some winter nights will require a jacket, and occasionally snow will fall in a central Italy hill town. (See chart, below.)

Italy's Average Daily Temperature & Monthly Rainfall

Rome	Jan	Feb	Mar	Apr	May	June	July	Aug	Sept	Oct	Nov	Dec
Temp. (°F)	49	52	57	62	72	82	87	86	73	65	56	47
Temp. (°C)	9	11	14	17	22	28	31	30	23	18	13	8
Rainfall (in.)	2.3	1.5	2.9	3.0	2.8	2.9	1.5	1.9	2.8	2.6	3.0	2.1

Florence	Jan	Feb	Mar	Apr	May	June	July	Aug	Sept	Oct	Nov	Dec
Temp. (°F)	45	47	50	60	67	76	77	70	64	63	55	46
Temp. (°C)	7	8	10	16	19	24	25	21	18	17	13	8
Rainfall (in.)	3	3.3	3.7	2.7	2.2	1.4	1.4	2.7	3.2	4.9	3.8	2.9

Naples	Jan	Feb	Mar	Apr	May	June	July	Aug	Sept	Oct	Nov	Dec
Temp. (°F)	50	54	58	63	70	78	83	85	75	66	60	52
Temp. (°C)	10	12	14	17	21	26	28	29	24	19	16	11
Rainfall (in.)	4.7	4	3	3.8	2.4	.8	.8	2.6	3.5	5.8	5.1	3.7

Information Service (☎ 131-232), or visit the government website at www. passports.gov.au.

For Residents of Canada: Passport applications are available at travel agencies throughout Canada or from the central **Passport Office** (Department of Foreign Affairs and International Trade, Ottawa, ON K1A 0G3; ☎ 800/567-6868; www.ppt. gc.ca). *Note:* Canadian children who travel must have their own passport. However, if you hold a valid Canadian passport issued before December 11, 2001, that bears the name of your child, the passport remains valid for you and your child until it expires.

For Residents of Ireland: You can apply for a 10-year passport at the **Passport Office** (Setanta Centre, Molesworth Street, Dublin 2; ☎ 01/671-1633; www.irl gov.ie/iveagh). Those under age 18 and over 65 must apply for a €12 3-year passport. You can also apply at 1A South Mall, Cork (☎ 021/272-525), or at most main post offices.

For Residents of New Zealand: You can pick up a passport application at any New Zealand **Passports Office** (☎ 0800/225-050 in New Zealand or 04/474-8100) or download it from www.passports.govt.nz.

For Residents of the U.K.: To pick up an application for a standard 10-year passport (5-yr. passport for children under 16), visit your nearest passport office, major post office, or travel agency, or contact the **United Kingdom Passport Service** (☎ 0870/521-0410; www.ukpa.gov.uk).

GETTING THERE

High season on most airlines' routes to Rome is usually from June to the beginning of September. This is the most expensive and most crowded time to travel. **Shoulder season** is from April to May, early September to October, and December 15 to December 24. **Low season** is from November 1 to December 14 and December 25 to March 31.

FROM NORTH AMERICA Fares to Italy are constantly changing, but you can expect to pay somewhere in the range of $550 to $1,580 for a direct round-trip ticket from New York to Rome in coach class.

Flying time to Rome from New York, Newark, and Boston is 8 hours; from Chicago, 10 hours; and from Los Angeles, 12½ hours. Flying time to Milan from New York, Newark, and Boston is 8 hours; from Chicago, 9¼ hours; and from Los Angeles, 11½ hours.

American Airlines (☎ 800/433-7300; www.aa.com) offers daily nonstop flights to Rome from Chicago's O'Hare, with flights from all parts of American's vast network making connections into Chicago. **Delta** (☎ 800/221-1212; www.delta.com) flies from New York's JFK to Milan, Venice, and Rome. **AmericaWest/US Airways** (☎ 800/428-4322; www.usairways.com) offers one flight daily to Rome out of Philadelphia (you can connect through Philly from most major U.S. cities). **Continental** (☎ 800/525-0280; www.continental.com) flies several times a week to Rome, Milan, Venice, and Bologna from its hub in Newark.

Air Canada (☎ 888/247-2262; www.aircanada.ca) flies daily from Toronto to Rome. Two of the flights are nonstop; the others touch down en route in Montreal, depending on the schedule.

British Airways (☎ 800/AIRWAYS; www.britishairways.com), **Virgin Atlantic Airways** (☎ 800/821-5438; www.virgin-atlantic.com), **Air France** (☎ 800/237-2747; www.airfrance.com), **Northwest/KLM** (☎ 800/225-2525; www.nwa.com), and **Lufthansa** (☎ 800/645-3880; www.lufthansa-usa.com) offer some attractive deals for anyone interested in combining a trip to Italy with a stopover in, say, Britain, Paris, Amsterdam, or Germany.

Alitalia (☎ 800/223-5730; www.alitalia.com) is the Italian national airline, with nonstop flights to Rome from many North American cities, including New York (JFK), Newark, Boston, Chicago, Miami, Washington, and Toronto. Nonstop flights into Milan are from New York (JFK) and Newark. From Milan or Rome, Alitalia can easily book connecting domestic flights if your final destination is elsewhere in Italy. Alitalia participates in the frequent-flier programs of other airlines, including Continental and US Airways.

FROM THE UNITED KINGDOM   Operated by the European Travel Network, **www.discountairfares.com** is a great online source for regular and discounted airfares to destinations around the world. You can also use this site to compare rates and book accommodations, car rentals, and tours. Click on "Special Offers" for the latest package deals.

British newspapers are always full of classified ads touting slashed fares to Italy. One good source is **Time Out**. London's **Evening Standard** has a daily travel section, and the Sunday editions of almost any newspaper will run many ads. Although competition is fierce, one well-recommended company that consolidates bulk ticket purchases and then passes the savings on to its consumers is **Trailfinders** (☎ 0845/058-5858; www.trailfinders.com). It offers access to tickets on such carriers as SAS, British Airways, and KLM.

Both **British Airways** (☎ 0870/850-9850 in the U.K.; www.britishairways.co.uk) and **Alitalia** (☎ 0870/544-8259; www.alitalia.it) have frequent flights from London's Heathrow to Rome, Milan, Venice, Pisa (the gateway to Florence), and Naples. Flying time from London to these cities is from 2 to 3 hours. British Airways also has one direct flight a day from Manchester to Rome.

GETTING A GOOD DEAL

The dirty little secret about flights to Italy (or most anywhere for that matter) is that passengers sharing the same airplane cabin rarely pay the same fare. Travelers who need to purchase tickets at the last minute, change their itinerary at a moment's notice, or fly one-way often get stuck paying the premium rate. And sometimes passengers who are simply unlucky also pay more than the fellow in the next seat: There's little logic to airfares. Here are some ways to keep your airfare costs down:

- **Fly in the low season.** June to September is high season for flights, with prices more than doubling over winter fares, often going well over $1,000 for a round-trip from New York to Rome.

- Passengers who **fly midweek** or during less-trafficked hours may pay a fraction of the full fare. If your schedule is flexible, say so, and ask if you can secure a cheaper fare by changing your flight plans.

- **Search the Internet** for cheap fares (see "Surfing for Airfares," below). Sales tend to begin on Wednesdays, so that can be a good day of the week to search. Additionally, American travelers can sometimes get a slightly better deal by booking airfare at around 2am (Eastern Standard Time). Why? Fares are based on a complex logarithm of supply-and-demand, and at midnight all unpaid-for bookings are flushed from the airlines' computers, leading to a steep, though brief, drop in demand.

- **Keep an eye on local newspapers** for promotional specials or fare wars, when airlines lower prices on their most popular routes. You'll rarely see fare wars offered for peak travel times, but if you can travel in the off months, you may snag a bargain.

- Look beyond the usual suspects for inexpensive flights. A new airline called Eurofly now offers low-cost fares from the U.S. to Milan and other northern Italian cities. KLM is also another airline to check when looking for airfares.

♦ **Consider a stopover** on the way to Italy. London is almost always the least expensive gateway to fly to Italy from the United States, and you may end up paying less by flying into that city and then hopping a **low-cost carrier** from there to one of the major Italian cities. **Air Europa** (www.aireuropa. com), **Meridiana** (www.meridiana.com), **EasyJet** (www.easyjet.com), and **RyanAir** (www.ryanair.com) have super-cheap intra-Europe flights, although usually to and from less convenient airports—but if you're flexible, you can get some amazing deals. *Note:* These airlines usually don't show up on consolidator websites, and aren't connected to any travel agencies, so you'll need to book directly through the websites above.

♦ Consolidators, also known as bucket shops, are great sources for international tickets. Start by looking in Sunday newspaper travel sections; U.S. travelers should focus on the *New York Times, Los Angeles Times,* and *Miami Herald. Beware:* Bucket-shop tickets are usually nonrefundable or rigged with stiff cancellation penalties, often as high as 50% to 75% of the ticket price, and some put you on charter airlines, which may leave at inconvenient times and experience delays. **STA Travel** (p. 587) has been the world's lead consolidator for students since purchasing Council Travel, but their fares are competitive for travelers of all ages. **ELTExpress** (☎ 800/TRAV-800; www. eltexpress.com) has excellent fares to Europe. It also has "local" websites in 12 countries. **FlyCheap** (☎ 800/FLY-CHEAP; www.1800flycheap.com) is owned by package-holiday megalith MyTravel and has especially good fares to sunny destinations. **Air Tickets Direct** (☎ 800/778-3447; www.airticketsdirect. com) is based in Montreal and leverages the currently weak Canadian dollar for low fares.

♦ **Join frequent-flier clubs.** Frequent-flier membership doesn't cost a cent, but it does entitle you to better seats, faster response to phone inquiries, and prompter service if your luggage is stolen or your flight is canceled or delayed, or if you want to change your seat. And you don't have to fly to earn points; frequent-flier credit cards can earn you thousands of miles for doing your everyday shopping. With more than 70 mileage awards programs on the market, consumers have never had more options, but the system has never been more complicated—what with major airlines folding, new

Travel in the Age of Bankruptcy

Airlines go bankrupt, so protect yourself by buying your tickets with a credit card, as the Fair Credit Billing Act guarantees that you can get your money back from the credit card company if a travel supplier goes under (and if you request the refund within 60 days of the bankruptcy). Travel insurance can also help, but make sure it covers against "carrier default" for your specific travel provider. And be aware that if a U.S. airline goes bust mid-trip, a 2005 U.S. federal law requires other carriers to take you to your destination (albeit on a space-available basis) for a fee of no more than $25, provided you rebook within 60 days of the cancellation.

budget carriers emerging, and alliances forming (allowing you to earn points on partner airlines). Investigate the program details of your favorite airlines before you sink points into any one. Consider which airlines have hubs in the airport nearest you, and, of those carriers, which have the most advantageous alliances, given your most common routes. To play the frequent-flier game to your best advantage, consult Randy Petersen's **Inside Flyer** (www. insideflyer.com). Petersen and friends review all the programs in detail and post regular updates on changes in policies and trends. Petersen will also field direct questions (via e-mail) if a partner airline refuses to redeem points, for instance, or if you're still not sure after researching the various programs which one is right for you. It's well worth the $12 online subscription fee, good for 1 year.

PACKAGES VS. INDEPENDENT TRAVEL

The major Italian cities, in particular Rome and Florence, are some of the top destinations in the world for travel packages—by which I mean travel products that bundle together airfare, hotel, and sometimes car at one reasonable price. Why? Because these über-developed destinations have hundreds of hotel rooms that need to be filled year-round. Though the cheapest of these packages traditionally use mainstream, somewhat dull hotels, booking a travel package can result in big savings, in some cases a $100-a-day or less vacation for airfare and hotel (not including taxes or security fees). No, you won't have the choicest of lodgings, but you will get a clean, convenient place to stay (always with private bathroom), perfect for those simply using their hotel as a place to crash after long days of viewing art and eating pasta.

Go-Today (www.gotoday.com) and **Virgin Vacations** (www.virgin-vacations. com) are the first two sites you should check, though in truth you need only search one as they offer the same packages. Deals are phenomenal in the off season (as little as $400 round-trip air from New York to Venice or Florence plus hotel for 4 nights) and still pretty good during summer ($1,400 for the same deal). Both companies serve nearly every gateway in the United States, and offer a number of well-priced options that include weeklong stays in one city, air/car packages allowing you to tour the countryside, and deals allowing you to stay in a couple of cities (Rome and Paris or Rome-Florence-Venice are two of their most popular offerings). Be sure to total all the costs when you're shopping around.

Gate 1 Travel (www.gate1travel.com) is Go-Today's fiercest competitor and often matches its rates (occasionally undercutting them). It, too, offers many permutations on the standard air/hotel package: air/car, air/train, and hotel/tour guide/ bus, among others. Midsummer 6-day packages for a two-star hotel and airfare have run a reasonable $1,200, which is quite good considering that's what many tickets go for.

1-800-FLY-EUROPE (www.1800flyeurope.com) is the best place to go for airfare/ car-rental deals. I recently saw a stellar 7-day Rome airfare/car-rental package for $448 (not including tax, or weekend and other surcharges).

Some other packagers to factor into the equation (though they rarely beat the four above): **TourCrafters** (www.tourcrafters.com), **Italiatour** (www.italiatour.com), and **Europe ASAP** (www.europeasap.com).

Surfing for Airfares

By far the best way to search for airfares to Italy is to use the **"aggrega-tor" websites**, so named because they don't sell travel, but simply aggre-gate information on what the other sites are offering (they then get a commission from these sites if you make a booking via their search). Because they usually take you directly to the airlines' websites, you bypass the fees charged by such online travel agencies as **Expedia.com, Travelo city.com**, and **Orbitz.com** (also the aggregators don't allow companies to pay for placement, yielding a more logical search). The top three within the United States are **Kayak.com, ITASoftware.com**, and **Sidestep.com.** If you can be flexible on your dates of travel, I highly recommend **Cheap Flights.com**, which works with small discounters, allowing them to post their lowest fares online with no dates attached (you then contact the site in question directly to book travel). Each of the smaller sites searched by CheapFlights.com has different business deals with the airlines and may offer different fares on the same flights, so it's wise to shop around.

Great **last-minute deals** are available through free weekly e-mail serv-ices provided directly by the airlines. Most of these are announced on Tuesday or Wednesday and must be purchased online. Sign up for weekly e-mail alerts at airline websites or check mega-sites that compile compre-hensive lists of last-minute specials, such as **Smartertravel.com.** For last-minute trips, **site59.com** and **lastminutetravel.com** in the U.S. and **lastminute.com** in Europe often have better air-and-hotel package deals than the major-label sites.

If you're willing to give up some control over your flight details, use what is called an **"opaque" fare service** like **Priceline.com** (www.priceline. co.uk for Europeans) or its smaller competitor **Hotwire.com.** Both offer rock-bottom prices in exchange for travel on a "mystery airline" at a mys-terious time of day, often with a mysterious change of planes en route. To be fair, these sites usually use only major carriers and allow you to limit your flight times to between 6am and 11pm. Hotwire tells you flight prices before you buy; Priceline usually has better deals than Hotwire, but you have to play their "name our price" game. If you're new at this, the help-ful folks at **BiddingForTravel.com** do a good job of demystifying Priceline's prices and strategies. ***Note:*** In 2004 Priceline added non-opaque service to its roster. You now have the option to pick exact flights, times, and air-lines from a list of offers—or opt to bid on opaque fares as before.

Untours

As the name implies, **Untours** (www.untours.com) is an alternative-travel company that specializes in booking airfare and 2-week stays at a local apartment, farmhouse, or cottage. You can save money by packing a few more people into a rented apartment. They have a near cultlike following from customers who enjoy a more concentrated, local-oriented vacation rather than a city-a-day-type tour. Untours books locations around Venice, Rome, Sicily, and Tuscany and Umbria.

A few other things to keep in mind when booking a package:

◆ Prices are always based on double occupancy, so these might not be good deals for solo travelers.

◆ Be sure to crunch numbers before booking: Look at the seasonal airfare to Italy at the time you'll be going (do a search on Sidestep.com or Kayak.com) and then subtract that to find out how much you're paying for the specific hotel room. If you can do better, book separately. Look up the hotel's reviews and check their rates online for your dates of travel. You'll also want to find out what **type of room** you get. If you need a certain type of room, ask for it; don't take whatever is thrown your way. Request a nonsmoking room, a quiet room, a room with a view, or whatever you fancy.

◆ Packages are usually only good for the major cities: Rome, Florence, Venice, sometimes Milan, and sometimes the ski resort areas. If you're hoping to go to Ravenna or Perugia, this method probably won't work for you. (Though there are fly/drives that may make sense, as car rental in Italy is the priciest in western Europe.)

◆ **Read the fine print.** Sometimes cancellation policies on packages are ugly. Consider getting travel insurance if you book a package but *never* buy it from the packager (if the company goes belly up, you lose all your money).

◆ Finally, look for **hidden expenses.** Ask whether airport departure fees and taxes, or fuel surcharges, for example, are included in the total cost. Particularly with the post-9/11 security fees, these charges can add up in a hurry to the $200+ range if you're going through multiple airports. Italian **car rentals** also can add a nearly **20% tax** on top of an already high rate. On a positive note, many places offer a **hidden savings**—a good 10% or more if you pay for the package with cash.

SAVING MONEY ON ACCOMMODATIONS

Throughout this guide, you'll find information on alternative accommodations—B&Bs, monasteries and convents that accept guests, vacation rentals, and so on. Here are three general money-saving tips for booking your accommodations in Italy:

SURF THE WEB   Such sites as **Sidestep.com**, **Hotels.com**, and **Quikbook.com** can be very helpful for zeroing in on "distressed merchandise": hotel rooms that have gone unsold and are therefore available at a discount. For last-minute travel, you can also find very good deals on the British site **LateRooms.com**. An excellent free program, **TravelAxe** (www.travelaxe.net), can help you search multiple hotel sites at once, even ones you may never have heard of, and conveniently lists the total price of the room, including the taxes and service charges. Another booking site, **Travelweb** (www.travelweb.com), is partly owned by the hotels it represents (including the Hilton, Hyatt, and Starwood chains) and is therefore plugged directly into the hotels' reservations systems—unlike independent online agencies, which have to fax or e-mail reservation requests to the hotel, a good portion of which get misplaced in the shuffle. More than once, travelers have arrived at the hotel, only to be told that they have no reservation. To be fair, many of the major sites are undergoing improvements in service and ease of use, and Expedia will soon be able to plug directly into the reservations systems of many hotel chains. In the meantime, it's a good idea to **get a confirmation number** and **make a printout** of any online booking transaction.

In the opaque website category, **Priceline** (www.priceline.com) and **Hotwire** (www.hotwire.com) are even better for hotels than for airfares; through both, you're allowed to pick the neighborhood and quality-level of your hotel before paying. Priceline's hotel offerings even cover Europe and Asia, though it's much better at getting five-star lodging for three-star prices than at finding anything at the bottom of the scale. On the downside, some users claim that hotels stick Priceline guests in their least desirable rooms (it hasn't happened to me, but that's the scuttlebutt). Be sure to go to the BiddingForTravel website (see above) before bidding on a hotel room on Priceline; it features a fairly up-to-date list of hotels that Priceline uses in major cities. For both Priceline and Hotwire, you pay upfront, and the fee is nonrefundable. *Note:* Some hotels do not provide loyalty program credits or points or other frequent-stay amenities when you book a room through opaque online services.

If you have a specific hotel in mind, be sure to check the big three on the Web: **Travelocity** (www.travelocity.com), **Expedia** (www.expedia.com), and **Orbitz** (www.orbitz.com). These monolithic sites offer a variety their competitors can't match, and while their lowest prices usually aren't quite as low, for midrange and luxury hotels they tend to be quite competitive.

LOOK INTO *AGRITURISMO*   Originally defined as more of a farm-stay program, the definition of *agriturismo* had expanded to include every building with a roof outside of a city, from B&Bs to luxury hotels, to cramped outhouses, to actual farms. In the past few years, regulators have imposed some standardization to this lodging category, requiring that anything denoted as *agriturismo* derive at least half its revenues from farm products. Still, this leaves over 2,500 establishments certified as *agriturismi* in Tuscany alone.

So how do you make a selection? The government has created a rating system, with one to five ears of corn (no, really) ranking the facilities, amenities, and rooms for each establishment. Decide what you're looking for in a "farm holiday," whether it be a rustic horse-riding ranch (Rendola Riding, p. 183) or a full-service hotel with swimming pool (Le Silve Hotel, p. 210). This book includes many *agriturismo* options; you may also want to also look at the following two sites for additional information:

- **www.agriturismo.regione.toscana.it**   A helpful, government-run site focused on *agriturismi* in Tuscany with a searchable database by sub-region.
- **www.agriturismo.com**   A privately run site with direct links to a number of "farms."

CONSIDER A HOME EXCHANGE   House-swapping is becoming a more popular and viable means of travel; you stay in their place, they stay in yours, and you both get an authentic and personal view of the area, the opposite of the escapist retreat that many hotels offer. Many people simply do this informally, staying at the homes of friends or friends of friends. If you don't know anyone in Italy, though, try **HomeLink International** (www.homelink.org), the largest and oldest home-swapping organization, founded in 1952, with over 11,000 listings worldwide ($75 for a yearly membership). A recent listing showed over 250 home owners across Italy specifically requesting exchanges with the owners in the United States. **HomeExchange.com** ($50 for 6,000 listings) and **InterVac.com** ($69 for over 10,000 listings) are also reliable.

RENTAL CARS

Italy has the most expensive car-rental rates in Europe, partially because by law you must purchase more insurance there than in other countries. But there are ways to get a good deal. I've always found that **AutoEurope** (☎ 888/223-5555; www.autoeurope.com) significantly undercuts the prices of the major international car-rental agencies, sometimes by as much as 30%. I would suggest pricing its vehicles before looking at the other sites.

Travelers should also remember that smaller cars are not only less expensive, but they'll also be cheaper to gas up (gasoline is heavily taxed and therefore quite expensive throughout Europe) and easier to drive in the narrow cobblestone streets of Italy's ancient cities. Keep in mind, too, that manual transmission vehicles are significantly less expensive than those with automatic transmission.

TRAVEL INSURANCE

Check your existing insurance policies and credit card coverage before you buy travel insurance. You may already be covered for lost luggage, canceled tickets, or medical expenses.

The cost of travel insurance varies widely, depending on the price and length of your trip, your age and health, and the type of trip you're taking, but expect to pay between 5% and 8% of the vacation itself. You can get estimates from various providers through **InsureMyTrip.com.**

TRIP-CANCELLATION INSURANCE   Trip-cancellation insurance will help retrieve your money if you have to back out of a trip or depart early, or if your travel supplier goes bankrupt. Permissible reasons for trip cancellation can range from sickness to natural disasters to the State Department declaring a destination unsafe for travel. For more information, contact one of the following recommended insurers: **Access America** (☎ 866/807-3982; www.accessamerica.com); **Travel Guard International** (☎ 800/826-4919; www.travelguard.com); **Travel Insured International** (☎ 800/243-3174; www.travelinsured.com); and **Travelex Insurance Services** (☎ 888/457-4602; www.travelex-insurance.com).

MEDICAL INSURANCE   For travel overseas, most health plans (including Medicare and Medicaid) do not provide coverage, and the ones that do often require you to pay for services upfront, and reimburse you only after you return home. Even if your plan does cover overseas treatment, most out-of-country hospitals make you pay your bills upfront, and send you a refund only after you've returned home and filed the necessary paperwork with your insurance company. If you require additional medical insurance, try **MEDEX Assistance** (☎ 410/453-6300; www.medexassist.com) or **Travel Assistance International** (☎ 800/821-2828 or 800/777-8710; www.travelassistance.com).

LOST-LUGGAGE INSURANCE   On international flights (including U.S. portions of international trips), baggage coverage is limited to approximately $9.05 per pound, up to approximately $635 per checked bag. If you plan to check items more valuable than what's covered by the standard liability (never a good idea), see if your homeowner's policy covers your valuables, get baggage insurance as part of your comprehensive travel-insurance package, or buy Travel Guard's "BagTrak" product. Don't buy insurance at the airport, where it's usually overpriced. Be sure to take any valuables or irreplaceable items with you in your carry-on luggage because many valuables (including books, money, and electronics) aren't covered by airline policies. Most airlines require that you report delayed, damaged, or lost baggage within 4 hours of arrival. The airlines are required to deliver luggage, once found, directly to your house or destination free of charge.

MONEY MATTERS

Italy is fully integrated into the euro system, and ATMs are readily available. Before you leave, be sure you're aware of your bank's fee policy for withdrawing money from foreign ATMs. Combined with local fees, you may pay up to $8 per transaction, but sometimes the whole process is free (like First Republic Bank of California's "refund all fees" policy; many credit unions also charge low fees for usage abroad). It's good to have backup in case a machine eats your card, your wallet gets stolen, or the like. Either bring an alternate ATM card, or bring two or three traveler's checks. Traveler's checks can be more hassle than they're worth, but they do offer the security of being replaced if your things are stolen (another option: the new check cards that can be used like credit cards, but are only good up to a limit and can be replaced within 24 hr. if lost or stolen).

Credit cards are another safe way to carry money. They also provide a convenient record of all your expenses, and they generally offer relatively good exchange rates. But try to never use them for cash advances, which carry a very high interest rate. Keep in mind that many banks now assess a 1% to 3% "transaction fee" on *all* charges you incur abroad (whether you're using the local currency or U.S. dollars).

HEALTH & SAFETY

Tourism is big business for Italy, so the authorities do their best to ensure that **heavily touristed areas are safe** at any time day or night, meaning violent crime against tourists is exceedingly rare. That being said, tourists are a target for petty theft, from pickpocketing to the theft of goods left in rental cars. Never carry large amounts of money on your person, keep your passport in a safe at your hotel, and consider using a money belt to better hide your money. Fanny packs are the worst place to keep money or valuables; they're easily opened and mark you as a tourist.

As for health dangers, traveling through Italy in the heat of summer brings on the threat of **heatstroke** or **sunstroke,** particularly for those determined to see a number of sights in a single day. A couple of basic rules: (1) Relax: Unless you're a guidebook writer on deadline, you don't have rush to cover every sight in town. (2) Stay hydrated: Keep a bottle of water with you, and replenish as the day goes on. (3) Stay covered: Wear a cap, sunglasses, and sunscreen to escape the blazing sun. Take some breaks in the shade, and take some breaks in the middle of the day—this is what the Italians do, and they've been living here for a couple of thousand years, so they should know.

SPECIALIZED TRAVEL RESOURCES

FOR FAMILIES

Italy is an extremely family-friendly country. It's not at all unusual to see children out with their parents for a night at a trattoria; there are playgrounds and parks in every city and small town; and the Italians simply love kids, meaning that if your baby starts to squall in a museum or restaurant, you won't get the evil looks you might in other countries. (In fact, you're more likely to get offers of help.) Of course, you're going to want to make sure that you approach the vacation in a sensible way: Mix and match museum days with days spent simply kicking back at the local park, and skip the wine tastings and instead go for a bike ride or a paddle on a nearby river. There's lots in Italy to keep the kids involved.

Recommended family-travel websites include **Family Travel Forum** (www.familytravelforum.com), a comprehensive site that offers customized trip planning; **Family Travel Network** (www.familytravelnetwork.com), an award-winning site that offers travel features, deals, and tips; **Traveling Internationally with Your Kids** (www.travelwithyourkids.com), a comprehensive site offering sound advice for long-distance and international travel with children; and **Family Travel Files** (www.thefamilytravelfiles.com), which has an online magazine and a directory of off-the-beaten-path tours and tour operators for families.

FOR TRAVELERS WITH DISABILITIES

Italy isn't the most convenient country for travelers with disabilities, with narrow sidewalks, uneven cobblestone streets, and historical-preservation laws that prevent certain old buildings from becoming barrier-free. But many museums and churches have been adding ramps and elevators to increase accessibility. The newer transit lines also have increased space and usability for those with disabilities.

In general, most disabilities shouldn't stop anyone from traveling. There are more options and resources out there than ever before. Many travel agencies offer customized tours and itineraries for travelers with disabilities. **Flying Wheels Travel** (☎ 507/451-5005; www.flyingwheelstravel.com) offers escorted tours and cruises that emphasize sports and private tours in minivans with lifts. **Access-Able Travel Source** (☎ 303/232-2979; www.access-able.com) has extensive access information and advice for traveling around the world with disabilities. **Accessible Journeys** (☎ 800/846-4537 or 610/521-0339; www.disabilitytravel.com) caters specifically to slow walkers and wheelchair travelers and their families and friends.

Avis Rent a Car (☎ 888/879-4273; www.avis.com) has an "Avis Access" program that provides such services as a dedicated 24-hour toll-free number for customers with special travel needs; special car features such as swivel seats, spinner knobs, and hand controls; and accessible bus service.

Organizations that offer assistance to disabled travelers include **MossRehab** (www.mossresourcenet.org), which provides a library of accessible-travel resources online; the **American Foundation for the Blind (AFB;** ☎ 800/232-5463; www.afb.org), a referral resource for the blind or visually impaired that includes information on traveling with Seeing Eye dogs; and **SATH** (Society for Accessible Travel & Hospitality; ☎ 212/447-7284; www.sath.org; annual membership fees: $45 adults, $30 seniors and students), which offers a wealth of travel resources for all types of disabilities and informed recommendations on destinations, access guides, travel agents, tour operators, vehicle rentals, and companion services. **AirAmbulanceCard.com** is now partnered with SATH and allows you to pre-select top-notch hospitals in case of an emergency for $195 a year ($295 per family), among other benefits.

For more information specifically targeted to travelers with disabilities, the community website **iCan** (www.icanonline.net/channels/travel) has destination guides and several regular columns on accessible travel. Also check out the quarterly magazine *Emerging Horizons* (www.emerginghorizons.com; $14.95 per year, $19.95 outside the U.S.) and *Open World* magazine, published by SATH (see above; subscription: $13 per year, $21 outside the U.S.).

FOR SENIOR TRAVELERS

Many Italian museums, and some bus and rail lines, offer reduced rates to seniors 65 or older (some have 60-plus discounts). To fish for discounts, mention that you're a senior: *un anciano* (for men) or *una anciana* (for women).

A number of reliable agencies and organizations target the 50-plus market. **Elderhostel** (☎ 877/426-8056; www.elderhostel.org) arranges study programs for seniors 55 and over (and a spouse or companion of any age) in more than 80 countries, including Italy. Most courses last 2 to 4 weeks, and many include airfare, accommodations in university dormitories or modest inns, meals, and tuition. **Grand Circle Travel** (☎ 800/959-0405; www.gct.com), in business since 1958, is one of the leaders in the field and consequently has greater buying power than many of its competitors. All its trips feature easygoing itineraries, perfect for older travelers or travelers with disabilities, and decently priced tours (in 2006, an 18-night, all-inclusive guided tour of Italy—with airfare—sold for just $1,895). Its "Discovery Series" events bring travelers into contact with locals in the areas visited with events such as cooking classes, visits to schoolchildren, and meals in private homes.

Recommended publications offering travel resources and discounts for seniors include the quarterly magazine *Travel 50 & Beyond* (www.travel50andbeyond. com); *Travel Unlimited: Uncommon Adventures for the Mature Traveler* (Avalon); *101 Tips for Mature Travelers,* available from Grand Circle Travel (☎ 800/221-2610 or 617/350-7500; www.gct.com); and *Unbelievably Good Deals and Great Adventures That You Absolutely Can't Get Unless You're Over 50* (McGraw-Hill), by Joann Rattner Heilman.

FOR GAY & LESBIAN TRAVELERS

While Italy is a traditional Catholic country in many respects, it has become more tolerant of homosexuality in recent years. That being said, aside from a few larger cities like Florence and Rome, there isn't much of a gay "scene." But Italy does have a national support group, **ARCI-Gay/Lesbica** (www.arcigay.it), headquartered in Bologna with "political and recreational" offices in 57 cities across the country offering information and welfare services.

The International Gay and Lesbian Travel Association (IGLTA; ☎ 800/448-8550 or 954/776-2626; www.iglta.org) is the trade association for the gay-and-lesbian travel industry, and offers an online directory of gay- and lesbian-friendly travel businesses; go to their website and click on "Members."

Many agencies offer tours and travel itineraries specifically for gay and lesbian travelers. **Above and Beyond Tours (☎ 800/397-2681; www.abovebeyondtours. com)** is the exclusive gay-and-lesbian tour operator for United Airlines. **Now, Voyager (☎ 800/255-6951; www.nowvoyager.com)** is a well-known San Francisco–based, gay-owned and -operated travel service. **Gay.com Travel (☎ 800/929-2268 or 415/644-8044; www.gay.com/travel),** is an excellent online successor to the popular *Out & About* print magazine.

The following travel guides are available at many bookstores, or you can order them from any online bookseller: *Frommer's Gay & Lesbian Europe* (www.frommers.com), an excellent travel resource to the top European cities and resorts; *Spartacus International Gay Guide* (Bruno Gmünder Verlag; www.spartacusworld.com/gayguide) and *Odysseus: The International Gay Travel Planner* (Odysseus Enterprises Ltd.), both good, annual, English-language guidebooks

---

Staying Wired While Away

Internet cafes abound in the larger cities in Italy, and the amount of competition helps keep prices down. Most hotels in Florence, Rome, and Venice will have at least one "Internet point," where guests can check their e-mail at no charge. Once you get out of the larger cities, things change: Hotels charge for access, upwards of €10 an hour. And Internet cafes are few and far between—those that exist charge higher (€3 for 30 min.) rates than cafes in the larger cities. The free wireless "hot spot" concept has yet to catch on in Italy, so don't expect to go to a local coffee shop with your laptop and get connected, although Starbucks is making some inroads.

focused on gay men; and the ***Damron*** guides (www.damron.com), with separate, annual books for gay men and lesbians.

FOR STUDENTS

Arm yourself with an **International Student Identity Card (ISIC),** which offers substantial savings on rail passes, plane tickets, and entrance fees. It also provides you with basic health and life insurance and a 24-hour help line. The card is available for $22 from **STA Travel** (☎ 800/781-4040 in North America; www.sta.com or www.statravel.com), the biggest student travel agency in the world. If you're no longer a student but are still under 26, you can get an **International Youth Travel Card (IYTC)** for the same price from the same people, which entitles you to some discounts (but not on museum admissions). **Travel CUTS** (☎ 800/667-2887 or 416/614-2887; www.travelcuts.com) offers similar services for both Canadians and U.S. residents. Irish students may prefer to turn to **USIT** (☎ 01/602-1600; www.usitnow.ie), an Ireland-based specialist in student, youth, and independent travel.

RECOMMENDED READING

Beyond this guidebook, you can increase your enjoyment of Italy immensely by doing some reading before you arrive. Here are some of my recommendations for fun, informative reads.

NONFICTION

To learn more about Renaissance-era Florence, pick up a copy of ***Brunelleschi's Dome,*** by Ross King, an entertaining account of the creation of the dome of the Duomo in Florence in the 15th century. It's a must-read before climbing to the top. ***April Blood,*** by Lauro Martines, is another page-turner about the Pazzi family's plot against the Medicis in Florence in 1478. For a straight historical text, try Harry Hearder's ***Italy, A Short History.***

The first of two wonderful biographical approaches to Italy is Norman Lewis's ***Naples '44: An Intelligence Officer in the Italian Labyrinth;*** one of my all-time favorites, it's the story of a British soldier getting his first taste of Italian culture during the chaos of World War II. The second is ***Pietro's Book*** by Jenny Bawtree, the biography of a Tuscan farmer that gives a much better feeling for the hard countryside life than do the slew of the "Oh, it's so tough to build a vacation home" books on the market.

A couple older Italy travelogues still have entertainment value as well as valuable insights about the country. Mary McCarthy's 1956 ***The Stones of Florence/ Venice Observed*** offers such sharp commentary it seems like it was written last year, not 50 years ago. And Mark Twain's 1878 ***Innocents Abroad*** is still a hilarious read, especially the chapters where he torments tour guides, complains incessantly, and rewrites history.

For an insight on contemporary Italian culture, try Tobias Jones's 2003 ***The Dark Heart of Italy,*** which skewers Italian politics, the Mafia, and the Red Brigade, with scathing criticism of Silvio Berlusconi's "might makes right" regime. A lighter modern tale is told by Joe McGinnis in his book ***The Miracle of Castel Di Sangro.*** An account of a year with a small-town soccer team, it takes you into the heart of Italian *futbol* mania.

A collection of Italy travel stories makes a good companion for a trip around Italy. Try *Travelers' Tales Italy*, edited by Anne Calcagno, which has 30 thematically organized stories about travelers' experiences across the country; also see *Travelers' Tales Tuscany* for stories focused there. *Tuscany In Mind*, edited by Alice Powers, is another nice compilation with 20 famous authors, from Dickens to Twain. For a women's take on the country, read *Italy, A Love Story*, edited by Camille Cusamano, in which 2 dozen women write about how their lives have been shaped by their experiences in Italy.

FICTION

The definitive Renaissance classic is Dante's *Divine Comedy* (Inferno, Purgatory, Paradise). The classic epic poem that practically created the Italian language also has biting political commentary, with Dante's enemies ending up in various levels of hell. The Penguin Classics edition translated by Mark Mura has good commentary (essential for understanding all the obscure references) and cool maps of hell from prior editions. Boccaccio's *The Decameron,* also from the 14th century, is a bawdy collection of stories taking place at the time of the Black Death. If you can get through the archaic writing, it's a good read.

Historical fiction is a fun way to learn about the old days without reading a dry textbook. *The Leopard,* by Giuseppe Di Lampedusa, is a 1960 novel recounting the last days of a fading aristocracy in Sicily counterbalanced with the political life of Italy in the 1860s. Irving Stone's 1961 *The Agony and the Ecstasy* adds drama and intrigue to the life and times of Michelangelo. *The Name of the Rose,* by Umberto Eco, uses the framework of a murder mystery taking place in a 14th-century Italian abbey to debate the essence of literature, history, and religion.

ITALIAN FILMS

One of the best ways to gear up for your Italian vacation is to rent an Italian film. There's none finer than *The Bicycle Thief* (1947), regarded as one of the best films ever made, or any of Fellini's epics (1963's *8½* and 1968's *La Dolce Vita,* among others). Recent Italian-language films that enjoyed success in the U.S. include *Cinema Paradiso, Medeterraneo, Il Postino,* and *Life is Beautiful,* with scenes shot in Arezzo.

THE CUISINE OF ITALY
by Bill Fink

Anyone looking for the quintessential Italian meal is likely to be disappointed. Why? Because there's no such thing.

To be sure, there's plenty of Tuscan fare. And Neapolitan specialties are available across the land. Then, too, a hearty Umbrian soup is just the answer for a cold winter night almost anywhere, while spaghetti *alla bolognese* is offered on most of the country's menus. But Italian cuisine? You may as well request "Earth Cuisine" or "The Table of the Northern Hemisphere."

REGIONAL TASTES, NATIONAL FERVOR

Like the history of the Italian provinces that spawned it, Italian cuisine has a highly regionalized, even localized, character. And these distinctions are serious. Ranging from the selection of the ingredients to the method of preparation to the ceremony of the meal, Italian dining could be considered the second major religion of Italy (after Roman Catholicism, and slightly ahead of soccer).

For the traveler, a chance to sample the regional cuisines of Italy can be the highlight of any trip. The vast majority of Italian eateries are family-owned establishments, labors of love reflecting several generations of local learning and lore. A dinner often turns into a multihour theater of courses accompanied by gossip, people-watching, and a spirit of community seen only at, well, a Catholic Mass or an AS Roma playoff match.

So how should you enter this culinary world? Open your mouth. Not just to eat but to ask your tour guide, your cab driver, and your magazine vendor where the best place is to find a bite (though don't bother inquiring at high-end hotels—they'll point you to the most touristy place in town). Italians always have an opinion about where and what to eat. This guide recommends the most local *trattorie, osterie,* and *ristoranti* at which a traveler can experience regional specialties in a homey atmosphere. Seek them out.

After entering an Italian restaurant, your job is not yet done. Keep talking (or gesturing, depending on mutual linguistic ability). Ask about the specialty of the house *(specialità della casa),* or the seasonal specialty *(specialità della stagione).* Ask for help interpreting the menu—waiters and owners usually enjoy showing off their knowledge of food (plus it's a good way to get some free samples). Try to dine with friends so you can order several courses and share. But if you're alone, eat up—there's plenty of hiking to be done tomorrow.

THE CHOICE OF RESTAURANTS

So where to go? The major categories of Italian restaurants are the bar, the trattoria, the *osteria,* and the *ristorante.* An Italian **bar** is more of a cafe (not to be confused with a pub), which serves coffee, sodas, and sometimes ice cream and snacks. Stop at a bar for a quick panino and a drink. But be careful: The prices usually double if you sit at one of their tables; if you're counting euros, it's best to chow down at the bar, or to wander off to eat in the shade.

The differences between *osterie, trattorie,* and *ristoranti* are less distinct than they once were. Traditionally, an **osteria** was a rustic and rudimentary open kitchen in which travelers could grab a plate of pasta and a glass of wine. A **trattoria** represented a step up the food chain, so to speak, offering multicourse meals with a selection of wine in a traditional setting. And a **ristorante** had a formal atmosphere, with linen tablecloths, wine lists, professional waitstaff, and a bit of ceremony in the presentation. But now *ristoranti* have added the words *"osteria"* or *"trattoria"* to their titles to seem more authentic, while the *osterie* and *trattorie* have been passing themselves off as *ristoranti* in an effort to jack up prices or draw a richer crowd. Regardless, the quality of food can be first class at any of these; try them all and reach your own conclusions.

An alarming development in dining in Italy is the insidious rise of the cover charge, the **coperto,** aka *pan e coperto* (bread and cover). This initial expense ranges from €1 to €3 at many places. Look at the menu displayed at the door, where the charge is often disclosed (along with a service charge of up to 15%) or else you'll find that your cheap snack of pasta and tap water has nearly doubled in price. Unless it's a particularly famous restaurant, try to avoid any place with more than a €1.50 *coperto.* A service charge of 10% to 15% (instead of a tip) is usual. Let the waiters keep the change for an extra tip, or add a couple of euros if the service has been particularly good. Request *"il conto, per favore"* to get the check at the end of the meal.

THE CHOICE OF PLATES

So now that you've found the restaurant and learned about paying, it's time to decide what to eat. In the countryside, you can't help being overwhelmed by regional specialties. In the bigger cities, you'll have more of a taste of the nation, with an increasing selection of Asian and European dishes. But you haven't come to Italy to try won-ton soup, so here's a quick review of Italy's regional specialties, moving from north to south.

Northern Italian cuisine has a strong flavor of the French, German, and Austrian traditions. **Piedmont,** to the northeast, serves Swiss-like *fonduta* (fondue), a concoction of melted cheese mixed with butter, milk, and egg yolks. *Bagna cauda* is a vegetable-dipping variation made with the addition of olive oil, garlic, and anchovies. Just west of Piedmont, in **Lombardy,** the locals like their *cotoletta alla milanese,* veal cutlets in egg and olive-oil batter. It took awhile for Marco Polo's pasta to make it up to these parts, so polenta (cornmeal) and risotto (rice) often serve as the starches for a meal. **Trentino** carries on the Austrian-German traditions of its neighbors to the north, with heavier meat-and-potato dishes, along with an endless selection of strudels.

Venice, as befits its maritime tradition, features seafood, and grilled fish is often served with the regional red radicchio. *Fegato alla veneziana* is a liver-and-onion entree served at most city restaurants, as is the traditional *risi e bisi,* a rice-and-pea dish. **Liguria,** on the opposite northern coast, also boasts menus full of seafood, including a spicy *burrida* fish stew resembling French bouillabaisse.

When pressed, many Italians outside the **Emilia-Romagna** region of Bologna, Ravenna, Parma, and Ferrara grudgingly admit that this area may have the best Italian cuisine; certainly, items like spaghetti *alla bolognese* (with meat sauce) will instantly appeal to visiting tourists. Most permutations of pasta shapes came from this region: tagliatelle (long strips of macaroni), cappelletti (little hat-shaped pasta), tortellini (small dough squares stuffed with meats), and lasagna (layered squares of pasta mixed with layers of meat or vegetable). Parmigiano cheese, of course, comes from Parma, which is also known for its hams. Ordering a simple ham-and-cheese sandwich in Parma can be a culinary highlight (though it's really better to sample the cheeses and the thinly sliced prosciutto hams on their own). The more adventurous might try Modena's specialty: *zampone,* pickled pig's foot with assorted stuffings (ugh!).

The tables of **Tuscany,** which is south of Emilia-Romagna, will always await you with a bottle of the region's fine olive oils (although sometimes less responsible eateries will "forget" to leave a bottle on a tourist's table—some locals think their expensive specialty will be wasted on a foreign palate, so request it if you don't see it). Tuscan dishes are characterized by hearty peasant fare, meats, and pastas with tomato-based sauces; some *brigande* (bandit-style) dishes are extra spicy. Penne and pappardelle are Tuscany's characteristic pastas. Florence is famous for its *bistecca alla fiorentina,* a thick steak of Chianina beef charcoal-grilled to juicy perfection.

Umbria, still farther south, is a center for truffles; be sure to sample some shavings of the local fungi on your pasta when in season. The thick *umbriceilli* pasta and *tagliolini fatti in casa* are two regional dishes you'll find homemade in nearly every establishment. Game dishes like hare, wild boar *(cingiale),* and venison dot the menus of many Umbrian countryside kitchens.

Rome, the largest and most central Italian city, offers the best chance for a one-stop experience of the country's cuisines. Located near the sea, Rome offers many seafood specialties, including dishes like *scampia alla griglia* (grilled prawns), *zuppa di pesce* (fish stew with white wine and spices), *zuppa di cozze* (mussels), and *fritto di scampi e calimaretti* (fried squid and prawns). Characteristic pastas include the stuffed tube-shaped *cannelloni* and the potato-flour dumplings of *gnocchi alla romana* (covered in meat sauce and cheese). Try the *saltimbocca alla romana* (thin-sliced veal and ham with cheese and sage) or the assorted fried items of *fritto alla romana,* which can include vegetables, seafood, or various cow parts or tripe. To continue this *"alla romana"* sampler, try *carciofi alla romana* (artichokes cooked in white wine with mint, garlic, and other herbs).

Southern Italian cuisine is well represented by the foods of **Naples,** including its thin pizzas, clam sauce pastas, and mozzarella cheeses. Across Italy, locals will usually point you to the nearest Neapolitan restaurant to find the best pizza in town, so don't miss a chance to try some in this center of the pizza universe. Fresh fried fish in Naples is also a standard dish. Try some *sfogliatelle* for dessert, a ricotta-filled layered pastry. On the other side of Southern Italy, **Puglia** features hearty fare, heavy on the vegetables and seafood, including such specialties as *orecchiette,* "little ear" pasta, with sautéed local greens.

The hot hills of **Sicily** have spawned a strong-tasting, often spicy cuisine. *Maccheroni con le sarde* is a traditional Sicilian spaghetti with sardines and olive oil flavored with pine nuts, fennel, and other spices. At smaller coastal towns, order fish fresh off the boat; swordfish is quite popular and tasty. *Involtini siciliani* are bread-covered meat rolls stuffed with egg, ham, and cheese. Or try the vegetarian *caponata* eggplant in tomato sauce. Sicily is also famous for its desserts. Its *cannoli* pastries stuffed with ricotta or chocolate, and *gelati* ice creams, are considered some of the best in Italy.

VARIATIONS

No matter what part of Italy you visit, one of the best ways to fully experience Italian cuisine is by taking a **cooking class.** Classes are offered in every variation, from an afternoon seminar at a restaurant, to an all-day trip to a country kitchen complete with wine tastings, to a multiweek (or multimonth) formal culinary education course certifying some of the best chefs in the world. Chapters 3 and 4 list a good sample of cooking classes targeted at the short-term visitor.

The Slow Food movement is gaining momentum in Italy. **Slow Food** is more than a type of cuisine—it's an attitude. It emphasizes eating in a more traditional manner: using genuine, local (usually organic) ingredients, encouraging traditional food education, holding tastings, and creating an organization of participating restaurants and food suppliers who share the same principles. Now there are "slow" hotels, tours, and many restaurants. Find out more about the 35,000-member Italian organization at **www.slowfood.com**, and then register to have access to their encyclopedic food descriptions, restaurant recommendations, and tasting events.

THE ART & ARCHITECTURE OF ITALY
by Bill Fink

You can't help but be awestruck at the sheer quantity and quality of over 2,500 years of Italian art and architecture. For students of Western art and culture, Italy is paradise. The country will even impress those whose eyes glaze over at the thought of marble statues and Madonna-and-Child paintings. It's one thing to see a classical art reproduction in a textbook, or in a sterile museum display, but it's something else altogether when these historical works are viewed in the context of the area in which they were created.

Photographs or reproductions can't produce the awe you'll feel while standing in the Roman Colosseum, gazing at the Mediterranean from the 2,000-year-old temple of Dionysus, or walking the eerily preserved streets of Pompeii. The majesty and mystery of historic Catholic Mass are best understood in the darkened *duomi* of Florence or Siena, their walls lined with Last Judgment frescoes threatening the wrath of God or the rewards of Paradise. Even Italy's museums give the artwork a context, housing pieces in Renaissance villas converted into museums, family palaces, or the elaborately decorated city "offices" of the Uffizi Galleries in Florence.

THE CLASSICAL PERIOD (500 B.C.–A.D. 500)

The art and architecture of the Roman empire is the highlight of the classical period. Statuary of this era in archaeological museums, architectural monuments such as the Roman Colosseum, the preserved city of Pompeii, and the Roman Forum, are must-sees on any visit.

The Romans borrowed their artistic and architectural styles from the Greeks and Etruscans. **Etruscan** relics from the era before 600 B.C. can be found in museums across the country (Volterra has an outstanding one, as does Rome in the Villa Giulia). Etruscan tombs are scattered across the Tuscan countryside, and some bronze statuary still survive in Florence's archaeological museum.

Greeks colonized Southern Italy in the pre-Roman era, and their works significantly influenced the Romans. Paestum's museum, in Campania, has some of the best surviving Greek works in Italy, and archaeological centers across the country have a variety of pottery, tomb carvings, and statue fragments. Many Roman statues are copies of the Greek originals (perhaps the "Classical Roman" era should really be called the "first neoclassical period").

Obviously, Rome is the best place for highlights of **classical Roman** art and architecture. For sculpture, look to the bas-relief carvings on the Arch of Constantine, and to the equestrian statue of Marcus Aurelius on the Capitoline steps. For mosaics, see the collection at the Museo Nazionale Romano. The massive Roman Colosseum displays not only the classic Roman arches, columns, and brick-and-concrete construction techniques, but the 45,000-seat stadium is evidence of the remarkable scale and scope of Rome's public works. For the engineering-minded, architectural techniques are on display at the Pantheon—a 1st-century marvel of scientific proportions, and an innovative dome construction that was not even attempted again for 1,400 years.

The city of **Pompeii** is another awesome display of Roman art, architecture, and urban engineering. The symmetry of the streets uncovered from the A.D. 79 eruption of Mt. Vesuvius shows the organization of the city, while interior mosaics and wall paintings show something of the artistic side. The area, one of the wonders of the world, also has a well-preserved amphitheater and temple. Naples's archaeological museum contains some transferred mosaics from Pompeii, along with a host of other relics, and Sicily boasts a fine collection of ancient mosaics in the villa of Piazza Armerina.

THE MEDIEVAL ERA (5TH–14TH C.)

Medieval art in Italy was wholly concerned with the Church. Nobles sponsored elaborate altars and artworks to atone for their sins and demonstrate their piety to their neighbors. Churches funded frescoes and statuary to educate the mostly illiterate parishioners about Scripture. Many medieval artworks take almost a comic-book form of progressive panel paintings illustrating the life of Jesus, the miracles of saints, and other teachings. The early part of this era had a strong Byzantine flavor. This was a time when the Eastern Church in Constantinople (now Istanbul) exerted the strongest cultural influence, all while Vandals, Goths, and other tribes were running amok through Rome and Italy.

Far removed from the realism of the classical period, **Byzantine** art had an iconic, symbolic feel: Two-dimensional, static representations were the norm.

Gilded figures were created to stand out in the dark, gloomy churches of this era. Facial features of saints looked somewhat Middle Eastern, with robes and backgrounds to match. You can see good examples of this era's art in the churches of Ravenna (San Vitale and Sant'Appollinare), Venice (Basilica di San Marco), and Sicily's Chiostro del Duomo, above Palermo.

With the **Romanesque** era of the early 1100s came some artistic fluidity, and the incorporation of many Roman architectural elements. Arches and columns characteristic of the era decorate churches in Pisa, Lucca, and Verona, including the Duomo of Pisa, the famed bronze doors of the Basilica San Zeno Maggiore in Verona, and the friezes of the Baptistery in Parma.

If you see something pointy, think **Gothic** art and architecture. The stylized creations of the late 13th to early 15th centuries were more natural than those of prior eras, but still characterized by a great deal of symbolism, exaggerated expressions, and stiffly posed figures. Architects of this era discovered that pointed arches could support more weight, so, presto, all arches became pointed, and points were added to the roofs for good measure. The extra support meant that roofs could rise higher and more windows could be added, making churches larger and brighter. The arches supported more downward weight of stone, but the walls began to buckle outward, a problem solved with flying buttresses; these free-standing stone pillars had spider-leg-like connectors and abutted the sides of the church. Examples of these structures are found at the Basilica di Santa Maria Novella and Santa Croce in Florence, and the French-influenced Duomo of Milan. Characteristic examples of art from this era include the Pisano Pulpits of Siena's Duomo and Pisa's Baptistery; the painting *The Allegory of Good and Bad Government* in Siena's National Gallery; and Giotto's frescoes, which begin to bridge the gap between the Gothic and Renaissance eras. Giotto's greatest achievements include his *Life of St. Francis,* in the Basilica of Assisi and Santa Croce in Florence, and his *Ognissanti Maesta* in the Uffizi.

THE RENAISSANCE (EARLY 15TH TO 17TH C.)

The Renaissance, meaning "rebirth," signaled a return to the classical depiction of the human form in art, and a refocus on more secular matters. Artists studied recently discovered Roman and Greek relics with scientific zest, copying perspective techniques and measuring ratios in paintings, in buildings, and in sculpture.

The most famous Italian **artists** worked during the Renaissance. Masters such as Leonardo da Vinci, Michelangelo, Raphael, Botticelli, and others competed for commissions from popes and princes, embarking on an era of creativity in the region not seen since ancient times—and really not seen anywhere since.

The Renaissance was most dramatically launched when **Ghiberti** unveiled his first carved panels for the doors of the Baptistery in Florence in 1401. Ghiberti created a scene from the biblical story of Abraham with such realism, depth, and clarity that he won a citywide competition for the commission and set off the use of a similar style by other artists. Visitors to Florence can see the original panels (and those of the second-place contestant, architect Brunelleschi) in the Bargello gallery.

Donatello did his part to launch the Renaissance in sculpture with his *David* (ca. 1431), the first free-standing nude since Roman times. The effeminate statue (popular with the Medicis) stands in stark contrast to Donatello's manly *St. Mark* statue of 1411, also in Florence's Bargello museum.

To gain some perspective on the early Renaissance, take a look at **Masaccio's** works in Florence. His 1427 *Trinità* fresco, in Santa Maria Novella church, was said to have "punched a hole in the wall" with its innovative use of perspective to create depth in a two-dimensional painting. Masaccio's fresco cycle, in the Santa Maria del Carmine church, with its scene of the expulsion from Eden, and his lively character studies, inspired an up-and-coming artist by the name of Michelangelo.

Michelangelo, along with Leonardo da Vinci, was the ultimate Renaissance man. The former is celebrated for his lifelong creativity and production as a painter, sculptor, and architect. His commissions came from princes and popes, and the battle over his hometown of record continued after his death, as the Medicis spirited his body from Rome and had it entombed in Florence's Santa Croce church. Florence is also the site of Michelangelo's 1504 *David* statue, a creation about which historian Vasari declared, "Anyone who has seen [it] has no need to see anything else by any other sculptor, living or dead." But Michelangelo didn't stop with sculpture; he painted the majestic Sistine Chapel in Rome, and designed the dome above it for good measure. His first *Pietà* statue, done at the age of 25, stands in St. Peter's Basilica as a soaring testament to the sorrow of Mary. His final, almost modern-art version, in the process of completion when he was 89, stands in Milan's Museum of Ancient Art, another example of the lifelong creative passion of one of the greatest artists ever.

Leonardo da Vinci added science and engineering to his masterworks. His *Mona Lisa* is in the Louvre in Paris, and his splendid *Annunciation* painting of 1481 is on display in Florence's Uffizi Gallery. His famous *Last Supper* fresco, an artistic icon in Milan's Santa Maria delle Grazie, has become almost unrecognizable with the passage of time. Da Vinci's combination of perspective, soft colors, innovative backgrounds, and realistic detail makes him one of the great painters. His mechanical inventions, including a machine gun, parachute, tank, and glider, are re-created in a series of "Leonardo Museums" across the country, a good place for kids to play with the wooden models.

Other titans of the era include **Titian** and **Raphael,** who both flourished as artists in the early 16th century. Raphael created a huge body of work featuring vivid colors in epic compositions. His series of frescoes in the Vatican include the famed *School of Athens,* with a who's who of artists of the era appearing in the painting. Titian added a focus on light and shadow to the vivid colors of the time. His 1538 *Venus of Urbino,* in the Uffizi, remains one of the most influential pieces of art, with its combination of realism, symbolism, and tonal subtlety. The churches and palaces of Venice are filled with Titian's works, including his battle scene painted in the Ducal Palace, and the altarpiece of Santa Maria Gloriosa.

Renaissance architecture followed the sweep of artistic creation with works by Brunelleschi (creator of Florence's Duomo—still the largest free-standing stone dome in the world), Michelangelo (the dome of St. Peter's and the Medici Library in Florence), Andrea Palladio (Villa Rotonda and Foscari of Vicenza), and Vasari (the Uffizi in Florence, the loggia, and others in Arezzo). Most of these architects studied the proportions of ancient monuments to create their own works. The brutal competition for commissions was such that Brunelleschi (admittedly a bit paranoid) wrote down all his measurements in cipher so that his rivals couldn't steal his building plans. Through the work of Brunelleschi and his peers, architects were, for the first time, considered to be artists.

BAROQUE & ROCOCO PERIOD (LATE 16TH TO 18TH C.)

Think of Donald Trump decorating Las Vegas, and you'll have a good idea of the spirit of baroque and rococo art. More is always better. If you're going to paint one angel on the ceiling, might as well add 10, cover them in gold, and surround with 2 dozen roses, frolicking doves, unicorns, and the Roman Fifth army. Puffy clouds in blue skies were painted on ceilings across the country. This era coincided with the decadence and decline of Italy's major families, such as the Medicis, whose heirs spent their inheritance on gold-encrusted bird baths rather than on sponsoring innovative artists. But despite the tawdriness that marked the era, some fine artists and artworks have survived the years with their reputation somewhat intact.

Rather than excess gold and decoration, **Caravaggio** painted with an excess of darkness. His noted *chiaroscuro* technique combined shadow with dramatic sources of light within his compositions. The destitute were his subject matter, a reflection of his own upbringing as a street urchin. The Vatican Museums display his famous 1604 *Deposition* painting, while the Uffizi devotes almost an entire gallery to his works.

Gianlorenzo Bernini represents the pinnacle of baroque sculpture and architecture. His dramatic, twisting, contorting statues represent some of the spirit of the era, a flurry of activity that never really moved anywhere. Nevertheless, his statues of *Apollo and Daphne* and *The Rape of Persephone* (works from the 1620s) are worth seeing in Rome's Galleria Borghese. Bernini's architectural achievements include the colonnade of St. Peter's Square in Rome, as well as the interior setting of St. Peter's Basilica, which contains the tombs of Urban VIII and Alexander VII.

For baroque aficionados, a visit to the Sicilian town of Noto, near Syracuse, is a must. The city was rebuilt after an earthquake in an all-baroque format, with the entire city center designed in the style of the era in 1693.

THE MODERN ERA (1800–PRESENT)

Art's modern age in Italy began with the neoclassical movement, whose spare, white-marble buildings and undecorated columns represented a backlash against the artistic fluffery of the baroque era. The 19th century featured the expansion of archaeological digs (discovering Pompeii, among others), and reignited an interest in the classical era. The unification of Italy in the late 1800s catalyzed a desire to return to the glory of Roman architecture, embodied by the excessive Vittorio Emanuele monument in Rome; it also culminated in Mussolini's "glory through marble" fascist architecture of Stadio Olimpico and other hulking monuments.

Italy's modern-art era pales in comparison with the Renaissance. But Amado **Modigliani** represents a triumph of early-20th-century art with his innovative portrait and figure painting and sculptures featuring elongated forms. Milan's Brera Picture Gallery and Rome's National Gallery of Modern Art display a good selection of his works, alongside those of his peers like the naturalist Giovanni Fattori and the modernist Gino Severini.

Additional Information on the Art of Italy

For more information on Italian art history, consult Gardner's *Art Through the Ages,* a very readable textbook on the history of European art. Giorgio Vasari wrote the world's first comprehensive art-history text with his *Lives of the Artists* in 1550, providing us with contemporary biographical information on the artists of the Renaissance; it is still an engaging (if not always accurate) read. The Oxford History of Art has a series of art-history books discussing every era from the pre-classical to the modern periods, which are well illustrated and instructive (and even affordable at about $20 a pop). For a "Virtual Museum" of Renaissance art, check out **www.wga.hu,** with its hundreds of high-quality reproductions and artist biographies searchable by site, artist, or time period.

A BRIEF HISTORY OF ITALY
by Reid Bramblett

One of the major reasons to come to Italy is to look at, live in, and walk through more than 2,000 years of vivid history. In a sense, the entire nation is a huge, open-air museum. You can hardly kick a soccer ball in Italy without hitting some kind of historical structure, from Roman amphitheaters to medieval castles or Renaissance statues.

The following history of Italy focuses on major dates and associated sights of interest to travelers. For a more detailed history, check out some of the books in the "Recommended Reading" section of chapter 15.

PRE-ROMAN TIMES

As many statues (and AS Roma soccer logos) commemorate, Rome was founded in 730 B.C. by the brothers Romulus and Remus. According to legend, a she-wolf discovered the brothers in the woods, and suckled them to good health. Remus's son Senius went on to found Siena, where additional statues can be seen.

If you're not buying that story, a slightly more reliable one has Etruscan tribes unifying across north-central Italy in the 8th century B.C. to create the first statelike entity on "the boot." The Etruscans defeated Latin tribes and made Rome their capital about 600 B.C.

The Etruscans continued to be a strong presence in trade, war, culture, and shipping, until first losing in Greek naval wars in the 4th century B.C., and then becoming subjugated and fully absorbed into the Roman empire by the 2nd century B.C.

Dateline

800 B.C. Etruscan tribes begin to consolidate control of north-central Italy, creating Italy's first nation-state.

510 B.C. Roman Republic is established.

250 B.C. Roman and other forces defeat the Etruscans, marking the beginning of the Roman empire.

50 B.C. Rome rules all of Mediterranean Europe.

45 B.C. Julius Caesar becomes ruler of Rome.

44 B.C. Caesar is assassinated.

continues

27 B.C. Augustus Caesar becomes Emperor, marking the beginning of Pax Romana and the Golden Age of Rome.

A.D. 40 Emperor Caligula declares himself a god and names his horse to the senate.

300s Rome's decline is scored with corrupt emperors, collapsing regimes, and armies losing control.

Early 400s Rome is sacked by barbarian hordes.

800 Charlemagne is declared Holy Roman Emperor, and his armies control most of Italy.

1200 Rise of power of Italian city-states like Florence, Genoa, and Venice.

1348 The Black Death/Bubonic Plague sweeps through Italy, killing from a third to half of all inhabitants.

1401 Giotto completes Florence's Baptistery doors, making a convenient mark for the start of the Renaissance.

1498 Leonardo da Vinci paints *The Last Supper.*

1508–12 Michelangelo paints the Sistine Chapel.

1527 Charles V of France conquers Rome and becomes Holy Roman Emperor.

SIGHTS   Etruscan ruins dot the country, with their largest concentration in Volterra, in Tuscany, and the necropolis southeast of Tarquina. Many Roman walls, wells, and roads across north-central Italy are based on Etruscan foundations. Etruscan tomb relics and tablets can be seen in many museums across Italy, including the Museo Nazionale di Villa Giulia in Rome.

ROMAN EMPIRE

The Roman Republic began in 510 B.C. when Latin tribes evicted the Etruscans from Rome. Through a combination of alliances, colonization, and efficient infrastructure-building, Roman armies expanded throughout Italy—building roads, aqueducts, and walled cities as they went. With Rome's triumph in the Punic Wars, and with the destruction of Carthage in the 3rd century B.C., Rome became the greatest power in the Mediterranean region.

The generals and armies of Rome expanded across Mediterranean Europe through the 1st century B.C. Julius Caesar conquered most of what is now France to the Rhine River, and invaded Britain. Pompey led armies to the east, conquering what is now Syria and Asia Minor. In 60 B.C., Caesar, Pompey, and Marcus Crassus (a leader in Rome) allied to create the First Triumvirate to rule the empire. Following Crassius's death in battle, a civil war broke out between Caesar and Pompey. Caesar defeated Pompey's armies in 45 B.C. and returned to Rome a hero. He seized power to effectively become dictator of the Roman empire, which now stretched from the Atlantic Ocean to the Black Sea.

Julius Caesar ruled for 1 short year. In 44 B.C., he was assassinated by senators eager to re-establish the Republic. Mark Antony (Caesar's top general) briefly shared power with Caesar's adopted son Octavian and Marcus Lepidus in the Second Triumvirate from 43 to 32 B.C. Naturally, they couldn't get along either, and another civil war broke out. Antony fled to Egypt, hiding out with his mistress, Cleopatra, until they both committed suicide as Octavian's armies and navies swept through the region.

The Golden Age

The rule of Octavian (now known as Augustus Caesar) from 27 B.C. to A.D. 14 launched the "Golden Age of Rome" and the 200 years of the Pax Romana—during which the Roman armies kept Europe and the Middle East free from any major wars. Art, architecture, and commerce flourished during the time, with the major structures being built, including the Roman Forum, Colosseum, and Pantheon, as well as the Roman roads crisscrossing Europe.

Not that all was quiet in Rome during the Golden Age. Succession battles raged following the death of emperors (rarely from natural causes). The Emperor Caligula famously married his sister, named his horse to the senate, had himself declared a god, and generally turned Rome into his personal nut-house until he was assassinated in A.D. 41. Revolts in Palestine and the rise of Christianity (and its subsequent persecution) created continuous unrest throughout the realm.

The Fall

By the beginning of the 3rd century, the Roman empire was wracked with civil wars, barbarian invasions, and domestic unrest. Following the death of Marcus Aurelius, in 180, the empire began its slow but steady decline. During the next 73 years, 23 different emperors "ruled" the empire. In 306, Constantine became the first Christian emperor, relocating the capital from Rome to Constantinople (now Istanbul). In 395, the empire formally split between the western section in Rome and the eastern section in Constantinople.

The barbarian hordes reached the gates of Rome in 410, with the Visigoths being the first to sack the city. Attila the Hun swept through Italy in the 450s, and the Vandals made a name for themselves with a savage destruction of Rome in 455. Competing groups battled for control for the next 100 years, leaving Rome a depopulated, crumbling husk of a city to begin the Dark Ages.

SIGHTS Virtually every construction in Italy has some foundation in the Roman era. Rome obviously has the bulk of the sights, with the Colosseum, Pantheon, and Forum being three of the top attractions. Roman amphitheaters cover the country, from Verona to Gubbio to Arezzo, and they continue to host performances. The National Archaeological Museum in Naples houses many relics from all eras of the Roman empire.

DARK AGES TO EARLY MIDDLE AGES (A.D. 475–1000)

As my grade-school history teacher liked to say, the Dark Ages was the era in which "the light of civilization was nearly extinguished." Competing tribal armies fought across Italy, with the Goths and Lombards carving out areas of control. For their own survival, the popes became temporal power brokers as they allied with warlords to protect

1602 Galileo Galilei is among the first to use a telescope to study the stars and planets, collecting data to help prove a sun-centered solar system.

1633 After the Inquisition threatens torture and death, Galileo says he was just kidding about all that science stuff, and agrees that the sun rotates around the earth.

1804 Napoleon declares himself Emperor of Italy after his armies conquer the country.

1861 A (mostly) united and independent Italy becomes the Kingdom of Italy.

1915 Italy fights World War I on the side of the Allies, but suffers huge losses.

1922 Benito Mussolini's fascists march on Rome, and Mussolini becomes Premier.

1935 Huge crowds in Rome cheer Mussolini and his army's conquest of Ethiopia.

1936 Mussolini signs alliance with Hitler.

1945 Allies march through Italy; Partisans kill Mussolini and string him up.

1945–95 "50 governments in 50 years": Rival factions of the Christian Democrat group compete for power in Italy.

continues

1960s–80s "The Years of Lead": Left- and right-wing Italian terrorist groups wage a low-level civil war across the country, with bombings, kidnappings, and killings.

1994 Billionaire Silvio Berlusconi is elected prime minister as part of "clean government" campaign.

1995 Berlusconi resigns as coalition dissolves, corruption trials loom.

2001 Berlusconi is re-elected prime minister with huge majority vote.

2002 Euro is introduced as the currency of Italy.

2004 Berlusconi transfers $400,000 to judge's bank account.

2004 Judges dismiss all corruption charges against Berlusconi.

2005 New corruption charges are introduced against Berlusconi.

the Christian realm. Pope Leo III crowned Charlemagne Emperor in 800, and the Christian king became a papal ally. After the era of Charlemagne came the Holy Roman Empire—the largest power base of the time. Battles between northern European forces, the Lombards, Normans, and various local groups created the decentralized, highly divided environment in which the Italian city-states arose in the Middle Ages.

SIGHTS   With one of the leading tribes of the time called the Vandals, it's no wonder there aren't too many historical relics from this era. Byzantine-styled religious relics (Ravenna is a center for this) and paintings are the bulk of art from this era.

MEDIEVAL ITALY (A.D. 1000 TO 14TH C.)

With the continual sweeps of competing armies through Italy, only the strongest, most self-sufficient Italian cities survived. The Middle Ages featured the rise of city-states including Venice, Genoa, and Pisa, with merchant fleets driving their economic growth. This era spawned the first of the merchant banks, whose money sponsored the armies and fortifications necessary to survive external attack. The era also featured the growth of the guild system, with artisans banding together to create cohesive economic and political groups within the cities. The crusades and pilgrim routes brought a number of travelers through the cities of northern and central Italy, further enriching the cities with trade. But southern Italy didn't experience the same economic progress, owing to Norman conquests and an extended period of feudalistic torpor.

As Italian city-states began to protect themselves from external invaders, they fell prey to internal strife. The rivalry between the Holy Roman Empire and papal forces created a multicentury family feud throughout Italy. While ostensibly a battle between the temporal powers of the empire and the spiritual powers of the Pope, it was essentially a fight between two groups who wanted to be in charge. The "team" names were the Ghibellines (the "whites," pro-Emperor, feudalistic) and the Guelphs (the "blacks," pro-Pope, merchant-class). The struggle between these groups involved such luminaries as Dante and Machiavelli, both of whom were exiled from their hometowns for supporting the wrong team.

The second major internal disruption of the period came from the Black Death of 1348. Fleas carrying the Bubonic Plague bacteria arrived on the backs of rats riding trade ships from Asia. Between a third and half of the population of Italy died during a 6-month period. Crowded cities with little sanitation suffered the worst, and many never fully recovered. Venice, Siena, San Gimignano, and Orvieto are among those almost frozen in time, with their 14th-century art and architecture (which is what makes them a boon for tourists).

SIGHTS Pisa, Venice, Genoa, and Siena reached their apogee during this period. See the Romanesque architecture of Pisa, the Gothic cathedrals of Milan and Siena, and the Middle Eastern–influenced architecture and art of Venice. In Venice and Perugia are guild halls from this period. Ruined medieval fortifications dot the countryside across northern and central Italy.

THE RENAISSANCE (LATE 14TH TO LATE 16TH C.)

The Renaissance, meaning "rebirth," signaled a second coming of the humanistic focus of the Greco-Roman classical period, as Italian thinkers started to study the works of that era. Michelangelo, da Vinci, Dante, Petrarch, and Galileo are just a few of the famed figures of this period. The unofficial beginning of the Renaissance might be 1401, with Giotto's famous carved doors of Florence's Baptistery. Florence itself is practically synonymous with the Renaissance, the entire city a living reminder of the art, architecture, and politics of the time.

Politically, the Renaissance was the time of the Medicis, a power-hungry family of bankers and textile merchants based in Florence. The family first leveraged their finances to control local, and then regional government, sponsoring and banking politicians and their armies. Soon, the Medicis took direct control of the city, essentially making themselves dictators, while installing their relatives as popes (Leo X and Clement VII) to expand their control nationwide. Lorenzo de'Medici (1449–92) is most tightly associated with the Renaissance, being a patron of Michelangelo and a Renaissance man himself: He had a career in art, politics, banking, hunting, and horsemanship.

As the era moved to the late 1500s, the Medicis, and others like them, tried to carry on their family fortunes through hereditary rule, rather than through legitimate business or political skill. Power-grabbing battles between (and inside) cities made them vulnerable to foreign invasion. When Charles V, King of Spain, sacked Rome in 1527, it marked the beginning of the end of Italy's reign as the economic, political, and cultural center of Europe.

SIGHTS Along with the Roman Era, the Renaissance is Italy's richest source for sights. Florence is practically a one-stop shop, with the city chock-full of artworks, buildings, and a spirit dating from the era, with the Uffizi Galleries, Michelangelo's *David* in the Accademia, and Brunelleschi's dome on the Cathedral. Rome's Sistine Chapel, da Vinci's *Last Supper* in Milan, and the National Gallery in Perugia are also emblematic of the progression of the arts through this period.

DARK AGES PART II, AKA THE COUNTER-REFORMATION (1500–1850)

With the end of the reign of the powerful merchant families, the Roman Catholic Church once again became the most powerful Italian political, social, and military force. And as during the Church's first reign in the early Middle Ages, Italy became a feudalistic, static region. The Church led the Counter-Reformation to fight the Protestant movement and the teachings of Luther. While there were some reforms introduced to reign in corrupt clergy, and the construction of a new generation of churches, Italy suffered through the Inquisition, autocratic rule, and a medieval mentality which put it at the mercy of northern European rivals progressing economically, militarily, and artistically.

For a couple of hundred years Italy became a plaything for Spanish, French, and Austrian invaders whose armies conquered wide swaths of the country, sacking towns and ensuring continued misery for the citizens of the countryside. Napoleon declared himself Emperor over the Kingdom of Italy in 1804, famously grabbing the crown from the Pope whom he commanded to come to France for the ceremony. When Napoleon hit his Waterloo in 1815, Austrian overlords moved in to fill the power vacuum.

SIGHTS   This period is noted for elaborate baroque and rococo art, embodied by Rome's Spanish Steps and Trevi Fountain, the entire Sicilian town of Noto, and the churches of Lecce, as well as many older churches across Italy remodeled during this period at the behest of the counter-reforming Church.

ITALIAN UNIFICATION (LATE 19TH C.)

Despite its long history, Italy is a young country—its myriad cities and provinces unified in 1861. Italian unification is the story of the heart (Joseph Mazzini), the head (Camilo Cavour), and the sword (Giuseppe Garibaldi). Mazzini led some of the revolutionary activities sweeping Europe in 1848, writing and publicizing his radical and romantic plans for the unification of Italy. Cavour, a career politician and prime minister of Sardinia in 1852, picked up on Mazzini's passionate writings, but modified them into a more practical plan, particularly in the face of the reactionary Church powers. Garibaldi, an Italian exile fresh from struggle for independence in Uruguay, led a military movement across Italy. Garibaldi's squadrons of armed "Red Shirts" coordinated with (or were manipulated by) Cavour's political element to unify nearly all of Italy outside of Rome and Venice (which were added after the Franco-Prussian war of 1870). The Vatican condemned the republic and remained in a cold war with it until a formal independence agreement was crafted in 1929.

SIGHTS   Garibaldi statues fill town squares across Italy, the most notable of which stands in front of an epic mountain view in Todi, Umbria. Piazza della Repubblica in Florence with its triumphant arch commemorates the brief period in which Florence served as capital of the new republic. The late 19th century featured many neoclassical monuments, particularly in areas under Napoleonic influence (like Lucca's main square).

20TH-CENTURY ITALY

During World War I, Italy fought on the side of the Allies, having conducted a secret treaty in London that awarded Italy the Trentino, the south Tyrol, Trieste, and some Dalmatian Islands as an incentive for victory. For the most part, Italians weren't enthusiastic about the war, and became less so after suffering large casualties on the northern front. Following the war, Italy suffered from the inflation and unemployment rampant throughout Europe in the 1920s.

Benito Mussolini took control of Italy with his Brown Shirt squads in the 1920s. Through ruthless executions and purges, he solidified his power, joining into an alliance with Hitler on the eve of World War II. His plan for a new Roman empire extended to conquests over two nearly defenseless targets: the farmers of primitive Albania and the poison gas–aided victory over the tribes of Ethiopia. While many Italians embraced Mussolini as a newfound symbol of national pride, an equal number took part in the anti-fascist Partisan movement. The Allies invaded Sicily in 1943, and the Italian army surrendered about a minute later, but remaining German troops and Italian fascists fought rear-guard actions through the country until 1945. The Partisans caught up to Mussolini in 1945 and strung his body (and that of his mistress) upside down from a gas station roof.

Postwar Italy provided a replay of prewar politics, with fascist- and communist-dominated parties fighting for control of the country, struggles that continue to the present day. Following World War II, the U.S. Marshall Plan channeled huge sums of money to anti-communist elements in Italy. While this led many die-hard fascists right back into the government, it also stimulated a rapid industrialization program that improved the standard of living across the country.

Since then, the saying is that there have been 50 changes of government in the 50 years after the war, but most of these were really different permutations of the same ruling party and shifting coalition partners. In the 1970s, a low-level civil war nearly arose, with communist Red Brigade terrorists kidnapping and killing politicians, and fascist power brokers staging civilian bombings and arrests. Beginning in 1999, Silvio Berlusconi's coalition government (including neofascist and racist groups) imposed some level of stability in the country, despite a series of corruption scandals. Because Berlusconi owns or controls seven of eight TV stations in the country, as well as Italy's largest publishing company, it's not surprising that many of these scandals don't get much play in the local press. In May 2006, Romano Prodi, of the center-left coalition, was elected prime minister.

Index

See also Accommodations and Restaurant indexes, below.

606　Index

608   Index

616　Index

620 Index